See You in Court
The Potts Family of Mannington Norfolk
1584 – 1737

William and Maggie Vaughan-Lewis

ITTERINGHAM HISTORY

Published 2009 by Itteringham History

ISBN: 978-0-9561795-0-0

Printed in the UK by The Lavenham Press Ltd, Lavenham, Suffolk

Contents

Part 1 Emergence and Rise

> *Cheshire and Sawston origins - Geoffrey Downes and Lady Ingoldesthorpe - earliest Cheshire Potts - a curious connection - James Apott of Sawston and the Campions - James Apott junior, Citizen and Grocer - James Apott, grocer: his will and estate - the Paris family*

> *Roger Apott and Katherine Boteler - Katherine and William Doddes - John Potts and the Grant of Arms*

> *The Bishop and The White Hind - The Maidenhead and Jasper Fisher - Tremel Street - St Bartholomew the Less - Roger Apott's acquisitions and The King's Head - St Botolph without Bishopsgate*

> *William Lumner senior of Mannington - Lumners in London - Aleyn the Grocer - Thomas the Mercer - Henry the Grocer - John Lumner the Grocer - Nobody Expects the Spanish Inquisition - Thomas senior of Sharrington - Henry the fishmonger - John Lumner yeoman of Sharrington - Thomas junior of Sharrington - William Lumner of Sharrington*

Part 2 Pinnacle of Success: Sir John Potts 1st Baronet

Family Notes

List of Illustrations

Acknowledgments

Our thanks must go first to Lord and Lady Walpole who have not only given us access to their home and papers but have encouraged and helped us from the beginning. Without them the book would not have been written. We hope it meets with their approval.

Particular thanks also are due to Dr John Alban and his ever patient staff at the Norfolk Record Office who have helped us with readings, references and source ideas. Special thanks go to Nick Sellwood, the Senior Conservator for assisting us with fragile documents. The Norfolk county archives are second to none and fortunately for all researchers, (despite some comments that are still occasionally made by the mis-informed) no documents were lost in the flames of the dreadful fire that destroyed Norwich library. We would also like to thank Elizabeth and Paul Rutledge for their encouragement and willingness to offer advice and suggestions; this book does not attempt to match their very high standard of editorial quality but nevertheless, we trust it will be useful to other researchers.

Thanks also to others who have dealt expertly with endless enquiries: Dr James Ross (TNA), Dr Stephen Roberts and Dr Hannes Kleineke (History of Parliament Trust), Ms Jacqueline Cox (Cambridge University Library), Robert MacLean (Glasgow University Library), Nottingham University archives, Michael Webb (Curator of Early Modern MSS, Bodleian Library), Dr Clive Wilkins-Jones of the Norfolk and Norwich Millennium Library and his staff; Cheshire County Libraries and Record Office, Dr Peter Webster (British History Online) and especially Dr D Ogier of the Guernsey Island Archives Service. Thanks also to M Britton, churchwarden of St Michael's and All Saints Church, Brooksby, Leicestershire, Derek Palgrave (Palgrave Society), and Mrs M Taylor, Eltham Parish Church, Eltham, Kent. Also, thanks to Ron Fiske for his help on some heraldry issues.

Acknowledgments for the illustrations are due to Lord and Lady Walpole, Mrs Theresa Courtauld, Mrs Donna McDougall, Mr and Mrs C Shippam, Mr Roy Precious who also made some helpful observations, Thetford Library (DS Collection) NCC Library services and we are very grateful to our friend Jonathan Neville for taking such excellent photographs in all sorts of lights and imperfect situations. And without the kind assistance of Ms Sheila Day, Mr Tim Harris and Bonhams of Ipswich, the pictures would not have been located at all.

Acknowledgements are due to the Bodleian Library for the Tanner letter extracts and to the British Library for extracts from the Harley, Egerton and Additional Mss. Norfolk Record Office has kindly allowed us to quote from innumerable deeds, wills, court rolls, quarter sessions papers, letters and family papers referred to throughout the book. For information from other referenced documents, we acknowledge: Cambridge University Library; Cambridgeshire Record Office; Cheshire Record Office; Derbyshire Record Office; East Sussex Record Office; Essex Record Office; Hertfordshire Archives and Local Studies; Hunstanton Library, Norfolk; Centre for Kentish Studies ; Suffolk Record Office (Bury and Ipswich); Nottingham University Archives; and of course The National Archives, source of much of the probate and all of the equity courts' material. For the digital access to the Journals of the Houses of Commons and Lords and other quoted sources from www.british-history.ac.uk our thanks to British History Online.

Our thanks too to Bill Byford and designer Lisa Spiking for seeing the book through the press.

And lastly we'd like to thank all our Itteringham friends and family who have waited patiently for this, our first, book. Every "how's it going? looking forward to seeing it" kept us on track when at times the task seemed overwhelming.

Abbreviations

APC	*Acts of the Privy Council,* HMSO
Bacon Papers	*The Papers of Nathaniel Bacon of Stiffkey* 1556-1602 *Vols 1 -4* NRS 46, 49, 53, 64, 1978-2000. Vol 5 forthcoming (typescript 2008)
Bod	Bodleian Library, Oxford
BL	British Library: Egerton Mss, Harleian Mss and others
Blom	F Blomefield, *An Essay towards a Topographical History of Norfolk* 11 vols, 1805
CPR	*Calendar of Patent Rolls,* HMSO
CRO	Cambridgeshire Record Office
CSPF	*Calendar of State Papers Foreign,* HMSO
CSPD	*Calendar of State Papers Domestic,* HMSO
CSPCAWI	*Calendar of State Papers Colonial, America and West Indies: 1675-1676* and *Addenda 1574-1674,* HMSO
CSPI	*Calendar of State Papers Ireland, 1647-60* and *Addenda 1625-60,* HMSO
CUL	Cambridge University Library
DRO	Derbyshire Record office
EAA	*East Anglian Archaeology,* Norfolk Museums and Archaeology Service
Folger	Folger Shakespeare Library, Washington, DC
Guildhall Lib	Guildhall Library, Dept of Mss (London)
HCJ	*Journal of the House of Commons*: Volumes 1-10 (1802) URL: http://www.british-history.ac.uk. History of Parliament Trust
HLJ	*Journal of the House of Lords:* Volumes 1-19 (1802) on British History Online (as above)
HMC	Historical Manuscripts Commission

HofC	The History of Parliament Trust:
	JS Roskell et al, *The House of Commons 1386-1421*, 1992
	ST Bindoff, *The House of Commons 1509-1558*, 1982
	PW Hasler, *The House of Commons 1558-1603*, 1981
	BD Henning, *The House of Commons 1660-1690*, 1983
	E Cruickshanks et al, *The House of Commons 1690-1715*, 2002
	R Sedgwick, *The House of Commons 1715-1754*, 1970
IGI	International Genealogical Index (Familysearch)
IPM	Inquisition post mortem: enquiry held after death of manorial landholder
K-C	RW Ketton-Cremer, *Norfolk in the Civil War*, 1969; *Forty Norfolk Essays*, 1961; *Norfolk Portraits*, 1964; *A Norfolk Gallery*, 1968; *Felbrigg*, 1962; *Three Generations*, Larks Press 1992
LPFD	*Letters and Papers Foreign and Domestic of the Reign of Henry VIII preserved in the PRO*, vols 1-21, HMSO
Mason	RH Mason, *History of Norfolk Vol 1*, 1884
NA	*Norfolk Archaeology*
NRO	Norfolk Record Office
NRS	Norfolk Record Society
ODNB	*Oxford Dictionary of National Biography* (online version)
SHC	Surrey History Centre, Woking, Surrey
Tanner	Papers and letters collected by Thomas Tanner, now in the Bodleian Library. M/f available at Millennium Library, Norwich
TNA	The National Archives, Kew
VENN	JA Venn, *Alumni Cantabrigienses ... from the earliest times to 1900*, CUP, 1922-1954; JA Venn, *Biographical Dictionary of Gonville and Caius College*, CUP 1897

For pedigrees of Norfolk families *The Visitations of Norfolk 1563, 1589 and 1613* and *The Visitation of Norfolk 1664* (Harleian Society volume 32, 1891 and Norfolk Record Society volumes 4 & 5, 1934), where possible with corroborative sources, have been used extensively but are not individually cited. Similarly, unreferenced local historical statements are usually taken from Blomefield.

Note on style and transcription

Dates before 1752 have been modernised to current years, ie January-March 1648 is shown as January-March 1649.

Many of the original documents have been modernised in part to allow for ease of reading. Although most are given at length, there is no attempt at full record publication.

Given the large number of names and places in the text, capitalisation of other words has been kept to a minimum even where traditional usage (eg chancery, puritan, parliament) would have used upper case.

Sums of money are given as £ - pounds, s - shillings and d - pence.

Family surnames inevitably have thrown up many variations: for each a standard form has been selected and all occurrences are indexed only by this form. Variations have been noted in the text or footnotes.

The three main examples are Potts (which includes Pot, Pott, Pottes), Apott (A Pot, Apotts, A Put, Aputt) and Lumner (Lominer, Lomner, Lomnor, Lomnour, Luminer, Lumnor, Lumnour, Lumpner, Lumpnor, Lumpnour, Limner and Lymnour).

As with all early historical writing, much of the work has to be speculation. We have been scrupulous in reflecting the gaps in documentary evidence and stating where we have made assumptions. The overuse of possibly, perhaps and may well have been should therefore be forgiven.

Introduction

In a lecture in spring 2007, Dr Hannes Kleinecke underlined the increased interest historians have in 'the lesser squires', the 'heart of how local networks worked'. For this interest to continue to be met, it is vital that detailed research on individual gentry families appears in print - a view expressed as long ago as 1956 by HJ Habakkuk. In his preface to Margaret Finch's work, *Five Northamptonshire Families,* Habakkuk wrote that case-studies of that type would 'have to be multiplied several-fold if sensible answers are to be given to the questions posed by the general historian'. Here is such a case-study, unashamedly full of detail on one extended family, helping to throw light on the fast-changing world of the sixteenth and seventeenth centuries.

As we started researching into the history of Mannington and Itteringham, two small villages in north Norfolk, we found that little had been written about the early owners of the major house and estate, Mannington Hall. The Potts family owned the estate from 1584 to 1737, spanning much of the early modern period, before their line died out and the property was purchased by Horatio Walpole of neighbouring Wolterton.

In writing their story, it became clear that they typified middle to senior level Norfolk gentry, never particularly famous, but exemplifying a number of themes that commonly emerge from studies of East Anglian, and particularly Norfolk, social and economic history. First, social stratification and mobility. The Potts worked their way up from farming and trade to achieve a baronetcy. Their family and social networks over the generations are fascinating and intricate. Their initial rise into manorial status came from using early family connections across London and the south-east. They had friends and relations at court. Later they were linked by marriage to most of the North Norfolk gentry families. Despite the efforts of Sir John Potts - baronet, deputy-lieutenant, JP and MP - like so many similar seventeenth century families, they failed to make the next step to the aristocracy. In 1737, with no male heirs, the Potts line ended. Second, the recourse to law. Norfolk was renowned for its numbers of lawyers and the litigious nature of its people. The Potts family are a stunning example of both - an extraordinary number of equity cases have been found over the whole period including acrimonious actions between family members adding spice and rich detail to the story. Third, the development of landed estates. The fortunes of each generation responded to effort - first in trade and in opportunistic purchases after the dissolution of the monasteries and later in the management of Mannington and their other estates. As was so often the case, property could be lost as quickly as it could be acquired. Mortgages, although a useful form of borrowing and raising cash, frequently led to land slipping away from the estate. Too many daughters and married sons often put pressure on the family's wealth. In the end, most of the gains had been lost, leaving only the old core of the manor. Lastly, the Potts family seem to be a striking example of the confident independence often noted as a characteristic of Norfolk families.

Their story, and therefore the book, falls naturally into three major phases: their emergence and rise, prior to their purchase of Mannington and in parallel the story of the Mannington estate itself during the fifteenth and sixteenth centuries; the pinnacle of success, both socially and politically achieved by the long-lived Sir John Potts the 1st baronet, 1592-1673; and lastly, the decline and fall of the family, in debt and no longer at ease with themselves. The lack of male heirs, as so often the cause of a family's demise, broke the connection with Mannington, resulting in the sale of all assets and importantly for historians, leaving no major collection of family papers.

The lack of a known corpus of material led earlier writers to say relatively little on the family and what was written unfortunately repeated some false information. The Harleian Society, Norfolk Visitation of 1664 had added an extra generation between John Potts esq and his father Roger. Others, including Francis Blomefield have confused John Potts (later Sir) with John Potts of Chalgrave, Bedfordshire and accredited the former with legal training. Blomefield did however assert correctly that the family had originated in Cheshire although that was presumably based on the seventeenth century adoption of the arms granted to John Potts by one member of the Cheshire Potts family. Close examination of early IPMs, wills, deeds and court rolls has allowed the origins of the family lines in Cheshire, Cambridgeshire and elsewhere to be followed with more certainty. The details of their London properties in Holborn and elsewhere have never been published and show a very different environment from rural Norfolk.

The entry for Sir John Potts in the History of the House of Commons volume covering his second election, in 1660, is acknowledged to be out of date (it adds a non-existent wife called Mebwoke) and will be updated in the forthcoming volume for the period 1640-1660. A very useful work, however, is the short booklet, *Mannington Hall and its Owners* by Sir Charles Sissmore Tomes, who lived in the Hall in the early twentieth century. Where material has survived, such as in the nationally-important letters collected by the Reverend Thomas Tanner, it has often been used in a wider context not allowing for comprehensive publication. RW Ketton-Cremer wrote an excellent introduction to the role of Sir John Potts in the civil war in *Norfolk in the Civil War* but given his subject had to be brief out of necessity. Other letters and the chancery actions have given us a chance to flesh out the man in a way not previously possible.

Later members of the family have been virtually invisible. Much more has been discovered giving each a chance to be seen taking part in the events of their day. Portraits, where we could track them down, are included to enhance the presentation of the characters involved. We hope that reading the last chapter will result in the re-appearance of those paintings that have gone to ground.

As for Mannington Hall itself, the major new find of a seventeenth century inventory has thrilled everyone who is fascinated by this lovely old moated house. New ideas have been generated with the help of Lord and Lady Walpole and some questions answered. Quite unexpectedly, we have found potential links between the Lumners - who built the Hall - and the Potts well before the period of the latter's purchase.

This has been a labour of love for us. We live within a few miles of Mannington and Wolterton Halls in a countryside little changed from the eighteenth century. Our love of working with archives, in the original, has taken us across the country in pursuit of new information. Our aim was not to produce an academic publication but one based on original documentary sources never before printed. A secondary purpose was to cast a critical eye over published information that was often frustratingly slight or teasingly unsourced in an attempt to set the record straight wherever possible. In this light, we recommend reading, in their own right, the footnotes where much of the detective work necessarily has to be placed. The end result is a book which we hope will be useful to local and family historians, economic and social historians, specialists and non-specialists alike. The new research is here to be used, challenged and added to by others.

Timeline

1460s	William and Margaret Lumner built Mannington Hall
1481	William Lumner died leaving Margaret a life interest in Mannington
1504	After the death of her next two husbands Margaret died
1508	James Apott of Sawston in Cambridgeshire died, leaving son James as heir
1510-1560	James junior and his son Roger built London grocery/property business
1505-1558	Mannington owned by William Lumner junior and his son Edmund
1530s	Edmund married first wife Rose Spring of Lavenham
1555	Edmund married second wife Katherine Wigmore, née Leighton
1558	Edmund died leaving son and heir Edmund junior
1559-1562	Edmund's widow Katherine remarried John Callard and then John Dodge
1563-	Katherine brought up children by all 4 marriages
1557	James Apott died, followed by his widow Margaret née Paris in 1567
1561	Roger Apott died leaving 4 children by his wife Katherine née Boteler
1562-1580	Katherine remarried first William Doddes and then Francis Flower
1578	Apott name changed to Pott or Potts
1578-83	John and Philip Potts attended Lincoln's Inn and John gained grant of arms
1584	John Potts married Anne Dodge and bought Mannington from Edmund Lumner
1596-98	Deaths of most of the senior generation of the Mannington and London families
1598	6 year-old John Potts, ward of court, became Mannington heir
1598-1623	Mannington run by Anne Potts's second husband Sir Christopher Heydon
1610-	John Potts married Barbara Godsalve and they had 3 daughters
1615	Barbara Godsalve died
1617-	John Potts married Ursula Spelman of Narborough and they had 4 children
1620s-1630s	John Potts active in running Mannington and in Norfolk local government
1640-41	John Potts knighted, made baronet and elected to parliament
1648	Sir John MP in Isle of Wight negotiations with the King; fell to Pride's Purge
1649	Sir John retired to run his and his brother's estates
1660-61	Sir John member of Restoration council of state and returned to parliament
1673	Sir John Potts senior died leaving Sir John junior as son and heir
1678	Sir John junior died leaving Sir Roger as son and heir
1678-1711	Family focus switched from Mannington to Sir Roger's Great Ellingham home
1689	Sir Roger stood for Parliament but not elected
1711	Sir Roger died leaving eldest surviving son Algernon as heir
1716	Sir Algernon Potts died childless and estate passed to his only brother Charles
1732	Sir Charles Potts died without issue
1737	Dame Mary Potts died and Mannington estate sold to Horatio Walpole

Part 1

EMERGENCE AND RISE

'In Chancery, one time when the counsel of the parties set forth the boundaries of the land in question, by the plot: and the counsel of one part said, "We lie on this side, my Lord", and the counsel of the other part said, "And we lie on this side": the Lord Chancellor Hatton stood up and said, "If you lie on both sides, whom would you have me believe?" '

Bacon's *Apothegms* as quoted in Eric St J Brooks, *Sir Christopher Hatton*, 1946

Chapter 1

Apotts Before Mannington - Their Ship Comes In

———————————————

The Potts name and family background began in Cheshire and Cambridgeshire; the Campion family, the Paris family and the Lumners, the family who were to build Mannington, are introduced demonstrating the influence of the Grocers' trade. The family made their first appearances in chancery.

The mystery of the origins of the Potts family was unlocked by a discovery in a late sixteenth century inquisition post mortem (IPM). Their surname had evolved during the century from a very different form, Apott. From further IPMs and a number of Apott wills, this unusual name allowed the Potts/Apott family to be traced back with absolute certainty to Sawston in Cambridgeshire where one James Apott died at his home in 1508 (see below).[1] His will showed that he had two sons, James and John, and two daughters by his wife Alice. From the list of executors and overseers, she must have been Alice Campion. The Campions were a mid-ranking family in Sawston of which several members were doing well in the grocery and other wholesale trades in London. He also left land to the church in Sawston and to a John Apott and his wife Jane in nearby Pampisford. The relationship to John was not stated but the gift of land showed a close family connection. John was probably his nephew. The gifts of land away from his direct family show that James was a man of at least some substance. However, substantial research into the Sawston area failed to find any earlier reference to a Potts or Apott family in this area of Cambridgeshire (see Family Notes 1: Apott for this and other possibilities for the origins of the Potts family). James's two sons were to make the first known appearance of the Potts family in chancery; for the next eight generations family members would rarely be out of it.

Cheshire and Sawston origins

The Cambridgeshire discovery did not at first fit with Blomefield's statement that the Potts family came from Cheshire.[2] However further evidence showed that the Apott family did indeed come from Pott Shrigley in that county. By 1633, a London member of this family, Edmund Pott haberdasher, had adopted the Potts arms first created in 1583 for John Potts of London, later of Mannington.[3] This showed that the Cheshire family was, by 1633, certain of ancestral linkage. However, with several Potts branches in and around Pott Shrigley through the sixteenth century it has not proved possible to create a definitive family tree back into the fifteenth century and thus to show the precise linkage of the Norfolk line to those who stayed in Cheshire. Some evidence was found in dispersed surviving manorial documents. The proof of James Apott's Cheshire origins lay in the supervisors of his will of 1508 - John Parys esq and Geoffrey Downes gent. The latter was also co-executor with James in the will made in 1503 by John Warde of Stapleford in which he was given as Geoffrey Downes gent of Babraham.[4]

Geoffrey Downes and Lady Ingoldesthorpe

Geoffrey Downes is to this day well-known for founding, with Lady Joan Ingoldesthorpe for whom he worked, the chapel and lending library at Pott Shrigley church. Both her will, made and proved in 1494, and his made in 1492, referred to the creation of the chapel and a number of documents relating to it have survived.[5] These materials include quite a number of references to the Potts family and in particular show that James Apott had made arrangements to sell and surrender his property in Pott Shrigley to Geoffrey Downes. James must have gone with him to London to work with him in the service of Lady Ingoldesthorpe who was of London, Burrough Green and Sawston. After her death, he continued to be closely involved with Geoffrey Downes, similarly living out his days in Cambridgeshire.

In the early fifteenth century Sir Walter de la Pole, nephew of Michael de la Pole Earl of Suffolk, was lord of the major manors of Pyratt's (Sawston Hall) and Dernford in Sawston.[6] He married the heiress Elizabeth Bradston (d 1423) and their daughter and heiress Margaret (d 1426) married Sir Thomas Ingoldesthorpe (d 1422). The Sawston manors passed into the Ingoldesthorpe family at Sir Walter's death around 1535. Thomas and Margaret's son (five years old at his mother's death) was Sir Edmund Ingoldesthorpe who married Joan (sometimes given as Jane) Tiptoft the second daughter of John Tiptoft Lord Powis and sister of John, Earl of Worcester. A receipt of 1453-54 has been taken to imply that the Ingoldesthorpes then lived in Sawston and Teversham's analysis of fifteenth century Sawston documents suggests that the Ingoldesthorpes spent at least part of their time living in Sawston. Sir Edmund was a Cambridgeshire JP and an MP in several parliaments in the 1440s and 1450s. He died quite young in 1456, seized of nearly 30 manors in eight counties, with particular concentrations in Cambridgeshire (at and near his main seat in Burrough Green between Sawston and Newmarket) and in Norfolk where he held Ingoldisthorpe and Raynham manors among others. He also enjoyed a long standing royal annuity of 500 marks granted to a Bradston predecessor of Lady Joan's which she continued to enjoy after his death. She was a very wealthy woman.

Sir Edmund and Lady Joan had a single daughter Isabella, aged fifteen at her father's death, who married first John Neville. He was the Marquis of Montagu and brother of Richard the Earl of Warwick. He died at the battle of Barnet in 1471 and his estates were confiscated, possibly explaining why so few documents relating to Sawston survive from the last three decades of the century. Dame Joan regained their lands for the family and held them until her death in 1494. There are indications that she continued to spend some of her time at Sawston. Isabella, by then the wife of Sir William Norris, died in 1575. One of Isabella's two Neville sons was buried in Sawston in 1480. The other son George died in 1485 leaving five daughters. One of these daughters Isabella Neville married, as her first husband, William Huddleston esq (d 1511), the third son of Sir John Huddleston of Millom Castle in Cumberland. She brought the Sawston manors to the Huddleston family, via a family settlement of 1502 between the five daughters of George Neville and their husbands and heirs. The Huddlestons' son and heir was John Huddleston of Sawston (d 1530) who married Elizabeth daughter of Edward Lord Dudley. Their son Sir John Huddleston (1517-1557) was married to Bridget the daughter of Sir Robert Cotton of Landwade.

Lady Joan is said in some older texts to have married again to Sir Thomas Grey, later Lord Grey of Richemount from Ridgmount in Bedfordshire, a younger son of the Grey family of Ruthin. However, the *ODNB* entry for this family shows Sir Thomas to have married a distant Grey cousin and he was attaindered and executed by Edward IV after the battle of Towton in 1461. He may have married Joan, but she retained her Ingoldesthorpe title throughout her life. If they had been briefly married she might have kept her previous title to distance herself from Grey and protect her own lands from his attainder. In any event, for the next thirty years or so she remained a widow.

Between 1456 and 1494 Lady Joan Ingoldesthorpe would have had a major task in managing her estates. It is believed that, from the early 1470s at least, the task fell to Geoffrey Downes who was probably her steward. Downes became her friend and the co-founder of the chantry chapel at Pott Shrigley.[7] The earliest reference to Geoffrey in the Cheshire Downes Papers was in 1472 and there is a rare sighting of him among the papers in the National Archives as a creditor of a substantial loan in a statute staple of 1473.[8] Geoffrey was probably the eldest son of his branch of the family, making him the cousin of the head of the Downes family in Pott Shrigley, not, as sometimes said, the brother.

The interesting story of the foundation of the chapel and lending library has been covered fully by a number of authors. In addition to his role in looking after Lady Joan's affairs, Geoffrey remained a land holder in Pott Shrigley obsessed with the creation of the chapel and the endowment of its furniture and priests. The various local property transactions necessary for this would have created an opportunity for James Apott to work for him, initially there and subsequently further afield. The indications are that James had left Pott Shrigley to join Geoffrey by the early 1490s and, since his children were born around the 1480s to Alice Campion of Sawston, it may have been considerably earlier. Geoffrey and James seem to have lived in London and the Sawston area - wherever Lady Joan travelled no doubt. Geoffrey was usually referred to as a gentleman of London and certainly wrote from there to his Cheshire family.[9] However, one of the key letters in the Downes Papers that links Geoffrey and James Apott was written from 'Sanstoun' [Sawston] where he was with his brother Thomas Downes.[10] This letter has been dated as probably from September 1494.

Geoffrey's will made in 1492 has been an important source for those writing on the foundation of the chapel.[11] While written as a last will and testament its text was wholly related to his arrangements for how the chapel and library should be run. As there was no mention of his family or real and personal estate, it is perhaps best treated as binding instructions for running the chapel. Nobody has been able to show that it was ever proved. As a result most writers gloss over when he died or assume it was near to that date, particularly since his co-founder Lady Joan died in 1494. However, the discovery of him involved in the two Sawston area wills in the early 1500s showed that he was still alive and had retired to Babraham, close to both Burrough Green and Sawston. There was another Geoffrey Downes, a well-known cleric later Archdeacon in York, but he would have been too young to take an overseeing role in these two wills and would not have signed as 'gent'.[12] From Downes Papers references, this clerical Geoffrey was almost certainly a son of the head of the family remaining in Pott Shrigley.[13]

The last reference to Geoffrey Downes gent in the Downes Papers dated from December 1495 and also referred to his wife Jane.[14] Like the late Lady Ingoldesthorpe she may have been Joan or Jane. Presumably by then the chapel and its funding were fully established and he had relatively little further business to conduct in Pott Shrigley. Indeed the priest there would already have been praying for the soul of Lady Joan. This document undermines the assumption by Earwaker in his *East Cheshire* that Downes and Lady Joan may have been married.[15] Lady Joan's relatively short will made arrangements for some further revenues to be allocated to the chapel of which she was foundress.[16] Downes was one of the executors. She also left 10 marks each to Joan, Margery and Maud Downes, presumably Geoffrey's daughters and probably with the eldest named for Lady Ingoldesthorpe. There were minor bequests to Joyce, Thomas and William 'Sauston' and John 'Parishe' and John and Thomas were witnesses. The Sawston family held the small manor of Dale in Sawston throughout the fifteenth century. John Paris was either the heir apparent of the family in nearby Great Linton or one of the Sawston Paris family, no doubt a junior line. The latter were evident at regular intervals in fifteenth century documents and earlier in the century a Thomas Parys had been Receiver General for Sir Walter de la Pole. These being Sawston people and possibly even in her household or working for her, this reinforces her connection to that place in her later years. The residue of her estate was left to Downes to 'dispose of freely after his pleasure as his own', demonstrating her friendship with Geoffrey.

Although speculation, Joan or Jane Downes, Geoffrey's daughter, could be the Jane who was wife of John Apott of Pampisford in 1508. Since John was subsequently of Babraham and became a man of some substance in both Cambridgeshire and London, it seems at least possible that he and Jane inherited a significant part of Geoffrey's estate.

Earliest Cheshire Potts

The Downes Papers yield Potts family references back to 1393 and no doubt before that they lived in the Pott township from which they were named. For details of this and other Cheshire lines see Family Notes 1: Apott. The Potts family were then at most yeomen farmers not gentry.

A court roll entry in May 1450 showed that John Pot was one of the stewards of the Hallemot of the Forest.[17] In 1472 two documents showed Nicholas Potte as one of the witnesses of significant Downes family transactions relating to the early stages of Geoffrey Downes's commitment to the chapel at Pott Shrigley.[18] The first of these in August that year is the earliest reference to Geoffrey and his brother Thomas. They also had a brother John and were the sons of John Downes, who was in turn the younger brother of Robert Downes senior the head of the family. Robert Downes junior was also a witness and was to become head of the main branch of the family when his father died in 1489. The 1450 and 1472 documents show that the Potts family were of some substance locally and closely involved with the Downes family. They reveal that Geoffrey Downes gent was not the brother of Robert junior as has been written into some pedigrees. With some family experience of the role of steward, perhaps James Apott was a natural choice for Geoffrey Downes to make when finding someone he could trust to help him manage Lady Joan's estates.

In January 1483 John Potte was one of the jurors at the Hallemot court and pledged a fine for the admittance to all William Downes's lands in Pott Shrigley.[19] In February 1493 the court roll showed Reginald Downes admitted to copyhold lands forfeit into the hands of the lord of Macclesfield: 'a croft called le lees in the township of Potshrigley, lately held by John Pot of Pot; and land adjacent between le Colclogh and the high road called le Rakes in Potshrigley lately held by John Pot and formerly by James Pot his brother; value 8d pa'.[20] The same month and no doubt in a related transaction Geoffrey Downes endowed the chapel with 10 marks a year to pay for a priest to pray for his soul and that of 'My Lady Jane Ingaldestorp'.[21] Presumably the Johns in 1483 and 1493 were the same man. It is likely that John was the elder brother and head of the family at the time.

This early 1493 transaction implied that a long undated letter from Geoffrey Downes to his cousin Robert must have been written within the previous few months.[22] The letter covered matters to do with timber and farming and, more extensively, arrangements for the priest and furniture in the chapel. Geoffrey was trying to make sure that the chapel was well-endowed with lands for income. Since his will was made in June 1492 this again supports a date of around this time for this letter. The first section of the letter dealt with the house that he had bought from James A Pot and for which there should be a surrender by John A Pott (presumably because James's brother John still occupied it). Geoffrey was vaguely critical of the behaviour of Robert's brother Raynald [Reginald] and was keen to protect the interests of James Apott in the dealings that had been going on in his property. It is clear that James was absent from Pott Shrigley and was with and working for Geoffrey and under his protection. The letter also mentioned the house that Roger A Pott then lived in. He was probably a brother of John and James.

A curious connection

At some date between 1493 and 1500 a William Aputt grocer of London was witness to a chancery submission.[23] By an extraordinary coincidence, this document connects the Potts family and the Lumners. The suit related to the execution of the will of Elizabeth Lumner of London, the widow of a grocer Aleyn Lumner (of whom more subsequently). Aputt and Lumner must have known each other, possibly quite well. William and Aleyn were probably of the same generation and at least middle-aged. Within a few years more Lumners and Apotts were active in a group within the Grocers' Company, so by the early years of the new century some were definitely good friends and colleagues.

A family relationship between this William Aputt and James Apott seems at least possible given the rare surname at the time and the coincidence of the grocery trade that was prevalent in the Apott family and the Campion family of James Apott's wife. It is of course possible that William Aputt was another Pott Shrigley brother and that John of Pampisford was his son not Roger's. The grocery trade connection makes this a distinct possibility but there is no corroboration of a William Pott in or around Pott Shrigley in the last decades of the fifteenth century. Another parent having children in the 1480s or 1490s would also help to explain the proliferation of Potts men in Cambridgeshire by the middle of the sixteenth century. For now William Aputt remains an unsolved puzzle.

James Apott of Sawston and the Campions

The grocery branch of the Campion family had its roots in the Sawston area and many family members were involved in grocery and other major trades in London. James Apott's will provides strong circumstantial evidence that his wife Alice was a daughter of one of the Sawston Campions. For the detailed structure of this large and complicated family see Family Notes 2: Campion. By the late fifteenth century the senior line of the Campions, headed by Robert who died in 1486, was in Sawston, but already had various younger sons engaged in trade in London. Robert's will made no mention of a daughter, a son-in-law or Apott grandchildren, so he was probably not the father of Alice. He seems to have had a brother Richard who fathered Richard, William, John and Alice Campion. The younger Richard may have remained in Sawston, but William and John were grocers in London. Through the Ingoldesthorpe and Downes connection to Sawston, Alice met and married James Apott. With all her Campion family connections there it is likely the couple would have remained living in Sawston. With a house but only modest lands in Sawston he might also have been involved in the saffron trade – a major crop of this part of Cambridgeshire and an important product for the grocery trade in London. Since James had a married daughter in his 1508 will, James's children must have been born in the 1480s, probably in Sawston.

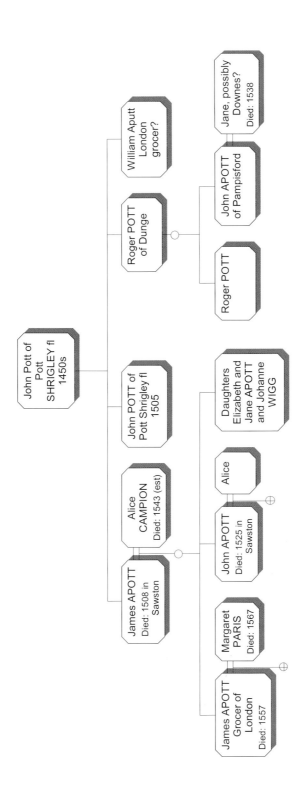

Early Apotts

Fortunately TF Teversham in *A History of the Village of Sawston*, published in 1947, did a remarkable job of cataloguing and commenting on local deeds and manorial documents that had survived in the Huddleston family papers and which are now in the Cambridgeshire Record Office. Sawston, just a few miles south of Cambridge, in the early modern period was in the saffron growing area around Saffron Walden, with a large acreage of common land supporting this activity and an animal husbandry oriented rural economy. There was relatively little freehold land outside the cluster of quite small manors in Sawston. Unfortunately document survival from these manors is poor and Sawston and adjacent villages are particularly hard to research back into the fifteenth century.

James Apott's 1508 will, made in April and proved in November, suggests that he may have been affluent, rather more so than his small land holdings would imply had they been his only source of income. He requested burial in Sawston church and left the usual godly bequests to the church. In addition he gave a close called Franklyns to the church wardens, one of the earliest of several charitable land bequests to the parish. This in itself implies a certain degree of affluence, since a modest monetary gift would have been more usual. Perhaps he was influenced by Geoffrey Downes's substantial endowment of the Pott Shrigley chapel. His eldest son and main heir was James who received £20 and John, the younger son, was to have £5. As there was no indication that they were under age, they were probably born in the 1480s. There were three daughters: Johanne or Joan who had married a Mr Wygg or Wigg, Elizabeth and Jane. They were to have 10 marks, £3 6s 8d and £3 6s 8d respectively. Had two of the daughters been named for Lady Ingoldesthorpe?

The sense that James was reasonably well-off is reinforced by his bequest to John Apott of Pampisford of James's lands that he held of the manors of Pampisford and Clovelly in Thripplow. If John were to die the lands would still go to Jane, which implies she mattered to James as much as his kinsman. John Apott of Pampisford is interesting. Obviously he was in some way under the wing of our James of Sawston. The assumption that he was a nephew would fit the circumstances of being given this leased or copyhold land which could easily have been passed to one of James's own sons. Without a will John's date of death is unknown. Jane died in 1538 when administration was granted to a John Holte of Sawston. Almost certainly he was related and, while Jane might have been a Holte girl, John Holte might have married another Downes daughter. The Holte family were previously of Sawston and headed up by William who had dealings with James Apott over James's Sawston messuage. Holtes, probably related, were also grocers in London. It would be perfectly natural for a brother-in-law to deal with an administration. In any event it is therefore certain that James Apott was not referring to his younger son John who died in 1525 married to an Alice, not Jane or Joan. John and Jane of Pampisford probably had sons William and Thomas, identified by the 1554 will of Thomas Potto butcher of Sawston. It is also possible that they may have had a son John who became John Apott (not Pott or Potto) of Babraham and London. However, on balance this John may have been the son of John Apott of Sawston. Without surviving wills for any of the Babraham line of Apotts/Potts, the precise linkages remain uncertain.

All the rest of James's lands and tenements were given to his wife Alice for her natural life. After her death they were to go to their son James, provided that he paid from the profits every three years £3 6s 8d each to Elizabeth and Jane. So, John the younger son apparently was left no land - a source of conflict to come.

The executors, supervisors and witnesses of James's will give us a strong clue to Alice's family and to James Apotts's status locally. Alice and son James were joined as executors by Edmund Campion a cleric (who held various livings in Essex and Cambridgeshire between 1498 and his death in 1536). The other supervisor (with Geoffrey Downes) was John Parys esquire. John Parys of Linton was one of the major gentry figures in the area at this time, with land also in Sawston and he may have been James junior's father-in-law or at least a close relative of his wife. The witnesses were John Sutton the vicar of Sawston, Robert Campion and Richard Campion. Richard was probably Alice's brother and Edmund and Robert their first cousins. The preponderance of Campions suggests that Alice must have been a Campion.[24] Most likely, in part because of the London connections, Alice was a daughter of Richard senior, rather than Robert senior.

William Campion, probably the brother of Richard junior and Alice, was to become Master of the Worshipful Company of Grocers in the 1520s. Several of his relatives, including his son William were in the company also. No doubt James Apott junior, the grocer, achieved success as a result of help and patronage from the Campions in the early decades of the sixteenth century. Perhaps under the auspices of William Campion, other Sawston linked families became involved as grocers in London. In 1480 William Gardener was admitted as apprentice of William Holte. Both were land-holding families in Sawston and many more Gardeners followed in the Grocers' Company. Indeed one might argue from the numbers alone that the Gardener/Gardiner and Campion families may have dominated the leadership of the Grocers' Company around the turn of the century. The young James Apott was in good and valuable company.

It would seem that James Apott senior's two sons may have fallen out over the family property in Sawston, since at some time between 1518 and 1529 John sued James in chancery for detention of deeds.[25] This was probably a genuine family squabble - John referred to James as his illegitimate elder brother, not something that would be admitted to in a collaborative action. However, the action may have simply been the easiest way of establishing title in the property before another deed could be written. It may even have been a precursor to the mortgage later referred to in John's will and which seems to date from shortly before his death in 1525. James, their father, when he died had been seized in his demesne as of fee in one tenement in Sawston. John argued that the property should have come to him as of right as the legitimate son. However he said that the charters and evidences had come into the hands of James Apott of London, who now pretended to the property.

The answer of his brother James has survived – badly torn and undated.[26] James related that the premises were held in fee simple by Robert Campyon, Thomas Campion, William Carter and others (clearly as feoffees) to the use of one John Glover otherwise called Bucher. Teversham showed that the 'Bocher' family was of long standing in Sawston and indeed were butchers in the early sixteenth century. For a certain sum Glover bargained and sold the tenement to James and John's father James Potte. The feoffees requested that Glover deliver estate of the premises to James the father and William Carter to the use of James and his heirs forever. James the father, William Carter and John Ward became seized in their demesne as of fee to the use of James but after this John Ward died. Here the document is illegible, but the premises passed to the other feoffees and were still to the use of James Apott the father and his heirs. Unfortunately none of these deeds and events was dated. The Wards were another family with Sawston and London grocery links. John Warde of nearby Stapleford, Cambridgeshire made his will in September 1503 which was proved in May 1504. He wanted to be buried in St Andrew Sawston and made his nephew John Warde his main heir. His two executors were 'Jefferey Downes of Babraham' and James Potte the elder of Sawston. His nephew may have been the John Warde of London who died in 1508 at the age of 17 or 18, the son of Thomas Warde of Agmondisham [Bucks].[27] He may also have been related to the John Warde, alderman and grocer of the City of London who died in 1501.[28] He included a legacy to Richard Hawkyns draper, which may well have connected him to Aleyn Lumner's family linked by marriage to the Hawkyns (see Chapter 2). The Stapleford Ward family were close friends of the Apotts and may have been related by marriage in some way (or another Downes girl marriage?). The 1503 will depicts James Apott senior as having a similar social standing to Geoffrey Downes, not simply a modest yeoman farmer.

James's chancery defence was that his father made his will leaving the property to his wife Alice for life and then to their son James, now the defendant, and his heirs. James the father died and the tenement accrued wholly to John Carter (not William Carter, but perhaps a son and heir was now feoffee) to the uses in the father's will. It seems that Alice, by sufferance, allowed the younger son John to use the premises and take the issues and profits from them for two years or more. But at this point, about 1510 or so if this was directly after James senior's death, James entered the premises and enfeoffed them to his own use through Thomas Gardener, John Rog__ [Rogers?] and James Hogan (of yet another Sawston family) who were at the time of the answer still trustees to the use of James and his heirs. James went on to say that he had various evidences and charters concerning the premises for the preservation of his inheritance. So, he argued, at no point had the premises descended to John.

His brother John seems to have remained a relatively minor husbandman farmer in Sawston. In his will, made in March 1525 and proved that year, John left two quarters of barley and two of saffron heads to James Campyon who may have been a son of Richard.[29] Given his first name, which was not used elsewhere in the Campion family, he may have been a godson of James Apott. This would reinforce the view that Alice was Richard's sister. With this extra level of concern for the Campion family, John Apott's wife, also called Alice, may also of course have been a Campion cousin and perhaps was the Alice who was one of the daughters of Thomas Campion (d 1502). To her, John left the use of the lands which he had of his brother James by mortgage deed which provided for payment to James of £3 in the next year and £2 for each of the subsequent four years. The will encouraged his family or friends to pay off the £60 principal of the loan and allowed whomever might do so the use of the land until the money was recovered from the profits.

After his wife's death all his lands were to pass to their son John. Unfortunately nothing definite has been discovered about him or their daughter Elizabeth. In a rental of 1561-63 John Pott or Pottes paid 26s 8d rent in Sawston and about £4 in Babraham. This John was probably John Apott of Babraham, probably the son of John Apott of Sawston. While this younger line is rather uncertain, fortunately the direct line can be tracked without any doubts.

James Apott's wife Alice lived to a good age. In 1513 she and Henry Clovell esq of Pampisford were fined in Sawston's Dale manor court for encroachment on manorial fields.[30] In 1516-17 she was admitted to lands in Dale manor. In 1519-20 and 1524-25 Alice Apott widow was referred to regarding Franklyn's croft. Coming before the death of her son John in 1525, the 1519-20 document confirms that she must have been Alice senior widow, not the wife of John. In 1541-42 Alice Potto (the spelling of the surname normally used for all family members locally by the mid-century) widow surrendered 3 messuages (Duntisyard, Monke's orchard and John Braddie's) and 16 acres held of the manor of Pyratt's and Dernford in Sawston. This was surrendered to John Campyon (again perhaps a son of Richard Campion and thus Alice's nephew). By this stage the reference could be to either Alice the elder or the younger. References to Alice stop around this time indicating that she probably died in about 1543, unfortunately not leaving a will and with no surviving court book entry which might have recorded her death.

James Apott junior, Citizen and Grocer

James and Alice's eldest son James became a substantial London grocer and was, as far as the records show, the first Apott or Pott to become a member of the Grocers' Company. In 1498 'Jamys' Pott was sworn in as apprentice to William Southworth for a 20s payment.[31] Normally he would have been admitted to the Company as a freeman about seven or eight years later. However there is no sign of this happening until an entry for James's admission in 1533, with no details of whether he was apprenticed. Perhaps there had been an oversight in the record-keeping in the early part of the century. Support for this comes from the number of admissions reported as simply 'during 1505-1512', without a specific year being given. James was probably admitted near the start of that period. Certainly he was working as a fully fledged grocer by about 1510. In the 1511-21 Book of Warden's Accounts of the Grocers' Company the 'bretherhedde money' of 2s each was paid in by a modest number of members who seemed to be involved in smaller group within the Company.[32] Among those names early on were Robert Campion, William Campion, William Campion junior and 'Jacobus' (James) Potte, probably in the year 1511 since the entry is at the front of the book. From their wills we know that Robert died in 1517 and William junior in 1519. Then, in July 1518, the brotherhood list of names paying 2s included Henry Lumnor, William Boleyn, William Campion and Jacobus Potte.

James was operating as a grocer in 1515-18, the date range for the action William Holt lodged against James Apott, citizen and grocer of London, for refusal to complete the sale of a messuage and land in Sawston, Foulmire, Pampisford and Babraham, partly paid for in saffron and partly in building and repairing the messuage.[33] The complainant said that the messuage and lands were all of Apott's lands in Sawston and nearby. Holt had leased them from Apott up to the previous year (no specific year was given) at which point Holt said Apott had agreed to sell them to him by bargain and sale for £200 to be paid in equal amounts at the City of London over 20 years: that is £5 at All Saints (1st November) and £5 at the Discovery of the Holy Cross (3rd May). If any payments were missed James would have the right to re-enter and enjoy the premises as if they had not been sold. Holt would agree to be bound in £40 for Apott's security and Apott would discharge Holt of the annual 40s which the property had to pay to Alice Apott for her life. Holt trusted Apott to prepare the indentures which the two of them would seal. On that basis Holt delivered to James in part payment and by agreement, one half pound of saffron at 8s the half pound and spent £5 in house building and repairs. Soon after, Holt, clutching his £5, came with his surety William Salston (Sawston) to London to be bound to Apott as agreed. However, James refused to make the bond and continued to refuse to convey the premises to Holt despite their verbal agreement.

It seems that Holt and Apott remained for quite some time at odds over whether the premises were sold to Holt or merely leased by him. Another action by Holt, this time in the court of the Star Chamber, showed how contentious such property matters could be and how close James Apott was to the Paris family of Linton.[34] Holt claimed again that Apott had sold him the premises (which were described in exactly the same manner as before). Now Philip Pareez [Paris] esq of Cambridgeshire wanted the property and was trying to force Holt out of it. He said that on 14th December 1527 Paris, James Apott, John Higham, one Cornett and others had ridden to the house armed with daggers, halberds and other arms. They had tried to take by force three horses, but Holt's wife stopped them and at that point Holt arrived on the scene. He refused to sell Paris the land and so Paris again told his servants to drive away the horses and to strike one of Holt's servants, which was done twice with a pitchfork. Paris himself struck the servant and, even though told by Holt to keep the King's peace, Paris also hit Holt's wife with a pitchfork. Clearly this accusation of riotous behaviour enabled Holt ready access to the Star Chamber court.

Philip Parys [Paris] answered that James Apott had been seized in the lands and had leased them to Holt at 40s a year, payable at Our Lady and Michaelmas.[35] At the time of the 'surmised' riot that lease had still not ended and the rent was 40s in arrears at Michaelmas 1527. Apott had sold the premises to Paris, not to Holt. Paris and his men had gone to the premises unarmed and peaceably to obtain the rent and when it was not forthcoming they intended to take three horses instead, as was lawful. Holt's wife refused to let them and was 'very importunate upon' Philip – presumably extremely rude. At which he pushed her away and gave her 'a little strype upon her fingers with his staff, by which she had no manner of harm'. He then went on to deny breaking in, using force or being armed.

How this ended is not known: Paris probably owned the property with Holt continuing as his tenant. Apart from the picture the action gives of the exciting episode, its value lies in showing that James Apott had effectively severed his ties to Sawston and was a London grocer through and through. The relationship to Paris is also very interesting. Holt's wording was absolutely precise: the named men were servants of Paris. This shows that even though Apott was a London grocer he was close to Paris. It may have simply been that he was there because he wanted to sell the land to Paris. But Apott was married to a Paris girl which would have created a closer relationship although exactly which part of the Paris family she came from is not clear. This action suggested the Paris line of Linton was the most likely, but as we shall see the related Paris family of Hitchin might be in the running.

James had quite a number of brushes with the court of chancery, using it as a speedy and fairly inexpensive means of enforcing trade agreements. Taken together these give some idea of the range of goods he was dealing in, the large transaction sizes showing that he was a wholesaler rather than (or as well as) a shopkeeper and also the risks associated with the grocery trade at the time. The number of bonds for trade debts shows that he was providing finance to enable smaller grocers to buy in bulk from him. It may well be that this financial side of the business was extremely lucrative - there are hints of very high rates of interest being charged for short term loans. All of these bills of complaint have to be treated with caution - they are one-sided and complainant or defendant could be lying through their teeth to protect their own interests.

An undated mid-century fragment of a debt bill showed that James Apott grocer of London sued William Nevell in the Six Clerks Office of chancery for a debt of £86 overdue on the purchase of 'vessels of oyle'.[36] In pleadings dated between 1538 and 1544, Richard Justice of Reading sued James 'a Pott' grocer of London over a bond given by Thomas Myrthe deceased for which the complainant was security and of which the terms were altered by the defendant without his knowledge.[37] This action showed that in May 1537, for £256, Apott had sold Myrthe 300 pieces of 'chamlette' (or chamlet, a cloth originally of camel's hair or a mix of wool and goat's hair but later a fine woollen or silk cloth). After a part payment, £233 was outstanding and had been loaned by Apott at the rate of 12% per annum. He appears to have extended the loan for extra years not in the original agreement or obligation. Justice was now complaining about the accumulated interest. Apott said Myrthe and his wife Elizabeth 'occupied the said chamlette for three years' and he was therefore, in about 1540, pursuing the surety for £233 plus interest.

Again in 1538-44 James's name appeared in chancery, albeit this time he was cited in a case in which a bond had been given to him by one of the parties. The surviving fragment says nothing more, but shows Apott engaged in handling trade debts.[38] More importantly, during 1538-44 Richard Grove another London grocer, sued James Apott and the sheriffs of London in an action over a debt.[39] Grove had borrowed £58 from Apott, for which deal Grove said that Robert Colte, another London grocer, had stood surety. Apott had pressed for repayment and Colte rather than Grove had paid Apott £56 in part payment from £60 which Grove had paid to

Colte. Grove did not know if the residue had been paid or not since Colte had taken to his house and refused to pay any of his creditors. Apott, 'a man of great substance', had commenced an action for debt against Grove in the sheriff's court and Grove wanted an order in chancery to stop him pursuing the debt. In this case 'Jamys' Apott's answer survives. In February 1535, he said, Richard Grove had bought from him £58 worth of pepper, cloves and sugar. The debt should have been paid a long time ago, but Apott repeatedly extended the repayment dates and even agreed to rebate £10 of the £58. Eventually he received just over £17 from Robert Colte, but Grove refused to pay any more and employed 'crafty delays'. He was now pursuing Grove in the sheriff's court for £53 - presumably including some interest on the original sum. Apott said he had no agreement with Colte regarding Grove's debts. A further action sheds light on Colte's circumstances and shows that either Apott or Grove might have been trying to take advantage of Colte's misfortune. During 1544-51 Robert Colte acted against James Apote grocer over a trade debt of some £116.[40] Colte was indebted to a number of creditors for great sums which he was unable to pay by reason of several great losses that he had suffered. Although he said that he had the King's pardon for his debts, two Frenchmen had him kept in prison in the counter (jail) in Broad Street. He hoped to be able to make an arrangement with his creditors, as we would say nowadays. Each would receive 8s in the pound and by implication the scheme would only work if all creditors agreed to the terms. Apott had already been paid £40 of the £116 with some £30 being offered on the residue. The bill of complaint said that Apott had initially agreed to the terms but had then changed his mind and refused. Colte hoped to force him to accept the terms offered. We do not know how this played out.

Another action showed that James Pottes and William Higby or Higbly had a creditor (the name has been torn away) imprisoned in Wood Street Counter (or Compter) for defaulting on a bond for £22 payable to them.[41] From the surviving scraps of this bill, it seems that the complainant was newly arrived in London from Herefordshire. No doubt to James this was irrelevant pleading - a trade debt was a debt due. In 1546 James Apott was sued in the court of requests by John Chandeler, a London draper, attempting to force Apott to have him released from The Fleet prison where he had been languishing for some months.[42] James had lent £100 in goods and money to Robert Handford who had involved Chandeler as security for the loan. Handford had defaulted on the repayment date but Apott agreed to let them have a further five months to repay since Handford was to be out of the country on business. But payment was not made and Apott went through due and proper process in the courts (recited in detail) and had Chandeler put in jail for the £100 due plus 20s costs. Chandeler pleaded that his wife and children were as sorrowful as he at the cruelty of Apott. He had used up all his money and substance and the imprisonment prevented him from recovering his former credit and trade. He argued that Handford was now back in London and should be made to pay for his own debts. Indeed between 1538 and 1544 Chandeler had pursued Handford directly in chancery over the Apott bond, presumably to no avail since this effort preceded the above appeal to the court of requests.[43] Though perfectly normal at the time, this action shows how imprisonment for debt, despite the relative flexibility of life at The Fleet, made it impossible for debtors to get credit and fully engage in trade. Without affluent family or friends Chandeler would have had no means of getting his liberty.

In the 1553-58 chancery papers is a short action by Edmund Redyng a London grocer who sued the mayor and sheriffs of London and James a Pott over a bond for £7, Apott having redeemed cloths of complaint laid in pledge and taken them into his own possession.[44] Redyng said he had lined up a purchase of 40 pieces of woollen cloth from Robert Semar at a price of £21 with a limited period to complete the deal. He needed money to do so and asked James 'a Pott' for a loan of the £21 for one month for which he would give him ten shillings interest (29% of the principal if he had paid this every month for a year - sounds like an early credit card bill!). James, with a neighbour, went to look at the cloth and then said it was not worth more than £18 or £19, but he would lend £21 if Redyng gave him a bond as surety for £7, as well as the 10s interest. James then bought the cloth and refused to part with it to Redyng. Instead he started proceedings against him in the sheriff's court for repayment of the £7 debt. Redyng said that he was but a poor man and Apott was a man of great substance. This action is typical of many of these trade issues. Apott may well not have been the bad guy here at all, with Redyng concocting a story to squirm out of an obligation.

James Apott, grocer: his will and estate

What more is known about where James lived and worked? In 1541 the London Subsidy Roll for Candlewick ward listed James Apott of the parish of St Clement Eastcheap as one of the petty collectors. He was shown as worth the huge sum of £800 and was to pay 20s in St Clement's parish.[45] A patent roll grant of February 1549 referred, in passing, to a messuage in the tenure of James Apottes in the parish of St Clement East Cheap.[46] This dwelling which does not appear amongst the properties owned later by the family, may have been rented. The parish register of St Clement Eastcheap however shows a burial of Jane Apott on 15th October 1543. She was probably James's unmarried sister Jane, mentioned in their father's will. She might have been living with her brother in London and her death would explain her absence from his will.

In addition, an action in the court of requests showed that James Apott held more property during his lifetime than can later be identified from his will and subsequent family IPMs.[47] He was certainly the one who built the family's property portfolio from his own trade profits. No doubt he, like many, was an opportunistic buyer at the time that many tenements came on the market after the dissolution of the monasteries. He was after all living and working very close to the belt of monasteries that ran down the western side of the city and several of the Potts properties would turn out to be ex-monastic premises. In 1544 he even acquired property in the north of England (see Chapter 3).

Between 1549 and 1553, Robert Beverlyes pursued him to complete a bargain and sale on the 'manor and lands of Grenesbury in Grenesbury Bedfordshire'. This would seem to be the small farm or manor of Greensbury, once Grymsbury, in Bolnhurst parish just north of Bedford.[48] The property had passed to a chantry of Pleshey in Essex and in 1521, by forfeiture from Edward Duke of Buckingham, to the crown. In 1549 Edward VI granted the capital messuage called Grymsbury to Edmund Clarke, Nicholas Vaux and Thomas Grendon. The first two seem to have been trustees for Grendon, who in his will made in 1549, left the property in tail successively to his sons Walter, Roger and Robert. He died in 1559. Presumably James Apott had secured a lease from Grendon. Beverlyes claimed that Apott had agreed to take 200 marks for the remaining term of the lease, which Beverlyes would pay after he had surveyed the property. He paid 'one grott' in part payment, carried out the survey and declared himself 'well pleased' with the result. He offered the 200 marks ahead of the due payment day, but Apott refused the money and refused to carry out the bargain and sale. This left Beverlyes without a house and farm to live in and in the meantime he had also lost the opportunity to take other good leases available to him. He sought £200 damages. This suit raises the interesting question of whether the Apott family was actively involved in property speculation as a sideline to the grocery business.

In his later years Mr James Apott sat in the Grocers' Court of Assistants. His regular attendance was recorded throughout the summer and autumn of 1556 with his last appearance in February 1557.[49] On 10th May 1557 the Court agreed that the £6 that Mr Apott had bequeathed 'to this mysterie' would pay for the Livery dinner held on Monday the 1st of May. We hope he had a good send off from his chums. The £6 gift was not included in his will which he had made a month before his last attendance. The will was an unusual one which has proved very helpful in understanding the structure of the family.[50]

It may not have been proved, possibly because of the extensive corrections throughout it. These might have been made at the time of first drafting on 13th January 1557 or over the next few weeks. James was buried in early March. Probably born about 1480, he was by now an old man in his mid-70s and was sick in body. His goods, chattels, plate, ready money and debts were to be divided into three. The first third went to his wife Margaret, 'according to the laudable use and custom of the City of London', in full satisfaction of her portion. Margaret must have been Margaret Paris, given the reference in his will to his wife's brother John Paris. The second part went to his two children Roger Apott and Anne Parker. The third went to the performance of his will. His wife was to have her jewels and apparel over and above her third.

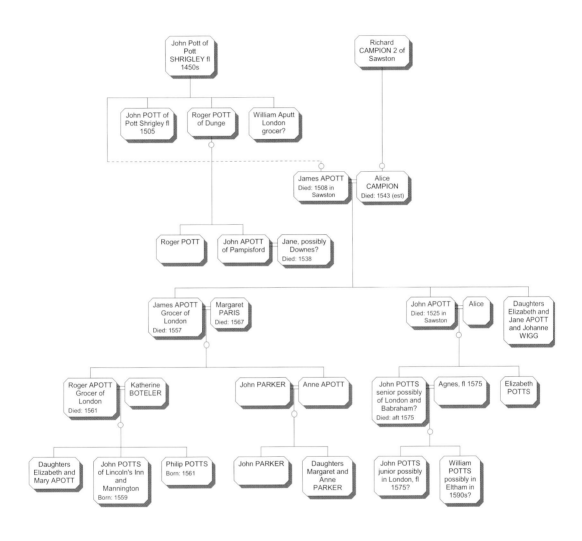

The Apott Family

His various charitable bequests and many of his other legacies were first drafted at quite generous levels and then were reduced. For example the Universities of Oxford and Cambridge were to get £50, which was amended to £30, then £20 and finally ended up as £10. It would seem he took stock of his initial largesse and realised he could not afford such generosity. No doubt, apart from genuine altruism for the protection of their soul, there was great social pressure among the merchant class of the time to outdo each other in generosity in their wills as a mark of their relative standing. Other charitable gifts included:

> ~~£50 or £40~~ to Christ Church Hospital and St Thomas Hospital Southwark (in fact with no final amount entered)

> The 'prisoners of Newgate Ludgate the two counters of London the King's bench and the Marshalsea in Southwark' were to get a total of £70 (reduced to £10)

> The mending of the highways within 20 miles of London £50 (reduced to £10)

> 20 marks for 40 poor maidens' marriages

> To 40 poor people 40 gowns at his executors' discretion

> Poor of Hitchin Hertfordshire ~~£5~~ (reduced to 40s). (This is an important first clue to the strong connection to Hertfordshire and the emotional rating of Hitchin as at least as important to him as Sawston)

> Poor of Sawston Cambridgeshire ~~£5~~ (reduced to 40s)

> Poor of Pawnsforth [Pampisford] ~~£4~~ (reduced to 30s)

> ~~'to every poor householder dwelling in the parish of St Peter in Cornhill 12 pence'~~ (not amended)

> ~~8s to every one of his poor tenants in St Bartholomew the Little in the ward of Broadstreet~~ (not amended)

While he did not give any more information about the Hitchin connection, he or his wife's family may at one time have held property there of some substance. Later Potts IPMs identify a residual holding of a tiny messuage in Bancroft Street. It was held from the Queen as of her Manor of Hitchin in common socage by fealty at an annual rent of 17d and valued at 5s a year. The manorial records and surveys in Hitchin show this property in Potts hands until about 1620.[51] It was in the old main street of Hitchin and adjacent to larger houses of the more substantial tenants, notably the farmhouse of John Mattocke. George Graveley gent also lived in Bancroft Street in 1591. But from the relative rental levels the Potts property was simply a very small cottage, probably with a poor tenant living in it - perhaps an old family retainer? Although the Hitchin property was not mentioned by James, his will was very concerned with the poor there and it is probable he already held this property. It remains a mystery as to why the family had it and why James felt such a strong connection to Hitchin. The property may have come in some way from the Paris family of Hitchin. It was next but one to a house that by the 1560s was in the hands of Robert and his wife Elizabeth who had children baptised in Hitchin in the 1560s. To this house 50 acres or more of land was attached, showing that this Paris family was of some substance. The 1545 Hertfordshire subsidy roll showed that in Hitchin there were three Paris or Parys family members but no Potts.[52] The arms born by the Paris family in Hitchin by the 1570s had the same main device (three unicorns' heads) as the Linton family, showing a close connection.[53] Beyond that the Hitchin story remains unsolved.

The will however continues giving family details. James's surviving sister, Johann Wygg, was to have a black gown. There was a Wigg or Wygg grocer in London with links to the Wiggs of Mentmore in Bucks, which may well be the right family.[54] Albeit subsequently crossed out, he left '£5 to John Paris my wife's brother'. This is the only clue to Margaret's family background (see below). He crossed out a bequest to Arthur Holte - of the family that had Sawston connections as well as history in court against Apott.[55] James gave gowns to his daughter Anne who was married to John Parker, also a grocer. The Parkers had a son John and a daughter Margaret, both under 21 and each left £20 on coming of age. John Parker had a servant Thomas Parker (perhaps a younger brother or nephew) and an apprentice John Jackson who was left 40s. James's own apprentice John Weston was left £6 13s 4d.

Three maid servants were next provided for. Margaret Paris was to get £10 on marriage providing it was with the consent of James's wife to whom she was presumably related. Katherine Browne (possibly a Parker relation) and Dionise were to receive 20s each. Margaret Bedall who was to receive £3 was probably also a senior servant who was to remain with the family and Robert Flussby, Roger's servant, was to have 20s. James's son Roger appeared at this date to have just one child, Elizabeth who was left £30 for when she reached 21 years or married if earlier. Roger and the widowed Margaret were named joint executors and he was to have the real estate after her death. Two clusters of property were specifically mentioned: lands tenements and cottages in West Smithfield and Tremel Street in the parish of St Sepulchre without Newgate; and a messuage with shops cellars and solars in St Bartholomew the Little. However, as is known from later IPMs, this was not the whole tally of James's properties. Some had already been passed on by deed to Roger.

The witnesses to James's will may indicate a circle of friends - Edward Atkynson merchant taylor, John Haustand grocer and Giles Swykson skinner as well as Thomas Atkynson notary public. The latter had probably patiently sat through the dictation of the will, writing and correcting away - James's original signature was poorly written and certainly not the fairly neat hand of the writer of the will itself. Perhaps he was very sick and these were effectively deathbed corrections. A useful reference in his son-in-law's will revealed where James was buried. John Parker, grocer of London in his will, made in April 1570 and proved in March 1572, asked to be buried in the south hill of St Peter Cornhill as near the grave of his mother- in-law that was Mistress Pott, as may be convenient.[56] The family burials there were as follows:

> The burying of Maister Jeames Apot 7th March 1557

> The burying of Misteris Pott widow 19th August 1567. (A later IPM recorded that Margaret died in Islington where she then lived with her deceased son's wife Katherine)

> John Parker buried 26th April 1572

> Mrs Anne Parker widow of Mr John Parker grocer buried in the south chapel 10th September 1581

And in 1606-10 a John Parker was churchwarden there - quite possibly their son.

The Paris family

All that can be discovered about James Apott's wife Margaret Paris, is the reference in his will to her brother John Paris.[57] There are several lines of the family to which she could have belonged. Paris wills for Cambridgeshire, London and Hertfordshire do not particularly help. Despite there being evidence for Paris in London, the two main contenders are the most substantial family line of Linton in Cambridgeshire and the Hitchin family.

The will of Robert Paris esq of Little Linton near Sawston was made in 1503 and proved in 1505.[58] He had a brother William and a sister 'Dame Emma'. William's 1520 will made clear that Emma Paris was one of the nuns of 'Hikelton' (the Cluniac Priory of Hickleton near Doncaster).[59] Robert's son Thomas was already dead by 1503 and his son and heir was John, presumably the John named in Dame Joan Ingoldesthorpe's will. Other than John's wife Margaret and Thomas's widow Eleanor, Robert mentioned no daughters in his will. John Paris married Margaret, one of the two daughters and heiresses of Thomas and Margaret Huntingdon of Sawston.[60] John and Margaret had son and heir Philip Paris (later Sir Philip) and second son William, both mentioned in John's will of 1517.[61] William Paris married Elizabeth Coningsby and his sister Joan married Thomas Cotton of Cottington. Another sister Margaret Paris was in their father's 1517 will and she could be a strong candidate to be James Apott's wife. However, if she was, her father John made no mention in his will of son John, her brother. This might be explained if John Paris junior was a cleric and not able to inherit any significant property. John senior's uncle William's will of 1520, among small legacies to family members, left a ring to 'Maister' (Magister, a cleric) John Paris. He does not seem to slot into the family tree other than as a son of John.[62] However, despite much research, this remains a theory.

The 1559 will of Sir Philip Paris of Linton provided no extra clues.[63] Pedigrees for the family are of dubious reliability and are inconsistent even on the sons in the main line.[64]

Surprisingly, given the proximity to Sawston and the involvement of James Apott and Philip Paris over the Apott property in Sawston, none of these Linton Paris wills included any mention of the Apotts. However the London and Hitchin Paris families similarly provided no results for Margaret.[65]

Thomas Paris of Hitchin Hertfordshire made his will and it was proved in the summer of 1518.[66] By his wife Agnes he had a son John, his executor, and other sons Thomas, Richard, Lawrence and Edward. He mentioned his daughters Johanne and Agnes, but there was no mention of a Margaret. If by then Margaret was married to Apott, her father may have not included her in his will. A number of other Paris wills from Hitchin survive but add nothing. The Paris family continued here through most of the century. The Robert Paris who held the large house in Bancroft Street in the 1560s may well have been the grandson named as heir to Sir Philip Paris of Linton in his will. Descriptions of the armorial bearings of the Paris family show that the Linton and Hitchin lines by the late sixteenth century shared arms distinctively based on three leopards' heads but how they were linked is not recorded. However, despite James Apott having a small messuage there and charitable ties to the parish, no direct link between him and his wife to the Hitchin Paris family has been made.

So the Linton line, with Sir Philip Paris as a brother-in-law seems the most likely. If so, this would produce one or two rather interesting connections. Sir Philip's second wife was Anne Eden, the widow of Robert Spring of Lavenham in Suffolk.[67] One of Robert's sisters, Rose, married Edmund Lumner of Mannington as we shall see. Sir Philip was actively involved in work on the dissolution of religious houses and as a result was no doubt able to influence the ensuing land grants of the properties to lay owners.[68] Was Sir Philip the source for the Apotts ex-monastic property? As a witness in 1551, then aged 59, at the trial of Stephen Gardiner Bishop of Winchester, Philip was shown to be a long serving servant of the Bishop.[69] He and his son had property leases from the Bishop, who also left Paris a small legacy in his will.[70] James Apott was certainly closely linked to him, even if he was not his brother-in-law.

Although the details of James's wife have proved hard to pin down, his son Roger, who thanks to his father was also a Grocer, was easier to track. After James's death there do not seem to be any chancery actions involving his son Roger and the grocery business. Perhaps James had always been the driving force both as a grocer and in lending money aggressively against riskier trade deals. James, who lived to his 70s, was certainly a character to be reckoned with and, not for the last time in the Potts family, the father overshadowed his son and heir.

Chapter 2

Buy One Get One Free: Roger Apott, Grocer

Roger Apott married well, his wife Katherine Boteler was of a good family; they had John their heir; Katherine married again and moved back briefly to Hertfordshire; John Potts gent was granted armorial status.

Roger, the only son of James and Margaret, was admitted to the Grocers' Company in 1547, as the son of James Apott and as a freeman of London. This date would indicate his birth in the early 1520s. Nothing else is recorded about his early life until he married. From later IPMs it appears that his father settled properties on him in 1552, perhaps indicating an approximate date of the wedding. A possible baptism of his eldest daughter Elizabeth (an Elizabeth Pott is given at St Michael Cornhill in January 1552) would add further support.[1] Four of his children are known to have survived infancy: the two girls Elizabeth and Mary (or Margaret) seem to have been the eldest. Margaret was still alive and unmarried in 1577 but whether Elizabeth had married or died by then is unknown. John Potts, the heir, was born in August 1559 and his younger brother Philip was probably born only shortly before his father died (or maybe posthumously).

Roger's wife was Katherine Boteler, daughter of Sir Philip Boteler of Woodhall in Watton-at-Stone in Hertfordshire. How did Roger and Katherine meet? The match was a good one for Roger and would help pave the way to the family's later armorial status. Apart from the tenuous link to Hertfordshire via the Hitchin property there was no obvious connection between Roger or his father and the Botelers of Hertfordshire. Sir William Butler - Boteler is also spelt Butler as one variation - grocer and alderman of London who was a friend of James Apott, would have been a possible link but unfortunately seems not to have been related to Katherine. Perhaps the explanation lay in the Paris puzzle.

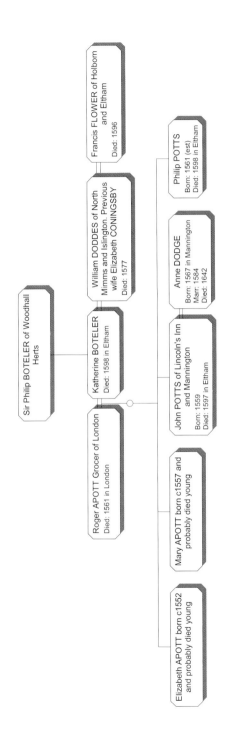

Family of Roger Apott

Roger outlived his father by only a few years, leaving Katherine with four young children to look after. He may well have lived rather in the shadow of his entrepreneurial father. Unlike James he did not appear in chancery, even for recovery of debts. Not a bad thing perhaps, but it might imply that he was not particularly adventurous as a grocer. Neither did he add very much to the property portfolio built up by his father. Although in 1559 shortly before his death, he is shown as of St Clement Danes parish, he may have spent as much time in Hertfordshire as London.[2] Roger Apott 'gent of London' made his will in July 1557 and it was proved in August 1561.[3] After the London custom, his personal estate including plate and household stuff after funeral charges and debts was to be split into three equal parts. The first third went to Katherine his wife. The next went to Elizabeth his daughter and any other child that should be in his wife's womb at the time of his decease. If more than one child they should split the bequest equally at the age of 21 or when married if earlier.

If all his children died their share was to go to the Worshipful Company of Grocers to build up a perpetual free school in the City of London. This reflected the well-known bias of the Grocers towards charitable support for education. The final third was to go to Katherine his sole executrix to pay his legacies. Among these, continuing the educational theme, was 20s for a ring to Mr Moore Schoolmaster of Ratcliffe and a requirement for Katherine to pay the substantial sum of £15 per year to the Grocers' Company for their school. Ratcliffe or Radcliffe, near Limehouse, was a free school for 60 poor men's children and 14 almshouses founded by Avice the wife of Nicholas Gibson grocer. Gibson, a contemporary of Roger's father, was admitted to the Grocers' Company in 1505-12, became Warden in 1527 and London's sheriff in 1539 (indicating that he might have been tipped to become Lord Mayor).[4]

Roger left 40s to poor householders of Hitchin, Hertfordshire. This showed again the strong family connection to Hertfordshire. By comparison he left 30s to the poor of Sawston and only 20s to the poor of wherever he was buried - no doubt expecting that to be somewhere in London. The gift to Sawston poor implies some continuing connection with his grandfather's home village. Perhaps he retained trading links - perhaps sourcing saffron there - and maybe as a boy he had been a regular visitor to see his long-lived grandmother. Whatever the reason it is clear that he retained the family tie and obligation to Sawston, perhaps encouraged by the continued presence of John Apott of Babraham in London. He also left a small bequest in traditional manner to the poor prisoners in London and its suburbs. Again quite typical of the period he left 13s 4d to the four houses erected in the City of London for the relief of the poor: Christ Church, St Mary Spitel, Bridewell and St Thomas Spitel in Southwark. He also left 20s to his poor tenants.

To Margaret Apott, his mother, Roger left £40 and a black gown 'price 15s the yard'. Minor bequests included 40s to George Butler his godson - more on the Boteler or Butler family shortly - and 40s to Mr John Michael of Codycote Herts for a gold ring with a death's head on it. The Michell family of Codicote was a well-connected one locally at this time.[5] Roger's mother's servant Margaret Paris was to have 13s 4d and his own servant John Weston was to have the same. As his father's apprentice we should probably assume that John Weston was important to Roger's grocery business and may have run it for him. His other men servants were to have a black coat worth 10s and the women a black gown only. Family ties, apart from the Boteler/Butler and Paris ones, were shown by giving his sister Anne Parker a black gown and his nephew and godson John Parker a small bequest. Similarly he mentioned his cousin John Apott of Babraham Cambridgeshire. Mr Thomas Mariot was made supervisor of the will and given 40s and a black gown for his trouble. Roger was more thorough than his father in describing his real estate, but even so it was a brief version compared to that in his later IPM. First he provided for his mother to continue to enjoy his lands messuage gardens and stables in St Sepulchre London, which she had held from July 1557, until her death. Katherine was allowed £40 provided she released her title to the property in favour of his mother after whose death she would inherit. All of the rest of his real estate was left immediately to Katherine for life and then to Roger's rightful heir, which of course would be his oldest surviving son. He listed London lands and messuages in the parishes of St Bartholomew, St Andrew Holborn and St Botolph without Bishopsgate. He also noted his three acre close in Lewisham and his messuage and land in Bancroft Street Hitchin. The estate is described in more detail in the next chapter.

Roger's will did not name his wife nor had he included his later children's names. Fortunately his mother's will gave more detail. Having outlived her husband and son, Margaret Apott made her will in November 1565 and it was proved on 27th August 1567.[6] She was a 'widow of London, late the wife of James Apott while he lived of London grocer', near to whom she asked to be buried. She left 20s to the Christ's Hospital. To Elizabeth and Mary Apott, daughters of her late son Roger Apott, she gave two of her silver pots but her grandsons were not mentioned. She left 6s 8d each to her maid servants. The residue was left to her joint executors her son-in-law John Parker of London grocer and to her daughter his wife Anne. The witnesses included John Edwardes draper of London.

Roger Apott and Katherine Boteler

Roger Apott's wife Katherine Boteler was far more interesting than her husband.[7] Her father Sir Philip Boteler (born by 1493, died in 1549) was the first son of John Boteler by Dorothy Tyrell of Gipping and was married to Elizabeth Drury. He was an MP in 1529, the year he was knighted, and in 1539 and held a variety of Hertfordshire roles during his life, including being sheriff of both Hertfordshire and Essex. His will, made in 1546, did not dwell on all of his many children but focused on his eldest son John. His two married and three unmarried daughters were also mentioned.[8] Anne and Dorothy, presumably married, only received a cup worth five marks each. Elizabeth, Mary and Katherine were each to have 200 marks 'towards their advancement of marriage' as long as they married with their mother and eldest brother's approval.

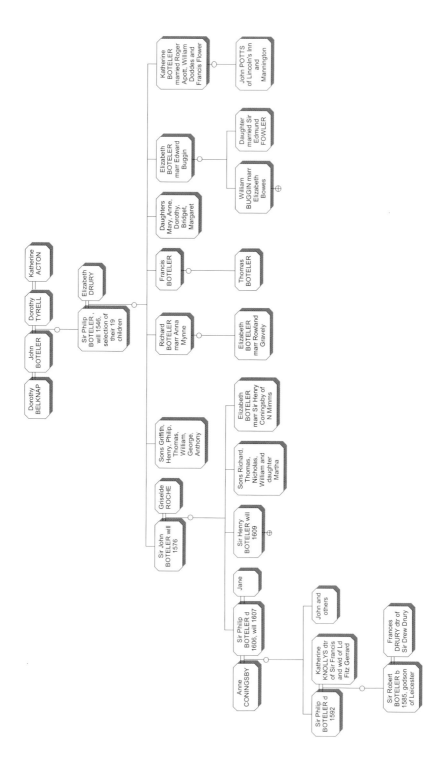

Boteler family tree

Katherine's mother was Elizabeth the daughter of Sir Robert Drury of Hawstead in Suffolk, just south of Bury St Edmunds. She had at least 12 sons and 7 daughters, many of whom died young.[9] Katherine's sister Anne married Leonard Hide esq, Dorothy married Anthony Brown of Rutland, Mary married John Harpham and Elizabeth married first, John Gale gent of London and then, Edward Buggin.[10] The Drury family link remained of importance to Katherine. Her mother's brother, Sir Robert Drury junior, had as his third surviving son Sir Drue Drury of Lyndsted in Kent, Gentleman Usher to the Privy Council of Queen Elizabeth and, with Sir Amyas Paulet, one of the keepers of Mary Queen of Scots. Before he died in 1617 at the age of 85, he had married first a Calthorpe girl related to the Boleyns and the Queen, and second Katherine Finch by whom he had children. One of his daughters, Frances, married Sir Robert Boteler of Watton, Katherine's great-great-nephew. Sir Robert's grandfather, Sir Philip, seems to have been a favourite nephew of Katherine.[11] Sir Robert's father, also Sir Philip, was married to Katherine the daughter of Sir Francis Knollys. Cecilia Knollys her sister was Maid of Honour to the Queen and another sister Elizabeth married Sir Thomas Leighton. This produced strong court connections for the whole family.

From this a family linkage between the Potts family and the Lumners of Mannington also emerged and may be one reason Katherine's son, John Potts came to know the Lumners and Dodges of Mannington. Certainly his mother and her family were very close to those involved at court. Through Sir Thomas Leighton, the Lumners of Mannington had similar connections. The Potts and Lumner families must have known each other during the 1560s and 1570s, expanding the grocery trade links that had existed at the start of the century. They may even have been friends.

Katherine's eldest brother and the next head of the family was Sir John Boteler who spent most of his life as a leading county landowner and office holder. He was an MP once in 1553. He died in February 1576 leaving a will that provided considerable detail on his family, but unfortunately only referred to his brothers and sisters collectively.[12] Katherine Boteler had five other brothers who survived to maturity: George, Anthony, Richard, Francis and William. Her particular favourite, from an affectionate mention in her will of which he was executor, appears to have been Richard of Stapleford, Hertfordshire who outlived her, dying in 1614. His wife was Anna Mynne of Hertingfordbury and their only child Elizabeth married Rowland Graveley of Graveley and Hitchin.

Katherine had probably been born either in the last group of siblings, in 1535, or in one of the apparent gaps earlier in her mother's almost continuous production, in 1521-23 or 1532-33. She was probably aged between 15 and 17 when she married Roger. Despite her family's status, as a younger daughter her marriage expectations would not have been particularly high. Katherine had her own ambitions.

When Roger Apott died in August 1561, Katherine was left with four children to bring up. The children seem to have lived in some combination of their own London property, a house in Islington and one of the Boteler Hertfordshire homes. Soon after her husband's death Katherine remarried to one William Doddes. They lived with the children and her Apott mother-in-law in Islington. Roger's IPM was not held until six years after his death and seems to have been triggered by his mother's death rather than his own. Again, this implies that he was not a high profile individual:

> And they say that Roger died 10th August 3 Elizabeth [1561] and that John Apott the son and heir of Roger is 8 years old at the Feast of St Bartholomew the Apostle last past [24th August 1567].
>
> And that Katherine late wife of Roger is in full life at Islyngton and that Katherine and William Doddes her now husband have received the issues and profits from the date of the death of Roger. And that from his death to 16th August last which day Margaret died at Islyngton [she was buried on 19th August 1567] and from Margaret's death, the profits go to Katherine and William, all by right of wife and guardianship of John.[13]

Katherine and William Doddes

While the sequence of Potts homes remains unclear, John Apott was surrounded by people of substance and influence from his mother's family and connections. Like the Botelers, her second husband William Doddes also had strong links to Hertfordshire. William Doddes's early life and family background have proved impossible to identify with certainty. The Dodds or Doddes name cropped up regularly among trading families in London and elsewhere. For example there were vintners of that name in London around 1530.[14] William's first known appearance was when he married the widow of John Coningsby and lived at the Coningsby seat in North Mimms, Hertfordshire.

John Coningsby had married Elizabeth Frowick daughter and co-heir of Henry Frowick of Oldfold and North Mimms and by 1529-30 they held the whole of the manor of North Mimms. They were clearly closely linked to the Botelers. Their eldest son Sir Henry married Elizabeth the daughter of Sir John Boteler (Katherine's brother). Their daughter Anne married Sir John's eldest son Sir Philip Boteler. John Coningsby made his will in 1543 but it is not known exactly when he died and the will does not appear to have been finally proved until 1554.[15] He may have died in 1547 as he was the first of two sheriffs of Hertfordshire that year, implying that he died while in post. Also a chancery document of between January 1548 and January 1549 included a passing reference to Elizabeth being a widow and as yet not remarried.[16]

Coningsby left his wife a life interest in North Mimms manor, conditional on paying their daughters' portions. Shortly after his death Elizabeth married William Doddes.[17] In the autumn of 1551 'William Doddys esq' and Elizabeth his wife were involved in a South Mimms property transaction and a second Feet of Fines entry for William and Elizabeth appeared in 1557.[18] W Berry in his *Pedigrees of Hertfordshire Families* gave William Dodd as being originally of North Mimms, but this may simply be a reflection of his status after marrying Elizabeth. The pardon roll of January 1 Elizabeth [1559] showed William Doddes of North Mimms and also as late of Kings Langley, Herts which may be another possible place of origin.[19] He also featured regularly in roles as a commissioner - such as in 1562, 1564 and 1568 and subsequently - and had also been mentioned in a patent roll entry in 1557. In these and in his role as sheriff he was clearly one of the leading group of Hertfordshire men. The sheriffs' list for the county shows particularly how dominant the Botelers and Coningsbys were: 1556 Sir John Boteler, 1569 Henry Coningsby (John and Elizabeth's eldest son and heir), 1570 William Doddes esq, 1578 Philip Boteler esq, 1582 Henry Coningsby esq, 1596 Ralph Coningsby.

William and Elizabeth were soon in chancery where they were involved in an action regarding the parsonage of North Mimms once held by the Prior of Charterhouse London.[20] In 1557 they were involved in sorting out the affairs of Robert Wrothe of Enfield who had died making his wife Jane (possibly a Coningsby by birth) and John Coningsby executors of his will.[21] The Wroth family also came into Callard property in Islington, which in due course gives another link of these London and Hertfordshire families to Mannington. Elizabeth had ended up responsible for Robert's affairs which her relations had not yet administered.[22] In 1557 they appear to be granted the North Mimms property for life, by Henry Coningsby esq.[23] With no early North Mimms registers surviving and no will found, Elizabeth's date of death is unknown but William must have married Katherine Apott within a year or so of Roger's death in August 1561. At Easter 1563 William and 'Catherine his wife' acquired the manor of 'Wyllyottes' or Wylottes and premises in South Mimms and Monken Hadley.[24]

William Doddes was one of the subsidy commissioners for Hertfordshire in 1566-67 and headed the assessment list, paying the most, for North Mimms. Interestingly this coincides roughly with the time when the Apott IPM recorded William and Katherine as being married and living in Islington. This would imply they used North Mimms (where William apparently had a life interest from the 1557-58 deed) as well as a town house in Islington.[25]

William Doddes esq of North Mimms died in 1577 leaving a will made in February that year.[26] Proved the following month, it included minor bequests to the parish church and poor and to his brother Robert Doddes. He also left £20 each at their marriage day to John Apott, Philip Apott and Margaret Apott his wife's children. Katherine's daughter Elizabeth may have already married or more likely may have died by this date. Interestingly as late as this the Apott name was used, although the very next year John signed in as Pott, dropping the A, at Lincoln's Inn and styled himself as of Hertfordshire, not London or Islington. William also made small bequests to his nephew Bartholomew Doddes (presumably Robert's son). He was also, specifically only from 1585, to have a messuage in North Mimms that Doddes had acquired from Edmond Darde. Katherine was to have the residue as executrix and also was given one year's interest in his manor of North Mimms after his death - presumably the earlier settlement on him had allowed for his estate to have the profits for a year after death to pay legacies. In her own right and to her heirs, Katherine was to have the manors of Mordannte als Mordens and Blackwell Hall in Great Chesham, Bucks which Doddes had purchased from John Cheyney esq and Henry his son. His brothers-in-law Richard Butler esq and Edward Buggin gent were to help Katherine as supervisors of the will and were to have a silver cup each. This underlines the close ties between the Potts, Boteler and Buggin families.

John Potts and the Grant of Arms

The young John Potts grew up under the influence of William Doddes and in a respected household that was fully engaged in local administration in Hertfordshire. While his origins were in London and in the grocery trade, he grew up in a landed county family and this no doubt set his expectations in life. John Potte[s] of Hertfordshire was admitted to Lincoln's Inn on 9th May 1578. His brother Philip Pott of Herts was admitted from Furnival's Inn on 1st April 1582. *The Black Books of Lincoln's Inn* show that on 16th November 1581 'Mr Potts junior' (an unrelated Thomas Potts of Bedfordshire had been admitted in 1567 and presumably was seen as the senior Potts) was appointed Steward of Christmas - he was to organise the Inn's Christmas dinner. On 25th November 1586 there was a note that John Pottes was among those to be called to the bar next term. On 30th January 1592 one of the stewards of the Readers' Dinner was Mr Pottes - probably John rather than Philip. On 30th April 1592, unusually commenting on a dinner, Mr Pottes was noted as having 'very liberally for his part performed the charge of the Readers' Dinner last past'. The same entry referred to him as an Utter Barrister. These entries imply that in the early 1590s John Potts was a practising lawyer, rather than merely a gentleman who had attended Lincoln's Inn simply as part of his general education. The possibility of course exists that it was his brother Philip who was the practising lawyer. John Potts's friend and cousin Mr [William] Buggin was one of the stewards of the Readers' Dinner for 1593-94, again showing that he too was a practising lawyer.[27]

In 1583 John Pott of Lincoln's Inn, son of Roger, was granted the family's first coat of arms thereby achieving a measure of public respect for his status.[28] His choice of arms adds another possibility for the family's earliest origins. Burke's *Extinct and Dormant Baronetcies* gave the Potts arms as: Azure two bars, and over all a bend or. Other sources sometimes give the horizontal bars as 'or' and the diagonal band as 'sable'.[29] The notes of the original grant show that both the diagonal bend and the horizontal bars were in gold on a blue background.[30] The arms were of a simple design and could not draw directly on the devices of the Boteler or Paris families since he was not of the male line of either. However, his choice of a leopard's head with a gold collar for his crest may have been prompted by the leopards of the Paris shield. When applying for a grant Potts probably provided the College of Heralds with the short family pedigree that remains evident in the early Norfolk Visitations. Proof was normally required that the family had been gentlemen for at least three generations. John had been educated as a lawyer; Roger had been styled gent and James had been in a London Company. However, the entry for his grant only recorded his father Roger, while in the Visitations his grandfather (or at least an ancestor) was shown as Sir William Pot.

The latter of course was certainly not true at least as far back as the Sawston generations. Indeed there is no evidence that a knight of that name ever existed in England and, if he had done, presumably his arms would have continued in his family. Perhaps John Potts created a story about his ancestors to justify his status and right to apply for arms. Why Sir William Pot and why the fairly simple design?[31] Besides a simple bare-faced lie, there could be two possible explanations of the inclusion of dodgy grandfather or earlier ancestor. Could John Potts (or the heralds) have been using word-play? In the late fifteenth century there is one scrap of a chancery document that seems to indicate there might have been a London priest called William Potts who may have been in John's line. He would no doubt have had the honorific 'Sir' (for qualified priests) as was common at the time and, since many lower level priests married and had children, he may have been the claimed or pretended 'Sir William Pot'. Probably unrelated but to illustrate the point, a 'Syr William Apott', curate of Nuthurst in Sussex, was witness to one Nicholas Hill's will in 1555.[32] Was he the stimulus for the idea?

The second possibility is more complex but has the virtue of providing a 'Sir William' and a not dissimilar coat of arms. In addition it is based on a Norman-French family background - always good for those trying to establish a long pedigree. While the following facts are all correct, the interpretation is entirely guesswork. All that would be required would be for the well-educated John Potts to have a little knowledge of French current affairs and a smattering of history. Or, perhaps, the College of Arms may have proposed the idea.[33] In 1578 Guillaume Pot de Rhodes was made a Chevalier or Knight in France. He was Provost and Master of Ceremonies at the foundation that year of the Ordre du Saint-Esprit. He served from 1585 as Grand Master of Ceremonies at the court of Henri III until his death in 1603. His shield was a simple design based on a gold background with a single blue band across the middle and a diagonal bar. The Potts arms were in a sense a modest evolution of this basic coat, with two horizontal bands and the colours reversed. These arms had been in the French Pot family for many generations. This was a famous senior Burgundian family with strong court connections, best known today for the glorious tomb of Sir Philippe Pot who died in 1493. Pictures of the tomb (now in the Louvre Museum in Paris) and its copious armorial decorations can be viewed on the internet.

In the fourteenth century, Guillaume Pot had been a well-known mercenary associated with the Count de Nevers. In 1403 Sir Régnier Pot the steward of the then Count acquired the Chateau de la Roche, near Beaune in Burgundy, and he and his grandson Philippe made major improvements to the castle, which became renamed Chateau de la Rochepot after the family. In between these two famous knights of the order of the Golden Fleece (Philippe also became Grand Senechal of Burgundy) was Jacques Pot who seems to have been an unremarkable member of the family.

Did our John Potts simply 'borrow' this family because of its name and invent his Sir William stimulated by his namesake in France? Or was there any evidence that our Apotts were descended from a junior line of this famous French family? This is doubtful but at very least John Potts tapped into this rich heritage. Whatever the basis for the heraldic device, John Potts had his grant of arms, reinforcing his social status. In 1584 he was to consolidate this by marrying and acquiring Mannington as his country seat. But would it be fair to include him as one of the targets of this diatribe of 1600?

> It cannot be denied but the Common people are very rich ... the gentlemen, which were wont to addict themselves to the warres and nowe for the most part growen to become good husbandes and knowe well how to improve their lands ... the yeomanry of England is decayed and become servants to the gentlemen ... I knowe many Yeomen in divers Provences in England which are able to despend betwixt 3 or 5 hundred pound yeerly by theire lands and leases and some twise and some thrise as much; but my yonge masters the sonnes of such, not contented with their states of the fathers to be counted yeoman ... But must ski into his velvett breches and silken dublett and getting to be admitted into some Inn of Court of Chancery, must ever thinke skorne to be called any other than gentleman ... a fyne daughter or 2 to be married after with 1000 pounds to some Covetouse Mongrell. Of these yeomen of the richest sort are accounted to be about 10,000 in Contry Villages besides Cittisens.[34]

Chapter 3

Buy to Let: Potts Properties In London

The family became London landlords after James Apott bought up former monastic properties; the Holborn houses were leased to Jasper Fisher. Roger Apott added to the portfolio and chancery actions ensued.

Writers on the Potts family have noted in passing that they owned a number of properties in and around London. The implication has been that the Potts were wealthy as a result of this property. The truth however may be that the property was not that extensive and that rebuilding and repair costs may over time have eaten up all but a rather modest rental stream. Some of the property was certainly sold towards the end of the sixteenth century quite possibly as partial funding of the purchase of the Mannington estate. Several parts of the property comprised monastic holdings which the Potts family had been opportunistic in snapping up as the London property market opened up after the dissolution.

Property was acquired in a number of ways: by purchase, as James Apott had done in Bedfordshire, and by grant. A grant of August 1544 showed William Buteler (presumably the London grocer and Mayor William Butler), James Apott and many others receiving lands in Yorkshire, Lincolnshire and Nottinghamshire, once the property of Roche Monastery in Yorkshire.[1] Coincidentally in a different grant of the same month Edmund Lumner, Surveyor of the Custom House of London (and of Mannington), also received a grant of Lincolnshire land. In December, Roger Pottes was included in a grant of lands in Wadingham, Lincolnshire, previously of St Leonard next Stamford and Durham Monastery.[2] These grants were not large, but do show the families actively accruing land.

Whether the dissolution led to any significant direct grants in London is not known but James Apott did make two large purchases in about 1545. One was a well-known property of long-standing and its history can be given in some detail. A large majority of the family's London property was acquired by James. Another handful of houses was added by his son Roger. Subsequently the holding was not increased and it diminished with later generations. The estate can be tracked through IPMs for Roger, John and his mother Katherine Flower, Roger's widow. James, Roger and John in their wills also added some further detail. Later information on the Potts's London property in the seventeenth century is all consistent with the portfolio as it stood in John and Katherine's IPMs of 1598 and 1599. Unfortunately the family settlements of 1552 and 1557 referred to in these sources have not survived nor have any deeds relating to these properties while in Potts ownership or immediately before. The reason for this will become clear later.

The best way to describe the portfolio is to follow each site or cluster of buildings through its sixteenth century history, starting with those acquired by James Apott, followed by those added by Roger. James acquired four clusters of properties in London, the first two being in St Andrew Holborn and probably acquired as a single parcel:

> The Bishop and 6 associated tenements, one of which being

> The White Hind formerly the Plough and Harrow, on the same site on the west side of Gray's Inn Lane at its junction with High Holborn

> The Maidenhead and 6 associated tenements in Gray's Inn Lane and probably adjoining the site of The Bishop and The White Hind

> Three cottages with gardens in Tremel Street in St Sepulchre parish (Tremel is the sixteenth century spelling of the modern Turnmill Street)[3]

> A large cluster of as many as 19 tenements, probably on a single site, in St Bartholomew the Less

The Bishop and The White Hind

The Bishop was a high profile site held by the Charterhouse Priory from the royal manor of Pancras. It can be traced back for 150 years or more before it came into Apott hands, probably in 1545. By comparing the sixteenth century 'Agas' map and the 1755 Stow's map (when The Bishop site was known as Bishop's Head Court) it can be seen that The Bishop, with its associated tenements, occupied an approximately square block with High Holborn and Gray's Inn Lane frontage. The George, its alley through to Gray's Inn, and a small tenement bounded it on the west. The White Hind may well have been within this block with Gray's Inn Lane frontage, with The Maidenhead probably adjacent or very close by, but further up the west side of Gray's Inn Lane.

The site of The Bishop, at the corner of High Holborn and the western side of the southern end of Gray's Inn Lane, is now a modern shop and office block. Even by the thirteenth century this was both a residential and a commercial environment. The opposite side of Gray's Inn Lane was a noted run of 36 shops and The Bishop site itself in 1298 was occupied by Adam Bedyk the King's Tailor.[4] Interestingly, in the 1580s some of the tenants were still tailors.

A number of Charterhouse Priory rental rolls have survived and show entries for The Bishop. In 1426 Thomas Nanseglos paid 9s free rent and in 1430 the entry shows he held 'Le Bychope', a tenement at the corner of 'Portpole', at a quit rent of 9s pa. This and other properties were held of the royal manor of Pancras. In 1478 the 'son of William Nanseglos' paid the same 9s rent for a tenement above the corner of Holborn called 'Le Busshop'. The property was shown in 1493 and 1500 (then described as a hospice or inn) but without the name of the holder. It was similarly shown in the King's hands in 1539-40, as a hospice without a holder's name and again in 1543-44 still with a quit rent of 9s as a 'tenement in Holborn called le Busshoppe'.[5]

So, The Bishop was held by the Nanseglos family for a hundred years or more prior to the Potts's ownership. From a family originally of Cornish descent, Thomas Nanseglos was a churchwarden of St Andrew Holborn in 1424 and may have already held The Bishop. He died sometime after 1436.[6] His sons Robert and William were both London merchants, with William inheriting and expanding the family's properties into the manor of Redfans in Shalford in Essex, perhaps on the back of profits from his role as Comptroller of the Great Custom in London in 1457. In his 1477 will William Nanseglos senior, gent of Shalford Essex, left to his son William his tenements in Holborn called The Plough and The Bishop. William in turn passed this property on to his son John who was a merchant in London. John, by then the elder, appears to have had severe financial problems in the 1520s given the number of chancery references and deeds mortgaging or selling London property prior to his death in the 1530s. These documents tell of the decline of the Nanseglos family; by about 1530 they probably sold their London property to their major creditor, Thomas Perpoynte, citizen and draper, to settle their debts. Even in the next generation John Nanseglos was still having debt problems as late as 1547 when his Redfans Essex property was the subject of court action over a mortgage.[7]

Through all the chancery documents the nature of The Bishop is revealed.[8] In the block were three named houses - The Sign of The Bishop, The Sign of the Plough (presumably what is later referred to as the Plough and Harrow or White Hind) and The Sign of the George - together with '10 other messuages or tenements lying within the said premises'. The Bishop appears to have been seen as the primary capital messuage on the site which included a brewery. A sheriff's inquisition listing Nanseglos goods and chattels on the site in 1524 included a great lead trough, a lead trough called a graunt leed, a horse mill, a quart measure, 18 barrels, 28 vats, 5 whole barrels, 13 firkins, an old batch and an old mash tun worth together £7 7s 8d.

The whole site generated £7 a year in rents in the early 1520s. However, during the mid 1520s Perpoynte demolished and rebuilt some or all of the messuages. Perpoynte's personal account, prepared for arbitration between himself and Nanseglos in 1529, included a sum of £240 claimed for new building of tenements in Holborn and for repairs there. This very substantial sum may have covered a complete re-building of the whole site. From his account, the rents from the site in the later 1520s seem to have risen to about £18 per year (whereas all the other rents received by him from the Nanseglos properties in Essex and Northants had remained unchanged from their historic levels). Later in the century there were more tenements on the site, so the rental increase would have come from both the improved quality of The Bishop's main building and from squeezing in more tenants.

The George was separated and sold off and was never mentioned in the later Potts IPMs. In September 1529, Nanseglos conveyed to John and Juliana Hogge and others a tenement with barns stables and courts almost adjacent to the western end of The Bishop block, being The Sign of The George to the south of Gray's Inn and adjacent to the access lane from Holborn to Gray's Inn.[9] The witnesses included an Edward Campion (presumably of the Essex family) and Jasper Fisher. This particular transaction was possibly part of a complete sell-off of Holborn property by Nanseglos. Fisher's presence as a witness is significant given that certainly in the 1560s and later he was the chief tenant for the whole block of properties here that were owned by the Apotts - possibly he already held the head lease and was witnessing in that role. The property abutting to the east of The George was the messuage or tenement in the occupation of Thomas Bontham esq. By 1552 The George had been conveyed onwards by Hogge's widow, the by now twice-widowed Juliana Romyng, to Richard Forssett gent as trustee for herself and Richard Cliffe gent, now her neighbour to the east, whom she was to marry. The Cliffes owned extensive properties in High Holborn and elsewhere in this area of London. The property between The George and The Bishop was repeatedly listed in wills, IPMs and court actions as just an unnamed small tenement. The Cliffe family did not hold The Bishop itself.[10]

No record of any sale transaction explicitly including The Bishop has been found. James Apott may have bought it directly from Perpoynte or the Nanseglos family, possibly with pressure for a sale from Perpoynte wanting the return of the £800 that the arbitration had concluded was due to him. With at least two grocers involved in Nanseglos debts, it seems likely that James would have known what was going on. However there is some evidence that the property first came into the hands of the Rest family. During Michaelmas term 1545, James Apott bought unidentified premises in the parish of St Andrew in Holborn from Edward Rest and Alice his wife.[11] At the same time from a different vendor he bought the Tremel Street property. These are the only evidence for the Apotts buying London houses. How did James come by the funds to make two substantial purchases at once? The most obvious theory would be that a major trade deal went well and that he was flush with funds to invest.

The case for the St Andrew purchase being The Maidenhead and The Bishop/ White Hind is strong. Edward was the son and heir of John Rest, alderman and grocer who had been Mayor of London. John's will, naming Edward as his heir, was proved in early 1523.[12] John also had two married daughters: Elizabeth the wife of Roger Pynchester another grocer and Mary the wife of Thomas Perpoynte draper. Roger and Thomas later that same year were overseers of John's widow Agnes's own will[13] Unfortunately there is nothing in these wills, family IPMs (Edward Rest's 1546 IPM of course made no mention of the property he had sold just before he died) or other documents to show the path of The Bishop from Nanseglos to Rest hands; presumably it came to Perpoynte as a result of the debt, who sold it to Edward Rest.[14] Perpoynte left no will or IPM, so he may have died childless having first sold his property to his brother-in-law.

The first reference to The Bishop being owned by a Potts came in Roger's IPM. The enquiry into Roger Apott's lands and tenements was held on 5th June 1568 at the lodging house called The Antelope in High Holborn.[15] The poor condition of the document means that a few key words are illegible, but the majority of the text is clear and gives a very good description of the real estate held by Roger and his father before him.

> They say that before the death of Roger, a certain James Apot
> was seized in demesne and fee in one capital messuage called
> The [Bishop] lying in the parish of St Andrew Holborn and in 6
> messuages lying there of which one was called The White Hynde,
> formerly The Plough and Harrow. And that James Apot on 22nd
> October 6 Ed VI [1552] granted all the said messuages to Roger
> Apot and Katherine his wife and heirs. Roger had the evidence.

A damaged sentence seems also to show 14 gardens, almost certainly associated directly with the 13 or 14 dwellings in The Bishop and The Maidenhead taken together. The Bishop was described as being held of the Queen's manor of Pancras (Priory of Charterhouse) at 9s and value ____ [missing].

However, in this IPM the tenure details for The Bishop and The Maidenhead were obviously sketchy and a follow up was commissioned years later on 15th November 1570.[16] The commission returned (among other things) that before Roger died a certain James Apot was seised in 6 messuages in St Andrew (one The White Hynde) and 6 in Purple Lane (called The Maydenhead) but the nature of the tenure had not been discovered. The inquisition was held on 13th February 1571 at High Holborn where it was said that 'the messuage now The White Hynde and formerly The Plough and Harrow and 6 messuages called The Maydenhead in Purpullane in St Andrew Holborn mentioned in the commission, were said at the time of the death of Roger Apott (Rogeri Apotto) to be held of the Queen as of her manor of Pancras lately a parcel of possessions of the dissolved Priory of Charterhouse, but by what services the Jurors did not know'.

James Apott had not specifically mentioned this property in his will because it had already been passed on by the family settlement. Roger's will mentioned property in St Andrew and the other parishes, but none was described by name or in any detail. It is worth looking ahead here to the next Potts IPM - that for John Potts held on 23rd January 1599.[17] The first section relating to London property referred to him still as John Apott, even though in all other documents and his own will the name was by then Potts:

> They say that John Apott gent at the time of his death did hold in
> fee of and in a capital messuage called Le Busshopp in St Andrew's
> Holborn and in 6 other messuages in the same parish, one of which
> was called The White Hynde or The Plough and Harrow; and of and
> in six other messuages in Purpool Lane als Greyes Inn Lane in the
> said parish called The Maydenhead, which were also previously held
> by James Pott and by James's deed of 20th October 6 Ed VI [1552]
> he gave to his son Roger Potts and Katherine his wife the messuages
> for their lives and to their heirs.

The section on tenure added more, including the key point that The White Hind site was adjacent to The Bishop:

> John Potts held the capital messuage called The Busshoppe and another messuage next to it called The White Hynde or The Plough and Harrow which were held of the Queen as of her manor of Pancras, recently a parcel of the possessions of the dissolved Priory of Charterhouse in Middlesex and at socage and annual rent of 9s and valued per annum after all reductions at £5.
>
> And that the messuage called The White Hynde or Plough and Harrow and six other messuages in Purpoole lane als Greyes Inn lane called The Maydenhead were held of the Queen as of her manor of Pancras but through what right they know not, and valued per annum etc at £3.

However, this is still somewhat confusing given the repetition of The White Hind in the valuations. Katherine's IPM as Katherine Flower, widow of Francis Flower, was held on 24th November 1599 at the Church House in St Clement [Danes].[18] By then The Bishop was shown to be apparently in 9 units. The IPM referred to the history of The Bishop, The White Hind and The Maidenhead together:

> And James had issue the said Roger Potts his son and the same Roger took in marriage Katherine; and the said James was seized in the messuages and all the premises by his deed dated 20th October 6 Edward VI [1552] and gave granted and confirmed to Roger Potts his son and Katherine his wife the separate messuages to have and to hold to Roger and Katherine and the heirs of their bodies and remainder to the right heirs of Roger, and they were seized in demesne as of fee.
>
> And Roger and Katherine had issue John Potts and afterwards Roger died at the parish of St Andrew and Katherine survived him and was seized

This was the only reference to Roger living in St Andrew at the time of his death and perhaps implied that he and the family were living in one of the family properties. Further detail explained the sub-division of The Bishop:

> They say before her death, a certain James Pott was seised as of demesne as of fee, of and in a capital messuage lately and still called Le Bushopp, now divided into [blank] separate messuages or houses ['domus manscional' translating as a mansion house or dwelling house] in the parish of St Andrew Holborn, lately in the several

tenures or occupations of Sir Adam Gwinne, Milo Holmes, John Puller, Wm Walker, Wm Colson, Radulph Aldr[in?]shawe, Matthew Hubbart, Robert Poole & Nicholas Wallenger.

And six other messuages in the said parish ... to the said capital messuage thus ... adjacent

The tenure section, however, continued the confusing repetition of The White Hind:

The Bushopp, adjoining messuages, The White Hynde (or Plough and Harrow) held of Queen as of her manor of St Pancras lately parcel of Charterhouse in free socage by fealty and 9s rent, value after outgoings £5 pa

Messuage called Le White Hynde or Plough and Harrow and the 6 messuages in Purpoole Lane called Maydenhead held of Queen as of St Pancras but by what service not known. Value £3 pa

Unfortunately the IPMs offer no further clues as to how the combined sites of The Bishop, The White Hind and The Maidenhead were divided up between large and small dwellings. It is not clear whether The Bishop was still operating as an inn in 1599. It seems most likely that by the end of the century The Bishop site had nine dwellings on it and The White Hind and The Maidenhead six each.

Fortunately, research by Mark Eccles into the playwright Christopher Marlowe found that The Bishop was still operating as an inn in 1588 and probably for at least some years after that.[19] Marlowe and his friend Thomas Watson were imprisoned in Newgate in September 1589 for the murder of William Bradley. Watson, with prior bad blood between him and Bradley, intervened to stop a sword fight in Hog Lane between Marlowe and Bradley. Bradley turned on him. Wounded and in fear of his life Watson managed to kill him with a single lunge to the heart. Their self defence plea was accepted and they were released in due course. Eccles, curious about Bradley, identified him as one of three sons, then aged 26, of William Bradley senior, a citizen and marbler of London and the innholder at The Sign of The Bishop on the corner of Gray's Inn Lane and High Holborn. He was buried at St Andrew's church on 19th September.

The use of these properties by any member of the Potts family is unclear but the under-lease of one of them was retained by Katherine. As a lawyer, John Potts would have needed somewhere to live that was convenient for the inns and courts. In 1587 money was raised for new bells for St Andrew's church.[20] On the long list of contributors were various of our later cast of characters (Mr Flower, Mr Dodge, Mr Buggins), one of the Potts tenants, Aaron Holland and 'Mr Pottes' himself. So, John Potts may have had rooms in one of the Gray's Inn Lane buildings.

The Maidenhead and Jasper Fisher

Roger's IPM of 1567 showed The Maidenhead as: 'six messuages in Purpullane in St Andrew's recently in the occupation of Jasper Fisher esquire'. Portpool or Purpool or even Purple Lane was the old name for Gray's Inn Lane, taken from the old name of the small local manor. The road was known by both names from at least the middle of the fifteenth century. Tenure was described in this IPM as of the Queen's Honour of Hampton Court and valued at £10. But as we have seen, the later IPM said that this site and The Bishop/White Hind were of the Queen's manor of Pancras. John's IPM showing it held of the Queen through Pancras manor was probably correct. These IPMs have been taken by other writers, wrongly, to mean that the family had lands in the parishes of Hampton Court and St Pancras. These were merely the royal manors to whom the underlying rents were payable.

As with The Bishop, this site had been in the 1552 settlement on Roger and Katherine and was simply mentioned in passing in Roger's will. The later IPMs and wills add no further detail. The Maidenhead seems simply to have been an investment property for rental. No early deeds or even references to such a building name in Gray's Inn Lane have been found but there were further buildings north of The Bishop before reaching the frontage of Gray's Inn itself. Most likely it was located there, probably adjacent to The White Hind.

The reference to Jasper Fisher esq witnessing one deed and renting The Maidenhead block connects the Apotts to one of the colourful Londoners of the Elizabethan era. Fisher was at various times an MP, one of the six clerks in chancery, a JP for Middlesex, the royal goldsmith to Queen Mary, an alderman and a governor of the grammar school of St Dunstan in the West.[21] Courtesy of Stow's *Survey of London* he is also remembered for Fisher's Folly - the affectionate contemporary name for the grand house with pleasure gardens and bowling alleys that he built in Bishopsgate. So extravagant was this house that it is said to have bankrupted him. In 1580, shortly after his death, it was bought by the equally extravagant courtier and poet Edward de Vere, Seventeenth Earl of Oxford.[22] He could not afford to keep it and was a forced seller in 1588.

Jasper Fisher's *ODNB* entry suggests his only child Alice married Richard Hanbury a successful goldsmith and ironmaster. Apparently she died in 1593 and was buried at Datchet, their country home. However, this is at odds with Jasper's IPM of November 1579 which clearly stated that his heirs were Katherine and Anne the married daughters of Cecily and Robert Taylor.[23] Cecily was the sister of Jasper's father John Fisher. Also, Jasper Fisher did not mention any children in his will made and proved in 1579.[24] He described arrangements he had made for his St Botolph's capital messuage to go to his then wife Margaret for life and then his executors and trustees should sell it. This would provide for the £1,600 left by Richard Blounte deceased to Richard's daughter Elizabeth by Margaret. Fisher on marrying Margaret, Richard Blounte's widow, had taken over her property and that of her close family. Richard Blounte of Colman Street had died towards the end of 1575 leaving Margaret very rich.[25] She was personally to receive £1,000 in money, £200 in plate and all the household goods and jewels at Colman Street. In addition she was to administer the money for her daughter until she was of age and a further £400 for Richard's nephew Richard Blounte. Blounte senior was closely connected to the widowed Lady Pawlet and had brothers (presumably in law) Bostock and Fuller. Among his friends were Vincent Pointer and John Glascock. The latter was one of the overseers of the will together with the solicitor-general, attorney-general, Lady Pawlet and others.

While Fisher had left Margaret his large house, his interests in the Holborn leases were to pass to John Mills (variously Mills, Milles or Mylles) and those in Hounsditch were to go to John's sister. John Mills, sadler, and Richard Bostock gent (probably Margaret's brother) were among the executors.[26] Margaret married her third husband, the well-connected Nicholas Saunders of Ewell esq whose first wife had been Isabel, daughter of Sir Francis Carew. She outlived him also and benefitted from his will proved in January 1588.[27] Saunders mentioned his cousin Vincent Poynter in his will, presumably the same man as Jasper Fisher's friend and feoffee Vincent Poynter alias Corbett.

The evidence that Jasper Fisher rented The Bishop and other Holborn properties is confirmed by the depositions of William Bradley senior (age 62) inn holder of The Bishop and others in a 1588 chancery action.[28] Humphrey Harding and his wife were suing Margaret Saunders widow and Richard Bostock esq of Tandridge, Surrey. Margaret was accused of wrongfully taking the rent and fines of the Holborn properties.

John Mills, citizen and sadler of London had died in 1584 leaving to his sister Jane (or Joan) Mayden a stake in any money recovered from Saunders and Bostock from the money owed to him by Fisher and the bequest of the lease.[29] When he made his will that year the rent arrears due on the lease were the subject of a suit in chancery, which presumably would have lapsed on his death, leaving his good friend and kinsman Humphrey Harding to pursue the matter as sole executor. The bill and answer of Mills versus Bostock and Saunders survives.[30] Although undated it must have been a 1584 action from the reference back to Fisher's last illness during which Fisher had borrowed just over £95 from Mills in two sums. Mills had pursued repayment but had been denied it by Margaret and Nicholas Saunders and likewise they were denying him access to the Holborn lease and its proceeds. Bostock answered that Fisher had died heavily in debt, particularly to Thomas Smith esq Her Majesty's Farmer of the Custom of Merchandise in London - a bond of £600 was cited. The exchequer had had an independent valuation of the Holborn lease done and it was sold for £50 towards the debt repayment. The lease had been bought by none other than Vincent Pointer who had sold it on for the same amount to Margaret. She said that she had offered it to Mills for a similar sum but that he had refused to take it at that price. According to her the lease was therefore legally hers and she suggested that since Mills had been an executor of Fisher's will he should have looked after himself regarding the £95 debt. The implication was that it was his problem if he had not done so! She went on to say that she had struggled to recover all Fisher's property, which he had conveyed to her before his death in recompense for having enjoyed her wealth. Harding had made enough progress in his claim on the lease to receive some rent from the tenants but the legal tussle with first Margaret and Nicholas Saunders, and then with Margaret, widowed yet again, continued.

Chancery decrees show how intransigent the widowed Margaret Saunders was in defending against Harding's suit against her and her brother Richard Bostock esq.[31] Harding clearly had a perfectly good claim to arrears of rent from the property. In October 1588 all those involved in the case with their counsel had attended and argued the case fully in front of Sir Christopher Hatton, Lord Chancellor, at his house. Perhaps he had made a special exception to try to arbitrate the case involving such a high profile and high status woman and put her at her ease by meeting in his house. Presumably Francis Flower, Sir Christopher's chief servant, would have been in attendance and it would certainly have been known that the properties in Holborn were owned by the Potts family, with Flower's wife Katherine holding a life interest in them. It is at least conceivable that John Potts himself might have witnessed this hearing. Hatton proposed that Margaret should resolve all matters at issue by paying Harding £195, £50 immediately and the balance in two subsequent six monthly payments.

She refused to agree to this! Sir Christopher very reasonably gave her twenty days to consult with counsel and friends. If she still refused, he would have the case heard at large and the loser would have to pay whatever was determined in court. In December Hatton referred the matter to two named judges to try to resolve the specific disagreement over arrears of rent due to Harding. In May 1589 it was noted that she still refused to accept the arbitration, which it was said Sir Christopher thought was a good one.[32] In June 1589 there was a full chancery hearing. The court heard that she had received rents and entry fines totalling £134 and that her late husband Saunders had received £184 rent and fines during their marriage. Since being widowed, she had had to pay £50 for a lease renewal (therefore a payment to Katherine Flower) and £30 in repairs. These were allowable expenses, so it was found that she had received £238 net. Also she had borrowed £95 from John Mills now deceased, for whom Harding was executor. She had 'pawned' jewels as security for this loan but had later retrieved them from Mills without repaying the loan. Presumably she had rolled over her husband's debt of this amount, making it her own.

Sir Christopher, hearing the case, ordered that she should pay Harding the £95 and £50 of the rent arrears received during her widowhood (the £130 less the £80 allowed costs). These were to be repaid in roughly equal amounts over eighteen months. Harding was given leave to start a further chancery action against Nicholas Saunders (deceased) and Margaret to claim the £134 taken by Nicholas Saunders, which he would obviously have had a very good chance of winning, given this finding. Entertainingly, in Michaelmas term 1589 the sheriffs of London returned that they had been unable to find the defendants (by implication Nicholas and Margaret Saunders) and a 'commission of rebellion' was issued against them.[33] There are no further decree references to this action and presumably at some point Margaret settled with Harding.

The 1588 depositions add a little further knowledge about the Potts properties in Holborn, even though at no point was the fact that they were held from John Potts and his mother directly mentioned. William Bradley said that he had paid rent for the inn named The Sign of the Bishop at Gray's Inn Lane's end to Margaret since Fisher's death and indeed had agreed a ten year lease renewal with her during that time and had paid her an entry fine of £16. Since then he had borne the cost of repairs. For the last few months he had paid the £12 pa rent to Harding, who had obviously by then persuaded the tenants that the rent should have been paid to him or his wife. This is not the only sighting of William Bradley. In an action of 1575 he was cited as improperly holding the documents relating to a lease of one of Jasper Fisher's messuages in Gray's Inn Lane, almost certainly one of the Potts properties.[34] Fisher had granted a lease to Agnes Thompson a widow with two little girls, Jane and Elizabeth. Agnes had remarried to Robert Powle, who would have become the beneficiary of the lease. She had entrusted the documents to Richard Bludworth. But she had died and the documents had now somehow come into the hands of William Bradley who refused to hand them over to the orphaned girls whom Powle had ruthlessly turned out of doors destitute.

Other local witnesses in the Harding/Saunders case gave their evidence. George Goodwyn, a 56 year-old chandler, was a tenant of a total of 13 of the disputed houses, for which he had paid £11 yearly to Margaret and for the last year to Harding and his wife. He had paid a £20 fine to Margaret then Mrs Fisher for a ten year under-lease on the house called The Maidenhead and the gardens and tenements belonging to it (ie The Maidenhead and 11 tenements). When she was Mrs Saunders he had also paid a £8 fine for a lease of another house and a great garden late in the tenure of 'Gillams a straunger'. He had since paid about £20 on repairs to the 13 houses.

Richard Owen, a 40 year-old tailor, was not and had never been a tenant of Mrs Fisher, but paid his rent as a tenant of 'Mr Flo[er] or his wife' - this reference shows that Katherine and Francis Flower ran at least one property here, not John Potts. It also shows that not every house was in the Fisher block of leases, but why they took the rent just for this one is unknown. Owen had spent more than £20 on repairs and 8 or 9 years ago Mr or Mrs Fisher had spent about £30, but nothing since. This implies Owen's tenement was probably directly connected to or part of the Fisher properties. Gryffin Owen, another tailor and at 47 perhaps a brother of Richard, rented 2 tenements in Gray's Inn Lane. From their rent of £8 and £4 pa respectively, these appear to be rather larger than most of the premises - perhaps including The White Hind? He had renewed his lease when Margaret was the widowed Mrs Fisher and had paid her a fine of £16 and 'a newe frenche hoode'. He had paid his own repairs since Fisher died.

Yet another tailor, Roger Ashemore aged 39, leased a tenement of a house in Gray's Inn Lane. The £2 annual rent had been paid to Fisher, then Margaret and recently to Mrs Harding. Fines and repairs were small. John Myles, a 70 year old baker, paid 20s a year for his house in Gray's Inn Lane and again minor payments for repairs to the house immediately behind his. Was he John Mills's father perhaps?

John Puller, or Poullard as he signed himself, a turnour or bale maker aged 48 of Gray's Inn Lane paid his £4 rent to Fisher, Margaret and Mrs Harding over the 12 or 13 years he had lived there. He had paid no fine and always paid his own repairs.

Thomas Mount, a 56 year old shoemaker, leased the house where he lived in Holborn from Andrew Holborne of Westminster, who held it of Fisher. The rent due to Fisher had been 26s 8d a year paid to Margaret and again recently to the Hardings by first Holborne and then one Jones, one of Fisher's men. A lease renewal had been granted during Margaret's management of the property. The location was not given more precisely as was also the case with James Fenton's dwelling house in Holborn. Another tailor, aged 47, he had been a tenant of one of Mr Fisher's houses for 5 years and paid 32s a year to Mrs Saunders. He also paid £8, probably as a fine, to Jones. Finally, Thomas Olyver another chandler aged 47, paid to Fisher, Margaret and now Harding 33s a year rent for the house he lived in.

This adds up to rental details on 23 properties and an annual rent roll of about £50, ignoring the intermittent entry fines at lease renewal points. It is interesting to note that the overall head lease had been valued by the exchequer at only one year's rent, making its recovery for £50 an attractive proposition. With the tenants generally responsible for ongoing repairs these properties were producing a respectable income for Fisher and his successors. Of course he may have paid a significant amount for his head lease arrangements with the Apotts, or even the Rests. The total number of properties roughly corresponds to the numbers from the late 1590s IPMs. These properties were lived in by tradesmen and probably at least some of those facing onto the main roads contained small retail shops. Variations in the rent indicated different sized houses. Presumably the lower rents were for smaller ones that had been built in courts at the back where once there had been gardens. That Jasper Fisher had the whole package in one lease supported the view that they were bought as a complete bundle from Edward Rest in 1545 and possibly even then had Fisher as leaseholder. The one property held directly of the Flowers cannot be identified any more precisely and its size cannot be estimated since the rental was not quoted. Probably one of the houses had been retained for use by the Apotts themselves at some point (where Roger died perhaps), but was now rented out.

Tremel Street

James Apott bought the cottages in 'Tremelstrete without the bars of West Smithfield in the parish of St Sepulchre' during Michaelmas term 1545 from John Thornton and his wife Joan.[35] This may have been the John Thornton, Merchant Taylor of All Hallows Broad Street whose will was proved in October 1559 but nothing more has been found about him.[36]

In Roger's IPM these are described:

> ... and of and in 6 cottages 2 stables and diverse small gardens adjacent and being in Tremel Street in ____ extra barras West Smythfeilde, Middlesex ...

> And Roger by his deed of 2nd July P&M 3&4 [1557] granted
> and leased to Margaret Apot, widow, mother of the said Roger,
> all tenements, etc and rents, reversions in St Sepulchre and in St
> Bartholomew ... for Margaret and heirs from date of indenture up to
> the end of 30 years if she live so long, at a yearly rent of 1 red rose ...

> And Roger was seized in July 1557 [after his father died]. And in
> 1557 he made his last will and testament as follows: After the death
> of my mother all my lands, tenements, stalls, etc in St Sepulchre
> shall remayne to my wife Kateryne for her life, and after the death of
> both, to my heirs ...

> And they say the lands were held: Tremelstrete in St Sepulchre by
> socage and value £15

The Tremel Street premises had not been in the 1552 settlement on Roger. They were passed on to him in James's will, explicitly after his mother's life interest. Roger and the widowed Margaret were joint executors and he was to have all the real estate after her death. Two clusters of property were specifically mentioned: lands tenements and cottages in West Smithfield and Tremel Street in the parish of St Sepulchre without Newgate; and a messuage with shops cellars and solars in St Bartholomew the Little. The reason for these two clusters not being in the 1552 settlement was not given but since James had Tremel Street by 1545 he may have been making use of them in his trading activities and did not want yet to release them to his son. The description of the St Bartholomew property supports this theory as this site was the only one with a specific mention of a shop. Perhaps the stable in Tremel Street was important to James especially if they had lived in Tremel Street at some point. Alternatively, Roger's mother may have lived there after James's death. In his 1557 will Roger provided for his mother to continue to enjoy his lands messuage gardens and stables in St Sepulchre London, which he had leased to her in July 1557 - ie just after his father's death - for one red rose a year (what a good son!). Katherine, Roger's wife, was given an incentive of £40 provided she released all title to these lands and hereditaments in favour of Roger's mother. After his mother's death this property was to go to Katherine. However, this might simply have been a mechanism to guarantee his mother an income and she may have lived elsewhere.

John's IPM adds little more: '... and of and in 3 cottages in St Sepulchre in the City ... and by his will dated 8th July 1557 the messuages in St Sepulchre were Katherine's for her life and also ... remaindered to Roger's male heirs ...'. It was closely matched by Katherine's inquisition: '... and the 3 cottages in St Sepulchre were held of the Queen in free burgage valued at 40s pa'. John's IPM also referred to John having the use of this property and conveying it to John Dodge and Edward Dodge in 1587: '... and John had the use of the three cottages [St Sepulchre given the context] for divers years [by deed of] 17th May 29 Eliz [1587] and on the same day he feoffed the three messuages to John Dodge and Edward Dodge, to be held of John and Anne Potts' [and then presumably back to Potts's male heir]. This was clearly some sort of trust arrangement by John for himself and his heirs. It might mark the birth of John and Anne's first son Drury - the date of which is not recorded.

Tremel Street in St Sepulchre was variously spelt as Tremyl, Turnemyll, Trymyll or just about any phonetic variation one can imagine. These all refer to Turnemyll Brook or Holborn Brook, as this section of the Fleet River was once called. Tremel Street ran parallel to the brook on its east side from The Charterhouse Priory towards West Smithfield and is Turnmill Street today. The Agas map of the 1560s clearly showed three water mills on the brook at the bottom of tenements on Tremel St.[37] The absence of any reference to Apott owning a mill makes it likely that his six cottages or messuages lay on the eastern side of the road, perhaps in the cluster almost adjacent to the Priory.

The reference to two stables there might imply some sort of commercial enterprise, even an inn, on this site right at the edge of the city. That the original six cottages had become three by the time of Roger's death may imply he sold some of them but more likely suggests they were made into larger units. No deeds for these properties, apart from the 1545 Feet of Fines reference, have been found.

St Bartholomew the Less

Similarly, the cluster in St Bartholomew the Less was acquired by James and passed on by his will, not through the 1552 settlement. It was a monastic parcel, no doubt from the Priory of St Bartholomew which dominated this area, but when James acquired it or from whom is not known. The 19 messuages were probably all in one block, since at no point was it described as multiple sites. The reference to shops there means that it may well have been James's primary trading location. In 1547 St Bartholomew's Hospital was re-founded by letters patent from Henry VIII.[38] One of the five medieval chapels became the parish church. The small parish itself shared its boundaries with the Hospital and the church, sitting on the east side of Smithfield, was particularly for the tenants and others living in St Bartholomew's Hospital. With no good description nor tenants' lists, the location of the Potts property is undiscoverable, now no doubt subsumed into the Hospital premises. But, as part of this tiny parish, the site must have been in Smithfield or perhaps Little Britain. It was probably a major site with retail elements facing onto Smithfield itself. This would have been a prime location for a grocer and merchant - adjacent to the busy Smithfield meat market and the huge annual cloth fair just around the corner in Long Lane.

James's will shows that he had a particular affinity to just two London parishes, the only ones to which he left money: 'to every poor householder dwelling in the parish of St Peter in Cornhill 12 pence' and '8s to every one of my poor tenants in St Bartholomew the Little in the ward of Broadstreet'. Roger had no such special affection for this area in his will. However, he did leave this property in a slightly different way: 'after the death of my mother, the premises in St Bartholomew to my male heirs, or [failing such heirs] to my female heirs, or to my wife Kateryne for her natural life'. In other words his son John was to have the property straight after Roger's mother's death and did not have to wait for Katherine's death. Maybe he thought his very young son might in due course follow him into the grocery trade and should have immediate access to this valuable commercial site.

Even though John did not become a grocer, the specific treatment in the will was important. John must have sold the whole parcel. There was no mention of it in his will, his IPM or in Katherine's. It seems pretty likely that John Potts sold it in 1584 as part of raising funds to buy Mannington.

Roger Apott's acquisitions and The King's Head

Roger added a small amount of property to the family estate. Of most interest, given later developments, was the purchase of additional messuages in Gray's Inn Lane. These did not feature explicitly in Roger's will or his father's. The latter was vague on property and Roger's bundled all his Gray's Inn Lane houses together. But these additional houses were in Roger's IPM and they do seem to differ from the Holborn property held by James and leased to Jasper Fisher:

> And Roger died at St Andrew's Holborn, Katherine surviving him leaving John as the heir. And when Roger died he held in fee of and in the 6 messuages then in the tenure and occupation of John Potts, Aron Holland, Elizri Bacon

The reference to John Potts, one of the occupiers, was not to 'the said' John Potts and so cannot have been Roger's son, in 1567 still very young. The tenant was probably Roger's cousin John Potts (by then possibly the younger) of Babraham and London, again reinforcing the close relationship between Roger and his cousins. The Holland and Bacon names recur in subsequent IPMs even though the number of messuages later dropped to three. Indeed three was probably always the case, the scribe earlier mistakenly simply repeating the 6 messuages phrase used for each of the other two clusters in Gray's Inn Lane. The IPM of John Potts at the end of the century clearly stated that there were three messuages in a separate cluster from The Bishop/White Hind and The Maidenhead. The reference to John Potts, the tenant was repeated from the earlier IPM:

> And that the 3 other messuages in Purpool lane recently in the occupation of John Potts, Aron Holland and Elisei Bacon were held of the Queen as of her Honour of Hampton Court valued at 40s pa

This was echoed in Katherine's IPM with a more up-to-date tenants' list:

> And they say Roger before his death was seized of certain other messuages in Purpoole Lane als Gray's Inn lane in St Andrew Holborn Middlesex, now or lately in the several occupations of Thomas Mill, Oro Holland & Elizei Bacon ... [and in the tenure section] ... three messuages in Purpoole lane in tenure of Thomas Milles Aron Holland and Elizei Bacon, held of the Queen as of Hampton Court by fealty and in chief [in capite] value 40s pa

The premises were most likely The King's Head plus two tenements together on the east side of Gray's Inn Lane which were definitely held by the Potts family in the seventeenth century. On the 1755 edition of Stow's *Survey*, The King's Head Inn was shown as number 58 on the east side of Gray's Inn Lane opposite the northern part of the buildings of Gray's Inn itself. This places the property in the sixteenth century, from the Agas map, as the very first major building in Gray's Inn Lane as travellers came south down this main road into London - a prime spot for an inn, one imagines. Did the Potts cousins run an inn there amongst their many activities in London and elsewhere?

Thomas Mills was perhaps a relation of the John Mills in Jasper Fisher's will. In his book on Marlowe, Eccles says that Aaron Holland was the builder and co-owner of the Red Bull Playhouse in St John Street.[39] His house in Gray's Inn Lane was broken into on 6th April 1592 and he and his wife Elizabeth were assaulted. Aaron had married Elizabeth Tomson in St Andrew Holborn in August 1581, quite possibly the same Elizabeth who had been mistreated by her stepfather Powle. Their attackers were George Orrell and Allen Starlinge, one if not both of whom lived nearby. The reason for the incident was not given but may have been about property. Captain Orrell, an attorney, was later in Essex's rebellion and forfeited his house which his father Peter Orrell had occupied and three other houses in Gray's Inn Lane. His houses were restored to him in 1607.

In February 1593 John Pottes of Mannington esq leased to Miles Helme citizen and grocer of London a garden near Gray's Inn Lane als Purpool Lane abutting the common sewer there for 24 years from Christmas 1593, at the rent of a peppercorn if demanded.[40] The nominal rent suggests an agreement for the tenant to undertake repairs or major rebuilding work on the property, as happened later within the Potts London property portfolio. Indeed the reference to the sewer reappears and may locate it as adjacent to the inn and two messuages called The King's Head on the east side of Gray's Inn Lane. It was perhaps originally part of a larger single site.

The two tenements were soon to feature in a legal action which had strong similarities to later disputes relating to the London properties that followed over the next half century. The story can be pieced together from chancery decrees starting in 1595 (lacking any bill and answer) with more detail in a subsequent action in 1602 where the bill and answer survive. This latter was the complaint of Ralph Lawson esq against Sir Christopher Heydon and Anne his wife as guardians of John Potts.[41] Lawson was probably the son of William Lawson, brother of Reginald Lawson gent of Gray's Inn with whom the story started. Ralph Lawson asserted that John Potts gent of Lincoln's Inn, deceased, had been seized of two messuages or tenements on the east side of Gray's Inn Lane 'als Pourpool Lane' in High Holborn (the tenants were named). He also held a garden probably adjacent to the tenements and by the common sewer there.

In July 1584 Potts had leased the property to Reginald Lawson for 30 years at £3 annual rent. This is a good indication of how little the rental value of the London properties was. At this level for two small tenements, the 40 or so in the Potts portfolio at this time, even allowing for some bigger units, could only have been generating some £200 a year or so (excluding entry fines on lease renewal) and certainly not enough to generate a surplus to invest in Mannington or other lands. As later, the new lease required building work to be done by the incoming tenant. In this case Lawson had to upgrade the site to three tenements by 1586, spending £200 on the work. If he defaulted on rent or building work Potts could re-possess. In 1586 Lawson contracted with certain named carpenters and bricklayers to do the building work and paid them about £260 and they became bound to him to complete the works.

Ralph Lawson claimed that his uncle saw that the work would not be completed in time and persuaded Potts to grant him a new lease agreeing that Potts would not sue him, nor would Lawson sue the workmen. However, in June 1586 Reginald Lawson died. Ralph claimed unlawful entry by John Potts, but in fact chancery orders from 1595 show that the case was rather more complicated than given out in his 1602 action. A chancery decree of Easter term 1595 showed that Reginald (or Reynold) Lawson had left two wills both of which had been proved in different courts.[42] His brother William as executor of one of them had proved his will in the court of the Bishop of London and had letters of administration and an 'extent' from that court against the executor of the other will. This was Cuthbert Parkinson, Potts's ally. He had proved a different will in the Prerogative Court of Canterbury and had administration from that court. This will, proved on 1st July, mentioned his brother William Lawson and made Cuthbert Parkinson his cousin his sole executor.[43] Ralph claimed that Potts and Parkinson unlawfully entered the premises in breach of the agreement with Reginald. They stopped the building work and then renegotiated the lease with Reginald's brother William. Ralph then referred to an 'ecclesiastical court case' resulting from Potts entering and dispossessing William, but before full process had been completed Potts himself died and the case lapsed. Presumably this was the chancery dispute over the wills which may also have been running in parallel in one of the ecclesiastical courts. Chancery orders seemed to be favouring Potts in 1595, perhaps the dates of the wills were declared and the Parkinson one was more recent. But the court had allowed Lawson the opportunity to try to prove his case.

Now, in 1602, Anne as Potts's widow and executrix had possession with her new husband Sir Christopher Heydon. William Lawson had also died and Ralph had become executor. He claimed that the Lawson family had had no recompense for the more than £300 paid to the builders and that the Heydons were now enjoying a rental of £40 pa higher than it had been before the 1584 lease, from a lease negotiated with William at about £43 a year. Ralph said they refused to make a new lease to him.

In their answer Anne and Sir Christopher said the property was only Anne's by jointure and belonged to her son John Potts. The original lease was taken out and building work was begun but was of very poor quality and no rent was ever paid. They claimed Potts re-entered after Lawson's death and, even though he was under no compulsion to do so, he had paid compensation to Cuthbert Parkinson as executor. £300 or more had not been laid out on the building and if it had, then Lawson should claim against the workmen. A new lease was not granted as Ralph alleged, nor were they receiving an additional £40 annual rent. They said they had heard there might have been a suit in chancery involving John Potts and Lawson but they knew nothing about it (and in fairness there are only fleeting traces of it in the decrees).

Lawson's replication showed that he believed Potts and Parkinson had conspired to create a false will in which Parkinson was made executor and by this and other means Lawson had been deprived of £300 and he should have the original lease at £3 annual rent. This might imply he now leased the property at approximately the alleged higher rent and the action was really an attempt at rent reduction. In the summer of 1602 Ralph Lawson was awarded a commission of enquiry.[44] The action continued into Easter term 1603, when both sides were told to produce their witnesses.[45] However, shortly afterwards only Lawson was under that same pressure and the action then did not reappear for a year when the cry was still for witnesses. Then the case went cold. Presumably Lawson could not find convincing witnesses and failed to bring evidence to the commission.

St Botolph without Bishopsgate

The descriptions of this cluster given in the family IPMs are unfortunately not wholly legible. It seems that Roger Apott probably bought three messuages in St Botolph, which at times were in multiple occupancy resulting in six tenants. There was no reference to these having been part of his father's estate. From Roger's IPM:

> And Roger by his deed of 2nd July P&M 3&4 [1557] granted and leased to Margaret Apot, widow, mother of the said Roger ... and also half the reversions and rents in one messuage in St Botolph lately ___ John Young, one reversion and rent of 3[?] messuages in St Botolph recently in six tenures (William Stevynson, ... , Phillip ___) for Margaret and heirs from date of indenture up to the end of 30 years if she live so long, at a yearly rent of 1 red rose

Further on, the IPM summarised the premises as: '... and of and in 6 ___ gardens in St Botolph extra Bishuppgate free burgage and value £20'. The wording relating to the John Young house is not clear. By the end of the century John's IPM recorded only 5 messuages here. So either one large house had been made from combining two or, less likely, the John Young house was additional to the original parcel and had been sold off by John Potts.[46] St Botolph being Jasper Fisher's home parish, the original acquisition of the properties might in some way have been facilitated by Fisher.

The Apotts also had minor properties in Lewisham and Hitchin. The latter has been covered in the context of the Paris family. Roger mentioned in his will his three acre close in Lewisham and his messuage and land in Bancroft Street, Hitchin. John and Katherine's IPMs also mentioned a small messuage in Hitchin, but not the Lewisham field. Perhaps the field had come as payment of a trade debt. Presumably it had also been sold by John and, depending on when and exactly where it was, it might have produced a good price as a contribution towards the Mannington purchase.

After the death of his grandmother Katherine, the young John Potts inherited the City of London and Middlesex properties set out in his father's IPM, albeit not in full until after his mother Anne's jointure interest. It has never been clear to writers on the Potts family what became of this property. In later chapters, we shall see how the properties' subsequent ownership caught Sir John, his brother Charles and their families in an extraordinarily tangled web.

Chapter 4

Mannington Before Potts: Nobody Expects the Spanish Inquisition

---

The story of Mannington before the Potts acquisition is essentially the story of the Lumner family. The Lumners owned the manorial estate from about the end of the fourteenth century. There is little in print about them with Blomefield offering only a handful of miscellaneous events and dates. There is no reliable family tree; those that have been published, such as by Walter Rye and Charles Tomes, contain fundamental errors.[1] The Visitations of the sixteenth century surprisingly did not produce a descent for the Mannington line. No relationship was made to the secondary line in Sharrington which was not extended back before 1500. The reason for this is the dearth of original sources. Few family wills have survived. Until the middle of the sixteenth century, the holders of Mannington manor did not have church presentation rights in either Mannington or Itteringham, so their arrival and generational changes cannot be traced through the Bishops' Registers. Despite bearing arms and being manorial lords or tenants only two Lumner IPMs were held - one for Mannington in 1558 and the other for Sharrington in 1542. Neither contained a reliable or full description of all the family relationships.[2] All of which has made the task of establishing a definite family tree all the more difficult. Researching the family is further complicated by the huge array of different spellings of the name. Here the spelling has been standardised as the modern Lumner, although of the many early forms perhaps Lomnour was the most frequent. Lomnor, Lomner, Lominer, Lomynour, Liminer, Lonmer, Lorimer, Lumnour, Lumpnour, Lyminor and others can all be found in both indexes and original documents. From the evidence of our wide-ranging research, it appears that most occurrences of this otherwise unusual name, certainly in Norfolk, and possibly even in London, during the fifteenth and sixteenth centuries, refer to this family. The history and pedigree of the Lumners add another dimension to the account of the Potts family and their ownership of Mannington. The two families developed along a parallel path in London from the late fifteenth century, with both being heavily involved in the grocery trade. The relationships between them can now be understood: the evidence suggests that the Potts and Lumner families may have known each other for about 100 years before John Potts bought Mannington. This, in turn, helps to explain how John Potts came to be in Mannington. In a future work, in preparation, on lands and lordship in the Itteringham area before 1700, more detail on the early history of the Lumners and their impact on the estate will be discussed.[3] This chapter concentrates on the later years of the family and the branches of the family in London and Sharrington, as well as the Mannington line. (See the outline family tree of the major characters.)

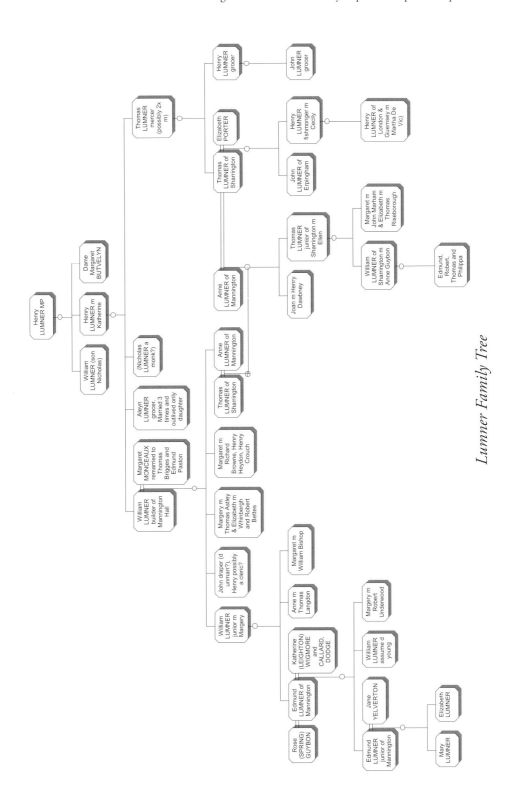

Lumner Family Tree

William Lumner senior of Mannington (c 1420-81)

The Lumners were wealthy and politically influential Norwich merchants by the late fourteenth century. Henry Lumner, the head of the family, was active in Norwich governance and a member of parliament. He had come into Mannington by his marriage to Margaret probably the only daughter of William Fewell junior.[4] Two generations of William Fewell had held Mannington, the first of whom had married the heiress of the Tyrells, the previous long-standing owners. Henry's son William, also a merchant, died in 1401. William's son Nicholas may have produced the cluster of Lumners in Barton Bendish.[5] By the time Henry the MP died in about 1410, his other son Henry junior inherited Mannington. Perhaps Mannington had been settled on Henry junior at his marriage, since there is no obvious surviving documentary evidence linking Henry senior to Mannington after the 1490s. Henry the MP also had a daughter Margaret who married Sir Robert Butveleyn junior of Flordon and Gissing in Norfolk and Cottesbrook in Northants.

Henry junior and his wife Katherine (who may have been Butveleyn's sister) had as their son and heir William Lumner, who must have been born before or around 1420. In 1436 William was named as an executor of the will of his aunt Lady Margaret Butveleyn.[6] This implies that his father, Margaret's brother, was probably dead and that William may even have been of full age. It may also suggest that he was a lawyer or training to become one. William became well-known as a long-standing and trusted 'servant' or supporter of the Paston family.[7] From his closeness to both John and Margaret Paston it seems that, certainly from the early 1450s, he was a sometime secretary and adviser. His role again hints at legal and administrative training. Paston letter references to William being at times in London also support this. Certainly there is very little documentary evidence of him leading a life simply as a Norfolk country gentleman. References to him in separate letters as 'brother' of Margaret Paston and 'cousin' of John Paston 2 and John 3 show that he was related although none of the Paston writers have explained how. Here we suggest that William's sister had married one of the Pastons as a second husband after the death of her first husband Roger Taverham in about 1461.

William prospered and married the young Margaret Monceaux, daughter and heiress of Thomas Monceaux of Wood Dalling. At Monceaux's IPM it was recorded that Thomas died on 7th May 1450, when he held the manor of Wood Dalling of Lady Isabella of Morley and some further lands directly of the Crown.[8] His sole next of kin was his daughter Margaret the wife of William Lumner and she was '14 years old and more' at the time of the inquest in October 1451. This implies that she was of marriageable age but still quite a young girl when she married either earlier that year or in 1450. She obviously was taken under the wing of the Pastons when William was in London. In November 1452 Agnes Paston (John's mother) wrote from Norwich to her son at the Inner Temple: 'recommende me to Lumnour' and tell him his best beloved fareth well but is not yet come to Norwich, for thei deye yet but not so sor as thei dede' [they die yet but not so sore as they did]. The plague was rife in Norwich and Agnes wanted to reassure William his young wife was not in danger. At first they lived at Dalling, her home, and William later had the role of steward at neighbouring Salle (see below). However as his income grew the couple could afford a home of their own.[9] During 1460-61, William Lumner built a hall at Mannington, that still survives today at the heart of the moated Mannington Hall.[10] The house almost certainly replaced an earlier Tyrell family house on the site, probably a small hall-house. Blomefield wrote that there was a licence to embattle from the King but gave no date. Pevsner and others have written that Lumner had a licence to crenellate in 1451 which would precede the work on the house by some nine or ten years. There seems to be no foundation at all for this often repeated statement.[11] William and Margaret's children would have been born during the 1450s and 1460s although information about them is scarce. Their eldest son was William junior, the heir to Mannington, and he had a number of brothers and sisters.[12]

William senior died in 1481 but infuriatingly his proved will only included charitable and religious gifts.[13] He had obviously made a prior family settlement in an earlier document, which probably had Thomas Brigges as its executor. Brigges referred to such a document explicitly in his own will, calling it Lumner's last will and testament. This Lumner 'will' has never been found. As a result no definitive list of Lumner's children alive in the late 1470s can be re-created. William and Margaret did have a younger son John, a draper in London about whom nothing more is known.[14] He was mentioned in Margaret's will, but there is no further sign of him or any issue. He presumably died unmarried since he was not mentioned in the later deed which created a complicated default sequence for the inheritance of Mannington. William junior came into Mannington fully after Margaret's life interest ended with her death in 1504 when she left her will as Margaret Paston, widow of her third husband Edmund Paston.[15] After her second husband Thomas Brigges's death in 1494, Margaret married for the third time to Edmund Paston a younger son of the family who had been married to the widowed Katherine Clippesby (daughter of John Spelman esq and wife of William Clippesby). Margaret also left a small bequest to her son Henry. From the modest nature of the gift he may have been a cleric or monk. There had been other clerics in the Lumner family and in the family of Thomas Brigges.[16]

Thomas and Margaret's wills require some interpretation to work out the structure of the family around the end of the century. Margaret's will made no reference to her already deceased daughter Margery who had married and produced sons for Thomas Astley of Melton Constable. Interestingly neither her will nor Brigges's went in for naming grandchildren. But Margaret did leave bequests to her 'daughters' Margaret Browne, Elizabeth 'Whymberg' (Whinberg), and Anne Lumner as well as her 'daughter-in-law' Margery wife of her son William.[17] Anne has been taken by some as an unmarried daughter and possibly even the Anne Lumner who married Thomas Langdon of Wolterton. From a careful assessment of all the families involved it can be shown that the Anne who married Langdon was a daughter of William junior not William senior.[18] The Anne in Margaret's will was in fact her married daughter, still named Lumner since she had married her first cousin Thomas Lumner of Sharrington. The Norfolk Visitations made a poor attempt at the Lumner families of Mannington and Sharrington and indeed of the Brigges background, causing confusion for subsequent writers. The first surviving visitation of 1563 was of course written after the death of the head of the Mannington family and two generations after the Brigges line had passed sideways to Thomas's brother and his heirs. The then head of the Sharrington Lumners was still a young man and may have known little of the family history. The Brigges pedigree showed Thomas's grandfather's name wrongly as John rather than Thomas. Blomefield indicated that Thomas Brigges had had a first wife also called Margaret and reported that there was a brass in Salle church that was probably for him and simply said 'pray for the souls of Thomas Briggs and the two Margarets his wives'. While he may have been right, the old brass may have referred to Thomas Brigges's grandfather who was certainly married to a Margaret as the 1494 will showed. Thomas junior himself was shown as married to an unnamed daughter of a Talboys and no mention was made of his ten year marriage to Margaret Lumner. While it is possible that he had married twice, the wording of his will makes it uncertain. He detailed a long string of Brigges, Monceaux and Lumner antecedents of himself, Margaret and William Lumner whose souls should be prayed for. He made no mention of a first wife in this list. The length and detail of his will makes it inconceivable that he had simply omitted a first wife particularly since he had done such a thorough job on Margaret's Lumner relations. The Visitation assertion in the Brigges pedigree that he died without any issue is probably correct as his IPM stated he had no issue by Margaret and confirmed that his heir was his brother.

However, the Lumner of Sharrington pedigree (which gave no details back beyond about the 1490s) showed Thomas Lumner senior of Sharrington as married to Anne Bridges. This has been taken to be a daughter of Thomas Brigges, with Bridges being a then frequent version of Brigges. Perhaps the folk memory in the Brigges family was that Anne had been described by Thomas Brigges as his 'daughter' which would have been common parlance for a stepdaughter as well as a natural daughter at the time. Later Lumner IPMs show that Thomas Lumner and Anne would have married in the late 1480s at which time Anne's mother and Thomas Brigges were married. Another possibility is that 'Anne Bridges' might have been a daughter of brother Edward Brigges. However this is not supported by the entries on the Visitation pedigree, which showed Edward to have had one daughter married to a Robert Turner.[19] Importantly, while Thomas Brigges made good provision for 'Thomas Lumner and Anne his wife' in his will, he at no point described her as his daughter or niece.[20]

Where did Thomas Lumner senior of Sharrington come from? He was the eldest son of Thomas Lumner the London mercer, brother of William Lumner senior, who died in 1492 leaving sons Thomas junior and Henry. Margaret in 1504 left Thomas, her 'nephew', a bed and bedding. Bedding was also left in the next clause to her 'nephew' James, which may be a scribe's error for Henry.[21] These nephews and their London origins and subsequent family developments in London and Sharrington will be described below. Many years later the descendants of the Sharrington line would make a determined assault in court to claim that John Potts had no right to the Mannington estate.

Interestingly Thomas Brigges was also a gentleman servant of the Paston family. He was apparently a wealthier man and a more substantial landowner than William Lumner senior, with manors around the Salle and Heydon area and elsewhere in Norfolk. Indeed there is evidence that William Lumner worked for him as estate steward for Salle Kirkhall manor in 1479-80.[22] Salle Kirkhall was leased to Brigges at this time by Margaret Paston.[23] William Lumner senior was probably a steward for Paston manors as well as Brigges over a long period leading up to his death.

William Lumner senior's three other daughters married well in the local context. Margery's marriage to Thomas Astley produced two sons (both confusingly called Thomas) and a daughter Elizabeth who married Thomas Moore gent the holder of part of Wolterton and who, as the major family of the village, occupied the old Wolterton House.[24] Elizabeth Lumner married first a Whinberg and may already have been widowed by the time of the sole reference to him in Margaret's 1504 will. Her second husband was Robert Bettes of Irmingland and Oulton. Margaret married Richard Browne of Thwaite, then Henry Heydon and finally Henry Crouch. These men will re-emerge at various points in the story.

Lumners in London

The Lumners have been considered a local Norfolk family, but to some in the fifteenth century they would have appeared more like Londoners than locals. William's father Henry junior may well have spent his life living and working outside Norfolk. There is little evidence of him here, whereas there are hints that he may have lived in Oxford and worked in estate administration.[25] William senior clearly spent time in London and was probably a trained lawyer. Reflecting the family's trading past, William's two brothers became citizens and freemen of London, Thomas as a mercer and Aleyn as a grocer. Both are interesting men - Aleyn in particular given the grocery trade connection.

Aleyn the Grocer

The admission register of the Grocers' Company shows Aleyn was admitted to the Company as a freeman in June 1456 as 'Aleyn Lymnoa apprentice of Richard Reede'; he was probably born therefore about 1430.[26] Indicating reasonable success as a merchant, he took on apprentices of his own: John Gryse in 1465, John Holme in 1470 and Robert Mille in 1475.

Aleyn Lumner was married three times as he described in his will of April 1491.[27] He asked to be buried in the church of St Stephen Walbroke in the place there where the bodies of 'Johanne and Johanne late my wyfes' were buried. His executors were to be his then wife Elizabeth and William Sutton clerk, with Richard Lee the elder as overseer. Some years earlier in August 1468 Alan Lumnour and Johanna his wife, daughter of Thomas Hawkyn had attended the Court of the City of London to acknowledge satisfaction for his wife's patrimony.[28] Previously in 1456 at the same court Thomas Hawkyn's widow and her second husband came to give a bond regarding Thomas's bequests of pieces of plate to his two sons and two daughters when they came of age. This means Joan Hawkyn was probably born in 1447 and unlikely to have married Lumner much before 1468. Their marriage provided a few more clues to Aleyn Lumner's history. Given that 1468 was some 12 years after he became a freeman, it seems likely that she was his second wife. She was the mother of his only child, Margaret Lumner who died without heirs before her parents. Aleyn crops up in one or two minor chancery actions over trade debts, but more interestingly in an action over one of his wives' inheritance. In the 1496 IPM of John Wille junior, 'Alan Luminour' grocer was cited as having married Joan the daughter of Thomas Hawkyns grocer of London and his wife Margaret Gaylor of Sandwich, whose sister Joan Gaylor had married John Wille the elder.[29] The point of the IPM was that with all the Lumners being dead, their ex-Hawkyns lands reverted to John Wille the elder who outlived John the younger (whether his brother or son was not stated).

The knowledge that Aleyn had no surviving children helps in interpreting his will. After minor religious gifts and payment of his debts, half his goods and chattels were to go to Elizabeth 'in name of her purpart and dower'; with the balance for a number of legacies. These included:

> A further £20 reward to Elizabeth
> 40s to John Lomnor draper
> 40s to Johan Hawkyn (see above for the Hawkyn and Willey connections)
> Plate and jewels to Jake Hawte and his wife and their son Henry (a relative perhaps)
> Further religious bequests and to the poor
> To Thomas Lomnor his brother his girdle and harness with silver
> To Thomas's son Henry a book in Thomas's keeping and to his brother Thomas a prymer
> To Richard Hawkins draper a ring value 13s 4d, William Spencer grocer 20s, John Willey 6s 8d and to William Sutton £5 if he agreed to be an executor

John Lomnor the draper was almost certainly the young son of William senior and Margaret of Mannington, mentioned in Margaret's will. John was made apprentice in 1485 and became a freeman and member of the Drapers' Company in 1499 (although this may have been a late registration for an apprenticeship finished seven years earlier). This would make him probably born about 1470 and about the right age to be a Mannington boy. The reference to Thomas Lomnor and his two sons gave the definite identification of Thomas the mercer and his son Thomas who started the Sharrington branch of the family.

Elizabeth Lumner's will was made the following year and proved in July 1492.[30] She also had been married three times and chose to be buried in St Sepulchre London, by the body of John Feres a previous husband. Apart from references to her other husbands John Foster and 'Alen' Lomnor, no other family was mentioned. After minor bequests the residue went to her executors William Johnson of the Temple Inn and Thomas Sharpearow citizen and draper of London. At some point between 1493 and 1500 William Johnson sued Rauff Lech gent (a witness to her will) in chancery for detention of a little black chest and plate to the value of £20.[31] The plate included a standing piece of silver and gilt with a cover and a low standing cup of silver and gilt and a plate and 2 goblets. This was in respect of 'burdeclothys' and towels bought from Elizabeth by Lech's wife. Since grocers also traded in cloth it is likely that Elizabeth had briefly continued her husband's business after his death. She may even have operated earlier than this as a draper if one of her previous husbands had been in that trade. This continuation of trade by the widows of freemen was not uncommon in late medieval and early modern London. One of the witnesses to this suit was William Apputt grocer of London. The clear implication was that William knew the Lumners but, as discussed in Chapter 1, he is an unsolved Apott puzzle.

Thomas the Mercer

Aleyn and William's brother Thomas Lumner was a freeman and member of the Mercers' Company. Although he did not hold high office, as a senior member of the Company he featured regularly in their court books.[32] Thomas appears in 1461 when he came very low down in a long list of mercers paying a grant to the King for the Earl of Warwick in the north. This may indicate that he had only recently become a member and freeman. Perhaps Aleyn, admitted to the Grocers' just a few years earlier, was the elder of the two? A few years later, in May 1467, Thomas was involved in a bet with Sir John Paston. He agreed to sell an ambling horse to Sir John with the price dependant on whether the marriage of Margaret, the King's sister and Charles, son and heir of the Duke of Burgundy would take place within two years.[33] If it did, Sir John was to pay six marks; if not, only forty shillings! This is another indication of the closeness of the Lumners to the Pastons, in London as well as Norfolk. Thomas's other connections in London included Anthony Woodville, second Earl Rivers and Lord Scales. In his eve of execution will of 1483, Scales requested payment of his debts due to Lumner 'mercer of London'.[34] The juxtaposition of these facts is deliberate. Anthony Woodville became Lord Scales through his wife; his sister married Edward IV. He was no friend of the Pastons and he played a significant part in the marriage of Edward's sister Margaret to Charles the Bold in 1468. Lumner got full price for his horse - he obviously had the inside story!

From 1461 onwards Thomas and Edmund Bettes also featured regularly in the minutes of the Mercers' Company. Bettes entries in the 1460s and 1470s showed them to have been senior men of the Company. A William Bettes was one of the four senior mercers representing the Company in Bruges. Other references showed both a William senior and junior; the relationships here are not clear, but no doubt this was a family group. In November 1505 a patent roll entry showed Edmund Bettes citizen and mercer of London involved in a claim over land in Little

Barningham, which gives a positive identification of Bettes the mercer with the Oulton and Irmingland family into which William Lumner's daughter Elizabeth had married.[35] The minutes also noted that in 1461 Geoffrey Boleyn, the London mayor just a few years earlier, was second from top of the list of subsidy payers by value. Did Lumner and Bettes get their chance in the Mercers' Company through family links to the Boleyns of London and Salle?

Many entries for Thomas Lumner have to do with the ceremonial duties so beloved of livery companies. He was often among those who rode out to meet the King on his returns to London. By January 1475 Thomas lived in 'Cordenerstrete Ward' and by September of that year he was a Warden of the Mercers' Company and had to be ready to ride out in livery. In October 1479 he was admitted to the office of Weigher of Silk in place of Nicholas Hatton. In November he was sworn in at the Guildhall, where he was given the necessaries for the office of weigher - the forerunner of the modern trading standards officer. All of the items belonged to the fellowship of the Mercery and the Weigher was responsible for keeping them in repair:

> First, a beam of iron closed in a case of leather and two laten [brass]
> basins with cords and hooks in a leather bag
> Weights of brass for raw silk of 21 ounces to the ll [pound] closed in
> leather - that is to say 8ll, 4ll, 2ll, 1ll, 8 ounces, 4 ounces, 2 ounces,
> 1 ounces
> Weights of lead for Paris and Venice silk of 17 ounces to the ll
> closed in leather - that is to say 8ll, 4ll, 2ll, 1ll, 8 ounces, 4 ounces, 2
> ounces, 1 ounces

An entry in April 1492 recorded that 'Thomas Lymnour Weigher of Silk' had died on 29th March and that he was to be succeeded by Robert Collett, who had received the best show of hands among the five candidates. When Thomas Lumner citizen and mercer of London made his will, he was a parishioner of St Peter Cornhill and left his wife Elizabeth as executrix with 'Maister' (Magister) John Brereton Doctor to help her as overseer.[36] His simple will gave a third of his net estate to Elizabeth and the balance equally to his unnamed children. Elizabeth may have been his second wife as Thomas and Henry were born some years apart. Thomas probably married in the early or mid-1460s shortly after he had been made a freeman of the Mercers' Company. His son Thomas (senior of Sharrington) would then have been born by about 1465 and married around 1486-87, with in turn Thomas's eldest son (Thomas junior) being born in about 1488-89. These dates are corroborated by later Norwich depositions and the 1542 IPM of Thomas Lumner junior of Sharrington. Some years after Thomas the mercer's death, lands in Sharrington were settled on his eldest son. These came from the Heydon family. The inference, unprovable though it is, was that Thomas the mercer probably had married either a Heydon girl (most likely) or a Boleyn girl (Sir Henry Heydon, at the heart of the land grant, had married Anne the daughter of Sir Geoffrey Boleyn). This might reinforce the possibility that it was a Boleyn connection that had got Lumner and Bettes into the Mercers' Company.

Henry the Grocer

The Corporation of London Letter Books show that Thomas Lumner mercer of London in 1492 left in the City officers' trust, via Richard Lilbourne gent and others, a £70 bond for his son Henry when of full age.[37] No doubt this was to provide capital for Henry's entry into a London trade of status after his apprenticeship, since it was clearly additive to the bequest in the will. If Henry was still so young in 1492 it is likely that his mother Elizabeth was a second wife. It seems that Henry followed his uncle's trade not his father's and was the Henry 'Lunor' admitted to the Grocers' Company in 1512.[38]

In July 1521 Henry Lumner citizen and grocer received a quitclaim of a 40s quitrent on a tenement in St Benet Sherehog parish, the property having the junction of Bucklersbury and Cheapside on the south, with a tenement in Poultry to the north.[39] This house on the east side of Bucklersbury at its junction with Poultry is likely to have been his home - just a few yards from the Hall of the Grocers' Company. In April 1541 a grant showed that Henry Lumner's house was formerly of the Priory of St Leonard Stratford and that he was under-tenant of William Rolte a serjeant at arms.[40] In April 1540 Henry Lumner and his wife Margaret seem to have taken a lease on a garden in Colman Street London, then in the tenure of Robert Studley mercer and Elinor his wife.[41] This would have been just a very short distance to the north of the property in Bucklersbury.

Nothing is known about his wife Margaret except that she had their son. No will survives for Henry and the Grocers' Company records are scarce at this date, but there is plenty of evidence that he was a busy and prominent grocer. On 12th February 1522 John Lord Berners and Raymond Gutturus (mayor of Calais) wrote from Calais to Thomas Wolsey, the King's chief minister, on a subject that showed one of the risks facing grocers and other major merchants of the sixteenth century - piracy. They said that a proclamation would be made in Calais and that all Englishmen who had been aggrieved by William Pendecherf and William Dacquebert on the sea should repair to Boulogne on Monday 17th to claim their merchandise. They sent word that the merchants in question were living in London and Wolsey must take measures accordingly. One of the claimants was specifically mentioned: Henry Lomner grocer and his cargo of figs, raisins and other grocery items.[42] One or two chancery items also survive which show Henry Lumner active in trade in London. At some point between 1533 and 1538 he sued Percival Ayres servant of George Colyns mercer for £42 owed to Lumner that had been assigned to Nicholas Cosyn, dwelling on London Bridge.[43] Various other actions in the 1520s and 1530s show Henry Lumner as a grocer, sometimes chasing trade debts, sometimes himself being chased.[44] In April 1537 he was one of three London grocers (with Robert Dean and John Lane) granted a 7 year lease on 6 acres in Newchurch Kent, presumably a trade matter rather than residential property.[45]

But Henry Lumner's name most often features in surviving records in matters relating to his debts. In June 1536 he was named with John Astley (a Norfolk cousin, grandson of Margery Lumner) and Edmund Harvey in a bond, owing £100 to the late Queen Anne Boleyn.[46] Recorded shortly after her execution, this item showed Lumner's closeness to the court although by no means heavily indebted to the Queen. His Norfolk family connections had given him a route to the Queen and the credibility to borrow money from her treasury. Sir James Boleyn, the Queen's chancellor, looked after her finances and would have been the person to tap for a loan. It may even have been a loan to finance the import of goods for the Queen. Astley's mother was probably Anne Wood of East Barsham, Sir James's sister-in-law.[47]

In 1540 Henry Lumner was sued by Sir Edward Boughton of Woolwich.[48] Sir Edward had been bound with Henry to pay £609 of Henry's debts and subsequently they agreed that this would be discharged by the payment of £20 yearly for life to Boughton by the Chamberlain of London - an agreement made in the Court of the City of London. But the annuity was no longer being paid. Henry's answer said that he had borrowed some £5,982 from Sir Edward's father and Sir Edward, that most had been repaid and that he was willing to repay the balance. He now asserted that Boughton's actions had been a major cause of his financial undoing and that Boughton had made various unlawful documents and had even suggested that Lumner should go into sanctuary at Westminster to avoid his creditors! He asked the court to investigate through an independent commissioner.

In his replication however, Boughton said that about 12 years earlier Lumner and he had done a reckoning of debts and that about £500 was then still due and that £400 of this had not been forgiven and was therefore due to Boughton. Henry had become indebted to several others including Richard Tailor pewterer and 'Mr Roche now the Mayor of London'.[49] Boughton had only received partial repayment and so the £20 annuity had been arranged even though it meant that he, Boughton, had had to sell lands to pay off the debts in which he stood bound on Henry's behalf. He asserted that Henry had not recompensed him for the debt of £5,982 and indeed said that no such sum had ever been reckoned.

Henry Lumner was now besieged with debts of a scale that would no doubt have made him well-known in the close community of the grocers in London. The next reference, in an action of 1544-51 by John his son and heir, is after his death probably in the late 1540s.[50] A letter from Anthony Cave of March 1545 referred disparagingly to one Lumner as a potential tenant of a house, preferring 'his cousin Blase or some of his friends'.[51] He may well have meant Henry Lumner, near the end of his life and when his debt problems were well-known. No such problems or stigma appear to have attached to his son John.

John Lumner the Grocer

Henry Lumner and his son John became embroiled in a long-running sequence of chancery actions involving Thwaite manor in Norfolk. The manor had come into the Lumner family through Richard Browne and his marriage to Margaret Lumner the daughter of William senior and Margaret. Richard Browne of Thwaite died in 1508 without children, leaving a complicated will first proved in July 1508.[52] Browne had lands in Erpingham and Thwaite. The former, with the sheep flock there, was to be sold by his executors to perform the will. His executors included Richard Pye of Erpingham from whose family a later bailiff or steward of Mannington was to come. The original family lands in Thwaite were given to his wife Margaret. Other legacies went to John Lumner (presumably the young draper, as it seems unlikely that Henry the grocer's son had been born by then) and to Margaret the daughter of William Lumner junior, who was about to or just had married William Bishop, a citizen of Norwich.

Margaret, Browne's widow, next married Henry Heydon esq the second or third son of Sir Henry Heydon and had no children by him either. After his death in 1536 she married Henry Cruche or Crouch, by whom again she had no children. The lengthy court battles stemmed from Crouch claiming that he had bought Thwaite manor from Sir Edward Boughton in 1540-41. Henry Lumner the grocer said he had been granted the manor by a fine of 1532-33 by his first cousin Margaret Lumner/Browne/Heydon/Crouch and it was still his. This was all tangled up with Henry Lumner's deals with Boughton over his own debts. Boughton claimed he had bought Lumner's interest in Thwaite from him in 1538-39 and that it was only a life interest after Margaret died. After Henry's death his son John Lumner, also a grocer, continued the battle during 1544-51 on the premise that it was a full interest, not merely a life interest to his father. Boughton and Crouch denied that John had any claim over it. Richard Osborne, another London grocer involved with Henry Lumner, even argued that Crouch was neither a close servant of the crown nor a poor man and so should not be allowed to use the court of requests for one of his actions. At one point Edmund Lumner of Mannington was drawn into the fight.[53] He was accused by Henry Crouch (and by implication Margaret), both resident in Gresley in Derbyshire, of having given Margaret bad advice on Henry Heydon's death, persuading her to grant Thwaite to Sir John Heydon in return for an annuity of £40. Seven years after her marriage to Crouch she claimed that Heydon had not paid her the annuity for that whole period. Edmund said he was sure Sir John had been paying the money and had receipts to prove it. He would not hand over the papers and obligations that he held on Margaret's behalf, in case Crouch should try to sell Thwaite to her disadvantage. Sir John had stopped payments because he had heard that Margaret had died. If this was untrue Edmund would have no hesitation in suing Sir John for non-payment. In the end the Lumners did not manage to make good their claim to Thwaite. [54] For more on Thwaite see Appendix 1.

'Nobody expects the Spanish Inquisition'[55]

Apart from his admission to the Grocers' Company as apprentice of Thomas Bowyer and as a freeman of the City of London in 1541, little is known about John Lumner. One small snippet shows that, like his father, he was an adventurous merchant not a stay-at-home shopkeeper. On 8th July 1540 John Lumner was one of 25 signatories to a letter of complaint to Roger Basyng of the King's Household about the treatment of the English in Spain.[56] The letter was from William Ostrych, the Governor of the English nation in Andalucia assembled at San Lucar. Lumner was joined in this complaint from sherry country by Blase Saunders, a major London grocer later well-known for his involvement in the Spanish wine trade. Blase was also a trustee in the marriage settlement of Edmund Lumner and Katherine the widow of the mercer Richard Wigmore.[57] The Englishmen were complaining specifically about the Inquisition imprisoning and torturing one Thomas Pery of London. But they were making a wider point that the English community was constantly harassed and lived in fear of the fathers of the Inquisition, having to face among others the tricky question: 'is the King [Henry VIII] a good Christian?' Four or five others remained in prison and some in England feared to return to San Lucar. Trade was suffering.

Despite extensive research in London parishes, John's year and place of death has not been found. The absence of any later references to children suggests he died unmarried or at least childless. Perhaps he spent much of his time abroad and may even have died in Spain (but not we hope on the rack). With his death, probably in the 1550s or 1560s, the three generation run of Lumner grocers came to an end.

Thomas senior of Sharrington

Returning to the 1490s, Thomas the mercer's elder son Thomas did not stay in London or go into trade but was described as Thomas Lumner senior gent of Sharrington. He was clearly taken under the wing of Margaret Lumner/Brigges/Paston. He was given lands in Sharrington by Margaret, possibly of course at the prior arrangement of his father, and also acquired land in his own right. The gifted lands may have been the Sharrington property willed to Margaret by Thomas Brigges which were to come to her after the death of John Sharrington and his wife.[58] The IPM of his son Thomas Lumner junior of 1542 showed that Margaret, previously the wife of Thomas Brigges, was seized as of her right with her then husband Edmund Paston esq in messuages and lands in Sharrington, Gunthorpe and Bately with a tenement and the liberty of a foldcourse for 50 sheep in Gunthorpe.[59] These premises had been granted in a charter of July 1499 to Edmund and Margaret by John Heydon esq (son and heir of Sir Henry Heydon) through a long list of feoffees, including Sir Thomas Lovell for the King, Sir Henry Heydon, Richard Southwell esq, Thomas Langdon, John Wynter junior esq, Thomas Cosyn clerk and Edward Calwe. The last two were later executors of Sir John Heydon's will.[60] While this might have been a marriage settlement on Edmund and Margaret, it seems unlikely for three reasons. Both were well-provided for, had married late in life (probably a few years earlier) and neither seems to have had direct or close Heydon relations. (Margaret's daughter did not marry Henry Heydon junior until after 1508). Why should the Heydon family grant them land earlier? As already suggested perhaps Thomas the mercer married a Heydon girl and Thomas Brigges, and then Edmund and Margaret all acted as trustees for the future Thomas of Sharrington.[61]

The Lumner of Sharrington IPM went on to say that the 1499 transaction had been followed by a fine, levied at Westminster at the Purification of St Mary 1500-01, between Thomas Lumner (senior), John Heydon, Francis Calybut and Richard

Browne plaintiffs and Edmund and Margaret defendants. Through this fine Edmund and Margaret recognized that the messuages and lands (described in round figures only as 100 acres of land, 100 acres of pasture and a fold for 500 sheep) were rightfully Thomas Lumner's by their gift (with John, Francis and Richard as his trustees) and quitclaimed themselves to him. Thomas outlived all his trustees and was fully seized of the premises by his death on 20th September 1525. The premises then descended first to his son and heir Thomas junior. At his death on 14th or 24th December 1541 the property went to his son, William Lumner of Sharrington, who in October 1542 was aged 11. The premises in Sharrington, Gunthorpe and elsewhere, being about 130 acres and several messuages were held under various lordships including the crown, the Duchy of Lancaster, Henry Dawbney of Sharrington and others. A further 10 acres or so were held as a result of Thomas senior's 1523 purchase from Thomas Davy senior of Gunthorpe and 2 closes and some land bought of Simon Mony and others in 1507. In total the estate may have covered about 200 acres.

Thomas Lumner senior of Sharrington married twice, probably with two children by each wife. As already discussed, his first wife was Anne Lumner. Thomas and Anne had probably one son and one daughter before Anne died in 1508, which date is recorded in a memorial inscription in Sharrington church noted in the eighteenth century by Thomas Martin.[62] A number of chancery actions show Thomas Lumner as executor of John Fuller of Sharrington.[63] These date from the period 1518-29, so therefore could relate to Thomas senior or junior. None of the actions adds anything significant about the Lumner family, other than that they were not shy of resorting to chancery when occasion demanded. Around 1514 Thomas senior married again. Elizabeth the daughter of John Porter of Warham was the young widow of Edward Yelverton. It would seem likely that Henry Lumner and his brother John were both born to Elizabeth. Elizabeth was still alive in about 1559, thirty years after her second husband had died.

Henry the fishmonger

The two younger stepbrothers of Thomas junior were Henry and John. Henry was involved in London trade as a fishmonger. The two children of Harry Lumner baptised in St Dionis Backchurch London - Mary on 24th June 1561 and William on 14th June 1562 - were probably the younger siblings of his first born son Henry.[64] William was buried the next day and there is no reference to Mary or any more of Henry senior's children surviving. Henry Lumner junior was active as a young man on Guernsey by the early 1570s as well as being a merchant in London. In December 1582 he and Henry Hussey were granted a royal licence to export 2,000 tuns of beer, paying only the customs as levied during the reign of Henry VIII.[65]Henry featured in chancery actions and can be tracked through them to Guernsey, where by 1584 he had a role as a tax collector as part of Sir Thomas Leighton's administration of the island. See Chapter 6 for his role on the island and his marriage to an islander.

Henry senior left no will but his administration in 1563 was granted to his then wife Cecily.[66] At this time the fishmongers were a wealthy company. Henry senior was an executor of his childless brother John's will in about 1560. In this role he was joined by Thomas Pye who was originally from Erpingham and probably after 1563 became estate steward at Mannington. There is every indication that even though a Londoner, Henry senior remained quite close to his Norfolk family connections.

In late 1561 or early 1562 Henry launched a chancery action against Alice Framingham widow and her son Robert Framingham.[67] This action was therefore after the death of his brother John Lumner and by implication after the death of Henry's mother Elizabeth since she was not party to the action. Henry recited that John Porter in his lifetime held various messuages, lands and a foldcourse in Warham and that in consideration of a marriage between Edward Yelverton gent and his daughter Elizabeth he had settled these premises on Edward and Elizabeth and their heirs. Edward died and Elizabeth held the property as survivor. The depositions indicate that this was about 1514. She then married Thomas Lumner senior of Sharrington. In 1536, some nine years after Thomas had died, she assured the estate to her son Henry Lumner and his heirs. He now complained that this deed had somehow come into the hands of the Framinghams and that he was being denied his lands.

Alice Framingham answered that Elizabeth had no right to the property and that William Yelverton, Henry Pagrave, William Woodcocke, William Inglyshe and John Wilkins were lawfully seized (as trustees for William Yelverton, presumably the elder). The premises had only been conveyed to Elizabeth for the term of her life, which Robert in his answer echoed. Elizabeth was referred to by the Framinghams as Elizabeth Swan or Swanne, having remarried perhaps to a member of the family of that name in Sharrington at the time. William Yelverton had good title through conveyances and he and his co-feoffees had assured the premises to Alice and her heirs. Henry replied, largely with bluster, that Alice had not shown what these deeds were. He repeated that Elizabeth was the daughter and heir of John Porter and that Elizabeth and her heirs were seized after Edward Yelverton died. Henry also tried the pitch that the co-feoffees had not protested in 1536 when the lands were assured to him.

The action went to the next stage of gathering depositions at Walsingham in September 1562 before Sir Christopher Heydon and others.[68] The interrogatories or questions from the Framinghams were simple and brief, asking witnesses to describe what they knew about the title to the premises of the various parties. William Yelverton esq of Rougham aged 58 said that he had the premises by conveyances from Thomas Skarlett and Katherine his wife (who by an ambiguous phrase might have previously been married to a Dowghtie). He did not know of Elizabeth Swan widow having any right or title to the lands. Thomas Skarlett a North Walsham yeoman aged 57 said that he married Katherine the daughter and heir of Edward Yelverton, by whom he had the premises. He had sold them to William Yelverton. While they would have had no value to the owner during Elizabeth's lifetime, the reversionary rights would have had value to those able to take a long view such as the wealthy Yelverton family. Unfortunately neither witness clarified whether Elizabeth was the mother of this Katherine or whether Katherine had been Edward's daughter by a previous marriage. The latter is perhaps more likely since the chancery action and other information made no reference to Henry Lumner having a half-sister by Elizabeth. This remains a bit of a mystery - how did Katherine have rights to the property if she was already alive when Edward and Elizabeth married? Was there a specific clause in the original settlement giving her the long term rights?

To Henry's questions, William Yelverton answered that his father William Yelverton enfeoffed Edward and Elizabeth and paid £20 to John Porter in a deed of 14th July 1511. His father had certain documents, he thought, because he was Edward Yelverton's executor after his death in about 1514. Since then Elizabeth had been seized of the premises until two years ago (by implication when she had died and when her life interest ceased). William Porter husbandman of Holkham aged 56 said he knew Henry Lumner well and knew that John Porter had the lands, which he heard that Elizabeth and Edward had at their marriage. He added that about 24 or 25 years ago (roughly consistent with her assuring the property by deed to Henry in 1537) Elizabeth came to Stibbard and complained to his father in front of him that she had delivered evidences to William Yelverton deceased and was seeking counsel how to retrieve them. Perhaps this was simply when William Yelverton senior died; but just possibly this was around the time she married Mr Swan and she was seeking to ensure that her son Henry would get what she thought was his right to the premises after she died.

Tracing John Porter the father of Elizabeth has proved difficult. There is a will of John Porter of Warham made in February 1520.[69] No mention was made of an Elizabeth, only his son William and a daughter Agnes Chory. He was probably the grandfather of the William who was a witness (his father was still alive in 1537 or so) and probably the grandfather too of Elizabeth, if her father had died by February 1520.

Seeing the Yelvertons in this action with the Lumners is a nice coincidence. Just a few years afterwards, William Yelverton's young daughter Jane would be married to Edmund Lumner junior of Mannington. All forgiven by then perhaps but Jane had learnt the game of chancery at a tender age and would use it later!

John Lumner yeoman of Sharrington

Back in Sharrington, Henry and Thomas junior's brother John Lumner did not leave much of a document trail. He was simply a yeoman farmer, with only a remote chance of ever inheriting Mannington. Documents place him in Sharrington in the 1540s and in 1550-51.[70] By March 1553 he may have been living in Erpingham where, with parish consent, churchwardens Thomas Pye and John Mason sold him a gilt chalice for 110s.[71] Fortunately he broke the family tradition by leaving a helpful will made in late March and proved in early April 1559.[72]

John Lumner, by then of Erpingham and seeking to be buried there, died unmarried and childless. The Erpingham register recorded that he was buried there on 2nd April 1559. He left his goods and corn in Smallburgh, where he must also have farmed, to John Marham (sometimes given as Martham) of Smallburgh and his wife Margaret and son John Marham. Margaret was Lumner's niece, the daughter of his eldest brother Thomas Lumner junior of Sharrington. Of the rest of his goods and chattels one third was to go to Thomas Rysebroke the husband of his other niece Elizabeth, one third to his brother Harry or Henry Lumner and one third to Thomas Pye. Henry and Thomas Pye were his executors and were charged with collecting debts due to John, with the proceeds to be divided four ways as above. The inclusion of Pye is interesting. Probably a son or grandson of the Richard Pye feoffee and executor of members of the Lumner family earlier in the century, Thomas was at some point to become the estate steward or bailiff at Mannington. In 1559 he seems however to have been living down in London. Perhaps he was working for Henry Lumner the fishmonger. Alternatively he may already have been a long-standing servant of Edmund Lumner and had remained in London after Edmund's death in 1558 working for his widow Katherine.

At some point presumably fairly soon after John Lumner's death in 1559 his executors launched a chancery action against John Marham of Smallburgh, the husband of one of John Lumner's two nieces.[73] Marham stood indebted to John Lumner for £52 16s 2d recorded in sundry writings. But he had now also got his hands on some of Lumner's goods and chattels. The executors, both then being down in London, claimed they had not heard about Lumner's death until a long time afterwards. No inventory had been made, nor any account of his money and Marham now refused to pay or deliver up the goods despite their requests. The executors were now charged with paying various bequests but without the money or goods to do so.

Poor Margaret had suffered at the hands of a rascal before marrying John Marham. Her uncle John Lumner was involved at the margins of the affair. Edmund Lumner esq of Mannington and others gave evidence to the Norwich Consistory Court in 1550-51 for a paternity action in which Margaret was the claimant.[74] The action of Margaret Lumner against Nicholas Poynter was effectively for breach of promise over a commitment to marry. In his evidence Edmund Lumner, aged 56, described Margaret simply as his 'kinswoman and daughter of my uncle's son deceased'. (He could, more accurately, have said 'great-grand-daughter of my great uncle'.) Her mother was Helen Lumner of Sharrington wife of Thomas Lumner junior of Sharrington. Nicholas Poynter was described just as 'a servant of the Earl of Surrey' and may well have been one of the large clutch of sons of the Poynter family of East Dereham.

Edmund gave evidence that Nicholas had come to his house saying he 'did bear good will to Margaret in the way of marriage' and that he had come to Edmund since he understood he would pay £10 at Margaret's marriage – a legacy left her in her father's will, of which Edmund was executor (almost needless to say, this will does not survive). But Edmund said that he had not taken up the executorship since the father had died a poor man and all his money had been taken up paying his debts. He told Nicholas either to marry Margaret without the £10 or it would be best to avoid her company. Apparently Nicholas visited Edmund again, at which time he said that in fact Margaret 'was already his wife before god' and that he had a Bishop's licence to marry her whenever the two of them wished. The implication here is of an existing formal betrothal which would then have been taken (by some) to be as firm a commitment of marriage as the final church service itself. Poynter had admitted to Lumner that he was only delaying the marriage to get what he could - a dowry of some sort.

As Poynter was living in the girl's house, Lumner advised Helen Lumner and her 'brother' (John Lumner, her deceased husband's brother) that they should put Poynter out of her house, 'less the maid should lose her honest name by reason the said Poynter did nightly lie in the house of the said Helen'. Lumner continued that Poynter had confessed to him several times that he and Margaret were sworn together and 'were man and wife together before god's presence at the premises'. It seems Poynter did leave Sharrington and Edmund had heard that he went to Norwich and had married a maid there. Doctor Shaxton had confirmed that Poynter and one Mary Dokking were married in the Hospital Church at Norwich.

The second witness was Walter Barwick, aged 40, the parish clerk of Sharrington. He said that he had chanced to be at Helen Lumner's house upon a working day at breakfast (presumably hoping for a free meal). At this breakfast Helen, John and Nicholas were sitting at the board together and since 'the common voice in Sharrington was' that Nicholas and Margaret would wed, he asked Nicholas: 'Goodman Poynter, when shall Mr Parson and I take pain to unite you two together'? Poynter answered: 'Mr Parson is very great and will not marry me without money. I trust some day to have a good fellow to marry us without money'. Barwick went on to say that Poynter slept at the Lumner house most nights for the space of half a year, while Margaret was there. And during that time Margaret became pregnant, he believed by Poynter, who he had heard paid for the nursing of the child. How the scandal was resolved and what happened to Poynter is not known but Margaret was fairly hurriedly married off to John Marham.

Thomas junior of Sharrington

Thomas junior was born about 1487-88 and grew up in Sharrington. He was certainly living there in 1505 aged about 17 as he later testified to being at a wedding there.[75] Thomas inherited the Sharrington property when his father died in 1525. His sister Joan married Henry Dawbney, the head of the senior family in Sharrington and lord of the manor, and bore him two sons and three daughters. Giles died without issue, but Christopher continued the Dawbney line and was lord of the manor there by 1565. One of his daughters Joan married into the family of the Bramptons of Brampton who will later feature in a small way in one of the chancery actions.

Although his land was in Sharrington, Thomas was not always resident there. In 1529 aged 40 he gave evidence in a case about a Sharrington contested will when he was described as of Itteringham where he had been resident for a year or more. The implication is that Thomas may have been looking after the Mannington estate for his cousin Edmund. It is hard to come up with any other explanation for why a forty year old Sharrington relative would otherwise be resident in Itteringham, 9 miles away, when he had, since his father's death four years earlier, been in possession of his own small Sharrington estate. Edmund only became visible in Norfolk around 1540 when he was in his mid-forties. He had come fully into the Mannington estate some 15 years earlier when his mother died. If Edmund was away in London until this time, Thomas was probably acting as his trusted steward possibly even running the home farm. When staying there Thomas probably lived in what is now Itteringham's Old Rectory, which was later in the century a high status house linked to Mannington.

Thomas was obviously seen as a reliable man of some ability as early as 1516 when he was given a power of attorney concerning some Cawston lands being conveyed to Henry Heydon esq and Richard Pye of Erpingham.[76] John Jannys of Aylsham and Henry Goodman of Cawston were leasing or conveying to Henry and Richard two messuages and lands in Cawston, one called 'Cayses' in a street called 'Sygate' with land in 'Boywodfeld' and the other 'Mowtynges' at Sygate with lands in 'Wyndemyllfeld'.[77]

Despite his inheritance, Thomas junior of Sharrington died in 1541, greatly in debt. His widow Eleanor or 'Helen' Lumner (described as 'Ellen from Kent' in the Visitation) as we have seen was left to cope with children and troublesome lodgers. He and Ellen, as well as their two daughters Margaret and Elizabeth, had also produced son and heir William, born around 1530-31.[78]

William Lumner of Sharrington

Perhaps because of his father's role, William was obviously close to his Mannington cousins. The link was strengthened when he married Anne the daughter of Thomas Guybon esq of King's Lynn. Most of Thomas Guybon's children were not by his second wife Rose Spring, but by Elizabeth Thorsby his first. Anne, though, may have been Rose's child, named after her mother. Unfortunately Guybon's will did not name any of his children.[79] Rose Spring, the daughter of the very wealthy clothier Thomas Spring of Lavenham, married again - to Edmund Lumner of Mannington. So William Lumner of Sharrington's wife Anne was the daughter of the first husband of the first wife of Edmund Lumner senior - in that sense, Edmund's stepdaughter!

Rose's will also was short, mentioning her first husband but no other relations. She simply left everything to her second husband Edmund Lumner senior.[80] William was later named as the main beneficiary in a settlement of 1555 should there be no male heirs in the Mannington line; that is, he would succeed to Mannington if Edmund junior and his younger brother (also, confusingly, a William) had no sons. There will be more about the Guybons shortly, but this shows just how close the linkage between the Mannington and Sharrington branches of the Lumner family still was by the middle of the sixteenth century. It also explains why the default sequence of heirs would have shifted from the Mannington line to Sharrington if necessary.

William of Sharrington also made a contribution to the legal theme. In May 1566 he was on the receiving end of a court of requests bill of complaint from Richard Davy of the senior family of Gunthorpe.[81] Apparently their fathers Gregory Davy and Thomas Lumner had had various dissensions and strife over the Lumner lands that sat on the edge of Sharrington field. This action focused on a sheep shack issue. Lumner argued it should be deferred until the same cause had finished its path through common law. More money for the lawyers!

William Lumner died on 12th August 1593, never, of course, having inherited Mannington.[82] His inventory showed him to have been a modestly well-off farmer. While styled gent, he was a yeoman farmer with mud on his boots. The total value of his goods was £50, including cattle. Only his best bedstead, cows, horses and 30 combs of rye came in at above the £1 per item level. With no will and no surviving Sharrington registers, relatively little is known of his family. William had two daughters and three sons. A later action referred to his eldest son Edmund, who probably died by the early to mid-1590s, by implication without issue and possibly before his father.[83] By that time William's heir in Sharrington was his second son Robert Lumner who died around February 1605 in Hindringham.[84] There is no evidence that Robert had a surviving male heir.[85] Robert had taken over their father's administration in 1597 from his sister Anne who had been granted it in 1593.[86]

William's other daughter, Philippa, had married Robert Rogers in 1589 in Itteringham. When Rogers died in Mannington in 1613 he was clearly working there as a farmer on his own account and may also have run the home farm of the estate.[87] Philippa, his widow, was granted administration. In his inventory he was described as gent of Mannington. The inventory made in November 1613 by Anthony Page (of Saxthorpe), Robert Eldyn, James Brigge and Edward Tynblerd showed that Rogers was not a wealthy man. His personal possessions were beds and bedding and a range of linen and household items, none of any great value. His only plate consisted of two teaspoons valued at 10s.

However, the inventory is most interesting as his beds were in two rooms - the 'little parlour' and the 'gatehouse chamber'. The former was the room in Mannington Hall in which seisin had been delivered to John Potts in 1584. It was the estate office or study of the head of the household. This implies that Philippa and Robert had a trusted role in the household. As he bore the title of gentleman, he may even have acted as steward. No doubt they looked after the Hall when the Heydons and the Potts children were not in residence. The Little Parlour was probably at the back of the northern end of the house.

The evidence for an occupied room above a gatehouse at Mannington is an exciting find. The gatehouse room contained an 'old featherbed' and old bedding, implying that it was no longer much used and the bedding was of lesser value than the bed and bedding in the little parlour. His other possessions were in the buttery, kitchen, dairy, boulting (in fact mostly brewing vessels) and baking houses and in the barns. All these were service rooms and buildings belonging to the main

Hall. His agricultural implements and a variety of stored crops (largely barley with some wheat and rye) and various animals (over 100 sheep - some welsh and some 'country' - plus some cattle and pigs) show him to be a yeoman tenant farmer in his own right, with well in excess of £100 worth of livestock and grain. The grain was variously in the 'rye barn', the 'barley barn', the 'other barn' and the 'hay chamber'. Withers, the butcher owed him £6 for 'fat ware'.

Where was the gatehouse? On the north side of the moat, the Mannington map of 1595 clearly showed an arched structure astride the driveway that runs over the moat to the north door of the Hall. It would have been large enough to accommodate a single room upstairs.[88]

The Rogers buried their daughter Philippa in Itteringham in June 1591. Much later a Robert Rogers was buried in Itteringham, presumably their son. Philippa and her husband probably looked after her brother Thomas before his death in 1604. 'Thomas Lumner gent' was buried in Itteringham on the 27th January. He may have been a tenant or servant of the Houghton family. There is no indication that he married or had heirs.[89] The same parish register also shows probable bad behaviour in the Rogers household with the burial in June 1599 of Edward Rogers begotten of Annie Richardson.

William Lumner's eldest son had been the Edmund referred to in the court materials. Although there is a possibility that he may have briefly been married to a young L'Estrange girl, he could not have had any heirs. If he had, his younger brother Robert would not have been able to pursue his claim to Mannington.[90] The Norfolk Lumners eventually died out without male heirs in any branch of the family. The last of the Sharrington male line ended with Robert, but not before he had made a good attempt at claiming Mannington from John Potts.

Chapter 5

The Matriarch of Mannington

_____

Margaret Lumner was the first of a series of notable women in Mannington's history who lived long lives. Their many marriages and children led to complex inheritance problems. Her grandson Edmund senior married twice. His widow Katherine, the next matriarch, lived through most of the sixteenth century. Her son Edmund junior, the heir to Mannington, died before his mother and Mannington lost its link with the Lumners.

In Chapter 4 the children of William Lumner senior, builder of Mannington, were introduced: his three sons, William (his heir), John the draper and Henry, and his four daughters (with their seven husbands!). Elizabeth's second husband Robert Bettes of Irmingland was important for his local land ownership, some of which later would be sold to the Mannington estate. Although she seems not to have had any children by her first husband Whinberg, Elizabeth Bettes gave birth to Margaret, Elizabeth and son and heir John.[1] Her husband had ambitions outside the county. In his later years at least, he had secured a role in London as well as his lands in Norfolk. In 1538-39 'Robert Bettes gent of Irmingland' was appointed to a post at the Tower of London to enhance the nation's capability in archery and firearms. Unfortunately Robert died in February 1559 without a will so no more is known about him.[2] Elizabeth lived on in Oulton until 1571 and her will gave some details about the husbands and children of her two elder daughters Elizabeth and Margaret.[3] Of her sons only John, the eldest, was mentioned and then only in his role as supervisor. From the Heydon and Irmingland parish register, it appears that a Thomas and a Robert were also sons of Robert Bettes and Elizabeth. However it seems that there was another son, William, who married Katherine Dodge's Wigmore daughter. The eldest son John Bettes married well. His first wife Anne was the widow of Thomas Fermour esq and daughter of Christopher Coote of Blo Norton. John and Anne seem to have had at least two sons one of whom died relatively young. Thomas was groomed as the heir and attended Gonville and Caius College in 1577. When Thomas died about 1588, John's heir became Henry, his second son. Henry, who may have lived in Saxthorpe, was still alive in the late 1590s when his parents sold Irmingland property to John Potts. The connection to the Coote family is also relevant since they held Coldham manor in Little Barningham, immediately adjacent to Mannington Hall. Thomas Bettes was to become the steward of this tiny old manor and its ancient site which, later, was to feature in acrimonious court actions involving the Cootes and Dodges. John Bettes's second wife was Margaret Gawsell, by whom he had a son Edmund and five daughters.

William Lumner junior of Mannington

As the eldest son, William Lumner junior was due to inherit Mannington after his mother's death. But she lived to a good age, marrying twice more and surviving until 1504. Prior to this William seems to have been impatient to inherit Mannington. As early as the 1480s he used a chancery action to establish Margaret's current right and his reversionary right to Mannington after her death.[4] Lumner sued his mother, her husband Thomas Brigges, John Cussyng chaplain, Thomas Gente and John Witton, the men all being feoffees to uses for his father. William junior's claim was that since his father's death the manor of Mannington should have been released to him by the feoffees. His action included a brief and no doubt formulaic description of the estate: 300 acres of land, 100 acres of meadow and 600 acres of pasture in Mannington, Itteringham, Saxthorpe, Barningham, Wolterton and Oulton. Even if the acreages are at best only indicative, they at least show that the estate had a very modest amount of arable and was then being run largely for sheep.

Brigges and Cussyng answered that the manor was left in his will by William senior to the use of himself and Margaret, or whoever lived the longest, with reversion only then to his heirs. This showed that there had been a separate will or testament by Lumner relating to his real estate, which has not survived. Since Margaret was still alive, William junior did not yet have any claim to the estate. There was sufficient disagreement between the parties for a commission of enquiry to be required, the writ being issued in November 1482:

> Commission to the King's kinsman Anthony, Earl Rivers, Henry Heydon, William Boleyn, Richard Southwell, John Fyncham, Henry Spelman and James Hoberd [Hobart], certain dissensions having arisen between William Lumnour on the one part and Thomas Brygge of Mannington, Co. Norfolk, gentilman and Margaret his wife on the other, to summon the parties and other persons and examine them and put their examinations in writing and to enquire by inquest into certain felonies murders trespasses and offences committed by the said Thomas and Margaret Brygge late the wife of William Lumnour and to certify thereon to the King and Council in the quinzaine of midsummer next.

The writ has been interpreted as meaning that Lumner (or Brigges) was being investigated for murder and other very serious crimes but this was simply the standard wording of the time when local senior gentry were commissioned to look into matters relating to a chancery suit. They were given wide powers to investigate anything concerning the parties that came their way. Presumably they found for the defendants. Since Margaret still had possessions in various rooms at Mannington when she wrote her will in 1504, William probably did not come into the manor until after her death as his father had originally intended.

Another chancery action dating from the period 1493-1500 showed that William 'Lomenour' gent of Norwich had sold 'Sir' John Porter, a priest, a grey horse for 20s but had reneged on the deal and sold it to someone else.[5] If this was young William Lumner he was then living in Norwich. However, although the reference to 'gent' is not specific enough to identify him absolutely, the link with the Porter family is interesting.

During these long years waiting to take control of Mannington, William must have pursued other sources of income, since he would have had no right to anything from Mannington unless specific provision had been made in his father's will. Given the preponderance of relations in trade, he might have operated as a merchant. However, no trace of him in such a role anywhere in Norfolk or in London survives, perhaps because he did not seek formal apprenticeship or freeman status in either city. His activities and place of residence from the mid-1490s to his death (before 1522) are unrecorded. As he left no surviving will and there were neither letters of administration nor an IPM for him, his date of death and place of burial remain a mystery. However, there is one clue that might suggest that William died quite early in the century and possibly soon after his mother.

In 1509 in the roll of pardons given at Henry VIII's accession, an entry showed 'Sir Philip Calthorpe of Norwich and Mannington'.[6] Five years after Margaret Lumner's death this raises all sorts of questions. Sir Philip's main house was near the cathedral in Norwich. Was he sometimes at Mannington, staying with William Lumner, or was he actually a tenant, resident there? Was William even still alive? Given that Sir Philip had also appeared in Lumner deeds of the turn of the century and later as a family trustee, had a Lumner married his sister (or daughter) or was he in some other way closely related? As the Visitation information on the Calthorpe family at this period is sparse and that on the Lumners non-existent, there are no easy answers to these questions.[7]

Equally shadowy are William junior's family circumstances. His mother's will gave his wife as Margery and the 1522 subsidy roll for Mannington showed Margery Lumner, widow, holding the manor on her own.[8] It is possible therefore that William may have died years before, at any time after 1504, leaving the Mannington estate in the hands of his widow.[9] All in all, little has survived about William Lumner junior and it is even possible that he did not spend any or much time at Mannington. He was possibly well into his thirties or even his forties when he finally inherited Mannington and he may not have outlived his mother by more than a few years. His widow Margery ran Mannington until her death in about 1525 when, with the end of her life interest, the manor passed to their son Edmund.[10]

Links with Sir Philip Calthorpe

Margery's maiden name is unknown. Might she have been a sister (or daughter) of Sir Philip Calthorpe? He was son and heir of John Calthorpe of Nettlested in Suffolk, who had come into the manor there through his wife Elizabeth the daughter of Roger Wentworth esq of Nettlested. His grandfather was Sir William

Calthorpe who died in 1495, but unfortunately Sir William's will did not detail any grandchildren.[11] Sir Philip was sheriff of Suffolk in 1499.[12] According to the Visitation Sir Philip had no brothers and three sisters: Anne who married John Cresnor esq and Edward Knevett, Agnes who married William Curson esq and John Crane, and Margaret who was Abbess of Bruisyard in Suffolk.[13] There is no mention anywhere of another sister Margery, but with so little written about the family and no long-term male line from Sir Philip to provide accurate pedigrees, there may have been other female siblings.

Sir Philip married twice.[14] When he died on 24th August 1534 his son and heir Philip was aged 50 or more, so born about 1480, and his second wife Jane and her 4 children were also alive at the date of his IPM in 1535.[15] These dates make it possible that Sir Philip might just have had a daughter old enough to be the mother of William Lumner junior's two children, since Edmund appears to have been born in about 1495-96. From this point onwards Sir Philip was certainly closely involved in Lumner affairs. For whatever reason, he became a Lumner/Browne trustee by 1495 and continued as such at least until 1516.[16] In 1516, at the request of Henry Heydon esq Sir Philip confirmed the demise of land in Cawston which he had as a feoffee for Richard Browne of Cawston - Margaret Lumner's husband - dating back to 1495, when he was co-feoffee with Sir Henry Heydon, Richard Browne and Thomas Langdon. The three other feoffees were all related to the Lumners by marriage (Henry Heydon esq and Browne were married to William's sister Margaret, Langdon to his sister Anne). This hints that Sir Philip might also have been related.[17] In passing it is worth noting that Calthorpe held Smallburgh manor which might give a clue as to why John Lumner of Sharrington had ended up with some land there and why his niece Marham settled there.[18]

Margery Lumner's children

William and Margery Lumner had a daughter Margaret and one son Edmund, the heir to Mannington. Margaret married William Bishop who is shown on the 1522 subsidy roll for Marsham as a gentleman with significant land and cattle. Bishop made his will in August 1543 and it was proved in January 1546.[19] While wanting to be buried in Marsham he also had strong connections to Aylsham, Tuttington and several parishes nearby as well as Crostwight near North Walsham, where he held the manor of Costeyns. He left small legacies to his kinsmen Edmund Bishop and Robert Bishop the younger. Margaret and William would seem to have had no children and he left all his real and personal estate to his wife whom he made executrix. Her brother Edmund Lumner senior was to be supervisor. The witnesses included Robert Clarke gent, who had been given Bintry manor in Itteringham by the Lumners in 1537.[20] He was a resident variously of Aylsham and Buxton (where Bishop also held lands). Margaret Bishop outlived her brother and died at some point between March and October 1566.[21] She was buried next to her husband in Marsham. Small legacies went to her godchildren, including the children of Robert Marsham, Margery (the daughter of Edmund Bishop of

Marsham her supervisor) and her 'nephew' Thomas Langdon (actually her great-nephew or cousin). She also left £20 (when he became 21) to her nephew Edmund Lumner (junior) of Mannington. Edmund was then, as she described in her will, the ward of Sir Christopher Heydon following the death of Edmund senior. Wardships were a valuable asset and the Heydons were nothing if not opportunistic. A later Sir Christopher would keep better hold of the heir of Mannington. Margaret's executrix was her niece Mistress Margery Underwood.

Edmund Lumner senior of Mannington: a major player

Edmund senior was the first to have a significant impact on the Mannington estate. While he was busy in Norfolk local government activities, Edmund also seems to have had a sustained presence in London, perhaps reinforcing the idea that his father may have been in London too. If his grandfather was the well-connected Sir Philip Calthorpe this too would go some way to explain Edmund's tax gathering role and the proximity of Henry Lumner his grocer uncle to the court of Queen Anne Boleyn. In August 1531, in his mid-30s, Edmund was appointed by letters patent to the potentially lucrative post of Surveyor of the Petty Customs and of the Subsidy of Tonnage and Poundage in London, following Thomas Palmer the previous office holder.[22] He was to hold this appointment until June 1546.[23] While he had staff to do much of the work it would seem likely that this quite high profile tax collecting role would have required his regular presence in London. Edmund Lumner, with most of the nation's gentry, was called up in early 1544 to 'attend the king at war in France'. He was to be on parade with 10 men on foot in the Vanguard - presumably Mannington and Itteringham men, but equally they might have been Londoners - but as Surveyor of the Custom House of London, he was one of those given a grant of exemption on 8th August 1544.[24] In June 1549, Thomas Coleshill of Chigwell, Essex was appointed to the same role and given a life grant 'as amply as Edmund Lumner held it' with £36 13s 4d yearly for himself and £10 yearly for his clerks.[25]

At home he improved the Mannington estate by building up the manorial holdings in Wolterton and Itteringham.[26] Edmund already held the whole of Mannington parish and a third of the land in Itteringham. To this he added half of Wolterton parish lands, a considerable area of closes and arable land acquired in 1540.[27] Throughout the 1540s major changes were made to the estate, with an open field on the west side of Itteringham probably converted into a single tenant farm and land allocated in Wolterton in recompense for loss of strips in the West field.[28] This, together with the estate's smaller holdings in Little Barningham and Saxthorpe, made up the estate that John Potts was to buy later in the century.

Lumner was also active in a variety of roles around north Norfolk and seems to have been well-connected to the powerful Boleyn family in nearby Blickling. In October 1553 Edmund Lumner, with Thomas Payne of Itteringham, the steward of all the Boleyn/Blickling lands, was made trustee in a licence to enfeoff the manors of Hevingham, Cawston, Kerdeston and Reepham.[29] The manors were for the use of

Sir James Boleyn and his wife Elizabeth for life and afterwards would revert to the Lady Elizabeth daughter of Henry VIII, the future Queen. The document bears the bold, clear signatures on it of Edmund and Thomas. Again, the putative Calthorpe link might help to explain this connection. In November 1553 Edmund 'Limmor' of Mannington esq was on a pardon roll.[30] Edmund served as Commissioner of Sewers for Norfolk from January 1535, with the senior men of the county: Sir James Boleyn, Sir Roger Townshend, Sir John Heydon, Sir Francis Lovell, Richard Southwell, Edmund Windham, Thomas Godsalve, Francis Moundeford, John Mynne and others.[31] Letters to Thomas Cromwell, the King's chief minister, by Godsalve and Southwell show that Lumner was very active in organising meetings relating to tax gathering - a keen workhorse for the county's leaders it seems. Edmund himself wrote to Cromwell in September 1535 from Mannington regarding first-fruits auditing matters.[32]

In December 1540 Edmund was one of the many Norfolk men who turned out to greet the arrival of Anne of Cleves in Rochester, where she was received by the Duke of Norfolk and all his senior supporters.[33] In October 1542, again with the senior gentry of the county, he was one of the commissioners of gaol delivery at Norwich Castle.[34] Edmund was also listed as a potential juror at the treason trial of Henry Earl of Surrey in January 1547.[35] In the event only the more senior men of Norfolk were sworn in to this all-Norfolk jury. That same month Edmund was granted the wardship and marriage of his young cousin William Lumner of Sharrington.

Edmund senior's first wife: Rose Spring

Edmund's first recorded marriage was to Rose Spring one of the daughters of Thomas Spring of Lavenham and the widow of Thomas Guybon. Thomas Spring 3 (to distinguish him from his father and grandfather) was a very wealthy clothier and one of the senior citizens of Lavenham at around the peak period of that town's cloth industry.[36] In his 1523 will he left a huge sum towards finishing the church tower. Alice his widow completed the tower and erected a fine carved wooden parclose as a memorial to him.[37] Thomas 3 had two sons, John (later Sir John) and Robert and two daughters Anne and Rose, by his first wife Anne King of Boxford.[38] Robert's wife Anne Eden married again after his death in 1549. Her second husband (she also married thirdly Justinian Champneys) was Sir Philip Paris of Linton, hinting at another possible networking link between the Lumners and the Potts. Thomas 3's daughters all married: Margaret married and had children by Sir Thomas Jermyn of Rushbrooke; Rose married first Thomas Guybon of Lynn; and his youngest Bridget, still unmarried in 1538 but subsequently married to William Erneley of Sussex.[39]

Reputed to have been the wealthiest non-noble man of his day in England, Rose's father owned a huge number of manors and lands spread across East Anglia. His house at the Grove in Lady Street in Lavenham was a substantial one. Rose's expectations from marriage would have been high. When she married her first husband, Thomas Guybon esq the son and heir of Gregory Guybon of West Lynn near King's Lynn, her father settled his extensive copyhold landholdings in Thompson, south-west Norfolk (with lands in Merton, Stow and Breckles; Bodney, Langford, Gooderstone and Croxton; Buckenham; Shipdham, Letton and Cranworth) on Rose.[40] Thomas had previously been married to Elizabeth Thorsby and already had a son and heir Thomas Guybon, a second son Anthony and married daughters Margaret and Elizabeth.[41] Thomas Guybon junior married as his fourth wife Agnes, or Anne, Clarke who may have been the widow of the Robert Clarke to whom Edmund Lumner had given Bintry manor in Itteringham in 1537. The gift, rather than sale, of Bintry manor has the feel of a marriage settlement (or trustee arrangement) and it is possible (but unprovable) that Agnes/Anne was a Lumner girl. If Edmund Lumner had in fact been married before Rose and had a daughter Agnes/Anne the dates would be right. No-one has found such a marriage but wives who did not produce sons are often air-brushed from history. It is rather unusual for Edmund, as an heir, not to have married until he was about 37. As a widow Agnes would have been marrying back into the extended family, a common practice. Anne Guybon, for example married her relation William Lumner of Sharrington. Anne must have been Thomas Guybon senior's daughter by Rose.[42]

Unfortunately Thomas Spring's will included a legacy of £20 to each of Rose's children without naming them. Similarly when Guybon died in 1531 his will made no mention of his children and simply provided for Rose.[43] Rose was now a well-set-up widow having not only her Thompson properties but also a life interest in all Guybon's lands and the flexibility to sell them if she chose. Edmund Lumner her next husband had a fine but old-fashioned house. With such expectations did she bring some of her money to help make significant physical changes to Mannington Hall? Architectural commentators all note that most of the windows on the main west facade are of mid-sixteenth century size and style and that probably at that time the original two storey-high main hall was floored over to make a more capacious and modern house. Rose was to live there for 20 years so had ample opportunity to add fashionable improvements. Their expenditure (if it was indeed Rose and Edmund who altered the hall) did not extend to the church. An inventory of church goods taken in 1552 described Mannington as 'Church in ruins, no inventory'.[44] This perhaps implied that the Lumner family held services in the Hall when at Mannington and may suggest that they were often away in London.

Edmund and Rose married within a year or so of Guybon's death, probably by March 1532. A court roll of that date showed the first court of Henry Fermour as lead feoffee for an unreadable holder of the manor.[45] Further details are scant, but it seems very likely that this was the inaugural court for Edmund and Rose. They certainly appeared in the roll for 1536-37, where again Fermour was the lead feoffee. Other feoffees included John and Robert Spring. Edmund and Rose were certainly both involved in a chancery action of the period 1538-44 relating to a debt owed to her late husband.[46]

How many children were living with Rose and Edmund is not clear. Her Guybon stepchildren would have been growing up and may have stayed around Lynn although her step-grandson William appears to have grown up around Mannington. Rose's own daughter Anne Guybon and her new daughter by Edmund would have been at home. Daughter 'Margaret' was left £100 towards her marriage portion in her father's will in 1558 when still unmarried. By May 1566, when Edmund's sister Margaret Bishop wrote her will, she described her niece as Mistress 'Margery' Underwood, the girl having by then married Robert Underwood of Hevingham. Given the dates, Margery was either born well into their marriage or married quite late in life.[47]

Rose's daughter Anne would have grown up with William Lumner of Sharrington, her future husband. His father had died when he was only 10 or 11 and he had become a protégé of Edmund of Mannington. The fact that his father Thomas had been living in Itteringham around the time William was born, reinforces the close ties of the two family lines. In effect Edmund of Mannington, perhaps around 1551 when William became of age, married off his stepdaughter and his ward. Sadly little more can be said about Rose. When she died in 1552, Rose left everything she had inherited from her father and her first husband to Edmund, including 'any goods beyond the realm of England and overseas'.[48] Later Edmund became an investor in a Merchant Adventurers scheme; perhaps they had made an earlier investment in some merchant venture. Thomas Guybon is thought to have been a merchant in Lynn; if so Rose may have maintained some involvement in mercantile activities.

Edmund's second wife - Katherine Leighton and the Wigmores

After Rose's death, Edmund married again. Katherine was the daughter of John Leighton esq of Wattlesborough in Shropshire (a few miles to the west of Shrewsbury) and Joyce Sutton the daughter of Edward Sutton the sixth Baron Dudley. The Leightons were one of the senior families of Shropshire. Katherine's brother was Sir Thomas Leighton, later Governor of Guernsey. From Mannington court roll entries and later IPM references to the age of their son Edmund, their marriage must have occurred in 1554 or 1555. It was to be short-lived as Edmund died in 1558. Katherine, who outlived Edmund by forty years, was to become a significant player in the Potts story later on.

In total Katherine Leighton married four times, had children by all four husbands with at least nine surviving infancy. They were:

> By Richard Wigmore – Thomas, William, Grace and Richard in the years to 1553
>
> By Edmund Lumner – Edmund and William between 1555 and 1558
>
> By John Callard – Emmanuel Callard in about 1560
>
> By John Dodge – Mary and Anne probably about 1565-67, with a son John who died as an infant in 1563

Her family background and previous marriage are very relevant to the story. Her first husband was Richard Wigmore a citizen and mercer of London. In addition to his trading activities in April 1545 Wigmore had been granted the office of a surveyor at the time of the major shake-up of the Mint in The Tower.[49] This would have meant that Wigmore and Edmund Lumner were working in public roles within a very short distance of each other in and near The Tower. Wigmore was a younger son of John Wigmore of Lucton in Herefordshire. William 'Wygmore' gent of Shobdon, Herefordshire (another of the younger sons from Lucton) left a will in 1540 which mentioned brothers Richard and Thomas.[50] It is no coincidence that Richard the mercer's sons were named Thomas, William and Richard. Richard and Thomas senior, in 1540 were left the customership of Abergevenny - consistent with a trade involvement. Despite being covered by the Visitations of Herefordshire, the Wigmore family is not well-documented.[51] With virtually no information in the pedigrees on siblings of the eldest sons it is not easy to see how the branches in Lucton and Shobdon fitted together. Lucton was the long-standing family seat of what had once been a more substantial and influential family than it had become by the middle of the sixteenth century. The Wigmore family tree shown here is more fully explained in Family Notes 14: Wigmore.

When Richard Wigmore died in 1553, Katherine was to be one of the executors of his will together with 'her father in law Richard Lee esquire'. They were to be assisted by Wigmore's loving friend Blase Saunders grocer as overseer.[52] Blase Saunders had been admitted to the Grocers' Company in 1541, having been the apprentice of Sir William Butler, the Mayor of London.[53] He had been in Spain with John Lumner in 1540 at the time of the Inquisition and he was to be a trustee in Katherine's marriage settlement with Edmund Lumner in 1555. No doubt as senior grocers, Saunders would also have known James and Roger Apott - yet another reason to believe the Potts and Lumners knew each other at an early stage.

In his will of 1553 Richard Wigmore left his great house or messuage in Mark Lane, All Hallows in Barking and two other tenements there to Katherine for life and then to his son Thomas, defaulting to his younger son William or to the 'child my wife now goeth with if a man child' (it was a boy named Richard) or ultimately to his daughter Grace. He also had lands in Beckenham and Winchester, which went to the sons.

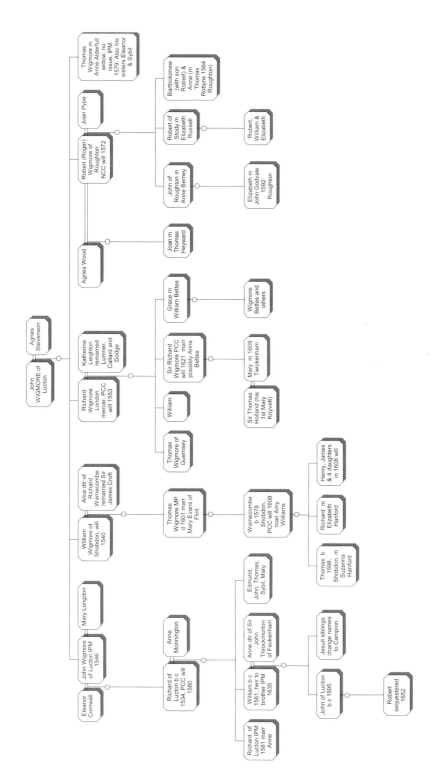

Wigmore Family Tree

What happened to Katherine's Wigmore children? They had no claim on Mannington, but all four would have spent some of their childhood there after 1555 when their mother married Edmund Lumner. In Grace's case she would most likely have stayed with her mother until she married a neighbour in north Norfolk. Edmund Lumner confirmed in his will that Richard Wigmore's children were to receive the portions left them in their father's will.[54]

The Wigmore Children

Thomas Wigmore had a military and governance career in Guernsey under the wing of, and for some years as deputy to, Katherine's brother Sir Thomas Leighton, Governor of the island. Thomas's story is told in Chapter 6, and includes his brother Richard's role in a murderous incident in 1587. There is no suggestion that Thomas married and had a family. William Wigmore although given lands in Winchester and Beckenham by his father, might have ended up almost anywhere in southern England or may even have died young. Richard was probably the Sir Richard Wigmore who was a member of King James's court. If so, he was the most successful.

Sir Richard Wigmore

It is generally thought that, being from Herefordshire when knighted, Richard was of the Lucton or Shobdon lines of the Wigmore family. However, perhaps surprisingly, there is no certainty about where he came from or whom he married. Venn tentatively identified him as a younger son of Richard Wigmore of London which would fit with his father being Richard Wigmore the mercer of London, the younger son of the Herefordshire family. Richard junior was admitted to Peterhouse Cambridge in 1568 and awarded his BA at Clare in 1571-72. He was probably also the Richard Wigmore admitted to Middle Temple in October 1573 from New Inn.[55] These admission and qualification dates would all be precisely consistent with Richard's being 'in the womb' of Katherine in 1553.[56] Richard Wigmore shortly afterwards appeared as a secretary to Francis Walsingham. In 1576 Walsingham unsuccessfully recommended him for office as Clerk of Fines to the Council in the Marches.[57] Again, the date would match a young man coming out of law school without having stayed the course to become a barrister.

In 1587 Richard was implicated by association in a serious crime (see Chapter 6). The relevant state papers relating to the incident contain nothing to indicate Richard was indicted or tried for his involvement. Was this because he was one of Walsingham's secretaries at this time? Intriguingly, in the middle of 1588, equipped with pages of instruction by Francis Walsingham, Richard was sent as an ambassador to Scotland with the aim of ingratiating himself with King James and then reporting back. He seems to have been successful on both counts, being later renowned for sharing the King's passion for all forms of hunting.[58] He was in Scotland for a number of years, not necessarily continuously. From 1596, when King James seemed to be vacillating over his religious views, Queen Elizabeth wrote a note in which she exhorted Wigmore to 'induce the King resolutely to profess himself a protestant ... and rely and depend upon the amitie of Queen Elizabeth and England'.[59] He may have been persuaded to accept the Scottish appointment rather than face criminal charges, but then found that he was good at the job. He seems to have been granted a prestigious post, perhaps as a reward for his successes in Scotland. Sir Richard's widow later married Sir Stephen Powle and as a result some aspects of Sir Richard's career have been well-documented.[60]

In 1594 Richard was appointed Constable of the Castle and Steward of the Manor assigned to the Earl of Essex.[61] Given Sir Thomas Leighton's earlier role looking after the Queen's favourite Robert Devereux, Earl of Essex in his 1591 military foray to France, this appointment frankly smacks of Richard's uncle's involvement in the nomination. In 1603 at Newark he was knighted by King James and made a Captain.[62] Sir Richard became a courtier at King James's court and he remained a hunting companion of the King. In 1614 he was a Gentleman of His Majesty's Privy Chamber. In 1609, Richard was made by King James his 'Marshal of the Field'.[63] The King and his entourage had been interrupted while hunting near Newmarket and there and then Sir Richard was appointed to prevent any but the King's followers attending him while hunting or hindering his sport. Other rewards came too. In 1612 he was granted a 21 year licence to import large quantities of cod and ling and in 1614 sought permission from parliament to extend his licence from loose bulk to allow packing the fish in barrels and casks.[64] That year he was also granted £1,000 by the King from sequestered recusants' funds.[65] References also survive to Sir Richard having been a justice of the peace in Middlesex between about 1613 and 1619.[66] Sir Richard along with many others was in May 1609 an adventurer investor in the second charter of the Virginia Company.[67] In 1615 Sir Richard Wigmore was with King James on a visit to Cambridge University when he was made MA. Not bad for a small boy whose early years were spent a long way from court at Mannington Hall, Norfolk.

Sir Richard's family

Sir Richard's wife's name was given as Anne when he made his will in 1621. His daughter Mary became the second wife of Sir Thomas Holland of Quidenham in Norfolk (whose first was Mary Knyvett).[68] The closeness of the Holland and Potts families was shown in a letter of 1619 from Sir Thomas to the young (Sir) John Potts (see Chapter 9). The kinship he claimed could only have come about through the Wigmore connection.

Who, though, was Sir Richard's wife? No sources have identified her but strong evidence suggests she might have been Anne Bettes of Irmingland, Norfolk. There are two reasons for this idea. Firstly Blomefield says that from 1579 John Dodge, one of Katherine's later husbands, was to receive for life an annuity of £40 a year from John Bettes of Irmingland, for a jointure. The implication of that seems to be that John Bettes settled this sum on one of his daughters on marriage to one of the boys in John Dodge's household. By this time Katherine had produced three more in addition to her Wigmore boys.[69] Who was involved in the marriage? Without parish registers for Mannington and Oulton and only patchy survival of Irmingland entries in the Heydon register it is hard to be sure. By his second wife Margaret Gawsell, John Bettes had five daughters about whom nothing is known but their names: Anne, Elizabeth, Margaret, Mary and Helen.[70] They may not have been born by 1579 but he may have had others daughters by his first wife Anne Cootes/ Fermour. Any one of these might have married any of Katherine's sons: Thomas, William and Richard Wigmore; William Lumner; and Emmanuel Callard. Of these, two can be eliminated easily. William Lumner certainly did not live to produce an heir, or the Mannington story would have played out differently. Emmanuel Callard married in 1588 and although this might have been a second marriage there is no hint that this was the case. Both would have been quite young to have married in or by 1579, although not impossibly so. Edmund Lumner junior had been married off very young with all sorts of problems arising from that leaving Katherine wary of marrying off her other children too young. That leaves the Wigmore boys. Of these, Thomas was probably unmarried. William Wigmore remains a complete mystery and (if he survived to adulthood) he could be a candidate but Richard fits the bill very well. The second support for the suggestion is that Richard's elder sister Grace married a William Bettes, probably John Bettes's younger brother. John Bettes was of course the son of Elizabeth Lumner, daughter of the builder of Mannington!

Sir Richard made his nuncupative will in May 1621 at his house in King Street Westminster.[71] He was buried at St Margaret's church in May 1621, when a sermon was delivered by Michael Wigmore.[72] Sir Richard left a ring to his only child, the Lady Mary Holland and a gelding to his son-in-law, Sir Thomas Holland. The rest of his estate went to his wife Anne, including his house. The will specifically said that he had received £1,000 (the recusants' money no doubt) but that it was no longer in his estate. He had invested it to produce an income of £200 a year for his and his wife's lives. Sir Thomas and Mary Holland were not to interfere with the arrangements in the will and were reported to have said they would not.

Dame Anne, his widow, married Sir Stephen Powle on 8th May 1623 at St Margaret Westminster, her parish church which was known colloquially as 'Ringingtown' for the quality of its bells.[73] Soon afterwards they moved from his home in Mile End to St Margaret's parish. The only sour note in the story is that Powle obviously disliked Sir Richard (whom he would certainly have known as both were senior investors in the Virginia Company) and described him in a diary note as being guilty of gluttony, drunkenness, chambering and wantonness. It may of course have been true! The Powles died in 1630-31 leaving no wills to help confirm Anne's origins.[74]

Grace Wigmore

It is pretty certain (but without parish register confirmation) that Grace Wigmore married William Bettes of Irmingland. The Bettes were a modest Norfolk family of similar scale to the Lumners and intermarried with them. Like the Lumners in the late fifteenth and early sixteenth centuries they had been involved in the merchant trades in London as well as holding Norfolk property. In the second half of the century the head of the family was John Bettes the son of Robert (d February 1559) and Elizabeth Lumner (d 1571).[75] John, his second wife Margaret and his heir Henry sold part of their Irmingland property to John Potts in the 1590s and the two manors and the rest of the lands to Thomas Catlyn of Lakenham in 1598.[76] In 1605 Catlyn (and his wife Judith a daughter of the Itteringham/Wolterton Houghtons) sold them to Sir Francis Bacon who built a splendid new hall, one wing of which remains in Irmingland Hall today.[77]

It seems that John Bettes may have lived elsewhere, perhaps in Oulton where his mother had lived, and that the old manorial hall in Irmingland (no doubt the worse for wear) was occupied by a younger brother. Blomefield found that there had been five different sets of arms in the windows of the old farmhouse at Irmingland which he assumed had been the old hall of the Bettes family. Each of the arms was Bettes impaling another family. Three of the others - Cobb, Banyard and Bardwell - can be identified from the Visitation pedigree as wives of the senior men of three of the generations before John Bettes. The unidentified fourth one seems likely either to have been Bettes impaling Lumner for the marriage of John's father Robert to Elizabeth Lumner, or perhaps for John's marriage to a Coote girl. The fifth, accompanied by the date 1585, showed Bettes arms impaling the correctly described 'three greyhounds courant' of the Wigmores of Herefordshire, presumably for Grace Wigmore. A William Bettes of Salhouse died in 1591 intestate and his widow Grace was granted administration of his estate.[78] Grace at this time was not a particularly usual name and certainly was not widely used in villages around Mannington. Grace herself died in 1600 in Salhouse where she was buried on 17th February, even though her husband does not seem to have been buried there. In a short and focused will, she left her goods and debts to Margaret Archer, her young granddaughter.[79] Grace made two local Salhouse men her executors and made no other reference to any family or friends. However, Grace and William seem to have had two other children. The tellingly named Wigmore Bettes of Irmingland died at the end of 1601 or start of 1602. In January 1602 administration was granted to his natural brother John Bettes and natural sister Mary Bettes.[80] All of these dates indicate that Grace married William Bettes about 1570, which would fit very well with her birth in the very early 1550s.[81]

Katherine Leighton/Wigmore and her Lumner sons

Katherine Leighton/Wigmore and Edmund Lumner senior would have met in London where Lumner's tax gathering role would have brought him into contact with the major traders. Katherine may have influenced Edmund to maintain his presence in London. In February 1555 the two of them, each named in their own right were founder investors in 'The Merchant Adventurers of England'.[82] Katherine's status was given as Katherine Lumner widow of Richard Wigmore perhaps reflecting her independent right to invest. Her business activities do raise some doubt on her later claim that she could not 'write any more than two letters for her name nor read any writing at all, be it in English or Latin' - an unlikely failing for a woman from a major family (see Chapter 7). Their friend Blase Saunders was also among the group who invested under the leadership and sole governorship of Sebastian Cabot in ships provided and rigged to 'discover isles and lands unknown ... sailing northwards ... to attain by this adventure both the glory of God and the increase of the general wealth of the realms of the King and Queen and of their subjects'.

Although Edmund was to live for only a few years after his marriage to Katherine, she bore him two sons Edmund junior and William. The younger, William, at his majority was to receive the messuage of Mannes in Aylsham with lands belonging to it and he would have been his brother's heir to Mannington if Edmund had not left male issue. But William did not feature in later chancery actions regarding the inheritance so it must be assumed that he died without issue, probably quite young. A chancery action in the late 1580s over the Mannes property made no reference to him at all. He may have died in Aylsham but unfortunately the early parish registers have not survived.

Edmund junior was to inherit, after Katherine's life interest:

> The manors of Mannington and moiety of the manor of Wolterton
> and Itteringham … with ten messuages; one water mill; a thousand
> acres of land; 100 acres of meadow; 500 acres of pasture; 100
> acres of wood; 500 acres of furze and bruerie; the liberty of fold
> course in Mannington, Wolterton, Saxthorpe, Little Barningham,
> Itteringham, Oulton, Blickling, Corpusty, Aylsham and Ingworth;
> the advowson of the church of Itteringham; and the moiety of the
> advowson of Wolterton.

This may still be a somewhat formulaic description of the estate with its rounded numbers, but the relative proportions of the types of land seem reasonable, including the large area of pasture and heathland in Mannington parish. The arable land had been substantially boosted since the 1480s description by Edmund's purchase of a large section of Wolterton. Edmund's will stated that the estate had been conveyed in a fine early in 1555, suggesting a marriage settlement for Katherine and providing a clue to the birth dates of their children. This fine was important as if both his sons died without male heirs Edmund willed that the estate should revert to those named in the final concord, being himself, his wife and William Lumner (of Sharrington) and others unspecified.

However his IPM taken in September 1558 gave more detail.[83] The 1555 settlement was cited with the default sequence in the absence of male heirs given in full: William Lumner of Sharrington, John the brother of William's father Thomas junior, their other brother Henry of London fishmonger, John Lumner the grocer and son of Henry the grocer brother of Thomas senior of Sharrington. Finally came Henry, son of Henry the fishmonger who was of the same younger generation as William.

The 1555 fine involved John Southcote and Blase Saunders grocer of London, presumably acting as trustees for Edmund and Katherine respectively. Other parties to the deed itself were the various extant Lumners named in the default sequence, except the youngest Henry.

The manor of Mannington, its lands and the Itteringham advowson were held of Lady Anne Heydon widow as of her manor of Micklehall in Saxthorpe by half a knight's fee. The manor of Wolterton and half the advowson there was held of the Earl of Arundel by unknown services. The manor of Burgleons with its 100 acres of land and woods in Reepham and elsewhere was held of Sir Christopher Heydon as of his manor of Sayes in Hackford by one third of a knight's fee. The 200 acres and 2 messuages in Shipdham and Bradenham and the lands and woods in Letton and Cranworth were held of Sir Richard Southwell as of his manor of Cranworth. Three messuages and 20 acres in Hoveton and Cromer were held of the Bishop of Norwich (these alone not being in 1558 in the possession of Katherine). Edmund Lumner junior the son and heir was precisely 3 years 5 months and 10 days old on that 20th September 1558 (therefore born on 10th April 1555).

By Edmund's will (also recited in the IPM), Katherine was to have Edmund's manor of Burgleons in Reepham, Salle and elsewhere and his lands in Shipdham, Letton, Cranworth and Bradenham until Edmund their son was 21 years old. Katherine and then Edmund were to have all the cattle on the estates. Similarly Edmund was to have all the jewels, plate and household goods when 21, with Katherine having custody beforehand. Finally Katherine was to have in her own right all his messuages, houses, lands, fishings, moors and marshes in Hoveton and Cromer. She was made executrix and the supervisor was to be the powerful steward or auditor of the Dukes of Norfolk, William Dix esq of Wickmere.

Katherine Leighton/Wigmore/Lumner and John Callard

After Edmund's death, Katherine married again twice. She probably had only a short period of widowhood when she ran the estate on her own. As owner of Mannington, 'Mistress Lumner' had been involved in a new lease of Itteringham's mill in about 1559 when her Mannington bailiff was John Doughty. By 1561 Doughty was a yeoman of Coltishall so he may have moved on after the death of John Callard, husband number three.[84]

Who was this John Callard to whom Katherine was briefly married from about 1559 to his death in 1561-62? He and his son by Katherine are hardly mentioned in the usual printed sources. John left a simple will made as 'John Callarde of Mannington esq' in May 1561 in which he bequeathed almost everything to Katherine.[85] It was proved exactly a year later, with Katherine as sole executrix and contains only one clue to his family background. A legacy of £20 was left to a sister Anne Dawes. The will was signed at Mannington with local witnesses Thomas and Christopher Knowles and John Doughty the bailiff. Katherine was pregnant at the time, as the will made different provisions for his lands 'in the realm of England' (implying in a variety of places) depending on the gender of the child she was carrying. Emmanuel was to be their only child. In October 1563 Emmanuel Callard was described as three years old in an entry in the Little Barningham court roll, which is roughly consistent with a birth in summer 1561.[86] Another later document referred to him being 6 months old in April 1561 (not consistent with being unborn in May 1561, but still close enough if months in the womb are included!).[87]

Further research points to John Callard having been a soldier and a younger son of a north Devon family. John must have been a man of some substance and standing as he was one of the executors of the will of Sir James Boleyn of Blickling in 1561.[88] A later court action (see below) in which his son claimed his father had bought a capital messuage in Booton, supports this idea. But, even if Callard had not owned the property, this action shows that Emmanuel's father was a man of at least some means and not just dependant on Katherine and her interest in Mannington. Where did his money come from?

The Callard surname is intriguing. Not only is it rare in Norfolk, but at this time occurrences were usually restricted almost entirely to Devon and Cornwall. As Katherine obviously had strong links with London as she met him there? A Richard Callard who was living in Islington at his death appears to have been John Callard's uncle. Islington was a popular village for residences with good access to London and the Potts family would also live there at some point in the late 1560s. Richard was clearly a wealthy man. In the 1541 London Subsidy Roll for Farringdon Ward Within for the parish of 'Seynt Fosters' or St Vedast in Foster Lane he was the most substantial parishioner, with property valued at £2,000.[89]

A chancery action of 1532-38 showed that Callard had bought a capital messuage with outhouses and lands in Islington from William Gardener citizen and grocer of London.[90] How well-connected to the grocery fraternity was he?[91] By 1538-39 a lease said that Callard's was a 'great mansion house', adjacent to which, on its western brick wall, was to be built an outhouse for a large lead cistern to gather water from nearby springs to pipe down to the Priory and Hospital of St Bartholomew. The lease contains wonderful detail about the plumbing for those interested in such things![92] He was paid £40 for the inconvenience of the building for the cistern and associated works on his land and was allowed to draw water for himself. Rather nicely, he left the same handsome sum of £40 towards building a road 'from the pales outside his house towards Walkers in the direction of Newington'. This money was left even if he had already started work on the road, which implies he was deliberately using the money from St Bartholomew's for good works. Presumably with all the springs there the road was frequently impassable.

Callard had also been involved in other Islington parish property transactions. Towards the end of his life, in 1542, he had purchased from Robert Foster esq and George Foster gent premises in Holloway and Tollington.[93] This was probably the last of a number of land acquisitions in the area.

As 'Rycharde Calarde esq of Islington' he made his will in April 1544 shortly before he died that summer.[94] His long will is full of interesting information and family clues. His first wife Alice was buried in St Vedast ('otherwise St Forster') parish, along with two unmarried daughters Joan and Margaret and one married daughter Alice Tucker. His unnamed father whose bones lay buried at the 'church of Our Lady at Strand' was probably a John Callard.[95] No mention was made of where his mother was buried or her name. He left 40s to the London fellowship of Painters and Stainers. Confirmation that he was himself a painter and stainer comes from a chancery action regarding a fishmonger, Thomas Pyrry, whom he had had imprisoned over security for a bond at some point between 1529 and 1532.[96]

Richard Callard was well-connected to, and no doubt directly involved with the work of, the top court painters of his era. He may even have held senior office in the newly formed Painter-Stainers' Company but their early records are scant. An investigation of the life of Vincent Volpe, who was paid for painting work from royal funds in the 1520s and 1530s, shows a cluster of senior painters including Callard living in the parish of St Vedast Foster Lane at this time.[97] These painters also decorated flags and banners, ships, armorial escutcheons for funerals and cloth for the battlefield and such conspicuous displays as the Field of the Cloth of Gold. There has been much speculation about the links of these men to Hans Holbein and other portraitists of the period.[98]

Richard's relatives included his daughter Elizabeth, her husband Thomas Hayes and their children. Elizabeth and Thomas were to be his executors and their children received large cash legacies. He had previously settled all his Islington lands on Elizabeth and her family, particularly her eldest son William Hayes. *The Victoria County History of Middlesex* gives substantial details of Callard's property in and around Islington and how it passed down through his daughter's heirs.[99] Unfortunately this does not include what happened to his main houses in Islington and St Vedast. Elizabeth married twice more after Thomas Hayes. Her next was John Wroth, brother of Sir Thomas, by whom she had sons Edward and William before he died in 1556. Finally she wed (very briefly as he died in 1557) John Clerke, the son of Sir John Clerke and Callard's second wife Dame Anne Clerke.

Richard left his brother, John Callard, £20 - 'when he chose to collect it' - implying perhaps that he was either wealthy or lived away from London or both. John Callard and Richard's son-in-law William Tucker grocer were to be overseers. There is no sign of Tucker having had children, nor specifically was there any mention of John Callard's children. Richard's second wife was 'Lady Anne' the widow of Sir John Clerke, knighted for his exploits in battle.[100] So far this looks like a typical wealthy Londoner's will. But Richard left an annuity for life to John Stephens the elder of 'Toryngton in Devonshire', his mother's brother and he noted that he himself had been born in Tavistock Devon. So, despite his father being buried in London, the Callards were a Devon family. Devon deeds and chancery cases show John Callard as holding land near Great Torrington and being of Burrington near Barnstaple.[101] John being the elder brother retained the family lands in Devon while his younger brother Richard made his fortune in London. John not only had a son called John but also a daughter Anne who married William Dawes gent of Cornwall - the sister Anne Dawes mentioned in John Callard of Mannington's will.

John Callard (of Mannington) did not however follow his uncle as a painter-stainer or in another trade in London. Indeed all three Johns (he, his father and grandfather) are somewhat elusive in surviving records. However, at least two of them were soldiers. During 1511, staying on after an uneventful English expedition had ended, Sir Henry Guildford fought on behalf of Ferdinand and Isabella in Spain.[102] He was knighted by them at Burgos and at the same occasion John Callard esq, one of his retainers, was granted a coat of arms for his bravery.[103] Guildford was the close companion of the young Henry VIII and his Master of Revels amongst other roles at court. He was routinely with Henry on his military excursions and played a significant role at the Field of the Cloth of Gold. All this placed Guildford at the heart of court commissions for the output of the painter-stainers. The Callard family presumably remained close to him from the Spanish fighting days onward and Guildford may have been instrumental in increasing Richard Callard's wealth as a painter-stainer. John Callard the soldier, as a brave retainer, may have enjoyed favour at court which might explain why a Devon man was buried in London. He would have secured his son Richard's prominence as a painter. While his eldest son John looked after the Devon country estates, grandson John may well have also made his career as a soldier.

It is very likely that the Callard and Clerke families knew each other because of battlefield prowess. John Callard senior, the same generation as Sir John Clerke, died around the same time: Clerke in 1539 and Callard before 1544. He certainly cannot have been the Mr Callard who was Lieutenant of Boulogne in May 1548.[104] In a list of trusted senior soldiers from good families who were being considered for an important post, Callard was said to be already in an equivalent role and could not be spared. He was clearly well-regarded. Others considered were Mr Henry Dudley Captain of the Guard at Boulogne and George Throgmorton one of the guards at Calais. The identification of Mr Callard as John of Mannington is supported by considering how Katherine Leighton/Wigmore/Lumner could have known Callard and come to marry him. Her brother Thomas Leighton (later Sir Thomas, the well-known Elizabethan soldier and Governor of Guernsey) was closely connected to his Sutton/Dudley cousins and by the 1550s had joined them in their abortive plot against Queen Mary.[105] Henry Sutton or Dudley as he was generally known was a central conspirator, who with a retinue of his own men, had fled to France. Most were allowed back by Elizabeth, some receiving rewards. Leighton certainly came back into favour. That Callard had served under Henry Dudley in France suggests that Thomas Leighton would have known Callard well and probably served directly with him in the various actions in France in the run up to the loss of Calais and Boulogne. Indeed it is quite possible that Callard served under Leighton in France and in the north of England. Leighton may have promoted Callard's marriage to his sister after the death of Edmund Lumner in 1558, around the time the soldiers returned from France. With no other evidence for Callard's livelihood, this identification is compelling.

Katherine's son Emmanuel Callard

Although he crops up briefly in a later Star Chamber action alongside John Potts (his half brother-in-law), John and Katherine's son Emmanuel does not feature strongly in the Mannington story. There are passing mentions of him in the Little Barningham court roll, but nothing of any note. In 1588 the 27 year old Emmanuel married Margery Underwood in Itteringham's parish church. She was the widow of Robert Underwood gent of Cromer. Despite the same names, this is unlikely to be Margery Lumner who had married Robert Underwood of Hevingham in 1566. Although she would still be alive, she would be at least 16 years older than Callard. Robert of Cromer was the son of Richard Underwood, the elder Robert's brother. The marriage in Itteringham implies that this Margery may have been a local girl. She and Emmanuel lived at Cromer (on the edge of the town) either in one of Katherine's houses or more likely in Margery's late husband's house.[106] Both in his own right and with Margery, Emmanuel was to keep up the tradition of the families by being no stranger to the local and London courts.

Prior to Michaelmas term 1583 Emmanuel Callard had sued Robert Harward of Booton (son of John and nephew of Thomas) and Robert's mother Bridget by then the wife of William Arnold.[107] Callard asserted that when he was six months old his father John Callard had bought from Thomas Harward a capital messuage with lands in Booton, Brandeston and the Witchinghams (a farm, not the manor of Booton itself) as confirmed by a deed of 18th April 1561.[108] The mid-1580s annual rent was about £120 so, using a standard multiple of 20, John Callard probably paid about £2,400 for the premises, a substantial estate. Or at least his son was led to believe he had the wherewithal to do so and must have gone into the chancery action with his mother's active support as she would have been a key witness for the transaction. He claimed that, during his minority, it had been farmed (leased) by the Harwards and had come into Robert's possession. The evidence for the purchase and for the repayment of a mortgage on the premises to Peter Read esq, Callard said, had fallen into the Harwards' hands where they had altered, defaced and burnt the documents refusing to give to him what was remaining. When, the previous year, at age 21, he entered the property to claim it, they had ejected him.

The hearing, in Michaelmas term 1583, found both sides' proofs of title dubious and suggested taking the matter to common law.[109] If such a trial found for Callard then he should be allowed to hold the property until such time as Harward was able to find proof to overturn such a verdict. But Harward came back in early 1584 with the argument that chancery had not focused sufficiently on the fundamental issue of the mortgage of the property by his father to Peter Read. He said the mortgage was not repaid on the due date whereas Callard said it was satisfactorily repaid. It was ordered that the mortgage issue should be heard by two chancery judges and their findings should be reported back. In Easter term 1584 it was found that Thomas Harward had sold the property to Emmanuel's father absolutely in 1561 and that, at his death that year, the property descended to Emmanuel then aged just nine months.[110] Harward and John Langdon had stood bound to perform the conveyance. However, the documents relating to the transaction had been snatched and burnt 'by the devise of' Thomas Payne gent (of Itteringham). Nonetheless one of Payne's clerks entered the details into the Booton court book - Payne was clearly steward for this manor at the time. The entry, which was recited, showed conveyance by bargain and sale of a messuage lands and tenements in Booton, Brandeston and Witchingham to John Callard of Mannington. John Langdon and other named men had been present. It seems that Harward did not deny this, but argued that the conveyance was only 'in trust or confidence of a mortgage'. He implied that Peter Read's money had not been repaid. However, the court seemed happy that Read had been present when Callard paid for the property, said he was fully repaid and returned the mortgage writings to Harward. Chancery found Harward's title not proved. They were troubled that it seemed that after John Callard's death and during Emmanuel's minority Harward had tried to convey the premises to Simon Bowden as a device to attempt to withhold the property from Callard. It was decreed that Emmanuel had good title and that from Michaelmas 1584 he should have the premises. He was also to receive the pro rata amount of the tenant's rent on the premises between the decree date and Michaelmas. Harward's only remedy was to prove at common law, if he could, that he had better title in order to overturn this decree. Until then the property was Callard's to enjoy. Harward did try to recover the premises at common law but Callard again won the case and had his possession re-affirmed.[111]

But that was not the end of it. The Harwards took up their option to pursue their claim at common law. Worse, they refused to pay the rent arrears for which Callard sued them in chancery. The Callard versus Harward (and Callard against Arnold in 1585) action rumbled on in chancery and it also continued on a grand scale at common law.[112] Callard was back in chancery in 1586 claiming that the Harwards had launched four different common law suits against him and that these were without substance and that they should be barred from hounding him in this way. They re-asserted that the mortgage had not been repaid on the due dates and that Read had therefore become seized. In some unstated way they said that the property had then come to John Harward and so by inheritance to Robert. In the summer of 1587 Callard won an order to limit Harward's suits at common law against his own witnesses.[113] By Michaelmas it was noted that Harward had brought no less than twelve common law suits against Callard and his tenants.[114] Of course Callard described them as 'vexatious'. He was particularly concerned about the suit against Baxter, one of his tenants, due to be tried in a week's time in King's Bench in London. Callard went to chancery to plead that Baxter was one of his key witnesses in the actions by Harward and that this King's Bench suit risked him not being able to call Baxter as a witness in other suits. Harward argued that because Baxter lived on the land at issue he was particularly keen to use his case against Baxter as part of his suit against Callard. He said that ten Norfolk men had been brought to London to form a jury. Since this was so far advanced, chancery permitted Harward to proceed.

This was a lifetime obsession between the two main protagonists. Certainly they popped up again in chancery orders in 1589 still battling over the same issues without clear resolution and with the implication that most of the action now took place at common law.[115] Arnold also remained a defendant in one of these orders. References were made to Norwich court actions, so presumably Callard was something of a fixture at assizes! Who was the long term winner - other than the lawyers from their fees? Were the Harwards trying to cheat Emmanuel Callard of his inheritance? Callard must have had a credible case given the early finding in his favour and possibly had the 1561 document. Perhaps he held an old counterpart of a mortgage, written as many were as a bargain and sale with provision for repayment on a certain date, in which his father had advanced money with the Booton premises as security. Probably Emmanuel had just one document that implied an interest but did not tell the whole story.

Most of Emmanuel's other London court actions related to helping Margery sort out Robert Underwood's affairs, particularly his creditors. Henry Brereton and others sued Emmanuel and Margery over a small sum that they denied was payable.[116] Reynold Foxe sued in 1589 again over a debt that he said he had repaid to Underwood.[117] He said that he and two members of the Shakle family of Great Witchingham had become bound to Underwood over the purchase from him of lands in Hevingham. Emmanuel and Margery said the money had not been paid and pointed out that Foxe had brought no witnesses to testify that he had actually paid the debt.

A third court of requests action was weightier, involving monies held by Underwood for a major repair of Cromer pier.[118] In short, Cromer had been granted a licence to export corn and use the profits to repair the pier. Underwood was obviously trusted by the town to manage the accounts of the whole exercise. It was claimed that he had sold an interest in the licence to Robert Cotterell for £300. Cotterell had obviously involved Thomas Baxter gent of Cromer in a claim that the £300 had been paid in return for the contract to do the building work and that Underwood had entered into a bond for 1,000 marks to stand by that commitment. Presumably with Underwood's death no contract for work had been forthcoming and Cotterell sued. But the answer by Emmanuel and Margery (all that survives of the whole action) made a more sinister issue of it. They said that before she remarried, Cotterell had persuaded her to give him access to the accounts (which he now kept from them) and he and Baxter had fabricated the whole story - licence, sale and bond. They were now fighting back in the civil court against the actions of Cotterell and Baxter in common law, where they were at risk of having to pay the 1,000 marks obligation.

As a character Emmanuel was rather an abrasive man. Whether this caused, or was caused by, so many arguments, he certainly seems a grumpy fellow. By 1596 he and distant cousin Robert Lumner were in court over a debt. Brief findings of an enquiry held on 11th September 1598, show that for up to ten years Callard had been in dispute with Nicholas Tompson of Roughton, Nicholas Smyth of Northrepps and Felicity Hogyne over their apparent sustained pasturing of their horses and cattle on his barley, enclosures and heathland (not to mention sheep-stealing).[119] They had caused damage by letting their dogs bait his sheep and had carried off ling and furze from the heathland. Various court actions had already taken place, including at that Lent's assizes. Some of the defendants had also previously successfully sued Callard and won damages against him which he now challenged as unjust. Several local men, presumably all his servants or workmen, gave evidence in support of Callard's claims: Roger Worstead, Thomas Colbye, Thomas Mendam, Richard Payne, Robert Fayer and John Smythe. At the Lent assizes Tompson had won damages against Callard's stepsons James and Thomas Underwood for their impounding of some of his cattle. This was unjust, said the defence, since the cattle were impounded by John Smythe as Callard's servant. (The Underwood boys presumably did not want to be embroiled in the row!) Since the encroachments had been going on for between three and ten years, why had the issue only recently arrived in court? Callard may have farmed his mother's Cromer lands for some time, but only very recently taken ownership of them on her death. He was now free to pursue legal action as he saw fit.

Evidence of a major falling out in 1604 with one Thomas Baker gent of Fakenham has survived in a court of the Star Chamber action.[120] The documents related to contested tithe payments in Cromer, but referred to other suits heard at Aylsham and Norwich highlighting various disputes between the two men and, even for the times, a high degree of public acrimony between them. Baker held a commission from the Crown through the exchequer to collect tithes and subsidies in Norfolk. If we are to believe Baker's evidence, Callard had been grazing animals on Cromer vicarage land and was due to pay about £4 to the exchequer, being part or all of the arrears owed by John Money, vicar of Cromer. Callard asserted that he did not hold the vicarage or any other ecclesiastical asset and said that he knew nothing about it. It seems Emmanuel was simply opportunistically using vicarage land and someone had split on him to a very assiduous tax gatherer.

In his defence, Callard said that he had been called, gratuitously, a traitor and assaulted publicly in Cromer's market place one Saturday market day in July 1604. On the same day, he said, Baker and his associates had attacked two of his servants with swords and seriously injured one of them. Callard sued Baker, John Spilman of Cromer and others in the Star Chamber and made a great fuss over his account of the various assaults and their lack of justification. However, Baker's response was that in fact he and his men had been assaulted by Callard at Callard's house (about a quarter of a mile from the market place) when he had come there with the local constable to arrest Callard for 'illegally and with force' repossessing the horses that Baker had taken in lieu of payment.

For those curious about Cromer people at this time there is much more detail in the arguments on either side. Also, it is clear that there had been common law suits between the two main protagonists. Callard had had Baker arrested for assault on his servants and for the felony of taking his horses. He had been taken to Norwich Castle prison by the constable of Aylsham. After the assizes had heard these actions, Callard had Baker arrested again; this time in Norwich over an action, unexplained, for the huge sum of £3,000. This was still pending in the summer of 1605.

Perhaps to the relief of his neighbours, Emmanuel Callard gent of Cromer died in May or June 1608, leaving Margery as executrix of his will and her son James Underwood gent as the heir to all their real estate in Cromer and Northrepps.[121] While most of the lands had been his father's, James Underwood may also have inherited from his stepfather the property in Cromer that Edmund Lumner had willed to Katherine in her own right. No mention was made of Booton or any inheritance from Emmanuel's father.

Katherine Leighton/Wigmore/Lumner/Callard and John Dodge

Emmanuel's mother Katherine meanwhile had moved on to husband number four. Next in line for this remarkable woman was John Dodge of Wrotham Kent. The marriage had taken place on 19th April 1563, two years after John Callard's death. Little Barningham parish register shows the burial on 26th October 1563 of John the son of John Dodge gent. With no evidence of a prior marriage for Dodge, the entry must refer to the infant death of their first child. Now nearing the end of twenty years of childbearing, Katherine did not have another son but did raise two daughters who are pivotal to the story.

What connection brought John Dodge to Norfolk? The sketchy entry in the Kent Visitation and the entry in the Norfolk Visitations give John Dodge of Mannington as one of two sons born to John Dodge of Wrotham in Kent, who in turn was the son of Richard Dodge of Wrotham.[122] Edward Dodge was probably the elder brother since he held lands there at his death. John Dodge senior achieved a grant of arms in December 1546.[123] No further ancestry was given in the Visitation and there is very little documentary evidence for the Dodge family in Kent before about 1520. There is however good evidence to suggest that the Dodges were descended from the Dodges of Cheshire where the family had been residents of substance in Stockport and surrounding villages since at least the early fifteenth century.[124] It seems likely that the Cheshire family adopted the arms of the Kent family at some point after 1546 and perhaps not until the Kent (and thus Mannington) line had failed to produce any male heirs. The parallel with the Potts family coming from Cheshire and achieving arms that were later taken up by distant cousins in Cheshire is of course intriguing. Had the two families known each other from Cheshire days? Was there a grocery trade linkage early in the sixteenth century? It seems there was.

Pott Shrigley is just a few miles from both Offerton and Poynton where yeoman Dodges had land. The parish registers show various Potts family events at Poynton. There is every chance that the Dodges and Potts of Cheshire knew each other around the turn of the century, if not before.[125] This connection also spread to Norfolk. A young Ralph Dodge became rector of Mannington in 1592, at the time John Dodge junior was lord of the manor. This was no coincidence. Ralph, in his 1610 will, made clear that he was the brother of Ottiwell Dodge (of Stockport) and that if his own son died his landed property should in due course pass to William the son of Robert Dodge. Although only distant cousins, the sense of family between Norfolk and Cheshire was strong. For more on Ralph Dodge see Family Notes 6: Dodge.

Exactly when or how the Dodges came to Wrotham is not known but it was probably early in sixteenth century. The only detailed reference to the Dodge family lands in Kent comes in a chancery action to do with a challenge to Edward Dodge's will at the end of the sixteenth century.[126] In this action Dodge was described as being seized of the manor of Lechlade in Gloucestershire and one capital messuage called 'Compelieng' (now Comp Farm) in Wrotham in Kent and other messuages and lands in Wrotham, nearby Leybourne and elsewhere in Kent to the clear yearly value of £240.[127]

John Dodge senior seems to have built up the family holdings around the 1540s and 1550s. The chapel near Comp was a chapel of ease of the church of Leybourne. This was presumably the chapel about which John Dodge wrote in September 1546 to Geoffrey Gates, brother of John Gates. John Gates was brother-in-law, steward and general 'minder' to the Right Worshipful Mr Denny, Henry VIII's confidant and fixer.[128] Dodge wrote on 5th September from Haveryng that the parson of Leybourne and his superiors would lease him a free chapel in Leybourne for as many years as the law will permit at 5 marks a year but needed the Gates brothers to push Denny to get the King's consent, as was then required for all leases made by archbishops and bishops. The implication was that it was forwarded in a letter by Geoffrey Gates to his brother John, in which he said he sent 'Mr Dogges bill to deliver to my master to be signed. If my master demur at the length of years, say he pays as much or more as any other would'. This letter must have been sent from Havering atte Bower near Romford in Essex, which adds credence to Blomefield's assertion that John Dodge senior married Elizabeth the daughter of John Carleton of Epping, one of the auditors to Henry VIII.[129]

John Dodge senior was one of the Kent gentlemen who fought, with the sheriff of Kent Sir Robert Southwell, on the side of Queen Mary in 1554. They and about 600 men routed about the same number of rebels led by Sir Thomas Wyatt, a fervent protestant. The main action is now known as the battle of Hartley Wood although the initial decisive fight took place at Blackesolle Field in Wrotham. No doubt Dodge was a key adviser to the sheriff on the local topography which was exploited to great advantage by their mounted men. Wyatt and many other rebels were subsequently executed.[130]

The earliest Kentish reference found for Dodge relates to a Richard. 'Richard Doge', previously apprentice of Robert Maye, was admitted to the Grocers' Company in 1527. Might he have been John Dodge's uncle and a second son of Richard of Wrotham? The identification is made plausible by two early chancery actions. A suit of 1515-18 showed John Edmoth of Hadlow in Kent (not far from Wrotham) and Johanna his wife, late the wife of John Benet, took action against her Benet relations. Johanna was the daughter of Richard Dogge of Wrotham.[131] Another action from 1538-44 possibly included a reference to the young Richard Dodge.[132] Richard was mentioned as one of several deceased husbands of Joan Porter who had held disputed bonds during his short marriage to her. Perhaps, as well as daughter Joan, Richard of Wrotham had two sons: John who became the head of the family in Wrotham and Richard who became a grocer but died shortly after getting married. If so, this would give yet another Grocers' Company connection in the story. At that time James Apott was of course very active as a London grocer.

The Dodge family may have really only made good in the second half of the sixteenth century. John of Mannington's brother Edward Dodge was active in London in business as a gentleman servant of Sir Christopher Hatton, rather than being a farmer in Kent. Katherine Lumner/Callard who was often in London may have met John through Edward's London activities. However John Dodge himself may have been known about town. After their marriage John may have been the Yeoman of the Exchequer who in 1568 acquired a twenty year lease of a tenement in New Windsor from Robert Dale gent.[133] If he was a minor exchequer functionary this would have been consistent with Katherine's connections forged as a result of Edmund Lumner's time as an excise collector in London. A real job in London would also help to explain why there is so little documentary evidence of John Dodge being active in Norfolk until the 1580s and 1590s. Interestingly a chancery action by John Dodge and Katherine at some point before 1579 merely described him as esquire and her as his wife and executrix of Richard Wigmore, with no residence given. It is interesting that Mannington was not given as their place of residence, perhaps hinting at a London or Middlesex sense of identity at that time.[134]

In the early stages of Katherine and John's marriage there was some contention arising from the earlier wardship of Edmund Lumner junior held by Sir Christopher Heydon of Baconsthorpe. A sixteenth century copy of a document tucked inside a Mannington deed quoted from an action of Dame Anne Heydon (of Thursford), Sir Christopher's mother, against Edmund 'Lumpner' and Katherine and John Dodge.[135] More substantially, Dame Anne's answer in an action has survived giving a November 1572 date.[136] Anne was answering the complaint of Edmund Lumner junior, who at 17, was, as she pointed out, still under age. While nominally referring to a close in East Bradenham called the Leys, in reality this action had more to do with Anne's claim to a third of Mannington's profits while Edmund was under age. Her claim was based on 'Fewelles' manor in Mannington being held of her Saxthorpe manor of Micklehall by knight's service. The name came from the Fewell family who held Mannington before the Lumners and perhaps she used the old name to show that her claim was based on very long-standing rights that preceded the Lumner tenure of the manor. She said she had effective wardship of Edmund through this involvement in the premises. (Her son Sir Christopher had certainly held the wardship of the boy earlier but whether this was from his mother's claim or by a purchase is not clear.) Her claim was that Edmund senior's settlement of the manor on Katherine was void in law. The estate should be partitioned, with Anne receiving a third of the profits until young Edmund was 21. The claim would have been quite a significant one - the estate probably generated some £300 a year and Dame Anne's claim would have totalled about £1,800 over the eighteen years of minority. Presumably the civil action by Edmund junior was to try to defeat her claim; but she argued that it should not be heard until her prior common law action had been heard and resolved. It is unlikely she succeeded. The cause would have died with her death in 1577 and her son's in 1580.

John Dodge versus Cookes over Coldham Manor

John Dodge was now becoming more active in Mannington. On 10th August 1570 he wrote from Mannington to Cecil Burghley about certain recusants in Norfolk particularly one Drythicke or Dirrich 'a rank papist' late chaplain to the Archbishop of Canterbury and gave particulars of other papists.[137] Records of three civil actions survive which show that John Dodge of Mannington was running the estate there in the late 1580s and 1590s, even after John Potts had bought Mannington and married his daughter. John Dodge seems to have had a major falling out with the Cooke family of neighbouring Little Barningham. They farmed largely in their parish with some land immediately adjacent to the Mannington parish boundary at Heckham Heath. As the 1595 map showed, one of the Cooke family had a house just north of Mannington Hall, at the site of today's Mannington Hall Farm and in the meadows just to the south and east of the old site of Coldham. They were perhaps too close for comfort and John Dodge accused them of being a difficult and quarrelsome family. The Cookes were however a family of quite some wealth and well-connected locally among senior yeomen families. For more information see Family Notes 4: Cooke of Little Barningham.

By 1583 John Dodge had, in his own right by lease, become lord of the manor of Little Barningham and with it the ancient small manor of Coldham, by now subsumed into Little Barningham.[138] After the Stafford family lost the manor at the attainder of the Duke of Buckingham in 1522, Little Barningham (then called Stafford Barningham) had been held by the Dukes of Norfolk for much of the sixteenth century. The Howards had used various trustees to hold the manor for them and from the 1560s their main estate steward for all their lands, William Dix, was resident in Wickmere. Little Barningham was under his watchful eye while the lordship was held firstly by John Stanley of Scottow in about 1562, then his widow Elizabeth Stanley in 1583 and then John Dodge, by lease, by November 1583.[139]

Coldham was a tiny manor sitting across the boundary of Little Barningham and Wolterton parishes just a short distance from, and almost due north of, Mannington Hall. The site of the manor was where Barningham Lowes Carr is today and in 1595 it had no house or building on it. Heckham Heath was in Barningham and abutted the Little Barningham and Mannington parish boundary just to the north of the present Lady's Wood. Coldham Beck no doubt referred to the small stream coming off the land at the old manorial site and feeding into Mannington's long lake, but not its moat - as shown on the 1595 map. The Dovehouse Close lay immediately to the south of the Cooke farmhouse and on the 1595 map was shown as having a cottage in its northern part and a dovehouse towards the southern end immediately across the moat and lake from Mannington Hall. So the land in contention was an arc along Mannington's boundary and was very close to the Hall itself. No doubt the Mannington estate had for some time wanted to incorporate it into the manor and in due course that is exactly what happened. In the meantime the manorial background of Coldham was shrouded in mystery and left ample room for different interpretations of land tenure in the area. For quite some time, it seems, Coldham had been held by the same lords as those of Little Barningham manor and while it technically retained its separate identity this was nominal and its business was transacted in the courts of Little Barningham manor under a common steward.

Entries in the court record of December 1587, made in Dodge's time, show that Thomas Cooke was asked by what right he held the 'scite of the manor of Coldham als Coldham Close'. He rather tersely replied that he held demesne lands 'sometime Pinchin's' by a lease from Mrs Cooke [sic].[140] He put forward three memoranda dating back to April 1579, from an unstated originator (but evidently Elizabeth Stanley who had remarried to become Elizabeth Coote) that granted him, for 21 years from Michaelmas, 1 acre of enclosed pasture or meadow at 30s a year; the Church Close 5 acres in three pieces one part being a meadow called Setyard; Coldham Close of 4 acres at 30s a year, being land 'sometime copyhold of my manor of Coldham'. As far as he was concerned that was all there was to say.

In March 1588 the manorial court ordered Little Barningham's bailiff to seize the 'scite of Coldhams lately in the occupation of Thomas Cooke and the meadow Setyards lately in the occupation of Richard Cooke'. This court also recited a lease of March 1549 for 21 years in which Thomas Cooke had been granted by Sir William Buttl___ and Henry Smyth 'the scite of the manor of Coldham with one grange built upon it and another parcel of land called Saxthorpe's farm als Hookham [Heckham]'. Also included were Dovehouse Croft of 2 acres to the south of Coldham Beck and 2 acres of pasture south of the beck and a parcel of meadow called South Meadows. The 21 year lease had been at £4 15s 8d a year. The intention of showing it in the court roll was presumably to show that the lease was long since finished and that it could not be cited by the Cookes as justification for retaining Coldham. In the subsequent court of requests action it became clear that Dodge was indeed arguing that the lands were not copyhold or customary hold, as the Cookes at one point said, but were straightforward leasehold. Not only that, they were leasehold of Coldham, not Little Barningham, even though in the same court roll. The court roll entry was critical to that argument.

An exchequer commission was set up in 1590 to look into whether Heckham Heath in Little Barningham was part of Her Majesty's manor of Little Barningham.[141] This arose from the claim by complainant Thomas Cooke that the Heath was his and leased directly from the Crown manor. John Dodge as defendant (with Elizabeth Coote widow and Thomas Wiggon) argued that a part of it had for very many years been known to be a parcel of the manor of Coldham Hall in Little Barningham parish and so was not part of the Crown manor.[142] Interestingly William Guybon gent, presumably Rose Lumner's step-grandson, sat on the commission of enquiry. He had been the first named witness to Christopher Coote's will in 1587 and, as a local man, he would have been quite knowledgeable about the Mannington/Barningham environment.

The commission's questions to both sides and the answers of all their witnesses make fascinating reading. Dodge's witnesses said that the 22-acre Heckham Heath pasture land had anciently been part owned by both manors and had been divided by a ditch. Cooke and his predecessors had paid rent for the Coldham manor part to whoever was at the time lord of that manor. The number and stature of Dodge's witnesses overwhelmed those for Cooke. William Guybon's evidence even claimed that Cooke's own father had been present at an earlier survey of the area and had made clear the ditch division and Coldham manor's stake in the heathland. Cooke and his father were shown to have paid rent to various lords for the Coldham's part since at least as far back as a lease made in 1567 for a 21 year term. Most tellingly, the action appears to have been prompted by Dodge's refusal after the end of the lease to continue to accept the old yearly rent of 22s since it was now costing him more than that in rent to hold the land himself.

In the early 1590s the issue of fixed rents - which, with increasing prices and poor harvests, were increasingly a problem for landowners - was raised again in the second action. In a complaint by John Dodge against Elizabeth Roades, wife of Francis Roades [sic] gent and previously the wife of Christopher Cooke [error for Coote] deceased, Dodge was questioning the rent payable on Elizabeth's 'manor of Coldham Hall in Little Barningham and lands sometime in the occupation of Thomas Bettes which were a parcel of that manor'.[143] By a lease made around Michaelmas 1587 he had agreed to rent the manor for ten years for £20 a year. Now he made out that the sum was above what it what was really worth. Dodge claimed that in the previous action he had gone to court effectively on Elizabeth's behalf to protect her title to part of Heckham Heath from the fraudulent claim of Thomas Cooke and by inference he had then succeeded. Now, after Thomas Cooke had died (in February 1591), his widow Maude and his brother William Cooke had gone back to court and got possession of the piece of land by a writ from the court of exchequer.

Dodge said that Elizabeth Coote had claimed good and full title for her lifetime to the freehold of Coldham manor and on this basis he had agreed to rent it. He also said she agreed to pay the costs of the earlier action. However she had only so far paid 40s and refused to pay more. Not only had the Cooke clan got back part of the land, but also a John Curson had succeeded with a writ in which he claimed half the manor. Curson obviously had a claim of some quality and as a result Dodge had to pay him half the rent.[144] However Elizabeth refused to reduce the rent payable to her. Further, she refused to give Dodge the writings which gave the breakdown details of the rent he should have from the under-tenants, which they were refusing to pay him. When he sought redress for this unfairness, Elizabeth's answer was that a deal was a deal. She was not obliged to warrant her title and she had paid the 40s of her own free will and saw no reason to pay any more. The outcome is not known.

It seems as if relations between the Dodges and Cookes had fundamentally broken down. The Heckham Heath affair returned to court with various moans between 1589 and 1592.[145] The rent action above, in one court, ran parallel with the further action in another court. Throughout Dodge had been arguing that the Cookes never had the site of Coldham and the other lands by copyhold or customary hold, but rather by lease. Since this had expired they had no title to the lands. These amazingly time-consuming cases provide a mass of detail.[146] They confirm the sequence of Coldham lordships from Stanley to Coote to Dodge by lease; they name Thomas Wiggon as steward there as well as for Mannington manor under Dodge's lordships. Thomas Bettes had been bailiff of Coldham as well as having leased some lands there prior to the Cookes. The famous Edward Coke was lawyer for Thomas Cooke. He may well have had a personal issue against the Dodges and Potts stemming from these actions by the Cookes. Probably he was keen on this action since a potential loss of land from a royal manor was involved - the same point of law that he was to make later against John Potts.

Thomas Cooke's widow Maud, by mid November 1591 had remarried to Fyrmyn Neave who had tried to patch up the disagreements. He prevailed upon the Dodges (and Elizabeth Coote) and the Cookes to go to arbitration to resolve matters. Richard Stubbes esq represented the Cookes and John Potts of Itteringham esq (then aged just 31) stood for the Dodges. Richard Stubbes 'late of Edgefield' was a friend and supervisor of Thomas Cooke's will made in 1590.[147] John Potts will shortly take front-of-stage in the Mannington story; for the moment he was a working lawyer and son-in-law of Dodge, with a particular interest in the estate.

The arbitrators met several times but failed to agree on an award by the deadline of April 1592. John Potts's deposition revealed that they fell out all over again debating whether they would all sign reciprocal obligations in £30 to stand by the award of the two arbitrators. So the action remained as it was, unresolved, and next we hear of it is in the court of the Star Chamber the following year. William Cooke, brother and heir of the late Thomas Cooke of Little Barningham, now sued John Dodge, Thomas Fenne his steward and others over riotous events in August 1589.[148] Only his bill of complaint survives. Without the defence and the decree, what actually did happen can only be surmised. It is interesting that this action referred back to events in 1589 which at no point were even hinted at in the earlier actions of exactly this time! No doubt, having lost the case from lack of evidence to overturn the lease description in the court rolls, the Cookes were having one last fling on an emotional pitch that Dodge had done them violence. Whatever the rights to the land, the events were said to be dramatic and show the potential for bad behaviour over property rights.

William Cooke said that his brother and their father and grandfather before him were lawfully seized of a 5 acre piece of copyhold land of the manor of Mannington located just over the parish boundary in Little Barningham. The abuttal given of 'Jessops Wong adjoining to the south' allows identification on the 1595 map as land a little to the north of Mere Farm in Mannington. The Cookes, he said, had ploughed and sown it with corn for some 50 years without any contradiction. William and Thomas's father Richard had died about 5 years earlier (about 1588) and the land had descended by right to his eldest son Thomas, who continued to grow and reap corn there through his farmer John Doo. In March 1589 they had sown oats and agreed between the brothers that they would have half the harvest each. By this time, they were, as the previous actions showed, outside the 21 year lease period for Coldham land but still arguing that this piece was copyhold of Little Barningham. On 8th August, according to William, he with several Cooke servants and Robert Eldinge his brother-in-law were reaping the oats. Horses and a cart were waiting to carry the harvest away.

But suddenly a band of 8 or 10 armed, 'ill-disposed and riotous persons' came to the field and made a 'riotous and forcible assembly'. Cooke alleged they were there unlawfully and at the procurement of John Dodge. The group included Thomas Fenne, Raphe Dodge (the future rector of Mannington!), Anthony Potter, Robert Rogers (who as a 'gent of Itteringham' had testified in the requests' action and became Mannington's estate steward later), Robert Lumner (from Sharrington and showing that at this time he was still very much persona grata at Mannington), James Gunton and others whose names Cooke did not know. Fenne had a long staff, Potter a brushbill, Dodge a pitchfork, Rogers a dagger, Gunton a cudgel and others had swords and bucklers. They made an assault and affray and struck Eldinge on the hand and William Harper on the head. They struck and beat Edward Smyth, William Camplyn and Thomas Willinson. Someone had obviously sent for Thomas Cooke, who was clearly ill and could not travel on foot but rode there and sitting on his horse was struck at by Potter with his brushbill - a long handled billhook and a lethal weapon. William Cooke said that Potter would 'very like have slain him if one of the bystanders had not met and borne the blow with a pitchfork'. The riot continued and John Dodge sent a messenger with a sword, buckler and pitchfork who said Dodge did not intend the band to beat Cooke and his men. But the attack was renewed and they 'sore beat and hurt divers of them until they were in peril of their lives'. In the end the attackers took away the cart and horses to Dodge's mansion house at Mannington where the horses were put in his pound. The cart was kept in his yard where his cattle were permitted to eat all the oats in it. Whereupon the rioters returned to the field and took away another load.

Cooke believed that this 'outrage against the laws of the land' should be punished to deter others from such riotous and unlawful behaviour. Since Star Chamber decrees have not survived, the story ends there. Within a year or so, however, John Dodge's ten year lease of Mannington from John Potts was to come to an end and Potts himself was to start taking a more disciplined grip of Mannington manor issues. The 1595 map already referred to, was part of that process and no doubt the long-running rows with the Cookes were part of the motivation to get local agreement to manorial boundaries, sheep shack rights and field tenure.

Edmund Lumner junior and Jane

In amongst the legal and physical carryings-on of his stepfathers Callard and Dodge, Edmund Lumner junior, the heir apparent of Mannington, was growing up. Katherine (perhaps pushed by Sir Christopher Heydon who may have still had the wardship of the boy) allowed Edmund junior to marry Jane Yelverton, daughter of William Yelverton esq of Rougham when they were both very young. As Edmund was born in April 1555, he was, at 14, just over the age of consent for a boy to marry. A court dispute of December 1587 over the will of Jane's father, gave Jane then as being about 29 years old. This would make her birth around 1558.[149] So in 1569 she was only 11 or 12 years old - 12 being the then minimum age of consent for girls. They married in Rougham church by a licence from the Bishop of Norwich dated 5th July 1569, on the following day.[150]

That pressure had been applied is quite likely. Within six months, on 9th February 1570, Edmund had appeared before William Masters, chancellor to John the Bishop of Norwich, where he renounced and disclaimed the marriage. Edmund recanted and sought annulment from the bishop on the grounds of being under age and not agreeing to the marriage.[151] During Trinity term 1575 there was a warrant of this act of renunciation and Edmund was held to be unmarried by decree of the court of Wards and Liveries. To wriggle out of the marriage he would have tried to prove he was under the age of 14, even though this was probably not so, and later there was a rumour that there had been some attempt to alter the records. Although the annulment was made, the couple rather bizarrely were reconciled and either remarried or simply agreed that the earlier marriage should stand. The exact sequence of events and dates is not clear and no re-marriage has been found. Did Jane, who later was clearly a devout catholic, not accept the annulment and insist their marriage was valid? Although she was afterwards legally taken to be Edmund's wife and certainly was the executrix and beneficiary of his will, others would use the doubts of her position in the courts. Later she was to become very assertive in pursuing her rights after her husband's death. She always claimed she had brought a good portion to her marriage as she was well-born. They were married for at least 16 years but despite their youth, no male heir was forthcoming. They had the first of their two daughters in 1579 and the second in 1582.

Little is known about the early life of Edmund Lumner junior and Jane. Later Star Chamber actions related that he went to London as a young man and built up debts there, which seems very likely. As early as 1577 he had mortgaged the lands he inherited from his father in Letton and Cranworth in Norfolk.[152] No doubt these had originally been part of the Rose Spring inheritance from her father. Having borrowed £220, he soon repaid the money and by 1580 had sold the property altogether. The rents and profits of Mannington would not be his until his mother died and there is no indication that he played any part in running the estate during Katherine's long marriage to John Dodge. After his marriage was annulled, he had been made a ward of Thomas Leighton esquire (his mother's brother) who received the profits from Edmund's marriage and custody of his body regardless of the prior dissolved marriage. Katherine may well have thought some role on Guernsey under the wing of her brother Sir Thomas Leighton, the Governor would be sensible and some time before 1582 he travelled to the Island. Jane went with him. Two pieces of evidence support this idea.

In his later nuncupative (spoken) and undated will (proved by his widow Jane in July 1587), Edmund Lumner (described as 'of Mannington esq' even though he had sold it) was certainly still travelling abroad:

> Being in or towards a voyage upon the seas … said: For as much as I know not whether I shall return again safely or not or what shall become of me, therefore my will and mind is that my debts shall be paid and that my wife and my children shall have that which I have amongst them. And I desire my captain Mr Bankes to look unto it. And as concerning my writings my man Searles can tell where they be. Then being present divers credible persons.[153]

This seems highly likely to be a reference to travel to Guernsey and, from all the references to his death in later court actions, it seems that he was lost at sea. Searles was probably John Searles of Itteringham who had some role in the running of the Mannington estate. The second clue was that one of Edmund Lumner's two daughters was born and baptised in St Peter Port church in Guernsey. This was noted in italic contemporary hand at the end of a very splendid and sumptuously illustrated copy of Lydgate's *Fall of Princes*:

> Marie Lumner was borne on Candlemasse Daye 1579 betwene the howers of twelue and one of the clock at nighte Elizabeth Lumner was Borne in the Isle of Gernesey vppon St. Thomas ye Apostles daye 1582: betwene sixe and seauen of the Clock at nighte. And these wer the Daughters of Edmunde Lumner of Mannington in the Countie of Norfolk Esquier which he had by Jane the Daughter of Williame Yeluerton of Rowgham in the sayd Countie Esquier.[154]

A poem written below, in a different hand, may well refer to the babies:

> As God hath lent them comely shapes And nature well disposde their mynde So ffortune graunte them (pretty Apes) An happy state on earthe to fynde Thus shall they lyue and prayse the daye That fyrst of lyghte hath gyuen them saye. [Then in the same italic hand as above]: Dos maxima fortuna.

The precision of the notes and the charming description of the girls, makes us believe this was probably written by a close relative. Intriguingly there is another entry in the same book opposite the first note in an older hand showing that it had been owned earlier by a member of or someone close to the Calthorpe family:

> Elizabet Calthorpe the dauter of Cristofer Calthorpe esquier and Jane his wife dawghter and one of the heires of Roger Rowkewoode esquier was Borne at Cokthorpe on Cristmas Daie being the xxvth Daie of December betwyn the howers of vij and viij at night A Dni. 1.5.5.5. Cristmas Daie being on the wednesdaie Jamys Calthorpe Son to the said Cristofer and Jane was borne at Starston the xxxjth daie of August being wednesdaie A Dni. 1.5.5.8.

The provenance of the book before the eighteenth century is not recorded but it could have belonged to the Drury family. There is a bible with many Drury family baptismal entries set out in a very similar form which is assumed to have belonged originally to Sir William Drury of Hawstead.[155] Sir William's mother was a Calthorpe. His daughter Bridget married Henry Yelverton and one of her half sisters-in-law was Jane Yelverton. Perhaps Bridget inherited the book and included Jane's two children.

Katherine, Edmund's mother, had used her connections to Guernsey before. As we shall see in Chapter 6 her son Thomas Wigmore, from her first marriage, was Lieutenant (Deputy) Governor and her cousin by marriage, the young Henry Lumner, was the Queen's Receiver of Rents and Revenues there from 1581. It would be natural for Edmund to enter this family enterprise hoping for a role with an income attached. Perhaps his mother had 'exiled' him there after he had got into debt. Perhaps she thought he could get into little trouble in a small community under the watchful eyes of so many family members. However, since he appears to have been on the island several years before he sold Mannington to John Potts it seems that this exile was neither permanent nor truly effective. Perhaps he was simply one of the many merchants operating out of London, Southampton and Guernsey and he failed to make money on his activities.

Jane Lumner widow

Edmund Lumner's undated will seems to have taken forever to administer. First proved in 1587 it was still active when in 1611 Jane Lumner, his widow, passed on her executorship to William Yelverton esq her eldest brother from whom nearly 20 years later it passed to Jane's daughter![156] Shortly after her husband's death in 1587, Jane, drawing on her Yelverton family experience (another family full of lawyers), turned to the law to maintain herself and her children. In 1589 she appealed to the Duchy of Lancaster over Edmund Lumner senior's property in the Duchy's manor of Aylsham. The warrant and her interrogatories and witness statements survive adding insights to her early marriage to Edmund Lumner junior as well as some local colour.[157]

The warrant for a commission of enquiry was issued on her behalf against Sir Robert Wood and Henry Pernell, who were accused of conveying the right and title to one half of a messuage with a building called Mannes in Aylsham, which with various tenements had lands there amounting to 260 acres of copyhold. They also had conveyed with it a shop and two stalls with a house on it - presumably in Aylsham market place. Mannes had been left to Edmund's brother William who may have died unmarried. Jane's six questions set out her case that she was legally married to Edmund and that as a result, by the custom of this manor, he should have inherited an equal part of the property and she was entitled to a part as her dowry. Effectively she was challenging Edmund senior's right to leave this property exclusively to his son William, ignoring Edmund junior's rights to half of it. She also asserted that, like the women of Kent, she should have part of the property after her husband's death, or else be paid compensation in lieu. Rather than putting forward a proposition, Jane asked what share she should be due but implied that it should be either a half or a third of what the copyholder originally had.

Her witnesses included members of the Barker and Soame families - long-standing Aylsham yeomen and husbandmen - and Edward Brampton gent of Brampton who was godfather of Jane's daughter Mary. Her star turn was Thomas Smythe of Massingham, a yeoman who obviously knew the major tenants on the

Mannington estate. All agreed that the custom of the manor of Aylsham was for copyhold to be inherited equally by all sons. Most agreed that local custom also was that a widow would have some right to her husband's share. Although they were not able to define standard practice, they were able to cite family examples where deals had been struck between a purchaser and a widow. As an example, the brothers Robert and John Soame testified that their mother Margery had received 10s from one Growte as compensation for her dowry rights in two tenements that her husband had sold to Growte. The outcome is not recorded but it seems that Jane had a plausible case for some compensation for the Mannes property having passed in its entirety to her husband's brother.

Certainly, nobody suggested that she and Edmund had not been legally married, although only Smythe actually addressed the question of Edmund's age at marriage and presumably he was there specifically to deliver his juicy story. He had heard that the wife of one [John] Searle of Itteringham (a tenant of the Mannington estate of some note and probably 'my man Searles' in Edmund's will):

> 'taketh upon her a certain knowledge of the age of Edmund
> Lumner ... affirms he was over 14 at the time of marriage and that
> the said wife of Searle says the church book where Edmund's age
> was registered was afterwards corrupted and that the party who
> corrupted it lived not a week after'.

Had the parish clerk of Mannington (or perhaps Itteringham, given Mannington's ruinous state) dropped dead unexpectedly at some time? Searles may have taken on the role of clerk later and his wife had had the inside story. Or perhaps the act of divine retribution was visited on the rector of the day? He, among others, would have had access to the register and could have altered Edmund's age to make him look younger to support his earlier appeal to the bishop to have his marriage annulled on the basis of being under age at the time. The forgery would have happened in 1569 or 1570 during the rectorship of Thomas Hill, rector of Itteringham 1557-58 and rector of Mannington 1563-77.[158] His survival after the date seems to let him off the hook and likewise Edward Atwood (1560-85) the relevant rector of Itteringham. If the marriage took place in the Hall, the register may well, given the state of the church, have been kept in the house. Anyone could have had access. As no early Mannington registers survive, whoever might have been struck down at this time for forging the register will remain a dark secret!

After Edmund's death, Jane and her two daughters Elizabeth and Mary went to live near her half-brother Edward Yelverton of Grimston. Yelverton had catholic sympathies and he and his sister were both separately recorded in the lists of presentments to the Bishop of Norwich between 1595 and 1615 as an 'obstinate recusant'.[159] In both 1595 and 1598 Edward was in Wolferton and Jane in Brandon Parva.[160] Jane's two daughters evidently shared her religious beliefs. During this period they apparently lived in three or four different houses, presumably with catholic family or friends who would give them support. From Brandon Parva, she and the girls moved to Rushall by 1600 (where only the Lumners were listed) and by 1605 they were in Hainford listed under 'John Drewrye gent' and possibly all in the same household. They stayed in Hainford between at least 1611 and 1615 but by now with Mary's husband Nicholas Everard.[161]

The lists show relatively small numbers of popish and 'sectary' recusants in the Mannington area. There were routinely two or three in Aylsham, the Brampton family in Brampton and Anne the wife of John Dix Ramsey of Wickmere. Anne, the wife of Francis Stubbes of Scottow, and her daughters were consistently listed as sectaries. Once, in 1598, John Bettes of Corpusty and Irmingland got a ticking off for not coming to church on prayer days, but he was not listed as a recusant. The family at Mannington were mainstream protestant. Jane would have become progressively poorer as a result of the fines imposed on her. No doubt this would have increased the determination of John Potts that Jane should not have more of his money than had already been paid to her husband.

Jane Lumner's story was not finished yet. She was to prove a thorn in the side for John Potts when she took both him and his mother on in chancery over the payments for Mannington.

First, however - a trip to Guernsey.

Chapter 6

Guernsey: No Picnic

Sir Thomas Leighton's governorship of Guernsey opened opportunities for three young men in his sister's family, including her son Edmund Lumner. However his life on the Island was not without its problems some of which were caused by two of those very same relatives.

Leighton origins

The 'matriarch of Mannington', Katherine Leighton/Wigmore/Lumner/Callard/ Dodge, had three brothers and five sisters. Her eldest brother Sir Edward Leighton inherited Wattlesborough Hall, the family seat near Shrewsbury in Shropshire. Sir Thomas Leighton was the second son of John Leighton esq and Joyce Sutton. Joyce was the daughter of Edward Baron Sutton of Dudley and his wife Cecily Willoughby of Dudley in Worcestershire and the granddaughter of Sir Edmund Sutton. The third brother, Charles, seems to have died without issue, being noted in the Shropshire Visitation simply as Captain Leighton.[1] Perhaps he served with his brother Thomas. Through her own bloodline and through her brother and his Knollys wife, Katherine was potentially extraordinarily well-connected to senior figures at court. By the Knollys connection the Leightons were also linked to the Botelers of Watton-at-Stone, the family of the other Katherine in the Potts story. Both families were heavily involved in the household of Robert Dudley, Earl of Leicester. Leicester's accounts refer to Leighton (who in 1585 sent him a gift of knitted stockings), his wife, Sir Philip Boteler and even Edmund Lumner.[2]

As shown in Chapter 5, Sir Thomas Leighton, as a young man, was part of the Dudley family group and he was implicated in the plot against Queen Mary led by his cousin Henry Dudley.[3] In 1559 Queen Elizabeth welcomed him and the other conspirators back to England. It may have helped that Robert Dudley, Thomas's relation, was then the Queen's favourite.[4] Although both rivals for the Queen's affections, Leicester and Sir Christopher Hatton were good friends and Hatton was overseer of his will. Sir Philip Boteler junior (Katherine Boteler's great-nephew) served with Robert in the Netherlands in the mid 1580s and in September 1585, on one of several visits to Boteler's house, Dudley stood godfather to Sir Philip's son and heir Robert. Sir Philip Boteler, Sir Francis Knollys junior and Sir Christopher Hatton were all senior attendees at Leicester's funeral in 1588.

Robert Dudley married three times: Amy Robsart, Douglas Howard and Lettice the daughter of Sir Francis Knollys and Elizabeth Carey. Lettice herself married three times: first to Walter Devereux the 1st Earl of Essex, second in 1578 to Robert Dudley and, after his death in 1588, to Sir Christopher Blount.[5] Her eldest Devereux son was Robert Devereux, 2nd Earl of Essex, who was promoted at court by Dudley and in due course became for a time the Queen's favourite. Essex will reappear later in the story. Leighton reinforced his close connections to the Queen by his marriage, also in 1578, to Elizabeth Knollys, Lettice's sister and a Gentlewoman of the Privy Chamber. He was knighted the following year. So, by both blood and marriage, Thomas was related to Leicester and by marriage to the Earl of Essex. Sir Francis Knollys was also hugely influential at court holding a long string of roles including Captain of the Guard, Treasurer of the Royal Household, Privy Councillor and he was a major player in negotiations with Mary Queen of Scots. He had been the leader of the government in parliament, a role which he passed on to Sir Christopher Hatton in the early 1570s. His wife Katherine Carey was a first cousin of the Queen through her mother Mary Boleyn, the sister of Queen Anne Boleyn. Although not acknowledged at the time it seems quite likely that Katherine may have been the illegitimate child of Henry VIII during his affair with Mary Boleyn.[6] Katherine Carey and Princess Elizabeth probably spent years together as children and as one of the four Ladies of the Bedchamber Katherine remained extremely close to the Queen. When she died, relatively young, in 1569 Katherine Carey was given an extraordinarily lavish funeral by the Queen in Westminster Abbey. Cecilia, another of the Knollys girls, was a Maid of Honour to Queen Elizabeth.

Sir Thomas Leighton was a trusted soldier even before taking on Guernsey. Soon after his earlier return to England, Thomas was Captain of a troop of 200 foot soldiers in the summer 1560 Scottish campaign.[7] Subsequently he served with distinction in France (at Le Havre with Leicester in 1562) and Ireland. He became a Gentleman of the Privy Chamber and was involved in 1568 in discussions with Mary Queen of Scots and the Earl of Moray. He served in Pontefract during the 1569 northern uprising. He had become a well-respected and trusted soldier with strong links to court and with a growing reputation too for his negotiating skills as a diplomat.

Demonstrating the Queen's patronage, extra revenues were granted to Leighton for his service in 1577 (a fishery in the Tweed in Northumberland) and in 1578 (corn and flax twelfths that had been of the Abbey of Mount St Michael in Guernsey).[8] The fisheries grant was somewhat of a double-edged sword. In 1578 he had to go to the court of requests to try to assert his rights to the revenues from which he had been evicted by a group of men who claimed a prior grant of at least half the fisheries from the Bishop of Durham.[9] In 1585 Sir Thomas was granted by the Queen his own estate of Feckenham manor, south of Redditch in Worcestershire, a result of the rough justice of Elizabethan times and the value of family links. Feckenham had been held by Sir John Throckmorton and his wife Margaret Puttenham.[10] His two sons Sir Francis and Thomas were heavily involved in the 1583 papist plot to remove Queen Elizabeth and install Mary Queen of Scots. Sir Francis Throckmorton was beheaded the following year, leaving a young son John and his widow Dame Anne. Why was the reversion of Feckenham, in which Dame Anne had a life interest, granted to Sir Thomas Leighton? Certainly for services to the crown but also no doubt because Dame Anne was a Sutton and Sir Thomas's cousin.[11] Their cousinship, however, did not prevent Thomas from using his royal patroness to guard his rights. On 16th March 1588 he was given an order to prevent Lady Throckmorton from cutting timber trees on the estate: 'Her Majesty was highly displeased'.

Leighton's life on Guernsey

He was appointed Governor (the older title was Captain) of Guernsey on 14th April 1570 by letters patent as successor to Francis Chamberlayne.[12] He was given a lifetime grant of the position without fee or fine 'for his service'. His primary role was building up and managing the main garrison at Castle Cornet and other fortifications on Guernsey and the other smaller Channel Islands. He was also given the widest ranging powers as the Queen's senior representative. His French language skills helped him in Guernsey and led to diplomatic roles in France and elsewhere in the 1570s. Leighton could receive the homage of men on the islands, appoint and pay officers and soldiers, collect tolls and issues due to the crown, give safe conduct to merchants and so on. He was to spend any surplus revenues on the safekeeping of the islands. He had a lieutenant who deputised as Governor when Leighton was absent.[13]

Taxation and administration was managed through the island's Bailiff and court of Jurats. These Guernsey men often had divided loyalties, focusing on historic customs and privileges which they demanded were to be honoured by the Governor. Between 1570 and 1600 these differences over the administration of tax, trade and both civil and criminal law were to be a running sore for Leighton and his officers, with major flare-ups in the late 1570s, 1580s and 1590s. As *de facto* court of appeal, the Privy Council in London had to deal with the major problems and Guernsey correspondence had a disproportionate amount of coverage in their papers. Throughout, despite aggressive accusations by the islanders against Leighton and his senior officers, he was supported by the Privy Council and it is clear that he was valued by them as a good Governor. Sir Thomas was a strict puritan with presbyterian views. This zeal was to bring him into conflict with the clergy on Guernsey who typically had rather stronger leanings to the old religion. Despite his firmness with the islanders, a couple of his requests to the Privy Council for pardons for Guernsey men show that he was a fair man. Among others, he asked that a felonious killing should not be treated as murder, which carried an automatic death penalty, since it was a tragic accident involving a horse and cart.[14]

Jobs for the boys

In his role as Governor, Sir Thomas Leighton employed one of his sister's Wigmore children and also a Lumner cousin. Katherine's Lumner son also lived on Guernsey suggesting he may also have had a role of some sort in his uncle's administration. Leighton had taken his nephew, the young Edmund Lumner of Mannington, as his ward in the 1560s, and it is quite likely he did the same for his nephew Thomas Wigmore. Certainly Wigmore was with him at the very beginning of his time as Governor. Wigmore, described as 'Maistre Wigmor' the Governor's lieutenant, stood as godfather ('parrain') to various children baptised in St Peter Port in February 1573 and in 1574.[15] At this stage, he would appear to have been Leighton's right-hand man although not officially the lieutenant-governor.

By the date of the baptism of Elizabeth daughter of Edmund Lumner ('Edemont Lhommer') in St Peter Port church on 23rd December 1582, her godfather Thomas Wigmore was described as lieutenant-governor and Bailiff 'pour lors'. The lieutenant-governor stood in for Leighton during his absences from the island in all military and civil matters - and his nephew had been appointed as such from 1580. From October 1581 Wigmore was also the Bailiff of Guernsey. Prior to 1617, the Bailiff worked under the Governor and headed both the legislature and the parliament on Guernsey - he was both judge and head administrator. In the 1580s, therefore, Thomas Wigmore was a man of great power on the island. However, his inability to speak French made him particularly unpopular on the island and meant that he was not competent to carry out all the duties of the Bailiff.[16] The implication of 'pour lors' - for the time being - perhaps showed the islanders' lack of confidence in him. Or perhaps in a time of crisis Leighton had made him Bailiff with some sort of statement that it was only a temporary appointment. His stepbrother Edmund Lumner might, at least for a time, have had a junior role in Leighton's administration but there is no evidence for this nor for how long he and Jane lived there with their young daughters. In 1584 they were in England but Edmund, as we know from his hastily spoken will, was still travelling when he died in 1586 or 1587.[17]

Henry Lumner and the de Vic family

Edmund's cousin, the young Henry Lumner son of the London fishmonger of the Sharrington family, was also with Leighton in the early 1570s and may too have been a ward after his father's death in 1563. Henry Lumner was heavily involved between 1570 and 1574 in Leighton's repair of Cornet Castle.[18] He was named as a clerk and in April-May 1574 he submitted expenses claims for 'riding into Dorset with a commission to impress masons and labourers in the said works'. On 17th November 1581 he was sworn in as Her Majesty's Receiver for Guernsey, appointed by Leighton, and that December stood as godfather at the baptism of Marie Trosbery.[19] In February 1582 he and Jean Effard were in court over Lumner's accusation that Effard had retained a Norman servant despite having been refused permission. Effard insisted he had sent the girl away and Lumner was forced to drop the action.[20] The people of Normandy were not popular on the island: the same year Leighton himself wrote crossly in a letter that he had ordered a female ass for Sir William More (of Loseley, Surrey) but had been 'abused by a Norman whom I put in trust which in the end brought me a male'.[21]

It would seem that Henry was one of the few senior Englishmen on the island to have a good reputation, being referred to as an 'Honneste Homme'.[22] He was still Receiver in February 1583, but by May 1585 he was referred to in an act of court as 'former Receiver'.[23] Thereafter there seems to be no record of Lumner living on the island although he did crop up in a case there in 1588. By this time Henry had been married for three years and may have returned permanently to England. There is no indication that Henry Lumner had been married before his wedding in London to a widow, Martha de Vic.

The de Vic (usual spelling in Guernsey) or Devicke (usual in London) family played a major part in island affairs. In the early sixteenth century a Louis de Vic had been an important islander. By his two wives he had three sons. The eldest, Thomas, by his wife Mary the daughter and heiress of Nicholas de la Mare, had a son John who, through Mary's inheritance, became Seigneur de Surville in Jersey and held substantial lands in St Sampson Guernsey. About 1550 John de Vic was described as son and heir of Mary Delamere in an action after her death in which he sued Clement Lemprière of Jersey over lands there.[24] He was also, as John Devicke gent of London, Secretary to William Paulet, 1st Marquess of Winchester (married to a de la Mere) and England's Lord Treasurer in the early years of Queen Elizabeth's reign.[25] In July and October 1571 Leighton wrote to Lord Burghley regarding improving the fortifications of Castle Cornet. He said, among other things, that John de Vic, who had 'fair lands in this country', would wait on Burghley and could be trusted to bring the money that Leighton had requested to begin work on the fortifications.[26] This was presumably the same John 'Devicke' of London who would have been known to Burghley in his secretarial role.

John de Vic married Martha Fouaschin and had five children (a son William and four daughters) by her before he died, in or before 1581.[27] Martha's origins are unclear since the Fouaschin family had several branches on Guernsey but this substantial island clan was much intermarried with the de Vics. Thomas Fashin (as the name became in England) who died in 1558 was a Southampton merchant and was involved in island affairs as a commissioner for the Privy Council. For more about Martha's relations see Family Notes 5: de Vic.

Thomas de Vic's brother Laurent had a son Louis who was Leighton's ally. Louis junior was the Queen's Procureur or attorney-general on the island and he replaced Thomas Wigmore as Guernsey's Bailiff in 1588. The Clement Devicke who features in the story below may have been Louis' brother. By his second wife Louis senior had a son Richard. Richard represented the island in a delegation to London in 1558-59. His son, by 'Thomasse' Fouaschin, was John de Vic (here called junior) who became Greffier or clerk of the court in the 1580s and Procureur in the 1590s and was the father of Sir Henry de Vic. John junior was married first to Anne Carey the daughter of Nicholas Carey, from another major family on the island. His second wife and mother of Sir Henry was Elizabeth Pageot. John was also linked with London. The Earl of Leicester's accounts for April and July 1585 noted payments to John Devicks (or 'Devyge'), Sir Thomas Heneage's man, for deliveries of wine from Orleans and 'Bargoin' which he had obviously brought over himself.[28] Heneage was the Queen's Treasurer of the Chamber and in 1586 was sent by Elizabeth to try to persuade Leicester to return from the Netherlands.

Martha must have married Henry Lumner quite soon after John de Vic senior's death. When her spinster daughter Mary Devicke made her will in May 1582 in

London, her mother was described as Mrs Martha Lomner.[29] An act of Guernsey's Royal Court of 20th June 1583 ordered Henry Lumner, husband of Martha, and John de Vic to deliver documents to each other to ensure that the money and goods in England and Guernsey of the deceased John Devicke were properly divided between his children, of whom John de Vic was guardian.[30] Mary's will also referred to her sisters Ursula, Anne and Jane and her cousins Maudlyn, Clement (and his wife Elizabeth) and Lewis Devicke. Clement was a witness and was granted administration as proxy for Mary's brother William in his minority.[31] William Devicke, of London, died in 1615 with lands in Guernsey and London.[32] There is no hint in either of these two Devicke wills that Henry Lumner and Martha had children.[33] Although it is thought that they had a daughter who was the first wife of the English Ambassador to Paris, Sir Thomas Edmunds, this has not been verified from published sources and it seems unlikely.[34]

Henry and Martha had a number of legal problems shortly after their marriage. Henry Lumner gent, as the Queen's Majesty's Receiver of Rents and Revenues of HM's Isle of Guernsey, and Martha his wife, as the late wife of John Devicke gent of London, took action in February 1584 to try to recover a London property.[35] Previously John Devicke and Martha had legally bought a tenement in St John's Lane, St John Middlesex from Samuel Cordall. Devicke had other tenements in that parish which descended to William, their son, on John's death. At the time of the marriage, Henry and Martha intended to go to Guernsey where Henry lived and had been uncertain when they would return again to London. So they left their writings with John Vawse, citizen and fishmonger of London a family friend. When they returned they requested their deeds but were refused due to the 'sinister intervention' of Clement Devicke. The action that followed was against Vawse and Clement Devicke. Clement's answer was that the complaint had not specified the property adequately and it might refer to property that was in Clement's charge as young William Devicke's guardian. The second bill in May 1584 added the current tenant Robert Chamberlain esq into the list of complainants. Since the guardian of John Devicke's children on Guernsey was John de Vic not Clement, sinister may have been right.

In Hilary term at the beginning of 1585 Henry Lumner and Martha won a court order for defendants John Vaux [Vawse] and Clement Devicke to bring to court all the documents relating to the lease of the premises in St John St.[36] Devicke's argument that they were trying to prejudice the interests of William Devicke was at this stage over-ruled. John Devicke was said to have been 'minded to purchase the inheritance of the house' and had leased it out to others for many years for the benefit and use of his and Martha's young son William. The defendants admitted they had the documents and that the lease was to William's benefit. Subsequently this admission excused them from producing the documents in court. An order in the summer of 1585 seemed to find in favour of the Lumners unless by the next term the defendants responded. There were no more decrees for this suit so presumably the Lumners won their right to deal with the property on William's behalf. This suggests that although he had a Devicke guardian, William must have been in the direct care of his mother and Henry Lumner.

Leighton and the 1579 Guernsey Troubles

During the summer of 1579 inhabitants of Guernsey complained to the Privy Council with a number of grievances about 'ancient customes' and the Council sent a commission of enquiry.[37] By late 1579 the four commissioners were operating on the island and it became clear that while some complaints by the islanders were not unreasonable, the islanders themselves were being investigated over potential improper behaviour in tax and judicial matters.

The state papers for October 1579 and immediately thereafter contain an extraordinary mass of items relating to Guernsey.[38] The commissioners were in danger of undermining the authority of the Governor and his officers, in part because the islanders had to pay the high cost of the commissioners' visit. There were major issues of principle at stake including the proceeds of wrecks, the cost of wheat sent from England and the right of Jurats to levy certain fines and penalties. There were also specific cases between various leading islanders and the Bailiff and Jurats. In these William and Henry Beauvoir, Nicholas Carey and Nicholas Martin featured. Thomas Fashin of Southampton complained that an earlier suit regarding his manors on the island had been overturned by the Bailiff and Jurats and his attorney had been put in prison for refusing to accept their decision. The Queen's revenue officers complained that they were not allowed to answer the complaints made to the commissioners about them. Louis de Vic, the Queen's attorney for Guernsey, interrogated Martin, Carey and Henry Beauvoir as to why they had imprisoned William Beauvoir (presumably junior) whom they accused of contempt against the Bailiff and the Jurats for refusing to join his fellow Jurats in answering the letters of the Privy Council.

Sir Thomas wrote to the Council anxious to answer the 28 slanderous charges presented to the commissioners by the islanders relating to imprisonment for sedition and rebellion, compelling them to fight against pirates, enforcing customs on strangers' ships and their goods, weights and measures, the administration of justice and more. He also refuted their additional complaints about the use of church bells for alarms, dancing at weddings, payment dates for rent and matters to do with the parsonage house and school building in St Peter Port. In December 1579 he requested a further commission to come and hear evidence, for his 'owne purgacion'.[39] Sir Thomas petitioned the Queen and Council:

> Accept my declaration of the state of the island. The disposition of the people has lately been disturbed by seditious persons, pretending the privilege of the isle, but really wishing the overthrow of Her Majesty's rights, and furthered by the Bailiff and Jurats

Leighton complained specifically about the behaviour of Nicholas Petevin, the Bailiff William Beauvoir and Jurats Henry Beauvoir and Nicholas Martin. His arguments for removing them from their places were that they had resisted his attempt to increase Jurat numbers from 12 to 24; they had imposed an unpopular and unacceptable general tax and they also contravened Council's orders that Nicholas Carey, Farmer of the Great Weight of the Island, should deliver rents and customs on strangers' wares to Her Majesty's use. The Queen's Receiver had tried to secure the revenues but had been silenced by these men. A general refusal to pay rents due had ensued. They had also seized letters from Council to Leighton and published falsified versions of them to islanders. Nicholas Petevin especially, he said, should be punished.

Leighton considered that if the Bailiff and Jurats were not 'sharply punished no English will be able to govern here without 300 soldiers to suppress these mutinies'. The commissioners apparently said that they were not at fault for the mutiny, nor did they exacerbate it. This may well have been true, but the troublemakers no doubt exploited their visit to the full to whip up anti-English feeling on the island.

A brief undated item is taken to be of the same period. The Minister of Guernsey wrote to Council to say that despite his 23 years' service he was being ordered off the island by the Governor. He refuted Louis de Vic's charges against him and wanted to be allowed back safely to sort out his household affairs.[40] If the date is correctly attributed it seems that Leighton had also believed that the ministers on the island had been inciting anti-English action and that he had secured the removal of the chief minister.

The orders, letters and appeals flew between London and Guernsey for two years. A good example of the tit-for-tat content is the response from the Jurats to the Privy Council. The council had written in January ordering them to allow Nicholas Carey, arrested by the jurats, to have bail so he could answer their charges:

> 26th February 1580 Bailiff and Jurats to the Privy Council. We will observe your orders on the complaints of the inhabitants, and also in not debarring the inhabitants from appealing to you. We have proceeded uprightly without malice. You bid us liberate Nicholas Carey, though John de Vic, the bearer of your letters, enticed by his father-in-law Nicholas Carey, tried to suppress them, to bring us into your displeasure. You ask the cause of his imprisonment. It arose from an action of debt brought by James Guile, a Jurat, against Carey who, being angry, called him thief and when required to prove his words accused him of detaining a rent of wheat from the Queen; failing to prove this he was fined 20 nobles to the Queen and 40 to the party offended. He appealed to the Queen and you and, as no appeals had before been permitted in such cases, we imprisoned him for doing so. Pray let us know whether all appeals are to be permitted; we think that the punishment of offenders and matters of small moment should not admit of appeals. Carey has spoken very contemptuously of the Bailiff and Jurats. We crave your directions.

Various annexes attached showed that William Beauvoir was Bailiff and Henry his brother was a Jurat. James Le Fevre Jurat and Nicholas Carey had been imprisoned for 7 months in the Marshalsea and had spent all their means. They also showed evidence that the custom of the island was only to allow appeals if both parties agreed and that if a party persisted in pressing for an appeal he was to be imprisoned.[41] In the end the Council told Leighton to sort it out! Leighton himself was again investigated in summer 1580 but most of the complaints were dismissed.[42] On 11th September 1580 the Privy Council gave him advice on governing Guernsey and how he might avoid the inhabitants having further legitimate grievances against him - they were getting fed up with the constant barrage of complaints![43] The Council could not stop appeals over property coming their way, however, and from November 1580 to March 1581 the Carey family were arguing in London over an inheritance and Thomas Wigmore, now the deputy governor was coping with the council correspondence.[44]

In September 1581 Louis de Vic, the Procureur wrote to Leighton regarding various matters and included a comment that 'Mr Bailiff is a good man but governed by the rest [the Jurats]. Let them know that you are the Governor for they presume too far. The Procurer [the writer] wishes to serve you and shall come if the Jurats come for he will deal for you and not for them'.[45] This may have been the trigger Leighton needed to make Wigmore the next Bailiff. The changes seem to have worked and the islanders turned their discontent against the church.[46]

By 1582 Leighton was surrounded by trusted men: Nicholas Carey as Lieutenant, Thomas Wigmore Bailiff, John de Vic Notary of the Royal Court of Guernsey and Louis de Vic as the Procureur. Louis sent the council some sensible suggestions regarding the prevention of abuses by Jurats and a question regarding the Jurats' right to imprison royal officers. Leighton, in return, supported Louis' claim to the council for his travelling expenses.[47]

Finally, on 30th July 1582, the Privy Council issued orders relating to Leighton's complaints against the Bailiff and Jurats. William Beauvoir the late Bailiff, Nicholas Martin and Henry Beauvoir were to be discharged from their offices as Jurats and others were to be elected in their place.[48] The fragile ceasefire was over. Now the ministers of the church sided with the islanders with old grudges against Louis de Vic. Leighton wrote to Secretary Sir Francis Walsingham to defend his faithful friend.

25th September 1582 Sir Thomas to Walsingham.

As the information against Louis de Vic proceeds from all the ministers here I have examined them and the ancients of St Peter Port thereon. I send you their depositions. I have examined the neighbours of the man said to be slain by him. It is 16 years since de Vic, then Constable, struck the man at the musters and he has had four children since, to one of whom de Vic was godfather. The charge of adultery could not be proved, being only brought by an ill woman. Some of the ministers protested a year since that either he would drive them out or they him, on account of his office of Commissary under the Bishop. Had he committed these offences Nicholas Baudouin would not have admitted him to the communion. I have always thought him honest and the best servant I have. I fear these troubles will overthrow the church here. Pray decide the case yourself, for if it come before the whole Council the unfolding of these evil doings may be hurtful to religion.[49]

Four annexes, in French, were attached:

Inquisition before Sir Thomas, Thomas Wigmore Bailiff and 7 Jurats on four articles sent by Secretary Walsingham against Louis de Vic for beating a man; committing adultery; doing violence to an ancient of the church; and troubling the ministry, with the depositions of the ministers in proof of the charges 5th September 1582

Like depositions of the ancients made at the requisition of Louis de Vic in disproof of the said charges 12th September 1582

Like deposition to the same effect as the former part of the proceeding 12th September 1582

Like depositions of the neighbours of Thomas Patron the person whom Louis de Vic struck 16th September 1582.[50]

Louis de Vic's own answer was that he felt 'himself unjustly accused and his life and goods endangered consented, though against law, to be inquested by his enemies'. Of the charges against him, he only acknowledged 'troubling the ministers because they preach against the authority of the Queen and Council, Bishops and the Government of England; they usurp the authority of the civil magistrates, disapprove law and justice, slander those that differ from them, and are always contentious and inventing new opinions'. He (a zealous puritan) entreated the council to ensure the orders for uniformity would be observed, and those who executed them were supported, 'for if men are allowed to do and say as they list dangerous effects will follow'.[51] On this occasion the malicious charges were not upheld and Louis was still in his job in October 1583, with Wigmore as Bailiff. Rather surprisingly the Jurats still included William Beauvoir.[52]

The next attack was on Wigmore: on 26th June 1585 Simon Alix and three other ministers on Guernsey wrote to Secretary Walsingham to complain against Thomas.[53]

As you have always listened to the complaints of poor ministers, we wished to send one of our number to complain that on 4ᵗʰ June Thomas Wigmore bailiff lieutenant [sic] and nephew of our governor, having sent to speak with us, ordered us to be taken prisoners to the castle, under a guard of soldiers with loaded arquebuses, endangering our lives and the lives of those who in pity asked if we wished to send anything to our wives. He then sent Louis and John De Vic, Peter Carey and others, haters of the ministry, to seize our houses and detain our families and followed himself with soldiers to search our studies, cupboards and presses, he sealing some and taking away what he would. Next day he sent us back to our houses. But when we wished to send one of our number to declare to you our misery, the lieutenant forbad him to leave. We beg your aid against such oppression.

By the mid to late 1580s another surge of issues found its way to the Privy Council.⁵⁴ The people of Alderney were again resisting Leighton's orders; trade issues with foreign ships were again sensitive and the Beauvoir family was again in the limelight. William Beauvoir had complained at length to the Council that he had been forced unfairly to pay an annuity to Louis de Vic and that he had illegally been prevented from appealing. In early 1587 the Council had taken his side and demanded that any money taken should be returned and that he should be allowed to appeal. Unfortunately William died suddenly leaving no will and in April his widow Margaret Delamarch complained that Henry and Peter Beauvoir, his brothers, had deprived her of her dower rights and were preventing her children from receiving their rightful inheritance. Nicholas Baudouin, minister, confirmed by letter that William had always said his brothers should have nothing to do with his estate. The brothers, without her involvement, had secured Prerogative Court of Canterbury letters of administration through the Court of Arches to pursue their own interests. The Council wrote to Leighton to make sure she received proper justice.

Military matters

Guernsey, being vulnerable to attack, was always watchful of its continental neighbours. The trial of the Queen of Scots had only served to add more reason for France and Spain to challenge England. On 1ˢᵗ February 1587 (a few days before Mary's execution) Leighton wrote from Castle Cornet to Robert Dudley urgently requesting him to ask the Queen to send 300 soldiers with supplies and munitions. He had information from St Malo that all English merchants there had been imprisoned and war against England was to be declared. If they did not send help 'the Islls will be lost'.⁵⁵

It is typical that trade matters still ranked important despite constant shows of aggression. In April 1587 the Council wanted to know 'speedily' why Leighton had seized French ships in Guernsey. In May they wrote to say that *The Greyhound* should be released immediately with all its merchandise. Although his letter does not survive, Leighton obviously wrote to complain of the high-handed tone of this instruction, as in June the Council replied that it was merely a standard form of words. However the Council did rescind the release demand, while reserving the Lord Admiral's rights over shipping decisions. This issue rolled on during the summer. John de Vic was sent from Guernsey to inform the Council of the full circumstances, as was Thomas Wigmore, arguing that island privileges were being ignored. The Privy Council referred the case to the solicitor-general and the Judge of the Admiralty. To discover what the ancient usage was, they called before them Richard Wigmore (Thomas's brother), sent by Sir Thomas Leighton and John de Vic. Sir Amyas Paulet was called in from Jersey to give his opinion on ancient privileges, that 'hitherto all merchant strangers had been received in Jersey and Guernsey safe from arrest'. The Council ruled the custom should continue but in times of hostility 'stranger' ships would need a licence from the Captain of Guernsey.[56]

Soon more pressing matters were to call on Sir Thomas's military expertise. The Spanish threat was still growing and by early December 1587 letters were going out to the county lieutenants in the south of England. They were instructed to respond to Sir Thomas Leighton who was to be credited for his advice as a man of experience trusted by Her Majesty in that behalf. Leighton was to be directly responsible for Hampshire, Dorset and part of Wiltshire and would be visiting them to ensure they had in readiness the required numbers of horsemen and foot for the defence of the realm. In 1588 Leighton was absent from Guernsey for an extended period while he took on a major role reviewing the fortifications in the south of England during preparations ahead of the feared invasion by the Spanish armada. As part of that he was specifically responsible for Essex, Suffolk and Norfolk work and was heavily involved in the major upgrade of Great Yarmouth's fortifications.[57] Leighton had always maintained a substantial London house at St Botolph in Aldersgate ward for when he was in England.[58] Now he travelled all over the south-east, spending time with the Queen in September 1587 and at Greenwich, Norwich and Yarmouth in spring 1588.[59]

While he was away from the island on armada duty and his strong hand was absent, the Jurats were at their most troublesome. Unfortunately Leighton and his right-hand man Louis de Vic were betrayed by the rest of the inner circle including his nephew. In October 1587 Thomas Wigmore, as Bailiff, and others were sent for by the Privy Council on a matter relating to Nicholas Carey, James Feaver [Le Fevre], John Effard and John de Vic. In January 1588 it became clear that Leighton had caused all of them to be sent for and was acting against them, even his own nephew. Louis de Vic showed that Louis Savarte (one of the French owners of the goods seized on *The Greyhound*), in front of all the Jurats, had spoken irreverent and reproachful words about Leighton. In response Wigmore, Carey as his lieutenant, Le Fevre and some others had set their hands and Her Majesty's seal, contrary to their oath, to a public instrument and other documents containing slanders against Leighton and his tyrannous behaviour. By this they sought to 'overthrow the estate of the whole island'. They also imposed an unlawful general tax without the consent of the inhabitants.

Attempted murder

Worse than all this, since coming to England for the hearing, they had 'unchristianly and mischievously' conspired with Richard Wigmore, brother of Thomas, to 'hire for money certain evil disposed persons to slay or mischief Louis de Vic'. One of these persons was William Rouswell an Englishman who had previously lived in Guernsey and knew the Procureur. He and one of Richard Wigmore's servants beat de Vic with a staff in the Queen's Highway at the Wool Staple in Westminster, hitting him from behind on his head and leaving him for dead. While de Vic had recovered, it was not clear that he would fully regain his hearing.

In January 1588 the Council found all this proved and immediately, since he was the ringleader, stripped Thomas Wigmore of his place as Bailiff and Nicholas Carey as lieutenant. With Le Fevre they were committed to the Marshalsea prison. Leighton had to choose a new Bailiff. Louis de Vic and Richard Lea, who had also been threatened by Wigmore, were allowed to demand bonds for good behaviour from whomever they saw fit to ensure their own personal safety back on Guernsey. Rouswell was to be sent to Guernsey to be imprisoned there and to be put in the pillory in the market place with a paper over his head reading: 'for treacherously beating and intending to kill the Procureur, Her Majesty's Officer, being hired thereunto for money by Richard Wigmore and his confederates'. The disgraced Thomas Wigmore was to pay compensation to de Vic and pay the costs of Council's messenger calling them all from Guernsey. John de Vic would be repaid his costs acting on behalf of the Council. It was made clear that those guilty should pay, not the islanders as a whole. The sums involved in these London hearings were not trivial; witnesses and parties were called to London, registered their attendance and were instructed not to leave England until allowed by the Council. Often, as here, they had to kick their heels in London for several months until the case was heard and resolved. Their business interests suffered and they had to pay their own costs and often those of others drawn into proceedings. The Council went on to require more rigorous application of the law in future in matters of debts and trade.

In early April 1588 the Council wrote to Louis de Vic and John Blundell (as judge-delegate of Guernsey) authorising them to call four honest men to help them try an issue between Henry Lumner, Thomas Wigmore and Nicholas Carey. The four men should only be picked when Wigmore and Carey arrived on the island. This shows that Wigmore and the others' stay in the Marshalsea had not been a long one. Now that Louis de Vic too was returning to Guernsey, the Council also wrote to give him protection from Thomas and Richard Wigmore, James Le Fevre, John Effard, Andrew Henry, and the Beauvoirs - Henry, Peter and William.[60] By the beginning of September 1588 Thomas Wigmore, Nicholas Carey and James Le Fevre, now simply 'inhabitants of Guernsey', were in trouble again. Leighton requested the Privy Council to order them to London to answer a complaint levied against them by John Jones, a merchant of Lyme. Carey and Le Fevre immediately petitioned Council to be allowed home to Guernsey and to be paid their costs on the ground that the matter concerned all of the Jurats not just themselves. They were dismissed from attendance and allowed a contribution towards their charges. Effard also was allowed to go home and reclaim his charges against such members of the Jurat 'as he had cause to'. It became clear that these guilty men were being allowed back to Guernsey and could only recover costs from those Jurats who had conspired with them. In February 1589 the issue of costs was back in Council with John Blundell, Edward Le Fevre and John Andrews complaining that Wigmore and the others were pursuing them for money even though they had not been involved in the conspiracy. This indicates that Wigmore had returned to Guernsey despite having no formal role there. The new Bailiff was instructed to protect them from any such payment.

John de Vic had not got off as lightly as it seemed. On 19th November 1589 the Privy Council wrote to Leighton requiring him to take bonds for the appearance before them of John de Vic, Clerk of the Court of Guernsey, and to send with him an informed person who could explain the charges against him.[61] In the meantime the council ordered that Nicholas Carey, father-in-law of John de Vic, who they had been told, was forced to stay in his house for fear of being acted against in the same way as de Vic, should be treated properly, by the due course of island law and custom.

Leighton did not act immediately. It was not until 9th February 1590 that Sir Thomas wrote to the Privy Council to say he had heard 'in a November letter' from the Council that John de Vic had complained to London that his house had been searched by Leighton and that he had been unjustly imprisoned. Leighton explained he had ordered the search by his soldiers. They were looking for the rolls of the island's court which de Vic refused to deliver into the custody of the Bailiff and Jurats while he was investigated for disorderly conduct and abusing the Jurats. De Vic had said he would not obey the Governor or the Queen and had then run off into hiding. After a search and proclamations he gave himself up four days later and he was put in the dungeon for two days. After that he was lodged in a good chamber. He also said Nicholas Carey kept to his house, not for fear of similar punishment but because he had gout! Although Leighton was not being soft - 'None that in word or deed disobey Her Majesty shall escape punishment where I command' - Leighton said he would not be de Vic's judge. As ordered, Leighton had bailed de Vic to appear in London by 29th March but he was sending evidence that he had not overstepped his authority in dealing with de Vic and seeking the Council's opinion. He ended by saying that de Vic had just made his submission and earnestly requested that the past punishment should suffice and that he should not be forced to go to England. 'I think he will not hereafter commit the like'.[62]

Later years

After that matters still routinely came before Council over the years, but none seemed to be of huge importance. The same core group of men were involved in all the actions. The French made occasional complaints about ships being seized. Perhaps the Privy Council rued the day when they had insisted appeals should be allowed to them! Louis de Vic seems to have transferred to Jersey to become

Procureur there. John de Vic was promoted to Procureur in Guernsey despite his earlier misdemeanour.[63]

A 13th July 1597 Privy Council commission to Sir Thomas Leighton Governor of Guernsey, Louis de Vic Bailiff (and later lieutenant governor) and John de Vic Queen's Procureur showed that the hierarchy had changed marginally once more. They and three others were to discover concealed lands tenements and effigies in the isle and grant them in fee farm to the Queen's profit. They were also to find noble tenures and their privileges and royalties and to conform good orders by advice of the bailiffs and jurats profitable to the commonwealth and agreeable to the ancient customs of the isle.[64] Another action involving bad behaviour by Nicholas Carey continued through 1597 and 1598, with the Privy Council again eventually finding in favour of Leighton and his senior officers.[65]

After 1589 Thomas Wigmore had disappeared from the record on Guernsey. While still in favour, in July 1586 he had been granted by Leighton the islet of Lihou and another fief with their revenues and some wheat rents.[66] Half of this grant was surrendered by an instrument dated 19th December 1596 by Thomas Wigmore esq of Shobdon Herefordshire, first cousin of the Guernsey Thomas Wigmore. The Shobdon man was a member of parliament, sometime sheriff of Radnorshire and father of Warnecombe Wigmore, named after his mother Alice's family.[67] As Leighton only held the premises for life - after which they would revert to the crown - Thomas Wigmore could have held them only as long as Leighton remained alive. The surrender showed that Thomas of Guernsey had assigned half his interest in the premises and rents to his cousin and by implication Thomas of Shobdon would still hold his part of the grant for as long as Leighton lived. Presumably Thomas of Guernsey had died at some point shortly before the surrender, although his date and place of death have not been found. He had probably needed to borrow a large sum against the security of the income. The assignment of half the grant would have capitalised the income stream and yielded him quite a decent sum of money. In 1596 the annuity value of half of the original grant was given as worth at least £30, so one could apply the typical 20 year multiple of rents used for land valuation to calculate a capital sum of £600. This might be a bit high as the two Wigmores would necessarily be betting on Leighton's likely longevity, but a reasonable sum is implied in any event. When Thomas Wigmore of Shobdon in 1596 surrendered his assignment in return for an annuity of £30 during Leighton's life, it was conditional on there being no chance of any earlier shifty acts of Thomas of Guernsey coming out of the woodwork. Leighton by then had no trust in his nephew's integrity. If anything untoward emerged he could stop paying the annuity to Wigmore.[68]

No doubt Thomas Wigmore of Guernsey had fallen significantly into debt - like his half-brother Edmund Lumner who, as we shall see, was deeply in debt by the mid 1580s. Guernsey had not made either of them successful despite Katherine and Thomas's efforts. In future Leighton would only favour his own children: his son Thomas Leighton esq married Mary the daughter and co-heiress of Edward, 11th Baron Zouche. In 1600-01, another time when Sir Thomas was absent, heavily involved in matters in the marches of Wales, Zouche was his lieutenant in Guernsey.

By 1616 Zouche was warden of the Cinque Ports and commanding officer of Sir Christopher Heydon's son John. See Family Notes 9: Heydon children. From 1604 onwards Thomas Leighton junior was his father's deputy. He died in St Peter Port in 1617, just a few years after his father.[69]

Leighton remained Governor until his death, after forty years of keeping the island in check with both help and hindrance from his family. He was buried in Guernsey in February 1610.

Chapter 7

Arms and the Man: John Potts of Mannington Esquire

---

*In the early 1580s John and Katherine Dodge, with their two daughters Mary
and Anne, were the owners of Mannington with the heir expectant Edmund Lumner
junior and his wife Jane waiting to inherit the estate. By late 1584, Edmund and Jane
had lost Mannington, Mary Dodge was married to Peter Houghton and Anne Dodge
was married to John Potts, a London lawyer. When Anne's parents died, John and
Anne would move in, beginning the 150 year-long Potts ownership of Mannington.
In this chapter, John Potts's links with Norfolk are revealed and the story of his mother
Katherine, the other matriarch in his family, is continued.*

How did a London lawyer from a grocery family with no obvious links to
North Norfolk end up in Mannington married to one of the daughters of the
lord of the manor? It could just have happened as a result of a chance meeting in
London between John Potts and Edmund Lumner shortly before the sale. But
previous chapters have shown that the Lumner, Dodge and Potts families may
have known each other quite well. The Potts and Lumner families in London had
been acquainted for years through family memberships of the Grocers' Company
and other mutual contacts. Blase Saunders, the Grocers' warden, appears to have
been known by both families. Potts, Flower, Lumner, Dodge and Houghton family
members were all drawn together in the circle around Sir Christopher Hatton from
1580 if not earlier. The linkage with Sir Thomas Leighton gave another connection
to court circles. It would be most surprising if our main characters did not know
each other by the 1570s.

Katherine Boteler/Potts/Doddes and Francis Flower

John Potts's desire to be part of the land-owning establishment must have been
deep-seated and fuelled by his mother's Hertfordshire origins and her marriages.
In Chapter 2, Katherine's marriages to Roger Potts and William Doddes were fully
discussed. At some time, perhaps shortly after 1577 when her second husband had
died, Katherine married Francis Flower of St Andrew Holborn and Eltham.[1] He was
the eldest son of George Flower, the sixth son of Sir Richard Flower of the long-
standing family of Whitwell in Rutland and married first Constance daughter of
John Cole and second Katherine Boteler. He is not known to have had any children.[2]

Flower stood for parliament several times and sat for Huntingdon in 1584, 1586
and 1589 and Corfe Castle in 1593, with the support of Sir Christopher Hatton
and latterly his nephew and heir Sir William Hatton. His stepson, John Potts, joined
him in the 1589 parliament. Flower sat on committees concerning appeals out of
ecclesiastical courts (he was active against recusants), subsidies, procedure and the

navy.[3] He was a servant of Sir Christopher Hatton by 1573 and was employed in the Court of First Fruits in 1587. A justice of the peace in Middlesex from about 1591, he was commissioner for musters in 1596. In that year, just before he died, he was also a JP in Kent and a Gentleman Pensioner, which latter role would have brought him an income of about £80 a year. Sir Christopher had obtained for him a monopoly in the printing of Latin, Greek and Hebrew books even though he was not a member of the Stationers' Company. His job in the First Fruits Court - 'the keeping of the books of entries and caveats for benefices' - gave him useful patronage in the administration of crown livings in the gift of Sir Christopher Hatton as Lord Chancellor. He kept a room in Hatton's house in Ely House in St Andrew Holborn (just around the corner from The Bishop, the Potts property) and died in Eltham where Sir Christopher had been a Keeper at the Palace.[4]

Sir William Hatton, to whom Francis Flower later attached himself, was Sir Christopher's nephew by his sister Dorothy and her husband John Newport. Sir William took his uncle's name of Hatton at Hatton's death in 1591. He is most notable for marrying the feisty Elizabeth Cecil the daughter of William Cecil, Lord Burghley. After Sir William Hatton's death in 1597, Lady Hatton went on to marry Attorney-General Edward Coke, a fiery relationship which ended badly. Coke took over Sir Christopher and Sir William's huge debts to the crown and also became resident in Hatton House in the grounds of the old palace of the Bishop of Ely, which stood in what is now Hatton Garden off Holborn.[5] Flower wrote one of the lengthy inscriptions for a pillar of Sir Christopher Hatton's tomb in Old St Paul's Church.

Part of Francis Flower's income came from assigning the life interest in the licence for printing the classics he had received in letters patent in 1574. The monopoly included all books and maps that contained these languages even if only in part. He received £100 a year for life from a partnership of five men who went on to buy paper, print volumes of grammar and 'accademes', hold stock and sell and merchandise them.[6]

Flower is also credited with being one of the authors of *The Misfortunes of Arthur*, a tragedy performed in front of the Queen in Greenwich in 1587. He is thought to have penned the chorus for the first and second acts. While much of the drama was written by Thomas Hughes, other collaborators included Christopher Yelverton and the well-known lawyer Francis Bacon.[7] His literary connections included Sir Philip Sidney whose 1591 publisher Thomas Newman dedicated his book of sonnets to Francis whom he described as of Gray's Inn and Gentleman Pensioner.[8] While his patron Sir Christopher Hatton had attended Inner Temple, he was not a fully trained or practising lawyer. When in 1587 Hatton became Lord Chancellor and sat regularly as a judge in the courts of both the Star Chamber and chancery he was known for ensuring that he was supported by experienced judges at all times. From the persistent visibility of Francis Flower in legal documents involving Hatton, particularly an important family settlement of 1579, it would appear that Flower was his principal in-house lawyer. If so, and becoming John Potts's stepfather just as John went to Lincoln's Inn, it seems highly likely that Flower was effectively a patron to Potts. How did John Potts rise so rapidly from admission to Lincoln's Inn in 1578, to be able to offer to purchase Mannington for several thousand pounds only six years later? Where did the money come from? The Potts London property was not so extensive that it would have produced significant profits, nor was much sold. Indeed we shall see that in the following century the long-term rental barely covered the major repairs needed from time to time. It seems much more likely that John Potts flourished as a lawyer working for Hatton and his household. Clients may have queued up hoping for favourable treatment if they used a lawyer close to such an influential man. Following his appointment to the Privy Council and knighthood in 1577, Hatton became a man of enormous and overt influence, rather than just a favourite of the Queen. Those immediately around him would have been sought out.

Sir Christopher Hatton and his servants

Francis Flower, as a Gentleman Pensioner of the Queen, was one of a band of gentlemen with at least notional duties in guarding Her Majesty. When not on business for Hatton (he went to Northampton for example in 1577 and 1584) he would have been routinely at court and his wife and stepson would have formed part of the large circle of people living and working close to the centre of power. Hatton of course was also a Gentleman Pensioner from 1564 and in 1572 replaced Sir Francis Knollys as Captain of the Guard of the Queen.[9] This gives a linkage with the Lumner side of the story. In 1565 Hatton, at a Dudley family marriage entertainment in London, with three others challenged all comers in the jousting lists. With him were Henry Knollys, Robert Colsett and Thomas Leighton. As we have seen in Chapter 6, Leighton was closely related to the Dudley and Knollys families.

Sir Christopher Hatton was Keeper of the Royal Parks at Eltham and Steward of Eltham Manor for the Queen from 1568. He was responsible for the management of the whole estate there. As a result he had the use of the Keeper's House in the Park. Also from 1588 as Lord Chancellor he had the use of the substantial hall house which still survives immediately outside the Palace moat in The Green Court.[10] As well as Francis Flower's rooms in Hatton's great house at Ely Place Holborn, his will showed that he had a house in Eltham - he left his goods there to his wife Katherine. As Eltham was a royal manor, the house was probably leased from the crown. His will certainly left no real estate of his own in Eltham. The possibility remains that Flower lived in one of Hatton's houses in Eltham. In later years the Queen regularly visited Sir Christopher at Hatton House and from other references it seems that major visitors were conducted into Hatton's presence by Francis Flower.[11] The chances of John Potts having been at the Queen's court at London and Eltham are high.

Edward Dodge and Peter Houghton

The role as one of Sir Christopher Hatton's 'followers' brought Francis Flower into very regular contact with two other 'servants' of Hatton. Edward Dodge, Peter Houghton and Flower were from at least as early as 1580 all working for Christopher Hatton. Francis Flower and a Henry (sic) Dodge were involved with Sir

Christopher Hatton in a release of certain manors and advowson rights in Warmingham in November 1580.[12] The previous month Edward Dodge was involved in a lease of the rectory of Plymouth, presumably on behalf of Hatton and in April 1581 Sir Christopher, with his servants Francis Flower and Edward Dodge, was involved in another deed regarding a rectory.[13] More rectory transactions can be found such as that for East Haddon in April 1581 when Sir Christopher, Francis Flower and Edward Dodge, servants to Sir Christopher were in receipt of the rectory there.[14] In September 1590 at Drayton and Ely Place, Francis Flower and Edward Dodge, two of his servants, witnessed Sir Christopher's instructions to his nephew and heir Sir William Hatton regarding settling his affairs after his death.[15]

Dodge was marginally connected to the Babington plot in 1586. Brooks noted that one of the conspirators was Henry Dunne or Donne who had been 'sometime a servant of Mr Dodge', probably from Dodge's role with Francis Flower in the First Fruits office.[16] Dunne was also described as a servant or secretary of Sir Christopher Hatton. Fortunately no taint from him spread to Hatton or his group of servants. Dunne confessed and was hung drawn and quartered for his involvement in the plot.

Edward Dodge has of course, already appeared, in Chapter 5, as the brother of John Dodge of Mannington. In 1588 and again in 1596 Edward Dodge esq of Wrotham and his nephew Robert Bathurst gent were involved in a number of transactions to do with the capital messuage called Hale and lands in Horsmonden and Lamberhurst, Kent.[17] In 1596 Robert Bathurst was then of Eltham and no doubt known to the Flower and Potts family group.

Dodge and Peter Houghton were closely connected in the wine trade as well as with Hatton. Who was Houghton? Sir Christopher Hatton was patron of Cornelius Ketel, the celebrated Dutch portrait painter. Ketel is known to have lived and worked in London from 1573-81. His contemporary Karel von Mander said that Ketel was introduced to Hatton by a young English merchant called 'Pieter Hachten'. Brooks assumed that he must have been a Peter Hatton from Cheshire, of a family with which Hatton was trying to establish pedigree linkage. However, this was surely Peter Houghton (the 'gh' providing the gutteral sound in the name, which was often written as Hoghton), the grocer and alderman who was involved with Hatton and Edward Dodge in the exploitation of wine import duties. Houghton presented Hatton with Ketel's allegorical work '*Force vanquished by Wisdom*' and through Hatton, Ketel gained access to court circles. He is credited with being the painter of the 'Winchilsea' portrait of Sir Christopher. This episode connects Houghton to Hatton by the mid 1570s, when Houghton would have been in his early thirties. Although Peter Houghton was quite well-known as an alderman of the City of London and a senior member of the Grocers' Company, his origins have been somewhat confused by earlier writers.[18]

Thomas, 'son of Thomas Hutton' was baptised on 16th April 1540 in the church of St Benet Fink in Bradstreet ward [Broad Street]. The same register had the entry for 19th October 1541: 'was christened the child of Thomas Hutton'. Even though Peter was not named, these must be Thomas and Peter Houghton. Thomas Houghton their father was Thomas Houghton churchwarden of St Benet Fink who, in that capacity, was involved in a lease of a brewhouse in March 1567. He was a citizen and grocer of London, which gives a clear link to Peter's trade and a home parish for the family at this time. The Grocers' Company provides another potential link to the Apotts.[19] Thomas Houghton was admitted to the Company as a freeman during 1560-65, a period when specific entry years have not survived.[20] Thomas the father would seem to have been a younger brother of Sir Richard Houghton kt, of Houghton Tower Lancashire.[21] Sir Richard's grandson Sir Richard was one of the first baronets created in 1611. One of his daughters, Anne, had married Sir John Cotton of Landwade in Cambridgeshire and they were to be seen as a safe haven for the young John Potts when at university in the early 1600s. Their portraits still hang in the dining room of Madingley Hall, seat of the related Hynde family.

Peter Houghton was admitted to the Grocers' Company in 1570 from apprenticeship under Francis Robinson.[22] If he was admitted in his late twenties, as might have been expected, he would have been born about 1540-45 which matches the St Benet register entry. Peter was elected to the livery on 10th April 1582 and elected to court on 20th November 1588. However, he refused to serve between 1589 and 1593, perhaps because he was so busy at this time running the wine import duty licence with Edward Dodge.

Wine seems to run in this story. Blase Saunders, the Grocer, had been heavily involved in importing Spanish wines, possibly with John Lumner, in the 1550s.[23] In November 1580 Edward Dodge and Peter Houghton were appointed for four years to run the collection of subsidies on imported French and Rhenish wines.[24] The two men again, in February 1585, were granted the England-wide right to collect all subsidies on French and Rhenish wines coming in to all ports, subject to some minor exceptions in favour of the Royal Butler and the Earl of Leicester.[25] This four year term was again renewed in 1588 when their rent on the various elements of the arrangement was increased to over £7,200 a year payable to the exchequer. On the renewal the exceptions were now in favour of the Earl of Essex - reflecting the arrival of the new royal favourite. Action on a trade debt relating to £314 due from one Marmaduke Spighte showed that the sums of money involved here were very substantial.[26] With over £7,000 at risk each year Dodge and Houghton must have been making a very considerable return on their investment and the lease shows that they were granted wide-ranging powers to use all the collectors and searchers around England to help them secure the revenues. Peter Houghton also provided wine for the court - 'a note of the service of wines for the Queen, exhibited by Mr Houghton servant to Mr Vice Chamberlain. December 5, 1583'.[27] Peter Houghton had his Collector's office in Fenchurch Street London by 1588 where payments were made.[28] In 1580 Edward Dodge appeared in a property deed, probably as a trustee, in the parish of St Gabriel Fenchurch St.[29] This was the home parish of Peter Houghton and it may be both men had property there.

Houghton also served as sheriff of London in 1593-94 and as alderman from 11th November 1593 until his death on 31st December 1596, with his administration being granted on 15th January 1597.[30] Initially he served as alderman for Castle Baynard Ward, but moved during his period of office although the second ward is not given. In passing it is worth noting that Lancelot Bathurst, grocer, also served as alderman between 1593 and 1596, reinforcing the Houghton/Dodge/Bathurst family connections.[31]

How long in total Houghton and Dodge operated the wine monopoly is not shown, but this evidence shows how closely connected the two men were. The start date for the first licence preceded by two years Peter Houghton's marriage to Mary Dodge, Edward's niece.

Peter Houghton married Mary, the elder daughter of John and Katherine Dodge of Mannington sometime in mid to late 1582, when Mary would have been about 17. If the marriage was held in Mannington Hall, no record has survived. The couple's first daughter Mary junior was baptised on 14th July 1583 in Wrotham in Kent, home of the main Dodge family.[32] Katherine and John Dodge would have been regular visitors to the family home in Kent, now his unmarried brother Edward's country place. Another Wrotham register entry in 1579, for the burial of 'Thomas Greene servant to Mr Dodge', shows that this was the Dodge family church at the time. By coincidence a branch of the Norfolk Houghtons (who were not related to Peter) also appeared in Wrotham at this time.[33]

Peter and Mary also had two sons but both died young. Hatton Houghton was baptised in St Gabriel Fenchurch St on 23rd April 1585 and Peter on 5th June 1586. Hatton was obviously named for Sir Christopher Hatton. The early death of these boys was confirmed in a wonderfully detailed burial certificate for their father of early 1597:

> Peter Houghton, esq, late Alderman and sometime Sheriff of the
> City of London, marryed Mary the doughter of John Dodge of
> Mannington in the county of Norfolk esq and by her had yssue
> two sons and two daughters, viz Hatton Houghton and Peeter
> Houghton; the first dyed at the age of 3 years and a quarter, and the
> second at the age of 8 years and a quarter; his daughters are Mary and
> Elizabeth; the first is of the age of 13 years and six monethes, the
> second is five years or thereabouts, and bothe living at this present.
>
> The sayd Peter died intestate the last day of December 1596,
> and was worshipfully accompanied (with the Lord Mayor, all
> the Aldermen, and many other citizens) from his house neer
> Fenchurche unto the parishe-churche of St Michaells in Cornehill,
> where he was worshipfully buryed (at the upper end of the Quier,
> on the lefte hand in a vaulte) on Tuesday the 8th of January
> following. Whose funeral was directed and served by Lancaster
> Herauld (deputy for Clariencieulx King of Armes) and Chester
> Herauld, officers of Armes.
>
> In witness whereof we, whose names are underwritten, have sett
> our handes the day and year above mencioned. Marie Houghton, R
> Wigmore, Edward Dodge.[34]

Mary was his widow, Richard Wigmore was one of her half-brothers (son of Richard and Katherine Wigmore and later to become Sir Richard) and Edward Dodge of course was Peter's business partner and Mary's uncle. Mary Houghton the widow subsequently married Sir Thomas Vavasour. On 23rd March 1597, just before she turned fourteen, Mary Houghton the daughter married Sir James Scudamore of Holme Lacy. The Earl of Essex, who had knighted James at Cadiz the previous year, was reputed to have attended the Scudamore wedding banquet.[35] Sadly the young bride was to die by August 1598 and Scudamore remarried to Mary Throckmorton. The younger daughter Elizabeth Houghton must have been born about the beginning of 1591. On 11th July 1609 at St Mary Magdalen in Richmond Surrey, she became the second wife of Sir Henry Bedingfield of Oxborough Norfolk, later a known royalist who died in 1657.[36] An affectionate letter to his wife from Sir Henry when in prison in the Tower in 1649 indicated that he had married Elizabeth 38 years previously. Before her own death in 1662 she bore several of his children including Henry his surviving son and heir. Her MI in Oxborough described her as the daughter of Peter Houghton esq of Houghton Tower in Lancashire, confirming the earlier Lancashire family link.[37]

There can be no doubt that Peter Houghton was a wealthy man. The Grocers' Company court minutes recorded that on 29th September 1597 he left £400 to the Company to be lent to young men at an early stage in the trade.[38] Had he agreed to purchase Mannington when it was offered to him by Edmund Lumner in 1584 the history of the house would have been very different. But presumably he had no interest in becoming a country gentleman and perhaps also his wife had no desire to return to life in Norfolk. Unfortunately Houghton died without a formal will - as with James Apott, the legacy to the Grocers must have been simply a commitment registered directly with them. Letters of administration of Peter Houghton alderman from St Gabriel, Fenchurch Road London were granted in 1597 to his widow Mary.[39]

In June 1602 Mary and Sir Thomas Vavasour, as Houghton's executors, were defendants in an action by Silas Tyto, a London merchant who believed that Peter Houghton had not fully repaid the sum due on an excess payment of wine duty.[40] The actions give a full picture of how the duties were collected on French wine brought into England and in particular into the Port of London. Tyto said he had (some 10 years ago) brought 'from Burdeaux in 3 several trips to the City of London 32 tonnes of Gascoigne wines; for the subsidy impost and composition money wherefore he was to have paid ... £76 5s. Before the landing of the wines, he paid ... £24 5s and also for the security of the rest of it entered into 3 obligations (£60, £60 and £12) and the wines were delivered to Peter Houghton in part payment (a tonne and half of wines at price of £30) so only £42 left to pay' with the bonds showing a total penalty of £60 if not paid on time. He missed the payment day and Houghton's men had him arrested on an exchequer warrant just before he was due to sail back to France and demanded the full £60. Unable to carry on his business unless released, he had no choice. He paid up but expected subsequently to recover his £18 overpayment. After more than two years abroad, Tyto returned. The Vavasours claimed that Houghton 'who was a man both of great abilitie and integrity, if he had made any promise [to repay the excess], he in all likelihood did perform it in his life time'. The debt had been cleared before he died and no money was owed. William Robinson, a grocer, and William Basse had both been servants of Houghton, involved in duty and presage collection, and now gave evidence that supported Tyto's claim that the £18 overpayment made to two other servants of Houghton (William Fells and William Harrington) had never been rectified. William Harrison a haberdasher, also involved in Houghton's affairs, gave a similar account. From Basse, Houghton's chief agent, we learn that Houghton had been a busy man, often away from home and often sick, even before the last sickness from which he died. Houghton obviously had a preference for employees called William. He could just call 'William' and someone would come running!

Edward Dodge's involvement in the wine trade also involved him in a venture in Ireland involving Sir Walter Ralegh.[41] On 18th July 1601 the Privy Council wrote to Sir George Carew:

> Whereas complaint hath been made unto us by our loving friend Sir Walter Ralegh, knight, Robert Bathurst, and Veronio Martens, merchant stranger, that they ... and Edward Dodge, esquire, deceased (who made the aforesaid Robert Bathurst his executor) having for ten years entered into co-partnership with Henry Pine, gentleman, now resident at Mogelie Castle in the province of Mounster, for the working and making of pipestaves and other cask-boards in divers woods in the realm of Ireland, and for the merchandising and transporting of the same to the common benefit of all the said partners. And likewise that they having been heretofore possessed of the said castle of Mogelie and of divers lands, tenements, and woods thereunto adjoining, whereunto (as they allege) they have lawful interest for many years yet to come.
> The said Henry Pine, contrary to the covenants of co-partnership agreed upon between them, having not only raised great sums of money of the said works and lands, and gotten into his hands other sums of great value taken up by the said partners and by Mr. Dodge in his lifetime for the use of those works, amounting to the sum of 4,000l. or more, but also holding the possession of the castle aforesaid, with the appurtenances, doth convert the benefit of all the said works and lands to his own particular use, and doth utterly neglect and refuse to account with his co-partners for any of the profits or sums of money made or received as aforesaid; whereby the said partners do sustain such prejudice as that Sir Walter Ralegh is like to be without recompence for his woods felled and consumed, Robert Bathurst, without remedy for the sum of 1,100l. and upwards, which he hath disbursed for satisfaction of moneys taken up upon Mr. Dodge his bonds, and employed about the same works, and Veronio Martens is (by this occasion) brought to such

distress as he is in some sort restrained of his liberty.

We ... therefore ... require your Lordship to give present order and direction that stay may be made of all the said works and transportations of the said pipestaves by Henry Pine or his assigns, and that he may be prohibited to proceed any farther therein. And in case he hath shipped any pipestaves in the rivers of Youghale, Shilligh, or any other ports or creeks of that realm, that they may be unladen again, and sequestered into the hands of some meet persons, until the right of the said partners may be farther considered; and also that the said Pyne may be forthwith sent over unto us, to the end he may account with the said partners and ... further order may be taken with him.

Court at Greenwich, 18 July 1601.

Signed: Tho. Egerton, C.S.; T. Buchurst; E. Worcester; W. Knollys; J. Stanhope; Ro. Cecyll; J. Fortescu; J. Herbert.

Addressed. Endorsed: Received the 6th of Sept.

John Potts, esq: marriage and Mannington

John Potts appears to have maintained an active London life before and after his marriage in 1584. He was called to the bar two years later and continued work as a lawyer. He fleetingly became a member of parliament, sitting for St Mawes in the 1589.[42] He would seem to have been selected for St Mawes via his first cousin William Buggin, another Lincoln's Inn lawyer. Buggin sat in the same parliament, also for a Cornish seat - he had Helston courtesy of his father's influence as mayor there. Both had benefited from the practice at the time for Cornish boroughs to seek out London lawyers to represent their interests in parliament at low cost.[43]

Other MPs in this parliament were Sir Philip Boteler for Hertfordshire and others who feature in the story: Francis Flower, Christopher Heydon esq - Potts's near neighbour in Baconsthorpe (and future husband of his widow) - Thomas Vavasour (later his brother-in-law) and Edward Coke the famous lawyer who later, as attorney-general, would sue Potts in the court of the Star Chamber. This post-Armada sitting was known for the magnificent opening speech of the Lord Chancellor Sir Christopher Hatton. The main purpose of the session was to vote the Queen an unusual double subsidy to pay for the defence of the realm. Having done this and passed a modest number of unremarkable bills the parliament was dissolved on 29th March 1589. Neither Potts nor Buggin are known to have made any material contribution to the parliament and neither returned to the House.

Why in 1584 did John Potts of London and Hertfordshire decide to marry Anne Dodge and how did Mannington come into his hands? So far a growing network of relationships has been demonstrated tying John Potts ever closer to the Dodge family in London and the south-east. However John Dodge was not the only link of this cotcric to Norfolk. Others may have drawn Potts to consider the county as a fruitful investment.

Botelers and Buggins in Norfolk

Around this time there is evidence that John's mother may have spent time in Norfolk even though she was to die at her house in Eltham. In Itteringham, Mannington and Heydon there was a grand spread of John Potts's senior relations as well as his younger good friend and cousin William Buggin esq. John and William's uncle, Francis Boteler of Woodhall manor Watton-at-Stone Herts, was born in about 1535 and on 25th September 1564 at Redenhall in west Norfolk married Katherine the daughter of Thomas Gawdy. Katherine's father, who died in 1556, was bailiff of Harleston and had three sons, all lawyers and all baptised Thomas. Two of them (one later known as Francis) became senior judges.[44] This family link to the Gawdys gave John Potts yet more valuable legal connections as well as a toe into Norfolk.

The Boteler and Gawdy families had other links. The eldest of the three Thomas Gawdy brothers had married first Anne the daughter and coheir of Sir John Bassingbourne of Woodhall Herts, the home of the Botelers. Anne's sister Catherine had married Sir Nicholas Hare MP, Speaker of the Commons and Master of the Rolls with a country seat in Suffolk but lands in west Norfolk.[45] So the Boteler/Potts Hertfordshire network linked into Norfolk as early as the 1560s. Francis and Katherine Boteler had their first children baptised (and sadly buried) in Redenhall: Gawdy Butler buried on 23rd September 1565, Gervase Butler baptised on 5th October 1567 and buried on 1st December 1567, Elizabeth baptised on 17th October 1568. Later they were to have a son Thomas who married Anne Gawsell of Watlington near King's Lynn, and three daughters, including Elizabeth who married John Moundeford of Boughton (who had sons Francis and John and by Francis, grandsons Francis and William).

Francis Boteler at some point came to live in Heydon, only a few miles from Mannington, where he made his will on 18th March 1596 and was buried five days later.[46] In his will, not proved until 1600, he left legacies for his Moundeford grandchildren, from the money that their father held from him. He advised his executor to ensure that it was paid since John Moundeford was a 'forward fellow'. His daughter Elizabeth Moundeford and his son Thomas also received legacies. Francis left 10s rings for his sister Buggin (ie Elizabeth Boteler/Buggin), his sister Flower (ie Katherine Boteler/Potts/Doddes/Flower), his brother Richard and his wife and cousin Graveley (ie the husband of Richard Boteler's only daughter Elizabeth), his cousin John Potts (newly of Mannington) and finally cousin William Buggin (Elizabeth's son and John Potts's friend) whom he made executor.

Apart from his interests elsewhere, William Buggin had Norfolk connections and interests. The auditor's enrolment books of the exchequer official John Hill, covering 1583-1603 for Norfolk, Suffolk and elsewhere in East Anglia and London, have a number of entries signed 'Buggin'.[47] Entries for 1586-87, for example, showed Buggin signing pages relating to Norfolk transactions involving William Dix of Wickmere the chief administrator for the Howard family (Thomas Duke of Norfolk and then his son Philip Earl of Arundel). John Hill was the brother-in-law of a Cawston man George Sawyer, the local surveyor responsible for creating the Mannington estate map of 1595. Sawyer's son Edmund was also an auditor with his uncle. Cawston and Heydon, where Buggin held lands, are very close. William's father Edward Buggin, apart from being an MP for Totnes in 1572, and from 1570 to 1584 Clerk Comptroller of the Revels, was also a clerk in the exchequer.[48] He had become a friend of Sir Christopher Hatton. Did William Buggin acquire an exchequer role through his father and then help his friends or was it the other way around?

Although not lord of the manor of Heydon, Buggin was a major tenant in Heydon. The 1597 subsidy roll showed him as the largest landholder and taxpayer.[49] Robert Kemp from Gissing, next on the list, held Heydon Hall, which he or his father had acquired from the Dynne family, possibly via the Colfers after the 1586 death of Henry Dynne. The parish register for Heydon with Irmingland shows Dynne and Kemp families present through the 1590s, so it is unlikely that Buggin leased Heydon Hall itself. However the Dynnes and Buggins families probably knew each other in London. Henry Dynne had been yet another auditor in the exchequer![50]

The other large manor and house in Heydon was Stinton Hall, now combining many of the earlier minor manors that characterised Heydon's manorial structure. Francis Boteler and then William Buggin may have rented it from its absentee owner Sir John Townshend. It seems that several of the Boteler clan were living in the area, no doubt making for a neighbourly group with John Potts and his family then in Itteringham and Mannington. Who moved in first? Katherine married Flower at a time when his friend's brother John Dodge was taking more interest in his Mannington estate. Did they visit Mannington when she came to see her brother Francis in West Norfolk? Or had her sister Buggin already moved into Heydon? Whichever way round Katherine would have encouraged the idea of her son having a country seat close to her family. After his marriage in 1584 she would often have spent time with John and Anne. Her sister's husband Edward Buggin died in 1590 and his widow Elizabeth remained in Heydon where she was buried on 9th February 1598, as Widow Buggin gentlewoman. On 10th March 1600 Johanna Gawdy widow was buried there, possibly a relation by marriage of Francis. With his west Norfolk connections Francis would probably have known the Townshends well and he may have been instrumental in achieving the original lease of Stinton Hall.[51]

Elizabeth's son William Buggin 'of London' spent less time at Heydon after his parents' deaths and disposed of minor lands there in 1613 and 1615.[52] In one of these deeds Buggin was referred to as 'late of Heydon' and the other recited that in 1598-99 William Buggin had purchased 3 rods of land in Heydon. In July 1610 William Buggin of Lincoln's Inn and his wife Elizabeth, daughter of William Bowes of St John Middlesex, sold various lands and woods in Irmingland and Heydon to Sir Nathaniel Bacon.[53] The deed, among a number of recitals, showed that four enclosures, including one named Spinkes Olland, had been sold in 1597 by John Bettes to Elizabeth Buggin widow of Heydon - William's mother - a year before she died. William Buggin died in December 1618 owning substantial property in London, particularly in St John's Middlesex and also in St Sepulchre. There was no record of any remaining Norfolk property in his IPM.[54]

The Dodge deal

Past historians of the Potts family and Mannington have given only sketchy details of what Potts bought, when and from whom. All bar one of the original documents relating to the purchase of Mannington have not survived, even though good subsequent documentation of much of the evolution of the estate survives in the Walpole archive. This appears to have been the result of carelessness by the very last of the Potts line in the eighteenth century. Unfortunately the sole surviving document is merely a short and rather unhelpful exemplification of a recovery of Hilary term (January/February) 1585 between Francis Flower esq and Edward Dodge esq (his step-father and uncle-in-law, presumably acting as trustees for Potts) of the first part and John Potts gent.[55] It used the same formulaic description seen in Edmund Lumner senior's will: Mannington and Wolterton manors with the advowson of Itteringham and half that of Wolterton and 10 messuages, 10 tofts, 1 mill, 1 dovehouse, 10 gardens, 1000 acres of land, 100 acres of meadow and 50 acres of pasture with 100 of wood and 50 of bruery or heathland. However, it does show categorically that Edmund Lumner junior was present at court in Westminster for this deed and warranted the manors and their lands to Flower and Dodge, thus letting go his claim on the property and so reinforcing other deeds that assured the estate to the ultimate use of John Potts and his heirs. It also showed that the recoveries of Dodge and Lumner and others referred to later in chancery had existed. The process was designed to strengthen the title created in the primary bargain and sale documents. A chance find in the Walpole archive at Wolterton shows that all the original deeds and writings had still been in the family's possession in 1721. A short note, possibly in the hand of the family lawyer Robert Britiffe, described documents and information that he had returned to Sir Charles Potts in 1727.[56]

He specifically noted that a conveyance between John Dodge and John Potts of the Mannington estates had been a marriage contract. This is the sole reference and has not been noted previously by other writers. Without the document itself, the circumstances of John Potts's acquisition of Mannington from Edmund Lumner junior must be pieced together. Most of the story was given in the later actions resulting from the change of ownership (see below). If the marriage reference had not been found, the sale of Mannington would seem to be a straightforward event. The details were given in John Potts's own IPM which followed the descent of the manor from Edmund Lumner senior to when Katherine married John Dodge. This extract has its spelling and punctuation modernised:

> And after the 19th April 1563 Katherine married at Mannington
> a certain John Dodge esq, by virtue of which John and Katherine
> were seised of the manors and other premises for Katherine's life,
> remaindered to Edmund and belonging to ['spectans'] John Dodge.
> Afterwards on 18th December [1584] by John's deed that same day
> at Mannington he surrendered all estate and title in the premises to
> Edmund Lumnor the son and so the son was seised and afterwards

on 19th December [1584] Edmund by his deed feoffed to John
Pott to the use of John Pott and his heirs, and after the octave of
Michaelmas [1584] a fine was levied … between John Pott gent and
Edmund Lumnor als Lomner esq for the manors of Mannington
and Wolterton with 10 messuages, 10 tofts, 2 mills, 2 dovecots, 10
gardens, 1,000 acres (then same), 100s rents, one liberty of foldage,
advowson of Itteringham and half of Wolterton. So John Pott was
seised and after Michaelmas [1584], Francis Flower and Edward
Dodge by writ of *ingressum super disseisin* [taking possession over
dispossession] before the Queen's justices recovered against John
Pottes the said manor, by exemplification [quoted, including Robert
Stanton as John's attorney]; John and Anne Potts stand seised.[57]

From this it was clear that Edmund Lumner junior, now in debt, had decided to sell
his estate and had done so with the Dodges' agreement. Katherine, when defending
Potts in a later action, explained that she had perceived that her son Edmund intended
to sell the manors of Mannington and Wolterton - 'compelled by necessity for his own
present relief and for the advancement of his wife and daughters'. Edmund had no
child or brother in a position to purchase it but he was desirous that Mannington
'should continue in his blood'. Katherine and John Dodge, before the conveyance of
the property, 'had been willing for Potts to have first offer on it before any stranger, in
respect of the marriage between him and her daughter, Edmund's sister. John Potts
accordingly paid and undertook to pay as much as any stranger would then give for
the property, being a great sum … . Thus far Potts had reaped no benefit from the lands
by virtue of his purchase of them'.[58]

The marriage and the purchase had gone hand in hand. The Dodges had
surrendered their rights to the title in the estate to Edmund junior the day before he
conveyed his reversion to Potts. Anne and John were married three days later on St
Thomas's day (21st December) 1584. An estate steward Thomas Fenne later recalled
that on the same day the 'livery and seisin', the old-fashioned ritual of taking
possession of a house, 'was made in the little parlour of the mansion house called
Mannington Hall by taking up a piece of earth in the floor of the said parlour'.

Naturally Katherine did not want to lose their comfortable home and income so she
must have been concerned when Lumner's first offer, to his brother-in-law the wealthy
Peter Houghton, his half-sister Mary's husband, was refused. Fortunately John Potts
was showing interest in Mary's sister Anne. According to Potts, Lumner voluntarily
offered the estate to him. What the exact deal was is not clear but Potts must have been
very keen to acquire both Anne and Mannington as he had to lay out a 'great sum'
with little expectation of return at first, both in terms of jointure and income. Potts
agreed as part of the transaction to lease the manor to John and Katherine Dodge for
10 years. He had no part in the running of the estate or in the rents and profits from it
during that time. As Katherine said he 'reaped no benefit'. No doubt this arrangement
was to reflect Katherine's life interest in the manor. The Mannington estate continued
to be run by John Dodge as lord of the manor by right of his wife Katherine.

Was John Potts an unscrupulous loan shark who enticed Edmund Lumner into debt and then took Mannington from him and his family when the debts could not be repaid? This argument was to be put forward in the next decade during a very aggressive action - the one in which Katherine, then nearly 70, stood up for John. Although he had become fairly wealthy quite fast, there is no evidence, except this accusation, to suggest any sharp practice. He was certainly a cautious man as a lawyer would be. He knew that with Katherine's life interest he would be taking the long view so he agreed to the purchase only on condition of paying part of the money in deferred payments. He took out bonds of obligation with Lumner, the first possibly on 2nd May 1584. Did he pay the going rate? At no point in the later actions was the whole purchase price given but Potts spoke of 'divers great sums' as did Katherine. In the main bond he agreed to pay £2,000 in two instalments but only after Katherine died when he would receive the income. The two £1,000 payments would be made in the second and third years after her death. The penalty for not meeting these dates would be his having to pay £3,000.[59] In the other, dated 8th November 1584 he agreed (on penalty of 1,000 marks) to pay Lumner £100 a year for his maintenance from Michaelmas 1588 while Lumner's mother Katherine lived, 'if Lumner lived that long'. Did he suspect something in Lumner's lifestyle? He described him as 'greatly indebted and decayed'.

Potts's foresight was remarkable as within two years Edmund was to die, possibly lost at sea. His widow Jane proved his will in the summer of 1587. But Potts paid out more than this: after the deal he lent further sums to Lumner totalling £280 presumably to help with his debts. To ensure he received at least £160 of it back, it was agreed that Henry Lanman (a yeoman of Greenwich) should hold the bond for the £2,000 'as a pawne' until the £160 was repaid after the death of Katherine Dodge. If Edmund or Katherine died within three years of the date of the deed the £160 should be repaid at the time of Potts's payment of the first £1,000 in the second year after Katherine's death. Katherine, however, outlived her son and so the £2,000 was not yet payable and the bond and deed remained in Lanman's custody until she did. The structure of the purchase deal as set out by John Potts makes sense and turned out to be far-sighted. It was wise to have a retention, particularly since Edmund Lumner had already incurred further debts at Potts's expense. John's shrewdness carried over to his deliberate strategy in all the later legal actions not to reveal what he paid, when and by what precise legal instruments. Perhaps he felt that giving any details would have allowed his opponents to try to make a case for unfair or even illegal practices. However, it is likely that a retention payment, then as now, would probably have been a small but noticeable part of the purchase price rather than the majority of it. If the later assertion that Mannington was worth £300 a year or more is correct, then at a standard multiple of 20, the estate might well have sold for £6,000, or even more if a deal was done to cover the value of timber. A £2,000 retention for delayed enjoyment of the profits would seem proportionate - 13 years after the purchase Potts had yet to get any benefit from it. Potts may well therefore have paid between £4,000 and £6,000 for his manorial status.

John and Anne were married in Mannington Hall. Sir Edward and Lady Clere with others were present at the marriage which was conducted by George Weeks, the long-standing parson of Plumstead (less than two miles away from Mannington).[60] There is nothing to suggest that this was just a marriage of convenience. John may well have already become a suitor before the offer from Lumner. If so Anne would have had little financial appeal being a younger daughter without expectations. Whether or not it began as a love-match, his affection for her was evident by the time he made his will. (See Chapter 8)

For the next 10 years, while his in-laws were still resident in the Hall, John and his wife probably lived in a high status house on the site of what is now Itteringham's Old Rectory just to the north-west of the church and lying beside what was in the past a lane that ran from the north-east corner of the churchyard directly to Mannington. See Appendix 2.[61] Several of their children (excluding their eldest son Drury) were baptised at Itteringham church rather than at Mannington which may still have been in a bad state. Frances was baptised in September 1588, Katherine in December 1589, John in April 1592 and Charles in July 1593. (Anne their last child was baptised there in January 1598.)

John made his will as 'of Itteringham' in 1593 which referred to the deed whereby his in-laws were to continue to live in Mannington Hall despite his purchase of the estate. He was, as seen in Chapter 5, the representative of Dodge in the 1591 arbitration with the Cookes. By May 1591 he was an under-steward of the Duchy of Lancaster (for Norfolk, Suffolk and Cambridge) and responsible for the Leets of South Erpingham hundred.[62] Apart from this there is little evidence for his having local involvement and he may still have spent much of his time in London.

1595 marked a turning point in John Potts's life. That year, at the end of the ten years, he took direct control of the Mannington estate, although he apparently allowed his in-laws to remain living in the Hall. On 1st May 1595 John Potts held his first court as lord of the manor of Mannington.[63] The court roll made clear that no formal court had been held since before the death of Thomas Payne of Itteringham (in October 1583) as his son John was now admitted to the small acreage the Payne family held of the manor. Thomas Payne had been steward for the Blickling estate and it is quite possible that this reference to him implied that he had also run Mannington's courts. Obviously John Dodge had not bothered with the formalities of his lordship during the ten year lease from his son-in-law. Apart from the attornment - where all the tenants came to pay their respects and a penny to the new lord - little other business was transacted in 1595. The senior free tenants that had not appeared were to be distrained by the bailiff. Various rental payments were of course overdue and to be chased up.

Unfortunately no other court rolls survive from the John Potts era. However, it is clear that by 1595 John Potts wished to assert proper manorial control and exercise his rights, in particular to sheep shack arrangements over the open fields during the winter. He commissioned an estate map, surveyed and drawn up in 1595.[64] The Cawston surveyor George Sawyer did the work and he called upon all the major tenants of the estate, whom he mentioned in a text panel as having agreed the contents of the map and the limits of the manor's sheep run areas. The map paid particular attention to the limits of the sheep shack area to which the estate had rights. Contention about this may have been a reason for drawing the map; there may have been a number of issues needing resolution after a dozen years of John Dodge running the estate without any courts. Indeed, with no court rolls surviving from Dodge's whole period at Mannington there may have been few proper courts even prior to 1583. The 1590s was a decade of poor grain harvests and animal husbandry became economically vital to estates like Mannington. No doubt the negotiations that led to the agreed shack areas on the map ensured the estate's right to the maximum possible winter grazing. This was perhaps the key initiative as John Potts took the estate in hand. As well as agricultural improvements, John Potts also started to add to the estate through purchase particularly properties immediately adjacent. Inevitably as John took a more active part in managing the estate and, as the map demonstrated, began to uncover old problems, the court cases started to increase.

Challenges in court: Edward Clere and Edward Coke

Sir Edward Clere his neighbour at Blickling enjoyed frequent recourse to the law and he and Potts began a long-running dispute as early as 1592. In Easter term that year a one-off chancery order, in an otherwise undocumented action, ordered a commission to hear answers in a case brought by Clere and William Payne (who probably worked for the Blickling estate) against John Dodge, Katherine his wife, John Potts esq and Lawrence Sargenson the rector.[65] As the statements of the Dodges and Sargenson were to be heard in Norfolk, the commissioners were to be drawn from local men John Bettes, Bartholomew Plumstead and Christopher Langdon gents. With the rector's involvement it seems likely that the issue over tithe payments (as opposed to other property issues) in Itteringham had been rumbling on for some time. As was often the case in chancery, one argument was then used to involve another more important dispute.

In this case John Potts sued Clere in 1594 nominally over the tithes as an excuse to enable Potts to assert his claim to Love's messuage in Itteringham. This in turn became a right royal row when Edward Coke the attorney-general took up what he saw as an attempt on Crown property. Things got nasty and led to the earlier case, quite bizarrely, being struck from the records on his orders. It is only from the books of orders and decrees that the evidence, such as it is, remained. The action was referred to commissioners, including Edmund Stubbes and William Guybon, in Trinity term in the summer of 1594.[66] Love's holding was based on a house in the centre of Itteringham, located where the barns of the manor house are today. The messuage also had a parcel of lands in the Broomhill area nearby and in the main open field of Itteringham just to the north and east. The 1595 map showed the site of the house marked as if it was Mannington manorial property and yet also clearly and correctly noted it as Sir Edward Clere's. Potts wanted to assert ownership or at least manorial control, but in fact Clere had bought the property from its previous occupants the Mortofts as if it was freehold. The house site was probably never Mannington's although arguably some of its lands in Itteringham's open field seem once to have been held of Mannington manor and may technically still have been copyhold not freehold. The holders of the neighbouring Nowers manor do not seem at any point to have made an attempt to claim Love's and its lands, which reinforces the view that these lands, whichever manor they were originally in, had become accepted locally as *de facto* freehold.

The map, with the visible support on it of all the main tenants, no doubt would have made a good impact at the local questioning of witnesses. Participation of all the main tenants in the area would have helped add credibility to Potts's stance as clear owner of the estate. Love's messuage appeared to be part of the royal manor of Nowers in Itteringham, previously held for a century and a half by the Mortofts, and at some point somebody tipped off Coke that Potts was possibly attempting fraudulently to steal crown land.

The old action was still going in Easter term 1596 when Clere seems to have been under pressure.[67] But in May 1596 Coke notified the court that John Potts's action chiefly claimed that he was seized of a part of an advowson of a parsonage and that he had a lease of the tithes thereof from the incumbent.[68] Potts said he also had a lease of a parcel of lands in East Dereham and elsewhere in Norfolk but he could not prove that he had a lease of the tithes, since the lease had come into Clere's hands. By this stage the parties had examined witnesses. Coke now argued that they had taken depositions relating to lands not specified in the bill. He also mentioned obliquely that Her Majesty and others had an interest in some of these lands and yet were not made parties to the action. His attack on Potts had begun. He and the solicitor-general were asked to examine all the case papers and documents and determine whether 'undue practices' had been made! The court warned of an exemplary punishment if this was found to be the case. From this point on the older case disappeared from view, as Coke later had it struck from the record as attempted fraud, but Coke was just getting into his stride.[69]

Who was Edward Coke?

Edward, later Sir Edward Coke the Queen's formidable attorney-general (1552-1634) was a Norfolk man through and through. Born and bred in Norfolk he made his name in London but continued to acquire Norfolk property for much of his life - at one time holding some 60 manors in the county.[70] As a result he was profoundly linked into the group of ruling families in Norfolk in the late sixteenth and early seventeenth centuries - Bacon, Cornwallis, Gawdy, Gresham, Townshend and Windham. Christopher Heydon was one of his antagonists in Norfolk politics and, in their youth, had competed with Coke for Bridget Paston's hand in marriage. He had become attorney-general in 1594 and through the decade his income has been estimated to grow from £100 a year to a staggering £12,000.

Coke married Bridget, achieving a great fortune from her family. Descended from the main line of the Paston family that William Lumner had served, she was the daughter of Anne and John Paston of Huntingfield Hall in Suffolk where Coke made his home for many years. One of Bridget's uncle's, Sir Thomas Paston, acquired Barningham Hall, just a short distance from Mannington. After her death in 1598, Coke rapidly married Elizabeth the widow of Sir William Hatton - a society beauty much younger than himself but equally strong-willed. As an up and coming lawyer with political connections and briefly an MP, he would have known Sir Christopher Hatton, the Lord Chancellor, well and those closely linked to him.

Coke's favourite young sister Anne (a notorious and staunch puritan recusant) married his Trinity College Cambridge contemporary Francis Stubbes, gent of Scottow.[71] Francis was the youngest of three sons of John Stubbes of Buxton, a Norfolk lawyer from a long line of lawyers.[72] His brother Edmund Stubbes had from Coke the living of Huntingfield but also acted as a lawyer, being involved in a number of actions involving Mannington and the Potts family. His name cropped up as witness on various Potts and Dodge documents. Coke no doubt procured chancery hearing commissions for him and Stubbes would have been a rapid conduit of communications to Coke. Edmund and John had no sons, but when Edmund died, he left bequests to Francis's younger sons Edmund and Francis Stubbes. But since his nephew John persevered with his vexatious suit against him, he would not now receive the annuity that he had earlier promised him at Sir Edward Coke's persuasion.[73]

Given all this, it is inconceivable that John Potts was unknown to Edward Coke - there are too many points of connection. Apart from the Hatton and Stubbes family links, Coke and Potts were both MPs in 1589. John Potts through his stepfather Francis Flower was in Sir Christopher Hatton's immediate circle when Hatton was Lord Chancellor, the senior figure in the equity courts. Coke and Potts must have known each other as practising lawyers in London. Coke was known for his 'inflammatory rhetoric' and 'overwrought language' but he was a man of prodigious energy and learning who both used precedent and created new milestones in the law. He had no time for the Earl of Essex (at whose trial he presented the prosecution) and would take on the lower gentry as often as the highest in the land. Even so, the language of the action was so harsh as to suggest that Coke strongly disapproved of Potts. How far did this go back? Coke had defended the Cookes of Barningham in their fight against John Dodge and Potts as early as 1592. He completely failed to acknowledge that Potts was a practising lawyer; or give any credence to the facts that he was married to Anne Dodge and that Mannington had been first offered to Peter Houghton the husband of Anne's sister. Why did he suddenly pick up the case in 1596?

Robert Lumner's claim

The Potts-Clere action had awoken other interested parties. However good Potts's claim might have been, he had now managed to open himself to attack by distant Lumner relations as well as Jane Lumner, the very disgruntled widow of Edmund. Their three actions became interwoven.

A brief appearance in chancery decrees, in 1596-97, of a suit by Robert Lumner, a son of William of Sharrington, against Emmanuel Callard, Katherine of Mannington's son, hinted at a possible cause of the animosity of Robert Lumner towards the Mannington families.[74] In Easter term 1596 a commission of enquiry was appointed to examine witnesses to their disagreement. By the beginning of 1597 an order noted that Lumner referred to a common law action between them relating to a debt of £500. He offered to pay double the bond if Callard's common law action against him for this sum proved to be true. Faced with this confident stance the common law suit was stayed and Mr Houghton (Robert Houghton the cousin of the Wolterton Houghtons) and Mr Hubbard (Hobart) of Lincoln's Inn were asked to hear the matter and report back only if they failed to agree on a resolution. Although for some years there were no further chancery decrees, the case probably continued at common law. Suddenly in Easter term 1601 the case reappeared in chancery and it was ordered that the plaintiff Lumner should pay 30s costs to Callard for the lack of a bill being produced. Perhaps this indicated the eventual lapse of the action and a win for Callard. No further chancery orders were made. Perhaps with this bad blood between Callard and Lumner, the latter had already by early 1596 taken revenge by informing Coke of the apparent risk to the manor of Nowers. Robert Lumner turned the Love's suit into a device to pursue his attack against Potts's tenure of Mannington. (These Star Chamber and chancery suits against him provided the details of his original acquisition of Mannington.) Robert claimed that he was to be the rightful inheritor of the Mannington estate after the death of Katherine Dodge by virtue of the male entail set out in her marriage settlement of 1555. Technically the 1597 Star Chamber action was not prosecuted directly by Robert Lumner. With his father-in-law William Franklin, a London lawyer, he had contrived to excite the Queen's attorney-general to believe that Potts had fraudulently seized the royal manor of Nowers in Itteringham.

Jane Lumner's first action

Jane Lumner, the widow of Edmund Lumner junior, twice attacked in chancery with a claim that John Potts had significantly underpaid her husband for Mannington and that she was due further payment for her and her daughters' maintenance. Robert's and Jane's first actions were both in 1597, which may or may not have been coincidental. It seems most likely that Robert's action had made Jane fearful that she would become ever further from any chance to make more money out of Mannington if he were to establish title. John Potts's will made on 4th November 1593 indicated that Jane Lumner was harassing him even then. Now Jane escalated her long campaign of requests and demands to formal legal action in response to Robert's machinations.

The 1597 Coke action

Coke's 1597 action was ostensibly to look into whether Potts had fraudulently taken possession of the manor of Nowers in Itteringham which had come to the crown on the attainder of the Duke of Norfolk. There is no evidence that Potts ever had any material involvement in Nowers Manor, other than in his concern to return to Mannington manor the copyhold land that had effectively been absorbed into Nowers and then mortgaged and later sold out of the control of both manors to the Cleres of Blickling. The reality of the action was the attempt by surviving members of the Lumner family to regain possession of Mannington or receive some extra payment for it. Coke was effectively acting unwittingly on their behalf under the guise of an action regarding a royal manor. It is likely that the accusations regarding Nowers were a fabrication by the Lumner contingent to draw Coke into acting on their behalf against Potts. The strong early connections of the Lumners with the Pastons, (Coke's wife's family) may have been invoked by Jane and Robert Lumner as they tried to secure his support for their claims.

As a result, much of the accusatory content of these Star Chamber materials has to be taken with a pinch of salt, particularly the vituperative recital of the earlier action between John Potts and Sir Edward Clere. Although the attorney-general had caused it to be removed from all chancery records he had no qualms about quoting from it when it suited him. Coke's bill started by reciting the story of Edward Lumner senior and his wife Katherine having Mannington with its 'annual value of over £300'. Edmund junior, he said, went to live in London where, at that time 'John Potts gent, now of Mannington, also lived in or about London, being a man of ~~bad~~ [deleted] large conscience' - the judgemental comment remains in the bill, regardless of the crossing out. Despite his being at Lincoln's Inn and working as a lawyer, Potts, according to Coke, lived by the 'hard gain and interest of loan money' and knew that Edmund would come into 'great and fair possessions and livings' after his mother's death. Allegedly Potts 'of his corrupt greedy mind endeavoured to make a prey of Lumner and to acquire to himself' the whole estate. Potts, he claimed, insinuated himself into Lumner's acquaintance and company and offered to lend him various sums of money for which he took assurances and bonds with great penalties. Lumner became entangled in an 'unconscionable plot' and was forced to convey to Potts, for a 'very small consideration', the inheritance of Mannington. After noting the common recovery of early 1585 and the death of Edmund junior with no male heir, the bill asserted that Edmund had only received about £300 (presumably a reference to the £260 additional loan) from Potts and made no reference to what debts had been written off, nor to any deferred payment. Instead it piled on the emotional pressure by saying that the timber on the estate was worth £2,000 if sold and even the lead on the mansion house was worth more than £300.

Coke then claimed that the inheritance of the manors came 'as it should' to William Lumner gent of Sharrington and his male heirs. He seemed to say that Potts understood that his assurances of the manors were not sufficient and effectual in law to bind William and his heirs as he said several writs of entry were brought against him by Lumner. Coke also agreed that Katherine had the freehold for her life. William Lumner had died and the inheritance went to his son and heir Robert. Potts, Coke claimed, allegedly tried to negotiate with Robert to strengthen his title to Mannington but Robert refused his offered great sums of money. Potts sought by 'all unlawful indecent and disorderly practices' to make himself secure in the premises and (the part Coke was really interested in) at the same time tried to acquire some pretended estate in Nowers manor and other royal lands in Itteringham and to defraud the Queen of them.

Coke continued with the accusation that, to that end 'on 20th May 1593 John Potts confederated to contrive certain writings' with John Dodge of Mannington, his wife Katherine and Philip Potts of London gent (John's lawyer brother), William Yates of Southwark, Thomas Fenne of Mannington (yeoman and almost certainly estate bailiff there), Emmanuel Callard of Cromer (Katherine's son), Leonard Batrye gent of London and a Mr Buggins (presumably William). Coke said that as her son Edmund was dead without issue Katherine would not have cared what became of the said manors! This putative deed may have existed. From the number of people involved (some of them being family members) it seems to have been some sort of transaction involving trustees for John Potts. By this date he had two young sons and perhaps, linked to his will of that year, he was making arrangements for the secure inheritance of his estate. Coke, though, said the purpose was to concoct a deed wherein before his attainder Thomas Duke of Norfolk had conveyed Nowers manor to Potts. Another, dated before Potts's two recoveries in 1585, in the name of the said Katherine in her widowhood (presumably referring to her claim on Mannington as Edmund Lumner senior's widow) granted Mannington to Potts and was endorsed on the back that livery and seisin had taken place. A third, again before Hilary term 1585, had John Dodge and Katherine together granting the manors to John Potts. These, as has been shown, were the deeds of the purchase of Mannington but Coke maintained they were created to take Her Majesty's manor of Nowers and to contrive a tenancy of the freehold in the Mannington estate. Coke went on to assert that to better publicise the claimed title, Potts in Easter term 1594 issued a bill of complaint in chancery against Sir Edward Clere of Blickling which showed that Lawrence Sargenson, rector of Itteringham in about Michaelmas 1589 had made leases to Potts of the tithe corn and hay in Itteringham for four years. However, Sir Edward pretended that a great part of the tithes had been concealed from the crown and he was granted a royal lease of them and took a great part of them from Potts. Notwithstanding a trial by court of common law Potts, apparently, would not cease from his pretended claim to them (ie he had lost the common law action). The new chancery action said that Potts had lost his writings during the actions and was thus remedy-less and could only come to chancery to pursue Sir Edward's breach of promise.

Coke had pressed for further enquiries and in Michaelmas term 1595 a chancery commission of enquiry had appointed seven potential commissioners to examine witnesses and review the whole issue by Easter term 1596. As before, Edmund Stubbes and William Guybon met to examine witnesses. Coke claimed that on 10th December 1595 John Potts unlawfully bribed Katherine, Philip Potts, Thomas Fenne and William Yates with gifts and rewards to depose falsely before the commissioners that the said counterfeit writings were true deeds and duly executed. On 19th December 1595 and again on 16th and 17th January 1596 Potts 'wickedly' held the three deeds in his hands and declared to the commissioners they were true deeds. But he was alleged to fear discovery and prevented the commissioners from seeing the detail of the deeds. Further, his questions of witnesses did not contain any details of the content of the deeds but simply asked if they were true copies of the deeds which had been sealed and with which livery and seisin was delivered. (Quite normal questions in this type of case!)

Coke then recited some parts of Potts's earlier interrogatories regarding Nowers. The manuscript is very badly damaged at this point and sadly whatever was recited about this aspect of the action is lost. Nowers manor had been held by the Mortoft family for many years and then by Sir Edward Clere of Blickling, who had a lease of Nowers manor from the Duke of Norfolk. At some point Richard Larwood had lived there as tenant. Previous debate about its ownership had in some way involved James Mason, the mid-century rector of Itteringham, and Thomas Pye yeoman and servant [probably estate steward] of Edmund Lumner senior. Potts produced as witnesses among others Christopher Langdon of Wolterton (a tenant of part of Nowers manor) and Mary Harrison, who may have been the granddaughter of Pye. Pye was probably the Thomas Pye of Erpingham who died in 1591.[75]

Coke refused to recite the responses of any witness. To do so would have been detrimental to the Queen's interests. Indeed Coke made clear that all these depositions had been suppressed by order of the court of chancery and were no longer a matter of record. So he simply complained of the manner of Potts's examination rather than about the content or any actions taken by Potts. Finally and directly he accused Potts of fraud likely to disinherit the Queen. Coke's set of questions followed, with the detailed answers of John and Philip Potts and general answers by the two of them and Emmanuel Callard rejecting all of the charges. John and Philip Potts and Emmanuel Callard submitted together tersely in writing that they were not guilty of fraud, counterfeiting and forgery.

In his general answer Philip rather pointedly stated that since the attorney-general had suppressed the action and depositions, they were not now of record, could not be used and he could not refer to them to consider their content. So he could not make any certain answer to Coke's charges of perjury regarding them. Philip said that he had not been told by his brother what to say to the commissioners, nor had any reward for testifying. John Potts testified that he had explained to the witnesses what the questions would be so that they would be able to answer them more easily. He had not told them what to say, but had simply asked them to tell the truth.

More family drawn in

The assiduous Edward Coke also launched a Star Chamber action against Katherine Dodge widow and Thomas Fenne and another against Emmanuel Callard of Cromer her son.[76] The Callard action gave the detailed date of 14th February 1597 and Katherine's answer is endorsed with a note saying that it was taken at Mannington on 22nd March 1597 by Isaac Astley esq, Rice Gwynne esq and Stephen Drury gent commissioners. This shows that all three Star Chamber actions may in fact have been launched during autumn 1596, given the time that usually was allowed for initial replies and then for commissioners to gather the facts.

The surviving Callard document is in fact just his answers to four interrogatories. His replies were very brief. He had not been procured at any time to set his hand to any deeds of feoffment, nor had he witnessed a deed between John Potts and the Dodges. He did not know whether Edmund Lumner was dead and did not know what John Potts had paid him for Mannington. Lastly he had not heard that Katherine Dodge was aggrieved and offended at Edmund Lumner selling away the manors and lands entailed to John Potts. Although brief, these answers imply that the suit against Callard was probably linked to the main action against John Potts (the Nowers manor accusation), together with improper payment for Mannington and an insecure title. This was certainly the case with the action against Katherine Dodge where both bill and answers survive. Her answer and that of Thomas Fenne covered some of the same points as John Potts, but added some further information from the fulsome replies.

Katherine in her answer to Coke's attack on her was described as a widow of Mannington then aged about 68 years. (John Dodge had died shortly before the enquiry.) She said that Coke's bill was based on false and untrue information and suggestions given to him by William Franklin, one of the attorneys of the Queen's Bench, whose daughter had married Robert Lumner. Robert 'pretends to the manors of Mannington and Wolterton' and Franklin's desire to know what conveyances had been made was to gain 'some colour to the said party's pretended title'. However, Katherine said, if they had put forward a bill in their own names and lost they would have laid themselves open to payment of costs and punishment for their false claim. They knew the attorney-general's zeal in protecting Her Majesty's inheritance and used that to persuade him to put forward the bill. She pointed out that one of the forgeries that John Potts, her son-in-law, and she were said to have produced showed him making an arrangement with the Duke of Norfolk. But at the time of Norfolk's attainder in 1572 Potts was of 'so tender years he was not then like to have been a purchaser'. He would then have been about 14. She asserted that John Potts never occupied Nowers, nor made title to the manor and anyway the Countess of Arundel was then in 1597 seized of the manor in her demesne as of fee (which we know to be the case as she had it as part of her jointure arrangements). She said that her counsel advised her not to answer the first eight questions which were all to do with the Potts versus Clere action.

Katherine robustly denied the charges of forgery, with a bereaved mother and widow's emotional intensity. Her son Edmund was dead without male heirs and neither that nor anything else would have induced her to consent to any forgery. And 'it is grievous to hear' that her dead husband was charged with such a crime 'whose good life and godly end she thought would have defended him from so hard and causeless an imputation'. She denied that she forged any document whereby the Duke of Norfolk would give Nowers to Potts. Indeed she pointed out that 'she cannot write any more than two letters for her name nor read any writing at all, be it in English or Latin'. She had not confederated with the long list of people supposed to be involved in the forgery. And she was therefore not bound to give any further details of the arrangements made between her and her husband and John Potts as to title to the manors. William Franklin and Robert Lumner had been making malicious speeches saying that she had forfeited her title by making the alleged writings. She followed the family line over the accusations regarding the Clere chancery case. The attorney-general had suppressed the depositions, so Her Majesty could not suffer from them and since they no longer existed she could not tell whether she deposed as this bill supposed. Intriguingly she ended by saying that she did not write or cause to be written the letter to her brother Sir Thomas Leighton, showed to her at this examination. How Coke acquired this (if it was genuine) or what it contained or even how it was supposed to fit into the allegations, was not stated.

Thomas Fenne, in his general answer, denied any part in anything unlawful. He too was questioned at Mannington on 22nd March 1597. He described himself as a yeoman of about 46 years of age and that John Potts was his master (he was probably steward of the Mannington estate). He had been a witness in the Potts versus Clere action but was not told what to say and could not remember the content of his deposition nor of all the manors listed in the documents shown then. But he did know that Mannington was included. He had seen nothing to suggest that the Dodges were upset by the sale.

No Star Chamber decrees survive, so this ends with a rather frustrating conclusion. John Potts had believed strongly that Love's messuage and lands in Itteringham in the occupation of Sir Edward Clere and his tenants belonged to Mannington manor, even though the house itself almost certainly did not. Potts had pursued the matter through a hybrid action involving contested tithes.[77] Love's had been occupied for many years by the Mortoft family or their tenants and early Mannington court rolls show Mortofts coming to court specifically and only as holders of Love's, presumably only in relation to their copyhold lands in the open field. The surviving versions of sixteenth century Mannington court rolls, which are late century contemporary copies, would have been made for this action (just as the Barningham rolls had been produced by John Dodge for the Coldham manor action). Coke had been wound up by Robert Lumner to believe that Potts had been trying to steal the Queen's manor of Nowers, where the Mortofts had been lords. There was no truth in this assertion.[78]

Jane's second attack

Shortly after answering the first round of questions from the Star Chamber, John Potts was sued again in chancery; this time Edmund Lumner's widow Jane brought a different but related action.[79] Jane Lumner's bill of complaint was dated June 1597 and John Potts's reply November 1597, when the Star Chamber action was still pending. In fact her complaint was also against Henry Lanman a yeoman of Greenwich who was involved as custodian of bonds and an indenture between Potts and Edmund Lumner. As the bill represented Jane's viewpoint and used a few tricks of twisting the evidence, further details are revealed about the circumstances of the Potts purchase of Mannington.

Her first complaint showed she either was misinformed or was deliberately misquoting the bonds her husband had signed. Jane claimed that Potts owed to her as executor 'the sum of £3,000 or some such great sum' in three payments. The first, she said, was to be made immediately after the death of her mother-in-law - and then £1,000 yearly. Having added a third thousand to the amount actually agreed, she then said she was due even more than this £3,000 since she had been well-born and had brought a good portion to her marriage and yet had no jointure assured her. She was desirous to provide for her maintenance and the advancement of her two daughters. She added that her husband had accordingly assured her that she would have £100 per year for the duration of Mrs Dodge's life (ie until the major payments would be made). But she claimed that Potts had 'so cunningly contrived the conveyance' that this £100 annuity was to cease upon the death of her husband. So she was now destitute.

She repeated that Potts and Lumner had agreed that the bonds for the '£3,000' and the assurance of the land (whatever that was) should remain in the hands of one Henry Lanman (sometimes given as Landman) of Greenwich yeoman, until such time as Lumner or his executors should demand them. Now, she said, Lanman and Potts were confederating together to prevent her having the documents and to prevent her having the sums due to her and her children. Potts retained and enjoyed the lands without any recompense to her. Potts, she said, recognised her claim but he reportedly said that Lanman was corruptly preventing her from securing what was due to her. So she sought a writ of subpoena on them both.

Henry Lanman's answer to this was succinct and very precise as to the dates and contents of the three documents he held and why he believed in law he could not yet release them. In November 1584 John Potts and Edmund Lumner had left the two obligations with him for safekeeping which he then described correctly. Lanman went on to describe the third document as a tripartite indenture of 8th November 1584 between Lumner, Potts and himself. Among other things, he said, it was agreed that if Lumner or his mother should die before three years after the date of the deed then the executors should repay to Potts £160 in the second year after Mrs Dodge's death (ie when the first £1,000 of the £2,000 was due). If this was not paid then the obligations should not be delivered to Lumner nor should he be able to sue for them. As Lumner had died within the three years but Katherine Dodge was still alive, he believed he 'was not compellable in law' to deliver the documents and should keep them until the £160 covenant was performed after the death of Katherine Dodge. Of course, he said, if the court directed him otherwise he would be only too happy to deliver the documents to whom they decreed. He went on to refute all the specific charges - he and Potts were not confederating, he had not been corrupt, there was no attempt to defraud and no bonds ever existed for the sum of £3,000. (He still held the bonds in 1602, when Jane tried once more to get hold of them.)

John Potts in his answer of 3rd November 1597 added yet more detail to the history behind the documents described by Lanman and also re-iterated the dates and contents. He pointed out the logical holes in Jane's argument. First, simply that she had said the main money was due after Katherine Dodge's death, who was of course still alive and 'god only knows if the complainant shall outlive Mrs Dodge'! Second, Jane herself had admitted that the £100 annuity was to cease on the death of Lumner, so he had no case to answer.

John then repeated how Lumner had made the offers to Houghton and then himself. Potts said he 'was then shortly after to marry and in truth did marry one other of the sisters of Lumner'. This again implied that Potts and Anne Dodge were already promised earlier in 1584. Potts added that his wife was still alive and that they had two sons and three daughters living. He had trusted that it was lawful for him to purchase the estate and shortly afterwards paid Lumner 'divers great sums of money'. He then explained how some of the payments were to be deferred until after Katherine Dodge's life interest ceased. Finally, Potts commented on the Star Chamber action of Robert Lumner gent. He 'pretended to Mannington or the remainder thereof' and was trying to undermine Potts's title to it. In this he had joined forces with one William Francklen or Franklin. Potts argued that if Katherine Dodge was dead, which she was not, the court of chancery would not take action until the pending Star Chamber action had been dealt with and title to the premises was resolved. This was particularly appropriate since he had paid great sums of money but had yet to receive any benefit from the estate.

End of the line for John Potts

Coke's Star Chamber action against John Potts was still pending in November 1597. Since John died that December the action probably did not get to a decree before it lapsed on his death. Robert Lumner did not start any further actions in chancery although he continued to hassle the family. The Potts family retained Mannington and in that sense won. But John Potts in the final codicil to his will made a passing comment about having less to pass on to his wife and children than he had expected. This might indicate that a decree had been given requiring him to make payments to either Robert or Jane or both; or perhaps he had been fined over the Nowers issue. Jane, however, returned to chancery later with a very similar action to her first, implying she had not won an earlier award. It is just possible that some sort of interim decree in favour of Robert Lumner had been given, leading to John Potts settling out of court with him as a device to ensure that at least he had an unchallenged title to Mannington.

Chapter 8

For Whom the Bell Tolls

———————————

The deaths of all the senior members of both John and Anne Potts's families and of John Potts himself ushered in a new generation and a new century. His widow started a new life on a sad note.

Sadly John Potts was in his grave within five weeks of his answer to the chancery complaint. He was buried in Eltham from his mother's house there on 11th December 1597 (the parish register shows this was about 10 days earlier than was stated in his IPM). Why Eltham and not Mannington or Itteringham, or indeed London? From a death-bed codicil in his will it is clear that he was then ill and in his mother's house in Eltham. His brother Philip died there shortly after John and it is possible both had an infectious disease and were being looked after by Katherine and her senior servant Frances Kettell. Since both men died in their late 30s or very early 40s their deaths were not really expected at this time. However, since John thanked Frances for looking after him in his illness it is possible that he had been ill for some time. Two of John's children, John junior and Frances were also living in his mother's household under her care. John would certainly have been keeping a close watch on the many court proceedings trying to disinherit him. Philip may also have practised law throughout his life, perhaps in partnership with his brother.

Then there were none ...

John's stepfather Francis Flower had been buried in Eltham on 1st January 1597. His wife Katherine remained in his house there which was probably rented from the royal manor of Eltham.[1] It seems that a number of the Potts clan had gathered there in 1597 and in the space of the two years after Flower's death all the elder generation died. The will of Francis Flower esq was made on 1st January and proved on 16th February 1597.[2] If the dates were correctly recorded the will was made on his deathbed and he was buried within hours. The implication of a plague death is hard to avoid. He described himself as 'one of the gentlemen pensioners to our sovereign lady' and asked to be buried in Eltham without any pomp or sumptuous funeral. He left sums to the poor of Eltham, St Andrew Holborn, Passenham Nottinghamshire and Stony Stratford Buckinghamshire. No children or immediate Flower relations were mentioned. Of most interest, among the very many small personal bequests were gifts of:

> A diamond to the value of £50 to Sir William Hatton [his last boss, nephew and heir of Sir Christopher who had died just a few years earlier]

> To Lady Hatton his gelding called Gray Butler [he had another horse named after a different family and presumably this one had come from the Botelers]
>
> Small bequests to one of Her Majesty's cooks and a footman [presumably reflecting his involvement in Eltham Palace]
>
> A seal ring value £3 to 'my old good friend Edmunde Dodge esquire' [an original transcription error for Edward]
>
> A coat, dagger and girdle to John Pott. [John was also one of the witnesses and may have done the drafting]

His executors were to be his wife, Katherine, John Potts's mother, and Richard Smith, Doctor of Physic. Smith was 'one of Her Majesty's physicians', presumably attending him when he made this death bed will. They were not to have any benefit themselves other than a chain of gold each to the value of £40 but his 'now wife' was to have all his 'plate and household stuff and implements of household'. This was to avoid any confusion with his first wife, Constance.

John Potts's will and IPM

John Potts was next to die, at the end of the same year. His original will was made on 5th November 1593 in Mannington with a substantial codicil added at Eltham on 7th December 1597, just four days before he was buried.[3] It was proved on 18th May 1598 by Anne Potts his relict and executrix. Anne was to have been supported by overseers - her father and her uncle Edward Dodge and John's brother Philip Potts - although by the time she came to prove the will all of them had died. The original will was witnessed by Lawrence Sargenson (Itteringham's rector at the time and as first in the list possibly the scribe), John Gallant and Edmond Nicolls, both good local Norfolk names. The witnesses to the codicil were Edmund Stuble (an original transcription error for Stubbes), James Twiste (then Eltham's rector), Philip Potts his brother and Henry Collinson.[4]

In 1593 he was 'of Itteringham' and asked to be buried in the church there; this strengthens the argument that, after the purchase of the Mannington estate and his marriage, he and his wife Anne had lived in Itteringham and not at the Hall. By 1597 he was 'of Mannington', perhaps implying that by this time he had taken up residence in Mannington Hall after John Dodge's death even though Anne's mother was still alive and presumably living there. Certainly he styled himself in that manner from 1595 at the end of the Dodge's ten year lease of the estate. His will and codicils reflected the growth of his holdings as well as his inherited lands. His IPM (which was not taken until a year later) was held at the church house in the parish of St Clement Middlesex, reflecting his London interests, and sealed on 23rd January 1599.[5]

After covering his London and Hitchin property as detailed in Chapter 3, the IPM went on to examine his Norfolk holdings. After the main Mannington section the enquiry detailed his holdings in Oulton and East Dereham:

> And they say John Pott was seised of and in 280 acres of land in Irmingland and Oulton recently of John Betts and that he was seised of all the premises in this IPM and by his will left to Anne his wife and male heirs when 21 years.

> And they say that before his death John Pott was seised of a third of a manor called Mouldes als Colburne and 400 acres in East Dereham, Shipdham Howe, North Tuddenham, Elsinge, Swanton Morley Westfielde Scaringe and Dillington which he leaves by will to Anne to the intent that she should sell for her better ease at not less than £650.

The final section detailed the original manorial dependencies of all the premises:

> The manor of Mannington, the lands [parishes given] and the advowson of Itteringham were held of Thomas Thetford esq as of his manor of Myklehall in Saxthorpe and elsewhere in Norfolk by half a knights fee and valued at pa 40 marks

> The manor of Wolterton and half the advowson of Wolterton and all lands and tenements in Wolterton were held of Sir Thomas Cecill, Lord Burghley as of his manor of Castle Acre valued at 5 marks

> And that he held the 280 acres in Irmingland lately John Betts, of Sir Christopher Heydon as of his manor of Woodhall in Baconsthorpe by half a knights fee and valued at £10

> And that the third of a manor called Moldes and 260 acres parcell of the 400 acres of land in East Dereham [etc, including Yaxham] were held of the Queen as of her manor of East Dereham and third part of the rent 53s and 8d and valued £10

> And that the said third of the 140 acres remaining of the 400 acres were held of Henry Gawdy esq as of his manor of Shipdam by one-third part of annual rent of 22s 8d

> And that John Potts was so seised, and after 20th December 40 Elizabeth [1597] died at Eltham, and Katherine recently wife of Edmund Lumner and afterward the wife of John Dodge, and Katherine recently wife of Roger Potts father of John Potts and the said Anne recently wife of John Potts, at the time of his death survived him and were in full life at Mannington.

In amongst the evidence was the fact that the two elderly widowed matriarchs, Katherine Leighton/Wigmore/Lumner/Callard/Dodge and Katherine Boteler/Potts/ Doddes/Flower, the pivotal players in John Potts's life, and his wife Anne Dodge/ Potts were, in 1597, all alive and well and living together in Mannington (at least some of the time).

To understand his will better, it is necessary to consider Irmingland, the small parish now part of Oulton, next to Itteringham.

Irmingland

In April 1593 Potts had agreed in writing to purchase from John and Margaret Bettes, a farm and 280 acres of land in Irmingland, adjacent to the Mannington estate, but the transaction was not completed by the November when John made his will. He drew attention to this in his will by stressing that he wanted the purchase to go ahead should anything happen to him. In his last codicils in 1597, he said the purchase had been made. He was obviously keen to take any opportunity to reinforce his rights to the property. While this may have to do with the general challenges to his Mannington title, the explanation may have more to do with the history of Irmingland.

The parish of Irmingland had originally been divided between two manors, which became known by the names of the families there in the fourteenth century - Hastings and Qwytfot or Whytfot [Whitefoot].[6] By the 1440s these manors had come into the common ownership of the Bettes family of Irmingland and Oulton and for 150 years they remained in the family, with occasional deeds conveying the property between family members and feoffees. By the 1590s the Bettes family was clearly intent on selling off the whole of their Irmingland estate. John Bettes was the grandson of William Lumner, the builder of Mannington and as such was part relation, part friend and neighbour. John Potts got in quickly with a bid for as much of the land as he could afford. Since Bettes was obviously selling all his Irmingland property, Potts may have been constrained by his finances from making a more substantial purchase here. Despite being in pocket by £2,000 (as Katherine Dodge was still alive) and not having to pay £100 a year to Lumner, other demands on him led him to write in his codicil that he was less well-off than he had expected to be.[7]

The farm that Potts bought was then known as The White House (now Elmerdale Farm) and it remained in the family until the sale to Walpole in 1737.[8] Unfortunately the purchase deeds have not survived but a later note of 1605 recorded that Potts had bought his Irmingland and Oulton property from Bettes for £860 on 3rd September 1597.[9] John did not have any other lands in that parish so he may have been looking ahead, assuming the agreement would go ahead, when he put the following clause in his will in 1593 for his brother Philip:

> 'Item. I bequeath to my said brother one annuity of £13 yearly during his natural life so that he convey and release to my wife and heirs whatsoever estate right and interest shall be in him at the time

of my death of in or to any lands tenements goods or chattels which either have been mine or procured by me to be conveyed or passed unto him in trust in confidence to my use for the which he hath not disbursed any sum of money and so that he become bound to my executrix in the sum of £200 to leave and bequeath at the time of his death the then residue of one term for 40 years which he the said Philip now hath of and in one annuity of £20 issuing out of certain lands situate in Irmingland and Oulton within the county of Norfolk to my younger sons or son.'

Presumably the purchase was to be made with Philip as trustee and he would receive, for up to 40 years, a lifetime annuity of £20 and after his death the residue of the 40 year term would pass to John's younger sons. By implication the land itself and the balance of its revenues would be part of the main estate going to his eldest son, John (later Sir John). There is no evidence that in the long term Sir John's brother Charles had revenues from the Irmingland property but this additional provision for the younger children may have contributed to Sir John Potts's much later decision to sell the London properties to Charles at below market value.

At the end of that will, he returned to the agreement to buy the Bettes lands in Irmingland:

> 'Item. Whereas certain articles of agreement dated the 8th day of April last past [ie 1593] are set down between one John Bettes of Irmingland in the said county of Norfolk gent and me the said John Potts for a sale to be made by the said John Bettes to me the said John Potts of certain lands lying in Irmingland and Oulton my will is that my executrix shall proceed with the said purchase as near to the meaning and true intent of the said articles as may be and either according to such draft of assurance as I the said John Potts have caused to be made for and concerning the same or by such other reasonable assurance as by the counsel learned of my executrix shall be devised.
>
> And if my said executrix shall not within one year next after my death perform the same then I will my said executrix within one year after her default or negligence herein shall pay to my supervisors £440 they executing sufficient bond unto her that they within three years after my death will cause good absolute conveyance and assurance to be made of the said lands in those articles mentioned to the use of my said executrix during her natural life and after to the heir male of the body of me the said John Potts forever.
>
> And my will and meaning is that the said last lands be conveyed to the same uses if the purchase thereof be despatched and performed by my said executrix as before touched.'

The implication is that he had £440 ready for the purchase, perhaps as a part payment still due of the total £860, and if Anne did not complete the deal, the supervisors should take over.

In December 1597 he added a codicil, to update the position:

> 'Whereas of late I the said John Potts purchased and bought certain lands and tenements of John Bettes of Irmingland in the county aforesaid gent in assurance whereof the wife of the said John Bettes and Henry Bettes his son joined in conveyance together with the said John Bettes at the denomination appointment and to the use of me the said John Potts to Mr Augustine Pagrave [sic] Thomas Asheley [sic] Edmond Stoble [sic] and Ralph Dodge clerk as by their several conveyances to them had and made may appear my will intent and meaning is and by these presents I do will devise and bequeath that the several conveyances of the said lands late John Bettes and the several feoffees and grantees of the said lands and of every of them shall be and shall stand seized of the said lands of the several uses and limitations in and by this schedule of addition to my last will and testament limited intended and appointed for the true performance whereof according to the intent and meaning of this schedule of addition to my last will and testament and according to the trust reposed of the said feoffees I earnestly entreat the said feoffees grantees and every of them to be ready at all times upon request to them made to execute all acts they and every of them shall be required unto for the accomplishment of this my schedule of addition to my last will and testament by reason of which purchase of the said lands and tenements late Bettes and by means of divers other things happened to the charge of my estate since my last said will and testament made and ordained whereby many alterations and changes have grown in and to my estate so as my said wife nor children cannot so sufficiently be provided for as in and by my said last will and testament my intent and meaning I expressed.'

The list of feoffees or trustees is interesting. Pagrave was Sir Augustine Palgrave of Barningham near Mannington and the family soon features in the story of the next Potts generation. Thomas Astley of Melton Constable was a distant relative through an earlier marriage of a Lumner girl. Edmond Stoble was the lawyer Edmund Stubbes - the argument for this identification given weight by this 'Stoble' acting as a trustee. Ralph Dodge clerk was the rector of Mannington and distant cousin of John Dodge. The acquisition from Bettes came at the time when that family was moving out of their Irmingland estate, the balance of which was sold to the Catlyns and from them passed to the Bacons who in the early years of the seventeenth century built a fine hall at Irmingland. Potts was probably aware of their intention to sell up and wanted to make sure his purchase was clearly separated from their tenure of the two ancient manors in Irmingland.

It is evident from the last few lines of the above clause that Potts's finances had come under pressure between 1593 and 1597 both from this purchase and 'divers other things', perhaps as a result of the suits against him. Or perhaps his legal practice had gone into decline after the death of his key contacts between 1590 and 1597 - Francis Flower, Sir Christopher Hatton, John Dodge, Peter Houghton, Edward Buggin, Francis Boteler, and others around him. (Edward Dodge was also out of the picture and would die a few weeks after Potts.) Or worse, had Edward Coke who was fast rising to the top of his profession so blackened his reputation that no-one wanted (or dared) to hire him?

The rest of John's will

John Potts's will is not wholly typical of the period, even though many other wills of the time show concern for the inheritance of their real estate. The will and codicil are manifestly the arrangements of a lawyer and one at that who was extremely concerned about the title to his various lands and tenements. Lengthy and repetitive legalistic clauses bind his close relations to perform his will and honour a number of pre-existing leases or other deeds relating to their interests in his estate. His concerns are easier to understand following the Lumner actions in chancery and Star Chamber. The will is of such interest on multiple fronts that some further complex sections are quoted here verbatim. Odd repetitions and minor errors occur, made by the original transcriber - hardly surprising given the wordy and complicated material he had to transcribe!

First John left all his lands and tenements to Anne until his male heir attained the age of 21. His East Dereham lands, bought of Edward Palmer, were to be sold - the freehold for not less than £660 and the copyhold and freehold together for at least £800. This money was to be equally divided among his younger children, not including his heir. If Anne did not sell within two or three years the lands were to be equally divided among the children at their full age and meanwhile she should use the profits for their maintenance. If she married without the consent of the supervisors or overseers then they should look after the lands until the children came of age. If the male heirs died before they were 21 then Anne had these lands until the daughters were 18 when they were to have them, Anne only retaining a £40 yearly annuity.

This £40 appears to have been bequeathed to her specifically by conveyance from the profits of the tenements in Gray's Inn Lane. Presumably this was the fixed sum paid to Potts or his mother for the head lease granted to Jasper Fisher and his successors. The reversion after her death of the £40, any surplus above it and the reversion of the Gray's Inn property itself was to go to their son Drury and to his heirs. If he had no issue then to John's second son and so on from son to son. If no sons survived then the inheritance of all the real estate passed to the daughters, then to John's brother Philip Potts and only finally would it default to Anne for life and then to John's right heirs.

Having warmed up with these clauses, which of themselves show that his arrangements for his wife were already subject to a formal deed, Potts moved on to his mother Katherine Flower (whom he didn't preclude from marrying a fourth time despite her third still being alive), Jane Lumner and the Dodges:

> 'Item. I will and bequeath to my dearly beloved mother one annuity of £20 yearly during her natural life so that she and whatsoever husband she shall be married unto for the time being within one year after my death by some good and reasonable devise in law by recognisance of a competent penalty or otherwise to give or make assurance to my executrix not to alter her or their or either of their estates or estate or interest of in or to any lands or tenements whereof she my said mother or they are possessed or seized in her right and that the same be not altered betwixt the date of this my testament and the hour or instant of my death otherwise than by lease for 21 years without reservation of a competent rent to her and her heirs.

> And that she my said mother nor any husband of hers for the time being do or shall avoid [void] any lease or grant [by] me made to her during her widowhood or coverture while the rents thereupon reserved to her [are] from time to time paid within the times in the said leases or grants limited during her widowhood or coverture.'

This must refer to his mother's life interest, by his father's will, in all the family's London area real estate before it would pass to John. It seems that John had come to a lease-based agreement to pay his mother an annuity of this £20 to buy out her interest and ensure the reversion of the property to him or his executor after his mother's death. The clause in his will sought to prevent her from breaking the lease while the rents due were being paid to her as agreed.

> 'Item. I will and bequeath to my sister Lumner 200 marks to be paid her within two years. And to each of her daughters £200 to be paid at their ages of 18 years.

> Memorandum I do give all these three last legacies upon condition that my said sister Lumner shall at the payment of the 200 marks given to her deliver in as her deeds into the hands of my wife to the use of mine heir for the time being and of his and her heirs a general release good and available in law of all actions and demands whatsoever.'

This clause was aimed at getting Jane Lumner to call off her actions. It strongly implies that by 1593 Jane Lumner was already, four years ahead of the chancery action, pursuing demands of Potts. She may have been made aware of the clause before her subsequent chancery actions but thought it too little and too late. It seems likely that Potts would have used it as part of his negotiations with her and it may have some bearing on Jane not going to chancery until 1597. If she knew about it she was sacrificing a certain benefit from his will in favour of the hope of a larger settlement from chancery.

> 'Item. I give to my very good father and mother Dodge £100 to be paid within one year after my decease so that all leases for years after my mother Dodge her death to him made of Mannington with their appurtenances and of all other hereditaments and lands therewith heretofore occupied be cancelled and surrendered or redelivered absolutely and freely to my executrix within the said time.'

Again he referred to the purchase deeds of Mannington having had within them formal lease arrangements for the Dodges to continue living there, reflecting Katherine Dodge's life interest in the estate. John Dodge had been granted a lease which would have enabled him to continue there even after Katherine's death. This clause enabled Anne, on payment of £100, to cancel the lease at the death of her mother even if her father was still alive and thus ensure the inheritance of Mannington for herself and her son - John Dodge's interest in Mannington was therefore effectively solely in the right of his wife while she lived. (In fact this all became irrelevant as John Dodge died about a year before Potts.)

Next Potts left a piece of plate worth 40s each to his aunt Buggin (his mother's sister Elizabeth), his cousin William Buggin, his uncles Richard Butler (his mother's brother) and Edward Dodge and to his brother and sister Houghton (Anne's sister Mary and husband Peter Houghton of London) or their two children at Anne's discretion.

To all his servants except Robert Butler that had dwelt with him for the year before his death he left a year's wages. To Robert Butler he left £10 so that he would remain his servant until John died. Robert Butler was the son of John's uncle William Boteler.

The poor of Itteringham were to receive 40s. The residue of his goods and chattels were to go to Anne so that she would give all his children an education 'answerable to their degree' and bring them up until the sons were 21 and until the daughters' marriages or full age. If she did not, then the supervisors were to spend £60 annually, equally divided among the children.

After noting various corrections in a few lines of the will it was signed. By December 1597 Potts was then sick in body and his codicil included a rather lengthier commendation of his soul to god, seeking forgiveness for his sins and transgressions. This annex to his earlier will was regarding his 'worldly estate for the advancement of my wife and provision of my children'.

The codicil went on to make rather similar arrangements for his wife, son and younger children as the original will, particularly regarding the Irmingland property. His emphasis on the non-Mannington manor lands showed his determination that they did not get swept up into the Robert or Jane Lumner actions.

'Now my will mind intent and meaning is and by these presents
I do will devise and bequeath that what benefit and advantage by
means of the change of my estate as aforesaid by any other way or
means whatsoever my said wife cannot now have take and enjoy
according to the intent and purpose of any conveyance or former
will whatsoever that she my said wife shall have take and enjoy so
much and as large and ample advantage and benefit out of all my
goods and chattels I do now possess and hold and out of all the
lands and tenements late as aforesaid purchased of Bettes as by any
former conveyance or will hath been to her out of any other lands
tenements goods or chattels limited or appointed.

And what shall be remaining and overplus of my said lands and
tenements late Bettes lands over and above that shall be by means
of this schedule of addition to my last will and testament due to
my said wife I by these presents do will devise and bequeath to
Drury Potts my eldest son and his heirs for the provision of my
younger children already born and of that child wherewith my
said wife is great with child my will and intent and meaning is and
by these presents I do devise will and bequeath to my said wife
all my Dereham and all other my lands in any other town there
near adjoining lying and being to the intent she my said wife with
convenient speed shall alien and sell my said lands to the best profit
and not under the sum of £750 current money and the money
thereof coming I will devise and bequeath shall be equally divided
among my said younger children living at the time of the said sale.'

While the East Dereham lands seemed by 1597 to be worth only £750, Potts
still left his Irmingland and Dereham lands or the profits from them to his younger
children, with the Irmingland property ultimately to pass to Drury his eldest son
and heir.

'And if it shall please god that my mother will vouchsafe to provide
for my children John and Frances now remaining with her then I
will devise and bequeath at the discretion of my said mother and
wife part of the portion of those two younger children then living
desiring my said wife in all the tender and true affection of heart
that is and hath been between us with a motherly care and duty
of a mother and wife tenderly and carefully to bring up in the fear
of god my hereafter fatherlies [fatherless] children providing so for
them and their maintenance being brought up as according to the
intent and meaning of this schedule of addition to my last will and
testament every of my children severally may have what to them is
limited and appointed.'

In such a stiff and formal will and codicil Potts's statement of love for his wife is very endearing and implies a loving relationship. Anne was pregnant with their daughter Anne who would be born just a month or so after Potts died. If Potts was too ill to travel to Mannington, his wife was clearly in no state to travel to his sickbed in Kent. Heavily pregnant, it seems likely that Anne did not travel to Eltham and that this was in a sense his farewell message to her. And perhaps at this emotional time he was having guilt feelings about his treatment of others:

> 'Further I heartily desire and entreat my said wife if hereafter it shall appear to her I have wronged or injured any person that she will recompense the wronged person what I have injured or wronged them in some part of recompense.
>
> For the travail and pains Mistress Frances Kettell hath taken with me in my sickness I give and bequeath to the said Mistress Kettell my cloth gown now remaining at Eltham at my mother's house in memorial of my true zeal and affection.
>
> To my well deserving friends I desire my said wife at her discretion to bestow upon every of my good friends here mentioned a ring with a death's head whereby to remember me deceased, viz: to Sir Thomas Vavisor [Vavasour] Knt and his lady [Mary, Anne's sister]; to Mr Augustine Pagrave [Palgrave]; to my cousin Mr Thomas Asheley [Astley]; to Mr Edmond Stoble [Stubbes]; to my cousin Mr William Buggin and to Mr Ralph Dodge clerk. The rest of my good friends who by infirmity of sickness I have omitted I desire to pardon me ascribing my omission of them to the infirmity of my sickness.'

For details on the Kettell family of Hertfordshire see Family Notes 8: Hertfordshire Families.

Philip Potts's will

Next to go was John's brother and fellow lawyer. Philip Potts gent of Eltham made his will on 26th January 1598 and it was proved on 8th March by his mother as executrix.[10] He may have contracted the same illness that killed his brother. Philip made no reference to any wife or children and his legacies went largely to his Potts and Boteler relations. To his mother Mistress Katherine Flower he left £100 owed him by a bond of Edward Dodge, his uncle. From his annuity from the Irmingland property he left £6 a year to his godson John Potts and £4 a year to his 'nephew Francis' Potts. This was an odd error for niece Frances - his brother having no son Francis. Odd because both the children, John and his sister Frances, were down in Eltham.

To Mistress Frances 'Kettill' he left £5 a year. To his goddaughter 'Phillipp[a]' Richardson two silver items that he had in London - implying a Potts residence was being kept up there, possibly a family home in The Bishop or nearby. To Richard

Richardson and his wife he left 10s each - presumably Philippa's parents. To his uncle Richard 'Buttiler' he left his great ring with a topaz stone. Minor bequests to friends and servants followed and then to a William 'Pottes' he left his cloth gown, best cloak, black rapier, saddle and bridles and one of his hats and a ruff band. William's wife was to have a shirt, a cap and a ruff band and their daughter Frances was to have a silver spoon that he had at Eltham. William Potts was also one of the witnesses to the will. He must have been a close relative, but not a son since no relationship was given by Philip. Nor did William and his children feature in Philip's mother's will unlike all her grandchildren by John Potts. See Family Notes 11: Potts of Eltham for further thoughts on William Potts.

Katherine Flower's will

The older generation of Potts all died out with Katherine Flower's death in December 1598, the same year as her son Philip. Her will was made on 21ˢᵗ December 1598 the day before her death and proved on 3ʳᵈ January 1599.[11] Although she described herself as of Eltham Kent and the widow of Francis Flower esq, one of Her Majesty's gentlemen pensioners, Katherine requested burial next to her father and mother Boteler at Watton-at-Stone and left £100 for her funeral charges - the will was clearly that of an affluent woman.

From her two manors of 'Blackwell Hall and Mordanntes Fee in Buckinghamshire', she left a number of bequests. Her executors (Sir Philip Boteler, her cousin Ralph Coningsby esq and her brother Richard Boteler esq of Stapleford near Watton-at-Stone) were to hold the manors for 21 years after her death and then any residue of rents and profits from them was to go to her heir and grandson - John Potts (Sir). To Frances Potts her grandchild and goddaughter she left £5 a year for life and to young Charles Potts £10 annually for life. If her heir apparent, John Potts (Sir), died without issue before the age of 21 then his sisters Frances, Katherine and Anne Potts were to receive £10 a year for life equally divided between them. Frances was also to have £200 at 18 or marriage; Katherine and Anne £100 and Charles £100 at 21 or marriage. She included a clause to the effect that nobody was to interfere with these legacies during the grandchildren's minority. She left various silver items to her brother Richard Boteler and his wife, her nephew Sir Philip Boteler, her cousin Sir Drew Drewrye [Drury], her nephew William Buggin and a number of other Boteler nephews and cousins. John Potts was to have her fairest basin and ewer of silver, various silver pots and £200 at marriage or 21. She also left £4 to Robert Boteler son of her brother William Boteler. This was presumably the Robert Butler in John Potts's 1598 will, with its implication that Robert was a servant of some status in the household.

Frances Potts who had been living at Eltham with Katherine was to be brought up by Katherine's niece Elizabeth Graveley, the only child of her brother Richard Boteler. Elizabeth was to have £10 a year until Frances was 18 or married 'for charge of her diet for as long as she stays with my said niece'. Elizabeth had married Mr Rowland Graveley in 1592, a younger son of the Graveley family of Hitchin and

Graveley, who was to have £20 for his pains and trouble. Sadly Elizabeth too was soon to be buried in Watton-at-Stone. After February 1601 little cousin Frances would have returned to her mother at Mannington.[12] The tradition of giving your eldest daughter a good start in their social life by setting them up in a wealthy household with good connections (especially court ones such as at Eltham) was a long-standing one and did not reflect a lack of feeling by their mother. To her daughter-in-law (John Potts's widow) by now the Lady Anne Heydon, Katherine left her 'best jewel which I shall own at the time of my death and my nest of gilt bowls promised'. Other minor bequests went to the poor of Watton, Eltham and St Andrew Holborn. Frances Kettell was to have £10 and all her other servants £4. Richard Howe her servant (also mentioned in Philip's will) and John Eyer goldsmith of Holborn were to have 40s a year each for life and Eyer a further '£10 for the pains trust and travail he is by me employed'. The witnesses included John Weston - possibly the former apprentice of her husband Roger Apott way back in 1560.

More sadness for Anne Potts

Just as 1596-98 saw the death of all the senior Potts family and the heir Drury Potts (see below), so the same period saw the death of Anne Potts's father, mother and uncle. John Dodge died intestate in 1596. Edward Dodge died in late December 1597. Katherine Dodge, the other matriarch, died in December 1598, eleven days before her namesake Katherine Flower.[13]

Anne's father John Dodge probably died in about October 1596 - he was certainly dead by March 1597 when Katherine answered as a widow in the Star Chamber action. However the administration of his estate was not immediately granted and it was not until July 1598 that it was recorded as being granted to Edward Dodge, Sir Christopher Heydon and Anne now his wife, daughter of John Dodge.[14] By this time however, John's brother Edward Dodge had also died, in December 1597, so the grant of administration was already well out of date in including him. Presumably he had been alive when the application papers had first been drawn up.

Although an inventory for John Dodge survives from December 1598, signed by Edmund Stubbes, Robert Gervis or Jervis and others, unfortunately Sir Christopher and Dame Anne did not credit her father with any belongings.[15] The inventory seems to have been overlooked, not being done until about two years after his death. Perhaps Edmund Stubbes the family lawyer reminded them of its necessity since John Dodge was shown to have had a legal claim on part of Mannington's profits. The inventory recorded, as his only asset, a lease of the manor of Mannington with three years left to run and worth 200 marks, presumably this being the total over the three years. This was the arrangement referred to in John Potts's will. A formal lease would typically have been for seven years or a multiple of seven years. So this particular lease would have been made in about December 1594 to run to December 1601 - entirely consistent with an annual pension from the estate of £50 after Potts had taken full control in early 1595. No doubt the Dodges had been permitted to remain in Mannington Hall rent free.

Further tragedy hit Anne in the summer of 1598, with the death of her eldest son Drury of whom little is known except his name. Drury had been named for the family of John Potts's maternal grandmother Elizabeth Drury the wife of Sir Philip Boteler and Katherine's mother. Elizabeth was one of the daughters of Sir Robert Drury of Hawstead in Suffolk by his first wife Anne daughter of Sir Philip Calthorpe.[16] The Drury clan was linked by marriage to many other substantial Norfolk families, including the Yelvertons. Elizabeth Drury's brother, Sir Robert of Hedgerley Bucks was the father of Sir Drue Drury of Riddlesworth Norfolk, a noted courtier and royal official who had for a time helped Sir Amyas Paulet as a keeper of Mary Queen of Scots. He was active in Norfolk administration and in 1606 was an executor for Sir Edward Clere of Blickling. Young Drury Potts might in fact have been named for Sir Drue who, if his godfather, could have been a source of patronage for John Potts's legal practice. Sir Drue was certainly close to his Boteler cousins - one of his daughters Frances married Sir Robert Boteler of Woodhall.[17]

Little Drury had not been given the opportunity of living in Eltham with Frances and John (the next son in line) so perhaps his health had always given concern. It seems likely that he died in or soon after May 1598. Unusually his baptism and burial may have been in Mannington since no parish register entry survives for him in Itteringham. (Similarly he did not appear in the Holborn register.) He had certainly died well before December 1598 when Katherine Flower made her grandson John her heir. Poor Anne, still mourning her husband's death six months ago and nursing the little baby he had never seen, had now lost her eldest child who could only have been about 8 years old.[18] She had also lost her father, stepfather and uncle so the two Katherines probably encouraged her to see their neighbour Sir Christopher Heydon of Baconsthorpe as a knight in shining armour (which only two years after Cadiz would have been quite appropriate). If Drury had been alive at the time of Anne's remarriage, no doubt Sir Christopher would have moved quickly to make the eldest Potts son his ward to guarantee the profits from the family's properties. There is no sign that Drury was ever a ward, although John was to become one immediately.[19]

No doubt Anne sought stability in her life amidst so much death and legal difficulty and Sir Christopher was a lively character. They were married on May 29th 1598 at St Andrew Holborn, where her late husband's property was.[20] Perhaps they felt a wedding away from the local gossips would be best. By the end of the year Anne's mother too was dead. The nuncupative (spoken) will of Katherine Dodge widow was proved on 22nd December 1598 only eleven days after her death.[21] Her witnesses - Edmund Stub[be]s, Elizabeth Page (no doubt of the major Saxthorpe family) and Dorothy Langdon (a half relation through the Lumner connection) - asserted that Katherine, from the beginning of October 1598, during her final illness, had repeatedly stated that she intended all her goods and possessions to go only to her daughter the Lady Anne Heydon wife to Sir Christopher and not to any other of her children. This perhaps was reward for Anne living in Itteringham and Mannington and remaining close to her mother. But even more likely it reflected the fact that the remaining £2,000 deferred payment for Mannington would fairly soon fall due to Anne's sister Mary and would have to be paid by Anne from John Potts's estate.

So, by the end of 1598, Anne Potts had lost her husband, both her parents, her uncle, her mother-in-law and her third husband, her Potts and Houghton brothers-in-law, and her eldest son. And now she and her new husband Sir Christopher Heydon had to continue the defence against both Jane and Robert Lumner's claims on the Mannington estate. At the same time Anne also had to deal with difficulties over reclaiming the Potts family deeds and writings regarding Mannington from the heir of her uncle Edward Dodge.

Back in chancery

In May 1598 a bill of complaint in chancery was lodged by Anne Potts, acting as widow and executrix of John Potts deceased, with her son 'Drewrie', the heir of John against Robert Bathurst.[22] Robert was the eldest nephew, main heir and sole executor of the will of Edward Dodge who had died on 23rd December 1597 at Lechlade in Gloucestershire where he had his main estate.[23] Unmarried and childless, Edward's will exclusively featured nephews, nieces and a grand niece. His IPMs showed that when he died his niece Dame Mary Vavasour (Mary Dodge/Houghton) was aged '30 or more' and her sister Anne Potts was '28 or more'.[24] His houses and lands in Wrotham and Leybourne in Kent went to his niece the Lady Vavasour. His Kent IPM described the property as the capital messuage called Comp, lands at Wrotham and Leybourne and 129 acres enclosed in Leybourne and Ightham called Little Comp and Ballocksmyths. Mary was to pay £50 a year to her sister and her Potts nephews. Anne was also to get another £50 annuity from Edward Clampard, another nephew by Edward's sister's second husband, who shared the proceeds after debts of the Lechlade property with Robert Bathurst. Other Clampard and Helinge or Heylyn nephews and nieces were mentioned as well as his (great) 'niece the little Elizabeth Houghton' - the younger of Mary's two daughters. See Family Notes 2: Bathurst, Vavasour and Clampards for more detail on the Dodge family and their Kent origins.

According to the chancery complaint, John Potts had entrusted for safekeeping to Edward Dodge 'a great part of the evidences writings and writing material touching and concerning the title' to his various manors messuages and lands in Norfolk, London and elsewhere. Dodge had apparently put them in a bag or box and written on it 'evidences concerning my nephew Pott'. But uncle Dodge had died within a week or two of John Potts's death. Since when Anne had 'gently entreated' Bathurst to produce the documents, but he refused to do so. She worried that this risked her and her son being disinherited from their property and had no remedy at common law and so hoped she would get a writ of subpoena on Bathurst to force him to chancery with the writings. Regardless of how much of all this was true, with the Lumner actions still continuing, Anne was right to be concerned about her ability to prove title. Interestingly Anne's lawyer who signed the complaint was Henry Hobart

- later a senior judge and in due course to become a near neighbour when he purchased the Blickling estate from the Cleres.

It wasn't long before Anne and her husband Sir Christopher Heydon had to answer a bill of complaint by Jane Lumner widow of Edmund.[25] While their answer was not explicitly dated, on the reverse it does have in a contemporary hand '29th January 1604' [ie 1605]. This almost certainly connects it to a chancery order of Michaelmas term 1602 when Jane Lumner, in her suit against Henry Landman (or Lanman), won an order to bring the bonds (which Henry was still holding in accord with the original agreement) into chancery, reinforcing a previous subpoena to do so.[26] Jane had wanted the bonds brought into court for Sir Christopher and Anne to be acquainted with their content. The court agreed to the bonds coming to court but said the bonds were to be safely kept by chancery rather than handed over to Jane. Once produced Lanman would then be discharged. If Jane wanted to take away the bonds she would have to make a separate action against the Heydons and prove cause why she should have them. This she clearly attempted since a chancery order of Michaelmas 1602 showed Jane Lumner being granted a commission to question witnesses in her action against Sir Christopher Heydon and Dame Anne.[27]

Presumably Jane Lumner had launched her suit fairly soon after the death of Katherine Dodge in December 1598 when the deferred payments for Mannington would have fallen due. By 1604 the Heydons said they had paid the sum due two years after Katherine's death. Unfortunately, Jane's bills of complaint against Lanman and the Heydons have not survived but presumably she was still claiming the maintenance money from the other bond, if not more.

The Heydons then brought up the whole question of her marriage! They pointed out that Jane was 'only involved' because she was the executrix of Edmund Lumner - a fact she had not made clear in her complaint. They accepted that it was generally said that Jane had at some time been Edmund Lumner's wife, but they claimed that it had been when he was 'under marriageable years' - under 14 years of age. So, the Heydons were arguing that the original marriage had been formally dissolved when Edmund was under 14 and that this had been reaffirmed when he was about 19 or 20. Being still a minor and 'unmarried' he was made a ward of court until his majority. By implication they were saying that Edmund and Jane may have had children together subsequently but were never legally married and that therefore Jane acted in chancery only as Edmund's executrix not as his widow. The suggestion that her children were illegitimate would of course weaken substantially the emotional strength of the case of an apparently defrauded widow with young children. It may also have been a calculated deeply wounding personal attack against this openly catholic woman.

Jane said she should have the bonds and the benefits included in them (ie, the bonds, deed and money described in the 1597 action, being the last deferred part of the payment for Mannington). The Heydons then introduced a completely new point by saying that this would be against the terms of a deed of 30th March 1586 wherein Edmund Lumner had granted the benefits to Peter Houghton gent of London, his half-sister's husband. Also a deed involving John Potts and Henry

Lanman concerning the 'baylement of the said obligations' showed that it was Edmund's intention that Peter Houghton should have the benefits and by implication that Potts had accepted the assignment of his bonds from Lumner to Houghton. So the Heydons claimed that Jane could not take the bonds from Houghton or Lanman or their executors and that she could not claim that any benefit ought to go to her, since Edmund had given away the benefits during his lifetime!

The reference to Peter Houghton having some or all of the benefits through yet another deed is intriguing. Dated well after Edmund's sale of the estate to Potts, it showed that Lumner had borrowed yet more money. This time he had tapped his brother-in-law Houghton, who had sought some security for the loan. Lumner had assigned his whole interest in the Potts obligations relating to the large deferred payment to Houghton. Jane would not be entitled to any payment until whatever Lumner owed Houghton was repaid. She would have to deal with Houghton as the bond holder for her money, if indeed any residue might still be due to her. It is of course very interesting that neither Potts nor Lanman made any reference in 1597 to Peter Houghton having any rights to the proceeds of the obligations, nor did they mention the existence of any such written assignment of the bonds. Perhaps Potts held back this information on the basis that since Katherine Dodge was still alive his defence was sufficient as it was and he was happy the full details of the arrangements should be kept secret. Something could be kept in reserve in case any further action emerged.

Jane Lumner was now up against a new problem. Peter Houghton had died on the last day of 1596 and she would have to deal with his executors over the assignment. His wife Mary, to whom the deferred payment would now be due, had married Sir Thomas Vavasour. So effectively, Jane was facing the challenge of trying to pursue two knights of the realm for monies to which she may not have had a legitimate claim. Jane Lumner faced formidable foes with what appears to have been a very weak case.

The Heydons concluded that if anything was due on the bonds it was not for them to answer for it. And although Jane claimed that John Potts had goods and chattels worth £6,000 or £7,000 at his death, they had had his goods valued by 'honest and indifferent persons' at only 1,000 marks (£666). Unfortunately the inventory, which would have been fascinating, has not survived. They also noted that 'the said bond of £3,000' had a payment day of two years after the death of Mrs Dodge and that they had fully administered that sum or thereabouts (presumably only the agreed £2,000) at that time. The implication was that there was nothing due to Jane as executrix and that they had paid the money due to Peter Houghton's executrix, Mary and Sir Thomas Vavasour.

The Heydons also said that John Potts in his lifetime was 'much troubled and impeached' about the manor of Mannington sold to him by Edmund Lumner (and for which the said money was to be paid) by Robert Lumner who claimed title to it. Robert Lumner had continued with his quarrels and claims since Potts's death and had made, or caused to be made, entries onto the manor. This implies that several years into the new century Robert Lumner had failed to make good his claim to

Mannington or some payment for his alleged stake in it. No formal equity suit by Robert Lumner against the Heydons has been found, but he may well have maintained pressure at common law. His challenge may have failed in his lifetime and would have lapsed with his death in 1604-05 in Hindringham.[28] Nothing further is heard of Jane Lumner in chancery. It seems that the lawsuits disappeared and the Heydons were left to enjoy the peace and quiet of Mannington. John Potts junior (later Sir John) would not, under his father's will, be able to take possession of the estate until he reached 21 in April 1613.

Plate 1. Dame Anne Heydon (1567-1642): born Anne Dodge, married first John Potts esq and then Sir Christopher Heydon.

Plate 2a.
Sir John Potts
1st Baronet
(1592-1673)

Plate 2b.
Dame Ursula Potts
(1588-1647): born
Ursula Willoughby,
married first Sir Clement
Spelman and then Sir
John Potts.

Plate 3. Francis Potts, second son of Sir John and Dame Ursula, died young in Naples c1642.

Plate 4a. Sir John Potts 2nd Baronet (1618-78)

Plate 4b. Ursula Potts, sister of the 2nd Baronet, married Philip Bedingfield.

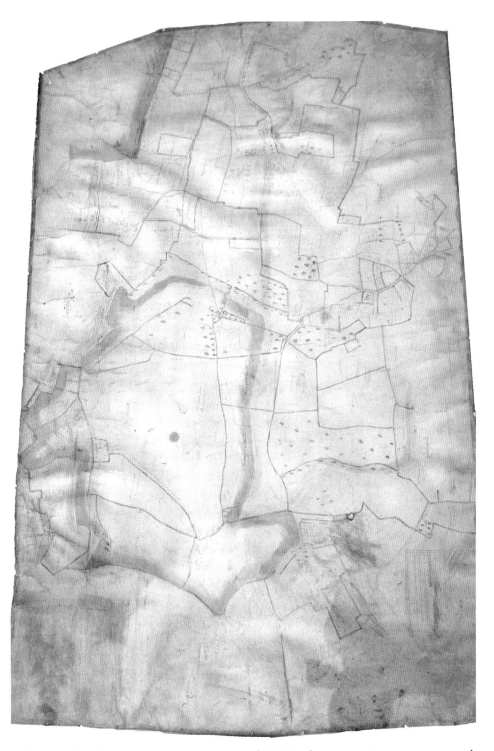

Plate 5. The Mannington estate map of 1595, showing Mannington parish within the green wash.

Plate 6a. Close-up of John Potts's house in Itteringham in 1595

Plate 6b. Close-up of Mannington Hall in 1595

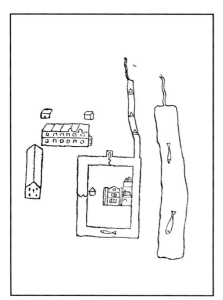

Plate 6c. Close-up from Tomes's sketch of Mannington Hall in 1595

Despite being now very faint, the 1595 map showed the high status house of John Potts at the site now known as Itteringham's Old Rectory. The moated site of Mannington Hall showed the Hall in elevation and a number of farm buildings and cottages nearby. Tomes's version of the map showed some details of the rear range of the Hall and aspects of the farmyard buildings not now legible. However, he omitted some of the buildings that were probably cottages for estate workers. The large building with dormer windows might once have contained the lesser service rooms and household servants' quarters.

Plate 7. Close-up from Mannington estate map of 1742, showing ground plan of the Hall and its extensive rear ranges and surrounding parkland with tree-lined walks.

Plate 8a. Watercolour, probably from the 1830s or 1840s, showing Mannington Hall North facade and its farm buildings.

Plate 8b. Mannington Hall West facade from the same artist and period, showing its partially closed-up state.

PART 2

PINNACLE OF SUCCESS: SIR JOHN POTTS 1ST BARONET

'And you Sir are the man'

Tanner 67.176

Chapter 9

The Heydon Years

John Potts was just 6 years old when his world turned upside down. His father died and in the summer of 1598 his mother Anne speedily remarried, to Sir Christopher Heydon. John was uprooted from Eltham in Kent where he had been living, with his sister Frances, in his grandmother's house. In a mirror-image of events in his father's life, the young child was to grow up in a stepfather's household of a higher status than his own. Now he was living in Norfolk, the heir to the Mannington estate and ward of the larger-than-life figure of Sir Christopher Heydon.

Sir Christopher Heydon 'the impoverished and eccentric representative of that declining family'[1]

Sir Christopher Heydon was born in 1561, the eldest son of Sir William Heydon of Baconsthorpe by his wife Anne, daughter of Sir William Woodhouse of Hickling.[2] Paid for by his grandfather, he attended Peterhouse College, Cambridge leaving with his MA in 1579.

That year Sir William Paston wrote to his aunt suggesting Christopher Heydon as a great catch for her daughter Bridget Paston: 'There is not the like young gent for his personage wisdom learning & staidness of his years in Norfolk Suffolk Essex or Kent and although it hath been reported unto you that his said father was above £6,000 in debt, I would wish you not to listen 'to such slanderous report … he oweth not more above 1000 pounds the which will soon be discharged'.[3] Bridget's mother wasn't impressed and married her daughter to the future Chief Justice Coke. Failing to capture Bridget Paston, and having travelled abroad for a while, Christopher married, in 1582, a Miss Mirabel Rivett, daughter of Sir Thomas Rivett, a London alderman, and Alice Cotton of Chippenham, Cambridgeshire. She brought a portion of £1,500 in their marriage settlement of that year.[4] It seems that she was very young, possibly under-age, at their marriage and the settlement may have indicated betrothal, rather than the start of the marriage itself. Although Baconsthorpe was the main family seat (Christopher was later responsible for refitting the inner gatehouse, dismantling and rebuilding other parts of the Castle), they lived at Sharrington while his father was alive but Saxlingham was to be his preferred home.[5] By Mirabel he had eight children including his two eldest sons William (baptised 19th Sept 1585) and John (baptised 23rd June 1588), both later knighted. Three more of her children were baptised at Saxlingham, Jane (24th November 1586), Miles (20th July 1589) and Thomas (18th January 1591). Sadly Mirabel died on 15th July 1593 aged only 22 years and 6 months, at Sharrington, and was buried at Saxlingham under an ornate tomb covered with symbols drawn from Heydon's great love of astrology.

In his youth, Christopher undertook the roles expected of his rank, apparently with some enthusiasm. He was High Steward of Norwich Cathedral, a Norfolk JP from about 1583 and a commissioner for musters in 1597. Although only 26, he stood for parliament in 1586 writing to Bassingbourne Gawdy to explain why:

> 23 Sept 1586
>
> Good Cousin, being incited by the imoderate bragges of Farmor [*Thomas Farmer*] I take uppon me to stande in election for one of the places in parliament which if my self I did never dreame on unty I was provoked contrary to my expectation; my suite is, good cousin, for yr furtherance upon Munday at 7 of clock at Norwich by the voyces of yr tenants and frends and if I might enjoy the companie of my cousins or of one of them then I doe think it shold do me so much credit as I would bind myself to ride a hundred myle to doe them any pleasure
>
> And this in last my commend to yourself and my cosine your bedfellow
>
> Chris^{fer}.[6]

Thomas Farmer, an enemy of the family, defeated him, but his father and his fellow deputy lieutenant Sir Edward Clere (apparently for once working together) appealed to the Privy Council and a new election was called at which Heydon was returned. However, the House of Commons rejected the second election as the Privy Council interfering improperly in their constitutional rights and seated Thomas Farmer. At the next election in 1588, with the support of the Gawdy family, Heydon was elected. He made some contributions to the work of the parliament when it sat in 1589 and although he did not return to parliament again, he retained a keen interest.

The fighting years

After Mirabel's death in 1593, Sir Christopher seemed to change. Despite the comments of his kinsman Sir William Paston, Christopher had a mercurial and adventurous nature too; this seems to have been a family trait. At the age of 30 Christopher was accused of attacking his great uncle Roger Windham's park and eating his Sunday dinner at Felbrigg (he claimed he and his 14 friends were deer hunting, killed nothing and they had been invited in for a drink by the servants).[7] He and his father, Sir William Heydon had long been at loggerheads. William was a hot-headed man as well as an extravagant one. His own father, Sir Christopher senior, seems to have found him a problem. Despite the fact that Sir Christopher had been a pensioner of Gonville College in 1538 and had granted land to the college when re-founded by Caius, he did not educate his son as would be expected. He had however arranged for his grandson to go to Cambridge. Sir Christopher senior had re-married as his third wife, Agnes Crane of Suffolk shortly before he died in 1580; after his death, Agnes (who had now seen off three husbands) married Sir Edward Clere of Blickling. The retention and use of the house at Saxlingham by his stepmother and her new husband, although legal, was greatly resented by William. As early as 1582 Agnes and Edward had to take William to court to obtain an injunction to leave them in peaceful possession of the properties in which Agnes had a life interest under her former husband's will. Edward Clere wrote to Nathaniel Bacon that 'my cosin Heidon' had made a vicious entry into Saxlingham House. (The house name varied between Saxlingham Hall, Saxlingham Place and Heydon Hall).[8] William, his wife Anne and Miles Corbett esq were named in the injunction. William's aunt Katherine Heydon had married Miles Corbett (later Sir Miles) and she may have claimed some interest in the Saxlingham goods. Interestingly by 1593 Sir William was writing from Saxlingham, so perhaps some accommodation was achieved.

Agnes lived at Blickling Hall, until she sold the estate in 1616. She lived to a grand old age probably dying in 1624. The problem was that Sir Christopher senior had excluded his son William from inheriting - probably wisely - so, after his wife's life interest, all his estates were willed to Sir Christopher his grandson. This could only lead to tension between Sir William and his son. In 1591 Christopher's mother Anne blamed Bacon for setting her son against her and his father because he had given him some advice but William's behaviour was quite sufficient without blaming others.[9] For Christopher's marriage settlement, his father had allowed him £800 a year but this had already been reduced by 200 marks to help with William's debts. The main quarrel arose in 1590 over Sir William's desire to sell estates to pay £11,000 owing to London money lenders. Christopher claimed his grandfather had entailed them to him and petitioned the Privy Council. His father reacted by saying he would raze Baconsthorpe, his principal house, to the ground. The Privy Council told him not to do this on the grounds that it was 'unnatural' and would create a bad precedent. In 1592 Sir William tried to break the entail by going to Star Chamber with minor disputes (Christopher had spoiled his pastures etc) and recording his claims to the estate in the court.[10] The lawsuit dragged on into 1593. Sir William then ignored the entail and made a will on 16th March 1594 bequeathing his real estate to his wife Anne, not his son.[11] However he provided for Sir Christopher to inherit if he, by deed, immediately after Sir William's death agreed to pay his father's debts and make provision for his mother and grandmother - the latter at Saxlingham. These arrangements were to be approved by Sir William's good friend 'Edward Cook esquire', the Queen's solicitor-general, who was also to be supervisor of the will helping Anne as executrix. A £40 legacy was left to 'Edmund Stubbe' to be a continual helper to Anne in the absences of Mr Coke. Stubbes witnessed the will and he may have been acting as man of affairs for Sir William.[12] It also showed the close connection between Coke and his brother-in-law Stubbes.

When his father died in November 1594, Christopher had to sue his mother over his father's will. She appealed to Queen Elizabeth and on her order the Lord Keeper resolved the dispute. Sir Christopher was granted the real estate but was also made liable for his father's debts of £11,000 built up by merchant speculation, as well as having to pay his mother £2,500 as executrix.[13] Dame Anne (who had been endowed with her own manors from Sir Christopher senior) was a strong figure in her sons' lives and, after the death of Sir William, there seems to have been familial harmony. In 1606 however she wrote to Sir Julius Caesar, lately Master of Court of Requests, now Chancellor of the Exchequer, and legal friend of Coke, at London to prevent her manor of Field Dalling being seised as her son had sold the reversion to John Smith of London.[14] Either she or Christopher would have the extra responsibility for ensuring the maintenance of Sir William's brother, Christopher, an idiot from birth who had been provided for by his father Sir Christopher senior.[15] By 1626 his annuities had fallen into arrears after the death of both his sister-in-law and his nephew; the younger Sir William, his great-nephew, whose duty it was to ensure this payment, was a soldier and would die the following year on an ill-fated expedition. No more is heard about poor Christopher.

Perhaps in an effort to make his fortune, Christopher courted his old friend from Peterhouse, Robert Devereux, Earl of Essex who was now the Queen's favourite at court. Another volatile figure, Essex was keen on the bold gesture, like his older rival Ralegh. In the summer of 1596 they planned an attack on Cadiz as part of the alliance with France against the old enemy Spain. The expedition crystallised the tensions which had built up over the preceding years and introduced open factionalism into high politics in 1596. Sir Robert Cecil and Essex were now violently opposed.[16] The fleet left on 1st June 1596.

Ralegh was the hero of the hour in this spectacular but short-lived success. One group was described as '300 greenheaded youths covered with feathers, gold & silver here'. Not all were young men: Arthur Throckmorton, who had gone to relive his soldiering youth, was now nearly 40. Christopher Heydon was 35 when he fought at Cadiz where he, along with over 60 others, was knighted by the Earl of Essex on 27th June after a sermon in San Francisco. The list of knights created at Cadiz added up to 64 although others give it as 66[17] and included Robert Mansfield, John Townshend, Arthur Throckmorton, James Scudamore (who a year later married the niece of Heydon's future wife), Edwin Rich of Mulbarton (who was Essex's brother-in-law), Miles Corbett of Sprowston and Henry Wriothesley.[18] The Queen was very annoyed at Essex. The creation of knighthoods had been restricted at home and yet he made full use of the ability to honour service in the field. By so doing he created a loyal band of grateful followers. It has been described as 'a rather pitiful example of men behaving badly'.[19] Certainly Throckmorton was knighted despite getting into a fight with another officer in a tavern brawl in the town. Most took the opportunity of the success to loot some valuables before their return home on August 5th. Throckmorton is known to have come back with books on astronomy and astrology. Perhaps Heydon did the same. He certainly seems not to have taken the much-needed opportunity to make himself wealthy although that may be partly due to Customs men at Great Yarmouth seizing three chests and two trunks of his on 4th September.[20]

Back in England their fighting spirit continued. Essex, never very emotionally stable, became ill afterwards and withdrew from court. He made up with Cecil at Ralegh House in 1597 and Ralegh led another expedition (the Islands) under Essex in 1597 with disastrous results. Essex tried to court-martial Ralegh for disobedience but failed.

Cecil (who was growing ever stronger and now had the lucrative post, Master of Court of Wards) pushed Essex into the hopeless Irish problem. In January 1599 Christopher sent his brother with a letter of introduction (and a present) to Essex. That spring and summer John fought in Ireland where in August he was also knighted by the Earl. (This time Essex knighted another 59!) Sir John was an experienced soldier having fought with Leicester in the Netherlands. Sir Christopher only absented himself from the Irish campaign because of 'the death of four of my wife's nearest friends and allies, all whose estates nearly concern mine'.[21] He was referring to the remarkable coincidence of so many Potts, Dodge and Flower deaths in the last three years of the century and the sustained legal actions by Robert and Jane Lumner. Sir Christopher's interests lay in maintaining his stake in the rental stream from the Potts properties. He tried to stay close to home that summer even though, in his role as muster commissioner, he was ordered to take his men to Brentwood. (He had been asked to help the muster commissioners in May 1598 'being a man of good experience in martial affaires'.)[22] He stopped at Newmarket and wrote hopefully to Cecil. To no avail, he was told to go on to London and had to bear the cost of his journey.

Essex lasted six months and returned with his men in September 1600, having failed to pacify Ireland. On October 2nd, outside Norwich half a mile from Barford Bridge, John Heydon fought in a rapier duel with Sir Robert Mansfield, the 'Elizabethan sea-dog' who had fought at Cadiz. John's second was Sir Edwin Rich, a Cadiz comrade. It has been said that he lost his hand in this fight but there is no contemporary evidence of this. The detailed accounts which do not mention a hand wound, were printed in a *Gentleman's Magazine* article of 1853.[23] The duel was a curiously elongated affair with several blows of rapiers and then dagger stabs. It would be difficult to sever a hand by rapier blade and if a dagger had caused such a serious wound as to need amputation, it was likely to have been reported. According to Mansfield, the affair ended with John asking for mercy. At which Mansfield offered him a paper to sign with pen and ink which would not be easy if John had just lost his hand! The severed hand which is on display in Norwich Castle Museum came from another John Heydon. See Family Notes 9: Heydon Children. Mansfield himself had been struck in the breast and, depending on which account one reads, had anything up to eight or ten wounds.[24] Indeed at first they were both reported as dead.[25] Mansfield, in a letter to Sir Bassingbourne Gawdy, said he was wounded in the arm but will have to go up [to council] 'as Sir Christopher is so earnest'. The exact run up to the affair is not clear. According to Batten and *ODNB*, John's duel with Mansfield happened first. When they were examined at Council on 26th October, because Sir John Townshend, follower of Lord Howard of Effingham, took Mansfield's side, Sir Christopher lost his temper and challenged him over 'his private value and public service'.[26] The two men, despite working together in official roles, had already been bound over to keep the peace with each other over an earlier argument. It is likely that Townshend was equally short-tempered as he was to die in a duel only two years later, having first killed his opponent. Perhaps fortunately prevented by the Council from duelling, Christopher was ordered to appear before them on 24th November.[27] Mansfield spent most of November and December preparing witnesses who would speak for him while Sir Christopher was preparing the case for his brother. Bassingbourne Gawdy took the depositions for Mansfield who allayed any fears Gawdy may have had about taking sides in a letter of December 1600: he said Sir John's friends asked him not to go public 'so Sir John may be able to show his head thereafter' and he 'need not regard any unkindness from the Heydons. People seek as much to shun the elder brother since the mortgage of Baconsthorpe as to talk of the younger'.[28]

John made a good recovery and was active by December. On 9th January 1601 messengers were sent to bring John Heydon and Robert Mansfield before the Council for the results where they appeared on the 17th and 19th.[29] Mansfield, having lost his commission as a justice, was later that year to stand for election to parliament for Norfolk, giving rise to an aggressive letter sent by Sir Christopher against the 'stranger'. Mansfield was from Wales and had only lived in Norfolk since his marriage to Nathaniel Bacon's sister.[30] In 1601 he wrote, probably, to Bassingbourne Gawdy:

> Sir
>
> Understanding that there is a Parliament expected, thought myself mean not to stand for the Shire of the county to be one of the knights yet to meet with the secret labour of some that more of a factious humour ... have underhand practised to transform the reputation of the place to a stranger from the gentry of Norfolk. I have thought good to praye you not to goe against your owne commitment but rather that at my request you and your frends wold houlde your voyce in suspense and reserve the liberty thereof until the election. I doubt not but we shall fynd of our owne countrymen more sufficiently than any stranger that shall unworthyle seek his owne glorye to our general disgrace withall hope fewe will shew themselves soe weak as to preserve any pryvat mans honor, whatever before his own particular inbredd love to the good of his native countie, assuring you that such will be propounded unto you, by deliberat advise and general approbation at the election as can not be misliked in your Choise and so being sorye that I and Others in a common care of the honor of our countie are enforced by the vayne ambition of some to enter into the apposite course, I repose upon your good affection and consideration together as to a case in this moment apyteyneth and so I commend me in hast
> Mannington 20 Jan
>
> yr assured loving frend
>
> Christo: Heydon[31]

Under Howard Sir William Heydon had lost his post as vice-admiral of Norfolk, a post now held by the young upstart Mansfield, so there was a history of animosity. Hassell Smith's excellent exposé of Norfolk politics at this time, shows Townshend was part of the Bacon faction (he was Nathaniel's son-in-law), with the Heydons aligning with the Heveninghams.[32] These alliances were not stable and family ties were often called on despite them. Charles Cornwallis (who was knighted a few months later in July) wrote to Sir Christopher:

> To my very loving cosen and friend 13 January 1603/4
>
> Sir, I pray give me leave to continue my claim to your promised assurance at the election of the knights of the shire for which places Mr Bacon and I have now full agreed to join & therefore on his behalf as well as mine own I require your best furtherance Yr kind care of us both herin I wyll for my pt ever indever to deserve in any office of frendship that I can And so with my right harty commendations to yrself and yr lady I wish unto you all the good fortunes you would & end this 13 of January... 1603
>
> yr very assured loving kynsman & friend
>
> Charles Cornwaleys[33]

(Sir Christopher Heydon's mother was Anne Woodhouse, whose sister Mary married Sir Ralph Shelton of Shelton. Shelton's second wife, Anne Barrow, after his death, married Sir Charles Cornwallis.)

Christopher earned a Privy Council censure for his threats against Townshend but worse was to come. The hearing at Council had been prolonged waiting for Christopher to attend as surety for John. This meant that John and Christopher were in London at the beginning of February 1601. On the 8th February 1601, Essex now even more distracted and tormented, broke into the Queen's bedchamber with armed men to speak against Ralegh and Cecil. Court officials, hearing of Essex's plans to act, had gone to his house but had been locked in the study, while Essex and 200 followers including many who had been at Cadiz, set off for Sheriff Smyth's house near the Royal Exchange. He thought the London Trained Bands would rise with him but they did not and the sheriff closed the City to him. A brief battle with the Trained Bands ensued and he fled back to the Strand by the Thames. On his return the house was surrounded. On the Queen's orders, Sir Robert Cecil confined him with his followers to Essex House on the Strand (near Ralegh's house). He was executed in March 1601. Both Christopher and John had found themselves on the wrong side; they were in Essex's house and led his company to Ludgate in the attempted coup. They were repulsed at Ludgate 'and after shifted for themselves'. Sir John fled to the Netherlands while Sir Christopher remained in hiding. A list of those 'not yet taken' on 26th February named both Heydons.[34]

An April 1601 inquisition into the possessions of the fugitive Sir Christopher (which included the wardship of John Potts) stated that he 'did after 10th Feb and before 1st March, without licence, depart and flee beyond the realm and for all that time was and is at his own freedom [in] contempt of the Queen contrary to statute'.[35] To avoid the loss of his goods, Sir Christopher surrendered on 6th April and was imprisoned briefly in the Fleet.[36] He opened a correspondence with Cecil in which he pleaded that he had been impulsive and had not intended to be part of a serious coup. He even proposed the eventually accepted remedy that he should be pardoned on payment of a fine although he said that massive debts and fourteen children would make it hard for him to pay anything substantial. His eldest son was running up debts at university which he had to pay his tutor to enable the boy to return in the autumn. During the summer, he was pardoned and was lucky to get off with a fine of £2,000 which only added to his financial pressures. His fine was the lowest listed; three or four of the rebels paid up to £20,000.[37] Sir John was not shown on the fines list as the £2,000 may have also covered him as the younger brother. Under threat of being outlawed, he returned to England on 2nd April 1602 and headed straight for Baconsthorpe, only to find his brother was at their mother Lady Heydon's house at Thursford.[38] By 15th April, he was under house arrest under bond for £1,000 to his mother and brother who wrote to Cecil to drop outlawry proceedings against John. Attorney-General Coke also lent his assistance to getting John a pardon. John was to stay a prisoner at his mother's house for a year. Cecil's letter shows a surprisingly sympathetic attitude towards the family.[39]

Over the next four years, Sir Edward Coke wrote several letters to Cecil asking for Sir Christopher to be granted the farm of customs in the county. But Heydon's financial affairs remained in bad shape. He wrote to Sir Bassingbourne Gawdy at West Harling on October 22nd 1602 from Baconsthorpe, at his usual length, but clearly with a sense of his family's declining reputation:

> Sir
>
> I am sorry my unhappy estate gives me occasion to become a suiter unto you in a matter of this nature but I have no other way to prevent executions that are nowe likely to come out against Mr Thetford as my surety but by your friendly forbearing to execute the same till the next terme, not doubting in the mean time but to satisfy the parties themselves. If I could have sold land I would not have suffered matters to grown to these extremities and before the time prefixed I assure you upon my honour faythe to provide some way for their contentment. And in the mean time I will not desire your undersheriffs loss but will most thankfully consider him for his fees which though it will be a charge yet by this favour I shall prevent much infamy, grefe and other inconveniences that will happen if my sureties should be molested and impeached by my debt. I most earnestly pray you that you will instantly give your

order by letter or otherwise to your undersheriff for the satisfying
of this my request, giving him contentment to the uttermost of this
due whereby as I shall acknowledge myself infinitely pleasured So I
pray you persuade yourself, you shall ever find me accordingly ready
to deserve your kindness at the present. so commending me heartily
to yourself, with my service to my lady in last I rest

your very assured friend

Christopher Heydon

And again on 2nd October 1604, banking all on procuring the customs:

Sir

Being in hope to farm the Customs of Norfolk of the King, I have
been bold with divers of my friends and the most of them not under
the rank, to undertake for me as surety to the king: I press them not
beyond one hundred a piece and if may entreat you with others to
do me this kindness as I not nedes take it for a friendly courtesy, so
you may well assure yourself never to be requited with danger, for as
I sue for this place for my benefit & good, so I will not live to have
both my judgment and honesty so engaged and overthrown that
neither yourself or any other shall be called in question for it. I leave
it to you kind consideration And so praying your answer in last I rest

yr very assured frend

Christopher Heydon

Did Gawdy help? Another even more desperate letter is undated but of the same
year, this time calling on kinship as well as friendship:

Sir

at this present my important occasions press me beyond my own
disposition to presume uppon my freinds, And although I can
challenge no interest in you by any one particular defecks; yet
having ever found you very affectionately well wishing to my estate,
I can rather emboldened to entreat you as my surety to join me
in the taking up of £100. I do assure you Sr it is for my good and
do as faithfully praise you to see you discharged at your day if did
not concerne me very nere I shall be I would neither press you nor
others as I am urged for a greater sum; But I hope in god this will
be the last time that ever I shall be driven to the like plunge, praying

you as wish me well so not to forsake and now where this money may be a means to enable me not only to discharge this but both to free and release my estate, so leaving it to your kind consideration, with my very hearty commendation

I rest

your ever loving kinsman and frend

Christopher Heydon[40]

(The kinship to Gawdy was complicated. Sir Christopher had called Bassingbourne Gawdy's 'bedfellow' a cousin in 1586 as did Sir William Heydon in 1593. Gawdy had married Anne Wootton the widow of Thomas Woodhouse, brother of William's wife, Anne.)

In 1607 Heydon even had the nerve to petition King James for the 'relief of his decayed estate ... for the sake of his own service and those of his father and grandfather' suggesting £45 a year to be raised from some pieces of escheated lands. It is unlikely that this was the last time he was driven to ask for help. His allies were no longer in power. Cecil died in 1612 and Coke was out of office by 1616. Baconsthorpe was further mortgaged and in 1614, his creditors closed in. Baconsthorpe was 'declared forfeit'.[41]

Marriage to Anne Potts

However, between the Cadiz expedition and the rebellion, Christopher had been lucky enough to make the match with Anne, the widow of John Potts of Mannington and claim the wardship of the young John Potts her son. He needed a mother for his numerous children but was not worried about taking on Anne's five despite his precarious finances. For more about his children see Family Notes 9: Heydon Children.[42] Further children were born to him and Anne, as he claimed in the 1601 Cecil correspondence that he had 14 children to bring up.[43] Anne was pregnant with either their first or second baby at the time of the London rebellion. On 13th February 1601 the Privy Council ordered the sheriff of Norfolk to seize both Sir Christopher and Sir John Heydon's houses.[44] With Christopher and his brother fled abroad, in late February 1601 she had to cope with 'a veritable army of under officers' - 16 men - occupying Sir Christopher's house.[45] Described as indignant rather than nervous, she was obviously a lady of some character and the Privy Council ordered her to be left in peace, with only '2 honest and discrete person to remain there' and to have all the goods necessary to her needs.[46] Was she not only a good-looking woman - even in her later years her fine features are clear (see Plate 1) - but also a good listener with her own intelligent opinions? Her influence may well have been a calming continuity for her son John and indeed perhaps on Sir Christopher after his release from the Fleet in 1601. They seem to have been very fond of each other; John's mother outlived Christopher by 20 years but did not remarry. Her memorial inscription shows that he was fond of her, wanting them to be buried side by side, a wish that her son was happy to carry out.

> Here lieth the body of Dame Anne one of the daughters and heirs of John Dodge esq. She was first married to John Potts of Mannington Norfolk esq and afterwards wife to the renowned gent Sir Christopher Heydon Kt who dying before her desired that she would be buried next to him. In memorial of whose conjugal affections and her own appointment in her last will this stone was laid upon her grave by Sir John Potts Kt & Bart eldest son of the said Dame Anne who died 28th January 1642 aged 75.[47]

We know little else of her. She went to visit 'my Lady Throckmorton' in 1619, probably Ann, the wife of Sir Arthur Throckmorton of Paulerspury, Northants who was knighted at Cadiz with Heydon. Her husband's sister was Bess, Lady Ralegh and she was godmother to little Walter Ralegh.[48] Arthur had also sat as MP in the same parliament as John Potts, Anne's first husband. Anne Potts's portrait was painted when she was in her 60s (see Chapter 24).[49] Her robust health may have been due to her husband's friendship with Dr Forster (the Earl of Leicester's physician). In a letter to Forster in January 1608 Sir Christopher wrote:

> 'My wife thanks you for her physik; she took the pills which wer three days in working but very gently two or three a day. She hath also used your plaster and losenges but fyndeth not so much good of the Plaster.'

John Potts's upbringing

How was young John affected by such a tumultuous childhood? Losing his father, elder brother, grandparents, and uncles before he was seven must have been bad enough. Finding himself with a new stepfather and uncle of such flamboyant reputations, and suddenly having up to another 7 or 8 step-brothers and sisters must have been quite extraordinary. Perhaps from his mother's steadying hand, John grew up with a surprisingly moderate and calm approach to life. His later concerns about the effects of war may well have come from his stepfamily's experiences. No doubt, as a 10 year-old, he would have been told tales of fighting, duels and derring-do by his uncle while the latter was under house arrest. He certainly seems the opposite of his hot-tempered guardian in this respect. In matters of learning and religion, however, he was better served by him.

His puritan beliefs were certainly influenced by his family. Sir Christopher is described as professing 'apocalyptic Protestantism' and as late as 1620 had reported a party of Norfolk recusants who were supporting the anti-protestant activities of the Hapsburgs in Bohemia.[50] Nathaniel Bacon wrote that [Christopher] 'William's son doth barre [bear] a good harte towards the church of God' and he had the honour of being High Steward of Norwich Cathedral. [51] John also would have been influenced by his college days. Like his grandfather, Sir Christopher believed in education and had sent his eldest son William to Caius College aged 12 in February 1597 and supported him until at least 1603. He arranged for John to study at Emmanuel College, Cambridge under Dr Samuel Ward, where he was admitted on 29th October 1606 at 14. Ward was a theologian, devoted to biblical studies and a man of great intellect. He was renowned in his day as a great scholar, a good administrator and a man of integrity in all aspects of his life. It is clear from a letter from Sir Christopher in February 1608 that he thought highly of Ward, 'his much esteemed frend', although his ever-increasing debts seem to have delayed his paying John's fees.

> Mr Warde,
>
> I have not leisure at this tyme to examine yr accompts But against I send next, I will certaynley sett downe out of yr owen accoumpts which of us is in the error, in the mean tyme I have sent you £3 by the Bearer and do pray you to let your pupill come home with him: for here are some of his friends that must needs se him;
>
> for any thing I know you shall see him at our lady or betwixt this and Ester agayne and then you shall understand more of my mynd concerning his disposing in yr Absence, for which I am unfaynedly sorry, holding you fitter for a University than for so remot a corner wher few of any understanding shall profit by you,
>
> And if so mean a stipend will give you satisfaction I cold have wished you wold have accepted of Baconsthorpe benefice which by Mr Wright's delays hath since bene chargeable & troublesome to me, but taken in Tyme wold have prevented the same, the living being worth £50 pa to be farmed .
>
> But I was not so happie & I trust god will provide better for you.
>
> And so till the retourne of yr Pupill I & my Wif commend us kindly,
>
> Resting, yr assured loving friend,
>
> Christopher Heydon

Sir Christopher was obviously concerned that Dr Ward was leaving Emmanuel for a lesser position and would have liked him to take the living of Baconsthorpe. However he had already promised this to Edward Wright who was presented in the same year. In the end Dr Ward had more influential friends, including Lady Anne Harington, through whom he received the post of master of the quite recently founded Sidney Sussex College. [52] He was later made Vice-Chancellor of the University.

It is clear that concerns for John's safety - as the Potts heir - exercised his mother Lady Anne while he was away. Heydon adds in the margin of his letter to Ward 'We heard at Christmas that yr pupil was forth, my wife desireth to know wer he was, for except it be to Sir John Cottons she doth not lyk he shuld be carried any wither'.

Sir Christopher's first wife, Mirabel Rivett had been the daughter of Sir Thomas Rivett and Alice Cotton of Cambridgeshire. Sir John Cotton of Landwade was therefore Christopher's uncle by marriage - and lived on the route from Cambridge to Norfolk.[53] John Potts's mother was related to Sir John Cotton's third wife Anne Houghton, through the Houghtons of Lancashire.

Emmanuel College was well-known for its puritan leanings while John studied there: Dr John Cotton was head lecturer, dean and catechist between 1606 and 1612. He became a preacher and emigrated to New England in 1633 with Thomas Hooker, another Emmanuel pupil. Ward was a Calvinist and puritan supporter although his views were not extreme. His moderate tendencies (he supported the continuation of the episcopacy but criticised royal behaviour) would later land him in difficulties but may have laid the foundations of John's own thoughtful, well-balanced beliefs.

Prior to going to Cambridge, the young John Potts may have been tutored by Sir Christopher's domestic chaplain, William Bredon. His stepbrother, William Heydon, had been tutored by a Mr Blackborne before college. Bredon later became vicar of Thornton in Buckinghamshire and William Lilly describes him as 'a profound divine' and 'absolutely the most polite person for nativities in that age'.[54] Young John would have had to put up with the smell of smoke when studying as Bredon was apparently 'inordinately given over to tobacco'. He was reported to have smoked his own bell ropes when he ran out of the 'fragrant weed'.[55] During his boyhood, John would also have gained great familiarity with the stars. Bredon, like Heydon, was an astrologer and was certainly helping Sir Christopher at Mannington with his great work *Defence of Judiciall Astrologie* which was printed in 1603 at Cambridge by John Legat, printer to the University.[56] Anthony Wood described the work, of over 500 pages, as 'of no common reading and carried on with no mean acquirements'.[57] Heydon said that 'some imperfect copies of my papers without my [permission] were spread abroad' so he felt obliged to consent to his work being published. The *Defence* was a detailed response to the treatise published in 1601 by Mr John Chambers, the Dean of Windsor, against astrologers and their superstitious, heathen ways. In defence of his statements, Heydon used extensive arguments quoting from Homer and other classics, and calling on the Bible as well as science. He disassociated himself from diviners, those who use divine instinct (augury and magic) to foretell events, relying rather on natural causes.[58] The publication led to a long controversy: George Carleton wrote a biting retort to the 'Knight's boke' *Astrologomania or the madness of Astrologers* but this was not published until 1624, a year after Heydon's death. Carleton called him a man of learning but said 'Now Sir wee charge you for abusing your Reader in writing so long a boke ... never once making offer to prove the thing in question'.[59] For Carleton astrology was Satan's work whereas Heydon placed it among the sciences, as natural philosophy and mathematics. Christopher also sent his astrological discourses to his friend Dr Richard Forster or Foster 'of London' the eminent physician, Fellow of All Souls, mathematician and astrologer. In Christopher's 1608 letter to Ward he wrote a postscript, his thoughts tumbling out on the paper, some words represented by only a letter:

> I wold be glad to heare what your university thinketh of the cold winter Turpa est Philosophe aliquid sine Ratione adferre; [*it is shameful to offer a Philosophy without reasoning*] Eyther we must mak it a Miracle and so a work above Nature, or ascribe it to chance, & so with the Epicure c … ete Templars so blynd for … Or we must fynd some reason out of the Principles in Nature for the same; the first 2: are unworthy a scholar & the last I do assure you in the word of an honest man I did forse by Astrologie, and accordingly writt a little Tracte in sum passage whereof I did sett downe my opinion thereof, which I sent to Mr Dr Foster of London, having written the same a yere since: certaine it is the planettes wer all this winter in the weekest conditions in respect of the Position that they cold be: Therefor I wd gladly hear whether any in Cambridge hath so much as endeavored to inquire into Astrologie for the Reson … After Mr Dr Foster Had receved my Tracte he was sent for into Sussex to the old Lady Mountague who being Dangerously sick held him almost six weeks in the country and my man retourning for the Terme he writte unto me that he cold hardly think that the case *[?cause]* of any cold this winter, whereunto I have replyed and do send you both his letter to read and my replye. Praying you w se yr Ephe*mci*rdus *[?Ephimedis or Ephemeris]* as you read my letter. For[ster] then m[ay] Red my tract when he will.[60]

Lively conversations would have filled the house when Christopher entertained his friends such as John Bainbridge and Edward Wright the mathematician, and John must have listened to his stepfather's long discourse on the effects of the conjunctions of the planets and stars, particularly on world affairs. His stepfather wrote important pieces on these topics and the phenomena surrounding the comet of 1618. Did John believe in astrology? There is no evidence at all to suggest it and his down-to-earth attitudes suggest he was not won over. His guardian's learning though was indisputable and widely respected.

In 1650, encouraged by his friends William Lilly and Elias Ashmole, Nicholas Fiske published Sir Christopher Heydon's *An Astrological Discourse (with mathematical demonstrations)*, having acquired the manuscript after the death in 1616 of Dr Forster, to whom Heydon had presented it after 1608. Fiske had tried to publish it before the civil war, but had been blocked by the clerical censors who had the role of licensing books of this kind.[61] He commended the work to the newly established Society of Astrologers, in the hope of an astrological renaissance in England. Fiske was painted by Cornelius de Neve in 1651, around the same time as de Neve painted Sir John (see Chapter 24). Is it a possibility that John arranged or paid for this as a thank you to Fiske for his determined efforts to see Sir Christopher recognised?

John's pattern of education would have a parallel in the life of his acquaintance Thomas Knyvett, of Ashwellthorpe who was four years younger. After being educated by John Rawlyns rector of Attleborough, Knyvett also went as a Fellow-Commoner to Emmanuel College, at the age of sixteen, graduating two years later in 1614. Knyvett's reports from his tutor, Elias Travers, to his grandmother survive and have been printed.[62] In the absence of any from Ward concerning John, they give a useful account of the expenses and trials of university life. John would certainly have needed at least the £40 allowance which seems to have been the norm.[63] Given his stepfather's finances he probably learnt the benefit of thrift at this stage of his life.

John would have certainly grown up in a house full of books and noisy debate. Or rather houses full of books: Sir Christopher now had Baconsthorpe and Mannington but is said to have preferred to live at Heydon Hall in Saxlingham.[64] In 1603 he was said by the rector Ralph Dodge to live 'sometimes' at Mannington and in 1600 two servants of Sir Christopher at Mannington were married in Itteringham.[65] Christopher who had himself studied at Cambridge had an extensive library which he had inherited from his grandfather Sir Christopher.[66] In March 1601 when his goods were being distrained, he or friends on his behalf, persuaded the Privy Council to order that 'there is a great library in one of his houses, & that the books are purloyned we require you to have care that none of them be taken away but kept together & locked up in the study where they are'.[67]

He corresponded with learned friends including William Camden (1610), Richard Fletcher mathematician and astrologer, from his eldest son's college Caius, and another eminent mathematician Henry Briggs, Savilian Professor at Oxford (also a friend of Samuel Ward).[68] In a letter of February 1619 to John (then aged about 26), Christopher's comments show that John may also have been in contact with Briggs: 'I am glad Mr Briggs has become a prophet: But I think [your] report wrongs him; for if he speaks by art he ought to ly[ve] himself by rules'. It would appear Briggs had warned of an impending disaster - Sir Christopher said humorously 'And I pray god Sir N Bacons gret feast be the worst it portends to this kyngdome'.[69] Sir Christopher also was involved in the printing of some classics. He told John that 'Jak Betes and I have already weried ourselves with the t[...] iorneys to Hamborough & Brem [*Hamburg and Bremen*] forward and back in the [*business*] of Mr Morisons books wher we know what to paye for our s[...] but not what we shall have for our mony nor how we sh[*all*] lodge. But the first verse in Homer hath a falt & w[*e*] may not therby be discoraged in procedinge. so great a w[*ork*] written by a scholar & so gret a tran..y'er [*transcriber*] cannot but pro[*vide*] some better recompense and it is but proportionable that, as it c[*ost*] him much payne & money to tell us so much, so his reder sh[old] have some patience to cracke the shell befor he shall tast the kernel'.[70] Was he referring to the 'great translator' George Chapman, whose complete original translations of Homer, had been published in English in 1616? Chapman had once also had the Earl of Essex as his patron but after 1600 his fortunes also went downhill and in 1605 he was imprisoned for debt. Heydon may have known Chapman through Essex (he was supposed to have been on military service in the 1590s) but in any case would certainly have heard of this poet and playwright.[71]

It is not clear why Heydon had to travel to Hamburg to achieve this as Chapman's works were published in London and should have been available. Perhaps 'Mr Morison' was involved in a wider distribution or just wanted a cheaper print.[72]

John may not have stayed much longer at Emmanuel after his stepfather had expressed concern for his care after Ward's departure from the college. He may have come home in mid-1608 or early 1609 at the age of 16-17. After University, unlike his half-brother Miles, there is no evidence of John having attended the inns of court. Venn confused him with John Potts of the unrelated family of Chalgrave, Bedfordshire who went to Gray's Inn.[73]

Keeler says 'John Potts spent some time as a young man in Norwich'.[74] This was based on the address 'at his house in Norwich' in April 1619, where he received a fulsome letter of thanks from Sir Thomas Holland of Quidenham. Holland wrote:

> The worthy testimonies of your true report obligeth me so farre that no time shall ever cancell it but all reciprocall affection doth and will tender a best endeavour of acquitall from mee Thate multiplicitie of profession the validitie whereof may many waies be doubted yet in the respect of the inward mind is to be deciphered by the outward behaviour and that the thoughts of men are to be explained by word or action give me leave to assure you that you could not have conferred your kindness upon a more thankfull creature who will ever in all respects remaine
>
> yours faithfully to dispose of Thos Holland
> yr feminine kindred desireth [to be remembered]
>
> I desire to be advertised whether Sir Christopher intendeth to prove a habeas corpus[75]

Holland called Potts his 'worthy Cosen' and referred to his feminine kin. Sir Thomas had married Mistress Mary Wigmore in 1609 at Twickenham, daughter of Sir Richard Wigmore of Westminster, John Potts's cousin.[76] Both Holland's new wife and John's mother Ann Dodge shared a common grandmother in Katherine Leighton (variously Mrs Wigmore and Mrs Dodge). At this time Sir Thomas was helping his late wife's sister, Lady Katherine Paston, in her legal affairs after the death of Sir Edmund Paston but it seemed John may have been helpful in a cause to do with Sir Christopher Heydon.[77]

In the market for a wife

Despite Sir Christopher's abilities and interests, John grew up in a family deeply in debt. It is clear from a 1619 letter from Christopher that John was fully aware of his stepfather's financial problems:

> Son Pottes, you have loaded your man Barrows with oysters and me
> with a double load of engagem[tes] both for them and your books But
> howsoever my condition is not so unhappie but that I may requite
> the value of these curtesies that which maketh me cum behind and
> in the arrerage [arrears] of your debt is the mynd from whence these
> kind testimonies of your love proced. And though my affectione
> be not any way defective or short of yours: yet here is my grefe that
> I am lyke an Artifficer without his tools; I have matter whereon
> to work but I n[ede] the means: And therfor my unfortunate estat
> doth lyvely ratifie the philosophers maxime that a poor man can
> not be happie: for he placeth felicite in the goods of the mynd
> and of the bodye & of fortune; And though a poor man may be
> accomplished with all virtue, and outward proper .. of the body yet
> saying the prayse of virtue conshst[rued/trained] ... in action, this is
> my unhappiness that I know not how to thank you in dedes as well
> as in words.
>
> It remaynes therfor that I must [word deleted] be your debtor
> both for these and your many other argaments of love which as I
> acknowledge with delight, so I pray you accept till my better destiny
> shall further manifest that I dissemble not.[78]

Christopher was grateful for the many 'curtesies' that John sent him, on this occasion oysters and books, but there were hints that John may have been supporting him more generously. Certainly there was a real affection between them.

By this time John had been married twice.[79] When his stepson was only 16, Sir Christopher was keen to set him up with a wife and John was seen as a good match. In late October 1608, Sir Nathaniel Bacon of Stiffkey offered the daughter of his younger brother, Edward, as a possible wife.[80] This was probably Jane Bacon, Edward's eldest surviving daughter who later married Francis Stoner in 1612.[81] Her younger sister Anne, who was about the same age as John, later married Philip Bedingfield. In November 1608, Christopher replied to his 'especiall frend' that the dowry offered was not sufficient and that he had had some better offers. Christopher's formal letters were still written without taking breath. To aid understanding here some of his more extreme spelling and style has been altered:

3 November 1608 Sir Christopher Heydon to Sir Nathaniel Bacon

Sir,

I pray you believe that I accept of your offered match with the kyndness and respect that your motion deserveth And although I have bene lately offered two other matches, the one of £2000 the other of £2500 yet I protest would my poor estate permit me, I would value your frendship and alliance which should grow to my sons house by the marriage with your brother's daughter before twice so much with any other of their condition that have bene in speech with me, which I do not accept of only because their condition and quality is not answerable to his birth. For be my wants never so great, I will respect him as well as my own sonnes, neither mean I to match meanly except it may be as well for his benefit as my owne and that in some good measure but if I could meet with a competent portion, I will sooner respect a gentleman with £2000 than a merchant with £3000.

Wherefore Sir I pray you think that my wife and I thankfully accept of your motion, though for so small a portion my wants will not suffer me to entertaine it; Protesting that if the £200 named by you would extend in any nearness to my need, I would never go further than your owne offer, if my wifes son could so from his liking being sorry [that] Mr Edward Bacon, being a gentleman of whom I conceive so very worthy, will not rise higher than the sum limited by you that I might have listened unto it.

I am this day toward my journey to London where if I may do you any service I shall be very redy & glad

And so with my wifes thanks and my own we commend us kyndly to my Lady & your self, resting your assured poor friend

Christopher Heydon[82]

A marriage between the two families would not have been surprising: whatever their past political allegiances may have been, Heydon and Bacon often worked together as justices and examiners.[83] The fact that the dowry was far too small may suggest Bacon was not too worried about the outcome. Perhaps, knowing Heydon's financial situation, he could not have expected Heydon to have matched a larger figure. There is no evidence that he offered more and relations between them remained cordial. Three months later Christopher wrote to his 'good frend' Nathaniel, about a court case. It opened in his usual creative style 'This morning as I was walking about my pastures, this bearer found me out, with his prisoner ...'.[84]

Barbara Godsalve

Instead of the Bacon alliance, Sir Christopher made a more pragmatic move and, despite his stated wish for John to marry 'quality answerable to his birth', chose the daughter of a merchant. The £3,000 mentioned in his letter to Bacon, may be an indication of the real offer Heydon had in his sights. John's chosen bride, was 19 year-old Barbara, eldest daughter of Roger Godsalve esq and his wife Barbara Cutts, of Buckenham Ferry and St Stephen, Norwich. The girl is usually described by writers as 'a favourite at court with a small fortune' following the entry in *Burke's Extinct Baronetcies* 1841. Burke said it was from 'an old writer' (not Blomefield for once) but the statement has not been verified and seems unlikely.[85] He also called her Goodsill, which although probably from the same root, is a separate name in Norfolk.[86] In fact, Roger Godsalve was a vital part of Christopher's financial survival. Some of the estate mortgage documents survive and show that John Potts's first father-in-law was one of the main providers of funds to Sir Christopher. On 28th September 1609 a marriage licence bond was issued for the marriage of John Potts, described as of Baconsthorpe, to Barbara Godsalve at Buckenham Ferry.[87] Roger Godsalve, together with one John Smyth (or Smith) and others, was actively involved in mortgage and other property arrangements with both the Heydons and the Cleres.[88] Smith, later of Arminghall but then of Blickling and Itteringham, was the son of Dame Agnes Clere by an earlier marriage and was involved in purchasing property with her. A deed of 20th May 1610 showed that Sir Edward Clere conveyed Thetford property to Godsalve and Smith in relation to a debt of £2,200 or more.[89] Additionally other property to this value was sold the previous day absolutely to Smith and Dame Agnes Clere. It seems that the Thetford deed was as security for the peaceable enjoyment of the other property and that Smith had paid off the £2,200 of debts. A mortgage deed of 1st December 1618 described Godsalve and Smith assigning their mortgage on certain Clere lands in Thetford.[90]

They certainly featured heavily in Sir Christopher Heydon's affairs. A Star Chamber complaint by Sir Christopher of 22nd November 1614 alleged misdoing by Godsalve, Smith and Owen Sheppard (or Shepheard) in relation to mortgage monies advanced to Sir Christopher.[91] The essence of his painfully long bill was that he believed that he had trusted Godsalve and the other two (who were justices of the peace) to lend him over £2,400 to pay certain debts and had mortgaged to them his manors and park in Baconsthorpe and Bodham. More property was added when the mortgage period and amount was extended. A deed of 4th November 1610 showed the debt at about £5,300 and Sir Christopher was in part challenging the precise amount. More importantly they tried to foreclose on 3rd November 1611 and take his property given his inability to repay the loan. He argued that they had added in bogus travel and legal costs to bring the amount due to over £6,000. They were, he said, trying to cheat him out of properties valued by others at £19,000 or more.

The interesting feature of this action is that events started in May 1610, just a few months after Sir Christopher's ward and Godsalve's daughter were married.

It is hard to avoid the conclusion that there was a major financial deal involving first a dowry payment to Sir Christopher and subsequently loans towards payment of his debts. Heydon even used a seven year lease to Godsalve of Mannington's rents to cover some monies. This seems to have happened around 1609 and was probably part of a complex marriage settlement on John and Barbara. John was given as of Baconsthorpe at that time, implying the Heydon family were not using Mannington.

From a later action of November 1617 it appears that Godsalve may well have actually taken up personal use and occupation of at least part of Sir Christopher's Baconsthorpe lands.[92] Heydon recited an earlier but undated chancery decree that Godsalve, Sheppard and Smith should have yielded Baconsthorpe Hall to Heydon by August or September 1615, via a settlement in trust to Sir Edward Coke, Lord Chief Justice and Sir Henry Hobart, Lord Chief Justice of the Common Pleas. Before the property was released to Heydon, Godsalve had, in Heydon's complaint, committed waste to the value of £200. Apparently Godsalve had taken away from Baconsthorpe Hall a very large brewing copper and hidden it locally. Heydon believed it was 'fixed to the freehold of the estate' and went to retrieve it. But Godsalve treated this as trespass on his close at Hempstead, particularly since he said Heydon broke in 'with force and arms'. This went to trial at the assizes at Norwich Castle and Heydon was found guilty and £35 damages and costs were awarded to Godsalve. Heydon argued that both the copper and the land on which it lay were his and that the witnesses had committed perjury against him regarding the true status of the land. Heydon now sought redress against the witnesses and Godsalve in the Star Chamber.

This yet again shows the impulsive and martial tendencies of Heydon - buckle on your sword, leap on a horse and ride off to do battle with perceived injustice! The sums of money were not huge, but the principle clearly mattered to him even if his son's former father-in-law was the problem.

For sadly, in March 1615, in the middle of this legal wrangling, Barbara died after only 6 years of marriage; her memorial at West Barsham church showed she had three daughters, Anne, Barbara and Willoughbia.[93] John and Barbara and the children lived at West Barsham until Barbara's death.[94] At the time of the 1617 action, Heydon was described as of Mannington. By his father's will, John would have come into his estate at 21 in 1613 but it is possible that he and his three girls did not go to live at Mannington until after 1615. (Mr Pottes gent was however described as the patron of Mannington in September 1612 when he would have been 20 ½).[95]

By now, Barbara's father Roger was himself having financial difficulties and well before his daughter died, he wrote of his problems. In a letter to Mr Mason in 1610, he described himself as an old man (although he was about 41) and said his circumstances were limiting his actions.

To my very good frend Mr Mason attendant to the Right Honorable
the Lady Bartlet from Roger Godsalve 26 Jan 1610

Mr Mason, I had knowledge by this messenger that my lady is
pleased there should be the forty pounds paid to Mr Tooly. it is
longe whence the money was borrowed and the bond hath been
put in suite so that the interest money and the charges of suite is
if not all so much within a st...e some as much more. I hope Sir
Robert will have more respect to me then I shall lose anything by
undertaking for him, my estate and present occasions inforce me
to look into all my courses with all possible labour to unburden
myself of all charges that possibly I can. I therefore entreat you to
be a means that all may be discharged that both trouble and more
charge may be saved and myself may have cause to be aserteyned of
my ladies favour towards me and of that love for Sir Robert which
from my heart I desire though my abilitie will not enable me to
this business as I would to deserve, if you please to take any course
herein this ould man will be [commanded] by you to tramitt [sic]
to Mr Tooly his attorney or otherwise as your shall please to imploy
him. Th..s desiring my duty may be remembered to my honorable
good lady and the like respective remembrance to Sir Robert
with my ... hearty commendations to yourself, I leave you to god
almighty his keeping this 26 Jan 1610

your frend

Roger Godsalve[96]

The letter is also interesting as it seems that Lady Bartlet was John Donne's friend,
in the service of Sir Robert Drury, Donne's patron. Donne was at Cadiz with the
Earl of Essex in 1596 so could well have known Sir Christopher Heydon.

What went wrong for Roger? His family had obtained manorial standing when
Queen Mary had gifted to her godson Thomas Godsalve esq and his male heirs, the
manor and patronage of Caistor Overhall.[97] Thomas, like his father Sir John, was
said to be a mercer and he died owning seven or eight manors. Roger, his eldest son
went to Caius College at 15 in May 1584 after being taught at school in Buckenham
Ferry, where the family lived, for three years and then Bungay for two more. He
was admitted to Gray's Inn in May 1588 when he was about 20, the same year his
father died.[98] He and his wife Barbara lived first at Caistor St Edmund and then
Buckenham Ferry. He was certainly of sufficient means to help Heydon and in a
report of 1615 Roger Godsalve was recorded as having the distinction of being one
of only two Englishmen to have their own herring-ships (haringbuizen). He had
'on the Stockes at Yarmouth, five Busses'. Most other deep-sea herring fishing boats
were owned by the Dutch.[99] Did he overreach himself? The cost of a summer season

for each boat could be over £400, but the catch could be worth £1,000.[100] He may have suffered a cash flow problem as this was a time of a great scarcity of herring and although prices were high, many boats were laid up in 1616 as no licences for export were being issued that year. Roger was also involved in the East India Company from 1609 and in June 1615 'Dr Rant's adventure' was set over to Roger.[101] Perhaps he lost boats or cargoes, for a letter written to Roger Townshend suggested Godsalve had either fled overseas or may even have been in prison:

> [Rog]er Godsalve to Sir Roger [Townshend] Bt at Raynham, Norfolk

> Sir

> Least through the want of words I should seem to suffer my necessitous disaster to transport me beyond the course of respect either by love or duty Because I am so forcibly sequestered from you, I have presumed to present you with a few word in writing therby only but to move you to have a care that you be able to hold in remembrance both what you truly and really are and on whom you do depend, that the common condition of all or calamity of mortality may make no greater impression in you, then to produce a salving Christian sorrow whereby to preserve you from the contagion of repose in temporal blessings and likewise to invest you in such a possession of those blessings which it shall please god to continue unto you as therby you may feel them to be the lively pledges of god almighty his will to possess you with eternal happiness. I know you shall at many hands have comforts worthy your keeping good Sir, bind them up together and be strengthened by them your health and happiness I heartily wish and my prayers to god to send both unto you, is all that I can render as recompense for your loving favours

> Gods chastisements are his unspeakable favours whereby his children are brought in this life into the kingdom of grace, that thereby they might be assured after this life of the kingdom of glory. Sir in all causes of your sorrow or joy, if I were but able by any action to manifest the truth of mine affection, my heart were much eased of grief that hitherto doth possess me through want of means to appear rightly thankful, But good Sir accept of my well wishings, for god he knoweth I do as heartily pray for all happiness to you both temporal and spiritual as for myself,

> this his hoping to hear of your good health and … your good mothers recovery I take my …

> … yr loving poor cosin.[102]

Unfortunately the letter was not dated. Despite his own predicament, rather than asking for help, he appeared to be sympathising with Roger Townshend. Was it for the death of Townshend's father, Sir John, in a duel in 1603 or his brother Stanhope in a duel in the Netherlands? Or perhaps for the loss of a child? Townshend's mother lived on to 1630. Godsalve's mother Elizabeth was Sir Roger Townshend's great-aunt (Roger may have been the godson of Elizabeth's brother, Sir Roger Townshend senior) so as usual in such situations, he reminded him of his kinship.

Certainly one Godsalve ended up in prison, for attempting 'to escape'. A letter from Thomas Godsalve to his cousin Sir Roger Townshend begged his help: 'for want of paying for my chamber, I am cast downe into the lower ward' [of the prison]. Unfortunately undated, this was probably Godsalve's son.[103]

Roger Godsalve definitely 'went beyond the seas in June 1619' having sold some of the Heydon lands cheap, leaving Sheppard and Smith £8,000 out of pocket.[104] Whatever had befallen Godsalve, by 1619, his wife Barbara was left to handle the consequences. Who did she turn to? Even after John Potts was married to his second wife, his first mother-in-law called upon him about her money problems. Having sold both Buckenham Ferry and Caistor earlier, Roger and Barbara had spent some time at Hempstead. Barbara was now living at Gorleston, above Yarmouth. Roger by this time appeared to be travelling and his creditors were anxious. John was already someone to be relied upon for advice and his sense of duty must have been strong (as with Sir Thomas Holland, and his stepfather) as he responded with concern. In July 1619 John wrote from Norwich:

> To the worshippfull my verye lovienge mother in lawe Mrs Barbara Godsalve give at Golstone
>
> Good Mother
>
> Since your being in Norwich, diverse have talked with me about my father Godsalve, & I perceive as well by their discourse, as also by some wordes which escaped Mr Smith that there is a purpose in the creditors to s[top] my father Godsalve with a writ of Bancrout [bankruptcy], if either he have not a sufficient warrant for his travells or that it can be reversed a thinge ordinary in these cases. This is a matter of many consequence & I thought fitt to give you speedy notice, for it extends to the inheritance which the Commissioners may sell notwithstanding all the conveyances made to Sir Tho Bendish. Redeem yourself by present counsailes, for delaye is dangerous neither indeed do I see how the mischief is to be [...].ated but by his retourne before this course be en[join]ed. This my intelligence I would have delivered [in] person but that other occasions hinder me, accept I pray my good will, as one that in best offices
>
> remain faithfully your loveinge
> sonne-in law John Potts[105]

Unfortunately Roger had fallen too deeply into debt. A single reference to Roger appears in the Acts of Privy Council for 19th November 1623 where a Robert Debden of London, gent tendered his appearance on behalf of Roger Godsalve of Gorleston. A final desperate letter from Barbara to Townshend in 1627 showed she was in danger of losing her home despite her husband having died some three years before:

> Barbara Godsalve to the Right Worshippfull Sir Roger Townshend kt & bt from Golstone 12 Aprell 1627
>
> I am bold to write unto you by this messenger which is my solicitor: that you would be pleased at my humble request to confer with him about my miserable estate as now it stands: for my great business being still delayed I am hopeless of present release towards the redemption of the lands where upon I now dwell which is all the maintenance for me and mine: for being run in arrear before Mr Godsalves death three years, and since three and more, that the time have been so long I can crave no longer forbearance: but the gentleman will enter and I must depart and so what will become of me I know not: yet good Sir if upon your advice and learned counsel it shall be thought fit that by petition to the Lord Keeper I may have order out of Court to obtain Sir William Campions money to pay my husbands private debts: which this Land being my joynter [jointure] stand engaged for part of them: that then I shall be able to discharge this debt and continue a poor living as now I do; this with my humble duty unto you and my hearty prayers to god to give you many happy days in this life
>
> I rest your poor distressed kinswoman
> Barbara Godsalve[106]
>
> For Sir William Campion see Family Notes 3.

Although the Godsalves had been living in Gorleston, a pleasant residential area overlooking Yarmouth, neither Barbara nor her husband chose to be buried there. When Barbara made her will in August 1633, she requested to be buried in the church of Steeple Bumstead in Essex 'by my good husband'. This parish was the home of the Bendish family who lived at Bower Hall. The Sir Thomas mentioned in John's letter had been High Sheriff of Essex in 1618 and was married to Dorothy Cutts, daughter of Richard Cutts. Dorothy and Barbara were sisters and so it was natural for her to turn to the Bendish family for help.[107] Her fortunes must have revived a little as when she died in December 1633, she was able to leave her two daughters, Judith and Anne, £50 each and her son Thomas received all her plate (except for one silver ewer). The plate was probably the heirloom plate that her husband Roger had been left by his father of which he was told to take good care and to pass it from heir to heir.[108] Somehow it had escaped the hands of the creditors. Thomas also had his parent's mansion house in Gorleston although most of the lands had been sold.[109] Barbara's servant Ann Bostocke was to have her wages and the Gorleston poor were to receive £3 at Christmas. She also gave 40s to a young goddaughter Barbara Godsalve for when she should marry. However her son Roger had to retrieve his money from Sir William Campion in whose hands 'ther is above £500 ... which he owes for land that was my jointure'. From this Roger 'shall pay himself ... whatsoever is due to him from me ... I leave it to himself hoping he will remember the rest of my children'. Her son Richard who was her executor seemed to have nothing and may have been reliant on his brother being successful in dealing with Campion.[110]

Perhaps John Potts felt that the Godsalves' decline might have been averted had Roger not become embroiled in the debts of his stepfather and Sir Edward Clere. Whatever the reason, he continued to offer help to the family in later years. He was present at the signing of an agreement in January 1648 whereby his wife's brother, Thomas Godsalve, would pay £10 a year to his uncle, John Godsalve, for life.[111] John, who was living on the Mannington estate under the aegis of Sir John Potts, did not enjoy the income for long as he was buried in Itteringham on 9th August 1648. To his death, Sir John retained some responsibility for the younger sisters of his first wife. For further details see Family Notes 7: Godsalve.

Marriage to Ursula

John Potts's next marriage, two years after Barbara's death, appeared to be his own choice. Dame Ursula Spelman was another Norfolk girl, from the fenlands - baptised on Christmas day 1584 in Hilgay where her family lived. She was the daughter of John Willoughby (later Sir John, of Risley, Derbyshire which he inherited from his uncle and aunt, Michael and Katherine Willoughby in 1594) and Frances Hawes of Norfolk. Ursula was named after her grandmother, Ursula Hawes and may have been close to both grandparents. Henry and Ursula were both buried at Hilgay, in 1592 and 1594.[112] Ursula was provided with 100 marks for her marriage (or at age 20).[113] For more on the Hawes and Willoughby families see Family Notes 15. Although her parents (with her brothers Henry and Francis) presumably took up residence at Risley Hall after 1594, Ursula married the Norfolk lawyer Sir Clement Spelman of Narborough. An older man, he had been sheriff of Norfolk in 1598 when Ursula was only 14. He had no children by his first wife Alice Kervile of Wiggenhall St Mary the Virgin.[114] Clement and Ursula had two sons, John, who was baptised at Narborough in March 1607, and Clement with whom she was pregnant when her husband died in September 1607. When did John Potts first meet Ursula? John's father's will, made in 1593, showed his close friendship with Augustine Palgrave (later Sir Augustine) who lived at North Barningham a few miles from Mannington.[115] Austin, as he was often called, married Elizabeth Willoughby of Hilgay and her younger sister Ursula would have visited often during her early teens to see her sister and her baby Mary (born before 1604). Did the 16 year-old John re-make her acquaintance when she baptised Clement in March 1608 at North Barningham church? He was at home from college (as we know from the letter of February 1608). Widowed with two small infants, the 23 year-old Ursula would have been staying with Sir Austin and Lady Elizabeth Palgrave, her sister, at their home at North Barningham Hall. Her late husband Sir Clement Spelman, as sheriff, had certainly been known to Sir Christopher Heydon.[116]

Perhaps there had long been an attraction between the two youngsters. In 1608 though, even if there had been a romance, Ursula would have had no dowry (being a widow). John's stepfather and guardian had to have money, hence the Godsalve marriage.

For whatever reason, Ursula, very unusually for the time, remained unmarried for ten years until she married John in 1617. They may have lived initially at her home at Narborough where their first child, John, was baptised in 1618. But we know that at least one of his children from his first marriage, Anne, was living with Sir Christopher Heydon in February 1619, quite possibly in Mannington. She pronounced on the oysters her father had sent home as 'very good ... both raw and Rost'. Sir Christopher, in his usual entertaining style, added, '& I allow her iudgemte but it being in the wane of the moon they are not so full as they wilbe in the new or full which is not your falt ... '.

Where John and Ursula had sent the oysters from was not given but it seems likely they were in Norwich as John received the letter from Sir Thomas Holland there two months later.[117] But this chapter of their lives, centring as it had around the magnetic personality of Sir Christopher, was about to end and John Potts's story would really begin.

Chapter 10

A Country Life

For most of their marriage John and Ursula Potts lived at Mannington with their family; daughters and sisters were married off and John took on the roles expected of a gentleman.

Home life

At 62, Sir Christopher Heydon died, intestate: Miles, his youngest son by his first wife, three years older than John, received the administration in February 1624.[1] This may suggest Miles, who had been admitted to the Inner Temple in 1610, was still in Norfolk in the early 1620s.

Although Mannington would have legally passed to John when he was 21 (in 1613), the property was subject to the lease Heydon had allowed Godsalve, which ended around 1616. As demonstrated in Chapter 7, the couple spent time at Narborough and Norwich until at least 1619 and may have used all three homes while Sir Christopher was alive. By 1621, John was being assessed for the subsidy for Mannington.[2] After Sir Christopher's death in 1623, John and Ursula were in permanent residence at Mannington with the children and most likely, his mother.[3] Ursula's last three children, Francis, Charles and Ursula, born around 1619 to 1625, would probably have been baptised there although this cannot be verified as, sadly, the Mannington registers are long since lost.

Ursula's two sons by her first husband, John and Clement Spelman, were already in their teens and would have been away at college. Sir Clement Spelman, perhaps surprisingly given that he was in his late forties and had two sons, had died intestate so there is no information on how he left his property. His eldest son John was to inherit Narborough Hall and, as the heir, was a good match; he and his stepfather John remained close throughout his life. Clement, training to be a lawyer, rose to be King's Counsel and was to make his name as Recorder of Nottingham.[4]

Dame Anne Heydon would have lived with John at Mannington Hall as Baconsthorpe was neither suitable nor hers, and no other property was hers by right. Did she see much of her other 13 children and step-children? John certainly helped his mother find suitable husbands for his now mature sisters, none of whom had been rushed into marriage early. Perhaps a lack of dowry prospects limited suitors; the girls would have come into their grandmother's legacies many years before. Learned and earnest puritan chaps were found for them. Of Anne's eldest brood, Frances died early in her marriage to Edmund Sadler; Katherine died, aged 41, in October 1631 only two years after marrying the well-to-do Thomas Lougher, rector of Letheringsett; Anne had died a few years after marrying the Reverend Thomas Case of Erpingham in 1631 and Charles was a London lawyer.[5] John, following his father's last wishes, had provided his sisters Anne and Katherine with a small dowry, an interest in a holding in Themelthorpe manor (lands and tenements scattered in Themelthorpe, Foxley, Bawdeswell and Hindolveston) which been held for the family by his brother Charles since 1622.[6] In 1632 Katherine's widowed husband, her sister Anne and her husband Thomas surrendered their rights in the property (apparently half of a messuage and 31 acres) to Edward Nabbs a gentleman of Hindolveston, who was purchasing parcels land all around that part of Norfolk. This action was presumably to raise a sum of money for Case and Lougher. (See below for the other moiety.)

John also extended this care to his niece, Frances Sadler, daughter of his elder sister Frances. Frances Potts senior had married Edmund Sadler, of Parndon in Essex, and their daughter was born around 1617-19. It may be that Frances Potts/Sadler died soon afterwards as Edmund Sadler was married to his third wife, a widow named Mary, when he made his will in 1634.[7] Edmund's first wife was Frances, the daughter of Robert Palgrave of Barningham, by whom he had a daughter Mary who married John Cory the Norwich merchant in 1631.[8] Edmund Sadler may have been the translator of '*Orion Republicae*', a humanist treatise which had been published in Latin in 1605. Sadler thought every man should be able to read it and translated it into English straightaway as the *North Star*. If the same man, he would have been known to Sir Christopher Heydon. Sadler altered the dedication (which had been to the King) to Sir Julius Caesar (someone well-known to Heydon's family and married to Anne Woodhouse, granddaughter of Sir Nicholas Bacon).[9]

Frances Sadler junior had therefore lost both her mother and father by 1635 and had only a £200 legacy from her father and a bond of £700 due from her uncle, John Potts. John and Charles were overseers of the will of Edmund Sadler who called them his 'well beloved brothers'. John received a pair of German pistols in cases and Charles was to chose '6 books of history in folio' from his study. Presumably to discharge his obligation, John bought, in December 1636, again with Charles as trustee, a relatively small package of named closes in Salle that had earlier belonged to Thomas Lord Knyvett.[10] Frances then married well, to George Hunt of Salle, in 1638.

Of Anne Potts's Heydon stepchildren, William had died in 1627, Miles was off fighting (or maybe dead), and John was a royalist working for the King (see Family Notes 9: Heydon children). Anne's last child Martha, from her marriage to Heydon, was the only one to outlive her mother. Martha had married rather late, in 1632, to William Crowe of East Bilney.[11] The Crowes were of Itteringham for some years before taking a lease of Baconsthorpe Park.[12] No doubt Anne, in her 70s, would have gone to Itteringham church for the baptisms of her Crowe granddaughter Anne (1638), and her great-great-grandchildren William Hunt (1639) and, if she were well enough, that of Anne Hunt in September 1641.

After the excitement of the Heydon years, John and Ursula lived more quietly in Norfolk during the next few years, looking after his estate which he extended by purchases. He made a number of modest acquisitions that added extra lands and a degree of cohesion to the estate. The ancient manor of Coldham in Little Barningham was brought in and various small closes and parts of the open fields in

Saxthorpe, Itteringham and Wolterton were integrated into Mannington's holdings. Even without deeds surviving for all of these, most can be seen at least graphically in annotations, in orange ink, on an earlier estate map of Mannington.[13] The deeds that have survived show John began acquiring lands from 1614 with the purchase of Coldham and increased his activities in the 1620s and 1630s when he had fully come into the estate. The detail will be covered in a future volume.[14]

At some point Mannington church, which had been in such decay in 1552, was renovated and made functional again.[15] From the description of his marriage by John Potts senior in one of his 1590s court actions, the Hall was used for the ceremony. His children had been baptised in Itteringham and he may not have felt the need to renovate the chapel. Were Sir John Potts and Dame Ursula the benefactors? As they were buried there it is quite likely they may have been responsible.

John's eldest daughters

John's first children, by Barbara, were growing up and their now very extended social network, through the intricacies of the earlier family marriages, included many of the major gentry families in Norfolk - Heydon, Clere, Hobart, Townshend, Bacon, Spelman, Holland, Knyvett, Wodehouse and Cornwallis. John's father had also regarded the Astleys and Palgraves as close friends. His brother-in-law, Sir Augustine, had been High Sheriff in 1617. The girls however were still only minor gentry and their matches reflect their status. There was however evidence of John Potts's growing reputation. Anne, who was old enough in 1619 to offer her step-grandfather her opinion on oysters, was the eldest and on 1st November 1627, aged about 17, married young James Scamler of Briston, at the desire of his uncle. James Scamler senior had obviously taken a strong liking to John Potts.[16] In about 1625 at a meeting of various gentlemen in Norwich, perhaps at an assize, James senior had proposed the idea of James junior being married to Anne Potts. He told John Potts that his wife Mary was sickly and would not live for long. Both of them had a great liking for young James, and Mary in particular was determined to leave him some of her property in Hickling to the annual value of £500. She also wanted him to have a 'very fair house' there called Hickling Priory, which he should have as richly furnished with plate and hangings and household stuff as the house of any or most Norfolk gents. She and James urged Potts to ride to Hickling to view the property, which he did.

After many meetings and letters, James senior finally came to Mannington, bringing the young James for his first meeting with Anne. He also brought all the documents that would show the title to the property and its annual income. Edward, James junior's father, was there too. Fortunately the draft agreement for a marriage settlement on Anne and James has survived in the Frere manuscripts.[17] Dated 26th October 1626 and probably written by John Potts himself, it was a record signed on the day of the meeting between John Potts of Mannington and James Scamler the elder of Hickling (the younger James's childless uncle, who made James the son of his brother Edward of Briston his main heir). This 'conference about a marriage intended … if the marriage proceed' agreed six items that would make up the marriage settlement. In summary, James Scamler senior would give James the younger and his heirs his messuages and lands at Hickling Priory and his manors in Happisburgh; and Edward would give him his manors of Briston Micklehall and Loundhall. In consideration for this John Potts would give James senior £900. James senior would give James junior and Anne £80 a year 'until cohabitation' and £100 a year thereafter during the lives of James senior and his wife Mary. The phrasing here strongly suggests a settlement on minors and possibly a betrothal and then a delay intended before an actual marriage. If James junior died before cohabitation the jointure would cease and Anne would be paid £1,000 by James senior. If Anne died before cohabitation then John would get his £900 back. The lands involved would be 'tied to pay' Willoughby Potts, John's younger daughter, £100 after the death of James senior and Mary. To ensure that Willoughby did not have to wait too long for Mary to die to get her bequest, the £100 would be paid after a period (left blank in the draft) of years from the date of the settlement. The marginal note by Edward confirmed that the £100 charge on the land would be void in the event that James junior died and Anne received her £1,000.

While the inheritance of lands from father and uncle can be seen from Scamler wills, this draft settlement showed the size of dowry that Potts had to provide for Anne. His daughter, Barbara was not mentioned. Although she was not yet married, she might have been betrothed. Edward however, involved as he was in James the elder's debts, decided that the portion offered by Potts was insufficient. So the deal was off. James went to see Sir Henry Buckman to see about the possibility of one of his daughters marrying James. This came to nothing and within the year, James renewed his campaign with John Potts. He was reported to have said that John could decide whether it should be Anne or his second daughter as he would prefer James junior to marry one of Potts's daughters than one of any other gent in the country.

The final marriage settlement was a little different from the outline agreement they had all signed. Fortunately it is recited in the chancery action that occurred some years after Anne and James had married. In a deed of 25th October 1627, James the elder conveyed to James and Anne the manor of Happisburgh Crispins and the Priory in Hickling and other lands. The arrangement was that the property should remain to the use of James senior and Mary his wife for life, before passing to James and Anne and their heirs. If they failed to have male heirs, the remainder would pass to Thomas junior, Edward's younger son. If both had no sons the property would default to their female heirs.

Potts said that previously he had stuck at offering a portion of £700 and had pressed for James and Mary to pay the young couple an allowance of £120 a year for life as a jointure on Anne and a further £80 a year for their present maintenance, before they actually took possession of the property. He raised the offer to £800 but Mary refused this and a new agreement was eventually reached with a different interim maintenance arrangement and apparently no jointure annuity. Potts had earlier lent James senior £200 (plus £8 interest), due for repayment in July 1626 and hence well overdue by autumn 1627. This debt would be cancelled. Potts would pay £80 a year interim maintenance to the youngsters until James and Mary died. Edward would pay £100 to James senior, presumably simply as a contribution to see his son well married, although there may have been some other more complex reason lying behind this. This time no reference was made to any side arrangements for Willoughby, any jointure sum or any one-off portion payment by Potts. This was the deal in the 25th October deed and the marriage took place a few days later on 1st November 1627.

The £80 annuity was to be paid out of the Irmingland property - a very early indication that it was convenient to use this property to secure Potts commitments and mortgages. John Potts's servant Christopher Body delivered the bond to be cancelled and the £100 from Edward to James the elder. Body might have been the Mannington steward by this time since these were large sums of money to entrust to a minor servant. It seems that this final deal enabled Potts to avoid paying the large portion that would be used to pay off James's debts, albeit at the cost of £80 a year. Edward then held in trust James senior's lease of the manor of Thurne Ashby and Oby as security for covering James's debts, which Edward said he thought totalled £1,000 or more. Potts and Edward agreed to pay off James's debts until such time as the Thurne lease could be sold. The solution came with the lease being conveyed to Potts and he in turn sold it on to Robert Houghton of Itteringham for £800, which was more than the minimum sum James had given him authority to sell it for. Both James and Potts were parties to the conveyance to Houghton.

So Anne and James lived in their 'fine house' at Hickling. But as with most of the members of the Potts family, they ended up in chancery. In May 1634 Adam Scamler esq of Honingham, as executor of the elder James Scamler who died in 1633, sued his Scamler and Potts relations.[18] The bill of complaint and the collective answer by John Potts esq, Edward Scamler of Briston and James Scamler the younger showed that James the elder had two other brothers apart from Edward - Thomas and Adam. Adam claimed that his brother James had meant various lands in Happisburgh and Hickling, including the 'scite of Hickling Priory', to pass in equal thirds to Adam's son and Edward's two boys. He also claimed that amongst arrangements to be made for clearing James senior's debts, James had meant his brother Thomas to have an income for life from the real estate. He claimed that the Potts marriage portion of £900 and the £300 from Edward were intended to pay off James senior's debts.

The Potts camp of course disagreed and displayed the 1627 settlement. At no stage were Adam or Thomas involved in the arrangements or default sequence for inheritance. James senior had a clause allowing him to lease the premises for ten years and it seems that after his death Thomas had found an unsigned and undated paper of James which implied he might have been considering leasing the premises to him. The defence noted, for added credibility in chancery, that Francis Bacon esq had drawn up all the papers, which after the October sealing were recorded in a fine at Westminster. Potts and Edward Scamler said that at no time had James intended to settle any property on anyone other than as described. Indeed James had explained to John Potts certain wickednesses done to him by Adam and said that even though Adam was a lawyer he would never give advice to his brother without first seeing that his bill was paid in advance! Presumably the action failed and the Scamlers were able to enjoy Hickling. Perhaps they outgrew the house or maybe the temptation to add a neighbouring property to the extended Potts family portfolio was the trigger. Whatever the reason, in October 1660 Anne returned to live next door to her old family home when husband James, now a successful lawyer, bought Wolterton Hall from Richard Houghton.[19] Links with Hickling were maintained and James left 12s a year to the church and poor there, in 1682. Anne appears to have been no fool; two summers running, she haggled with hired help over the wage rates and if they didn't like it, told them where they could go. Two servants walked out, Edward Mack in July 1663 and Philip Harvey in July 1664.[20] Their son James Scamler inherited Wolterton.

John Potts's next eldest, Barbara, named after her mother, married a local gentleman John Hills of Wood Dalling.[21] John Hills's father, Edmund Hills esq, of Wood Dalling Hall also had property in the same part of London as the Potts. When Edmund made his will in October 1626 neither of his sons appeared to be married. John, the youngest son, would inherit his lands called 'The White House Rentes in Holborn', the elder son having Wood Dalling after his mother's death.[22] Barbara and John were probably married around 1628 or perhaps after John had come into his property in 1629, when Barbara would have been around 16 or 17.[23]

A marriage settlement must have been agreed in which John Potts also gave London property to John and Barbara. Barbara's jointure 'of estate and houses in St Andrew's Holborn' was later mentioned in John Hills's will of 1662.[24] Although they had London property, Barbara and John Hills stayed in north Norfolk. At Cockthorpe, north of Holt, they buried daughter Amie in 1639 and baptised another Amie in 1640, Edmund in 1641 and Barbara in 1648. Certainly John was of Cockthorpe in 1662 where he was buried and had his brother-in-law James Scamler, by then of Wolterton, as one of his executors. Their daughter Barbara married Daniel Green of Felmingham where her mother, who outlived her husband, is reputed to be buried.[25] Of their sons John and Francis (who inherited the London lands between them), John had 'been set up in trade'. Francis, who also married a Barbara, died a yeoman of Itteringham in 1690 with his (step) uncle's Mannington estate steward Daniel Muddiclift, as a witness to his will.[26]

Some of the Hills that were in the Saxthorpe/Corpusty area and were also tenants of the Mannington estate later in the seventeenth century were descended from Barbara's marriage. John and Barbara also had a 'dear and sweet granddaughter' called Anne Jessup. Their daughter, Anne Hills, had married the minister of Colkirk church, Mr John (Jonathan) Jessup. Anne had died on February 28th 1660 and her husband was buried on 25th June 1662, leaving the child an orphan.[27] The little girl survived and by 1683 was married to William Wiggott of Tuttington.

Willoughby, the third daughter, was the youngest of John Potts's first three daughters. She married Jeffrey Ward, son of Thomas Ward of Brooke in south Norfolk, around 1635/6. They had a son John, baptised in Itteringham in December 1643.[28] Sadly for Willoughby, her husband died young and insolvent, in August 1647. He was buried in Brooke four months after his grandfather, for whom he had been named.[29] In February 1650 Willoughby buried their daughter Elizabeth. It would seem that none of Willoughby's Ward sons survived as Brooke descended to her brother-in-law George.[30] One daughter Anne lived to marry Edward Earle of Cawston.[31] Whether in an attempt to deal with Jeffrey's debts which, as his executrix, Willoughby had to settle or just to assist with his granddaughter's provision, John Potts and his brother Charles, the lawyer, became trustees in a conveyance.[32] On 1st September 1650 the advowson of Brooke, parcels of land there and a messuage and inn called The King's Head were conveyed by Thomas Ward esq (Jeffrey's elder brother) and Willoughby, the daughter of Sir John Potts and widow of Jeffrey Ward gent to Sir John and Charles Potts in trust to provide for Willoughby for her life and then for the benefit of Anne Ward her daughter until Anne had received £1,100 profits from it, with ultimate reversion to Thomas's heirs.

The parish register for Brooke noted that, in Bungay, on the last day of October 1654 Willoughby Ward, widow, and daughter of Sir John Potts, married Thomas Burghill gent. Their first born, Thomas was buried at Kirstead, near Bungay as a baby. Another son also called Thomas must have been born soon afterwards: he was aged 9 in the Visitation of 1664.[33] The couple later returned to Brooke where a daughter Willoughby was baptised in June 1657 and, sadly, she was buried in June 1659. Arabella their daughter was baptised in January 1659. Thomas senior was a JP in 1664 in Suffolk and had the second largest house in Bungay in 1674.[34] He and Willoughby appeared in chancery in 1666 sued by Anne Earle, her daughter by Jeffrey Ward. Anne, not content with the £1,100, now accused her mother of settling property rightfully hers, from her mother's original jointure from the 1630s, on her son Thomas Burghill junior.[35] Thomas junior later lived in Earlham.[36]

How did John Potts find the dowries for all his daughters? The extensive London holdings helped with Barbara but at some point in the 1630s he sold the remainder to his brother Charles. However at this stage John was reasonably solvent, with no major drain on his income so some marriage portions could have been in cash.

County roles

Apart from dutifully assisting friends and family, and building up his estate, John was active in his late twenties and thirties playing the role expected of him in the county. Norfolk was unusual in not being dominated by a single great family; the Howards were in decline here and the lord lieutenant was a rare visitor. The opportunity to influence affairs in the countryside was eagerly fought over; the places for the knights of the shire, the sheriff, the deputy lords lieutenant and the justices of the peace were filled by ambitious local families, all competing for a share of the power. Unlike Ketton-Cremer, we believe this atmosphere made the kinship network of even greater importance than elsewhere. Every string that could be pulled was used. John certainly kept up with all the major county events. On January 27th 1624 he wrote (the letter is unaddressed but probably to Lord Townshend of Raynham) giving the results of the chaotic election for the two knights of the shire held the day before. Sir Thomas Holland, Sir John Corbett and Sir Robert Gawdy were standing; with Holland clearly elected, the sheriff declared the other winner to be Corbett. Potts, who had backed Corbett (a relation through the Heydons), told how Gawdy's supporters tried to prevent the result being approved by carrying him and his son 'downe into the markett place in triumph'. Even Potts had been swept up in the action.[37] Subsequently on February 26th they sent a petition with 300-400 freeholders' names to parliament claiming the sheriff's return was invalid because he had broken off the poll and declared for Corbett. In the end parliament heard that Gawdy had been so put out not to win the first position - Holland received over 1,500 votes - that he had refused the second, leaving the sheriff no choice but to elect Corbett.[38] John's experience of these local political battles was to stand him in good stead.

He was named on the first Commission of the Peace for Norfolk of Charles I's reign in 1625 although he had been appointed a justice as early as 1622.[39] His attendance on the bench is difficult to quantify as early sessions records are patchy.[40] His first known work was to help two senior justices, Sir Anthony Browne and Sir Thomas Hyrne, with collecting poor relief tax in Heydon, Salle and Dalling in 1622.[41] He had grown up knowing these parishes well; his aunt Boteler and his father's cousin Buggin had lived in Heydon, the latter until around 1615. In Salle, he would have known Thomas Cletheroe (or Clitheroe), a reluctant tax payer. He worked closely with Sir Thomas Hyrne who as MP for Norwich in 1623 and 1625 would have needed reliable young justices to carry out business in their areas. Hyrne, of Haveringland, was himself a shining example of a man who rose quickly through public service. His grandfather had been a yeoman and Thomas was knighted by 1609.[42] The two families remained friends for many years. In 1625, John wrote a curt letter to a local attorney, Richard Bond, who had failed to come to a meeting set up by Potts:

> Dec 9 1625 Mannington hous
>
> Whereas I lately gave you knowledge by writtings, of a reference to me directed from Sir John Dodgyge [Doddridge] knt one of his Majesty's Justices of Assises for this County, requiring you to [pursue] an order heretofore made by Sir Thomas Hirne kt & myself between you and Henry Beane by vertue of the like Reference. And that I had appoynted this present day by 9 of the clock in the forenoone to mett for that purpose at the howse of James Grymer in Itteringham which accordingle I have performed And the said Henry Beane with others, to whome the business doth appeare, have there attended this day to noe purpose by resons of your absence.
>
> These are to signifie unto you that I have yet further appoynted the 15th day of this present month by 8 of the clock in the morning to be at the signe of the Black Boy in Ailsham for the hearing of the said business ... Requiring you then & there to be present ...
>
> And so I bidd you farewell
>
> yr loving frend
> Jn Potts[43]

The wasted meeting that had been at 9 o'clock had been re-booked for 8!

One suspects he had little time for those not as conscientious as himself but may have been a just man. Over the year of 1629, he committed six men and women to Little Walsingham gaol who were all then discharged. Two, George Sparke and Agnes King, unfortunately did not learn from this experience and re-offended. The second time they remained in prison.[44] His understanding of the everyday work of county government increased during this period; now in his 30s, his reliability and diligence earned him respect among his friends. A letter (which survived only because it was re-used by Sir John Hobart to jot down some notes) written by Potts to his 'very much honoured friend Sir John Hobart at his house in Chapply field, Norwich' is a good example of his concern for justice. Instead of leaving a clerk to update Hobart on the sessions cases that he had not been able to attend, Potts wanted to give him a personal account. He was concerned that one poor man may be treated leniently and another, an accomplice to murder, who was claiming Hobart had let him off, should be properly tried. Dated before 1630:

Noble Sir

I am glad of your health & that you had a will to be at your Country service though impedimented by greater occasions; I had Sir Austin Palgrave's assistance & we dispatched the business, whereof, though your man could [have] sufficiently informed you, yet I did you rather borrow tyme to give you a short account, because some persons brought before us seek to shelter themselves under you, whom I know too just & worthy to countenance any disorder. Thornborowe is punishable for selling beer without licence but as a poore man the mony may given him back, farther help may be afforded him as you please & that there be cause;

John Stanton of Sparham shews licence under your hande, Sir Charles Groose & Sir Robert Kemp, but I suppose it was surreptious, for I pray, take notice from me that this man hath been often suppressed for great disorders, make him uncapable but especially when Hamond did barbarously murder Tompson in Stanton's house, this Stanton & his wife did blaunch & daube their testimony, being present in the roome & Stanton himself was suspected to hold the door;

Sir, let me as a mere frend advise you not to lay so much guilt upon yourself, as to give licence, or permitt a man notorious. Either be pleased to command the license into your own hand or else signifie your mind & consent unto me to do it; for I protest it is my love to yourself that makes me write thus & leave the right to be done by your selfe, els I would done it; So with my service to yourself & your hon'ble ladies, I rest

yr faithful frend to love & serve you

Jo Potts[45]

He was confident enough of his relationship with Sir John to tell him what course of action he should take, to undo Sir John's mistake in letting Stanton slip through the system.

In other duties of the justice, John took his place alongside the senior men. In August 1620 his name appeared on a memorandum from the Norwich assize; his was among eighteen names, including Thomas Wodehouse, Christopher Calthorpe, Arthur Heveningham and Charles Cornwallis, who were to make a return of those subscribing to a collection for King James's daughter Elizabeth in the Rhenish lands.[46]

As early as 1622, he was signing letters sent to the Privy Council about the survey of crop stores, levies and other returns, along with John Smith, Owen Sheppard, Anthony Hobart, the two Heveninghams, Corbett and Drury. Aware of the growing concerns over the King's demands for money at a difficult economic time (the harvests had been bad for several years and corn prices were very high), he reported on a meeting held to discuss a collection (probably the second levy for Elizabeth) in 1623, the outcome of which was that 'People do not want to pay more than was formerly collected'.[47]

As commissioners for the raising of loans for the King for the defence of religion, Potts and Adam Scamler were working together in December 1626 with William Denny and John's future parliamentary colleague Edmund Moundeford of Feltwell.[48] Moundeford's grandmother was Bridget, daughter of John Spelman of Narborough so he would have been aware of Ursula through her first husband. Edmund and Potts became close friends. When Ursula's grandson was baptised Mundeford, around 1640, Edmund was no doubt his godfather. Edmund's stepmother was Thomas Knyvett's aunt Abigail and another cousin, Elizabeth, married Miles Hobart of Intwood.

By August 1628 Potts wrote as one of the commissioners of subsidy in Norfolk, the last name in an impressive list (William de Grey, Anthony Hobart, Thomas Wodehouse, Charles Cornwallis, John Hare, and Owen Sheppard). Was he the one who undertook the paper work, organising fact-finding and letter writing? Their letter talked of the problems of corn, the harvest, the difficulties on the seas, the French: all the issues of the day.[49] The situation worsened; the poor were really suffering from the corn prices which were now at 50s a quarter and by 1630 the Privy Council asked for detailed reports. The signatories of a letter about the price of corn, sent on 24th January 1631, were John Hobart, Roger Townshend, Richard Berney, John Heveningham, Hamond L'Estrange, Anthony Drury, John Potts, Thomas Derham, Owen Smyth, Edmund Moundeford, Anthony Hobart and John Cooke. Potts was working again alongside his friend, Edmund. Thomas Derham of West Dereham, had only recently been made a justice and wrote to Potts, as his 'cousin', on July 29th 1630 thanking him and his cousin Spelman: 'Although I am very unfit for the execution thereof yett I will doe my best service to his majesty & my countrie resting thankfull for all my worthie frends'.[50]

In June a detailed return was sent by Hobart, Owen Smyth and Potts adding to that already sent in for the hundred of South Erpingham by Adam Scamler.[51] Their comprehensive survey on 5th May revealed that there were no more than 3,697 coombs of any sort of grain available to feed 6,215 people until harvest time. In line with the measures to diminish consumption as suggested by Francis Mapes, the Sheriff, to the Council in March, they had ordered that strong and small beer be sold at a set price; that the strength be lessened (which had reduced drunkenness) and were watching a good crop growing. They hoped 'our poor might continue in some reasonable order' but feared that the weavers and combers would pass on losses in the stuff trade by lowering the wages of the 'poor women and children spinners', a large section of their community.

As a justice, John was always engaged with the system of relief for the poor: during the 1630s, surviving papers show that he had to arrange and attend monthly meetings for the hundred of Eynsford (not his own hundred) at Mr William Stumpes's house at Reepham where he sat with Sir John Hobart and Sir Thomas Hyrne. There they heard from the petty constables about poor apprenticeships, the churchwardens for lists of landowners and the overseers to receive the poor accounts. The organisation alone took time. The warrant to the chief constables on 7th February 1633 ordered the meeting of all churchwardens on Wednesday 19th February. At the bottom was added, probably by Potts, 'Lett Sir Thomas Hirne be acquainted with this meetinge and intreat his Clerkes to prepare some warrants to be delivered to the churchwardens to collecte by according to the tenure of the commissions'.

These meetings would have taken all day: John would ride to Reepham to be there early in the morning and hear the business of every parish in the hundred before riding home. By 1635, Sir Owen Smyth, John Potts and his stepson, John Spelman were arranging a meeting for the hundred of Eynsford on 23rd April 1635 at Mr Stumpes's house in Hackford giving only six days notice:

> To the Chief Constables of Eynsford
>
> For as much as the season of the year requires our care for the appointment of overseers for the poor in every parish ... we charge you to cause all overseers for the poor to be and appear before us at house of Mr William Stumpe gent in Hackford on Thurs next 23 April by 12 o/clock to present to us in writing, names of six or four of the most sufficient inhabitants of their towne to be by us appointed overseers for their poor this year and to deliver us in writing distinctly and fairly written a true & perfecte accompt, approved & subscribed by their minister & chief inhabitants, of all such money as they have received or assessed towards the relief of their poor and their disbursements and what stock remains
>
> Under our hand and seales 17th April 1635[52]

Other parts of Norfolk would also call on the justices to give aid: in 1636 Lynn suffered terribly from an outbreak of plague (busy trading ports were very vulnerable) and asked for relief. A letter from Norwich signed by Hobart, Owen Smyth, Miles Hobart, Robert Kemp, John Holland, Mapes, Windham, Talbot and Potts was a masterpiece of apologetic refusal.[53]

Another role was added to John's career when he became a captain for the musters of trained selected forces of horse and foot. In 1627 he spent Friday 13th July on the Ollands at Heydon, organising his 120 men for the Holt hundred, for viewing by Sir John Hobart. The next year it was Friday 8th August and every summer this would be a regular fixture for him.

John was now one of the local gentry who could be relied upon in litigation disputes. In September 1627 he was one of the commissioned panel sitting with Sir Thomas Hyrne and two officials at Aylsham hearing the enquiry following the death of his neighbour Sir Henry Hobart, the chief justice. Potts was able to give information on Dame Agnes Clere (his guardian's step-grandmother) and the Hobart holdings in Blickling and Itteringham.[54]

When Sir John Hobart took over his estate and found himself in a dispute, in 1630, over a sheep foldcourse in Oulton, Mannington was used as a venue for cross-examining witnesses in the case.[55] Hobart later leased to John the holding of the Leet and View (of Frankpledge) for Itteringham, Wickmere and Little Barningham for 31 years from 1638. After John paid his annual rent of 6s 3d, any fees or fines above that would be his profit.[56]

In January 1631 the cause of William Bladwell v John Richers and Henry Richers was referred for arbitration to John Potts, Robert Houghton, John Duke and William Hill.[57] This is an interesting group. John would have known the Richers family of Kent both as a child from living at Eltham in his grandmother's house and as an adult in Norfolk. The Richers of Wrotham had inherited lands in Swannington, a few miles from Mannington, from a cousin and John Richers was lord of the manor in 1612. His son Henry Richers was a Norfolk JP married to Elizabeth Corbett, daughter of Sir Miles. Henry was given as of Aylsham in his will in 1636 so Potts would certainly have known him well. Robert Houghton was Potts's neighbour now at Wolterton.[58] He also knew the Richers both locally and through the marriage of a cousin, (Sir) Robert Houghton the lawyer to Mary Richers in Wrotham in February 1581.[59] John Duke might have been one of the Duke brothers that attended Caius College in 1605 after having been at school in Norfolk. The action must relate to the sale of Swannington from the Richers to William Bladwell esq, who died there in 1642.[60]

In 1639 Robert Mapes, the legally trained brother of Sheriff Mapes, and John Potts were given a commissioners' warrant by the court of chancery to examine witnesses in a cause between James Scamler esq, complainant and John Calthorpe gent, one of the defendants.[61] Here we have Potts hearing witnesses in an action brought by his son-in-law James which today would be a conflict of interest but in those days was seen as appropriate for the local knowledge that the examiner brought to the proceedings. This turned into a long running cause with claim and counter claims.

Ursula's family

While such duties kept John busy, he and Ursula continued to enjoy their extended family celebrations locally. A wedding in September 1628 in Norwich brought together Ursula's nephew John Palgrave (her elder sister Elizabeth's son) and Elizabeth Jermy, a daughter of wealthy lawyer, John Jermy esq of nearby Gunton.[62] In 1629 Ursula was a godparent at the baptism of little Austin, first son of this marriage. On 14th December, Lady Spelman (as this was still Ursula's status then) stood in North Barningham church with her sister's husband, Sir Austin Palgrave, John Jermy esq (the two grandfathers) and Lady Sydney from Walsingham.[63] John was next to be a godparent - in November 1630 he was at the baptism of Elizabeth, John Palgrave's daughter. At the church in North Barningham he stood with the baby's two grandmothers, Dame Elizabeth Palgrave and Mrs John Jermy. Sadly Ursula's sister, Dame Elizabeth, died only four years later in July 1634. Her likeness, in marble, in North Barningham church is not unlike Ursula's portrait (see Plate 2). In December the same year, her daughter-in-law, the young mother Elizabeth, was also buried. Two years later, John Palgrave married again, to the widow Anne Gascoigne of Illington. The families were now linked with the de Greys of Merton (Anne's maiden name) and the Guybons (her sister was Lady Barbara Guybon).

Later the Potts would have attended the baptism of baby Anne, the daughter of John's younger stepsister Martha Heydon and her husband William Crowe, at Itteringham church on 16th April 1638. John probably also accompanied his elderly mother to her great-great-grandson's baptism in the same church in October 1639. Baby William Hunt was his late sister Frances's grandchild, son of Frances and George Hunt of Salle.

John and Ursula had made a good match for her Spelman son, John. In 1632 the heir to Narborough married Anne Heveningham, daughter of Sir John Heveningham of Ketteringham, another long-standing Norfolk and Suffolk family. This link led to the marriage, seven years later, of Anne's sister, Susan Heveningham, to John and Ursula's own heir, John Potts (later the second baronet). Susan and Anne were the sisters of William and Arthur Heveningham, and the granddaughters of Sir Arthur, sheriff and deputy lieutenant, who had been so influential in Norfolk politics in the late 1580s and 1590s and with whom Sir Christopher Heydon had sided against the Bacon/Gawdy set in the bitter local disputes of the time.[64] The family was later to be split by the civil war. Potts was now linked more closely to another major group of families - the Heveninghams were intermarried with the Pastons, Knyvetts, Sheltons and later John Carey, fifth Baron Hunsdon.

Francis Potts

John had been fortunate that all his children had survived infancy; sadly he and Ursula were to lose their second son, Francis, while still a young man. Francis's life remains a mystery. He was probably born about 1620 (after 1619 and before 1622) when the family were then living either in Norwich or Mannington. There is no record of his having a university education or legal training. The best clue to his life comes from a surviving three-quarter length portrait showing Francis, aged 18, seated on a bank, with a pointer dog, a fowling gun, a plan, a gold compass and, behind him, a waterfall and hills (see Plate 3).[65] This distinctive painting, probably dating to around 1638-1640, contained far more colour, content and background detail than the other Potts portraits and could have been painted abroad. For more details of the family portraits see Chapter 24. It has a motto which has been read as 'Utraque Minerva ducit' and translated as 'Minerva is the guide in her double capacity as goddess of War and of the Arts'.[66] This would imply that Francis was perhaps already making his way as a military surveyor or map maker or even an architect, as well as a traveller with a keen interest in the arts. Was he influenced by the travels of William Paston who, ten years older than Francis, had spent many months in Italy and further afield after he finished his education? He had travelled after 1627, returning probably by the mid 1630s.[67] In the 1664 *Visitation of Norfolk* Francis was said to have died in Naples, presumably information supplied by the family at the time. No date was given. So far no documentary record of his time abroad has been found, despite research in the letters to London of the British Consul in Naples in the second half of the century and in travel diaries of the time.[68] Assuming that he did travel in his early 20s, Francis would almost certainly have been in a like-minded group of young gentlemen furthering their education and their artistic interests. Naples was certainly a magnet on the European tour with very many workshops and many famous artists working there in the first half of the century. With whom did he travel? One possible answer, given his mother's relations and his father's contacts is made here.

Through his mother's first marriage Francis was a kinsman of Sir John Spelman of Stinton Hall, himself a noted politician, antiquarian and writer and the son of the famous antiquarian and collector Sir Henry Spelman. In the 1640s Sir John and his wife were living at Salle and visited Mannington and other houses locally.[69] Spelman was one of a select group of collectors and artists in the circle of Thomas Howard, the Earl of Arundel, himself a noted visitor to Italy and collector of art.[70] Arundel had long been a patron of Inigo Jones, whom he had taken with him to Italy for a year in 1613-14. Inigo Jones was until 1643 the Royal Surveyor among his other architectural roles. In November 1640 Sir John Potts consulted Jones in his committee work concerning a city church.[71] Another in the Arundel group was John Selden, the lawyer and learned scholar who, in addition to his artistic interests, served alongside Potts in Parliament and was a lay member in the Westminster Assembly of Divines. The Earl himself left England in February 1642 and travelled until his death at Padua in 1646.

A fourth in the Arundel circle was Sir Robert Cotton (1571-1631) the traveller, collector, antiquarian and politician. The Cotton manuscript and book collection in the British Library comes from his acquisitions and those of his grandson, Sir John the third baronet. Surrounded by this intellectual network, it could be that Francis Potts may have been a travelling companion of the young John Cotton who is known to have journeyed widely across Europe, of course including Italy. John and

Francis were of much the same age. John Cotton was born in 1621 and is known to have travelled, after his father's death, between 1639 and 1642 - precisely the right time for the 18 year-old Francis to have been abroad. Francis's cousin Elizabeth was shortly to marry his father's friend Sir Simonds D'Ewes who had known the late Sir Robert well.[72] There may have been other connections too between the families.[73]

How Francis died is not known but disease must be a likely contender. A letter to Secretary Thurloe of August 1656 reported that 170,000 had recently died of plague in Naples.[74] While Francis had died well before this (as he was not mentioned in his uncle's 1649 will), he may well have succumbed to an earlier attack of plague in Naples.[75] The 1664 Visitation also indicates that he may have had descendants but no names were given and there was no mention of him or any such family in any of the later Potts settlements, wills or legal actions, including the 1673 wills of his father and sister.[76] The first of the only two deed references to him was in the default sequence of heirs in the October 1639 marriage settlement of his brother John.[77] The second was in the manor court book for Themelthorpe.[78] Charles Potts, of Middle Temple, still held the other half of the family property in Themelthorpe (half a messuage with thirty or so acres attached) and in February 1642, acting as trustee for Sir John Potts and his second son Francis Potts of London, he conveyed this to Edward Nabbs.[79] The entry also referred to a deed of the same day in which Sir John and Francis had covenanted unidentified actions, but which clearly included the transfer of the second half of this property to Nabbs. This unexplained deed had Sir John, Dame Ursula, Charles and Francis as one party and Nabbs as the second; could the family involvement hint at a marriage settlement? Or was the sale just to raise some cash for Francis to go travelling? All these events would have been happily agreed to by the lord of the manor of Themelthorpe, George Hunt of Salle, husband of Sir John's niece Frances. The Hunts were originally from Hindolveston and his father William had held the manor in 1632. Edward Nabbs was from an Oxfordshire family before he appeared in North Norfolk. By his death in 1645 he had become the constable for Eynsford hundred.[80] His source of funds is unclear, but he may have been in trade or the law in London.[81]

One other clue adds to the possibility that Francis Potts was to marry into the Nabbs family: when Edward died, in 1645, he left a gift of 40s to Ursula Potts, Francis's sister. As he had made his will in November 1643 and all the other legatees were his children and grandchildren, Ursula seems to have had a special place in the Nabbs family. Had she been particularly supportive to them in their mutual grief at Francis Potts's early death abroad? Perhaps the young people had just been favourites in the house, godparents to the grandchildren: Edward's son and heir John had called his son Francis and his daughter Ursula. His sister Margaret had a daughter, Frances.[82] We may never know more than the fact that Francis was alive in February 1642 and living in London. This at very least supports the possibility of his having informal architectural training (architecture not yet being recognised as a profession with apprentices) - perhaps under the leading man of the day, Inigo Jones. His untimely death must have occurred, far from home, sometime between spring 1642 and 1649, perhaps even before the end of 1643.

Evidence of John's belief

Proof of John's strength of belief in presbyterianism was called upon during the campaign of Bishop Wren in 1636. Wren was keen to bring local incumbents back into conformity with the Laudian church and stamp out the puritan tendencies that were now widespread. Potts supported several non-conforming clerics against the zeal of Bishop Wren. Paul Amyraut (also spelled Amirant, Amyrault etc) was Potts's man. It is not known how this German puritan from the Palatinate, educated in Oxford, came to John's attention. He had been licensed to teach grammar in the diocese in 1626 (he taught with Mr Tallis probably at Holt) and was instituted to nearby Irmingland in 1627.[83] Whether John had a hand in that presentation - his stepfather had held the advowson earlier- is not clear but Amyraut appeared in 1630 as rector in the Wolterton register, presented by John Potts. An odd surviving snippet from the Mannington register showed he also held that parish: in 1631 he wrote 'Whereas John Potts esq, and the lady Ursula Spelman his wife, being under my charge and cure, in the parish of Mannington, are persons very sickly, and cannot eat flesh ... without great peril of their health: I, Paul Amirante rector of the parish above named, do license the same ... to eat such kind of flesh meats, as by the law are tolerated and allowed during the time of their sickness and infirmity. In witness whereof, I have set hereunto my hand and seal, the 3rd day of February 1631. Per me Paulum Amyrant, rectorem de Mannington'.[84] He and his wife were probably living in Itteringham, as on 4th Sept 1631, John son of Paul Amyraut and Mary his wife was baptised at Itteringham church.[85] He was a well-regarded teacher in the village between at least 1630 and 1633: he taught young Richard Houghton, Robert's son, who had been born in Itteringham. Like others, Richard spent five years with Mr Knowles in Aylsham and two with Amyraut before going up to Caius in 1633. Richard was a boyhood friend of John's first son and it is very likely that Amyraut taught the young John Potts as well. Another pupil was Francis Alman son of William Alman gent, who went up in 1632; this might have been the same Francis Halman of Mannington who in 1628 wrote a very well-written letter regarding timber from Edgefield for his 'master'.[86] In 1633 Amyraut was confirmed rector of Irmingland and Wolterton and in 1633 their son Christopher was buried at Wolterton.[87]

An energetic man of fervent conviction, Amyraut was said to '[run] up and down to private houses crying out of Popery and timeserving'. He was suspended by Wren in May 1636 for 'contumacy'. Despite Potts's efforts, Paul was deprived of his livings on 30th March 1637.[88] It is said that over the next few years he went to Holland but returned to Essex by 1639. Here he was solicited by the Providence Islands of Massachusetts but he turned them down.[89] He or his wife was back in Wolterton in November 1639 for the burial of their daughter Elizabeth. On 25th November 1640 he appeared before the Commons committee and said his suspension by Wren had been for not bowing to the name of Jesus. In early December 1640 the sub-committee of the Committee of Religion gave an order [to the Bishop] authorising 'Paul Amirant clark to be allowed to inspect the bishop's register at Norwich and transcribe what he wishes'.[90] His petition was due to be heard in late January 1641. Had Potts helped him get a hearing? At the time he appeared to be living in Guestwick where he and his wife Mary baptised their son Joseph in 1642.[91] By July 1645 he was the intruded minister of East Dereham (in a signed letter of inhabitants of 6th July to the Mayor of Norwich) and in November 1647 he complained to the Indemnity Committee.[92] Thereafter Amyraut worked in Essex and, with his son Joseph, in Ireland.[93]

Potts's brother-in-law was another victim of Wren. A fiery young man, Thomas Case had been ordained in Norwich in 1626. He became curate at Northrepps to a man who was to be a life-long friend, Richard Heyrick. Presented to the rectory of Erpingham in 1628, Thomas Case had married John's sister, Anne, in Itteringham on 24th March 1631.[94] Had she lived, Anne would have had a roller-coaster life with Case but she died before he left Norfolk. Despite being similarly defended by Sir John Hobart of Blickling as well as Potts, Thomas was ejected from the living. He departed and moved away to Manchester, before being cited in the Bishop of Norwich's court in November 1637. His fame grew and in 1637 he was already worrying the authorities in Salford by his zealous preaching. In 1640-41 John Potts would have heard him deliver his apocalyptic sermons to the Long Parliament. A fervent anti-Laudian, by the late 1640s, Case like his brother-in-law, came to believe the revolution had gone too far. He was removed from his London living in 1651 by the Independents. In the same year he and Heyrick were accused of plotting against the regicides and arrested. Case was later released and enjoyed a further preaching career under Charles II. He wrote to Potts's friend Lord Wharton hoping for a place in Lancashire in 1661 but he remained in London until his death.[95]

Political awareness

Living in north Norfolk was not a barrier to communication about national affairs. John had already become a man of letters and he received the news of the day. A clerk who wrote to him on 28th June 1631 assumed Potts would already have heard the news of a treasonable plot of which he was bursting to tell the details (although nervous of speaking so boldly). For ease of reading the style has been modernised:

> To my most Honored frend Jn Potts esq Norfolk
>
> Sir
>
> The occasion of the Lords close sitting in Councell, which I presume is come to your Eares before this time (for I heard of it upon the way), is now come to light. My Lord Rez [Reay] a Scotchman, out of an Inveterate hatred to the Marquess Hamblert' [Hamilton], and the feare that this journey of the Marquess might eclipse his credit with the King of Sweden (under whom he has had a regiment

a long time) has in the absence of the Marquesse in Scotland,
[pressed] the King of his unheard of Treason & disloyalty, that he
had a Intent to kill the king, and that Roxebourgh & his lady should
dispatch the Queene and my lord of Dorset, the prince; and that
those forces now being raised were but to strengthen the design; &
that Marquesse Huntly for the North of Scotland and some dozen
more of the Nobility of Scotland were of his Confederacy to make
him James the second.

The council were confined to six (3 English 3 Scotch) ... the Kings
words in his bedchamber - "What death must I die?" ... I am sure
[that] at my boldness not should speak much more to write this
nature, but I imagine be generally known before, And a great Lady
that I met told me, she thought all things would blow over with
some punishment to the Lord Miches [Mackay] viscount Res the
malicious Authour and this will be the end of almost 20 days secret
Counsel. The Marquess's Drums beat up here still yet they cannot
drive out of my head my promise of the [duty] with which I send
you my truth of affection bound under the Termes of,

ye servant

Jn Plumstead[96]

Donald Mackay, 1st Lord Reay, talked up a treason plot by the Marquess of
Hamilton, who had gone to Scotland to raise troops for protestant Europe; Reay said
the troops were for England to overthrow King. There was no plot and matters did
blow over although one poor chap spent 20 years in Blackness Castle for his part.

A major conduit for news and gossip was the holding of the assizes which as
a JP he would have been expected to attend. These were a great opportunity for
business and socialising between gentlemen, for he would not have presided on
these occasions. The assizes were not at a fixed venue, the judges being on circuit,
and the Norfolk winter (Lent) session was usually held in Thetford.[97] There was
some expense involved in travelling and staying over and attendance was always a
matter of contention as his stepfather's family had shown. In 1577 the absence of Sir
Christopher Heydon senior and his son William was explained by their kinsman,
Francis Windham in a letter to Nathaniel Bacon: they 'did not go to Assizes by
reason of sicknesses of my auld Lady Heydon though they were within 10 or 12
miles of Thetford'.[98] In 1579 Bassingbourne Gawdy sent an order for Heydon,
Sir William Butts and others to attend the assizes without any excuses. Heydon
replied, from Saxlingham, that 'for the reason he is far distant from that place he is
accustomed to be absent' and cheekily added that if Gawdy used the proper form
of request he would of course come.[99] Poor attendance continued to be a problem,
even though there were business deals to be made. In a letter of March 1633 from

Thetford, Thomas Knyvett described to his wife how the assizes 'hath bene the poorest that ever I yet sawe' except that it was graced by Henry Howard and his brother Sir William.[100] Knyvett was 'invited to goe with the Judges in ther coach to Berrye' and joked he would be too proud to come back to 'you poore countrye gentleweomen'. He admitted he was going 'more to Accomplish my owne business then in compliment'. It may be John would have been a better attender had they been held in Norwich. In March 1640 Sir Thomas Wodehouse wrote to Potts: 'I was enforced to find excuse for your absence at this late assizes in Thetford where I wish you had been for divers good respects'. On this occasion the elections were again the subject of hot debate and Wodehouse had good reason to want him there.

So John Potts's busy life revolved around his work and his family but with a growing role in county affairs. Despite his interest in national affairs, he could not have foreseen how his world was about to change. He was to be on the world's stage, for all his private desire to keep a low profile. In 1639 he would have been astounded to know that, within a few years, he would be working closely with future regicides, writing letters to the King and at the end trying with all his strength to persuade both King and Cromwell to make a peaceful resolution to a bloody revolt that was to turn Britain upside down.

Chapter 11

Duty Calls

John Potts was elected to parliament in 1640 and made knight and baronet in 1641. Ketton-Cremer's work Norfolk in the Civil War *is an excellent introduction to the story that unfolded in the 1640s and he was the first to highlight the role of John Potts. He published several of the letters mostly in part, which are shown here in full.[1] The story of the civil war itself is well-recorded so what follows here is an attempt to show the period through the eyes of John Potts, using his own words and experiences and those of his close friends. The letters and other original materials are used to give a sense of those extraordinary times and to round out his character and previously underestimated importance.*

At the end of 1639 there was great excitement: the first parliament for 11 years was to sit in April 1640. The two knights of the shire for Norfolk were to be elected and one candidate was already selected. Sir Edmund Moundeford, of Feltwell, was an experienced man who had been a member of the last parliament and someone John knew well.

1640 Representing the Shire

John Potts was encouraged to stand for the other seat by Framlingham Gawdy and Sir Thomas Wodehouse, the two chosen members for Thetford. Framlingham was three years older than John and had sat for Thetford since 1614. Why did they ask John? He had shown himself to be a sound man but it may have been as much to do with the fact that Sir John Holland of Quidenham was the other candidate. Holland was a little too influential in their part of the county and, although a puritan, he had a catholic wife which was now seen as a distinct disadvantage. Potts, now nearly 48 and ten years older than Holland, had no previous experience of parliament but was known as a moderate puritan and reliable man of good standing. Sir Thomas Wodehouse described himself as Potts's 'true loving kinsman'; as always there were several lateral links. Ann Wodehouse daughter of Sir William of Hickling had married Sir William Heydon and her son was Sir Christopher. Thomas's grandmother was Mary Corbett, related by marriage to the Heydons and his wife's sister Mary Carey had married William Heveningham and so was sister-in-law to both John Spelman and John Potts junior, two of Ursula Potts's sons.

Wodehouse had first asked his 'cousin' John Spelman to suggest Potts should consider standing and he then wrote directly to him on 13th March 1640:

> To my worthy respected friend & kinsman John Potts esq at his house in Norfolk Thetford March 13

Sir

I doubt not but you have heard of my desires (amongst many
others) that you might be elected to serve our Countie as a knight of
this ensuing Parliament and so I wish't it might be intimated to you
by your son-in law [stepson] my cousen Spylman long before the
declaration of those that now ryse up to be solicitors for the same;
since which tyme I have had much conference and approbation of
your iust merits by a confortable number of honest men, so there
is probable hopes you may carry it, if so be you would express your
willingnesse to undertake the worke and not neglect such ordenary
wayes as may be fayrely used by laws of modestie.

In theis bad tymes all good men ought to seeke such meanes as
might enable them to enterprise good matters; and you Sir are the
man, by serious observation, accounted one of those few we now can
fynde to setle our hopes upon for this employment; wherefore it is
not reasonable you should delay us any longer without divulging of
your willinge fowardness herein.

I was enforced to fayne excuse for your absence at this late Assises
here in Thetforde, where I wish you had been present for divers good
respects; I had some full occasion given me there, besydes what else I
tooke to tell your competitors of my own devotions unto your selfe,
which I doe not now tell you to beg a thankes, for thus I would have
done unto my open adversarie, if I had thought him so sufficient to
serve his countrye, which consideration hath made me and others to
resolve upon our best endevors for your election

[in margin] and therefore we wilbe confident (until you say the
contrarie) that you will not refuse the suffrages of many honest men
nor of myself

who am, your true lovinge kinsman[2]

Whether Spelman had broached the subject with his stepfather we do not know,
nor what John's initial reaction would have been. He clearly had not thought of
standing but perhaps he was moved by Wodehouse's words 'you Sir are the man'. His
reply was gracious and agreed that if it be God's will, he would undertake it:

That I have not sooner acknowledged the favor of your good
opinion was my unwillingness for an undertaking too heavy for my
strength. I must confess my own unfitness ever deterd any thought
of Parliament , especially in this high road, so full of every [K-C
gave 'envy'] toile and hazard, and more than ever had I cause to

decline it, when all in me grows weaker, save my affections to the
publicke good this consideration made me refuse all ... [though]
I shall be ashamed to accept a charge much above my abilities &
should have been much more ashamed to begg it, yet your noble
offer prevailes & since it pleaseth you & my friends, to cast the
uninvited honour of your votes upon me, I will [not] ungratefully
neglect the opportunity of service, not be wanting in a modest way
to further your god aims, soe for ... its a faire declaration ... & the
best husban[dman] ... of my freinds labours now ... when all stones
here [are] turned, the Dye is [cast] and we come to the Trial, wher
I expect [the] strongest opposition, which cunning, skorne & anger
can invent, to disgrace my self or defeat [others] freedom; But the
myschief is forseen & the remedy spared; If the work [be god's] he
can effect it; if it be not his will (more than my won) to imploye me
[I shall] finde ease on the loss & comfort in discharge of my duty;
The issue I [leave] to my master & whatsoever the success be I hope
still to approve myself [an] honest man to all the world

& to your self sir

yr humble kinsman & servant

Jo Potts[3]

His statements that his 'own unfitness ever deterred me from the thought of
Parliament' and that now he was older, 'more than ever had I cause to decline it,
when all in me grows weaker' have been taken by Keeler and others to mean he had
poor health; there is no other evidence for this and his modest self-effacing reply was
much more about his concern that he would not be able to do a good job.
Wodehouse replied on 23rd March warning that the election would be a hard fight:

Sir

I found your letter newly come to my house on Fryday night last
returning here out of Norwich where I had bein negotiating for
you or rather for my selfe and country which are the only objects of
our endeavores for your Election; It is likely there wilbe the greatest
noyse and confluence of men that ever have been heard or seene on
Norwich Hill for never doe I thinke was there such a workinge and
counterworkinges to purchase vulgar blasters of acclamation.

I have not bein necligent in preparinge mynds and mouthes about
those partes imparted by your letter, yet I fynde that some people
ever ravished a way by strenous importunities, so as you must expect
a Rivall of high Stomacke as well as stature, and yet I cannot fall in

my beliefe, but doe assure my self (by Gods good favore) we shall obtayne a prospirus wynde to bringe you to our wished port of Parliament.

I had some conference [K-C 'correspondence'] with my Cosen Heveningham at the Assises, he seemed but cold, my hope is, it was cunninge, and discretion not to discover his intentions to me; as I remember he sayd that Sir John had sent unto him, and that he never heard from you at all about the businesse.

If you plese to persevere by your self and freinds in divulging your intent & willingnesse, I will not dread nor doubt the influence of any infatuated Procyon that may be elevated.

Sir I shall not fayle (by Gods permission) to meete with you on Saturday at your house before dinner, where we may freely comunicate our thoughts and direct our course for a fayre preceedure according to his holy pleasure who will and only can conduct us to an happie issue,

I remayn Sir

your entirely loving kinsman to serve you

Tho Wodehouse[4]

John and Thomas would have hatched their campaign, perhaps in the parlour, at Mannington before joining Ursula and the family for dinner that weekend.

However, at the election, although Potts was well supported, Sir John Holland was returned with Moundeford for the first parliament. This lasted only a month from 13th April to 5th May when the King angrily dissolved it. In November 1640 when parliament was recalled (later referred to as the Long Parliament), Holland stood for Castle Rising, a less prestigious seat, allowing Potts to be returned as knight of the shire with Moundeford. Holland was chosen by Lord Arundel, whose borough Castle Rising was; although at first sight the choice may seem unlikely for the royalist lord lieutenant, his family, the Howards, had long favoured the Hollands and had close connections with them. Did Holland step aside willingly or was he nudged? Holmes suggests Holland had been worried about the bitter divisions in the county.[5] He was obviously influenced by Moundeford as in a letter to Framlingham Gawdy in November, he wrote that for his part, he strove to pass by the 'discourtecies and injuries' received from many, in part to satisfy the desire of Sir Edmund Moundeford and also to avoid 'sidings and factions among the gentry'.[6] He might have agreed that Potts, a distant kinsman, would be a popular candidate. Was he influenced by the favour that the young Potts had done for his father Sir Thomas Holland in 1619? It would certainly imply that Arundel was willing to support the arrangement, regardless of Potts's puritan leanings. Presumably John Potts's known protestant zeal countered any similar concerns which may have been held by parliament regarding his own wife's family. The Willoughbys and the Hawes, Ursula's grandparents, had apparently been suspected of catholic sympathies at an earlier time when Richard Willoughby became a seminary priest.[7] Potts was elected on 12th October and within a month left for London.

From 3rd November 1640 onwards John was at Westminster although perhaps because he was the junior partner, he did not make speeches to the House. Edmund Moundeford as the senior knight, presented the Norfolk freeholders' petition on the 7th and Sir John Holland, an experienced member, spoke regularly during these moderate sessions. The first time, on 24th November 1640 was to clear himself: 'Sir Jn Holland desires to clear himself from any opinion that might reflect on him of being a papist upon the consideration that his wife was: And whole House rested very well satisfied'.[8]

As John sat in the chamber, he would have recognised many faces: obviously Wodehouse, Holland and Moundeford but also the other member for Castle Rising, Sir Robert Hatton, William Heveningham (his son's brother-in-law) sitting for Stockbridge in Hants, Anthony Bedingfield (uncle of his son-in-law to be) sitting for Dunwich, Suffolk, the two Norwich members Richard Harman and Richard Catelyn, Framlingham Gawdy for Thetford and the other Dunwich MP Henry Coke, son of Chief Justice Coke. His relative through the Heydon line, Miles Corbett, was chosen by Yarmouth borough. He would have known most of the Suffolk members, such as Frederick Cornwallis and Sir Robert Crane, and many others by name and reputation.

Almost immediately John became aware of the scale of the cost that being a member of this parliament might entail. On Saturday 21st November, he was named on the list of people offering secured bonds for the parliament. Probably a safeguard in the face of the rumoured threat that Charles would break up the House again, the sums were large. John offered £1,000 as did Sir John Holland. This was to be the first of such proposals; 'loans' were to be levied on a regular basis.

So John's days settled to a regular routine, in the mornings the House sat after prayers were said between 9 and 10 and, in the afternoon, the committee work was undertaken. It must have been novel and interesting to be involved in matters of state, even if some were at first very minor. His absorption in the debates in November and December would have helped him ignore the very cold and wet conditions in which they worked; the House had been unloved for eleven years and many windows were broken. They would not be mended until early January.[9]

The afternoon of Thursday 26th November saw him sitting in the exchequer chamber (Westminster was quite compact and all rooms had multiple uses). As one of a small committee with Mr Hampden and Sir Dudley North, he was 'to take into Consideration the Parishioners Complaints of the Parish of St. Gregorie's by Paule's, concerning the pulling down of their Church, by Force of an Order from the Council-board: And are to think of some Way of Redress for them: And have Power to send for Inigo Jones, and any other Person, as they shall think fit'.[10]

The following week he sat with friend Moundeford, in the court of chancery, in a different, larger group discussing some petitions and seeing witnesses. This may have been the first occasion he and Mr Oliver Cromwell were able to observe each other at work. The subject matter of these afternoons was very varied: on 11th December he sat, in the Star Chamber with yet another set of members, discussing the plight of prisoners and captives of Algiers and Tunis under the Turks Dominions. The following week his Cambridge college, Emmanuel, was under examination by his committee sitting in the court of wards. John on this occasion would have become better acquainted with Sir Simonds D'Ewes, the voluble member for Sudbury. By mid-December Potts found himself able to join in matters even more to his interest: he was added to the sub-committee of the Grand Committee for Religion. He and others were 'to consider and inquire of the true Grounds and Causes of the great Scarcity of preaching Ministers, through the whole Kingdom; and to consider of some Way of removing of scandalous Ministers, and putting others in their Places. And it is further ordered, That all the Knights and Burgesses for every County, be required from this House, upon their own Knowledge, and upon Information from the several Counties, where they dwell, within Six Weeks, to inform this House of the State and Condition of their Counties, concerning preaching Ministers, and whence it ariseth, that there is such a Want of preaching Ministers'. He heard testimony from Northumberland, Cumberland, Lancashire and Wales widening his understanding of religious variations across the kingdom.

On 30th December, after a very short break for Christmas, he was debating a question arising from the second reading of his first act of parliament - for the yearly holding of parliaments - with Mr Pym, Mr Holles, Mr Hampden, Mr Cromwell and others. This old bill, re-discovered from the fourteenth century, was a necessary defence against the King's preference for doing without parliament.

The next afternoon, New Year's Eve, he heard Lady Hatton's petition with Denzil Holles, Sir Henry Vane, Sir Robert Hatton, Sir Robert Crane, Sir William Lewis and 'all the lawyers of the house'. John Potts's big moment came on Monday 25th January 1641 when he presented the Norfolk petition calling for the abolition of bishops. This was one of several coming in to the House and John would have been disappointed that it was noted but not read.[11] John Pym did not wish to debate issues at that critical time which might split the moderates and give the king a chance to call support to him. The petition had over 2,000 signatures and had been the subject of controversy in the county. Dr Edward Franklin, rector of Great Cressingham and a fan of Wren, had spoken out in opposition to 'such as gave their voices with Mr Potts at Norwich'. Franklin was to attend the House on 16th February. But again the matter was not taken up.[12]

John was however allowed to assist Mr Francis Rous, Pym's stepbrother, an experienced committee man and an outspoken reforming writer, in organising the conference for the impeachment of Mr John Cosins, a prebendary of Durham Cathedral. Cosins had worn a cope, openly displayed idols and used great candlesticks on an altar to beautify his church. Rous was praised for his anti-Popish speech to the Lords on 16th March. Potts, no doubt having organised the business, sat quietly by, watching the Lords' response to the Devonshire theologian.

By now he had been bound for a loan: not the £1,000 first suggested, but for £500, as were Sir John Holland and Sir Edmund Moundeford. Although being bound was a very usual occurrence for a gentleman, this might have concerned him. It would not have been clear in early February 1641 when the loan might be repaid.

His workload now increased; he was in committee on the last Wednesday and Friday of January (act for limiting Michaelmas Term and the Bishop of Bath and Wells), 11th February (act against exporting wools), 17th February (act for the Abolishing Superstition and Idolatry - an open debate), 22nd February (an appeal against a decree in chancery), three days later (the abuses of the court of wards and of the officials) and the following week (act re tillage conversion into pasture). On second of March he was preparing 'Reasons and Grounds of a Conference to be desired with the Lords, concerning the Putting of Clergymen out of the Commission for the Peace', for which he and Moundeford also had to bring all the names of justices in Norfolk by the next Wednesday.

In his spare hours in the evenings and weekends, he would have written many letters, not only on such business but also to Ursula, other family members and his estate steward. Not a single one from this period has survived so his thoughts and feelings can only be imagined. Tired from long hours in the House followed by the committees, sermons to be heard (including his son-in-law Thomas Case), work to be prepared at his lodgings, he must have wondered when he would be able to see Ursula and Mannington again. On the other hand, he would have loved the long and lively private discussions on the incredible changes that were taking place - with the shift of power moving away from the King towards parliament, the growth of radicalism, the trial of the Earl of Strafford. The sheer buzz of being at the heart of events was an antidote to being away from home. The one survival of evidence of John's sense of humour comes from one of these friendly evening get-togethers. Nicholas L'Estrange in his collection of anecdotes related that 'Francis Russell, at an ordinarie with some of his brethren of Westminster, where much discourse was about the Presbyterian and Independent ways in religion, borrowed some bold metaphore or allegorie about horse–racing (in which he was well versed) … "Well said Franke" says Sir John Potts, "thy simile is most proper: for thou hast e'ene as much religion as thy horse" '.[13] L'Estrange's use of the word 'ordinarie' is humorous; these were the famous gaming-houses of the early 1600s where young men wasted their time. Francis was the young son and heir of Francis, the 4th Earl of Bedford who sat in the House of Lords at this time. The Earl's cousin Edward had taken part in the 1601 Essex rebellion with the Heydons and John was later to know Robert Scawen, then the Earl's servant, and his favourite, Oliver St John. He would have also have heard talk of the Earl's great scheme for draining the fens. Sadly both the young heir 'Franke' and his father the Earl died, in April and May 1641.

The spring passed with more work on acts (usury and reforming elections); at the beginning of the summer, as talk of plot and counterplot surrounded the King and the army, the government made their allegiances clear. Following the speaker, Mr Potts joined others in making 'the Protestation' on 3rd May. In doing so he declared he would live and die for the true protestant religion, the liberties and rights of subjects and the power of privilege of parliaments. Two weeks later, any hope he had of a return of his £500 now vanished as the commons ordered that the loans due for repayment should be lent again. 'Mr Potts continue ... £500'.

John was probably in the House on 19th May, a week after Strafford's execution, when a 'sudden cracke' and shower of dust unnerved the members who, thinking they were under attack, rushed in unseemly haste outside. He would have then seen his uncle's old duelling partner, Sir Robert Mansfield, now in his seventies, sword held high, rushing into the empty Hall, alone, to fight the unseen enemy. Fortunately for him, this turned out to be merely some broken wooden slats and wall plaster which had surrendered to the weight of a member leaning forward![14]

There are no entries for June so he may have had time at home but in late July he was debating an act concerning printing and importing books, a matter that would have been close to his stepfather's heart. Joining him and others, on this Tuesday afternoon were Sir John Evelyn, Sir John Corbett, Mr Pierrepont and John Selden from Oxford University; the day before, he had been working on an act about the trained bands and trained soldiers, at this time still under the control of the king. Of his comrades, Sir John Holland was still doing his share but Sir Thomas Wodehouse had fallen ill and remained in Norfolk in 1641. He wrote to Potts (who had been keeping Thomas up to date by regular letters) thanking him - 'there be so few who will descend to love their lame and decrepit friends' - and adding that being assured of such as Potts sitting in the House 'gives no small content to us in your county'.[15] Wodehouse was one of many who would come to value John's steadfast character.

Knighthood and baronetcy

It was while the lower House still had moderate tendencies and Pym's leadership was by no means supported by all, that the King attempted to win over such men and at the same time to add some money to his purse. During July and August he dropped favours on over two dozen men. On 9th August 1641, the day before his journey to Scotland where he hoped to rally support, the King knighted John Potts at Westminster, the only Norfolk man among the 12 knights to be honoured between the 8th and 10th August. He was created Baronet Potts of Mannington five days later on 14th August.[16]

No Norfolk baronetcies had been created since 1629 but eight were made in mid 1641 and early 1642. Sir John Holland was already a baronet but of the eight Norfolk knights given baronetcies, Sir William Paston of Oxnead, Sir Thomas Pettus of Rackheath, Sir William Denny of Gillingham and Sir Robert Kemp of Gissing were known supporters of the King. Sir John Potts was the only one to be an MP at the time but neither he nor his neighbour and nephew, Sir John Palgrave of North Barningham (created 24th June 1641) were swayed by the honour. Sir Isaac Astley of Melton Constable, despite being the nephew of Sir Jacob, who fought for the King, was a firm parliamentarian. Sir Ralph Hare was not active for either party.[17] Of course a substantial fee had to be paid: a baronetcy normally cost over £1,000. On this occasion, given the King's urgency, the normal payment was reduced, falling to £350 in July.[18] This may seem a curious action for John Potts; he was not particularly wealthy and certainly not in favour of the King's beliefs. He was not, though, a republican and would have hoped that the relationship between monarch and parliament could be stabilised. He also may have felt it his duty as a gentleman to take the honour, for him and for his family. Accepting knighthood had always been expected of those would could afford it.[19] The rank of baronet was still quite new, having only been introduced in 1611 as a money raising scheme for James but it was hereditary, through sons, and was superior to the lifetime rank of knight. At £350 it was a bargain. Sir John Potts, kt and bt, had now reached the highest status his family had ever or would ever achieve. Every letter he now received, however brief, would always bear these abbreviations.

The King left behind a London suffering in the summer heat from one of the many outbreaks of plague. Many abandoned the House early but hard-working Potts stayed on.

Sir John now stepped up on to the committee for disarming recusants; they met on Saturday 21st August 'to prepare an Ordinance of Parliament, and Instructions for the present Disarming of Recusants: And have Power to nominate such Persons in every County, as they shall think fit to do this Service, though they be not Members of the House; and to present them to the House'. By now the hours of parliament were being extended to complete the business before the recess; the following Tuesday, John was sent up to the Lords to tell them that the Commons would be sitting in the afternoon and he had to 'desire their Lordships would do the like; if it may stand with their Conveniency'. He was probably not very popular. The next day he was considering the state of the navy - its defects and debts and how to set it out 'in a good posture'. He must have been very relieved to travel back home and enjoy the cool breezes and healthy air of September and October in north Norfolk. Many neighbours would ask for news and reassurance; his estate needed his attention too. All too soon his holiday was over. He would have heard rumours about the rebellion in Ireland and this was officially reported to the House on 1st November. The next day, he was plunged right back into work, sitting on the committee for the Irish affairs which was to last as long as necessary and meet at such times as they thought fit. Two days later, meeting late in the afternoon and into the evening, he was also on the committee discussing the act to levy soldiers for the defence of Ireland.

On the Saturday, he would have listened to Cromwell's speech urging that the Earl of Essex be given overall control of all the trained bands in the south; he knew how vital it was that parliament, not the King, took control of the army in this emergency.

The last week in November saw the King's return from Scotland amid a sea of scares and rumours of his involvement with the Irish rebels. Matters reached a head in the House on 22nd November, when the list of grievances against the King was publicly debated well into the night. The vote to send this statement of no-confidence to the King was passed by a majority of 11. Sir John must have been very weary when the house was adjourned at 2 o'clock in the morning.

Both the King and Pym were manoeuvring support. The King commanded all absent members (many his supporters) to attend the house by mid-January; he did not respond to the Grand Remonstrance and when he did go to the House on 2nd December he did not mention it. Under the surface the crowds in London were being stirred by both sides. Tensions rose throughout December and John would not have been able to get home for Christmas as they had only two days off. The climax was the King's attempt to charge Pym and four other leading men with treason; his mistake was to storm the House on 4th January and try to take them by force, breaching the privilege of parliament. That Tuesday morning, John would have sat under the angry gaze of the King while he looked at the empty seats. Did he wonder what this crisis would lead to? It must have been an extraordinary moment.

1642 Keeping the peace

After the abortive attempt to arrest five MPs from the House, the King left London on 10th January 1642 and parliament assumed authority, with all of London clamouring in the streets. A few days later, Sir John joined a joint Commons and Lords Committee to debate the 'Privileges of Parliament and a Petition to his Majesty'. He was at the house on 27th and 28th January, caught up in a minor fracas about an affront made to the guards who stood at the entrance. Members' footmen hung about on the stairs awaiting instructions and obviously the temptation was too much for one of the young men. Sir John, who had been there at the incident on the 27th, had to resolve what was said or not said and whether someone encouraged the footman to abuse the guard on duty. How vexing this trivial matter must have been: John needed to travel home as his beloved mother was ill. Sadly she died the next day while he was giving evidence. The death of Anne cut the last of his links with his father and the Potts past. He made time to organise her memorial stone in Baconsthorpe church where it was her wish to be buried next to Sir Christopher Heydon. Two weeks later he was back, sitting in the Painted Chamber, hearing the contents of letters intercepted from Holland. Lord Digby, one of the King's advisers, was advising the use of force.

On 18th February, yet again John's £500 was repaid to him (out of the subsidies raised) and immediately re-secured for the Irish Affairs. Only this time there was a promise that, when the war was over, the lenders would receive confiscated rebel lands in Ireland. Parliamentary business now engulfed John again. On 14th March, John was head of a list of members sitting on the Committee for Gunpowder. An early Monday morning meeting, presumably before the House sat, this was chaired by Sir John Evelyn. The two men, only a year apart in age, would have known each other at Emmanuel College. The manufacture of gunpowder had been the foundation of Evelyn's family's wealth and he was still smarting over the loss of the monopoly a few years before. Potts's next job, ten days later, was to write to the lord lieutenant for Norfolk and Essex with the names of those deputy lieutenants recommended by the House. This may have caused Potts some misgivings. The lord lieutenant, the King's representative in the county, that he had served under for the musters had been the ageing Lord Arundel, with the help of his son Lord Mowbray. Arundel had just left England for good but Mowbray was still in the role. With the shift of military power, parliament had a few weeks ago elected their own lieutenant, Robert Rich, Earl of Warwick, an Essex man who also had naval experience. It was to Rich that Potts had to write with the names. The 26th saw him ordered to work with the Lords committee - 'This being a Business of great Weight' - on the petition of the Merchants Strangers of the Netherlands residing in London who felt that they should be freed from paying the subsidies and fifteenths. Soon the whole country would be feeling the pressure of the continuous taxes levied by parliament to pay for their wars. A huge sum was necessary for the Irish war; parliament needed up to a million pounds quickly and more subscribers like Potts were being lined up. A staggering £42,000 was promised by a House only quarter full on 26th March, as Robert Reynolds, MP for Hindon, wrote excitedly to tell Sir John:

31 March 1642

Sir

Upon Saturday last it was mooted to those members which had a mind to subscribe might openly in the house declare themselves and thereupon though not a 4th part of the house were present yet in half an hour £42,000 was underwritten besides £20,000 in Wat [Walter] Long his paper where your hand is; they come in very fast at Gealdhall so that this day the house hath voted that additional forces shalbe sent that the Adventurers shall make choice of the officers etc which doeth much quicker the work, tis thought the million wilbe made up before Easter. I am in £1200 what is to the estate in proportion £40,000, the king hath sent us a round message in so much that now things being at the highest we are in great hope of a happy & suddene change. Sir [Edw] Deering Mr Spencer Sir Roger Twiseden & Sir George Stroud are sent for as delinquents for p'ferring a seditious petition at Kent Ass[izes]: to be sent to the Parliament by 4000 men, he is fled to Yorke from the messenger

in all hast service yr frend & servant

Robt Reynod

If you or one for you underwrite at Guildhall before 20th of April by a late short act past both houses & sent to the king, he shall pay an 4th part down & hath three 3-months for the reste. I pray present my service to your noble lady & pardon mee for the great haste at 11 at night you will suddenly heare of a change to better or worse/the rebels are beaten dailie come in apace so that wee are in great hope to end the warre this summer[20]

Such was the hope of moderates like Reynolds that the Irish war would be over soon but in the same letter he referred to the Kentish strength of feeling against parliament's religious reforms which did not bode well for a unified England.[21]

In the afternoon of 5th April Sir John worked on preparing the declaration vindicating the (puritan) doctrine of the church and how to ensure a preaching ministry was maintained. Early the next morning, jointly with the Lords, he was listening to lawyers' statements concerning 'Tumults and seditious Pamphlets'. Now, however, came the start of orders from parliament concerning the militia which would affect men in all parts of the country. The fight for control of the militia was inevitably to bring the war forward. On 8th April Sir John carried the new forms of commission for officers and other militia papers up to the Lords for their agreement; the next day he brought their answer into the Commons. Now much of Sir John's work was concerned with the supply of arms: an order about salt-petre men on 12th April, the attempt to move the magazine of arms at Hull to London (16th April) and how to furnish the kingdom with gunpowder, of which there was a shortage (11th May). Ironically, his half-brother Sir John Heydon, as Lieutenant-General of the Ordnance, was frantically attempting to ensure the King, in whose service he was, had access to the arms and ammunition in his care. Potts wrote to ask Heydon to call on him one afternoon. Heydon replied 'to his Hon'ble & much esteemed brother' as 'your faithfull brother & servant' that he would attend Potts if the latter could spare the time from parliament.[22] Was this a last ditch attempt on John Potts's part to warn his Heydon brother of what would happen if he went with the king? Heydon left London on 4th August. See Family Notes 9 for more on Heydon sons.

The new commissions for the militia were now to be put in place. Parliament decreed on 5th May 1642 that the ordinance was to be acted upon, that is men who were captains in the musters would take up their roles under parliament's orders. The King countered by sending out orders forbidding them to obey it.

Potts was now instructed to enforce the militia ordinance and attempted to comply: a few days after the decree, he and Moundeford met Thomas Knyvett (of Ashwellthorpe) in the street in Westminster and told him to take up his command of his company. Knyvett, very concerned by this new action, asked for time to consider and was more confused when he shortly afterwards received the King's direction to ignore the ordinance as illegal. His letter to his wife on the 18th May 1642 shows he was planning to keep out of the way 'of my newe masters till these first musterings be over' adding 'I wish myself in thy Armes every night … and all the Potts in Christendome shall not keep me from the[e] long'.[23]

Whether John was concerned about this turn of events and wished to confer with his Norfolk neighbours or whether he was just in need of a break, on 17th May Sir John asked for a leave of absence 'to go into the Country'. He appeared to remain there for a month or so during which time there was no evidence that he attempted to introduce the militia orders. He kept up with the news from the House through letters from Moundeford. Potts seemed to have been the driving force and had obviously left instructions for work in his absence. Edmund's spelling and style is hard to read but it seems worth printing:[24]

London 24 May 1642

Honored Sir

I received from Sir Thomas Woodhouse an intimation of something you desired but I herd you left a later will at your departure which I could never see & feare it hath lost its way; therefore if your memory can tell you agayne what it contayne, renew the [request]. Your Poll rowles shall be & ar redy for the Committee: Mr Willowby I will be careful of, as directed, so of Peter Murford in its tyme, the official names ar not yet returned from the Committee upon Friday last these votes & parti'[culars] wer sent from the sessions house where wer soone their passed. Sum gesse the Lor' rayther nurses their parents to them. They ar sent to York but not yet in Print:

1. That it aperes the King being seduced by wicked counsell intend to make war against his Parliament, who in all there consultations & actions have proposed no other end to themselves but the care of his Kingdoms & performance of their duties as lialtie to his person.

2. That whensoever the King maketh war upon his Parliament it is a breech of the trust reposed in him by his people contrary to his Oath & tending to the Desolution of his Government

3. That whosoever shall serve or asist him in that war ar traytors by the fundamental lawes of the Kingdom & ar so iudged by twoe acts of Parliament & ar to suffer as Traytors (11 Ric 2 & 1 Hen 4)

[he then recited the Humble Petition of Lds & Commons]

Mr Hall of Norwich is the man named for one of the assemblies, other I know not but so much I was biden tell you & I am very glad of it: Saturday ended or [our] second remonstrance: it may be thought long yet I doubt we shall finde it fall short. The first I send you printed. This day our letters from York say that on Friday 120 horse apered 50 wer lefted & the rest returned Sir Robert Strickland his regement of foot ther yet remayne. Capt. Duncome the prime agent. On Friday next all the free howders copie houlders & farmers of valew [value] ar summoned to be at York: the cause not declared but it seem new & better hopes appear in Linconsheir, therefore it is sayed the Court is removing to Lincon & now the face set that way; Norwich begins to be againe on Westminster parle, Mr Perpoynt much laments your absence, he as a sad man, pities the blinde & the lame but knowse not how to deliver. I wish all wer satisfied & secured but know not how to hope for it. They must be good gamsters to make the after so fayre as was their foregame.

I send you twoe orders the one, the shorens dillegence sending to
all collectors will expedigt, the other I am lost in for we should give
estimates of the Recusants estates into the Committee appoynted to
draw a bill to tax them toward the Irish War.

Mr Mart: mooved to take sum propositions from them concerning
sum lawes which now truble them but wh looking towards a
tolleration Mr Hambden did second it, saying it might be fit in its
proper tyme to think of such an offer. I have one pettie newse more
for you which wills not you, to turne a new leafe but to read &
wonder

[Next page]

Upon Saturday last late, the Ld Keeper received a command from
the King forthwith to attend him at Yorke which he so fully obliged
that early on Sunday morning he began his journey not aquaynting
any of his Lordships with it; if he had the day of rist [rest]
intervening, he would had barred a Command of the house to stay
him. Of this now is all our talke until sum new thinge proffer it self.

The second remonstrance is past the Lo[wer] House, I think we shall
never get money by the paper commoditie The Lo's have named
a Committee to consider of sum way for a better understanding
betwixt the King & parl: This ends your truble if you will have any
more of it & can read this command,

your affectionate frend & servant

Ed Moundeford

My services to your Lady Brether sister & all[25]

William Pierrepont, another moderate MP hoping for peace, was missing John's
presence already after six days. John must have been a good committee man, able to
put across a cogent and persuasive argument. Pierrepont did not perform so well.

Edmund wrote again at length, a week later, despite being ill with a cold. John
appears to have been recalled. This very long rambling letter has been partially
modernised and shortened for easier reading:

To his honoured frend Sir John Pot k & b at his house Mannington
in Norf

Leave this at Mr Cory his house in Norwich to be sent with speede

June 7 London

Sir, I have now received yours telling me my last weeks [illegible].
Mr Ash's attorney called to leave you the unwelcome subpena to
appear the 16th: the next day we received letters from our Cttee
in Lincolnshire expressing the great hope ... [news about Lord
Lieutenant, the Earl of Lunsie and the magazine], Lincoln town for
a work of superarogation have raised and trained many volunteers.
Essex Dep: Lts, doubting their own strength, procured a letter
from the Lords to the Earl of Warwick being upon the Downes to
come to animate his countrymen: he came to London on Saturday
& doubt not but all will be of one piece in Essex: he returns from
... Burntwood to look after the Denmark ships which he as little
expects as fears. He has given me half a promise that when our turn
comes he will be in Yarmouth road & grace us with a visit if need
require. I am glad we shall have so [many] good examples, the best
tutors. Murford is Captain. Our Ld Lt, upon your letter, readily
consented to Murford his deputy. ... It pleaseth God still to continue
the wonted wonderful success in Ireland. Thos Derham hardly
was persuaded to accept his Commission for Capt; therefore at the
Earl's coming, I moved him to grant the Commission to Sir Robert
Bell's eldest son, dwelling the midst of the hundred, believing Greg
Gawsell would not have thanked us for it, or I will keep the Comm
until you come that we may consider of it. The house of peers
acording to the weather hath very thin linings. A letter out of Ireland
Munster saith the King is theer suddenly expected, the Castle of
Dublin preparing for him: a Parl' is to be called & so the businesse
accorded & the scene changed, but this was hearsay. I have got or
rather a cold hath gotten me, with which I fear I shall hard by part
on fair terms.

This day we received letters from York by our nimble Mercury,
Mr Rushforth. Our Committee delivered our propositions to the
King on Friday morning, & had only answer that he would take
tyme to consider of them. [He then recounted the King's actions
in York]. The King ... went into Haywood more abought half a
mile from York where he caused to be read in several places among
the company this inclosed speech & scattered many copies of it
& with little stay or further saying returned. The freeholders &
some Knights & Gent' had prepared a petition for him ... they
had first agreed to meet & sign it in the Castle yard, but notice
taken of that intention the King commands they should not be
there admitted. Then they began to subscribe it in severall places
of the grand throng. Sir Thos Fairfax was appointed to deliver it, 4
knights reading of it to some of the Committee the Earl ... with his
troops did come to him & asked what pamphlet he was reading &

snatcht it out of his hand swearing they were traitorous rogues &
Rascalls. ... Notwithstanding the affray, Sir Thos Fairfax endeavors
to deliver the petition to the King, but he would not receive it,
the freehoulders petition the parliament for justice ... & that they
would desire the king to accept their petition. The Parl: ... voted
their opinions that the two Lords are public enemies to the state and
incendiaries between the King & his people. [He then told John of
an attempt by a parliamentary messenger to arrest one Beckwith but
the King intervened and the messenger ended up in gaol instead.]
... We have passed a declaration to shew the illegality of the
proclamation concerning the Militia; it is put to the print, if it come
out before tomorow at night you shall have it, if not soone after, for
order is taken for the publishing of it as also for the declaration. It
is now new come news that Salsbury & Clare are come from York.
It is thought many more will follow if former determinations be
not Changed at York; all such intelligence is but a dim light to see
the bias of the generality although by the most conjectured to be
strongly inclining to the Kings counsell at Westminster, rather then
to his Counsell of war. The redy having a strength of horse is now
come into agitation in our house & 5 this afternoon is appointed
the hour to determine of it, the severall members of the house upon
voluntary offers to give example. The printer hath now overtaken
me, while I was transcribing the defective copies of somethings ill
written in my bad memory with which I shall now stuff your lettcr.
That of the Scots is worth the sending. The City of Exeter have
given a fair precedent to other Corporations & have underwrit for
the Irish adventure the sum of £11,450. A new bid for new time is
past both houses. City Merchant Strangers, Officers & Physicians
are sent out to borow money. London has now lent £100,000
presently to be brought in: this excedes the expectations of those
at York. I have sent you the names of the Lo' at York, upon all
symptoms & discourse I can make they have an ill game & play it
worse, God keep their Counsell from being & make ours wiser, thus
prayes and ends,

yr affectionate frend & servant

Ed Moundeford

My humble service to yr good lady brother & sister

[margin] In Lancashire the King is raising a troope of horse & the
two galliuns imployed in the service are sent for under safe custody [26]

It is clear that John was already using a route for his letters that he regarded as safe. Correspondence was easily intercepted (as both sides knew) and he used the house of his friend John Cory in Norwich as a central drop point. Here also we can see the speed with which the House used the printer to spread their decisions and orders to the country. The King did the same, scattering copies of a speech in York, one of which Edmund obtained and sent to John with this letter. Moundeford and Potts were engaged in finding officers to accept commissions in west Norfolk; John's cousin Derham was not keen to accept and so Edmund had found a replacement.[27] The Earl of Warwick had been happy with another appointment after reading a letter from Potts.

'The voluntary offers to give example' of which Edmund spoke were delivered to the funds over several days from 10th June onwards, by members of the Commons. His friends gave as follows: Mr Holles £300 4 horses; Mr Heveningham 3 horses £100; 'Sir Thomas Woodhouse will bringe in two horses & two hundred pounds in Plate or money'; Sir Edm Montfort 2 horses; Sir John Holland 2 horses £100; Mr Gawdy £50. John must have written to make his offer: his £100 appeared on the last list.[28]

John does not reappear in the Journal until 9th July. On Saturday afternoon he was charged, with Holland, Moundeford, Pierrepont and others with preparing 'a Declaration to prevent any Obstruction or Discouragement that may be occasioned to the Execution of the Ordinance touching the Militia, by Reading of the Bill for Ordering of the Militia: And are to bring it on Monday Morning next'. A busy weekend for at least four of them; Potts must have been considering how he was going to comply. By Wednesday he was working only with Mr Corbett and Mr Lisle, member for Winchester, to draw up 'a general Order for the Preventing of Garisons to be put into Towns in any Parts of the Kingdom'. The next day Mr Richard Catelyn, Harbottle Grimston, Sir Robert Crane and others were working with him to tighten up the framework in which tax collectors operated to 'prevent any Inconvenience that may happen to that Service, by the Collectors neglecting or refusing that Service': £400,000 was at stake here and people were feeling the pressure. John was already finding life expensive: he paid his second payment (of four) to the Irish Adventure, £150, on 19th July.[29]

On Monday 25th July, Sir John joined in the long debate with Mr Waller and others 'speaking for an accommodation to be had with his Maj. and that a civil war might be avoided but Mr Denzil Hollis, Mr Strode and other fierie spirits would not heare of it … it was voted they could not yield to his Maj.'.[30] In the afternoon, he spent time looking at the actions of those taking up the King's Commission of Array but two other things happened that day which shifted the direction of his daily life again. His partner knight of the shire, Sir Edmund, asked for leave to go into the country for his health, and the House ordered 'That the Knights and Burgesses of the County of Norfolk do consider what is fit to be done for preserving the Peace of that County; and bring it in with all Speed'.

Potts had more to do before leaving, so the next day he was in the house carrying up orders to the Lords, completing work on the removal of Hull magazine and supplies of arms in other towns, and setting up training in Lynn. Now all those long afternoons in committee were behind him; after nearly two years in London with only a few months at home, he was now to go back to reside at Mannington. He would be busier than ever.

On Monday 1st August he was ordered home. The full order of the Lords read:

It is Ordained, by the Lords and Commons assembled in Parliament, That Sir Thomas Woodhowse, Knight and Baronet, Sir John Holland, Baronet, Sir John Potts, Knight and Baronet, Sir Edmund Mundeford, Knight, Willm. Heveningham, and Framlingham Gawdie, Esquires, do forthwith repair into the County of Norff, and possess that County with the Declaration of both Houses concerning the Illegality of the Commission of Array; and that they, or any One of them, together with the rest of the Deputy Lieutenants of that County, with such others of the said County as they shall think fit to use and employ therein, do propound the Propositions concerning Contribution of Horse, Arms, Money, or Plate, for the Defence of the Kingdom, in the several Parts of that County: And it is further Ordained, That the said Sir Thomas Woodhowse, Sir John Holland, Sir John Potts, Sir Edmund Mundeford, William Heveningham, and Framlingham Gawdy, or any One of them, shall and may require the Sheriff, and all other Officers, and the Trained Bands, and all other Persons whatsoever in the said County, to preserve the Peace, and to be therein aiding and assisting to the said Sir Thomas Woodhowse, Sir John Holland, Sir John Potts, Sir Edmund Mundford, Willm. Heveningham, and Framlingham Gawdy: And it is further Ordained, That they, the said Sir Thomas Woodhowse, Sir John Holland, Sir John Potts, Sir Edmund Mundeford, Willm. Heveningham, and Framlingham Gawdy, shall take care and provide, that the Magazine of the said County be put and kept in Places safe and fit for the preserving of them, for the Peace of the said County.

The five were given the supervision of all the hundreds between them (up to 8 each) so that they, along with the deputy lieutenants (who Potts had helped to select) and the justices, could organise the collection of horses and money (often given as plate, being the moveable wealth of the time). Seven of the hundreds were given to Moundeford and William Heveningham of Ketteringham jointly, as Moundeford was now seriously failing in health.

This command galvanised Potts to rise to speak in the House and Sir Simonds D'Ewes recorded this second rare occasion.[31] 'He desired that whereas he himself was shortly to go into the Country, by the appointment of the House, that ... Mr Harman might likewise goe down to give thanks to the City of Norwich in the name of the house, and he further showed that there was great need for all the assistance that may be there, for [divers deleted] one deputy lieutenant which had been formerly appointed did refuse to meddle with the militia And some Captains also who had received commissions were likely to faile; hee further shewed that divers gentlemen of the county had been lately with his Maj. and were returned back and that it was likely that they would bee ready to assist my Lord Matravers who was shortly expected in that County with the Commission of Array, and that the papists there also who lately expressed much feare began again to grow very confident, especially Sir John Hobart and others who stood well affected [sic] to the parliament being put out of the Commission of the Peace; and therefore he desired that he, living in the Citie of Norwich, might be nominated a Deputie Lieutenant for the countie or that citie'. D'Ewes ended 'which was agreed to', but another five months would pass until the office was conferred on John.

His speech, typically matter of fact and practical, showed that he was fully aware of all the news from home and of the imminent crisis created by the Array. His perceptions were sound and August 1642 was to be Potts's greatest challenge. As usual his colleagues looked to him to take the lead. He left for Norfolk immediately (the orders were sent to him via Norwich on the 7th) but Sir John Holland remained in London.[32] This seems to have been a genuine partnership; Holland was sure of Potts's commitment and judgement and believed he could handle Norfolk without him. They had agreed at a private meeting that the militia ordinance would be put aside and held back in case: Holland had written to his friends on the other side, to persuade them not to enact the Array either. On 4th August he updated Potts on their situation, referred to his speech in the House, and as ever, talked of his health.[33] This from a man who was to live to the age of 98:

> Noble Sir,
>
> I ame gott since yr departure upon my leggs aganne which carryed mee to the House upon Wednesday last wher (as my Health which I find much impayn by my late Journey would permit) I have ever since attended. Will Stroude last day was soe uncharitable to me as he moved to have mee sent downe after you in advancement off the peace of the country for the preservation whereof I would willingly hazard my Health, I protest my life. But I know in whose hands that worke is now, not can my assistance bee wanted. I ame att this time in that condition as the House upon the true Acount I gave thereof, was pleased to despence with my service. Sir, I know yr wisdome & nor wayes dout off your prudent carriage in this business committed to your trust. I am confident you alter not that resolution you were plesed to comunicate to me when last you afforded mee the favour off a visite. And which still appears to mee to be the sence off the most eager-bent off our Country men remeyning heere - Nott to have the ordinance putt in Execution but in case. All I studdy Sir &

which I shall still with a faythfull hert, is the peace of my Country; & in order to this end, since my to the House upon the ocasion of Captain Treswell (who is committed) I adventared to move that in respect of the present constitution of our Country that the House would in their wisdome take order that upon noe comisions or directions whatsoever the noise of a drum might for the present be heard in Norfolk. And which I could nott perseve but was well taken. Sir, I have this weeke writt to most off thos frends in whom I have interest & such as I thinke are lyklest to be called to Councell in the Execution of the commission of Array to perswade all they possibly may the suspension off the Execution therof, as the only meanes for the preservation off the peace of their Country. How unsatisffyed so ever I may be less in the particular carrige off [*torn*] ... men, I neither must nor can ever depart from the duty of an Honest man nor for[sake] those Principles that renders a man faythfull to his Conscience & Country. Nor will I, Sir, at anytime fayle in any office of frendship wherein you may still receive an assurance off that intent you have in the affections of

Sr, yr most faythfull frend & servant

J Holland

It's now whispered that Colonel Goring is resolved [to] have diserted the Parliament & rended himselfe & Portsmouth into the fre dispose of his Majesty have turned out off the towne all disaffected to the designe & have receved (as sayd) many Recusants for the secure defence thereof against such as shall attempt it.[34]

Potts was now carrying the burden of the work: his friend Edmund had set off with good intent but his health, unlike Holland's, was failing. Potts received a letter, better written so probably dictated, explaining his whereabouts:

To his much honoured frend Sir John Potts ... at his house att Mannington these present Norf.

Sir

I am hartily sorry that your endeavours, having the strength of iudgement to back them, are inforced to yeilde to the headstrong curreere of passion & ends: I know not what your Commands are, I feere not such as you, or I wish it, if the event be not prosperous, were are onely passively accessory; it is easir to believe that the cause of my absence from you is not taken upp by choice; whether the agitation of my body in the coach to Newmarket or the change of so much differing Ayers increased my former ill disposition being sure of the effect. I needed not dispute the case, my cough there much increased, with spitting of some blood; in the afternoons the invasion of a fever hectickally inclined; my Phisician durst not prescribe, untill with some time of acuter observation he had made a further discovery of my estate, & which carried me to Cambridge, where if it be enabled to come & serve you, expect nor excuse; for as in my iudgement I am confirmed that you dare doe nothing but by Command of reason signed by a good conscience, so I know you are resolute ever to give my selfe the lye by discerting the path you tread, though Bugbeared by all the Newtralls [Neutrals] in the Countrie [K-C: County]; I am here in a place as malignant to the Parliament, as reporte can render it; if these fountaines be not purged wee are like to have bitter streams run all the kingdome over. The Colledges have alreadie sent to the King £6000 And are now sent to send their Plate to make shrines for Dianies Temple. Magdalen Colledge plate beginning the march, was seized by parliament Authority and is deposited in the Maiors Custody; St John Colledge conceived a better secrecy by water & that way conveyed their plate but having intelligence of a discovery they loaded it in the night into a dung cart & returned it to the Colledge; it is said now they expect a convey of horse. Keyes Colledge refuse to send plate, the Master affirming that it is directly against their oath, binding them in expresse words, not to alienate the plate of the Colledge; if he be not deceived in his iudgment it will be a problem for the rest of the Masters, if times comes to admitt the dispute; I am likely to be in this Purgatory an Apothecharies house where my Phisitian lives until about the 16th of this month. I crave the favour to heare from you in the meane time, if I can then craule [sic] to second you with anie serves, undertake for the willingness of

yr reall frend & affectionate servant

Ed Moundeford[35]

Again, the trust put in Potts's judgement, knowing his actions to be driven by conscience and rational thought, was very clear. Even on his sickbed at Cambridge, his old friend was supporting John when he was under pressure from the headstrong passions of their Westminster colleagues. If further backing for his course of action was needed, John must have welcomed a hastily written note from Sir Robert Crane of Suffolk, with whom he had sat in many a committee. On 9th August he was about to travel but wrote:

I am at this instant for my voyage ... [talks of the campaigns & declarations etc] ... if you can escape the Militia & the Commission of Array you are hope free from danger: where either of them meet there is no securitye. I wish you would be pleased to take better information of the court proceedings for it is of much consequence to know the truth. I am in such extraordinary hast. I must needs beg pardon for my scribbled letter having only time left me to present my best respects and service to my lady with my love to my cosen, assuring you of the most faithfull service of

your most humble servant

Robert Crane[36]

John the matchmaker

Now we have Potts's own letters containing a curious mixture of family matters and his thoughts on the political crisis. His colleague Sir Simonds D'Ewes, MP for Sudbury, had been created a baronet at the same time as Potts. He had asked Potts to speak for him with Ursula's brother, Sir Henry Willoughby. Simonds had married his first wife, Anne Clopton, when she was not quite fifteen (some say only 13 ½) and, after many tragic infant deaths, she had died of smallpox, leaving him with no son. Simonds had now taken a passionate fancy to Henry's youngest daughter, Elizabeth who had just turned 14 in June and was still considered under age.[37] Potts obviously was happy to promote the match although Simonds was much older and Henry was very uncertain. Henry's sister-in-law, Lady Anne Wynn, was Potts's ally in this matchmaking.[38] Henry wrote one of his confused, worried letters to her in early August:

> I know not what to ... or what to think of your loving kinde letter ... I had thought you would rather have preferred your goddaughter rather than her younger sister....[reference to her being underage] but the offer of the gentleman is so faire I have no reason to dissent ... [he was concerned that undue pressures] have wrought her to take a lyking of this gentleman [and that it may not be of] her owne free will which neither she nor her sister your goddaughter shall justly say ... I desire to see the gentleman recommended by my brother Potts before I give a full consent to the consummation of the match.
>
> Were we not all in these parts in a continuall combustion ... I would have now come up to London.[39]

Living in Derbyshire at the family seat in Risley, Sir Henry said he was too nervous to travel to London at such a time but this may have been an excuse to put off making a decision about his beloved little girl. Henry was an emotional man especially about his little co-heiresses: a few years before, he had been equally perturbed by a proposed marriage for his elder daughter, even though it was a royal suggestion:

> 1638 Nov 27 Only for Sir Henry Willoughby, though he be a
> man of great estate, yet I dare not recommend him [for Sheriff
> of Derbyshire]; and if you call to mind how he showed himself
> both in court and about the town, about 2 or 3 years since, when
> his Majesty recommended Sir John Suckling to have married his
> daughter, you will not hold his discretion very capable of that office
> in these times[40]

On 11th August 1642 John wrote from Norwich to Simonds in London: he mentioned in passing that the affair seemed to be going well but moved quickly on to more pressing matters. The King's lord lieutenant, Mowbray, had arrived suddenly in Norfolk to rally the royalists to take their commissions but Potts was relieved that there was a considerable apathy among the likely supporters:

> Sir I had yr letter & the inclosed, being glad of the prosperous
> success in your particular affaire, wishing a happy period to yr
> desires & the gret distractions of the K'dome; wer are yet ... heer free
> from blowes but not without divisions. My lord Mowbray came with
> the Commission of Array but did not put it in execution because the
> gentlemen of your side held it not serviceable, perhaps not feasible
> in this County: or not by his presence; I labour to preserve peace &
> give speed for those supplyes expected hence by legal rates towards
> relief of Ireland and discharge of the Scots. And this short account
> (with thanks for your favoure & desires of the continuance) shall
> serve to subscribe myself
>
> yr affectionate frend and servant
>
> John Potts
>
> Heer hath been practiz but the issue of it is another weeks taske[41]

We learn more from Holland who came home to Norfolk on Sunday the 18th and immediately wrote to John for his advice. His own house was right next door to Kenninghall, the Mowbray's family seat:

> Noble Sir,
>
> This last night brought mee to Quidenham where I heare of my
> Lord Moybreys [Mowbray] seating neare me. I know what sleepes
> in his Hand, the Commission of Array, & I hope it will still doe so.

You know, Sir, those relations our have had with the family I cannot but give him a visite & by such correspondence I persuade myself I shall be the better able to advance your & mine owe Aymes. The Countryes Peace [K-C: county]. But I pray your opinion herein which is very persuasive with me.

Sir, I gladly find the quiet of this country soe well preserved I attribute much to your temper & wisdom herein. And assure yourself Sir that I shall be ready to contribute all I can that may any ways bee in order to the end.

What progress, Sir, you have made in what was intrusted in your Hand, touching the Militia I desire to know & your intentions therein for hearby I shall bee the better able to frame & fashion my carriage here to the advantage of what owes every Honest man to endeavour to the Peace of his Country. [Asks for copy of instructions]

yr most affectionate frend & servant[42]

Potts's answer survives in two drafts, written apparently in two different hands. His meticulous care in redrafting this letter is worth printing. The choice of his words showed a much more cautious communicator than any of those who wrote to him:

A

Sir I am glad of your arrival in Norfolk where your presence may help to continue what your p[er]swations helped to procure the peace of this Co; I can give you little account of my self more than that I remaine in the same temper you left me, studious of peace; My Lord Mowbray was not at Assises nor the gent. of Array then with him but were sithence appointed to meet him; some of them told me at Norwich that my Lord was willing to forbear executing his Command if I would undertake the Militia shold not be set on foote nor preporacion of Arms be privately made, to which I was not authorised in way of bargaine to answer, but bad them judge of my actions which shold rather hazard the censure of slackness than my Country's [K-C : County] quiet; My Lords propositions to raise hors amongst our gentry & the great recourse to his huntings may give cause of suspect to weake judgements & perhaps did beget thos passages in Norwich concerning him, [K-C *printed only to here*]

Sir I shall ere long send you your copy of thos instruments for the Mili. which I brought down, your man's hast & my want of a clark not permitting now to be written being very longe; if occasion require I can at any time meet you in Norwich & comunicate in thes business, in the mean while Sir, ever you may be confident that as I have not acted rashly, soe I now shal not doe anything without acquainting you, relying upon your better judgement in publick services, & in all private frenship, remaining

yr affect frend & humble servant[43]

B [very crossed out, probably the first attempt]

Sir I am very glad of your arrival in Norfolk not doubting but your presence will continue the countryes peace as yr advice procured it; my Ld Mowbray being [was] not at the Assises but required divers Commissioners of the Array [then] to give him meeting at Kenninghall [inserted] which as they told me they then forbare, to avoid misconstruction but have since performed; it seemed by them would have me undertake to stop the Militia, & that noe preparation of Arms should be made underhand and [inserted] 'for this better acount to the King' I could give no answer to such propositions, it was sufficient for me to hazard a chiding [censure written above] for my own slacknesse, [inserted] 'without discouraging any to prepare for their own defence of case of stirring' [& leave others to their own acount] Yet Sir I assure you no man doth more desire the quiet of the Country, if it may be preserved safely, but the leveyes of hors amongst the gentry which my Lord endeavours & the great concours observed to accompany his huntings, doe give occasion of suspect to weake judgements; the people are [well] generally affected to the Parl: [hither too, until triall]

I wish ther may be noe occasion of triall; Sir I shal send you a copy of the instructions which I brought down (I am sory that the want of a clark will not afford) concerning the Militia which being long by reason of yr mans hast & my want [repeated and deleted] of a clark could not be now got ready (but will shortly send them); if need require I shall meet you at Norwich on Saturday next or any other time wher you may ples to comminicate what you hold useful of the publick; In the meane tyme Sir ever you may be confident that nothing in matters of this importance I ... not without advice & proper shall [rest obscured][44]

He was particularly careful over the words relating to what was said and done by the Array gentlemen who were equally trying to avoid their orders. For himself, he risked a 'chiding', altered to 'censure', for being slow to execute his ordinance. Holland's man was in haste to take the message back to his master and Potts did not have a clerk at Mannington at that moment so the long militia instructions that Holland wanted a copy of would have to wait.[45] Copying out papers by hand - these orders contained 1,213 words - must have taken many hours when so much information was being sent around the country.

The very same day John wrote to Simonds D'Ewes at London. Simonds had forwarded a letter addressed to Potts from Henry Willoughby and was anxious to know what it said. After he allayed his friend's fears over the match, John made some remarks which showed uncanny foresight:

> Sir , I had your kind Avisos & in yr letter inclosed one from Sir Henry Willoughby which according to your injunctions I keep safe by me till God afford us a happy meetinge; the contents of it are, that if this storme blowes over my brother will come to London to satisfye himself in all points & in the meane tyme is so well pleased with my information as he gives me thanks & warrant to continue your faire treaty in a waye of proceedings which is as much as I expected from him & gives my neice his daughter ground enough to hope for a good issue of hir discreet choice; myself need not add any persuation but wishes of Gods direction to you both for yr accomplishment if yr desire, according to his will;
>
> I concur with you in the fears of ungovernable numbers, from whence my thought always apprehended the most remediless dangers, which God avert. My own endeavours heer have been for peace & hitherto wee are quiet, whensoever necessity shall enforce us to make use of the multitudes, I dere not promise myself safety;
>
> I pray Sir let me enjoy the continuance of yr advertisements & present my affectionate respects to yr dearest, from, Sr
>
> yr faithful frend & servant[46]

John's comments on the dangers of uncontrollable mobs being deliberately used as a weapon were spot on. Just two days later, the Stour Valley riots broke out in Essex, apparently provoked by the discovery of royalist Sir John Lucas trying to smuggle out arms to the King. This was almost unprecedented popular violence against the persons and property of royalist gentry, catholics and unpopular ministers (even elderly ones). Attacks were targeted widely and inconsistently wherever old wounds had built up resentment, and spread through Essex and Suffolk up to Lavenham and near Bury. Even Sir Robert Crane, John's parliamentary friend, had to keep a trained band at his house in Chilton (he had helped Countess Rivers, a 61 year old catholic, to escape harm when she was pursued from Essex to Long Melford, so was unpopular). Three days later, when Harbottle Grimston, MP for Colchester, arrived from London to try to calm matters, the crowds still numbered around 4-5,000 strong. Potts and his neighbours would have been worried for their friends and family in Suffolk and in Kent which was also affected; fortunately the attacks did not spill over into Norfolk but the newsbooks and printed pamphlets which were now so widespread sent scare stories around the country. The House had learned of the troubles on the 23rd and Simonds picked up Potts's fears in his speech, warning of the loss of clear-cut boundaries between 'them and us' and noting later that 'we hear of a 100 lies in a day'. John would have suspected that the rebels had not risen independently: Essex was Warwick's home county and parliament was very concerned to stop men and arms reaching the King.[47] He might have been alerted by the order from the House on the 17th that he was to ensure the 'settings of strict watches at the several bridges between Norfolk and Suffolk'.[48] John's problems were however closer to home that week. While trying to hold off Mowbray, he found pressure on him from his own side. The next day, 20th August, he received the following:

> For my much respected frend Sir John Potts
>
> Sir, I presume soe much upon your favor as I intreate your furtherance off this service in particular I knowe your interest is greate in the County of Norfolk. And iff you please to laye itt oute in this, itt may have a very happy operation. Unles there bee a considerable strength speedily gotten together, we shall neither prevent the evill which wee feare, not obtene the good and iust ende wee hope and labour for. I desire to go to Lynn after I have bin att Bury which shalbe on Tuesday next god willinge iff I may heare from you and that I may have the honour off your company thether I shall take itt as a favour. Sir I desire to be esteemed by you as
>
> yr frend & servant
>
> Manchester[49]

Potts would certainly have known Edward Montagu at Westminster. Montagu, as the Earl of Kimbolton, sat in the Long Parliament as a radical puritan peer and had been impeached by the King at the time of his abortive attack on Pym in January. He was often speaker on the days when Potts was bearing messages.[50] He was married to Warwick's daughter, Anne Rich, and became the Earl of Manchester in November on the death of his father. His lands lay in Huntingdon and he may well have been under instruction from Warwick to keep an eye on Norfolk for him. This very civil note, typical of Manchester who was 'universally acceptable and beloved', was a direct command for Potts to get off the fence and raise the militia immediately according to his orders.[51] It was clear that the King was about to raise his standard (which he did at Nottingham on the 22nd) and time was of the essence. In Norfolk the town of Lynn was a worry for both sides, being politically split. John could hardly have turned down his 'request' to join him the following week. He must have needed all his famous coolness when the very next day he had a letter from Mowbray, who was still in Norfolk:

> To his very loving friend Sir John Potts k&b
>
> 21 Aug 1642
>
> Sir, I have received information that Certaine letters directed to me were intercepted at Lynn & sent to you if it be soe I doubt not but you will send them to me which I desire you to doe by this messenger & soe I rest
>
> yr very loving frend
>
> Mowbray & Matravas[52]

John was being pursued by both sides! Did Mowbray know Potts was about to go to Lynn with Manchester? The constant worries over letters being diverted by the opposition now led to Potts being suspected. He wrote back within 24 hours acquitting himself of any blame:

> My Lord,
>
> there were not any letters which concerne you brought unto me, neither doe I know of any intercepted at Lynn, which being soe remote it is unlikely they should send ~~bring~~ them hither; my self having noe acquaintance in that towne; If it had been as yr Lo' was informed you ~~so yr Lord~~ need not to doubt of such respect as is fitt to be performed by me as such with
>
> Yr Lordship's ready frend & humble servant
>
> John Potts[53]

Once again the survival of his draft showed his care: in making Lynn sound as far away as possible, he changed 'bring' to 'send' when talking of letters. With his stepsons at Narborough and his wife having grown up at Hilgay, it is hard to believe he knew no-one at Lynn but it might have been true. This was the closest Potts came to being in disfavour with both camps. Manchester's friendly warning was probably sparked off by the rumblings of the more militant members back in Westminster.

Manchester may have realised that Potts had done extremely good work in staving off the Commission of Array. Mowbray left Norfolk having accomplished little in the way of recruiting support for the King.[54] Potts himself did not apparently take any credit for keeping 'the noise of a drum' out of Norfolk for as long as he did.

Potts's next letter to Simonds D'Ewes showed he was careful to avoid post going astray. Simonds was not so sure and tantalisingly had not written down some secrets he wanted to tell John. John was desperate to keep their channel of news open and for Simonds to speak up for him against the 'scandalous tongues' who were questioning his loyalty:

> From Mannington 2 Sept 1642
>
> To my honored frend Sir Simons D'Ewes kt & bt one of the members of the hon hous of Comons in Westminster
>
> Sir, I had yr letter of 30 Aug for which I humbly thank you & am sory your doubting the safe conveyance, did deprive me of those secrets which you mention, for ther hath not hitherto any of yours miscarried. If you please but to add upon the superscription these words ('leave this with Mr John Corye of Norwich merchant') it would give sufficient speed & security to the passage;
>
> I shall be glad to heere of accomodation & wish we had the honour to have done our buisines without our neighbours help but why with aide they should give us lawe and binde our Kdome to conforme to their government is beyond my understanding; yr private affair is in good hands, my brother Willoughby late gone from hence, think his neice very young & small to couple, in all things else was wel pleased & not a backward frend to the match;
>
> I pray Sir continue the favoure of yr intelligence, & does to yr frend right against scandolas tongs which I heare blast me with report that I decline the service of the hous & encourage the Commission of Array; Sir I assure you my conscience leads me to uphold the Comon wealth to which I will prove noe changeling nor to my frend but rest:
>
> yr faithful servant
>
> My wife, sonn & daughter in law commend to you in exchange of yr salute[55]

The proposed match with Elizabeth was progressing; Francis Willoughby, Ursula's younger brother had been on a visit from Derbyshire and had thought it a good idea in principle, although she was 'very young and small'. D'Ewes was on tenterhooks and wrote again to Potts next week, hoping to have heard from the Willoughbys. Poor Francis had barely got home. John replied on 10th September with words of wisdom, telling him to be patient. As she was so young, the marriage could not have taken place even if the betrothal was agreed:

> Sir I receyved yr letter & can give you noe other account of Risly than formerly, the gent heere could doe noe bad offices in that buisness for I suppose he never wrote & is but lately arrived there; it is the ardency of yr affections that makes you impatient; Rebus sic stantibus, you need not spur on soe fast, for neither hir age nor the conjunction of the tymes doe afford an actual enjoinment. I hope my brother Willoughby will meet in London ere longe if the ... date of things give leave for treatys & in the mean while he hath delivered me warrant to continue it in the same faire terms as I presented it;
>
> Sir with thanks for yr favours expecting to heere from you weekly, I remain
>
> Sir
>
> yr faithfull frend and servant
>
> John Potts

In promising to continue his friend's suit, he made it clear he expected D'Ewes to continue to write to him once a week with the news from the House. If Simonds had waited a couple of days, he would have not have needed to worry: Francis wrote on the 15th from Risley with encouraging words:

> I received so faire a character of your worth & nobleness from Sir John Potts at my being in Norfolk as I ... gave a famile consent to what you desire; but since it pleased you to honour me with yr noble letter and to request my consent and furtherence, I doe tender it respectively unto you & give up the interest I have in my neices disposall, whose happy bestowing is a good part of the worldly comfort I have now in this life.
>
> I have spoken with my brother & have dealt with him as earnestly as I could concerning the ensealing of those bonds but I finde him unwilling to it till he comes to London which I hope may be this next terme if the tymes prove quiet. Thus with my true respects & service
>
> humble servant
>
> Francis Willoughby[56]

Henry was still putting off the evil day, waiting for quieter times before coming to see D'Ewes for himself. The next day he wrote, in a scrawly hand and very odd language, to his little girl, agreeing to the marriage despite his own misgivings and hoping she will change her mind:

> 16 September 1642
>
> to my Lady Elizabeth
>
> Why how now my little sparke of ... grace, how hath you only that wrought upon you to make you fully [*illegible*] Sir Simon has bewitched you ... but if there is no remedie, I have written to your Aunt Wynne to have it solennised at [*illegible*] or [*illegible*] where you shall like the better
>
> your dadde
>
> I am sure you will repent at more leisure & I my selfe will continue your loving auld dadde

Elizabeth may have been living with her aunt Lady Wynn as Henry seemed to be leaving the arrangements to her. Sir Richard Wynn had sat, as member for Liverpool, in the Commons with Potts and D'Ewes until a couple of weeks earlier, when he was suspended.[57] They had houses at Brentford (his wife's home) and Wimbledon as well as in the Strand. Henry presumably offered the choice of London or Derbyshire as the venue for the wedding.

In the end the marriage went ahead quite quickly and by November D'Ewes was calling Potts 'uncle'. The vision of Elizabeth, who may have been as young as fourteen or fifteen and the 43 year-old man who was later called 'that great Presbyterian bore' for his long speeches and equally long diaries and memoirs is slightly depressing.[58] However, he was wealthy with a large estate in Suffolk, would have been at Westminster most of the time and in his study writing at others. He died after they had been married five years and the young Elizabeth married another MP, Sir John Wray of Glentworth who later would join the family in court.

Chapter 12

Pull up the Drawbridge

From late 1642 to the end of 1643, Sir John's time was increasingly spent in Norfolk implementing parliament's orders; his efforts focused on keeping the war out of Norfolk and assisting his troubled friends wherever possible.

Sir John Potts now entered the next stage of his career: as a member of the Norfolk Committee. With his neighbours and kinsmen (four of whom were MPs and the rest were deputy lieutenants), John Holland, Thomas Wodehouse, John Hobart, John Palgrave, Robert de Grey, John Spelman and Framlingham Gawdy, he was to attempt parliament's bidding while trying to maintain the precarious state of peace within Norfolk. Most of their meetings were at Norwich and are well-recorded. On 6th September the meeting passed resolutions for the preservation of peace in Norfolk by organising their plans for the militia (in case of attack) and the raising of funds. On the 15th they persuaded over two dozen gentlemen to sign up accepting their commissions for the trained bands under the leadership of Warwick as their lord lieutenant.[1] This included some like Paston, de Grey, Richardson and Doyley who would later favour the King. John Potts, his mastery of committee work having been honed at Westminster, now took on the role of co-ordinator and able administrator.

Donating the family silver

On Monday 22nd September 1642 Potts met with Richardson, Paston, Holland, his nephew John Palgrave and Palgrave's brother-in-law Robert de Grey, to divide the work of the hundreds between them as the August orders had set out. John had seven: the two Erpinghams, Holt, Eynesford, Happing, North Greenhoe and Tunstead. They would have the help of the deputy lieutenants in their home districts and one able gentleman would be appointed to receive the horses, money and plate that had to be raised. It was agreed that the plate would be taken to New Hall in Norwich 'to be carried by carts with a guard of dragoons to London'. First the Norwich goldsmith Mr Scottowe would weigh the items (on Tuesdays, Wednesdays and Thursdays) with Richardson and Hobart overseeing the work. The scale of the operation would take weeks, first to persuade people to pay up, to handle those claiming exemptions or other excuses, to move horses, to count and weigh the money and ensure its safe arrival (with a proper paper trail from Norfolk to London); then to hear appeals and return horses if a case could be made for it. All recorded by letters and minutes of meetings for scrutinisation. They also resolved that members of the committee would be the first to subscribe in order to encourage others. At the same time, the militia must be raised with the captains in place and the troops viewed.

The next day 23rd September, Sir John Holland wrote a full letter detailing how hard the committee was working. This was addressed to Miles Corbett one of their most militant colleagues who needed to be assured Norfolk was behaving:

> To my very worthy frend Myles Corbett esq London
>
> Sir, I am newly returned from Norwich where I met with some of my associates in the publick service, but I have scarce time to tell for we ther agreed to put the propositions in present execution & for this purpose have allotted to every member of the House here present, together with one other Dep Lt a particular division who together are to call to their assistance such Justices & other persons of quality within the said division as are well affected to the service and that they then lead in the subscription by way of example & encouragement. I intend for the ease of the Country & the better advancement of the service to have a meeting in every respective Hundred committed to my care & that a list of all able persons inhabiting within every Hundred be brought to the us at our meetings, by which means the service will be more advanced & the affections of people discovered ... pray inform me what rules have been observed in the Nomination of Receions [receivers] in other Counties - whether security have been taken of them & if so what & whether any allowance for harm - we are at some stand-off I pray let me hear from you herein with what expedition you may. ... [story of Sir William Denny] ... All or most of the Captains have subscribed - I hope we shall at length repayre the reputation of our Country almost lost amongst you. And I pray Sir give us a good worde for oure incourage
>
> Sir, we thinke we deserve it for I assure you we doe not sleepe heir[2]

It was not long before the hopeful letters started as some gentlemen tried hard not to contribute. A week later, on the day appointed for the first subscriptions to be taken, a lawyer from Kerdiston wrote to John with mixed emotions. Edward Heyward, a close friend of John Selden's, had sent off a letter, perhaps rashly, which had contained his views against getting involved. Now he was hoping that Potts would keep his matters 'private'. Heyward would not be the last trusting to Sir John's reputation for fairness:

> Sept 29 1642 For the right worth' Sir John Potts bt
>
> Honour'd Sir
>
> I do not upon my saddest thoughts repent me of what I wrote to you in Monday last though on the Suddayn. In my free election of your self I trusted the House of Commons by you with all that

was at my disposall in matter of Ayde, as I suppose, the rest of the comons did by their Respective knights and Burgesses. I will not by any after act of mine endeavour to reuse alter or be wanting to that Trust. Only I beseech you, (as my former Answere inplyed) give me leave to keep my self (that am unfitt for action) meerely passive in this great difference. When any, how subordinate soever, imployed by that Honorable House shall come to me to that ende, I shall cleerely expose all the money and plate I have to their viewe and accesse, without any restraynt by me of proportions, or conditions but only of my being meerely passive: my vote and therein my will as well as my iudgement being by representation (as I conceive) already involved in the Votes of that Honorable House.

Thus Sir I rest in what I might be commanded by you

E Heyward

[added] Sir, the valewation you require now under my [hand] is this, my plate is worth £20 or £30.

[My] ready money is only sufficient to supply my present occasions but not to pay my present debts, my rents and debts owing me being at my command in these times.

yr Humanity Sir makes me presume this shalbe private[3]

That day at Aylsham the gentlemen of the area, including four of John's family, queued up to sign the following, a rather shorter and less fiery version of the Declaration than parliament had issued:

We whose names we hereunto subscribed do promise to lend the several sums underwritten to be disposed by the two Houses of Parliament (according to certain Propositions by them sent forth) for the maintenance of the Protestant Religion, the kings Authority, his person in his Royal Dignity, the free cours of Justice, the Lawes of the lande, the Peace of the Kingdome and the Priviledges of Parliament [4]

John led the way. In some cases minor alterations were made to the conditions - the use of the word county instead of country for example - which were a way of persuading friends that this was only for the defence of Norfolk, not for the general use of an army:

Sir John Potts of Mannington in money or plate to be sent up to Parliament one hundred pounds & for defence of his country 'not to be sent out' [*inserted*], two horses furnished & ten foote armed

Sir John Palgrave of Northwood Barningham in money or plate to be sent up to Parliament ... one hundred pounds & for defence of this County two horses furnished & ten foote armed

Edw Colfer twenty pounds & six foote well armed for the defence of this countye 'when occasion is offered'

James Scamler of Hickling esq in money ... for the intents & uses above said fifty pounds

Roger Townshend of Horstead esq ... fivetie pounds

George Hunt of Ittringham gent in plate to be sent to Parliament fifty pounds

William Crowe of Ittringham gent in plate to be sent ... sixty pounds[5]

Meetings were held around the county: at Holt, his brother-in-law, Thomas Lougher the rector of Letheringsett, offered £50 plate or money. On 5th October letters were sent to all the Captains to prepare their men for 'present service' and on the reverse of the Aylsham list above, were the notes for warrants to be sent setting up local review dates. The hundreds mentioned were all under John's care so it is likely these papers were his own notes. He would have been at Aylsham on Saturday 8th October, Roughton on the Monday, Walsingham on Thursday, Holt on Saturday 15th and North Walsham on the following Thursday.

At Aylsham, on the 8th, while he checked over the South Erpingham troop, he also persuaded others to sign up to subscribe. Sir William Paston offered £200 and six horses although like Palgrave and Windham he did not want them to go out of Norfolk.[6] Thomas Leman also signed up.

During the week this was all happening, the House sent orders to Sir John Potts and the rest of the committee and deputy lieutenants authorising them 'to have power to disarm Sir Nicholas Le Strange Bt, Sir Hamon le Strange, Sir Rbt Kemp, Sir Jn Spelman kt, Erasmus Earle, Edward Heyward esq for not contributing with the rest of the good subjects ... in this Time of imminent danger'.[7]

It had not taken long for the House to pick up on the absent names: Edward Heyward was named but Potts may have spoken up for him as requested. [8] By 1645 Heyward was actively involved in helping to raise money for the New Army. The L'Estrange family was a different matter. On the Thursday, while Potts was checking the men at North Walsham, a letter was delivered from Narborough, Ursula's son's house. Framlingham Gawdy was working with Potts's stepson, John Spelman trying to cover another five hundreds and they were in difficulties. As always Sir John was asked to help:

Narborough Oct 20 1642 to JP Much honored friend at
Mannington

Worthy Sir,

my cosyn Spillman and I wrote to Sir Hamond L'Estrange to
assist in the hundreds of Brothercrosse, Gallowe & Smythedon,
who hath absolutely refused. We have proceded with Marshland,
Clackclose & Freebridge and to morrow weere for South Greenhoe.
I believe we shall not have above a £1000 in the four hundreds.
What the remayne will bring in I know not. Therefore I shall take
as much paynes as any yett such is the couldness of the people as
I am like to receyve a checke. If you and my fellowe labourers doe
not help to excuse me, Sir Thos Hoggan, my cosyn Spillman & my
selfe entend to proceed with [Launditch] & as for Brothercrosse,
Galloe and Smythedon I beseech you Sir to put them (according
to your promises) into such hands as are better knowne in the
hundreds which will advance the service and to excuse my
attendance in those more the remote 3 hundreds for which I shall
remayne your

affectionate freynde to serve you

Framlingham Gawdy[9]

For all of Potts's efforts it was clear there were pockets of resistance and that some
families would be, at the least, disarmed to avoid any chance of rising for the King.
These actions against defaulters may have speeded up the payments from other
reluctant payers. By early November John was in Norwich overseeing the transfer
of monies. On the 3rd he was at a meeting where his friend John Cory the merchant
was appointed Receiver General for the monies collected on or before the 17th.[10]
While there he received a letter from Sir Charles Le Gros of Crostwick (MP for
Orford and Knyvett's brother-in-law)) apologising for his tardiness:

Nov 3rd 1642

To my honoured freind Sir Jn Potts Baronet at Norwich

Sir

I received a letter from you lately by Sir Wm Paston and desire your
pardon that the satisfaction I am to give you to what you required
in it, coms no sooner; I am willing towards the maintenance of true
religion, the safety and honour of the King and Kingdom etc to
lend £50 in plate which, to whom you plese to assign to receive it,

shall be delivered at Norwich upon 2 or 3 days warning given me at Crostwight. Sir it is an addition to what I suffer that I canot be yett able to attend the publick service upon occasion and to assure your self that all good offices shall be thankfully acknowledged by

Sr your assured freynd to love and serve you

C L Gros[11]

Potts himself had now made good his promise of £100 and he received a beautifully written receipt from Timothy Scottowe on 8th November:

Received the day and year above written by me Timothy Scottowe (being Treasurer ordained) of Sir John Potts of Mannington, kt & bt.

6 silver candlesticks, 2 banqueting dishes, one preserving ladle & dish, eight plates, one bason, one Broath standing Bowle, one Chafendish, one vinegar Creuet, A closet candlestick, a poranger & three trencher salts weighing together 300 3-score Eleaven ounces a halfe & one dram of Touch plate Troy weight amounting in value with the fashion at Five shillings 4 pence an ounce (together with eightyone shillings 4 pence in money) to the some of one hundred pounds which is to be imployed according to the said propositions

I say received by me

Timothie Skottowe[12]

On top of his previous expenses John (and his wife) must have felt the loss of this latest outgoing but could not have made any comment. He was ordered to lead others by his example. The following month he had a receipt for his two furnished horses, another £40 in value, that went off to the troop of Capt John Fountain of the Norwich Volunteers. John returned home to attend the full muster, held on Heydon Ollands (the heathland) on 13th November as 'captayne of a company of foote within the Hundred of Erpingham' in response to the call from the deputy lieutenants.[13]

John's role in acting as a go-between, smoothing paths, now started to show itself. The order to disarm the non-payers was slowly being implemented but a curious letter from the Earl of Manchester revealed not only the extent of their friendship but Manchester's desire to keep honour among gentlemen, a trait that would later be held against him:

Lyn[n] Nov 22

For my esteemed frende Sir John Potts these

Sir

I have receaved your letter and I was sorry when I founde that any
ill cariage had bin used towards Mr Spylman and therefore as soone
as I came I gave order that his arms and horses should be sent back
with him and soe I sawe itt dorne; in all things I shall desire to
express my selfe tender off the reputation off those that are for the
service off the publick in particular I shall assure you thatt I will nott
be wantinge in givinge you just cause to owne mee as

your frend and servant

Manchester[14]

   John had obviously made a plea on behalf of Sir John Spelman, a kinsman
through his stepsons' family, living at Stinton Hall, between Salle and Heydon. At
this time Sir John, a scholarly man, the son of the antiquarian Sir Henry Spelman,
was still just about defendable. It would not be long before he would put himself
beyond Potts's circle of care.[15]
   In the meantime John Holland was still actively working the county being heard and
seen where he thought he could count; he excused himself, to Potts, from a meeting at
Norwich so that he could be at Lynn (probably as Manchester was there). He hoped to
meet with John Spelman of Narborough on the way. The letter is badly damaged:

Nov 22 [overwritten 21] 1642

Sir

The certeynty off our danger & the incerteynty of our provision
for our remove, carryes mee this weeke to Lynn which pleads my
excuse at Norwich. Tottenhill Heath I intend in my passage, where
I hope to meet with Mr Spilman & to desire his assistance further.
The inclosed I found left for mee heere at my last returne from you;
which fortefyed my Resolutions nott to see Walton [West Walton?]
wher certeynly ther was an apparance much to the disadvantage
off our worke. I heere these parts grow ... dayley. The inclosed
I pray Sr d ... Noble Associate. I would nott h... fall under any
misconstruction; [rest illegible]

yr very affectionate frend & servant

J Holland[16]

Tottenhill Heath was on the main road to Lynn, within a few miles of John Spelman's home at Narborough. It is possible they were to meet at Gregory Gawsell's house at Watlington which backed on to the heath. Gregory, a parliamentarian, justice of the peace and committee colleague was related to both Potts and Spelman.[17]

There seems to have been a disturbance at Walton, perhaps West Walton far over on the fens, which Holland felt was not helpful. Unfortunately the 'enclosed' has not survived. Holland also sent a draft of a letter for Potts to send to a new arrival in Norfolk - no-one could escape the payment to parliament:

> My Lo:
>
> Wee understand your Lordship have brought yr familie into Norf & setled at Hindringham where this poor Country is likely to receyve benefit in yr abode; & therefore taking yr Lordship as an inhabitant amongst us, we canot but acquaint you with the proposition of Parliament delivered us in charge, & doe desire to knowe what assurance (in money or plate) yr Lordship wil be pleased to subscribe, for maintenance of the true Protestant Religion ... [fren]ds & humble servants[18]

On the reverse of Holland's letter however is a rare note by Potts. His to-do list shows some of the many pieces of administration he had to undertake:

> Write - To Mr Jerome Bloefield
>
> To Sr Will Paston
>
> To my sonn Spelman send Clem letter
>
> Prepare agt Thursday propositions
>
> Call for Rows [Rous] mony, gett Hen: Elmer to choos my weathers
>
> Try Covil for Sr Rich Bernyes troope or any other fit man
>
> nomt'[nominations] for the subsidy meetinge
>
> [ap]point the volunteer agreement spedily
>
> inquire whether Hamond did call his company or presented them at Musters
>
> Send for all defaulters at Musters both hors and foot

It seems that Sir Hamond L'Estrange still had not called his men to muster.

The amount of work that Potts had on his plate was recognised by the recently wed Sir Simonds D'Ewes, now his nephew. John wrote to Simonds on 26th November from Mannington when the latter had returned to parliament:

> Sir I recyved your kind letter and am glad yr health & that of my dear neice, with these frends whence you left hir; since you are returned to Parliament I shall expect more cleare relacion of affairs from thence by yr hand than otherways, for I need not be jealous of any miscarriage, however the post boy one night was knocked off his horse by rogues when he rode very late, yet those letters were after found unopened to come safe; I pray Sir continue yr accustomed panies [paines] & let me understand all particularly worthy your observation, which shall much oblige,
>
> yr affectionate unkle to
>
> serve you
>
> John Potts
>
> Sir you are serviceably saluted by all yr frends heer[19]

Potts, as brief as usual, still took time to reassure D'Ewes of the safe passage of mail so that his conduit of news would stay open. Two days later he received a reply from Westminster, as usual badly written (he had no clerk with him) but bursting with feeling:

> To the right wor' my verie much honoured unkle Sir John Pots kt & bt at his house neare Norwich these. By the Norfolk post
>
> Sir I am sorrie to heare that you beginne already in Norfolk to send for commanders and that the face of things beginne to looke after an hostile manner amongst you. This day we had a draught of an Association brought in by your neighbour Corbett for Norfolk Suffolk Essex Cambridge & Hartfordshire & we voted to send upp not onlie for all these sheriffs in safe custodie [but] ... for all the others sheriffs alsoe of England ...Thus is the whole kingdom like to be sett ...[com]bustion at once & Ireland to be lost in th ... time of those bloodie murtherers are like ... upon us like a swarme of caterpillars & ... that which the sworde of civill warre shall ... . I have neither of my servants at this time ... mae[?] who must be my manuensis when I ... long unles I write to my learned freind heere or beyond the ... in another language; & then I enlarge myselfe as well for exercise; as for correspondence I should much ioy to see you

heere to communicate to you many secrets of my past business; but
I feare you have a twelve months sadd & fatall worke in Norfolke; if
an higher providence beyond all expectation prevent not those sadd
desolations which are comming upon us.

Pardon I pray this brevitie; I tender my affectionate respects to your
self my noble Aunt & all my cousens.

I hope you received my last sent to you with the two enclosed
directed to my cousen Clement Spelman

your faithfull nephew & humble servant

Simonds D'Ewes[20]

It is clear John was not expected to return to parliament, having at least a
year's 'sadd and fatall worke' to do in Norfolk. This was also the first mention of
the Eastern Association in which Potts was already playing a part. The idea of an
Association had been agreed by Thomas Richardson, John Hobart, William Paston,
Thomas Wodehouse, John Potts and John Palgrave at Norwich on 27th October
between three counties, Norfolk Suffolk and Cambridgeshire, for the mutual
defence of one another. The House, particularly Corbett, thought a larger grouping
would bring the errant East Anglians better into line and agreed the decision on
10th December. At this meeting too, more resolutions were passed tightening up
the restriction on popish recusants (disarmed and to remain within 5 miles of
home) and those suspected by the committee of parliament of being disaffected to
parliament. The last phrase had the word 'justly' inserted but the tone would still
have been of concern to those at Norwich. Any captains of the trained bands who
did not subscribe plate were to be replaced and anyone who refused to pay could be
disarmed with the help of justices and soldiers as the deputy lieutenants thought fit.
Specifically, 'Sir Wm Paston shall be entreated to take upon him the command of
such horses as shall be raised voluntary within the County of Norfolk' (Sir William
was present so presumably had not yet agreed) and that 'if Lieut Col Knivet shall
not subscribe to acept his charge as Capt, under the Parliament authoritye then
it is agreed that Sir John Holland shall cause the Chief Constable to present that
company before him'. Knyvett who had avoided Potts many months before was now
clearly not going to join the parliamentarians. The last decision was that they would
meet weekly at the King's Head upon Thursday by ten of the clock in the forenoon
for the service of the deputy lieutenancy.[21] Perhaps with hindsight, the choice of inn
of that name was unfortunate.

At this time, despite all his work, Sir John was still not himself a deputy lord
lieutenant but was listed as one who united with them 'to preserve the inhabitants
from all kynds of Plunderers'.[22]

His previous experience in the House with arms and supplies was now called upon: on 2nd December 1642 he was authorised (by his nephew and friend) to purchase the necessary supplies for Norfolk:

> Whereas Sir John Potts hath bin by us requested to sende for & procure divers proportions of armes & powder for the necessary defence of this county by ordinance of Parliament refered to us & others the Deputy Lieutenants of the County, we have authorised him to give the warrant & directions for the payment of such sums of mony & unto such persons as he hath... at London to buy & convey the sd armes & powder unto the custody for the country's service
>
> J Palgrave Wm Paston[23]

Things were hotting up - at least on paper. On the 3rd John and his colleagues sent out a letter of alarm to call the gentry to a meeting on the 7th:

> Whereas we have received intelligence from the Earl of Warwick Lt of this county That there are foreign forces upon the coast of Norfolk Suffolk Essex and thereupon are required that the Trained Bands both of foote and horse should be put in readiness That upon Alarumes given we may be in a posture of defence to oppose their landing whereupon being desirous to do what in us lieth to prevent the ruine of this Countie, doe request you to give us a meeting upon Wednesday next being the 7th of the month at the sign of the Kings Head in Norwich by tenn of the clock in the forenoon There to advise and assist for the better prevention of the eminent danger hanging over this Countie, the neare approach whereof we are much more sensible of by the advertisement Importunitee and example of our neighbour countrys And in the mean time we desire you not to be wanting on your partes (as we will not of ours) to use all possible meanes you may for the Common safety And so in very much hast we rest your respective friends
>
> Tho Wodehouse Will Paston [*deleted* John Patterson?] John Potts John Holland John Palgrave Jo Hobarts

With a number of royalists present, tempers flared and pro-royalist statements were made which Palgrave, Potts and Holland 'took great exceptions unto; whereupon Sir John Spelman, Mr Hamon L'Estrange and others were commanded to depart the meeting'.[24] Was Potts beginning to lose patience with these outspoken stirrers? Either he or Holland reported this affair and on 10th December the House took action:

Persons affronting Committees.

Resolved, upon the Question, That Sir Jo. Spilman Knight, Sir
Wm. Doyly, Captain Crane, and Hamond Lestrange, Esquire, and
Francis Cory of the County of Norfolke, be forthwith sent for, as
Delinquents, for affronting the Committees, when they were met
upon the Service of the Parliament; and thereby, as much ... in them
lay, obstructing and prejudicing the Service of the Commonwealth.'[25]

Following the meeting, on the 8th, his friends, the deputy lieutenants sent him,
as one of the captains, an urgent letter, which was based on the earlier information;
Warwick wanted the militia to be ready at one hour's warning:

To our worthy frend Sir John Potts kt Col of a Regiment of foote
these Speed

Sir

Whereas you formerly received directions from us to call your
Company before you and to take exact view of the men and armes
and to supply the defences and then frequently to trayne and
exercise, of which directions we hope of your carefull performance.
But now having received intelligence from the Earl of Warwick
Lord Lieutenant of this County, that there are divers foreigne forces
seene upon the Coasts of Norfolk, Suffolk & Essex which threaten
danger to this County, for the preventinge whereof our sd Lord
Lieut' hath required us to call out the trayned bands of this County
as well of horse as foote, to be in a readines to answere any Alarum
that shall be given upon the Coasts and to drawe downe the said
forces to oppose the landing of any Enemies, in performance of
which Command and performance of that duty wee owe to our , we
have thought fitt to desire and require you that you forthwith put
your band or company in such a position as that they may be ready
to *March** to such Rondevouze as shall be appoynted by us in one
houres warninge, and that you cause every Muskettere presenting
to provide himself of two pound of powder four pound of Bullet
and one pound of Match, for the present defence of themselves
their wives, children, religion & Country , and that you faile not to
returne us a duplicate of your Muster rolle under your Hands upon
*thursday next the Fivetenth of the Instant december at the Kings Head
in Norwich** together with the names of those that shall refuse to
appears att your Musters or be otherwise materially deficient in The
Service soe necessarie for the present defence of this County, to the
end that they may bee delt withall according to their demerritts as
persons disaffected to the peace and satisfaction of the County

Not doubting of your speedy care, wee rest

yr affectionate freinds*

John Hobarts, J Holland, Thomas Woodhouse, John Palgrave, Miles Hobart[26]

*added in another hand

Sir John - a deputy at last

On 10th December 1642, five days before he presented his muster rolls at the King's Head, he was at last named in a list of deputy lieutenants:

> Resolved, upon the Question, That this House doth nominate and approve of Sir John Hobart, Sir Tho. Richardson, Sir Tho. Woodhouse, Sir Jo. Holland, Sir Jo. Potts, Sir Jo. Palgrave, Samuel Smyth, to be Deputy Lieutenants for the City and County of the City of Norwich.[27]

No doubt his health was drunk at the meeting, even if just the one glass. The same day he heard the news that one hundred dragoons were on their way to Norfolk for the county's defence for him personally to dispose of. Presumably he had to hand them over to others to arrange their billeting and food. Two days later he was in Norwich to take the oath of allegiance (which would become such a hot issue in 1648) as a bachelor of arts; his nephew John Palgrave was shown on 6th April 1643 as master of arts.[28]

Quite rightly, John was one of those congratulated in December 1642 on raising £40,000 for the army by loan by the committee for the advancement of money. This was an enormous sum (millions in today's money) raised within a few months. In Norfolk this had not led to open opposition but in London feelings were running high. D'Ewes reported on 11th December that the London companies were coming to blows about taxes and demanding peace be made. For once it was well-written and he remembered to send it by Mr Cory:

> To my very much honoured uncle Sir John Potts k &b at Manington These be [delivered] neare Norwich I pray leave this at Mr John Cories house in Norwich to be sent as abovesaid
>
> Westminster 11 Dec 1642
>
> Sir, Ther are propositions or articles past the House this instant monday which I feare will sett our two neighbouring counties into a combustion instead of joining them by an association. I beseech you beware of that fierie spirit & African face to whom you write so often.

269

For newes, in the first place all particulars in this cittie doe tend to a speedie confusion. Most trades except some 4 or 5 have lien still for about 3 months [since] last past & though they wanted many conveniences yet hoping for peace in the issue & enjoying quietly that little which was left them, they sate silent & patient But as soon as they saw that one [?] chute with 30 moore had prefered a petition to the House of Commons not to admitt of any further treatie or an accomodation & that ordinances of Parliament were past to lay taxes upon them, they supposed ther case miserable & desprate & have therefore about 4000 citizens already subscribed a petition for peace which though it were not delivered by some of the subscribers into the House yet it was read ther last weeke & is now in print. This afternoone ther hath been not onlie hott words but many blows amongst the citizens about it; & divers of those wounded who are for the petition because they came unarmed to the guildhall where the Ld Mayor & common councell were attended with armed men; This will but exasperate them moore then formerlie & give example to the counties alsoe to consider well whether anie tax cann be levied upon them but by an Act of Parliament. The poore towne of Marleborough Wilts which respected the Kings forces on the 25th day of November last past was on Monday last the 5 day of this instant December taken pillaged & plundered by them & yet being but 62 miles off we had no certaine newes of it till this day with newes that ther is a great fault somewhere that we have noe better intelligence. Sir Ralph Hopton hath an armie of about 1000 horse & foote in Devonshire & doth what hee please in taxing & plundering; but hee canot yet gett Plymouth nor Exeter; Sir John Norcot is come upp from Ireland post & tells me he is almost undone. The Lords do not agree to allow Mr Speaker to sitt in the Rolls but have been verie earnest these two or three dayes last past for propositions of peace; which god of his infinite mercy send with a full passage of the Truth

my service ... yr humble nephew

Simonds D'Ewes

Who was the 'fierie spirit' that D'Ewes warned Potts about? He said Potts wrote to the man often but we have no surviving letters to suggest another regular correspondent. The phrase of 'African face' ought to be helpful but as yet the identity is unknown.[29]

Potts, despite being a captain for the musters and organising the logistics of men and supplies, was not himself a soldier and may have deliberately avoided potentially violent situations. He certainly did not attend the disarming of royalist supporters. Of the original six named by the House, he had protected Spelman and Heyward;

he may also have persuaded his neighbours Kemp and Earle to sign up and that just left the L'Estranges. A letter, unsigned but probably from him and others, was sent the day he was in Norwich, to Capt Gilbert Parker & Chief Constables (Hundred of Smithdon):

> 15 Dec 1642 [addressed] To his worthy freind Isaac Appleton esq at Mr Prestons house near Norwich Leave this at Mr Bendishe his house a mairchant neare St Andrews Church in Norwich to be presently sent with all speed

In it the Constables were told to disarm Sir Nicholas L'Estrange and Sir Hamond L'Estrange leaving a few arms at Sir Hamond's house for defence; 'they [the writers] are too far away and have had many meetings in Norwich to go themselves'.[30]

On the last day of 1642 Potts, Hobart and Palgrave recorded another meeting at Norwich. Amongst the decisions was the appointment of adjutants for the captains: 'Capt Knivetts shall be adjutant of Sir Miles Hobart Regiment; Captaine Tough shall be adjut' of Sir John Potts his Regiment; Capt Carey for Sir J Hollands regiment; Capt Parker for Col Calthorpe regiment'. They also ordered scouts to go from Lynn, one to Lincolnshire to see if the enemy was there [Lord Newcastle] and the other to Peterborough and Northampton (directions and satisfaction were to be agreed with Mr Spelman and Mr Toll). Thomas Toll was the member for Lynn and was also in the process of transporting twenty papist horses which had been seized, from Lynn to London.[31]

As the year ended, John could not have been in any doubt that the war was going to escalate, despite so many moderate voices still hoping for peace. His role in Norfolk was now radically changed. He had worked hard to avoid open violence and upset. He and the Committee, based in Norwich had managed their work well, raised monies with as little parliamentary rhetoric as possible, and gently rebuked those who defaulted. But he and his friends had stood up for those in trouble, such as Sir William Denny and Dr Coleby, rector of Cawston: such tolerant ways had led them to be distrusted. For Corbett and Cromwell, Norfolk was backsliding. From now on the Committee work would be overseen by others, hardliners based at Cambridge. The days of the moderates were numbered.

1643 Spies and rumours

Although John was not attending the House, he did apply to it for assistance for a local widow. On 13th January he was allowed to take £10 from the Irish monies collected in Norfolk, 'to be disposed of to the Widow Olly, and her Company, lately come out of Ireland'. The use of funds in this way would ameliorate the feelings of locals increasingly worried by the constant demands of parliament for its army, demands which seemed reminiscent of the King's old methods.

The absence of both Potts and Moundeford from the House at this time was a great worry to their colleague William Pierrepont who believed they were needed there. Pierrepont, whose home was in Huntingdon, was obviously a great fan and had nothing but praise for John's judgement:

19 January 12 o'clock 1643[32]

to my noble frend Sir Jo Potts

I receaved you letter of the 16th of Jan this morning; what you write shewes your great iudgement or your affection to thes kingdomes, and I pray God when wise men know, and tell others may beleeve theyr owne good and follow.

The propositions are sent down from the Lords with amendments; we hope this day to [report] them, and the sooner we can dispach them the better; the Springe comes on & good success of late may make them more passable at Oxford. If your county can spare you, the service that you & Sir Edm. Moundeford can doe here is <u>very</u> great, and indeed, commands your coming if extraordinary occasions hinder not. The town of Saltash in Cornwall we heere is taken with the Ordinance, and all Sir R Hopton carriages, his foote all left him he retired with his horse to Pendennis castle, Coll. Godwin and the forces at Aylesbury have taken ... Capt Crofts his troope of horse, and all the troop men and horses armes; ther hath been some difference betwixt the Lord Fairfax and Mr Hotham which is sayd to be reconciled. A great rumer is of earl of Newcastles army to be 13000 strong but I beleve it not. A letter of intelligence is intercepted wherein the acts of the houses and the Cttee of the defence of the kingdome are sent to Oxford; ther was also a letter of Sir Robert Pye of our house wherein I am tould he give [intelligence] seekes his own peace, and did cause a Lady to be struck for £3700 for Sir Nic Crispe for secret services done; That Sir N Smyth was for money lent when the King went last against the Scots. I was not in the house when thes letters were read. Sir Nic Crispe is prisoner with the serjeant of our house and that business is referred to Cttee. I heare this morning that gret [store] of the forces from Oxford and thos parts are come near Aylesbury and it is imagined they will ascault that towne, wherein are Coll Godwin, Coll Bulstrod theyr regiments, and some others. Its sayd also that Dayntree in Northamptonshire is plundered by the kings forces.

my service I beseech you to Sir Ed Moundeford,

yr most humble servant

Wm Pierrepont

Letters such as this with their excited outpourings of the latest rumours and news were vital to John. Sir Nicholas Crisp, a devoted royalist, had remained in London spying on the parliamentarians for the King. The £3,700 was his pay-off. Crisp was a survivor: originally a rich trader with a monopoly along the west coast of Africa, he had a glass bead factory in Hammersmith which he used as barter for goods and slaves. He plotted and spied throughout the war and the Commonwealth period and was rewarded with a baronetcy after the Restoration. His heart was buried in Hammersmith under a monument to Charles I. Sir John's grandson, Philip Bedingfield, would later come to know this story well when he married Elizabeth Strode. Her two aunts Anne Crisp and Rebecca Hervey both suffered great financial losses at Crisp's hands. The story of the black sheep would have often been recounted.[33]

Back in the House, Sir John Holland was doing his best for the county. On 17th January he presented a petition from Norfolk to the House to request a peace treaty. He took part in the general debate in the House the following month but although he spoke fervently of his concerns that if the treaty were not to happen he believed 'it would bee occasion of much discontent in [Norfolk] which had long and earnestly desired for peace', the motion was lost, 73 to 113 votes.[34] The hardliners wanted the King to disband his troops and agree to all the propositions.[35] The draft petition to the House survives in part but with a petition to the King in draft on the other side![36] It hoped the King would 'entertaine those propositions of accommodations which shalbe present to your most sacred hands' and ' to abhore the bloodye Councell of a Civil Warre'.

A draft of a letter probably sent to Lord Grey of Warke (at that time in command of the forces of the Eastern Association) showed that Norfolk was now feeling threatened. One edge of the letter is unreadable:

> We think fitt to let you understand that many Papist and their ...
> [adh]erents of our County hereof late given out severall report to the
> disservice of Parliament advancement of some dessigne to br[ing]
> forces into our Countye: which wee conceyve cant be effected
> without an equal hazard to your County & Cambridgeshire lying
> between us & the danger; & nowe we heare that twenty gent have
> assembled themselves at Thetford, on Suff[side]in a kynde of warlike
> equipage well hord with pistols & the like company or more are at
> Barton Mills come out Cambridgeshire and other neare parts. That
> the heath is full [of] their Scouts daily crossing & posting up &
> downe for discord
>
> And that some of the gentry are gone to Oxford to solicit [more]
> - forces they expect or give intelligence of our unpreparedness Sir,
> Thes considerations makes [us] send this messenger to under - what
> you doe in the business of Association or what other course ...
> taken for your own safety & your neighbours that wee may proceed

jointly; If you please to take account of these assembly – Barton
Mills & Thetford on your side, surely we will end ... to prevent
your inconvenience which may arise from such mee ... here; soe not
doubting your worthy care, with our best respectes & desire of your
answer we rest Sir

yr true frend & servants

[Written up on the lower edge - the numbers were not explained]

Sir Thos Richardson 2
Sir Jo Hobart 6
Sir Thos Woods 2
Sir Jo Palgrave 2
Sir Jo Potts 2
Sir Miles Hobart 2
Rolf Hasset 1   [probably Blennerhasset]
Mr Smythe 2
Mr Spelman 1
Hen Yaxley 1
Capt Founteyne[37]

In response, they received two letters: the first a very cordial letter from the
Cambridge committee, written by Sir Miles Sandys and signed by Cromwell in
January addressed to 'Our Noble Frends Sir Jn Hobart Sir Thomas Richardson Sir
John Potts Sir Jn Palgrave k&b John Spelman esq & the rest of the Dep Lts for
Norfolk' which expressed that now parliament and the Lord General were there 'they
had taken into their care the peace & protection of the Eastern Counties'. That must
have sent a shiver down the spine. A meeting was requested 'at Mildenhall Tuesday
31 Jan' [1643] and the Norfolk committee were to have in readiness a considerable
force of horse and foot 'for we have certaine intelligence that some of Prince Rupert's
forces are come as farre as Wellingborrow in Northamptonshire and that the
Papists in Norfolk are solicited to rise presently upon you; thus presenting all our
Neighbourly & loving respects'.[38]

This letter had been awaiting the post to Norfolk when their letter arrived. With
this came a second which had an unmistakably threatening tone despite the friendly
words. It lacked the normal civilities and used scaremongering rumours about the
King needing another fertile county to plunder for feeding his army:

To our worthy frends Sir Jn Hobart Thos Richardson Sir J Potts Sir J
Palgrave Sir J Spelman

Gentlemen the grounds of your jealousies are real, they concur with
our Intelligences from Windsor ... from a prisoner taken by Sir

Samuel Luke (one Mr Gaudy a Capt of Dragoons) this confession was drawn: that Papists by direction from [the King at] Oxford should rise in Norfolk; whereupon it was desired from thence that Sir Henry Bedingfield and Mr Gaudy, their persons should be seized and that we should do our endeavours to make stay at the person and letter which contrived this encouragement to them, he being described by his house and clothes: but we believed was past us before we had notice, for our scouts could not light on him: as for the other consideration of his Majesties forces being invited into these parts, we have confirmation thereof from all hands and there is this reason to doubt it will be so because his Majesty is weary of Oxford, there being little in those parts left to sustain his army, and surely the fullness of these parts and fitness of them for horse are too too good arguments to invite him hither; thus we agree in your grounds of doubt and fears. The next thought is of remedy and in this we account it our happiness to consult with you of common safety to be had wither by the association you speake of or by any other consideration by communication of assistance according to necessity, wherein I hope you shall finde ... all readiness and cheerfulness in us, to assist you to break any strength shall be gathered or to prevent it if desired, having timely notice given from you thereof. The way will be best settled if you give us a meeting according to our desire by a letter particularly prepared ... before we received yours, and now sent unto you for that purpose together with these. This is all; we can say for the present but that we are your friends and servants

Miles Sandys

We sent to Sir Wm Spring to offer him our assistance for the apprehending Sir H Bedingfield etc. We have not yet received any answer. We know not how to address our selves to you. It's our desire to assist you in that or any other public service

The deliberate inclusion of the description of a confession being drawn from Mr Gaudy (who may well have been related to Framlingham) must have appalled Potts and his family. The Bedingfields were vulnerable, being catholic, but Potts's daughter Ursula was married to Philip Bedingfield (the protestant branch) and the relationship was a distinguished one. However worried Potts and friends had been, this reply must have produced greater feelings of the loss of control in their county.

Despite having help, Potts was still busy with meetings and organisation. The seizing of arms and horses from recusants was still slowly moving forward; by 11th January they were lagging behind and Potts asked for an authority that could be sent directly to the captains who were executing the business and likely to meet opposition.[39] A letter was sent to the deputy lieutenants to warn them:

Gentlemen

Whereas recusants horses taken about yr parts of the county, some
were left (with DLs permission) with the owners 'upon pretence of
necessary use for husbandry & promise of delivery whensoever they
should be required' - now Capt Frances Fines [Fiennes] is coming
with letters from Earl of Essex to take those horses - so they [the
Gentlemen] are entreated to send to the owners that they may bring
their horses to them for Capt F to assess & those fit for service will
be taken to London & not discharged

yr very loving frends[40]

On the 26th Essex's letter from Windsor authorised them to assist Capt Frances
Fiennes take the 30 horses.[41]

There was nothing to be done but attempt to lessen the hardships of their friends
as much as possible. They covered for those who had not subscribed promising to
show arms and horses when necessary (Moundeford promised for Mr Anguish of
Moulton, Edward Paston was recorded as never having any horse). The Association
was put in place and the ordinance finally executed and read to all.[42] Potts and the
others had to arrange more musters, 'Mr Browne of Fulmodestone having authority
to exercise such volunteers as willingly come themselves to preserve the peace of the
Country in the Hundreds of Holt Eynsford South and North Erpingham and North
Greenhoe'.[43] Accounts showed the men were properly armed; dragoons were being
sent for and paid for; the bridge watch was maintained.[44] James Tennant and Thomas
Cutlacke (a Northrepps man) were appointed to assist Palgrave with the paying and
arming of the trained bands in North Erpingham. The men had to muster in mid-
March on a Thursday morning by 10 o'clock fully armed with a 'knaphacke' and
4lbs of bullet, 3 yard of match and a 1lb of powder (1lb less than the orders had
specified).[45] All this had to be kept dry and safe somewhere: South Erpingham's was
stored in a chamber over the porch at Hevingham Church. The clergy must have
prayed all the more fervently with 6 barrels of gunpowder above their heads.[46]

Perhaps the strangest letter, showing how nervous gentlemen were at this time
was from Sir John Spelman. His precarious situation, having now been named in
the House, meant he was carefully watched. He obviously felt very vulnerable and
wanted to keep on the right side of Potts whose duty it was to report on any errant
behaviour. In February 1643 he wrote a long defensive letter to his kinsman to
explain why he was hanging around their mutual neighbour's house late at night.
The letter, which was printed in full in Ketton-Cremer, is addressed from Wolterton
'in haste', possibly written to assuage the anxiety of the neighbour, Mr Houghton
of Wolterton Hall (barely two miles from Mannington).[47] First he declared he was
unjustly charged: 'Sir If I was not uniustly & without all coulour publiquly defamed
for a malignant & Popishly affected, I should never entertain any jealousy that I
might be meant any share in such charges but being by that crimination now made

capable of partaking of every calumnation, in that kinde, I hold it my duty even to Christianity to protest my innocence'. In rambling detail Spelman explained that he thought his wife (Sir John Townshend's daughter) had gone to call, with Mrs Houghton in her coach, on Sir John and Lady Potts (the civilities of life continued) and then returned to Wolterton with her, it being dark and after 6 o'clock. Spelman therefore rode to Wolterton to find her but 'what by fetching about and missing my way made it so late that I found Mr Houghton in bed and much troubled at my so late coming to his house: as for my wife I found she neither was, nor had been there. I was sorry, that I had exposed myself and my neighbour ... that such a nightly coming to him might (in these times) insinuate.' He claimed he did 'at my Lo Mowbrays appearing with the Commission of Array ... realy endeavour the surcease of it'. He said he was as anxious as Mr Houghton and, he believed, Potts was, to avoid the war coming into the county.

Ketton-Cremer identifies Mr Houghton as Robert but it is quite possible that it was his son Richard. Robert had just completed Earlham Hall and Richard and his wife moved into Wolterton, having been living in Itteringham.[48] Although Mr Houghton 'has ever concurred' in sharing Spelman's views, he was connected to the arch royalist Richard Catelyn of Norwich who was Mrs Robert Houghton's brother. What is not clear is where Spelman's wife Ann was or had been and why he took so long to ride from Salle to Wolterton, about 5 miles! Sadly Sir John Spelman's worries were to end by July that year as he was summoned to the King at Oxford at the time Camp Disease had broken out and he died suddenly.[49]

Potts himself had been at yet another meeting in Norwich on the day in question discussing the Association meeting of deputy lieutenants in Bury the following week. Two of them would be asked to meet there and the other six (including Potts, Palgrave and Spelman) promised to go unless some extreme necessity prevented them. On the back of his notes of this meeting is a reminder to give Mr Bayfield a copy of the parliament order for the £10 of Irish money for the Blickling poor, presumably the Widow Olly. At the Bury meeting on 9th February, the Norfolk committee as ever looked for ways of mitigating the more extreme parts of the ordinance. However they had no choice but to tell their neighbours to be prepared; two days later and one day after the debate in the House, on 11th February, Potts, Palgrave, Richardson, Hobart and Wodehouse set up a meeting at the King's Head on the 16th explaining:

> whereas we received letters from the Dep Lts of Suffolk and Cambs
> much importing the safetye of this countie, We requested some
> gentlemen from hence to visett them for the better understanding
> of that Business, who being now returned, we thought itt necessary
> to communicate the substance thereof to the gentleman of our own
> Countie that we may together consider what shalbe fitt for our
> common good and safety. Desiring hereby that you will not faile to
> afford us your presence

This was sent to 'our loving frends Mr Wm Doughty Mr Robert Doughty Mr Geo Gimie Mr James Tennant Mr Robert Browne and Mr Samuel Malchitt', the gentlemen who were increasingly taking on duties for the committee. William Doughty's papers, as the collector of monies subscribed in the hundred of North Erpingham, were signed by Palgrave and Potts and have survived. They show the large number of warrants, accounts and orders that must have been produced all over Britain. Doughty himself gave £20 in plate and was still taking subscriptions at Widow Tanner's house in Roughton in January.[50] Potts may have been the one to notice a slip in the drafting of the orders which allowed them to give the gentry a choice in how they raised the men and to set a rate for raising the money rather than by personal subscriptions taken under the controversial oath. Anything that helped keep the lid on Norfolk was worth pursuing.[51] Apart from such trips to Bury, Potts remained at Mannington with his regular Norwich work.

The week before the Spelman outpouring, John had written to D'Ewes and he explained in detail why he had to stay in the country. For once he allowed his own emotion to creep in:

> Sir,
> I am glad of your and my neice's safe returne, where I wish myself
> for the service of Parliament, if the country would spare me; but the
> truth is, heere is need of more and wiser men then myself to keep
> all quiet, for the Parl's freinds are jealous and apprehensive, and the
> Papists side are indiscreet and bold, soe as I feare much the different
> tempers will breake out into some violence upon a small occasion.
> And though I move slowly in every thing, yet to me there seemes
> noe meanes of safetie, unless the countryes can be united. For what
> wee have pleased ourselves withall, the quiet and connivence would
> keep those wasps from stinging, will at the last deceyve, as they have
> all this tyme acted by their toungs, inventing and publishing all
> manner of disgraces. And when their own strength and forces sent
> them (which now they boast of) shall be able to doe noe more, wee
> may feel their malice, for it appears they care not to fire their own
> houses, soe as they may burne their neighbours. God send us peace
> and truth, soe, with retourne of all true respects, heer rests,
>
> Sir,
> Your affectionate unckle to serve you,
> John Potts.
> Mannington, 28 Jan. 1643.
>
> Sir you are serviceably saluted by all yr frends heer[52]

His annoyance with his royalist neighbours being indiscreet and the fearfulness of the parliamentarians is clear. His modesty stopped him from claiming he alone was holding it together but he obviously felt, at the end of January, he could not leave. However perhaps he was feeling he should have been at the major debates in February or maybe the hijacking of the local association now under the close scrutiny of the Cambridge committee grew too much. Lord Grey of Warke came himself to Norwich to demand the troops were raised and arrests of the disaffected be made. The dilatory Mayor of Norwich was arrested and moved to Cambridge. Others had already escaped (or were heading for the ports) but six others were named. They included Sir William Denny whom Potts and Holland had previously defended against Corbett. Most surprisingly, their fellow deputy lieutenant and committee member Sir Thomas Richardson, who had been working with them right up to this point, admitted to being a royalist. When Grey left on 2nd March, Potts had changed his mind. Keen to get back to London he felt he could do no more in Norfolk. He wrote on the 3rd:

> To honoured nephew Sir S D'Ewes
>
> Sir I receyved yr kinde letter & doe not only wish my self with
> you to understand the truth of things but have a kinde of purpose
> to come up the next weeke & discharge my Dutye there, seeing I
> cannot doe the Services heer which was my aime to preserve the
> Country in peace; yet in case want of health or necessity should
> detaine me, I desire you will afford me one letter more, wherein you
> may freely express your thoughts & be assured of safe convoy if you
> direct it to Mr Daniel Collins merchant at the George Inn Lumbard
> Street, to pass in his packet to Mr John Corey at Norwich.
>
> This with my harty prayers for the longed peace, I salute you & yr
> lady from all heere by the hande of Sir yr much obliged
>
> Onkle & servant
>
> John Potts[53]

Simonds was still not happy to trust in the post but Potts used a carrier he obviously could rely on. John Cory, the merchant and alderman, whose Norwich address he had always used, was married to Mary Sadler through whom Cory could claim kinship with both Sir John and Sir John Palgrave. Mary's father Edmund, had first married John's elder sister Frances Potts; Mary's mother, Frances, was one of the Barningham Palgraves.

Cromwell in Norfolk

But he did not manage to stay in London more than a few days. The effects of Grey's visit had ended the fragile peace: Richardson and others had barricaded themselves in Augustine Holl's house at Heigham hoping for royalist support to rescue them. The Norwich volunteers pointed their heavy guns at it and on 7th March, a surrender took place. Richardson was to die in custody five days later. A royalist journal said his only crime had been to be 'well-affected the King' and that he died 'partly with grief in being so unjustly handled but principally by the ill usage which he ... received'. This might have just been propaganda. On the whole prisoners were not mistreated, except for being kept in unhealthy gaols; seizing their arms and hitting them with large fines was usually enough. Wentworth kept his liberty by offering £1,000; Cory describes how another of the backsliders, deputy lieutenant Sir Richard Berney, had paid Cromwell £50 directly and had given Cory the receipt for safekeeping. He hoped Berney would 'be quiet henceforth, and study to conform'.[54]

Had Richardson's apparent willingness to perform his parliamentary duties been a cover for secret royalist plottings - a spy in the camp? Who gave his name to the House? Perhaps his betrayal of his position of trust on the committee did lead to some retribution at Cambridge. However much Potts was upset at Richardson's volte-face he would still have been appalled at his treatment; but worse was to come. Cromwell, whose headquarters was at Huntingdon decided to visit Norfolk himself after hearing Lord Grey's report. The county's biggest event of the war happened 10 days after John's letter. It was recorded in detail in a long letter sent to John at Mannington from his friend John Cory, who was now one of the most senior men in office in the city and would be elected sheriff two years later.[55] He started writing on the 17th but forgot to send it until the 20th so overwhelmed was he by the affair. It was clear he had seen John at Norwich, on his way home, and assumed he would already have heard about the events. Fortunately, he could not hold back telling his version. On 12th March Cromwell came to Norwich with five troops; on Monday 'old Mr Castle, Mr Loudon of Alby and Captain Hamond' were brought in with their arms. Stories of royalist groups at Yarmouth and Lowestoft reached the Colonel's ears and more arrests including Sir John Wentworth were made. Norwich was kept locked all night and early in the morning Cromwell marched on Lowestoft. Although there was a defence drawn up, it was easily broken and they entered the town asking for any 'Strangers' to be handed over. A few escaped but Thomas Knyvett of Ashwellthorpe and Richard Catelyn's son (and possibly his father) were taken. Cory's own cousin who he wished 'would have been better persuaded' was also arrested.[56] Sir John Palgrave, their mutual relative and friend came through Norwich on the 16th on his way to Berkshire but Cory did not see him. Sir Robert Kemp of Gissing, formerly Gentleman of the Bedchamber to the King, who had long been allowed to stay unharmed, was said to have surrendered to Palgrave although Kemp may have already fled abroad.[57]

As the country was polarised by the war, more of Potts's circle were being imprisoned. Corbett, who may have encouraged Cromwell in his move on Norfolk and Suffolk, pushed for those captured to be jailed and for an enquiry into the Lowestoft 'rising' to be held. Thomas Knyvett, who was now under guard at The Rose inn in Cambridge wrote to his wife that he feared being taken to Windsor. The gaol there in the Lower Ward was known for its lack of comforts. He maintained that his presence in Lowestoft had nothing to do with any plot and all were 'damnable lyes'. He had been waiting for a passage to Holland where so many of those who had refused to take up their commissions or subscribe to the ordinance had already gone. His letter of 24th March 1643 added that: 'Olde Dr Ward is in prison, and the proctor of Pembrooke hall. And many more country gentlemen comes in every day so that we shalbe a goodly number shortly'.[58] The colleges were used as holding areas: Samuel Ward was placed in custody in St John's College (the front court of which had been converted into a prison) for refusing, like most of the heads of colleges, to contribute to the parliamentary cause.[59] Potts would have been saddened to hear of his old tutor's arrest but he could have had no influence at this stage.

John now headed back to the House and on 22nd March was back in committee work there chasing up where and how the money for the army had been raised and spent. The House was looking for more ways of bringing in cash and at the end of March, Pym succeeded in pushing for a general order for the sequestration of all royalist estates. Each county would have its committee to undertake the work; this scheme was to create a mountain of paper-work and an upheaval in property ownership which would rebound for years.

John stayed up in London during April and was involved in a joint Houses group writing instructions to the King at Oxford who was not responding well to their First Proposition. The House was still concerned that, despite the shake-up in March, Norfolk was too slow. At the end of April, John and Framlingham Gawdy were ordered back to Norfolk to complete the execution of the ordinance, both raising money and troops: this time they were to send weekly accounts of their progress. They, with Sir John Holland, were also told to write at once to Suffolk and 'quicken them' in the raising of their money until they could meet them in person. Holland was still managing his precarious position well and the House allowed him time to dispatch 'his Lady beyond seas' before getting back to the Norfolk work.[60] Holland sent Lady Sandys, his catholic wife, to the safety of the continent.

Determined to sort out remaining doubters amongst members of the Commons, Pym and Corbett now had the new Oath and Covenant debated in the House. On 6th June, Potts and Holland joined in the clause-by-clause construction of an oath which all members were to be asked to take. John Potts was among many who stood up and took the oath that day. Holland was recorded as one of seven who asked for more time to consider. They were given a few days. Holland now was in difficulties.[61] He, Sir John Potts, Wodehouse, Heveningham, Hobart (John and Miles), Spelman, Thomas Windham, Francis Jermy and Palgrave, were named to be on the new Norfolk committee to sequester the estates of those delinquents 'as have been the cause of the public calamities'.[62] They were to have 1s in the £1 that they raised for their expenses and if delinquency was proved, the victim lost the whole estate. One fifth would be allowed for a wife and children and another fifth was given to the informer. Personal belongings were sold at auction and the real estate let out to tenants. How this must have weighed on Potts; like him all his friends and neighbours owed their lifestyle and their status to property bought, inherited or married into. To have to value other gentlemen's estates in order to seize them to pay for an increasingly radical Cromwellian army with whom he was clearly feeling less in tune, must have been against his better judgement. However being a main player would at least give him an opportunity to see malicious informers were not given credence and to ensure families were not left destitute by over-valuation. Yet again many were to be greatly in his debt.

Poor Thomas Knyvett, after two months in Windsor, was released but one condition was the sequestration of his estate. In July after having dined with his cousin Holland, he wrote to his wife, 'I hope I shall find favore amongst the sequestrators. I can get no great comfort from Sir John Potts who is coming down' but he felt 'he has no great mind for the job'. Potts apparently had sight of this letter and was affronted by the sentence, for two weeks later Knyvett wrote that 'he meant him nor any the least hurt & what I sayd was occasioned by some discourse I had with him concerning sequestration'. Potts had good reason to be worried about any loose writings about his commitment to the cause; Miles Corbett was ever on the lookout for shows of reluctance. July 6th saw the last order to Holland when he and Potts were told to go straight to Norfolk and assist the deputy lieutenants in meting out 'severe punishment' on the 'late mutineers in Sir Robert De Graye's company'. Holland claimed sickness and was excused going to Norfolk with Potts. His regiment was handed over to Lt-Col Wilton. Holland had been recuperating after a course of treatment at Epsom at Petworth, home of the Earl of Northumberland.[63] Now he took the precaution of moving to Utrecht, excusing himself from parliament for 6 weeks on acount of his wife's pregnancy. It is normally suggested that he stayed away for two years but in fact he went to and fro during the period.[64] Abroad, he would no doubt have met up with his cousin Sir William Paston of Oxnead (also Knyvett's cousin). Paston had left the Norfolk committee in February and, after spending May in London trying to find a legal solution to the conflict, had left England for the Low Countries. On 14th June the House accused Paston and others now at Rotterdam of ill offences against the parliament and ordered them to return within a month or lose all their estates.[65] Paston, the wealthiest man in Norfolk at the time, held out, hoping the King would be successful. Paston's relative, John Paston, who was Potts and Palgrave's neighbour at Barningham Hall paid his dues in June 1643 giving £150 and in goods £100.

The mutiny of Sir Robert de Grey is little known. He, like Richardson, had worked as deputy lieutenant along with the others up to 1643 with little evidence of his royalist tendencies although Sir John Palgrave, married to de Grey's sister Anne, may have been well aware of them. His initial arrest had been ordered in May but he still controlled his militia men in June. His estates were sequestrated but Potts must have persuaded him to conform as he later took the Covenant and the order was suspended in 1644.[66] As the brother-in-law of Sir John Palgrave, Sir Robert would have been foolish not to have stayed under the Potts-Palgrave umbrella of protection.[67]

Palgrave was now not just an experienced Norfolk committee man working with his uncle. He was a commissioner of the army in Norfolk and unlike Potts, actively led his men, four companies of whom were still seconded from the trained bands in June 1643. Col Palgrave's papers do not survive but he was a good paymaster (in mid-September the men, who numbered over 770, had been fully paid up to 12th August) and some of this was from his own pocket.[68] Like his uncle, he was most concerned with the defence of the county and his company had been based at Wisbech with that of Sir Miles Hobart from Little Plumstead.[69] On 13th June Cromwell complained to the Association at Cambridge about Palgrave's reluctance to join him in the midlands despite a direct order from Essex: 'Let him not keep a volunteer at Wisbech ... this is not a time to pick and choose for pleasure. Service must be done'.[70] Palgrave's reasoning was that if he left Wisbech the enemy might, as his Lt-Colonel Sir Edward Astley put it, 'soone ... breke into Norfolk'.[71] He and his men were suspected of not being completely committed to the cause and he was accused of poor discipline and even of being timid.[72] Astley himself told his wife their soldiers did what they liked.[73] However the regiments acquitted themselves well in July at Peterborough.[74]

John Potts was now working without some of his old friends. Framlingham Gawdy had also refused to help with sequestration but was ordered to go to Norfolk in late June to do his duty; Holland was away for long spells, Richardson dead, Paston abroad, and Palgrave was often on military duties. Sir Edmund Moundeford and Sir Robert Crane both died in 1643. Some familiar faces could be relied on but increasingly militia work would be passed on to men in the next level of society, younger and more radical, some of whom were not so keen on the old school network. However in August, John Potts, Palgrave and Hobart were still heading a hasty letter sent to Essex organising an urgent meeting as the King's army was sweeping down through Lincolnshire towards them:

Aug 11 1643

Signed by Hobarte, John Potts, John Palgrave, Miles Hobarte, Valentine Pell, Isaac Astley [sen], Franc Jermy, Phill Calthorpe, Thos Hogan, Greg Gausell, J Sheborough, Sam Smythe, John Coke, Thos Sotherton

Gentlemen

Approach of Northern Force so near threatening to all that ought to be dear to us makes us very sensible of the communicable misery that's like to befall us [so] not only as neighbours but being associated, [we] hold it our duty ... [do] desire a speedy & full

meeting of some 7 or 8 of the DLs of each of the 6 counties and as
many other gentlemen as please ... [so we] may resolve of a present
way and means to stop if not repel so formidable yet Popish enemy -
Bury Thursday next ... Urgency of the needs ... no further invitation
to meete.[75]

The raising of the now weekly tax was a major burden, both on the payers and the
collectors. The rate which was assessed on a percentage value of lands was supposed
to have been paid by 24th June. It was painfully slow despite demands, such as
Thomas Cutlack's on 29th June - 'all that were assessed at the last meeting concerning
the 5th and 20th partes to bring in their moneys to the said commissioners at the
Dukes Armes in North Walsham by tomorrow at nigh[t] at the utmost peril ... as
they will avoid the charge and troubled of sending troops to gather the same'.[76]
Between late April and mid June 1643 Norfolk paid in £350 out of £1,000 due to
the Treasurer of War.[77] On 8th August an ordinance was issued to the local MPs to
form a Committee of the Associated Counties to go after the disaffected and see that
the monies were regularly collected. From October Norfolk was to pay £1,250 and a
special committee, including all the usual suspects, was to expedite the collection.[78]
The Earl of Manchester replaced Grey of Warke as commander of the Eastern
Association in August, a move that pleased Potts and his military colleagues.[79] At
this stage the Association was still locally driven and had not been superseded by
the national army. On 18th August the House complained to Manchester that the
monies were too slow in coming from Norfolk, Cambridgeshire and Huntingdon
and that the ordinance for sequestration must be put in execution. They also desired
him to take care that Sir Thomas Wodehouse did 'forthwith send up [to London]
the plate jewels & other goods lately taken at Kenninghall in pursuance to ordinance
of sequestration as belonging to persons in activities against the Parliament and to
popish recusants'.[80] The rate of progress was still too slow. Orders now were sent
direct to Norfolk on 23rd August that non-payers must be sent up to the Commons:

> Ordered, That Sir John Hubbard [Hobart], Sir Tho. Woodhouse, Sir
> Miles Hubbard [Hobart], Sir John Potts, Miles Corbett Esquire, and
> Mr. Owner, or any Two of them, do call before them such Collectors
> as have been appointed by Act of Parliament, or by Ordinance of
> both Houses, to collect Monies in the County of Norfolk, and
> require an Account of them; and to commit such of them as refuse,
> or can give no good Account, and send them up to this House, in
> safe Custody[81]

With Corbett breathing down his neck, Potts must have felt very little room for
manoeuvre. The first of their joint progress reports has survived. Many of the first
phrases sound more like Potts than Corbett:

Norwich 28 Aug 1643

Mr Speaker

According to our duty, we present you with a short account howe
the State of affaires stand heer; you may plese to knowe that the
proporcion of horse & foote set upon this County of Norfolk, for
defence of the Association are likely to be got togither in convenient
tyme, there being already some good appearance & willingness;
although the charge falls out heavy in this barren County, at such
an expensive season (as harvest) & when divers other leavyes [levys]
are in hand; But wee are sory that this service must be mixed with
an unpleasing relacion of the town of Lynn, which after many
serious protestacions of fidelitye to the Parliament, hath been
seduced by practices of straungers; soe that at this instant whisl the
Earl of Manchester our major General, with careful endeavours
was labouring our Comon safety, whereof his Lo: gave the Mayor
of Lynn a very respective intimacion; they have not only returned
uncivil answers, but drawn into the town divers malignants,
disarmed the well-affected inhabitants & restrained some principal
gent' of the Committee, sent by his Lo: to expostulate their ill
Cariage; yet wee doubt not his Lo: wisdome & forces will reduce
them & doe what shall be fitter requisite for safetye of the whole
Association, if the forces there, nowe raisinge , be not diminished or
diverted contrary to his honorable intencions; His Lo: hath sent out
Coll. Cromwell to impeach all access on Lyncolnshire side, & hath
taken such cours both for sea & land gards, as by Gods blessing wee
hope this will be a speedy & good account of that Place

which is all wee can add but the respects of

Sir your humble servants

John Potts and Miles Corbett

However Corbett was unhappy with the lack of sequestrations and general
reluctance and stormed back to London. In Potts's absence he attacked the Norfolk
committee in the House on 13th September 'as remiss and careless'.[82] D'Ewes was
appalled on behalf of his friends and recorded Corbett's speech with his own reactions:

Mr Miles Corbet ... a most violent spirited fellow who was latelie
come out of Norfolk to make complaint of those worthie gentlemen
& lovers of their countrie who were appointed, and many of them
without their knowledge, to be committees in that countie for
the ordinance of the weekly assessment & for the ordinance of

sequestration that they were remis & careles in putting the same in execution ... He averred also that there was the same remissness in Suffolk ... some men calling on Corbet to name who were negligent ... he said that the other gentleman were much disadvantaged because Sir John Holland and the other member on the other side viz Mr Gawdie (who sat in the house on the north side towardes the lower end) did not iurne into the cuntrie as they had been formerly ordered to do. But he said that offence was especially taken at Sir John Holland because he did neither attend this house (for he was absent by licence of the house to recover his health) nor the service of the countre ther which made them have some suspicion of him; but he said that he hoped he would clear himself of that suspicion; whereupon many spake somewhat bitterlie & uncharitablie of sir John Holland & the speaker especiallie contrarie to the duty of his place who is not to deliver his opinion unless it be required of him much less to censure anie member of the House; for he spake to this purpose, as if Sir John Holland had but counterfeited himselfe sicke, to free himselfe from this implement. And for the said Mr Gawdie he fell twice or thrice verie fowlie upon him; first he said that ther had been 5 orders made for his departure in to the countuire but he disobeyed them all and yet afterwards he confessed, after another gentlemen had first declared it to the house that he said Mr Gawdie had been dispensed which [sic] all from going into the countre upon his promise to take care for returning of such monies as should be collected upon the ordinances ... if Sir John Holland still be so sicke again tomorrow morning another motion for his further stay ...

The House decided that Holland, who had returned to England, and Gawdy, were not to be let off the hook:

> Resolved, That Sir Jo. Holland and Mr. Framlingham Gawdy
> be enjoined forthwith to go down into the County of Norfolk,
> to put in Execution the Ordinances, of the weekly Assessments;
> the Sequestrations; the Twentieth Part; and the other Services of
> Parliament: And that from time to time, weekly, an Account be given
> of their Proceedings; and that none do move against this Order, but
> between the Hours of Ten and Twelve: And that they take especial
> Care, that, in particular, all those Gentlemen's Estates, that were in
> Arms against the Parliament at Leystoffe [Lowestoft], at Mr. Austin
> Holl's House, and that are now at Linne; and that the Estates of
> those Gentlemen that are in Holland, and other Parts beyond the
> Seas, and have had Summons left at their Houses, according to the
> Order, and have not thereupon returned; be sequestred: And that the
> Serjeant give Sir John Holland notice of this Order.[83]

Holland had begged to be excused from the Sequestration Committee partly because he had voted against it in the House but also because of his close relationship to Knyvett and 'obligations of friendship' to others. Within a few months Holland would be abroad again. Corbett issued a warrant for Thomas Knyvett's possessions.

King's Lynn, referred to in Potts and Corbett's report, had, encouraged by the nearness of the royal army, declared for the King on 13th August. Led by the L'Estrange family, parliament's own defences and arms there were turned against them. Manchester quickly barricaded the town temporarily while the militia of the Association were raised. Being harvest time, and far away, the southern counties like Essex were hard to organise. The siege dragged on; the King's army did not relieve the town from the north and Manchester's sporadic bombardment did not have the desired effect. On Saturday the 16th he threatened to storm the town and gave warning so women and children could be sent out. The surrender was swift. Sir John Palgrave and his cousin John Spelman of Narborough, two of the eight commissioners, went in to negotiate the terms. The fact that there was no retribution or looting but a generous amnesty, was typical of Manchester's reputation and of those influenced by John Potts. The 'gentlemen strangers' were allowed to leave with horse, pistol and sword. The town was rated for a levy (to prevent looting) and L'Estrange was held until the terms were met. So ended the only real battle on Norfolk soil. Manchester stayed at Lynn as Governor for a while and, when he and Cromwell left to retake Lincolnshire, the General's brother-in-law Col Valentine Wauton became Governor. The county was now secured for parliament. John was increasingly less involved in the Association which had reformed its committees under one sitting at Cambridge, to which each county sent two representatives, who would be regularly changed. Potts appears to have left that work and its travel to other, newer men.

He and Ursula would have been reassured by a visit from her brother Francis in October with news of the family in Derbyshire. He spent some time with Ursula and her sister Elizabeth Palgrave's households. It is clear from a letter from her elder brother, the ever worried Henry, to his son-in-law D'Ewes that life in that county was very different:

Risle [Risley] 6 Nov 1643

Honoured Sonne

By the opportunitie of this messinger I [wish] to let you know that we here are in good health that are heere together. My Brother went into Norfolk about [a] month since and is not yet retourned; for other newes there want thereof, this towne where I live fifteen hundred horse under the command of Sir Wm Fairfax & fifteen hundred men went by under the command of Sir Thomas Fairfax; how long they are to continue here I know not ... six score of those horses billeted here in Risle under command of Capt Aymes who lodges in my house

remembrance best services to you & my daughter

yr assured frend & father in law

Henry Willoughby

Potts was still occupied with the other local committees for assessments and sequestration. He was now involved with the fall-out from the new Committee for Compounding. This was introduced to allow landowners to pay one large fine by which the sequestration would be discharged, or if half was paid, it might be suspended. Another huge paper trail was created as the local committees valued the estate and gave a certificate of valuation to be taken to the owner to Goldsmiths' Hall in London where the compounding committee sat. The owner had to present a petition, with all the details set forth at length. The committee then reported back with an amount on which he would be assessed. Long disputes arose from this process as fines were taken unevenly from more committed royalists and catholics, anything from one-tenth to two-thirds of the value. Most cases were between £1,000 and £2,000.[84] Other fines were raised by the Committee for Advance of Money.[85] By October 1643 Hamond L'Estrange's estates were finally fully sequestrated. After his actions at Lynn nothing could have prevented this. Similarly Potts could not help his own stepbrother Sir John Heydon. His relationship with both his stepbrothers, William and John, seems to have been far from close. Since his meeting with John in 1642 in London, Heydon had left to join the King at Oxford where he used his considerable skill in organising the royal military supplies. No evidence survives to suggest Potts gave, or was asked for, help when Heydon's estates were compounded in 1643 to recover them from sequestration. However, the sum paid, £294, seems very low. It has been suggested that Baconsthorpe castle was demolished (from 1650) to recoup the losses.[86] More likely it was the last straw for a family in decline. Sir John and his brother Sir William had lived in London when not abroad so the Baconsthorpe house may have been unused. The inventory assessing the goods totalled £37 which was negligible (his 63 books accounted for £5 13s) and may refer to their belongings in the Minories.[87] For more on the Heydons see Family Notes 9.

Potts must have been pleased not to have any involvement in the fate of Baconsthorpe. In 1642 his half-brother John had been chased for an annuity outstanding on the property. Material from the old Baconsthorpe Hall was used to repair the 'New Buildings' in the park in the 1650s and 1660s. Potts's brother-in-law William Crowe of Guist gent, quarrelled with Charles Heydon (son of Sir John Heydon) over the lease of the new house and the park which Crowe had held from 1654.[88] Potts would have his own battles with Crowe to come.

Winter 1643-44 and the Pastons

Others, however, looked to Potts to assist them through the financial and political upheavals. With Manchester's help, Potts now responded to the plight of the Pastons. Sir William was still abroad and now, with little hope of the King's success, asked his wife Lady Margaret Paston (still at Oxnead Hall) to approach Potts for assistance. In December 1643 he arranged for her to surrender plate to the value of £1,100 for the Earl of Manchester's troops:

> For my Esteemed frend Sir John Potts kt & Bt these
>
> If the £1100 paid in as the ladye Paston pr'mised to pay, send it upp forthwith to Cambridge to paie the Charge belonging to your County. I shall trust your Countrymen here to see it disposed accordingly. But if it bee not, I am not fairely dealt with and doe thereupon order that all the plate bee sent up to Cambridge so as I may have the money upon the security thereof. And I shall rest beholding to you and desire you not to faile therein
>
> your assured frend
>
> Manchester Cambridge 6 December 1643[89]

Potts had organised a deal whereby, in return for the large offering, Sir William would receive a safe passage guaranteed by Manchester. The plate was entrusted to John Cory. Lady Margaret placed all her trust in Potts's ability to win such a favour for a known royalist. The plate was not easily given up though and she was determined not to give a penny more than the agreed amount:

> To my much honoured frende Sir John Potts present this
>
> Sir, I conceave Mr Cory having taken charge of the plate upon him and I satisfieng him with the alowence of his large demands acording to his note, shall not need to troubell my self any farder therein requiring my Lords asset or in giving his Lordship any accoumpt of the disposal of it. Mr Cory being to dispose thereof as hee pleases without my farder ceare or hezard. I shall desire your favour in letting him understand so much. Sir I beseech you also obleage me so fare as to gaine me my Lord's protection for the remainder as sonne as you can so with my serves and many thanks for all your favours I remaine
>
> Sir your frend & servant
>
> Margaret Paston

[margin] Sir this much I acknowkleg concerning the price of the plate that if it sell not for so much a nounce [sic] as they have valued it, I will make it good; if for more, Mr Cory is to be responsell to me for it.[90]

In reply Manchester sent the vital pass from Cambridge on December 8th [1643]:

For ... my ... respected friend Sir John Potts

Sir, I have received your letter and am very sensible of your respects I am glad to have any occasion to expresse any respecte to persons of quallitye and esteeme itt a great happiness to be understood as one that desires to win by civillitye then by harshness. I have sent you the passe and protection according to your desire and shd be ready to serve my Lady Paston

Sir I shall desire you to esteeme me in the quallitye off, your frend and servant,

Manchester,

I shall desire you that the plate may be putt downe particularly least [lest] others should coulor their plate either in the passe or in the protection[91]

William Paston's plate was ten times that which Potts himself gave to the cause: three horses were also collected for the Earl, one of which Potts was allowed to have the use of:

To my esteemed frend Sir Jhon Potts these

Sir I have received your letter and whyte Geldynge and the baye nagge. I have taken and shall despose off them; as for the other, you may doe by him as you please for your owne use. I have received the note off the Lady Pastons plate Sir I am very sensible off your respects unto me and I shall desire you to be confident that I shall studdy to expresse my selfe upon all occasions as

your frend and servant

Manchester

Cambridge 21 December[92]

Despite the encouraging news from Potts, Paston did not rush back. He wanted to be sure of how he would be received. Sir William Paston wrote from Rotterdam on 15th February 1644 fulsomely thanking Potts and asking him to help him further to find a way to live free and on his estate:

> To my Honourable frend Sir John Potts kt &bt at His, Mannington
>
> Much Honord Sir
>
> I doe infinitely acknowledge your manifold favors to me & my Pore wife, for which Sir I shall never forget to be most thankfull, Sir I have a verie great deale of reason to esteeme you my verie noble frende for your late advice to me by George to which Sir I assure you I am very much inclinable; if you wilbe pleased to labor to sett me out a way how I may make my Peace upon reasonable conditions with the Honourable House & to be assured of my liberty & estate (paying my proportions) I should gladder visitt my owne country then Oxford, and be subject to that authority under which I shall live, with fidelity and Honesty; Sir I have given George Directions how your letters shall come to me in which he pleased to give me the proceed of this my Biusenes & the most fayfthfull servis of your frend servant shall never be wanting to expresse my self upon all occasions
>
> Sir your most faithfull & Humble servant.[93]

Potts must have promised him that it was safe to return: Paston was back a month later. Now it seems likely that Potts had also asked Manchester to clear Knyvett's name: his sequestration had been pursued doggedly by Corbett. Over the winter of 1643-44 Manchester had obviously spoken to Cromwell and written to the Norfolk committee: in January 1644 he assured them of Knyvett's innocence in the Lowestoft affair and asked for his estates to be restored.[94] However, unlike Paston, Knyvett was not an easy man to help. Potts would now find vital friends losing their influence at the centre. His own position would rely on his ability to work away quietly, not upsetting the radicals but calmly pushing for a peaceful outcome.

Chapter 13

The King and I

As religious and political attitudes in the House hardened, loyalties changed; Potts lost some of his closest allies and in 1647, his beloved wife. His burdens culminated in a last ditch attempt to treaty with the King himself but all his efforts for peace were doomed.

Spring 1644

In helping Paston and Knyvett, John had used the Earl of Manchester's expressed wish to handle people with civility rather than harshness but a letter from his friend Lord Denzil Holles warned that the Paston affair should not be raised again as the sequestration was only a suspension. Manchester was losing support because of his tolerant attitude. However like others, Holles was very happy to do what he could for Paston purely because he was a friend of Potts. Paston's estates were finally cleared on 3rd June 1644 for a total already paid of £1,376. Later in the year he joined his neighbours on the local committees again.[1]

> To my honored frend Sir John Potts these
>
> Sir I am glad of this occasion to hear from you and send to you: both are a happiness to me, & I have bene long without them: you putt me in hope to enjoy shortly a greater then either, to see you here. I beseech you lett it be as soone as you can: for your frends here have long desired it & wee shall shortly have more need of you then ever. I need not enforme you of the busines of the House, you have it from better hands; This only, by the way, upon Friday sennight the Committee of the Two Kingdomes are to bring in Propositions for peace. The sooner you come before that time, the more you shall meritt; & I believe you will here find Sr John Holland, who writes word wee shall see him with the first passage; concerning Sir William Pastons busines, his frends were of opinion it was best not to stirr in it, in regard my Lord of Manchester had suspended the execution of the Sequestration; so as he enioys his estate; & to move it might but raise a spirit, which is easily done in our House.
>
> Yet as I write to him, what he will have me doe in it I shall readily act; so shall I for any whose name I find mentioned in a letter of Sir John Potts to whom I am,
>
> A faithfull and humble servant
>
> Danzell Holles, Covent Garden April 16 1644[2]

It is clear that Sir John Holland, who in January 1644 had been excused attending parliament (no reason given) until the spring, was also returning to England. Holles had missed Potts's letters and presence; he had more need of him than ever now. Holland and Potts returned to the House in May to find a very different atmosphere. John Pym, with whom Holland and Potts had worked well, had died in December. Denzil Holles, a charismatic if impulsive presbyterian who had pushed for peace negotiations, would have been a natural successor. However more radical men, such as Sir Harry Vane junior and Oliver St John, were intent on moving power away from the Earl of Essex and Holles. The new Committee of Both Kingdoms, set up with the Scots in February 1644, was to change the way the war was waged. Holles was not elected to the committee. Many familiar faces were absent; the drop in members' attendance had led to a committee being formed to investigate in September 1643. Some new people had been admitted. Sir John's partner knight of the shire, Sir Edmund Moundeford had died in May 1643 but had not yet been replaced. Potts must have felt alarmed at the domination of more radical members and the strength of the independents in the House.

Religious extremism

Another friend and neighbour who became grateful to Potts was Thomas Windham of Felbrigg, a lawyer and former High Sheriff; like John he was a moderate supporter of parliament and like many in north-east Norfolk did not suffer loss of his lands. However, like all the gentry, he had to give heavily in taxes and horses to maintain the army and was always nervous that extremists would make life really uncomfortable. Following the levy that Potts was involved in raising, Thomas wrote to him at Mannington in December 1643 to thank him for his support. Windham had undervalued his estate and Potts, as the supervisor, had stood up for him. Thomas said:

Honoured Sir

I thank you for those kinde favours which I lately received from you in way of Justice to rescue me from the Iniurie of that Monster Reporte which in this wicked Age often takes the upper hande of Truth; Our joynt affections (leaning on the same pillar of Constancy to Religion and the Common Wealth), I doubt not, shall always preserve our Neighbourhood unto the mutuall comfort of our families. My personall Estate I have given up at £2000 which is one more than I knowe that I am worthe [no bracket] my estate in land to the uttermost) during my fathers lieff. The oppression practised by Jubs and his Associatts is very odious, their fury in Churches detestable. Mr Cooke and Mr Satterton [Sotherton] are in the morning for Cambridge to represent those grievances which nothing but our owne firme Union (who have turned the skalle [scale] in

times of moste danger) can withstand. In this as I shall continue ever
to serve my Cuntry soe god willing Entirely remaine

yr servant to be disposed

Tho: Windham[3]

Sotherton and Coke were the two Norfolk representatives going to Cambridge at
this time; their grievances would be unlikely to be received with sympathy (except by
their neighbours).[4] Corbett and others would have kept a constant watch. The 'fury
in the Churches' was the result of the growth of the independents, far more radical
puritans than the presbyterians. Windham and others would once again play a game
of balance, happy to enforce the ordinance for taking the covenant in 1644 but
keeping safe many brasses and other items at risk.[5]

Miles Corbett, the radical member for Yarmouth was a constant thorn in Sir
John's side. Miles was a younger son of Sir Thomas Corbett of Sprowston; his
grandfather Sir Miles had married both the widow of John Spelman of Narborough
and the sister of Sir Christopher Heydon of Baconsthorpe (great-aunt of Potts's
guardian). He upset the moderates as much as the royalists, who had no time for
the 'bull-headed, splay-footed, bacon-faced Corbet'.[6] As we have seen, Corbett
was involved with all the Norfolk committees and had been their main critic since
1642. As head of the committee of religion he was far more extreme towards the
clergy than his Norfolk colleagues as they constantly were made aware. The bishops
were among the first to be sequestered and it was the duty of Potts and Thomas
Wodehouse to hear the case of Bishop Hall, the Bishop of Norwich, in 1643.
Unlike Wren, Hall was known for his tolerant views on puritanism and the two
men sympathetically allowed the Bishop sufficient of his lands to raise £400 a year
to live on and the rest was sequestered. But before Hall could draw any income,
Miles Corbett, on the central committee in London, heard about this and reversed
the decision. Mrs Hall was eventually allowed less than a fifth part of his estate for
support of the family.[7] Potts must have been furious not only at this interference but
at his inability to prevent it.

Although few lesser priests were harmed, if they were outspoken in their beliefs
there was little the moderates could do. Miles Corbett ill-used the Reverend Thomas
Reeve of Aldborough (near Erpingham) and Colby; he was examined in November
1642 and then went into hiding for two years, refusing to take the 'Scotch covenant'
and his estates were sequestered, in his absence, in May 1644. The story of the
family's harassment by Major Reymes is told in full in Ketton-Cremer. Reeve hid
for another year, tried to reach the King but was taken to Corbett who threatened
to have him hanged. He imprisoned him until 1652, when Mrs Reeve managed
to get him freed.[8] The more shocking story of Thomas Cooper, rector of Little
Barningham, who had taken part in a local rebellion in Aylsham in the spring of
1643 against payments to parliament, will be told in the next chapter.

Corbett had an ally in Norfolk, one Nathaniel Beadle. Beadle was the solicitor
to the sequestration committee and it was he who fed information about the

delinquents to Corbett. Thomas Knyvett had been hopeful that he would be left alone, as the committee of the covenant were busy with Paston and de Grey; but, unlike the others, Knyvett delayed taking the oath until late March by which time Beadle had been building a case against him. Cromwell said he had been tricked and Beadle attacked Manchester for his leniency. Potts and others had been holding off the execution of the sequestration order but a packet of very indiscreet letters from Knyvett's son was intercepted. The same day as Corbett threatened Knyvett with this incriminating evidence Thomas saw John Potts who was 'very courteous' to him. Potts had gone to put in a good word for him with Corbett but at this late stage he could no longer obstruct the London committee, described by Holles as worse than the Spanish inquisition.[9] In May the sequestration order was renewed. Beadle conducted a vicious campaign against Manchester and listed all the suspended or unclaimed sequestrations in Norfolk in July. Yet despite this level of animosity, Potts, Holland, Miles Hobart and John Palgrave (the last two had been in London on army business) and others, had worked hard enough to ensure that, in August, Knyvett's sequestration was discharged.[10]

Potts's family marriages had given him a wider network than just East Anglia. His son's brother-in-law, William Heveningham, although of Norfolk where he regularly helped Potts, was sitting for Stockbridge in Hants. He married Katherine Yallop, the sister of the member for Andover. A letter from Robert Yallop survives indicating how Potts worked closely with both members:

> 2 April 1644 Covent Garden: For my honored frend Sir John Potts Bt
>
> Sir, in my Brother Heveninghams absence your letter was brought to mee. I take it as a favor to receave any commands from you and shalbe very ready as occasion is to doe you what service is in my power being
>
> Sir, your affectionate frend to serve you
>
> Ro Wallop[11]

Wallop was to suffer a similar fate to that of Heveningham for his later support of Cromwell but, at this stage, the gentlemen were working together to achieve a peaceful end to the situation.

John and his moderate friend Thomas Wodehouse now stepped in to calm matters in Norwich. Francis Cory, the Recorder and cousin of John's good friend John Cory, had already been in trouble with parliament in December 1642. In May 1644 the assembly voted him out (though not all were against him) and Samuel Smith, a deputy lieutenant replaced him. Cory threatened to make trouble and Potts had obviously managed to assure parliament (through Corbett) that he would behave. They sent a letter to the Mayor Tooly (who had supported Cory) to ensure the city also would not cause trouble:

> To the Right Wo' & our very good freinds John Tolie esq Mayor and
> the Aldermen
>
> June 28 1644 As we have desired to preserve the Quiet of the City
> by our advise to Mr Corrie the late Recorder, whose inclosed answer
> hath satisfied us for his future carriage and we believe will give us
> satisfaction, so we must likewise endeavour that no disrepute be put
> upon him by his compliance ... or disturb his peace
>
> your very loving frends
>
> Richard Harman, Thos Wodehouse, John Potts and Miles Corbett

Potts spent the summer working at the House on some rather humdrum
committees. In July, Norfolk sent in a petition and he was told to stay for the debate
and then go home to give an account to his county. A summer break at home was
always welcome; it gave time to catch up with family and friends, and to judge the
mood of the county.

In October, Potts returned to the House where much time was devoted to raising
money for the army campaigns where they were in great need of provisions. He
joined the committee for the Army at the end of October which decided that the
associated Counties under Manchester would advance £1,200; another £1,000
would be advanced out of the monies appointed for Cromwell's army; and £800 by
the associated Western Counties for Sir William Waller's army.

Two days later John agreed to committ £1,200 in money or credit 'so much as
he may ... be enabled to receive the same again out of the weekly assessments'. The
order that went to the Lords on 1st November shows that he was being asked to
stand for nearly half of the £3,000 needed for army provisions.

> Whereas it is found necessary, as well for Relief as Encouragement
> of the Parliament's Army about Newbury, as also to prevent all
> unlawful or disorderly Taking of Provisions upon the Country, that
> some good Proportion of Victuals and Horse Meat should speedily
> be sent thither from the City of London: And whereas, upon Order
> of the House of Commons, Three thousand Pounds is appointed for
> furnishing of the same Provisions; whereof Twelve hundred Pounds,
> allotted upon the Counties associated under the Earl of Manchester's
> Command, is to be undertaken by Sir John Potts, a Member of the
> House of Commons, and paid unto Mr. Bond, Commissary of the
> Victuals, for Provision to be delivered and sent to the said Earl of
> Manchester's Forces: The Lords and Commons do hereby Ordain,
> That the said Sum of Twelve hundred Pounds shall be satisfied
> unto the said Sir John Potts, out of the first Monies raised by the
> weekly Tax, for the Maintenance of the said Forces under the Earl

of Manchester's Command: And that it shall be lawful for John
Cory, of the City of Norwich, or any other High Collector of the
Monies or weekly Assessment so rated and gathered in the County
of Norfolk, to ... stay the said Sum of Twelve hundred Pounds; and
the same to pay unto the said Sir John Potts: Whose Receipt shall
be a sufficient Discharge for the same; and shall be so answered
in Account to the Treasurers of the Association by the said High
Collectors; any Words, Limitation, or Direction, in any former
Ordinance notwithstanding.[12]

Sir Gilbert Gerard did the like for the second sum, of £1,000; Mr. Trenchard
undertook to supply £400 and Sir Richard Onslow and Mr Browne undertook to
supply the other £400, most of which was to provide horse-meat for the troops.[13]

Potts and Cory would of course have to ensure the tax was collected or Potts
would be left high and dry. Did he offer voluntarily or did Corbett and others
on the committee see this as a way of making Norfolk do its duty? The money
was for Manchester's forces so Potts may have felt a strong sense of duty. His
creditworthiness must have been widely recognised for him to be able to undertake
such a sum. He may also still have had cash reserves of his own and been sure
enough of Cory and his neighbours that the collectors would see him and his
creditors right as soon as possible. Cory was a very assiduous man so despite the
pressure to organise this major financial undertaking, Potts remained in the House
right through November and December.[14] He would have been loathe to leave as
the House was in the heat of discussing proposals for the unification of the English
and Scottish churches, as debated by the Westminster Assembly of Divines. The
Assembly, which included John Selden, was writing a replacement for the Book of
Common Prayer. In late November, John was on a committee with Sir Henry Vane,
Mr Rous and many others considering clauses relating to the administration of
the sacrament. He would have enjoyed furthering the cause of presbyterianism but
whether he would have supported the full Scottish Kirk model is doubtful. That the
committee was split was highlighted by the vote on 29th November over whether the
phrase 'as in the Church of Scotland' should be kept in the new Directory for Public
Worship. It was rejected 57 to 34.

Time and again he was working alongside Corbett; in early December the two
of them had to write an order for safeguarding passage by sea between Yarmouth
and Edinburgh.[15] However on the afternoon of 16th December, it was Potts and not
Corbett who sat with Cromwell and others from the Commons and the Lords, in the
Painted Chamber. Carefully arranged around the tables, with the Scots commissioners,
they received the King's Lords, the Duke of Richmond and Earl of Southampton,
who sat on a form 'at a little distance'. The two had brought the King's answer to the
latest propositions for peace. In principle he was not ready to give much away but was
very keen to find out how deeply parliament was now divided. The members who
sat before them were well chosen to show unity: the smooth-talking Vane and Holles
apparently working together, a mix of new men and old conservatives such as Potts

and D'Ewes. Potts would have given nothing away but sat pondering on what 1645 would bring, now that orders had been put forward that would remove Manchester and Essex from holding military office and effectively create a new army, control of which would be pivotal for whichever faction was to dominate.

Shortly before Christmas, he and Corbett were giving evidence to the House on the arrest and escape of Henry Bedingfield.[16] Christmas Day 1644 happened to fall on the last Wednesday of the month, a day of fast; parliament decreed that it should be observed as such and not as a feast. The House sat on the 25th as it would for the next 12 years. It seems ironic that the churches were to be closed and the shops kept open. Much of the country, though, still took a day's break from work. The festival was officially banned in 1647 and in Norwich the apprentices petitioned the Mayor at the beginning of December to keep the observance of the day. Violence ensued when he refused. Thomas Jackson, Itteringham's rector also signed a petition that year to have Christmas day reinstated suggesting Sir John's family would have tolerated the action. Despite the ban, in many areas, people managed to continue its celebration, albeit low-key, for another few years.[17]

1645 - out with the old order

Potts was back in London by mid-January and on 29th January heard the second reading of an order to repress sinful behaviour (incest, adultery, whoredom, drunkenness, swearing and blaspheming).[18] On the same day he and five others, including Sir John Evelyn junior and Sir William Drake, subscribed to the Solemn League and National Covenant, which was then ordered to be read in every congregation on every fast day and to be hung in full view in every church. The Covenant was the result of the Scottish alliance and was to upset many who did not feel that the presbyterian model was the answer. For many though it was just another oath to 'be taken like pills, swallowed whole'.[19]

On the 31st John Potts and William Heveningham advanced £250 each for the garrison of Newport Pagnell. They were to be reimbursed from the collectors of Suffolk and Norfolk respectively. Potts would then have been owed nearly £1,500. Parliament put pressure on the collectors of the 'Scotts money' from the Eastern Counties with letters in early February being sent from Potts to Norfolk and Heveningham to Suffolk, letters which they would have been happy to write. At the end of February, John Potts was given the task of telling his friend Manchester of the order to turn over Captain Poe's troop to Sir Thomas Fairfax. He was also the messenger the day the Lords agreed Fairfax should take over the army, 11th March 1645:

> Sir John Potts brings Answer, That the Lords do concurr in the Ordinance for enabling Sir Thomas Fairfax to put the Lieutenants, and other Officers and Soldiers of my Lord General's, the Earl of Manchester's, and Sir Wm. Waller's Armies, into the Army under his Command.

His friend no longer held any power; Manchester resigned in early April. The new army was marching to a different drum. No-one could claim his or Essex's protection now as Captain James Hobart discovered. Even name-dropping Sir John Potts did him no good as Anthony Hobart explained in his affidavit sworn on 3rd March 1645:

> Whereas Captain James Hobart, upon Saturday last was a Sevennight, being the 22nd Day of February, was employed in the Parliament Service at Norwich, in which City the said Captain Hobart was arrested, upon a Billet, at the Suit of one Rookewood Robinson and Elizabeth his Wife, by the Prosecution of one Thomas Turner, an Attorney or Solicitor: Now Anthony Hobart Gentleman deposeth, and faith, upon his Oath, That he, being then present, at the Time aforesaid, did tell Thomas Barrett and Barnard Church, the Sheriffs of the said City, that the said Mr. Hobart was a Captain in the Parliament Service, by Commission under the Hand and Seal of his Excellency the Earl of Essex, a true Copy whereof this Deponent did then deliver to the said Sheriffs; yet they obstinately refused to discharge him, giving a slight Answer thereunto; so they caused their Serjeants, or Officers, to carry him to their Gaol, where he now is: Moreover, the said Thomas Turner said to this Deponent, 'That he did not care a Turd for the Earl of Essex's Commission, nor any Parliament Lord of them all; for he said, that if the said Sheriffs would send the said Captain Hobart to the Gaol, he would enter Bond or Security of One Thousand Pounds, to save them harmless' or Words to that Effect. And this Deponent further deposeth, That the said Captain Hobart went purposely at the Time aforesaid to Norwich, for to deliver a Letter to the Committee of Sequestrations, under the Hands of Sir John Potts and Miles Corbett Esquire, Two of the Honourable Members of the House of Commons, which Letter was written in the Behalf of the said Mr. Hobart, and to raise Monies for the Parliament Service; and, at his Return from the Committee House at Norwich, the said Sheriffs Officers arrested the said Mr. Hobart, and carried him to the Gaol as aforesaid.

Anthony Hobart.[20]

The money-raising work for Fairfax was relentless; through March and April, Potts spent his days debating how to secure another £80,000, how to improve the excise system (far less money was coming in than previously) and inquiring into the sale of delinquents' lands to pay back those to whom parliament was indebted. Potts would certainly put his mind to the excise issue: he and seven others had been asked on 23rd April to procure another £1,000 between them on their personal credit, to safeguard the Isle of Ely. It was to be repaid to them out of the excise money.

Two weeks later he went in a party of seven, to the Lord Mayor and Common Council of the City of London, to press them to pay the three months' assessment due to the army and explain the necessity of sudden payment.

Parliament was now pushing again. Suffolk and Norfolk were still lagging behind and on 9th April 1645 Potts, and others on the committee for the army urged the Suffolk committee to contribute men, horses and money.[21] The following month on 12th May 1645, John was one of the signatories to a letter from the same committee 'for hastening with moneys for Sir Thomas Fairfax' sent to Norwich to complain that although 'the Committee had been very instant' with them, nothing had been received for three whole months. They reminded them that collectors could be punished and suggested they meet every week to deal with delinquents.[22] He was signing in the company of three lords lieutenant as well as Cromwell's brother-in-law Valentine, and Arthur Haselrig leading light of the independents.

He had an uncomfortable afternoon on 26th May, when he was sandwiched between Corbett and Toll, two of Norfolk's hardliners, discussing raising the promised £1,000 for the soldiers at Ely. Presumably matters were not progressing fast enough.

Five days later Potts was allowed to go to the country; he could not avoid Corbett for long though. On 1st July the House ordered:

> That Mr. Corbett do write to Sir John Potts, now in Norfolk, to acquaint him, That it is the Order of this House, That he do take special Care, that the Committees and Deputy-Lieutenants for that County, do speedily raise, as well the old Levies, as new Recruits, for Sir Thomas Fairfaxe's Army: And that they do put the Ordinance for Punishing of such imprested Soldiers as have run away from their Colours, into speedy and due Execution: And that he do give a weekly Account, to this House, of their Proceedings herein.[23]

The new army was not a happy one: pressed men were reluctant to fight and soldiers who had fought under Essex and Manchester were not all impressed by Fairfax and the new regime. The following week the order was repeated and enlarged:

> That Mr. Gaudy do go down into the County of Norfolke: And that Sir John Potts, who is now in the Country, do join with him: And that they do take care for the speedy Sending in of the Proportion of Horse assigned upon that county, to be employed at Grantham, and those Parts, for the Defence of the Association against the Newarke Forces: And, It is further Ordered, That they do take care for the speedy Bringing in of the Recruits, and old Levies of Men, and of the Monies assessed upon that County, for the Maintenance of Sir Thomas Fairfaxe's Army.[24]

In Norfolk Potts anxiously kept up correspondence with friends in London; events were moving fast; rumours of the Queen summoning help for the King from the continent had reached his ears:

June 30 1645

To my noble frend Sir John Potts

lieave this at the George Yard, in Lombard Street with Mr Cory to be sent as above

I have receved yours of the 26th, the 28th instant; for that you mention of French fleet. The King and Queenes letters taken at the last sight are full of it: our foreign letters import most earnest endeavours in the Queene for the Duke of Lorraine's forces which are called 8 or 9,000 and for what other forces shee can procure other particulars and wher to land, from what parts to come I yet know not.

The Intercepted letters are to be reported at a a [sic] comon hall on thursday next and are to be printed which make mee omitt thyr further contents, the heads of them I assure my self being already communicated to you .

We heare Massey was at Blanford on thursday last with 2000 horse and dragooners that he will this night be at Lynne.

We have not heard from Taunton of a weeke we have sent severall persons to them to satisfie them of success comyng; Sir Thomas Fairfax is with his whole army marching thither; we suppose he will be this night about Salisbury. The king is still about Hereford pressinge soldiers but the whole he yet hath wee cannot heare to be above 3000 horse. Gorand [Goring] with his men is returned into Pembrookshire; the houses of parliament and the Cttee of both Kingdoms have writt several letters to the earl of Leven for the speedie advance of the Scottish army into Worcestershire. Wee hourly expect an answer.

yr most assured humble servant

Wm Pierrepont[25]

Pierrepont, the second son of the Earl of Kingston, was the member for Much Wenlock in Shropshire although his estates lay in Huntingdon and his family was from Nottingham. His elder brother was a royalist but William was a loyal parliamentarian who had sat with Potts through many a long committee meeting and who had lamented Potts's absence back in May 1642. He assumed that Potts would already have heard from others of the intercepted letters. As they had not yet been made public, this suggests he knew the efficiency of Potts's information network.

Potts also had to maintain his work for the Army Committee and an interesting letter survives from the man just put in charge the committee's day-to-day affairs, Robert Scawen. Scawen had been put in as member for Berwick by his employer the Earl of Northumberland and was now to prove himself a very able administrator. He was a Cornishman of undistinguished family, hence his mode of address to Potts. His master was a friend of Sir John Holland and was well-disposed to Potts. The letter was written from Suffolk House the earl's house at Charing Cross, soon to renamed Northumberland House:[26]

> 17 July 1645
>
> To my honorable frend Sir John Potts knight, these Norfolk
>
> Noble Master
>
> I beleeve my self last [lost?] in your opinion, & to be under the notion of a negligent servant with you, & I must be content with sorrow to suffer itt untill I may have an opportunity to kisse your hands. In the meane tyme I beseech you to receave the inclosed & consider, what we have had to do since you left us, the more Victories wee have, the more troubles to us, how to gett supplies & I doubt not but you do Perticipate with us, in making up the Reciewts, which wee expect. I have no newes to impart you but that our affaires are in a most excellent condition, [This] last blowe upon Goringe is very greate, 1800 horse & 1000 foote & 2 Peacs [pieces] taken in summe a total Route & could wee agree heere & attend the Publique we might hope, God blessinge us, to see an end of much of our miseries before October be att an end, I have no more to say but to begge your pardon & to assure you that I am Really,
>
> Master, yr humble servant
>
> Robert Scawen[27]

The work had grown since Potts left; the more the army engaged, the more the supplies were needed. Scawen, who had also signed the letter to Norwich urging the collectors on, also had a little dig at Potts about the money they were waiting for. Given his grovelling apologetic manner, with hand-kissing gestures, there seems a little of the Uriah Heep about him.

Potts still endeavoured to keep both sides happy; Francis Neave of Witchingham House was in hot water for not taking £100 to the Standing Committee at Norwich.

On 18th July his 'assured loveing' friends, Potts, John Hobart, Richard Berney and others sent a copy of the order to him again with a postscript 'We expect your answer without delay after receipt of this letter or other wise we shallbe enforced to returne up your name and neglect to parliament which may turne to your trouble'. William Paston, who also signed this, knew only too well what trouble that would be.

An intriguing note reached John in Norwich on 2nd September from Robert, Earl of Warwick, now in Bury. Warwick had also been ousted, from his command of the navy, by the Self-Denying Ordinance that had toppled his son-in-law Manchester. He had involved himself in witchcraft trials in Suffolk during the summer attending the assizes there. What he and Potts were hatching with a Mr Garrat was unfortunately not made clear:

> Robert Rich, Earl of Warwick at Bury, to my worthy frend Sir John Potts
>
> Sir Jhon [sic]
>
> I receved yours and have confered with Mr Garrat whom I finde to have honest intentions. When you come up wee will confer how to doe any good to our County of Norfolke in the meane time I commend you to Gods protection, and rest, your assured frend
>
> Warwick[28]

John may have been on his way to London as he was obviously expected there. An equally tantalising letter shows his correspondents used all avenues to reach him, including his brother-in-law Willoughby. Henry wrote to his son-in-law D'Ewes at Westminster:

> Honoured Sonne
>
> I have receved yr letter & my daughters and am glad to heare of both your good healthes but should have [been] much more glad to have seene you both heere in Derbighshire; I have [been told] to inclose this letter unto my brother Potts, within yours, earnestly desiring you you take special care for the speedie sending the same to him because it is of some importance and requires a speedie ansire, and so with membrance of my kind love & best respects unto you & my daughter I rest
>
> your loving father-in-law
>
> Henry Willoughby   Risele 8 Sept 1645.[29]

Who sent the urgent missive we do not know. Whether Potts made it to town is doubtful. The speaker of the House, William Lenthall, sent a letter to him, Framlingham Gawdy and Miles Corbett, dated the 10th, informing them of yet another committee to which they had been appointed. They were to levy more money, this time for the recruits being assembled at Reading for Fairfax's army. If they had any trouble with the collections, the Army Committee was to be told.[30] Potts was certainly still in Norfolk on 8th October when he received news and a plaintive plea for his return from Pierrepont. The carrier system was still working well through Mr Cory (who relied on his kinsman William Cory to handle letters and money at the London end) for letters coming to Mannington but one sent to London a month before had only just arrived:

1645 8 Oct from W Pierrepont

to my noble frend Sir John Potts leave this I pray you with Mr Corie at his house in the George Yard in Lombard St to be sent as above.

Yours of the 1st Sept I received not till this 8th of October 1645

Sir I did hope to see you here before this, only because I would ever gladly attend you and that I conceved your busines in the parts you are in would not cause your stay. But whilst publiq' affaires detaine you, I submit I see the service entrusted with you hath been sutable to the rest of your actions, and that you will never be wearie to doe well.

You know the king is at Newarke; 2000 ... horse came with him near half enarmed ... we heer his forces such as are left in all parts and Earl of Gorman's army draw together as the [intent] conceived to have to relieve Chester if he can.

The houses have sent to the Scotch Commissioners the house of commons several times to desire the Scotch army to besiege Newarke; their first answer, they had not the power to direct that army but had writ to your Cttee on the plece whose concurrence they hoped for, as the season would permit. This day we had another answer from them that the Ctte of the estates of Scotland had a meeting in the borders cheifly to reforme what is amiss, in their army for the good of both kingdoms and doubted not of their p'complying with our desires. Our letters are that the headquarters of the Scotch army is at Stokesby in the north part of Yorks, theyr artillarie come into Newcastle. We hope by this Sir Thos Fairfax and Marrie are joyned ... in Devonshire etc

There are about 14 new members sett in the House. We heare of very many new elections made. Sir John Holland can obtain no further time to stay out of England then for 2 months from the 26th September last.

From your affectionate humble servant

W Pierrepont[31]

Pierrepont's belief that Potts would 'never be wearie to doe well' suggests that many were feeling the strain of the war but trusted him to maintain his commitment. After assisting Knyvett in the summer, Holland had gone abroad again to see his wife but was only allowed short breaks of 2 months before reporting back. With the parliament being in continuous session without new elections and with several members having withdrawn, the House was suffering a loss of numbers. The new members that Pierrepont spoke of, known as the Recruiters, would now soon include the elderly Sir John Hobart of Blickling. Hobart was elected as the other knight of the shire in December 1645, two and a half years after the death of Potts's last partner. Potts knew the former sheriff and his distinguished family well as they lived only a few miles away, at Blickling Hall. As a JP, he had worked alongside Hobart on the bench in the 1620s and 1630s and they had both attempted to prevent Thomas Case losing his living at Erpingham. More latterly of course, they were both deputy lieutenants. Hobart was also the brother-in-law of Sir Robert Crane, the late MP for Sudbury. They were joined by another Recruiter, John's stepson, the 38-year old John Spelman of Narborough, son of Ursula by her first husband Sir Clement. He was elected to represent Castle Rising near Lynn, a seat now free from catholic Howard control, replacing the royalist Sir Robert Hatton who had joined the King early in the war.

Potts would have felt relieved to have more support against the increasingly hostile Corbett and the new, often younger, radical members.

The continuation of the assessments across the country was taking its toll. In late October, John's poor brother-in-law Henry, on top of having troops billeted in his manor of Risley and in his house, wrote to D'Ewes for advice on how to cope with the additional demands that had been placed on Derbyshire (another £1,600 every month had to be raised; goods and land could be taken to enforce payment). Ordered in May 1645, this was to last for over a year.[32] 'The rate' he said, 'will be so chargeable no person will be able long to endure it'.[33] Norfolk had yet again fallen behind with its returns. In December 1645 Sir John, as a member of the army committee, had to sign another letter to the Norwich committee this time charging them with 'the sense we have of your extreme neglect, if not contempt' of their orders. Their return dated 28th November 1645 was £350 short of the sum ordained on 3rd September. His name appeared with Thomas Dacres of Hertfordshire, William Masham of Essex, Valentine Wauton (Cromwell's brother-in-law), John Sayer (the new Recruiter member for Colchester) and Samuel Luke (MP for Bedford).[34] They ended by threatening that the committee must 'speed up or we inform the House of your carriage therein'.[35]

1646-47 pressure, health and bereavement

Straight after the New Year Potts was back in the House on 1ˢᵗ January discussing the proposed execution of martial law. On 6ᵗʰ and 7ᵗʰ January 1646, in the Duchy Chamber, Potts had to sign orders, as a member of the joint Lords and Commons committee for the Eastern Association, to chase the local committee of Bedford. Their assessments were four months overdue and their money had to be sent to Cambridge for the urgent need of Major Gibb's regiment of horse. As this had no effect, further letters had to be sent later that month and in February, with new Recruiter members, Francis and Nathaniel Bacon (sons of Edward Bacon), now taking on some of the work. Potts knew the Bacons well; their sister Anne's son Philip Bedingfield had married his daughter. After several weeks of long wintry days, John was granted leave to go in to the country on 14ᵗʰ March. Two days later he was named to a committee but presumably he was excused.³⁶

He was certainly still in Norfolk at the beginning of May when he received news that Corbett and Col Wauton were coming. They had been given *carte-blanche* to take over Lynn, to 'search for, disarm, and secure all Delinquents such have come out of the Enemies Quarters, and other Persons of the Counties of Norfolk and Suffolk, and City of Norwich, as they, or either of them, shall have in just Cause of Suspicion' and to 'take in any of the Trained-Bands of the said Counties of Norfolke and Suffolke as they think fit, for the Securing of the Town of Yarmouth'. All the sheriffs, deputy lieutenants, and committees, of the counties and towns, and the Mayor and trained-bands of Lynn, were to aid and assist Corbett and Colonel Wauton. Sir John Potts and the rest of the Members of the House, that were in Norfolk and Suffolk, were especially told to be helpful.

His presence was still being missed in the House; his nephew D'Ewes wrote to Mannington in August to say that at a recent session, his one vote might have been critical. His views would be needed in the discussions of how to handle the King's refusal to sign the propositions. With his usual evasion, Charles had asked for a personal treaty in London:

> Aug 4 1646 Westminster To my very much Honored Unkle Sir John Potts
>
> Sir
>
> Your lines weare very welcome to mee but I should have been gladder to have seen you heere for but on Friday last the safetie of these three kingdomes, was, I thinke, much endangered for want of your single vote. The King I heere (being I feare misled by evil Counsell) denies to grant as yet the whole Propositions or anie parte of them. High counsels must thereupon follow. I hope therefore that all private affaires sett aside you will hasten upp. My wife I blesses God is very well and like to prove an exemplorie Nurse. Wee both tender our due respects to your selfe your Ladie & all yours

I am

your faithfull nephew & servant

Simonds D'Ewes[37]

Ursula would have been delighted to hear that her little niece Elizabeth had survived the birth of a child and was coping well as a mother.

Potts returned to Westminster, although he was not active there. It may be he was unwell as the last entry for him in 1646, on 17th September, was that Sir John Potts 'shall have Leave to go into the Country, for Recovery of his Health'.[38] Certainly he was not involved in the ongoing battle to get Norwich to raise their dues, which had caused the joint committee for the Eastern Association to summon Mr Peckover and Mr Parmenter before them earlier in the year and who were still, in late October, owing £400.[39]

Whatever the cause of his extended stay, John would have been in Mannington during the terrible flood that autumn which destroyed the bridge over the Bure at Itteringham. He responded generously to the village disaster:

14th November 1646

The said great bridge was broken down by a great flood of water
the like flood hath not been known in the memory of any of the
inhabitants there. The said bridge was made passable the next month
at the charge of Sir John Potts and afterwards repaired at the charge
of the whole county by an order granted at the general sessions.[40]

How John passed the winter we do not know but in the spring of 1647 he was involved in a local blasphemy case. He and Hobart had rallied to the cause of a local tanner who had been foolishly loose in his speech and thrown in prison. They wrote to the presiding assize judge who had heard the committal on 15th March. Thomas Trevor, one of the barons of the court of exchequer, sent his reply to them at Norwich on 27th March from Huntingdon:

Worthie Sir[s]

Your letter concerning one Newman, a Tanner, dated 25 March I
receved here yesterday here at Huntingdon and because the offence
of the said Newman may the more fully appeare unto you, I have
here enclosed sent you a true Coppie of the present[ment] of the
grand inquest of the County of Norfolk against the said Newman,
testified to them by the testimony of two witnesses uppon their
oathes, that the said Newman had maliciously and publiquely said
that Our Saviour Jesus Christ was a Bastard. These words being
hatefull to god and man, I in my opinion, held fitt to comitt him

to prison and not to bayle him but to lett him rest safely until the next Assises for that County of Norfolk which is likely to be held in July next and in the meane time I did then publishe that I would make it known to the Parliament for directions therein, it being soe rare a case, and I did this to my best discretion and not without acquainting my brother therewith. Your request, by your letter, is that I would permitt the Justices of the Peace by my leave to bayle him or els to report his cause to the Parliament so that he may be speedyle tryed or upon good services to enjoy means to follow his trade. This last request of yours I will carefully performe at my returne to London, which I hope wilbe upon the fifth of April next, and then I purpose to acquaint both the Speakers of the honorable houses whoe (as you know) are for the present the Commissioners of the Great Seale desiring directions therein which shalbe by me Carefully performed, for all partyes in this Cause are Strangers to mee, and desire in Charitye that Newman may quite [acquit] himself from so odious a Blaspheinge as he is Charged with and presented publiquely by the Grand Inquest. And so with my love and service remembered, I rest

yours, Most assured to serve you

Thos Trevor

Huntingdon the Saturday morning 27 march 1647 ready for horse toward Bedford.

This morning the messenger shewed me a Certificate my hands to it without date and somewhat worne and not directed to any in particular which I have delivered him backe for before I heard not of it.[41]

Trevor was keen to have Hobart and Potts's views and sent them the case papers from the Thetford assizes where Newman had been jailed; it seems they asked for William Newman to be bailed so he could go on working and for his case to be tried soon so he could clear his name. Trevor, a fair man, did not know the parties involved and hoped the man would be acquitted but at this time he would not take action without parliament's approval, this case being 'so rare'. A petition was sent to Trevor and the two speakers of the House. With it was a certificate taken on 5th April, signed by John Martin (minister of Edgefield), Thomas Jackson (minister of Itteringham), James Bond (minister of Holt), Edmund Brown (minister of Southrepps) and Richard Allison (minister of Cley) and 30 neighbours of Newman's around Hunworth and Edgefield.[42] Six of the local justices, John Hobart, John Palgrave, Francis Jermy, Robert Jermy and John Potts countersigned to say all were 'most pious, godly men'.[43] William's accusers, Gooding and Bougin had apparently been arguing with Newman since December 1645 about the observation of Christmas Day.

The Lords heard the matter on 21st April and Newman was to be bailed until the Norwich assize. For so many clerics to have been willing to stand up for him, at a time when blaspheming was seen as a serious sin, suggests William was indeed a victim of a grudge especially as his accusers had waited over nine months before reporting him. Tanners often did excite arguments and were not always the innocent parties, but on this occasion Newman had wide support.[44]

By this time Potts was back in the House involved with committee business, spending 27th May discussing the weaving trade in Norfolk and Suffolk. The next day the House appointed him and three others to a joint committee with the Earl of Warwick, who were to 'assist' Sir Thomas Fairfax in the disbanding of the army regiments.[45] As this was urgent, the following day he had a helpful note from the Committee for Irish Affairs at Derby House:

May 29th 1647

The Houses have appointed you one of the Commissioners for disbanding the army at the severall places of rendezvous. The first whereof is to be at Chelmsford on Tuesday next. Your Instructions for that service are ready. And wee thought it necessarie to give you this Intimation thereof, that you might bee in a readinesse for that service at the time & place appointed by the house

So wee rest

your affectionate Frends & Servants

T Lyncoln, J Willoughby, Denzill Holles Chatworthy [etc]

John had to pack up and dash off to Chelmsford to face an army recently returned from Ireland who were due back-pay and were not in a good mood. He and the others were to declare thanks for the soldiers' gallant and faithfull service and give a general amnesty for any misdemeanours before telling them to go home, with a small amount of back-pay which the committee were to carry with them.

He must have known he had been given a poisoned chalice. Before he even reached Essex, the army officers had discussed the terms offered and told Fairfax at Bury what he could do with the offer. Eight weeks pay was not going to satisfy their arrears. Fairfax could see the danger looming. Potts and Harbottle Grimston signed Warwick's letter on 31st May explaining that having reached Chelmsford by six in the evening they found Fairfax was still at Bury and that there was no hope of troops being brought to Chelmsford to disband. Two hours before Potts had arrived, a company (without orders) had broken in and taken their colours and ridden off towards Newmarket. They met their officers on the way but others were also on the move. The group said that their being there at that time was useless but would await further orders. The security of the money was obviously a major concern.[46] The next day they wrote again saying orders had been given to some of the captains to read the declaration to the troops: Captain Wolfe and Lt Heydon and others refused.[47] A further letter from them told of soldiers running amok, stealing ammunition and heading off to Suffolk, breaking into a house on the way.[48] Harbottle must have thought back to the events of August 1642 in Essex and Suffolk. At the same time Thomas Hoogan, governor of Lynn was having trouble with mutinous soldiers wanting their pay.[49] Warwick and the commissioners, their journey having been to no end, were recalled, and the money sent for the disbanding was ordered to be returned. Waller in his memoirs said 'Those summs, that were carried to Chelmsford, had the great good fortune to finde the way home again, but all that was sent to Oxford, not withstanding the protection of the Parliament, was arrested by the souldiers'.[50]

Potts must have been very relieved to return to Westminster despite the fact the army had now taken the King and was marching southwards towards London. On 5th June he was in the Painted Chamber, again in a joint committee, to hear the Scots Commissioners who, although keen now to get back to Scotland, were still negotiating over arrears of pay due to them. On the 14th he was working with Sir John Evelyn of Wiltshire and others preparing a declaration which would explain parliament's intentions for the future and how they would bring ease to the people, satisfaction to the army and peace and safety for the kingdom. Quite a manifesto! Fortunately, given the nature of the task, they were allowed to 'adjourn from time to time'. By the next day Potts and three others were told to withdraw so that they could write a letter:

> to be sent to the Commissioners with the Army, to satisfy them, that there are no Forces raised here; and further to signify unto them, that, for the other Particulars in their Letter, this House can give no Answer unto them, until they receive the General's Resolution of marching back Forty Miles from London, according to the former Direction of both Houses.

The work had been taking a toll on him again: on 17th July it was resolved that Sir John Potts should have leave 'to go into the Country, for Recovery of his Health'.

Whether he himself was ill or whether his wife had fallen prey to a serious condition is not known but around the end of September 1647 his beloved wife Ursula died. John appeared (in a long list of names of members most of whom were sick) as excused on 9th October 1647 but no reason is given. On October 20th, he wrote to Sir Simonds D'Ewes:

> I need not write of my unhappiness, One known evil comprehending many others; It hath pleased God since the lose of my dear wyf to give me other troubles amongst which one is a lameness in my left arm by a straine too longe neglected which at

last hath put me under surgery to prevent more paine; I cannot dress
or undress my self without help & can but make an untoward shift
to write with my other hand, which I now use to serv my nephew
Sir Jo Palgrave; you may know the day of choice for knight of this
shire [grows] on; it is the first of November; his adversaries either
to wronge or amuse him report that he shall be shreive, which were
an insufferable wrong to him in several respects; This devise is only
to defeat him of the election which cannot I suppose be otherwise
taken from him; I pray Sir use all your frends to stave off this blowe
if the appointment of Shrieve come before All Saints in the Hous,
for that day will end the question; I may commend my service to my
niece yr lady & daughters soe rest Sir

yr assured frend & servant J Potts

I hope Sir you will deliver my just & unwilling excuse at next calling
of the House[51]

It is typical of Potts that despite being in mourning and great pain, and having
to use his other hand (presumably not having a clerk near to write it for him), he
was most anxious that D'Ewes would help Sir John Palgrave of North Barningham
(nephew to both of them by marriages into the Willoughbys). Sir John Hobart had
died during the year and Palgrave, another conservative who had been doing sterling
work on all the local committees and was a great friend and helper to his uncle, was
a natural choice to partner Potts. Thomas Windham had been prepared to stand for
parliament at the election for knight of shire but was not overkeen and was perfectly
happy to see Palgrave chosen. Palgrave wrote twice to his friend William Doughty
of Hanworth telling him of his resolve to stand regardless of 'the clangerousnesse ...
of the times' but asking for his company on the day.[52] Others, though, had started
scurrilous rumours that Palgrave was being lined up to be sheriff (in which case
he would not be allowed to stand for parliament) in order to scupper his chances.
Potts wanted D'Ewes to ensure that talk of the sheriff did not occur before 1st of
November, the date of the parliamentary elections.

His writing does not look too bad - perhaps being left-handed he was reasonably
ambidextrous - but his problem was recognised by others; Sir Jacob Astley his
cousin and neighbour at Hindolveston, wrote in December 1647: 'At my coming to
London I first visited my Lord of Northumberland who ascked verie kindly for you I
told him that you wer verie lambe [lame] of your Arme'.[53]

Unlike his son-in-law Edward Astley (who had fought alongside John Palgrave for
the parliamentarians), Sir Jacob, Baron Astley from 1644, was one of the exceptions
in Norfolk who had stood firmly for the King and commanded his soldiers
throughout the war, before being taken prisoner in March 1646.

Under the Articles of Oxford, Astley was allowed to return home to Hindolveston in July and his estates (in Kent) were withdrawn from sequestration. Instead they were compounded - he was charged a sum of twice the assessed annual value - a business that took two years to complete. In the same long letter, he related his problems in trying to get a decision on his estate despite having dropped Potts's name to various friends. He was still technically Fairfax's prisoner and rather bizarrely seems to have been accused of having burnt down a Mr Stevens's house. It is a splendid example of idiosyncratic spelling and has not been modernised here:

Dec 14 1647

Nobell Sir

... after I had visited other frends I first went to Sir Thos Fairfax at Windser who gave mee his letter to Mr. Speaker the coppie whereof I send you. His letter I delivered to the Speaker, Sir Thos Alcocke being with me. Mr Speaker perused it and gave it me back & bad me first go ther with all to Goldsmiths Hall, for as it ther was no time for him to Move the house on it.

When I cam to Goldsmith Hall, I put up a petition to them but founde but littel scivillitie from them, Mr Stevenes being by, presced his action mulch against me for birneuinbge [burning] of his house. The conclusion was first I must take the Covenant and the negative oath; the first they would exame me in but the last was their order & ... which beyond they could not or else they must committ me. I tould them I was a prisoner to Sir Thos Fairfax alreadie; as for my estat they must have the halfe of it. I told them that my estate was but mine for term of life and I could not sell it. And that it was verie hard that there would keepe my estate from me which I had sought this 3 quarters of a yere redeme, by a reasonable feine & now would sticke upon my conscience to, and this I presented to them. I returned to Mr Speaker, Sir T A being with me, and would have given him backe this ... letter. But he replied, thru the great business in sendinge the 4 proposalls to the kinge, nothing could yet be done this 12 or 14 daies but gave me the letter backe againe that it ought not be laied aside & promised that he would move the house for me very effectuallie, remembering very well the aceptabell scervices I did the Parliament in the North when I was entrusted ther by them & used many other good expressions of his willingness to do me advantage. As truly I wish this Army now could be as peceable disbanded as it was wherein I dar presume to say for the factte whatsoever ... I had the ... princsipallest hand in actinge of it.

I have given Sir Thomas Fairfax letters to Sir TA to attend Mr
Speaker at his convenience & full time to move the House for me.
And Sir I lefte the Cittie.

Beffor I appered in Goldsmiths Hall I went to Mr Ash & delivered
your letter to him, he said you were his nobell good frende but I
perseive Mr Stevones [Stevens] is so Hoisted with him in frendship
& fellow commissioner, as he is extremely partiall for him And
indeed I must commend Mr Stevens for he was the scevelist man to
me ... I wish the fine I must give the Parliament maie be given him,
but he must not have anything from me for birnenge, that was ...
ascenting [assenting] into moyther [murder] directly or indirectly.

Thus I have troubled you with a long discours & give you Manie
thanckes for your extreordenarie frendship which the presentation of
my humbell respectes to all your famelliee

And my wife and all this House to you & ther

I rest alwaes, yr affectionnated kinsman & most humbell servant

Jacob Astley[54]

Regardless of his loss and illness, it would appear John must have returned to the
House at some time after the 14th as, on 23rd December, he was ordered to go into
Norfolk along with Erasmus Earle (his neighbour from Heydon, now member for
Norwich), Framlingham Gawdy and John Spelman. Certainly there was no sign of
him in Westminster over the rest of the winter which he may have spent quietly at
Mannington with his son John and his family.

Even by April he was not in the House when the roll was called on the 24th at
which he was excused but Sir John Palgrave was absent without leave. On the 28th
Sir Jacob wrote to update him on the progress of his estate fines which had finally
been settled on 8th February with a £400 fine on his Kent estate. It is clear that John
was still unwell from time to time:

Apr 28 1648 Hilderston [Hindolveston]

Much honoured good Cozen,

We wear all hopefull to have sceen you heare this daie & an hartelie
sorie that an Agowt hath troubled you and disappointed us but I
hope & wish it maie not last but as tacken in the [?]suringetirne
[sure return?] to better health, Cozen I shall hartelie wish you a
god Jurnie & an authour to a happie peace. I thank you kindlie
as for London & my business ther I well hope hath bidden it

farewell for a longe time. Ondly my dughtie full respectes to my
Lord of Northumberland I praye present; Conserning £400 that I
owe in London against August next I have alreadie taken order for
the paiments of it; And shall not mayk use of ane money out of
Hollande, being my wife's, which I am verie loth to deminish. It was
very strandge to us to her [hear] the sad Newes at Norwidge of the
Losse of so manie men as Sir Edward Astley is geve theather this daie
& this myhte we shall better understand the scircumstances theerof
by his returne: But it is agreater wonder to her that the Duke of York
is escaped. I praise god, it maie not [rebound] ane waies to my Lord
of Northumberlands preiudis The discourse spred, by som my last
being at [reles?]

your servant will show you letter from the Inkeeper ther, what it
was, as it troupe, I never saw or speeke which all to my knowledge

My wife, selfe, sister & daughter right affectionately salutes you, all
of us wishinge you a god Jurnie & a happie ... of peace Mackinge,
All our respectes to my Cozen your son & his ladie & all prs And so
I rest

yr most humbell servant [55]

The letter is full of interest. Although Sir Jacob's main concern was for his estates
and his wife's money, safely tucked away in her native land, he was full of the
rumours of 'the Great Blowe' at Norwich which had occurred four days before.
Unrest over the campaign by hardline puritans on council to replace John Utting, a
popular Mayor, had led to a petition being presented on Sunday 23rd April to have
him stay. The city gates were locked; by midnight a crowd of 2,000 in Market Place,
shouting God and King Charles, would not disperse even at Utting's pleading.[56] Too
much drinking led to attacks on puritan aldermen's houses and so the cavalry, under
Col Charles Fleetwood, was summoned from Dereham. As they approached around
3 pm on Monday, the mob tried to steal more arms from the City Storehouse and
a boy was shot; the building was stormed. With spilt gunpowder and lit torches
the inevitable happened and the whole arsenal exploded. Forty people died in the
huge blaze, many more were injured, houses were destroyed. The explosion blew
out the windows of St Peter Mancroft and St Stephen's churches. Most rioters were
ordinary men; 300 were arrested as troopers regained control about a third of whom
were kept in prison for several months. Most were fined but eight were executed
as ringleaders on 2nd January 1649. Utting surrendered to parliament and was
imprisoned and heavily fined. This shocking event would have later consequences.

Astley was also concerned for their friend in the Lords, Algernon Percy, Duke of
Northumberland who had earlier been so solicitous about Potts's health. Percy had
been given the care of the King's three children the eldest of whom had just escaped.

1648 Sir John and the King

Astley also hoped that Potts would have a good and successful journey but what this mission was we do not know; John had no House of Commons journal entries from December 1647 to April 1648. Although it would fit with his later Isle of Wight journey, it is far too early to be a reference to the autumn treaty. Potts's main work in the House in early May was the petition of the City of London; there had been serious rioting by the apprentices earlier in April and the house was very concerned about its security. On this John was working with John Crew (later Lord of Stene, whose daughter married a cousin of Manchester) and Sir Harbottle Grimston. He and Sir Henry Vane junior joined the committee who went into the City to meet several times in May with the council, to discuss how to prevent further risings. He was also working on the latest propositions that would be put to the King concerning religion and the militia; the presbyterians were urging talks to take place. June saw John busy with the insurrection in Kent, the order to abolish all deans and chapters and sell their possessions, and the problem of ships which had taken against parliament, as well as working with the Lords. On the last day of June, he was heavily involved in the debate about the process for voting on how the peace propositions would be handled and what the Houses would demand of the King before a personal treaty could begin.[57] He and John Bulkeley, a former independent, were the tellers for the procedural motion (on whether to debate the question of the treaty) which was passed on 22nd July by 48 votes to 35.[58] In July, troubles in Surrey had to be investigated, delayed sequestrations followed up and the Scots declaration had to be prepared. Potts was among 7 asked to manage a conference with the Lords who had voted against Major-General Skippon. Skippon, who was firmly parliament's military man in charge of the safety of London, was a Norfolk man who had lived at Foulsham earlier in life.

The business with the City dragged on into August. Worrying developments from some of his old Association colleagues in Essex came with the news that some members of the committee including Sir William Masham had been carried off from Chelmsford to Colchester Castle. Now however matters with the King were moving. The commissioners who had gone to the King with the offer of treaty talks wrote on 7th August of the breakthrough: 'After a foule journey and stormy passage, by the protection & guidance of a gracious god, we arrived Saturday late in the Isle of Wight'. They had seen the King immediately and the Earl of Middlesex presented the vote to the King as their return had to be within 10 days of their setting forth. At this stage the King was told no names had yet been put forward. The King said he was willing to treat.

On 16th August Potts (with Grimston, Holles, Crew, Swynfen, Bulkeley and William Lewis) were to report on the conference between the Lords and Commons about the letter the King had sent back. Potts, speaking for the committee for peace, himself gave the report to the house on the 17th, read the King's letter and said how the Lords had voted. On the 23rd it was agreed that, further to Potts's report, so many days would be allowed for setting up the treaty and for its completion. Potts was leading the group of managers of the conference with the Lords on the 24th and gave the report back on the 25th. They had also discussed the request for funds that Manchester had proposed for the Earl of Northumberland who had care of the Royal children. By now it would have been clear to Potts that he was going to be given a chance, probably the last, to achieve a peaceful settlement with the King.

On 1st September, on his report from the committee, the House passed the instructions for the nominated treaty party. From the Lords, his friend Algernon Earl of Northumberland, Philip Earl of Pembroke and Montgomery, James Earl of Middlesex and William Fiennes, Viscount Saye and Sele were chosen. Of the lower House, Thomas Viscount Wenham, Sir Henry Vane junior, John Crew, Samuel Browne (whose daughter would later marry his son), John Glyn, John Bulkeley and his friends Denzil Holles, William Pierrepont and Sir Harbottle Grimston joined Sir John Potts. Potts was one of only nine presbyterians chosen.

They were instructed 'to repair to Newport in the Isle of Wight, and there to treat personally with his Majesty upon Propositions for a safe and well-grounded Peace; where you, or any Eight of you (whereof some of either House of Parliament shall be present) to treat with his Majesty for the Space of Forty Days, from the Beginning of the said Treaty, upon the Propositions which were presented to his Majesty at Hampton Court concerning the Kingdoms of England and Ireland, and for the Taking away of Wards and Liveries, now delivered unto you, and such other Propositions as by both Houses of Parliament shall be agreed upon'.

Having heard what the King first offered they were to 'proceed to treat upon the Propositions for recalling Declarations, &c. the Propositions concerning the Church, the Propositions concerning the Militia, the Propositions concerning Ireland'. Everything was to be in writing and they were to 'give frequent Advertisement to both Houses of Parliament of your Proceedings in this Treaty'.

Before that however, he and some of the others had to go straight to the Lord Mayor 'to desire the City of London, for the necessary Carrying on of this Treaty, to lend the Sum of Ten Thousand Pounds, to be paid by Two Thousand Pounds a Week, upon such Security to be given from the Parliament as the City shall make Choice of, either on the Excise, in Course, or the Moiety of Goldsmiths Hall Receipts, in Course, or the Estates of such Delinquents as are excepted, and not pre-engaged; or such other Security as they shall propose, being in the Power of the Parliament'.

Next, also on 1st September, Potts and Nathaniel Fiennes were told to prepare a letter informing the King of who the commissioners were to be and when they would come, which would be taken to the Isle of Wight with haste. He hurried up to the Lords to sort out the details and the simple letter was written the same day telling the King they could not be there within the ten days originally suggested. Now everything was a rush; other work such as the business of managing the compounded estates of Clement Paston of Thorpe had to be left to Spelman, Palgrave and Sir William Paston. News had spread; his appointment put him in the public eye. His daughter-in-law's brother and fellow MP, William Heveningham wrote to him on 4th September shortly before the party set off, asking a favour for

Edward Calver, his neighbour in Suffolk. Calver was probably from Wilby near Stradbrook (Heveningham would have felt able to ask Potts as he had supported him in his first candidacy in 1640 for parliament against Holland, and worked with Potts on the County Committee for Norfolk as well as that for Suffolk).[59]

> Sir This bearer Mr Calveir my neighbor in Suffolk I have known him a long time & he is a very Honest man & very well affected to the Parliament & the Poeticall; & desires to present a Littell booke of his own workes to his majestie as Hoping it may be some advantage to the Publicke; & also no prejudice to his own perticuler therefore for by better opportunitie to present it to his majestie He desires me to write to you that you would doe him the favor as to owne him as one of your attendance into the isle of Wight; you & the rest of the Commissioners being to goe therein there the middle of this week so with my respects & service to you I remayne
>
> yr loving frend
>
> W Heveningham
>
> If you plese you may see one of the Books[60]

John would hardly have had time to read the poem, probably entitled Royall Vision. Calver's poetry has not been well remembered: he 'mistakenly tried to combine Puritanism and poetry and wrote such dull books as *England's sad posture* (1644) and *Divine passion piously and pathepatically expressed* (1643)' according to Richard Pennington.[61] Potts was in lodgings 'right over against the Kings Head in the Strand' preparing for his journey and what would be his last chance to influence the course of events. We do not know if Calver was able to present it to the King but the poem has been attributed a date of 11th October 1648 which suggests Potts might have generously allowed him in his retinue and promoted the poet to the King's presence.

The following week on Wednesday 13th September, the party left London for the Isle of Wight and the serious work of talking and writing began.[62] On 16th September the first of the formal reports to the speaker William Lenthall was sent saying they were safely arrived and had seen the King. Charles had been removed from Carisbrooke Castle and was staying at the house of Sir William Hodges at Newport where the treaty was to take place. The formal reports were usually signed by most of the Commons' commissioners and always by Potts.[63] Two days later the talking started and on the 21st the next report was sent back: clerks and messengers must have been hurrying to and fro, trying to attend all those needing scribes and posting letters across the country. Newport would have seen an increase in business of all kinds during these weeks.[64] Potts was working hard, not only in the negotiations but also writing to his network of friends in the House. It was clear to him that many at home did not want the treaty to succeed and he needed to spur on those left behind to carry the debates. He also seems to have been the driver for ensuring funds were sent to the island for their expenses. On the same day as the next report was written, the 26th, one of his correspondents wrote back:

> From Francis Drake For my honoured frend Sir John Potts at Newport IOW
>
> Noble Sir
>
> Your great work about the first proposition and preamble as it had many fear before hand, so when it came it was received with many joys. The busines of the money yre presintly upon, your first got dispatched for £4000, to be immediately sent. This day a very full house & I am hopefull we shall have ease in setling things heer as well as you hope wher you are.
>
> I and the rest of your frends retourn you many thanks for your intelligence, praying the continuance thereof. I pray disirs Sir Jo Pal: to conclude if it be possible Sir J A Businesse for very many threaten that way. I shall obey your commands furthring to my power a good reception of all that is don by you whose endeavours are fallen out in a good climat, by Gods good providence
>
> I am
>
> FD[65]

Drake, the MP for Amersham, was hopeful of holding the House steady at this time; he also updated John on the progress of Sir Jacob Astley's estate affairs suggesting Sir John Palgrave should help complete matters in case others, perhaps in Potts's absence, disadvantaged Astley further.

Potts also received a letter privately from the speaker. He and Lenthall seem to have had a close friendship. Not only was Potts sending him private versions of the reports (which Lenthall found more helpful than the formal ones) but he had also undertaken to look after Lenthall's nephew while he was there, as part of his entourage:

> 1648 Sept 27
>
> Noble Sir John
>
> I do hartily thanke for kinde remembrance I will assure you letters, for these are very acceptable, a little passage in prevat [private] shewes much more respect, then many in publicke. I pray excuse

this messenger for I have kept him heere hopinge to have sent you
an answer of that letter he brought. it was presently committed but
as yet ther is noe returne & because the time is not certainly knowne
to me when it wilbe, I would keep him noe longer. I presently
move the House about your money & I can assure you I wilbe
your importunat sollicitor upon all occasion. I thank you for kinde
acceptance of my nephew. I know by your good instructions he wilbe
able to doe you service what paynes or countenance you bestow shal
not be forgotten by your assured frend & humble servant

Wm Lenthall[66]

Edmund Warcup was the son of Lenthall's sister Anne and Samuel Warcup. He
had been briefly at St Alban Hall Oxford and was back from a trip abroad. His uncle
had thought it useful for him to be employed helping the commissioners as their
secretary. It shows the trust that Potts's character engendered that the young man was
to be his protégé. A few notes from his pocket book have survived and give a glimpse
of the nature of his work for Sir John:

29 Sept This night received one from him [Speaker Wm Lenthall]
with enclosed for Mr Pierrepont, Sir John Potts, Sir Harbottle
Grimston, the Recorder Glyn and Mr Bulkeley

15 Oct I rec'd a letter dated the 13 Oct from Mr Speaker with one
enclosed for Sir John Pott Sir Harbottle Grimston Mr Browne and
Mr Glyn

1 Nov Rec'd a letter from Mr Speaker with one for Sir H Grimston,
Sir John Potts Sir Henry Vane Mr Crewe Mr Browne and Mr Glyn

[between 6-8 Nov] I must write to my Lord Say, to Mr Glyn, to Mr
Henry Vane, to Sir John Potts and to send him the papers put in this
day to the King

9 Nov I wrote to...........Sir John Potts ...& sent them copies of the
King's finall answer to the Propositions

11 Nov I wrote to the Speaker, Sir John Potts Sir Henry Vane Mr
Glyn & Mr Bulkeley by Mr Hendrick

18 Nov as above

17th at night I rec'd by Mr Blackeborne a letter from Sir John Potts:
[and from] my father, my mother, Bro, some other friends etc[67]

The boy suffered from a common childhood affliction, scrofula (a tuberculous infection of the neck skin) known as the King's Evil; it is said he was cured in the 1640s.[68] Perhaps he came to the island hoping to be touched by King Charles, the traditional if superstitious remedy.

Warcup went on to have an interesting life: he fell from grace (as mentioned in Pepys's diary July 1666), recovered, held a wine licence commission, became a London justice of the peace, a deputy lord lieutenant, translated a 3-volume work on Italy in 1660, helped to foil a popish plot against the king in 1690, was knighted, owned an estate in Oxford and died in 1712. He was, one hopes, grateful to the man who gave him a good start.[69]

While the commissioners were working their way through the propositions with Charles and sending reports back on the 7th, 9th, 10th and 11th, the House was debating the episcopacy.[70] The King's answer to the second clause, that the bishops should be retained, was voted as unsatisfactory on the 13th. Another letter from Potts sparked the response from Sir William Lewis, MP for Petersfield:

> 1648 Oct 12 for my honor' frend Sir J Potts Baronett
>
> Sir
>
> I receved your favour of the 9th and you will understand by the vots [votes] of our house, that we doe not like of your church worke. I must confess that his Majestie having so farre justified us by his consent to our first proposition, and secured us by the Militia, that ther is a great judgement upon these kingdoms, if we should differ upon the rest, soe as to become liable to the miseries of a future warre, though I finde you farre from any accord, in the business of the church, thorough thesides whereof, men will by so divers wayes, drive at their divers ends, God if his mercie direct, a good issue therein
>
> All letters will bringe you, our vote for the large cutt of servants, the filling up of the Benches, and therby the preferment of some of our worthy members
>
> If I heare of Mr Cresset I shall not fayle him of the little I can doe, to further his dispatch as you desire, without wh[ich] your attendence can not but be lease pleasinge Sir I wishe your return with the olive branch,
>
> remayning yours to serve you
>
> you have many remembrances here, I pray present my service to Mr True
>
> William Lewis[71]

Despite not agreeing with Potts on every issue, Lewis wished him to 'return with the olive branch'. Lewis and Sir William Waller had successfully saved Portsmouth for parliament early in the war but both had been disabled in January 1647 by charges brought by Fairfax and the new army. The order had been revoked in June 1648.

Six days later, Potts received a letter from his friend Sir John Evelyn, who agreed with Potts's view of the Scots and advised that whichever way the church proposition went it would be unpopular:

> 1648 Oct 18
>
> Sir If you have worse thoughts of the Scots than you had, I will assure you I have no better & we very like to agree on that Poynt. Let them appeare, for kirke or kinge, it is all one to me they are still Scots. I am very glad of our Justification & shalbe as glad of our security hoping you find cause there to believe me is freely & cordially granted & resolved to be kept, such an assistance from you will much encourage me. But promise not your selfe too much from the House upon that soore [score], for though I never layd weight on the 2nd proposition, you will finde your old brother Prist doe & that you shall heare on both earrs if you worke not his Majesty to a better understanding. I heare of this abroad but truly know nothinge & hope better, else we shall be left a pretty thinge that neither, will nor can, keepe promise with any sort of men. Lett things fall how they will
>
> I am sure I am & wilbe
>
> Sir yr affectionate humble servant
>
> J Evelyn[72]

On the 10th the commissioners had asked for the rest of the £10,000 to be sent and Potts had obviously asked all his friends to keep the matter at the top of the agenda in the Commons.

One of these was Sir Henry Vane senior, father of the Sir Henry Vane junior who was on the island with Potts. Both were members of parliament and it is interesting that Potts felt it necessary for him to write to the father, rather than rely on the son to do so. The reply to John reflected Vane's wish for a reconciliation with the King and his own private joy of being a grandfather:

> 1648 Oct 19
>
> Sir Henry Vane from 'my house in the Strand'

Sir

I was come to Parl. on Monday last and was very glad to understand
that by your publique transactions, the Treatie to be in soe hopeful a
way; your private letter gave me fuller satisfaction therein and of the
success thereof; for the Supply of yr moneys Mr Siderfield moved
but I know not what success he had, I hope well: when I hear it
spoken of, I shall serve you the best I can. It is expected here that
the Treatie at the rate his Maj: and the Commissioners goe, should
be finished by saturday sennight, at least his Maj: should declare
how far he would goe if he sticke at any of the propositions, it being
conceived he will pass all.

I doe much apprehend the busines of the churche but the
propositions touching it will yet entertaine muche debate before
agreed, but this is my private opinion & thereupon I hope I may be
deceived. I have presented my service to Sir Thomas Pallen [Pelham]
whom God hath given a lusty boy; and my daughter far[e] as well as
a woman in her case can be

Sir I am

yr most humble servant

Hvane (sic)[73]

More reports of the proceedings were sent on 14th, 17th and 21st October all
signed by Potts and Vane junior. They had been told to re-negotiate the episcopacy
question and were reporting the King's final answers: it was not going according to
plan. The forty days were running out.

A few days later, Potts heard that the House was increasingly unhappy and must
have suspected failure was looming. The letter was from a close friend, one who was
doing errands for him but was also in the House. This could be John Swinfen who
was a close colleague and friend of John Crew, one of the commissioners. Swinfen
was obviously coming over to see them:

1648 Oct 24

For my much Honoured frend Sir John Potts Newport

Sir,

yrs I received & the inclosed is conveyed & order is taken that the
£2000 be presently pd; Mr Doddridge moved for it; the debate is
put off till Thursday, I receyve of a few are very zealous to return the

last answere as unsatisfactory, more presbiters now than formerly, & yet some that I had thought were moderate will not see it of which Sir I: Jr & Mr D: are not the least; the house this day very full; a letter from the General complayn that the commander in chief against Pomfret [Pontefract] will not obey orders; Sir H Ch [Sir Henry Cholmley] complained last week that a Junior Col was sat over him, we have now voted that he doe obey. Your cloth was not then sent, we wilbe with you before Saturday

I shall pay the £20 according to direction

 I am Sir, your humble servant

JS [intertwined][74]

Potts would have been relieved that finally the last of the City money had been approved. Mr Cressett was ordered to take care of it for delivery.[75] They also had been allowed to discount 14 fast days and Sundays from the 40 days allowed so giving them a little more time.

A final apologetic letter came rather belatedly to Potts by a friend who had been away in the country and therefore had not seen Potts's earlier letter requesting help in the House:

1648 Oct 30

Sir Dudley North MP for Cambridgeshire, from Westminster to 'my much honoured frend'

Sir

 ... I cannot but say, that you, the commissioners (& something else) have wrought wonders, in bringing the matter of the treaty to the condition which it is now in. Yet I find, by those that pretend to have preserve the temper of the house, that unless there be a yielding in terminis, there is no great hope of a happy winding up within doors ... I hope you will neither want diligence, nor success in your future proceedings, so as to put the blush all those that shall endeavour to continue the miseries of this kingdom, by an absolute frustration of this treaty which hath given so great an expectation to the people. Sir, I am not able to serve you, in any thing mentioned in your letter but in the making knowne yr remembrance of the frends of both houses which you have named, some if which I have spoken with all already & I shall seeke opportunities to doe it with the rest & sorry I am, to have noe other ocasion to expresse how ready you shall be served you on all occasions by yr affect frend

Dud North[76]

North expressed his faint hope that Potts could still succeed against all odds. Within three days, it was all over: without agreement over the abolition of the bishops, the House refused to continue the treaty. Parliament recalled the commissioners who were to decide which three of them (one lord and two commoners) were to stay with the King. Lord Wenman, John Crew, Denzil Holles and William Pierrepont stayed. Potts took the last report, dated 6th November, that bore his signature, back to London and on 9th November the Commons journal entry read:

> A Letter from the Commissioners in the Isle of Wight, of 6 Novembris 1648, delivered in by Sir John Potts, one of the Commissioners, was read, with divers Papers inclosed, giving an Account of their Proceedings upon the late Vote and Instructions they received touching the Church, and other Matters.
>
> Resolved, &c. That the hearty Thanks of the House be returned to the Commissioners employed in the Isle of Wight, for their great Pains and Industry, and very faithful Discharge of the Trust committed unto them.
>
> And Mr. Speaker, accordingly, by the Command of the House, gave the Thanks of this House to Sir John Potts, Sir Henry Vane junior, Mr. Recorder, Mr. Samuel Browne, and Mr. Bulkley, now present; and was ordered to give the Thanks of this House to the rest of the Commissioners, as they shall come into the House.

Crew, and Swinfen who was staying with him, also sent a letter on the 6th, 'having the opportunity of this bearer Mr Cresset', which showed there was concern that the presbyterians would be blamed for the situation.[77] On 13th November, the day Potts and others were debating the King's future care, parliament wrote warning of the King's plot to escape from the Island within a few days. The remaining commissioners and Warcup took their final leave of the King on 27th November.

Sir John had been in the King's presence for over 6 weeks; he had worked tirelessly to fulfil his role in the negotiations and at home. Had he believed the King was listening? Charles had agreed to several of the propositions but had all along been planning an escape attempt. In fact there had been little hope of his ever agreeing to the main issues. John must have been tired, disappointed and apprehensive about the future. Now, at the end of November, Potts, Palgrave and Corbett were told to ride into the country to bring in the assessments for the army, an army which was becoming increasingly radical. He must have been content to get back to Norfolk leaving a House that was at boiling point. One faction of the radicals proposed the enforced dissolution of parliament but this was too slow for the army and the independents. On 5th December a plan was made to use force to purge the House of Commons of the 143 members they thought were hostile to the army. On Thursday the 7th, Colonel Thomas Pride stood with the list of names on the steps to prevent them entering the House; any resisting would be arrested. Most went away but 45 were taken and held in a local tavern for a few days before being let out.

Sir John and his nephew may still have been in Norfolk when they heard the news. The list included both of them, along with his stepson John Spelman, Sir John Holland and Framlingham Gawdy (thereby reducing Norfolk's representation to three). It also named William Pierrepont, Denzil Holles, Harbottle Grimston (who was arrested) and the other Isle of Wight members except Sir Henry Vane junior. There were many others of his friends, the other moderate presbyterians who were clearly not going to align themselves with the independents and the growing radicalism of the army. Sir Thomas Wodehouse was not named but, now an old man, may have already stopped attending; Sir Simonds D'Ewes withdrew from the House. John and his family were not amongst those who were imprisoned but they were allowed to continue to support the army in Norfolk. Potts would not attend the House again for 12 years. The few remaining members, who included Miles Corbett, known as the Rump parliament, now held power. On 25th December, a working day, a petition, ostensibly from the gentlemen of Norfolk and Norwich was presented, presumably by Corbett, requesting the King be brought to justice. Manchester, acting as speaker for the 16 remaining Lords, refused to be involved. The Commons resolved to act alone. Corbett, no doubt with great satisfaction, was chosen to attend Windsor to tell the King that he was to be tried. Potts and his circle, hearing all with disbelief, could do nothing to stem the tide.

Chapter 14

The Enfield Chase

Sir John's life in the 1650s has not been covered by other writers; he left Norfolk and dropped out of political life. His family and their property suits now started to take all his time and energy.

One can only wonder what Sir John felt, back in Norfolk, hearing the news of the King's speedy trial and execution. Mannington church would have heard many prayers and the hall must have been a sombre place. He was no regicide, but family and members he had worked with were now deeply embroiled. William Heveningham (whose two sisters Susan and Anne had married Potts's son and stepson who had supported the army and survived the Purge) was called as a judge in Charles's trial. Sir John may well have felt a personal grief caused by a sense of guilt. He was a man who believed absolutely in duty. Over the last eight years he had spent so much time and energy, firstly in keeping the peace in Norfolk and latterly attempting to reason with the King on one side and the extremists on the other. The feeling of his failure being partly responsible for the death of his King may well have been overwhelming to such a man. Whatever the depth of his sorrow or his anger, his life was now changed.

Sir John on his travels

A few weeks later, on 14th March 1649, the Commons recorded his request 'for his health-sake to go beyond Sea for six months'.[1] Was it really his health that caused him to request leave to travel or could he not bear to be in England anymore? We do not know where he went in those dark months. It may been to Holland where so many of his countrymen were, perhaps staying with Sir John Holland's family. Whether he returned around September 1649 is not known but he did not pick up the Norfolk life he had previously known.

Certainly at this time (after 1648), he was not on the Commission of the Peace.[2] Why is not clear, as Potts would seem to have been well placed to continue as a JP; parliament needed continuity in local affairs and with the removal of some of the King's supporters there would have been vacancies. However, members who had been evicted in the Purge were unpopular and were passed over until later in the 1650s.[3] While his colleagues Hobart, Windham, Earle, Miles Corbett and Bedingfield all appeared in 1650, Potts was not listed in the frequent Norwich sessions during 1649-54.[4] His nephew Sir John Palgrave, similarly secluded in the Purge, re-appeared later attending quarter sessions at Little Walsingham and Fakenham six times between October 1654 and January 1657.[5]

Certainly when a petition from Itteringham inhabitants came to the justices in January 1655 reporting that yet again the bridge was in disrepair, John Potts no longer came to the rescue and two other local justices, Edward Bulwer and William Steward esq, were to examine and assess the charges.

If Sir John had been on the bench in 1655, would Margaret Steward, the poor widow of a parliamentary soldier, a labourer, of Itteringham, who had died from his wounds, have had to fight so hard, going to quarter sessions twice, to try to get some of her husband's back pay? Like Widow Olly in 1643, it is probable she would have found assistance at a local level had Sir John been around. Out of £17 pay owed to this casualty of war, his widow was allowed only 40s.

Although Potts apparently reappeared on the Commission of the Peace from 1656 he was not listed as on the bench in the Norfolk QS Order books from 1656 through to 1676.[6] Neither did he appear to be acting as a committing justice at this time. Perhaps he felt that the King had been right when, forbidden the usual right to speak before execution, he had warned that if he was so treated, others could not expect justice to be upheld in future.

Had he been around, could he have influenced the capture and trials of Thomas Cooper and William Hobart? As part of their work for the committee for the army, John Potts and John Palgrave had examined and signed the accounts of the monies due from the rectory of Little Barningham for July 1645 to July 1646.[7] The third signatory was [Col] Robert Jermy of Bayfield near Holt. Jermy was the brother of Palgrave's first wife Elizabeth and was a zealous puritan. The accounts were drawn up for sequestration by Edward Cooper of Edgefield, gent. He was the brother of the Reverend Thomas Cooper, born in Edgefield, who had been instituted to the rectory of Little Barningham, alias Stafford Barningham, on 26th May 1631, presented by John Dix Ramsey, lord of the manor.[8] Thomas was an active royalist, and seems to have taken part in a local rebellion in Aylsham against payments to parliament in the spring of 1643. Edward had been administrating the sequestration of the rectory from 1645 by order of the Standing Committee and of the total £54, sums were listed for '8 months pay for Sir Thomas Fairfax', 'towards the Reducing of Newarke', 'the Brittish Army at Newport Pagnell', '8 months pay for the Scots army', 'for the Eastern Association & Brittish Army' as well normal parish affairs (4s 6d for the overseers of the poor). Thomas had held a post as usher at Holt School since his expulsion in 1643 and his wife received a fifth part of the rectory income.

Unless, even then, he knew Col Jermy's strength of feeling against Cooper, Potts would not have believed that, on Christmas Day 1650, Thomas Cooper, cleric of Little Barningham, would be sentenced to death at Norwich.[9] His offence was that he had joined the royalist branch of the Hobart family (of Holt) in November 1650 in an affray in Norwich in which, although no blood was spilt, the unrest and the sheer numbers forced the authorities to call in troops that had been raised in expectation of trouble.[10] The mob broke up and fled. Parliament decided an example must be made. Despite his petition for a six week respite for 'his poore wife and four small children', Thomas was part of a show trial where 'three judges were sent down to Norwich by the Parliament'. No local justices would have convicted and sentenced the artisans and tradesmen so severely for such a minor uprising, although this was only two and a half years on from 'the great Blowe' in which over 40 people died as a result of a mob protest, for which 8 had been executed on 2nd January 1649. Indeed the Court of Mayoralty later entered a note referring to 1650 'that it may appear to posterity they were not executed legally, nor for any notorious crimes'.[11] The judges 'sat at the New Hall as a High Court of Justice on Friday Dec 20 in great pomp with the sword, mace etc; on Saturday they condemned six who were executed on Monday, on Tuesday six more, on Wednesday being Christmas day they passed sentence on one Mr Cooper minister at Holt who was hanged there', 'before his own school door'.[12] William Hobart turned evidence against Cooper but that did not save him. The next day Hobart was condemned and executed at Dereham and his body buried at Holt on 4th January 1651.[13] Colonel Jermy was lampooned in a contemporary song: 'To sacrifice to his Fears and his Pride, He cause'd a Church-Champion to be murder'd and try'd'.[14] Potts and his moderate friends could not have restrained the zeal of Jermy and the Army. John remained friendly with Thomas's brother Edward, as is seen by a letter from John Potts to 'my loving friend Capt Edward Cooper theer at Edgefield' 23rd April 1654:

> Capteine Cooper
>
> My sons boy brought me word that you would be heer about one of the clock but in regard that my self shall not be then at home I have purposely sent this messenger praying you do defer the time until evening about 7 or else tomorrow what hour you will, for this day I am riding out upon appointment and shall not return til evening.
>
> I remain your loving friend
>
> J. Potts[15]

This letter also shows that Sir John still occasionally stayed at Mannington although by now he was living elsewhere. His last daughter, Ursula, his only daughter by his second wife, had married late but well. Some time after her mother's death, probably around 1649, Ursula married Philip Bedingfield of Ditchingham the son of Philip Bedingfield (whose father descended from the Oxborough family) and Anne Bacon. As one of the Bacon girls (either Anne or her sister Jane) had once been proposed as Sir John's wife perhaps he felt some connection should be honoured.[16] Philip junior was also the nephew of Anthony Bedingfield MP, his colleague in the Long Parliament. Ursula Potts may have brought stronger genes to the Bedingfield/Bacon family, as her husband was to be the only one of Anne's eight sons to leave descendants. Poor Anne had had 13 children in all.

Middlesex life

Whether he still deeply felt the loss of his wife Ursula, or whether he was restless, having no role to play in Norfolk affairs, Sir John only remained at Mannington with his son John, Susan his wife and their three children for a couple of years. During this time he got to know his grandson, who had been born around 1643 and had grown up while John was mostly in London. Now about eight, Roger and his grandfather spent time together for the first time and a bond formed between them. When in 1652, Sir John's brother Charles died, John found he was needed again. Charles, as we shall see later, left his estate in Essex, Middlesex and London, in need of active management, so John decided to move to Enfield, in Middlesex, which was conveniently close to the Essex border and to London, but far enough outside it to be able to retain a low profile.[17] Enfield at this time was a very fashionable, well-heeled place, popular with parliamentarian and senior trade families; John would have been made very welcome by old friends from the Commons. Sir Thomas Trevor, who had been made a baronet the same year as Sir John and had also been secluded from the House in the Purge, had his seat at Enfield Green. He was the son of Sir Thomas Trevor, the judge who had helped John with the local William Newman case a few years before. He had owned the old royal manor house of Enfield and Thomas junior may have lived there.[18] He was also auditor of the Duchy of Lancaster. Trevor, who died in 1676, was part of a lively intellectual set which included Thomas Fuller the church historian (whose widow died there).

The parish was also known for its presbyterian leanings: the eminent presbyterian divine, Edmund Calamy was to die at his house there in 1666. Calamy had been in the Westminster Assembly of Divines while Potts had worked with them and John would have often heard him preach in London. Trevor as we shall see was a friend who became involved in John's attempt to help his brother's family. The location of the house where John resided, presumably rented, is unknown. He had left all his household belongings for his son to use at Mannington. He may well have chosen to live in the centre of the town, near the church although there were a number of large houses including lodges in the Chase. Potts soon realised there was an excellent school at Enfield under the headship of William Holmes and decided to take over the education of his grandson Roger, the only son of John and therefore the heir to Mannington. He seems to have enjoyed a relationship with Roger that he never had with John, who may have been a disappointment to him. He brought Roger down to live with him and paid for his maintenance and education at the school and subsequently through Caius College, Cambridge and the inns of court.[19] He gave him an 'exhibition' of £100 a year as long as he accounted for his expenditure to Sir John. He also paid for Roger to be admitted to a chamber in Inner Temple, where Roger later lived. From other evidence, it seems that Roger may never have spent any further significant time at Mannington (see Chapter 20).[20]

Tomes's booklet on Mannington contains a curious reference to Sir John's supposed engagement to be married in 1654 to a widow of Enfield.[21] The source of this statement has not been found, suggesting it may have been an observation made by Rye or another antiquarian friend. Tomes knew nothing of Potts's living in Enfield so one explanation may be that he had found evidence of banns being read. Did he or Rye have sight of the now-lost Mannington parish register which may have survived at least until 1845 and which might have had a marginal entry relating to the banns?[22] The widow, Mary Hanger, did exist and was living in Enfield. Her late husband, George Hanger, merchant of St Dunstan in the East in London, made his will in July 1647 and it was proved in May 1649.[23] He asked to be buried either there or in Enfield's parish church, wherever he died. His wife Mary was sole executrix and received the main part of the estate, apart from his hoped-for lands in Ireland:

> Whereas I did venture upon the proposition for Ireland £200
> jointly with my son in law, George Buller esq deceased, late
> husband of my daughter Mary, who adventured £400 ... but all
> £600 was entered in his name with no mention of my £200 ... my
> £200 to Mary my daughter

George Buller was probably the MP for Saltash in Cornwall in the Long Parliament and like Sir John, he would have 'invested' in the Irish adventure, probably in 1643 when he married Mary Hanger. He persuaded his father-in-law to put in £200. Buller had died in 1646. As to Hanger himself, there is very little to go on. A single chancery action survives from 1657-59 involving a George Hanger merchant, who may be George's son.[24] Relating to trade matters dating back to 1642, it shows George Hanger was then living and working as a merchant dealing in cloth in Smyrna. This shows once again how widely the merchant traders travelled.

The mystery of John and Mary remains unsolved. As far as we can tell the marriage never went ahead - there is no record of it in the Enfield register, nor of Mary marrying another or being buried around that time.[25] Maybe they had a cooling-off period. All the evidence suggests Sir John remained a widower until his death.

Everything points to John spending about 10 years in Enfield, certainly until 1661 when Roger finished school and maybe even later. He did not have a local role at first (and was never a justice for Middlesex) but towards the end of his stay (1660-1661) he was a Middlesex county assessor for taxes. The last sighting of him there is as a commissioner on the well-known enquiry into matters on Enfield Chase, in which Trevor, as auditor, was also involved.[26] This large expanse of common and woodland had been heavily used in the Civil War to quarter soldiers, who remained there even after the Restoration. Much timber had also been felled and by 1660 there was a considerable quantity cut but still lying on the Chase. On 4th June 1660 parliament made two orders to halt the cutting of wood and lopping of trees and to stop any cut wood being taken away, since these activities were against the custom of this royal manor.[27] Six local landowners were appointed to look into the matter and put the orders into effect. With Sir John Potts were Sir Thomas Dacres, Sir Henry Wroth, Nicholas Rainton, John Huxley and John Wilford of Hadley.

John had worked closely in the Commons with Sir Thomas Dacres, MP for Hertfordshire (also unseated in Pride's Purge) who lived in Cheshunt, bordering on the north of Enfield. Of the six appointed, Wilford was to be the most active, but this assiduousness brought him into conflict with the soldiers still quartered there and by the mid-1660s this dispute was taken to arbitration. Unfortunately the surviving Duchy of Lancaster materials relating to Enfield manor and Chase do not give any further information on Sir John's role in local affairs.[28]

However Sir John's life, much as he would have enjoyed it, did not revolve around Enfield and Roger. He was now to embark on the most litigious period of his life; he would spend much of the next twenty years defending himself from law suits, about property and increasingly debts. Most galling of all were the ones which involved family that he dutifully tried to help. Rarely was he the plaintiff and indeed in many cases he seemed to seek arbitration and settlement out of court rather than suffer the costs and antagonism of sustained court action. This would be very much in character for such a conciliatory man. But when he thought the other side was being unreasonable or untruthful, he fought doggedly in court.

Apart from Mannington which he had built up in earlier years John had acquired lands as an 'adventurer', investing in parliamentarian land ventures. The Irish loan of 1642 resulted in an allotment of land in 1653 which he immediately assigned to his son Charles (see Chapter 17). His other venture was to lead to major disputes after the Restoration. This was the huge fen drainage scheme known as the Bedford Level.

The Fenlands

Two chancery actions show rather briefly that Sir John Potts and his son John Potts esq had an involvement with the Bedford Level drainage scheme in the 1650s and 1660s.[29] Subsequent research has found that the two Johns were in fact 'adventurers' or investors in the scheme at some point by 1653.[30] John Potts the son will be described as John Potts esq from here on to distinguish him.

The great fen area on the western fringes of Norfolk and westwards into Cambridgeshire was no distance from Narborough, home of Ursula's Spelman sons. Ursula herself had grown up in Hilgay a large parish half of which was fenland. The two manors, Woodhall and Modney Priory, both owned by her family, were surrounded by the low lying fens, drains and rivers. Southery lies to the south. Major drainage of summer lands had begun in 1634 with investors under the leadership of Francis Earl of Bedford and with the expertise of Cornelius Vermuyden. The Crown received an allocation of land as part of the means for getting parliamentary approval to proceed. Their first scheme was completed in 1637, but subsequently deemed to have been inadequate as not providing year-round drainage. During the Civil War the fens were allowed once more to flood fully as part of the defence of East Anglia against possible royalist invasion.

In 1649 interest in a more substantial drainage scheme was resuscitated and eventually won Cromwell's support. An act of parliament of 1649 enabled William Earl of Bedford and in due course Sir Cornelius Vermuyden to lead the charge. A group of investors, the new 'adventurers', became involved and were granted rights to part of the acreage that would be reclaimed. Work was somewhat slow to start and all plans and finished works had to be scrutinised by a panel of commissioners to ensure proper regulation and respect for local interests in the local lands and waterways. At an early stage the Earl of Arundel and a few other adventurers sold out their interest and the original group of thirteen investors blossomed to thirty or more by the early 1650s. It seems that Sir John Potts, not in the original thirteen, bought a modest stake in the venture in about 1651 or 1652 as one of these secondary investors. Potts had known the 4th Earl of Bedford and his son Francis before their deaths in 1641 and no doubt was known to William, the present Earl.

The company minutes for 3rd February 1653 listed Sir John among a group of adventurers charged with the preparations for a major meeting with the adjudicators regarding plans for works to the south of the Bedford River. During February and March John attended another four meetings, as the group prepared for the big meeting in Ely on 24th March.[31] The minutes showed that Sir John was no passive investor but was playing an active part in this, successful, attempt to get permission to proceed on major works. No doubt he was valued for his local knowledge and contacts, and of course he knew many of the other commissioners, including Sir Gilbert Gerard, member for Middlesex until the Purge. With Cromwell taking an active interest in the Bedford Level, this indicates that Sir John had not fallen fully from favour with Cromwell, despite having been purged from parliament. If he had, it is unlikely he would have been chosen for this leading role at such a sensitive time.

The attendance records also showed that Samuel Smith esq was an adventurer. Smith was Samuel senior, of Colkirk, who earlier had been recorder of Norwich and was married to Potts's niece, Urith Palgrave. Smith's involvement was relevant for what followed in chancery. John Potts esq was also listed, in his own right, alongside his father. John was present without his father at a couple of meetings, showing that he too played some active role in the adventurers' activities. However later meeting notes and membership lists carried no sign of either Potts.

In 1660 Charles II took an interest in the drainage works and reclaimed the Crown's original acreage, appointing by act of parliament new commissioners to manage the Level and its works. At this time Sir John Hewitt became one of the two bailiffs actively controlling fenland affairs. By May 1662 the Commissioners for Sewers for the Fens, among a long list of members, included Thomas Lord Culpepper, Samuel Smith and John Spelman esq. Sir John Hewitt, Lord Culpepper and others made successful claims under the allocations of the original participants who had been 'disseised' in 1649. As a direct result various adventurers lost their land allocations.

It is likely that Sir John Potts had foreseen the risk of this happening. For this reason and possibly also to pay for arrears of taxes he, his stepson John Spelman and son John Potts had sold their allocation of drained fenland to Samuel Smith esq senior. Sir John commented at one point that, as a lawyer, Smith had known the risk of repossession and that the two of them had included a compensation clause in their arrangements for just that eventuality.

What more can be learnt from the chancery actions? One piece of information arises from a separate action from within his wife's family.[32] In April 1658 Sir John Wray of Glentworth Lincolnshire brought an action against a huge cast of defendants who included several local subtenants as well as a rare grouping of Ursula's four surviving sons Charles Potts, John Potts, John Spelman and his younger brother, Clement.[33] Why was he interested in the lands in and near Hilgay and Southery? Wray had become the second husband of Elizabeth Willoughby, the niece of Potts's wife Ursula, in the early 1650s. He claimed that he and his wife (named at the time from her previous marriage as Dame Elizabeth D'Ewes, widow of Sir Simonds D'Ewes) had had the manor of Woodhall in Hilgay and lands in Southery settled on them at marriage by Elizabeth's father, Sir Henry Willoughby. Most, if not all, of this was old manorial land, not new creation from drained fens. Elizabeth had died around 1656 and now he was pursuing rent due to him; he also sought discovery of certain documents from the Spelmans and Potts.

It seems however that the Spelmans had a prior claim on the land, from an indenture of 1649 between Willoughby and Clement Spelman (then of Middle Temple). The deed had created a lease of the premises for 21 years from Lady Day 1651. Spelman did not dispute Wray's ultimate tenure and had been paying rent to him, but claimed his long lease of the premises predated the Wray marriage settlement. By the lease, extensively recited, Clement was allowed to sublet to his brother, which he had done. In turn, John Potts esq, their half-brother, had for a short period also become a subtenant of part of the premises. It seems that the two Johns were actively ditching, draining and improving properties in the area for letting to under-tenants. Wray claimed he had paid another tenant Hannah Sampson, for the surrender of her lease which she had had from Sir Henry Willoughby. The process continued through 1659, with Wray and Clement Spelman being the main protagonists. By 1660, George Purefoy esq had joined Wray as plaintiff; Clement Spelman was losing the case. No further orders appear in the ensuing few years and it seems that Spelman lost his claim to the premises. The action (really just a Wray/Spelman family squabble) is of little further direct interest, except that John Potts esq said that he had sold his interest in the lease to two named men and that the only interest he now had in lands in the Hilgay area was in lands leased to him by Samuel Smith, who had 'purchased them of the adventurers'.

This leads into the second chancery action. A chancery order of Easter term 1669 showed that Samuel Smith junior was suing John Potts esq for ten years' worth of rent arrears that Smith claimed was due from his father's lifetime.[34] In response, John Potts esq complained against Samuel Smith in an action over the lands in Hilgay and Southery that Samuel Smith senior had bought from Sir John Potts.[35] Smith senior had died in February 1664.

The story had begun in September 1653 when Sir John Potts and his stepson John Spelman had sold 360 acres of fenland in Hilgay and Southery including two plots, one of 142 acres and the other of 76 acres (known as Abbotts Fen) to Samuel Smith senior, who had leased back just the last two parcels to John Potts esq for 17 years. Smith now said the property had been purchased by Samuel Smith senior from Potts for the sum of £80 a year and that by agreement Potts was to have taken out a 21 year lease of the lands at the same amount. This rent Smith junior now, in 1669, claimed was in arrears. Potts argued that no allowance was made for reasonable repairs and other deductions. He would come to account if these were allowed. It was noted that Potts had long since been evicted from the premises. The case had been tried at common law where Smith had won a judgement that Potts should pay him £220 of rent arrears. Chancery now ordered Potts to bring this into chancery within several days and only then could he present his evidence against Smith.

Next term James Scamler, as Potts's counsel, came to court to argue that Smith had not revealed the fact that his father had agreed a £20 a year rent rebate on the premises, which he should have revealed in his answer to Potts's bill. The implication was that this had not come to light in the common law action and that the award of £220 had been calculated at the full level of £80 annual rent. Chancery ordered the £220 to be brought into court but allowed Potts to proceed with his action once this was done. That autumn the case reappeared when John Potts esq was given permission to add to his case a new deposition from his father whose testimony had thus far been excluded.[36] This was allowed as long as the two of them went on oath that the contents of the first set of depositions from other witnesses had not been revealed to Sir John or anyone else.

The surviving interrogatories and depositions from October 1669 clarify why the rents had dried up. The annual rent of £80 had been paid up to Michaelmas 1660. That year the King had passed the new act of parliament and subsequently the 218 acres had been seized under its terms. In 1662 Lord Culpepper had claimed and entered into the parcel of 142 acres and Sir John Hewitt entered the 76 acres - specifically on the basis of original 1630s allocations to Francis Earl of Bedford as described above. They had threatened to sue John Potts esq for all the rent on the land due since the act of parliament, presumably therefore from 1660 to February 1663 until when the rent had been paid to Potts (and possibly onwards to Smith). Apparently at some time at or after Lady Day 1663 John Potts, as Smith's tenant, had tried to get his latest instalment of rent paid at Mannington by his under-tenants Robert Sayer and one Woodward. They refused to pay as they were now paying rent to Culpepper and Hewitt and could not risk paying twice. The Potts and Smith families were out of pocket for large amounts of rent and were claiming what they could from each other in the aftermath.

From the construction of John Potts's interrogatories he needed to have his father's testimony allowed so that the two of them together could show that Sir John had involved his son as a trustee and that Sir John Potts and Samuel Smith senior had a very clear understanding between them of the risks they ran in their Bedford Level transactions. Since both were adventurers in March 1653 that would seem to be true. If so, Potts argued it was unfair of Smith junior to claim rent from him when he had been unable to secure it from his under-tenants since the premises had been seized. So the issue was all about compensation for the seizure losses and who had paid what rent to whom from 1660 onwards, with several hundred pounds at stake. Potts argued that Samuel Smith senior had well understood the risk to himself as well as to Potts when he included the eviction clause in the purchase deeds. By implication therefore Samuel junior had to bear some of the pain of the eviction. Samuel senior had also allowed Potts a £20 annual rebate from the rent as an incentive to stay, when in 1660 John Potts had discussed his desire to quit the tenancy. The Potts family knew earlier that there was a risk even in holding a lease of part of these lands; but by the 1660 act it was crystal clear that a big risk of seizure was imminent. John Potts's mistake was in not actually getting out of the lease if he could. Now, by inference, Samuel Smith was ignoring this agreed rebate and claiming the full £80 per year.

The papers showed that Samuel Smith junior had secured from the Potts the £180 eviction rebate, at 20s per acre, that he was due under Sir John's sale to his father of the original package of 360 acres. At least he had some protection from the seizure by Culpepper and Hewitt.

But Smith had, at the previous assizes in 1669, achieved a writ against John Potts for rent arrears, showing that he was trying also to get the rent under his original head lease. Smith had probably sued for at least the years 1663 to 1668 at £80 a year. He may even have included 1661-62, if Potts had then been in arrears, and possibly 1670 in advance. The timing of this action would have been prompted by the 17 year lease ending in 1670. In which case, his total claim might well have been as high as £800. Potts, probably not unreasonably, was now resorting to a court of equity to overthrow the assize judgement, having received no rent himself for 8 of those 10 years. Disputed liability for some years' worth of parliamentary fen taxes may have taken the claim even higher. Potts had also spent £300-400 building houses, improving the lands and planting trees. These were to the long-term benefit of the landowner after the initial 17 year lease period. However Smith's questions argued that his father had already paid Potts the agreed £80 one-off payment for his share of improvement costs and the additional spend was at Potts's risk.

The rationale behind the Potts case seems to be that Culpepper and Hewitt had received £560 for 7 years' rent directly from the under-tenants since entry. To claim 2 further years' prior to entry was unreasonable. Potts had spent extra spend on improvements and should have some share of any 1660s rent available, at least at the discounted rate of £60 a year. Smith had received the earlier rents from 1653 to 1660 (and possibly to 1662) and had only had to pay out £80 for improvements. Potts had paid fen taxes to June 1664. So Smith should not be entitled to all the 1660s rents. Potts would be the one to suffer most since he had not been able to collect any rents from 1663. Shared pain was probably quite an effective platform to take to an equity court.

The depositions taken on behalf of Potts, at the Black Boy Inn Aylsham, on 8th October 1669 were from relatively minor witnesses and, in the end, did not include Sir John Potts. Confirming testimony was given on the Potts expenditure for building costs and land improvements, including by Thomas Burton carpenter of Oulton who had done much of the building work. John Bullymer of Bradfield and William Grand of Itteringham noted the quantity of trees planted. Daniel Muddiclift of Itteringham, the Mannington steward, affirmed the original lease and other points. The precise dates of the lease came from Smith's witness Richard Jessop gent of Fakenham, who had probably been involved in its drafting. Thomas Spurgeon gent of Matlask, who acted as a 'servant' of Sir John Potts, probably as his local representative in Norfolk when he was elsewhere, confirmed various points including that rent arrears to Michaelmas 1660 had been paid that December to Samuel Smith senior. He confirmed that John Potts had paid all relevant taxes while he held the lands. Further process orders were recorded in the first part of 1670, but they do not make clear which way the case ended. Once again the action then disappeared from chancery orders, leaving the final outcome unknown. An equitable result would have been for the losses to be shared between John Potts and Samuel Smith; but it is not known if that was decreed or if any deal was negotiated. If John Potts esq lost, as he had at assizes, this episode would have been a considerable contributor to his debts and later mortgage problems when he became the second baronet in 1673.

Modney

Ursula's family lands led to other actions in which her husband and her sons were inevitably involved. Of her two brothers, Sir Henry and Francis Willoughby, Francis died without issue and Sir Henry had no sons. The family's property affairs in due course involved various chancery actions as Sir Henry's granddaughters and their husbands fought over the property. As relations and tenants the Spelmans were involved and Clement Spelman was executor of Francis Willoughby's will. For the background to her grandparents and parents holdings of lands in the Fens, and for her son Clement Spelman's problems with Ursula's niece Anne and her children, see Family Notes 15: Willoughby and Hawe.

As a child, Ursula may well have lived at Modney, a house at the old Benedictine Priory site in Hilgay, inherited by her parents from the Hawes, after John's marriage to Frances Hawes. Her brother, Sir Henry, as the male heir, inherited the Hilgay and Southery properties that had come into the Willoughby family. Various of these were leased at different times to Willoughby relations, including James Hawes, John Spelman and Sir John Potts and John Potts. By the second half of the seventeenth century some of the property was at the centre of a family feud in chancery. On 21st January 1650 Ursula's brothers Sir Henry Willoughby and Francis, both still of Risley, leased to her sons John Potts esq and John Spelman esq, a cottage or tenement called Modney Coate, by then in the occupation of widow Pratt, and the large parcel of fenland on the west side of the river.[37] The lease was for 21 years at £42 10s yearly rent, with an option to renew the lease for a second term of 21 years at £85. Provisions were included to allow drainage and improvement of the land.[38]

The family relationship was made clear in the deed of 18th October 1652.[39] Modney Coate and the fenland were conveyed by Sir Henry Willoughby to Henry Smith and William Sampson gents, both his servants, to his use for life and then to his grandchildren Magdalen and Mary Aston, the children of Sir Henry's daughter Anne, now the wife of Anchetil Grey esq.

A deed of 13th September 1655 recited the previous deeds as a preamble to Sir John Potts, John Potts esq and John Spelman esq conveying the Modney Coate and fenland property to John Francis gent of Narborough and James Muston gent of London.[40] This seems to be a straightforward outright sale, for £500, of the remaining term of the lease and of all the grain, cole seed, rape seed and hemp flax on the premises and in the ground. On the reverse is Sir John's signature receipting for the £500.[41]

The following month on 31st October 1655, Modney Coate and its fens were assigned to John Spelman for £500 paid by him to John Francis and James Muston, with his lease term still being the remainder of the 21 years from Michaelmas 1650.[42] So, Sir John and John Potts had extricated themselves from the property and John Spelman had regained it as his exclusively, effectively through a very short term mortgage arrangement to manage the conveyance. On 12th July 1659, two of Sir Henry Willoughby's sons-in-law, Sir John Wray of Glentworth Lincolnshire (second husband of Elizabeth) and George Purefoy esq the younger of Madley Berkshire (second husband of Catherine) renewed the lease of Modney Coate and its fenland to John Spelman.[43] Spelman had by now 'banked drained sluiced and made dry the fenland'. The deed now confirmed that Wray and Purefoy would lease the property to Spelman from 1671 for 21 years at £85 annual rent. Two days later, on 14th July 1659, it was agreed that for £5,300 John Spelman was to purchase from George Purefoy and his trustees the manor of Southery, albeit with certain named lands excepted which included the Modney site which Spelman already had by lease.[44] After Spelman's lease ended, on 22nd March 1671, a new lease was made by Thomas Lord Viscount Fanshaw and the Lady Sarah, guardians of Elizabeth Wray the daughter and heir of John Wray late of Glentworth.[45] (Sarah had been the second wife of Sir John Wray). The property leased for 11 years to James Theodoricke of Norwich was: Modney Coate cottage and its six acres; the fen grounds late of Sir Henry Willoughby deceased; another 300 acres of fen grounds also on the west of the Ouse called the Lords Piece (abutting Lord Culpepper and Arthur Towers's adventure lands); and 25 acres also west of the Ouse in the occupation of Clement Spelman, being part of Hilgay Common assigned to Modney Coate when the Common was enclosed. From the description it is not clear how much of the original fenland was included. The lease was at just £28 a year rent which seems to imply a considerable reduction in acreage. Perhaps the Willoughby fenland also suffered the incursions by Culpepper and others that had afflicted the Potts family in their fenland adventure.

And the Modney Priory site? In 1681 Nicholas Saunderson and his wife Dame Elizabeth (née Elizabeth Wray) sued her step-cousin, Mary Aston spinster, in a chancery action.[46] It seems that Mary Aston (Sir Henry Willoughby's granddaughter) had her title to the lands approved at Norwich assizes in 1681, against the complaint of George Saunderson Viscount Castleton. George's son Nicholas pursued the case in chancery. The surviving depositions show that this action concerned the scite of Modney Priory and 1,000 acres of lands and fenlands thereabouts known as Helgay Severals held from the manor of Woodhall in Hilgay. The priory lands and the severals had been let separately, the latter to John Potts esq. Sir John Wray had become owner through his marriage to Sir Henry Willoughby's daughter, Elizabeth. Sir Henry had died about 1654 and his daughter the following year, leaving Sir John in possession. Sir John Wray died in 1664 and Elizabeth the complainant was his sole daughter and heir. The details of Sarah her mother's two subsequent marriages were also given. William Graver yeoman (who had been John Spelman's servant at Modney Hall for some ten years) testified that before John Spelman took on the severals they were valueless and covered with water until he drained and improved them. He had witnessed the September 1655 indenture signed by John Potts and John Spelman and the October 1655 indenture signed by John Francis and James Muston. Clement had died about four years before (he died in 1680), some sixteen years after his brother John Spelman (died 1663).

However, the fenland disputes were nothing compared to the problems Sir John found when he took on his late brother Charles's estate.

Chapter 15

Where There's a Will There's a Way

Charles Potts (1593-1652) the lawyer brother of Sir John Potts senior lived in London and Essex and held the London Potts properties; he married Susan Wright who later married the wastrel Francis Drake; Charles's daughter the feckless Anne Potts and her husband William Villiers led her uncle Sir John a merry dance in the courts.

To understand the domestic difficulties Sir John faced in the 1650s and 1660s it is necessary to take a closer look at the life of his brother Charles. Baptised in Itteringham in July 1593, a year after John, Charles grew up under the wing of Sir Christopher Heydon when his mother remarried. All credit for his education as a lawyer must go to Sir Christopher. Charles became a practising lawyer of Middle Temple where he was admitted on 18th May 1614. He was called to the bar on 23rd November 1621 and became a Bencher on 31st October 1645. When he died in 1652 he was buried in the Temple Church.

Charles lived in and around London all his life and it may be through him that the family's arms were later taken up by another branch of the family. The Visitation of Cheshire of 1613 showed that the Potts family there did not at that time bear arms. Edmund Pott, who had left Pott Shrigley in Cheshire and dropped the final 's' from the name, was a haberdasher of London.[2] Did he and Charles meet? Edmund, rather than the Potts who stayed in Cheshire, seems to have been first to identify a family linkage to the Potts of Mannington line, as shown by his adoption of their arms, with small additions for difference, in the London Visitations of 1633-35. The same arms were shown in the 1663 Cheshire Visitation for Edmund as head of the Pott Shrigley family.[1] Edmund senior was certainly a contemporary of Charles Potts. Was Edmund's son Charles named for Charles the lawyer? Charles, son of Edmund Pott the haberdasher, was baptised on 26th November 1637 at St Lawrence Jewry. He was buried on 23rd October 1639. The parish register, Edmund's will and later deeds listing family members show no further use of the name Charles by this family.

Charles Potts the lawyer

Various documents and court actions show Charles Potts busy and successful as a lawyer and he acted for the family in several Norfolk property transactions and mortgages. By a strange coincidence, Charles Potts provided a mortgage on what seems to have been earlier the Dodge family house and lands in Wrotham Kent in August 1640.[3] At that time he had lent £2,000 (at a yearly 'rent' of £200) to Sir John Howell of Wrotham on the security of the capital messuage of Comp and other lands in Wrotham and Leybourne - previously the Dodge estate. The estate was fully described with tenants' names in a later court action.[4]

Potts paid out the loan by instalments over the first year, the details of which later emerged from a dispute over whether the last instalment of £200 had been paid before Sir John Howell died in August 1641. The issue re-emerged in 1661 when Sir John Potts was sued by a younger member of the Howell family on much the same grounds.[5] Disputed bonds and receipts were at the heart of the actions, which are of interest more from the Dodge coincidence and the ability of Charles to make a loan of £2,000 than for the issue itself.

As seen in Chapter 10, Charles was involved as a lawyer in a trustee role for the family but there is no evidence that Charles had any material property of his own or a house in Norfolk. His Norfolk connections were however no doubt at the heart of his legal practice. On 10th May 1627 he wrote from Middle Temple to Sir Roger Townshend at his house in Barbican to tell him that he had finished work on the 'book for the joynture' (presumably for one of his five daughters) and that Townshend and Mr Calthorpe could look at it the next day if they wished.[6] In 1635 Sir Thomas Wodehouse was granted a licence to alienate the manor and advowson of Hingham to Charles Potts.[7] Since the Wodehouses continued to have the presentation there after 1635, he appears to have been acting as trustee.

Charles Potts esq married Susannah (usually given as Susan), the eldest of five daughters of the affluent London merchant, alderman and furrier Nathan Wright, and his wife Anne Fleming of Warley Place, Great Warley, on 9th April 1646 'at Mary White Chapel' St Olave, Hart St London. Through her he came into the Wright family lands in Essex and subsequently they split their time between London and Essex. Five years later, in 1651, Charles was made a justice of the peace for Essex.[8] Their only son Charles was baptised on 3rd October 1649 in St Bride, Fleet St, but was only three weeks old when buried at St Olave, Hart St 'brought from Fleet St Chancel', on 24th October.

Two daughters, Frances and Anne, survived childbirth, but Frances died when just a few years old. Anne, baptised on 7th September 1648 at St Olave, was to become Charles's heir.

After his death Susan, left with two very young daughters, married a friend of theirs, Francis Drake and so the family became embroiled with a man renowned for his indebtedness. Nothing but trouble followed for the rest of the Potts family!

What is known of Francis Drake and his background? Although not related, the famous Elizabethan Sir Francis was godfather to Francis Drake of Esher, Surrey. His son, Francis Drake junior of Walton-on-Thames Surrey, married Susan Wright/Potts as his third wife.[9] Francis senior was MP for Amersham in 1625 and died in 1633. His PCC will showed him as Francis Drake esq and Gentleman of the Privy Chamber to King James. He was buried in Walton leaving two surviving sons, William and Francis.[10]

Sir William, his eldest son, was born in 1606, educated at Amersham and went to Christ Church College Oxford, Middle Temple and Gray's Inn. At Middle Temple he may well have known Charles Potts, twelve years or so his senior. In 1633 he inherited his father's estate in Esher but sold it by 1637 and used the proceeds to consolidate his estate near Amersham with the acquisition of Amersham manor for

£7,500 from the Earl of Bedford. He was MP for Amersham in 1640 and knighted and made Baronet in 1641 - a precisely parallel track to Sir John Potts whom he knew in the Long Parliament. Between 1643 and 1660 he spent much time abroad, particularly in Italy. In 1661 he was again an MP. He died unmarried in 1669.[11]

Francis Drake, the younger son, was to prove a disastrous match for Susan. After reducing her to a life of debt, he vanished from the scene after her death in July 1664 leaving her young unmarried daughter to be cared for by her mother's family. Documents show him alive and of Walton in 1672 and 1674, but little else is known about him. His brother's will made in 1667 left a bequest of £100 to be paid quarterly for life but only if 'he does not seek to disturb my will'.[12] The will is interesting also for his desire to see Francis's eldest son Francis 'forget all the miscarriages and undutifulness towards me ... of his father'. Francis had created mayhem with all about him.

Sir John Potts and Francis Drake

Sufficient details of Francis Drake's indebtedness have survived to piece together a reasonable assessment of the scale of his problems. Sir John was involved in Susan and Francis Drake's financial affairs from July 1655 at their request. This would seem to have been agreed to formally in a deed of 16th July which presumably gave him power of attorney and which was later referred to in chancery.[13] The chancery actions from 1666 onwards, which are detailed below, repeatedly said that Susan Drake and her daughter Anne were imprisoned in the Fleet for a debt of either £2,000 or £2,500. Sir John Potts secured their release.

In 1658 Drake used his Walton-on-Thames manor as security on a loan of £1,200 from Sir Thomas Trevor of Enfield and Arthur Trevor of Middle Temple.[14] The deed stated, without giving a name, that others were involved on Francis Drake's side. Sir Thomas Trevor was a friend of Sir John Potts at Enfield and he and Sir John were jointly bound with Drake in a penal bond of £2,400 in the event of non-repayment of the debt. The date fits firmly in the period when Sir John was deeply involved in trying to sort out Drake's affairs. Again a later reference to a deed between Drake and Sir John of 20th May 1658 was probably related to resolution of some of Drake's debts. It may have linked to this secured loan or perhaps to the debts Sir John paid directly in return for up to £1,000 worth of jewels and other goods of Drake's.

In his complaint of December 1660 against Sir Ralph Bovey and John Fountaine, Sir John Potts recounted that in May 1656 at Francis Drake's request he had jointly with Drake and Bovey become bound in an obligation to pay interest on Francis's debt of £1,000 to John Fountaine or incur a penalty of £2,000.[15] Potts did not enjoy any benefit of the £1,000 and did not know whether it had been repaid. But Francis Drake had since fallen into decay and was at this time a prisoner in the Fleet prison and not able to make any payment. Apparently Fountaine, a serjeant at law, in Hilary term 1659, had issued a warrant of attorney to pursue Potts for payment of his £1,000, which he said was part of his daughter Ellinor's portion. Fountaine was also pursuing Bovey. In Easter term Fountaine had achieved a judgement against

Bovey and Potts, which, now later in 1660, he had revived on Bovey becoming a knight and baronet. Potts said he had often promised to Fountaine that he would pay half the £1,000 and his share of the interest as long as Sir Ralph, who was very able to, paid his half. However, despite Fountaine trying to persuade him, Bovey had refused to pay his share. Fountaine also said that he would 'extend' Bovey's house and goods where he lived in St Giles in the Fields. Fountaine briefed Mr Gervis Elwes to deal with the Middlesex sheriff to secure £600 from Bovey. But instead Bovey paid the Fountaines, father and daughter, the full £1,000 and in exchange now held the original bond and was trying to get Potts to pay the whole £1,000. Potts could not prove all his conversations with the various parties but hoped that Bovey would confess and that the Fountaines would accept £500 and the matter would be ended.

The Fountaines answered that Drake, Potts and Bovey were equally bound to pay interest of £30 per half year on the bond started in December 1655 (consistent with first interest due in May 1656). Interest had been paid for some time, but seeing Drake in prison Fountaine had called the principal in. Fountaine agreed to Potts's request to be patient since he would be paymaster and ensure interest and principal would be paid. Initially Potts paid the interest but in December 1659 with interest unpaid (presumably for that half year) and Potts and Bovey at issue with each other, Fountaine put the matter into court in 'Hilary 1659' ie the beginning of 1660. He suggested that Potts pay the whole sum and pursue Bovey for half. Potts refused, but said he was happy to pay his half. Obviously the same offer was made to Bovey, who under pressure of the extent on his Warwickshire and London property paid £1,000 and took over the bond. Bovey, in his answer of January 1661, said that in 1659 he had sued Drake regarding the bond. Potts had told Bovey that Drake had or would convey to Potts and one John Wolfris (sometimes Wilfrids and Wolfreys) merchant, the manor of Walton Leigh and other properties in Surrey. Later this deed was cited in chancery as being of 11th January 1659 between Drake and Sir John with John Wolfris merchant of the City of London.[16] Wolfris was the husband of Susan's sister Alice. Other sums of money amounting to £5,000 had been bequeathed by Nathan Wright to Drake's wife and these would be used in trust to pay Francis Drake's debts. Drake's debts were listed in a schedule and this particular one was included. Bovey said he thought Potts was going to deal with the whole matter and he denied making any deal with Fountaine to discharge the judgement against him. He had had none of the £1,000 for his own use.

In 1664 Sir John was pursued a second time in court over matters relating to Francis Drake.[17] William Dalben of Inner Temple and William Gardiner of Bernard's Inn took action as administrators of Nicholas Nicholls gent of London who had died intestate. Sir John owed £1,100 principal money on a bond. In Easter term 1663 judgement in the King's Bench had been given against him for £1,400. Since then Dalben had died and the money had not been paid. Gardiner claimed that the Potts family had made a number of secret deeds relating to the substantial family estates and were trying to use this family settlement to argue against payment. Gardiner argued that, whatever the settlement details were, this money had been to

Potts's use and the £1,400 should be paid. This action has given us a good snapshot of the Mannington estate and its major tenants in or about 1659, crucial since the family settlement documents themselves have not survived and are only hinted at in later Potts chancery actions.[18]

Sir John answered that he had not dealt with Nicholls, but had only become bound jointly to him at the request of Francis Drake. The bond was for £700 principal not £1,100. He suspected some underhand dealing between Drake and Nicholls and that the bond was designed to entrap him. It was particularly suspicious that, even though Drake defaulted in Nicholls's lifetime, he had not pursued Potts for the principal until Drake was in prison and being besieged by others.

Dalben and Gardiner had then pursued Potts aggressively for the money, which he did not have since he had only a modest personal estate after the settlement of most of his property on his son John at his first marriage some 25 years earlier. Sir John Potts had a great debt of his own, from his time in parliament to 1648, that preceded the Nicholls bond and was still unpaid. This had built up from taxes, neglect of his estate while in parliament, bad tenants and having to make substantial provisions for his children. So in 1659 a large part of his residual estate was handed over to cover this debt of some £2,700, for which his son John became bound and much of which was still unsatisfied. Most of Sir John's annual income was thus set aside to pay the interest and principal of this debt.

In November 1662, still struggling to pay off the remaining £2,200 debt at a fast enough rate, he had wanted to save his son from this debt and had entered into a mortgage on the Mannington estate together with John Potts esq, Clement Spelman, James Fountaine of Salle and James Scamler of Middle Temple. This was to run for 8 years and mortgaged Mannington Hall and certain named farms within the estate. The rental from the lands was in trust to pay the debts of £2,200 which were detailed in a schedule attached to the mortgage (this has not survived and was not included in the chancery papers). Sir John hoped and expected that at the end of the 8 years the debts would have been paid off. As a result of this arrangement he had no spare funds to pay any other debts.

At the enquiry at Mannington in December 1664, John Potts essentially repeated his father's answer. At an earlier hearing in June, Roger Potts had denied detailed knowledge of the Nicholls debt, but added some nice extra detail. He had been young when Nicholls died, since he was now not much over 21 years of age. But he did remember about four or five years previously being sent by his grandfather with one Phineas Taylor (worthy of use by Dickens in his trawling of old chancery documents in search of names!) to Fleet Street to pay money to Mr Nicholls. He had heard that it was for a debt of Francis Drake. He had not bothered to know about the rental details of the Mannington estate as a whole, since it would only descend to him after the death of both his grandfather and father.

But Gardiner, 'disgracefully', would not accept this and had had Sir John arrested twice. He had offered to pay his half of the bond and if they had pursued Drake for the other half they would have been likely to recover a good part of his half. But they refused to do this. Now Potts was no longer in a position to find the money for even half the bond. Sir John then went on to deny he owned various parts of the Mannington estate which had been transferred to his son and second wife. He denied he had other property near Lynn or in Clippesby (again already transferred to John and Roger) except a rent of £100 from Repps with Bastwick, which could not be counted as a result of the recent sea breaches.

Francis Drake had been a terrible drain on Sir John, both financially and personally. Sucked into paying off some of his debts, he had become jointly bound with him in others. He had managed to find a large sum of money to release Susan and Anne from the Fleet and would seem to have had only partial recompense for his expense. He had only received £1,085 from his brother's personal estate. Some of the bonds continued to haunt him in court actions as an old man. The £20 left to Sir John in 1669 by his old MP colleague Sir William Drake, who seemed conspicuously detached from his brother Francis's troubles, can have done little to help.

Sir John Potts and his nieces

While all this had been going on Sir John had also had trouble with William Crowe gent of East Bilney, married to his stepsister Martha, daughter of Sir Christopher Heydon and Sir John's mother Anne.[19] When in November 1632 Martha and William married, John Potts had been involved in their marriage settlement. £350 had been paid to Crowe and he was required within seven years to acquire property worth £60 a year to settle on Martha for life as her jointure. It would then pass to their heirs. Crowe was bound by an obligation with a £1,000 penalty to perform the articles. By November 1661, Crowe was a widower (Martha had died in 1648) and Potts believed that he had not fully carried out the settlement requirement and that Crowe's son and daughter would suffer as a result. Following procrastination by Crowe, he went to common law calling for the penalty. Crowe responded with the chancery action, in which he said he had already paid his daughter £400 towards her portion and would sort out the rest if only Sir John would release to him the articles. But he said Sir John had taken some displeasure against him. This was clearly a result of a parallel issue over monies owed to Sir John on behalf of his niece Anne, daughter of Charles Potts.

Sir John's brother Charles, sometime before 1652, had acquired a parcel of ex-crown fee farm rents and tithes in Norfolk and had appointed Crowe as receiver of the rents on his behalf. Crowe's lease as farmer had been renewed in 1652 despite Charles having found him a slow payer. The lease was for eleven years, but would become void if the crown recovered the fee farm which of course happened at the Restoration. Crowe claimed that by late 1659 he was up to date with payments and had expected to hear nothing more about it after the Restoration. Sir John said that after Charles's death, he and others had been responsible for collecting these rents from Crowe on behalf of Charles's daughter Anne to whom they had been left by Charles. At one point Crowe had come to Sir John's house at Enfield and he had agreed that arrears totalled about £100. Of this, £70 had been paid to Sir John, but about £30 plus interest remained overdue. Sir John by 1661 was determined to recover the final £40 through mediation by a lawyer, but Crowe had refused and so Sir John had taken the matter to the King's Bench. But this was a minor issue compared to other aspects of Anne's inheritance.

Charles's daughter Anne was to become a continuing thorn in the side of the Potts family. After her father's death in 1652 she was looked after by her mother Susan and no doubt lived with her and Francis Drake after their marriage. But Susan had died on 15th July 1664 when Anne was still a young girl. 'Susannah' Wright/Potts/ Drake was buried in 1664 in Cranham church Essex where there is a memorial inscription for her and her father Nathan Wright who had died in 1658.[20] After Susan's death, Anne went to live with her aunt, Susan's sister Frances, who was married to Edward Hudson esq. In May 1666 on Anne's behalf (she was still under age at 18) they started what was to become a ten year or so run of chancery actions about Sir John's management of Anne's affairs and in particular the earnings from the Potts family properties in London and Charles Potts's lands in Essex.[21]

The Essex property that Nathan had settled on Susan was a small cluster of manors and lands in what is now Beaumont-cum-Moze and Great Oakley just to the east of Colchester, near the marshes there. It also contained a farm called 'Skighaur', still called Skighaugh today. No doubt these were bought as an investment; Charles and his family do not appear to have ever resided there. The London property bought from Sir John, as described in the first Anne Potts action, was houses and tenements in St Andrew Holborn in the tenancy of Valentine Heyward, Andrew Hodson, _ Dawson, _ Capcote, Widow Blith, _ Bromfield, _ Sholmer, John Bayly, _ Freeman, John Ganner and several others unnamed. There were also several tenements in Turnmell Street in St Sepulchre occupied by Francis Meverell and Thomas Cutts, _ Benfield, _ Bayly and _ Bullock. There was also an unspecified number of houses in St Botolph Bishopsgate in the occupation of _ Woodward apothecary.

So, from all the chancery paperwork (15 surviving items, many of quite some length), the story of the Potts properties and much of the drama of the Potts/Drake household in Walton-on-Thames can be retold.

The will of Charles Potts was central to all the legal action that followed his death in December 1652. It turned out that Sir John, perhaps as early as 1629-30, had sold the London and Middlesex property portfolio to his brother Charles for something less than their true market value. How much Charles paid is not known but, based on the rental stream, Sir John may have received £3-4,000. Charles was a successful man and his brother still had to find marriage portions for their sisters and his daughters. As a result of this good deal, Charles felt indebted and so in his will left the reversion of the houses to Sir John and heirs. First, however, Anne was to have the profits from them for 30 years following her mother's death. His decision was going to cause great problems. In his will, made on 4th February 1650, he left £400 a year for life to Susan, half from his London and Middlesex property and half from Essex, to be administered by the joint executorship of his father-in-law Nathan, Sir John Potts and John Potts junior.[22] The lands were then to go to his male heirs, or if none then they should be used to provide £2,000 each to his two daughters (and proportionately less if he had more than two). His children were to have their maintenance. If he had no son and only one daughter she was to have the London property for 30 years after Susan died and then the property should go to Sir John and his heirs. If he had a single daughter she was to have a portion of £3,000 and the manors and lands in Essex. The balance of his personal estate was for the executors to use for legacies which included gifts to his mother-in-law, Doctor Wright, Sir William Drake and his 'dear friend' Francis Drake. The gold in Nathan Wright's cabinet was to go to Anne. His nephew Charles Potts was to have £200 and niece Ursula Potts £100. Every other child of Sir John and their children were to have £50; as were his mother's children by Sir Christopher Heydon and their children. These clauses clearly differentiate his half-relations from direct kin. So, this wording makes clear that by February 1650 his nephew Francis Potts had died without any children.

Codicils were added. In December 1651 he amended the disposition of his real estate to take account of his recent purchases in Essex. If he had no sons, all his lands wherever they were should go to his daughter for 30 years and then revert to Sir John and heirs. But if the Essex purchases went through without question (there was obviously a potential problem of some sort with the conveyance) then the original disposition of the London and Middlesex lands was to stand as long as his daughter was adequately provided for. In August 1652 the will was amended following the birth of his second daughter Frances, but he still had no son. His 'inheritance that had been his ancestors' in London and Middlesex was to continue in the family of his father's heirs male. He now introduced a clause which would prove infamous. To that purpose he advised that his eldest daughter should be married to Sir John's grandson Roger Potts! If such a marriage happened then his eldest daughter was to have £500 and all the London and Middlesex properties. She and her sister were to share the Essex lands as was the law. If he had no sons and there was no such marriage then the arrangements should revert to those in the original will in the clauses covering having two daughters. His aim, clearly, was to ensure 30 years' provision for Anne and Frances with the properties ultimately to come back into the Potts family. Unfortunately this made no reference to the previous codicil and therefore the intent over the reversion of the property was confused. On 1ˢᵗ November 1652, not long before his death, he re-signed and witnessed the will and codicils. In December, as requested, Charles was buried in Temple Church. The three executors were still acting as late as 1655 when they assigned a lease of the manor of Southall in Rainham to Edmund Fleming of Warley, nephew of Charles's mother-in-law.[23]

Soon after his death, Anne's little sister Frances died leaving her as Charles's only eventual heir. Initially from December 1652, Sir Nathan Wright as one of the executors took Charles's papers and ran the estate for his daughter and granddaughter. Certainly he and Susan were entirely responsible for Charles's personal estate. However in 1655 it seems that Wright was happy for Sir John to take over the task, which Susan had requested. From later comments that the properties were very run down, perhaps Wright had not put in the effort required to get them modernised and re-let. Sir Nathan died aged about 65 in early 1658. His will was made in February and proved in April that year.[24] Among other clauses, Nathan noted that he had married his three daughters and all had been given 'competent portions': Susan to Charles Potts and then Francis Drake, Mary to Robert Burdett esq of London and Alice to John Wolfris the London merchant. Susan as his first born child had in fact been given a larger portion, so now he was not obliged to give her anything more. Legacies were provided for his grandchildren: Nathan Drake, Nathan Burdett, Susanna Potts, Ann Wolfris and a general provision for any others. The list is interesting both for the rare evidence that Susan had at least one child, Nathan, by Francis Drake and for showing that 'Anne' Potts had been 'Susanna' to her grandfather (unless the original transcription of the will into the register was in error).[25]

Susan died unexpectedly in July 1664 and from that point on there is no hint of Francis Drake remaining involved in any of the family affairs. Instead Sir John was imperiously sent for by the young Anne, then about 16 years old, to sort out (and pay for) her mother's lavish funeral. After her mother died, Anne said that she wished to run her estate herself since Sir John Potts then lived 100 miles away.[26] She wrote to her tenants accordingly, but was affronted when they did not follow her wishes and when Sir John refused to let her manage her own property - as was his right as her guardian until 21.

Anne's first action, in 1666, claimed that in total Charles's properties were worth £800 or more per year. His will had provided for Susan to have £400 a year (half from London and half from Essex) for her jointure. The rental residue should accrue to Anne until she was of age, when she should have the residue until her mother died and then should have the whole rental value for a further 30 years. In her court actions Anne accused Sir John of not passing her the full value of the rental stream and of refusing to give her a full financial account of all that he had received on her behalf. She said he refused to pay her sufficient for her education and maintenance and had made long leases to his own benefit in the properties but that he also pretended to have some document in which she as a minor had released all right and title in the properties.

To this first action Sir John, now in his mid-70s, and his heir John Potts replied in some detail to the effect that the properties were not worth what Anne claimed and were in a bad state of repair, requiring new leases with building covenants to bring them up to scratch and protect the rental stream. Even in late 1666 they were not worth more than £706 a year, which was £129 more than when Charles died, nowhere near the amount Anne was claiming. In fact the Essex estate continued until Michaelmas 1665 to be let at just £265 a year and it was only recently through his endeavours that Sir John had gained the extra £129 from spring 1666. They estimated that the London estate at Charles's death was only generating about £310. By implication that is all that was coming from it in 1666.

Sir John had clearly, as executor, been drawn into Charles's debts and had himself paid about £1,200 against a detailed list of personal bonds which included £212 to Francis Drake, £100 to Mr Spelman, £183 to Sir John Howell's executors and a variety of others including an agreed rental rebate to a tenant in Essex who seems to have been responsible for gathering the rents there. Potts also believed that Wright had made various payments to Susan from the rents, prior to Sir John acceding to Francis and Susan Drake's July 1655 request that he run the estate. After 1655 Sir John had paid Susan £400 and Anne £100 each year even though the estate could not afford such a level after repairs, parliamentary taxes and the costs of quartering soldiers and stabling their horses. It is clear that Potts had borne the additional costs himself between 1655 and 1664, only partly covered by a residual £44 a year from the rent. The court order later agreed the £400 was a properly allowable expense from the estate.[27]

Potts went on to detail the rent he had received from each tenant since Susan's death and said that he had paid £300 to Anne from this for her maintenance. He also rather discreetly said that he had helped Susan and Anne when they had got into trouble from Francis Drake's 'entangled estate'. In fact he had raised £2,000 or more to free Susan and Anne from imprisonment in the Fleet in the late 1650s where they were incarcerated for Drake's debts. At the time Susan and Anne had apparently declared how much they were in his debt and Anne had promised to see him repaid.

But in this first action Potts merely went on to deal with his difficulty in delivering all the documents that Anne had called for. He had left them with Anthony Webb a silkman or mercer in London at his premises at the Sign of the Golden Anchor in Fleet Street. This was Webb's business and home address at the time of the 'late dreadful fire' of September 1666. Potts's hopes that the documents had been preserved were sadly dashed. Webb was a close relation of his grandson Roger's new wife Mary Davy and had been entrusted with the deeds.

To this quite reasonable answer, the two John Potts attached two schedules relating to the London property, which detailed a little more about what the family still owned.

The First Schedule

A lease by John Potts to Adrian Matthews 30th November 1627

A lease by Charles Potts to John Shaw 20th January 1626

A lease by John Potts to Francis Meverell 12th December 1620

A lease by Charles Potts to Adrian Matthews 30th October 1652

A lease by John Potts to Francis Meverell 26th March 1622

A lease by John Potts to Charles Potts 20th January 1631

This last entry might be taken as the date of a large transfer of property to Charles; but the 1626 and 1627 leases (the dates are certain having been given in regnal years) also show that the two had an overlapping involvement, which implies perhaps a gradual sale of the properties by John to Charles.

The Second Schedule

A lease by John Potts, Francis and Susan to Henry Cat of a cottage and two tenements in Holborn of 12th November 1657. Made without a fine, but with a requirement for £20 to be spent on building costs and then to continue at the old rent of £26 13s 4d.

A lease by John Potts to John Benfield of 30th November 1657 of various cottages and gardens in Tremel Street, with a £60 fine, £100 to be spent on building, at the former rent of £7 6s 8d.

A lease by John Potts to Arthur Hollingworth and William Carter of 23rd March 1659 of 'Maidenhead Ally in Greys Inn Lane', with a fine of £175, £230 on building costs and the old rent of £20 continued, 'the houses being very ruinous' (This, from the larger sums involved and the name, seems to have been the main house and its subsidiary tenements in the old Maidenhead block)

A lease by John Potts to Valentine Heyward of 1st December 1659 of the King's Head in Gray's Inn Lane at a fine of £250 and a covenant to make good the buildings, 'most of them ready to fall' and needing at least £400 spent on them. At the former rent of £10

A lease by John Potts to John Bayly of two cottages or tenements in Gray's Inn Lane of 12th May 1658 at a fine of £15, of which only £10 was paid, and covenants to make good the tenement within a year since it was in great decay. Old rent of £10.

A lease by John Potts to John Gardner of a tenement in Gray's Inn Lane of 3rd April 1661, with £10 to be spent and the old rent of £8 to continue.

A lease by John Potts to William Carter of two cottages or tenements in Angel Alley in Gray's Inn Lane 'ready to fall down' of 20th June 1662 at a fine of £5, £120 in building costs and then at the old rent of £4.

A lease by John Potts to Ann Beedle widow of two tenements in Holborn of 28th March 1663 with a fine of £60 and for 'wainscoats and other goods to be left in the tenements' at the former rent of £24.

No lease terms were given, but they would have been for at least 21 years given the building cost requirements and there was an example in another document where Potts gave a 42 year lease on the King's Head. These two schedules seem to show most of the original Holborn and Tremel Street houses. However, there is no sign of The Bishop, which surely would have been referred to by name. Perhaps that was the Holborn property that he had settled on his daughter Barbara at her marriage. The old White Hind or Plough and Harrow was also not referred to by name. Was it still called that, or had it simply become one of the unnamed houses in the schedule? Or again, it may have been given to Barbara. The remaining properties were to be argued over for many years.

Anne seems to have been a grasping girl and despite this credible response by Sir John to the first action, she persisted with her claim in 1667.[28] That year she pursued him and his grandson James Scamler over a £500 mortgage that Sir John Palgrave had originally in 1658 taken out with Thomas Harris of Inner Temple.[29] On Harris pressing for repayment in 1663, Palgrave had assigned the loan to Sir John Potts who had paid Harris the money due. Anne's bill of complaint asserted that the £500 was in fact her money and that at the assignment in March/April 1663 she had been shown papers including Scamler's name which she had refused to sign. Sir John, she said, persuaded her that the property (in Barningham) was to be in trust for her and so she signed. Potts had then taken the papers from her and now would not release them to her. Scamler's answer was that he had been involved in the reassignment but that in return for acting as trustee for Sir John, he had given him a bond in £100 to save him harmless from any consequences. He could remember no details. But he could remember Sir John at Mannington receiving interest from Palgrave's servant and having it given to his son John Potts. Palgrave answered that in April 1663 he had asked Sir John to take on the mortgage, but did not know the source of the money.[30] This was certainly not the first time Sir John had helped Palgrave with a mortgage. As early as August 1647 Potts loaned Palgrave £500 on the security of lands in Great and Little Dunham and nearby.[31] The survival of this item from so much earlier shows that Sir John Potts had always been approachable by family wanting access to funds.

Anyway, Sir John Potts confirmed that he had taken on the provision of funds to Palgrave and was persuaded by his lawyer to assign it in trust to Scamler. However, he had second thoughts considering his own great age and in case he should die before the repayment date in 1665. He was worried that the property might be taken to be Scamler's in his own right. So he asked Scamler to sign a note in which the property was assigned to Anne merely as a convenience to Sir John. She was not involved in the transaction or shown the documents. The arrangement was purely for Potts's convenience and could be altered as he saw fit. But Sir John left the note and the mortgage together with other items in the custody of Susan Drake and left for Norfolk. These other items included plate, jewels and household stuff to the value of £600-700 and more which had been sold to Potts for debts (presumably Francis Drake's), as well as a casket with £80 of gold in it. Here he also described how he had freed them from prison following the £2,000 of debts and how Susan and Anne had both felt deeply obliged to him. At her mother's death, Anne got hold of all these items including the mortgage and had entirely misunderstood the nature of the mortgage and its assignment. John had named her in the assignment in trust and as her guardian and, she being under age, he was to all intents and purposes assigning it to himself. He also explained that he had paid Anne some £600 after her mother's death, including her funeral charges. These had been considerable since Anne desired 'to bury her mother with reputation although it cost her £1,000'. In other words Anne wanted to make a real splash with the funeral despite, or perhaps because of, the earlier imprisonment for debt. Potts had paid the bill. A chancery order made during Michaelmas term 1667 confirmed the London properties would be Sir John's in 30 years and ordered all documents to be held in chancery until the end of that time.[32]

The young Mrs Villiers

On 16th April 1668 Anne Potts of St Martin's in the Fields married William Villiers esq, son of Sir George Villiers, at Chelsea Old Church by licence:

> 15 April 1668 William Villiers of Brookesby Leicestershire esq
> age 22 and Anne Potts spinster age 20, her parents dead, she at
> her own disposal and living with Theophilus Parkyns of Bunny,
> Nottinghamshire esq, who alleges; at Chelsea or St Martin in the
> Fields Middlesex or at the Temple Church London [where her father
> was buried] [33]

With the marriage Anne's actions lapsed but the couple started with renewed vigour as Villiers versus Potts, with Anne claiming a staggering £5,635 from her uncle. This equated to about 14 years at £400 a year - roughly the period from her father's death to her action starting - and implying she had had no benefit at all from the claimed available surplus over her mother's annual £400. There was no recognition of Sir John's help in getting her and her mother out of jail, the funeral and his other expenses. No wonder Sir John was driven to describe her as 'insensible' to how he had been 'beneficial to her favour'.[34]

Having first tried another attempt on the Palgrave mortgage, to which Palgrave and Potts answered as before, they next brought the London properties back in the limelight, drawing in one of the tenants.[35] By 1669 Valentine Heyward of St Giles in the Fields had started to act in chancery against both Sir John Potts and William Villiers to protect his interests.[36] Heyward's complaint asserted that Sir John had been empowered to dispose of one great messuage called The Sign of The King's Head in Gray's Inn Lane and other messuages or tenements attached to it, lately in the occupation of Andrew Hudson. He said that in 1659 he had taken a lease on the premises from Sir John. This was a complicated deal in which Heyward took over the remaining 16 year term of the previous tenants (Hannibal Dawson and _ Blyth). Heyward paid an entry fine of £250 to Sir John in return for an agreement to spend a large amount on rebuilding the premises. He would then have a lease for 42 years, with the first 16 being at a peppercorn rent and the final 26 being at £10 a year. This would have given Heyward the chance to make a profit on his rebuilding investment before the property reverted to Sir John. The two leases (of 1st September 1659 and 4th May 1660) confirming these arrangements were made out to William Lawes, Heyward's nephew and trustee. He assigned them to Heyward who claimed that he then spent £800 on repairs and rebuilding, since the houses were in a ruinous condition and heading towards being unfit for habitation.

But now, with William Villiers and Anne Potts having married, Sir John's role as *de facto* part guardian of Anne had come to an end. It seems that Villiers and his advisers set about reclaiming all of Charles's London properties. Villiers, as he saw it, was entitled to do so, given that he believed Anne was to receive them under Charles's will. It seems Villiers paid no attention to Heyward's leases, saying that Potts had not been entitled to make them and, through the services of one Joseph Evans, set about evicting Heyward and his under-tenants from The King's Head site. Heyward accused Potts of confederating with Villiers in this intrusion into his peaceable enjoyment of the property and the prevention of his having the whole lease term to recoup his investment.

There are always two sides to every chancery action! Sir John answered that he had made the leases and received the £250 but his title was only through the term of years stipulated in his brother's will and on behalf of Anne. The leases were made with Anne's consent and the explicit agreement of Susan Drake her mother and guardian since Anne was under age. (There was a further £250 from a similar re-leasing). Susan knew the properties were unlettable unless the rent was at a low level to reflect their poor state and to allow the major repairs to be paid for by Heyward as tenant. The rent was to go to Anne, through him as guardian. Sir John, having viewed the premises, said he did not believe £700 or £800 had been spent on repairs. He was due to give Anne and William Villiers an account of all sums due to her. Finally he had not in any way disturbed Heyward's tenure of the premises.

In their January 1670 separate answer to the complaint, William and Anne said they knew nothing of Sir John's title to the property and that they were strangers to everything to do with the leases, the ruinous state of the property and rebuilding costs. They did not know by what right he had granted leases. They certainly were not confederating with Sir John; indeed they were openly critical of him and were pursuing him in chancery to give them an account of monies due to them. The premises were lawfully Anne's by her father's will and so they had started eviction proceedings. William Villiers denied having taken any rent from Heyward, as he had asserted, and Anne said that she had not yet had an account from her bailiff. They refuted his claim that they were now enjoying rent levels much higher than the property had yielded before his work on it. Villiers also said that Heyward, knowing his leases were not good, had solicited Villiers's agent and cousin Thomas Roper (sometimes given as Rooper) for a new lease. Apparently an agreement was reached to issue a new lease on 10th July 1669. Heyward would pay 120 shilling pieces in guinea gold on 24th October and he would then receive a 23 year lease on The King's Head at the old yearly £10 rent. Villiers confirmed that he was willing to make such a lease but that Heyward had not produced his 120 shilling pieces. Villiers's answer was witnessed by Thomas Roper and Francis Nedham.

That autumn Villiers argued that since Easter 1669 Heyward had taken no action on his bill against them, despite Villiers having followed due process.[37] As a result he was granted dismissal of the case. But that did not stop Heyward, who brought a new case against Sir John Potts and William Villiers as noted in chancery orders of Hilary and Easter terms 1672.[38] By the same terms the following year Heyward got court support in applying pressure on the defendants to provide a full answer to his bill.[39] In Michaelmas 1673, on 21st November, a writ of subpoena was issued for the defendants to appear.[40] But it was too late. At the start of 1674 the Norfolk sheriff reported that Potts 'could not be found'. The machinery of chancery had ground on regardless for nearly a year after Sir John had died!

No doubt the concurrent action by the Villiers pair against Sir John Potts, referred to in this action, would have determined the outcome of the Heyward action. Frustratingly the bill and answer for the Villiers v Potts action has not been found. The only means of understanding the action comes from the interrogatories and depositions taken in January 1669 at The Black Boy Inn in Aylsham.[41] Heard before Edmund Britiffe, Nicholas Wilson, Francis Annyson and Thomas Roper (representing Villiers despite a clear conflict of interest) only the questions posed by William Villiers and Anne and no answers have survived. Their seven questions imply a very weak case. They focused on mortgages and bonds put in Sir John's hands by Anne and the extent of his involvement in paying Charles's debts and funeral charges. They asserted that Anne had given to Sir John for safekeeping bonds she clearly thought were due to her, although the precise terms were not clear. The context clearly implied that they were old debts due to her father and whether any would ever pay up was also not certain. Some 16 years after his death it seems very unlikely that there was any value in them. The bonds were £100 from Mr Bestoven, £200 from Mr Dormen, £500 from Mr Williams, £200 from Sir Thomas Player and £100 due from Mr Rowse, together with the £500 Palgrave mortgage documents. They were presumably trying to show that Sir John had not dealt properly as executor of his brother's will; or that he had paid out very little personally in executing Charles's will, paying his debts and subsequently managing the estate for Susan and Anne.

Sir John's fifteen questions were altogether more robust and fortunately answers to many of them have also survived. The thrust of his questions, which in themselves set out his case, was that first Nathan Wright, and then he, had administered Charles's estate for many years on behalf of Susan as Charles's widow, then as wife of Francis Drake and after her death on behalf of Anne. Throughout Sir John's involvement Susan was paid £400 a year and Anne £100 a year. This left the estate with barely £75 a year residue from which taxes, repairs and other charges had to be met, including the agreed payment to Nathan's agent Mr Francis Rowland for his work.

In addition Sir John had clearly paid further sums to Susan and Anne and had been involved in paying Charles's debts. It would seem that proving the will had taken a remarkably long time and that subsequently Sir John had stayed in the London area for 'many years' at work on Charles's estate affairs and to the detriment of his own in Norfolk. Questions specifically covered repairs needed to the London and Middlesex properties and to houses, fences and marsh walls at the Essex properties. Without all this work many of the premises were effectively unlettable. The references in Charles's will to unexplained complications surrounding his Essex property reinforce the idea that his affairs were in a very difficult state at his death. Francis Drake had also been part of the problem. John repeated that when Susan was imprisoned for his debts, she had asked Sir John to get her freed, which he had done at considerable cost to himself. Anne had promised to repay him even the whole £2,500 and Francis sold to Sir John in return for debt repayments and personal debts to him various jewels and other goods of great value. But after Susan's death, Anne had asked Sir John if she could have these items and he had agreed this as an offset for what he had received from her estate.

Questions also covered the lease arrangements made by Sir John. But his defence was really that the leases on the London property were but a minor part of the whole situation and that fair resolution of the case could only come from the much broader picture of Charles's estate and Susan's finances. His questions also show that Susan in 1662 had signed a deed requesting Potts to grant leases in the various properties and that after her death in 1664 the document had similarly been endorsed on the back by Anne to give her approval. He also had a deed of June 1659 in which Susan and Francis acknowledged that all rents and other payments due to them from all the properties had been paid up to Lady Day 1659.

Additional texture came from the answers first of Roger Potts, then aged 25. Shortly after Susan's death, Anne had written to Sir John from the Drake home in Walton-on-Thames to ask him to come to her to 'take orders about' her mother's funeral. Sir John was not able to go personally but sent his grandson Roger and his own servant Thomas Spurgeon to sort out with Anne what should be spent on the funeral. Roger laid out about £500 and Anne took £30-40 for her own use, which he had since heard Anne thank Sir John for (thus acknowledging the debt). Roger went on to say that Sir John had spent many years sorting out the estate and had incurred nearly £1,000 at his own cost in so doing. He had seen the sheriff's writ citing Susan's imprisonment for her husband's debts of £2,500, although he could not say exactly how much it cost Sir John to get her freed. But Anne had promised to repay the whole sum.

James Scamler [senior] esq of Wolterton aged 58 (Sir John's son-in-law, not the younger James involved in the Palgrave mortgage) was next up. He confirmed that Sir John had spent years working on the estate. But the real purpose of his testimony was regarding the codicils to Charles's will. He had known Charles and his handwriting very well having corresponded with him and worked with him in Middle Temple. On seeing the originals of Charles's will and codicils, he confirmed that the main text of all three elements was in Charles's own hand, as one might expect of a lawyer's own will. One phrase though he said had been added which was definitely not written by Charles: 'And that the breath or denial of the said desired marriage be not on the part of my said brother's heir'. He was implicitly accusing Villiers and Anne of fraud by inserting this phrase that they were relying on to prove that the London properties were not to revert to Sir John and his heirs. The full significance of this point emerges in a subsequent action.

Thomas Spurgeon, yeoman of Matlask aged 31, was next and testified in great detail about debts and monies paid to Susan and Anne. From his familiarity with the detail of Sir John's financial affairs it is clear that this trusted 'servant' was intimately involved in Sir John's business and it is likely he represented Sir John's interests in Norfolk. He confirmed the annual payments to Susan and Anne and testified to receipts by Susan. Leases made by Sir John were at rentals of the same level as the previous leases - there had been no extra money for Sir John to take as the bill had inferred. He himself had paid various sums to Anne since Susan's death. Sir John had incurred over £700 in direct expenses on Charles's estate. He also confirmed that Sir John had got Susan released from prison and that Anne had promised to reimburse him. He cited a £830 debt to Sir Ralph Bovey and £760 to the executors of one Nichols in this context. Sir John had been jointly bound with Drake in various bonds and Spurgeon had seen various cancelled bonds which Sir John had paid for Drake. He knew that Potts had instructed Dunker the jeweller who held the jewels and Mrs Webb (no doubt the wife of Anthony Webb) who had the other items to release these to Anne.

Spurgeon was then presented with a very long sequence of indentures and bonds and receipts. He identified Susan and Drake's signatures as their handwriting. Among these was a 1662 deed with a 1664 endorsement signed by Anne relating to her and Susan's approval of Sir John making leases for them and committing to confirm them. The rest of his testimony is extraordinary detail on over 20 payments by Sir John to Francis Drake from 1656 to 1664 and to Susan from 1661 to 1664. These items alone totalled to more than £1,000. Additionally he said that after Susan's death, he and Roger had laid out £400-500 more on the funeral and Anne had spent £80 on a coach and horses and a footboy's livery. And for an emotional twist he confirmed that Sir John had also paid about £50 for maintenance of one Wilkinson, widow of London, who said she had been laundress to Charles Potts.

After all this it is hard not take sides. It seems that Charles had left his affairs in a mess. Susan and Francis Drake had made matters far worse leading to a spell in prison for her and Anne. The Drake household spent at a great rate, substantially supported by Sir John, and Anne carried on the tradition after her mother's death. Villiers appears to have stoked the fire and the chancery complaint was, in the circumstances subsequently revealed, a mean-spirited and probably fraudulent attack on Sir John and his family.

The King's Head lease

The issue of the London property remained a problem for the Potts and Villiers families. Sir John was still being pursued by Heyward the year before he died. In July 1672 Valentine Heyward was back in chancery complaining again about the behaviour of the Villiers and Potts families.[42] With all the same background recited he went on to claim that Sir John had encouraged him into a deal with another tenant Robert Hudson who had a lease of part of the King's Head premises, being access to the yard and a 'lay stall for dung' at the back of the premises. This in turn linked into his attempt in 1669 to secure a lease from Villiers. Potts denied the specific allegations and in his answer went back over the history of the lease to Adrian Matthews, the grant for little or no consideration to his then unmarried brother, the 30 year provision for Anne and so on. Heyward had got his 16 year lease from Dawson and Blyth and had gone to Sir John's house in Enfield to try to sort out a deal after Villiers's intrusion into the property. Potts had been persuaded to grant him a new lease through William Lawes. Now Heyward was in suits with the Hudsons, first Andrew and after his death Robert. Potts said that the issue over the laystall was a contrivance by Heyward. Matthews had been intending to convey it to Potts as obviously part of the King's Head site, but had died before doing so. Heyward claimed it had come into his possession and he conveyed it to Potts as part of the lease extension on the whole premises. However it had since become clear that Heyward did not have good title to it, Potts was therefore not involved and Heyward must sort it out with Hudson. Potts also noted that the Villiers had pursued him in court for 2 or 3 years. Diplomatically he said he did not know why. It was clearly implied that by 1672 their action had ceased, almost certainly because they had failed to overturn the 30 year reversion to Potts. Potts said that he had, while the action was pending, submitted a full set of accounts to Sir Nathaniel Hobart of chancery and that he and the Villiers had come to a full agreement about all matters between them. The Villiers had given Potts a general release. Afterwards Heyward had asked Potts to mediate between him and the Villiers over his lease. Potts said that it was perfectly proper for the Villiers to charge a fine and agree a new lease, but that as far as he knew Heyward had failed to pay the full 120 shillings fine. Potts knew no more about it and could not get involved and would not recompense Heyward for his part payment of the fine.

It seems that after Sir John's death in 1673, when his suit lapsed, Heyward changed his tactics. First he tried an attack on the second Sir John Potts and Roger in January 1674, in which he claimed that a creditor of the first baronet, one John Shackley had made some sort of claim against Heyward.[43] The Potts's response was that they had never heard of the man and that Heyward's assertion that Sir John had died intestate was simply wrong. It seems likely this suit did not succeed.

Then followed a sequence of actions between Heyward and Lawes and Hudson, spanning 1675 to 1680.[44] These add relatively little, other than that Lawes seemed to have sublet the whole King's Head site to Hudson and that Heyward considered that illegal and against the spirit of the trusteeship. In fact it turned out that Lawes had been going to marry Heyward's daughter and he believed the premises were given to him as part of her portion. But that is someone else's story!

Villiers versus Roger Potts

The Villiers however had not given up. After Sir John's death they too started again and raised the whole issue of the long term reversion with Roger Potts. Just prior to their attack, in 1673 Roger and his wife Mary, the daughter of William

Davy, were in chancery suing the widow of Anthony Webb and their children over Davy family matters.[45] William had been the executor of his brother Henry Davy who had also been a successful London silkman and mercer who had gone into partnership with Webb in 1642. The partnership had been successful for more than twenty years and Henry lived in the Webb's house (also their business premises) until his death unmarried in about 1664. William had since died and now Roger and Mary were the executors and were trying to reclaim possessions, money and documents that they said had been left with the Webbs for safekeeping. The Webbs denied any such money existed and said that in 1664 they had done a final account in writing with William Davy and they considered the matter closed. A few old bonds left with the Webbs, now after the death of both Anthony (possibly in the 1666 plague) and Henry, they judged to be uncollectable. Roger had taken other scheduled trade debts to try to recover the money, but they had not heard any more from him about them. They said that it was possible that other documents may have been consumed in the great fire which destroyed their house. Webb had also held documents for Sir John Potts, including his brother Charles's papers and it does seem very likely that a significant part of the Potts archive including most of the original title deeds to the Potts London and Middlesex properties was destroyed at their house in the fire of 1666.

Between 1674 and 1676 Roger Potts and William and Anne Villiers were at it all over again.[46] The actions hinged around which will of Charles Potts was valid and what it specified in terms of the enjoyment and final reversion of his London properties bought from Sir John. The actions bring out yet more of the earlier events.

Roger asserted that Charles's will clearly bequeathed the property to his daughter for 30 years after the death of his wife and that after that the reversion would be to Sir John and his heirs.[47] Sir John had recently died (in 1673) and Roger was his main heir and executor. Sir John, via a fine, had subsequently barred the entail and settled the London property after 30 years on Roger. Roger now asserted that the Villiers had got hold of title documents and were attempting to create new documents that would give them the right to the reversion. In particular he said they were claiming that there had been a new codicil to Charles's will only discovered in Susan's trunk after her death. This had effectively annulled the 30 year clause and willed the reversion to Anne not Sir John. He said they claimed they had all the documents from Sir John. Most significantly Roger said that, in a fine of Hilary term 1674, the Villiers had conveyed (implying fully sold) 60 messuages and 20 gardens in the parishes of St Andrew Holborn and St Sepulchre and 'of fine messuages one curtilage and one garden in St Botolph's Without Bishopsgate'. This very clearly represented the lion's share of the historic Potts holding in London and had been sold to none other than Thomas Roper gent and William Wollaston (or Woolaston) esq, both cousins of Villiers.[48] Roger called for all the documents and the codicil to be produced and for the witnesses to them to be interrogated.

William and Anne replied that they knew of nothing that prevented her full inheritance of the property. Sir John had been her guardian after Susan's death and had shown her a document that he said was her father's will which he had found in one of Susan's trunks and which he said contained the 30 year limit on her right to the property. But Anne asserted that there was in fact a codicil to the will phrased:

> Whereas I have lately another daughter and no son I desire that
> so much of my inheritance as was my ancestors in London and
> Middlesex may continue in the family of the heirs male of my father
> in manner as I shall hereafter express ... [here followed the clause
> that his eldest daughter should marry Roger Potts and if so all the
> property would go to them] ... if the marriage does not take place
> then the houses should go to my daughters, paying £200 pa for
> 30 years to my brother and his heirs and with the reversion to my
> right heirs [ie his daughters] ... providing that my daughters are
> competently provided for and that the denial of the said desired
> marriage be not upon the part of my said brother's heir.

Their claim was that if Roger had refused to marry his cousin, as they asserted he did, then he should immediately forfeit the eventual reversion of the property and that it was all therefore theirs to sell. This codicil wording effectively reversed the final ownership of the London properties when compared to the probate version. Frankly it looks odd if their rendition of it was true. His will and codicils had repeatedly aimed at ensuring the property was kept long term in the Potts family, whereas this apparent death bed codicil suddenly completely reversed that, leaving the property fully to his daughter and by implication her husband if she were to marry. Suddenly also he introduced bizarrely 30 years' of income to go to Sir John - at no point had he shown any intention of the kind. Was he persuaded in his final illness by Susan to adopt a contrary course? Quite possibly it was a forgery or maybe he foolishly had not destroyed an earlier incorrect draft. This would make it a possibly unsigned and undated document, but one in his own handwriting. At no point in the chancery materials was a specific date given for this codicil. The only issue would be whether it was his last codicil or an earlier superseded one. Roger should probably have attacked it head-on as an early mistakenly drafted version. His choice of tactics, however, went down a different path.

Anne said that Roger should be deemed to have refused her since shortly after the death of her mother he married another 'of his own voluntary act' and that she had not made any wilful refusal of him. They said that they were not aware of any other will or codicil of Charles Potts having been proved in any court; despite the earlier depositions showing the clause to be an addition in a different hand and despite having reached a full settlement with Sir John senior.

There were probably a number of claims and counterclaims, since it does not seem likely that Roger was the initiator of this round of litigation, yet his bill above is the earliest surviving item. Roughly in parallel, Villiers claimed against Roger in July 1675, probably just after Roger made his first complaint.[49] Roger's answer of October 1675 was met with reiterated writs by William and Anne in 1675. The Villiers' claim contained little new - the reversion should be theirs. They restated their vague claim about a phrase in a codicil regarding the denial or refusal of the marriage. Surprisingly, since they seem to have had the documents, they could not quote the phrase exactly. They said that Roger now had documents which he was not prepared to disclose to them, including a pretend will of Charles of 1649 which had been used to block the entail on the premises and give the reversion to Roger. They worried that their claim to the reversion might be blemished and that their purchasers (Wollaston and Roper) should not 'be affrighted ... from disposing and improving the premises to their best advantage'. They asserted that Anne never refused Roger in marriage. If at any time Roger had spoken to Anne about marriage, it had been only by design and contrivance when she was very young and immediately after her mother's death when Roger was already in league with another woman. If he had spoken of marriage it was only to surprise Anne into a breach of the condition (the reversion) and give him some pretence to the premises by asking her at an 'unseasonable time in her grief and mourning'. She did not answer him and he did not ask again, but married the other woman.

Roger's answer quoted heavily from Charles's main will of February 1650 and codicils of 30ᵗʰ December 1651 and 23ʳᵈ August 1652. All his quoted extracts match exactly those proved at Canterbury on 27ᵗʰ April 1653.⁵⁰ There does not appear to have been any further will or sentence entered into the PCC records.

Roger of course went on to assert that, although he could not remember exactly what was said between them after Susan's death, Anne in fact had refused his proposal of marriage and that she had at that time offered to write him a note to that effect. He had indeed married another but only after Anne's refusal and he had not previously been in league with her (ie Mary Davy his wife). The only documents he had he would produce in court, but they were only the will, codicils and some old leases (presumably the leases Sir John Potts had recited in his two schedules years earlier).

Finally there is a gem in the last item, the interrogatories and depositions taken in January 1676 at Melton Mowbray where Edward Hudson, Anne's uncle, now lived.⁵¹ Much of the information is repetitive. What is new is that both sides were trying to establish Anne's maturity and state of mind when her mother died and when Roger may or may not have asked her to marry him. Hudson said that he remembered that Roger had told him at the time of Susan's funeral that he had no intention of marrying, but rather planned to travel. Later when Roger visited Anne at Hudson's house in Walton, he told Hudson he did not intend to marry Anne and was already a suitor to Mary Davy. Hudson said that Anne was still very childish, though aged 'about 13 or so' when her mother died. In fact she would have been nearer to sixteen than thirteen but had the court realised that, the argument about her behaviour would hardly have held water. Hudson continued with the pretence: with her mother still unburied, Anne played at a 'childish or feined burial or christening' and invited the local minister Mr Ruddell to join in and served him with wine and sweetmeats. He had known several children of 11 or 12 who were ready to be married but Anne was not one of them.

A string of Hudson's household servants also testified that Anne was very childish at this time, despite being 'about 13 or 14'. She played with 'babies' or dolls, cut up paper and wanted to be wheeled around in a basket and wheelbarrow as if in her own coach. No wonder the purchase of a coach was such an adamant requirement of hers at the time. Most of the servants speculated as to whether Roger had intended to marry Anne. They concluded she and her mother had been keen but Roger had already set his eyes on a 'proper lady'. The overall impression, at best, is of an immature and very self-centred teenager.

Roger's questions focused more on dealing with the inserted words in the codicil and then went on to the implication that he had offered to marry Anne and that she had refused him. Depositions on his behalf were taken in Norwich in October 1676. Yet again Thomas Spurgeon, now described as 'gent' of Matlask, aged 46 was a key witness for Roger. In 1664 he had been present at the assignment of the London property by Anne to Sir John. On this occasion Sir John had said to her that she would probably soon have them back on marrying Roger. She said that Roger could marry whoever he chose since she had no intention ever of marrying him. Spurgeon was also present when Roger made a 'courtly application' to her as lovers used to do. In answer she scratched his face with her nails until blood ran. He had heard that she had also said to Roger to the effect that he deserved it for meddling with her. In short he believed Roger had asked to marry Anne as his father and Charles had wanted but that she was averse to it. Did Roger deliberately behave badly to her or was Anne a bad-tempered little madam?

James Scamler senior testified again that he knew the handwriting of Charles and that the key clause in the codicil was not in his hand. His son testified that Sir John had been keen on the match and had asked him to keep track of Roger's approaches to Anne. He had done so and Anne was very averse to the match. William Crowe gent of Bittering aged 70, Roger's great-uncle, also testified that he had known Charles and his handwriting and that of his clerk William Dawes who had died before Charles. The clause in the codicil was not in their hands. He also said that he had been with Charles in the days before his death and indeed at his request had stayed until he died and saw him buried. When he was very sick Charles told him that he had given his brother the London houses. They had talked about Roger and Anne and Crowe had advised that near matches 'do not usually do well'. Charles said that in any event he had given the houses to his brother as he would rather they were spent by someone with his own name. Isaac Preston esq of Lincoln's Inn aged 35 testified that in December 1674 he and others had gone with Roger to enter and claim the King's Head in Gray's Inn Lane and some other houses in Bishopsgate Street and elsewhere in the City and Middlesex. John Frost of Ellingham aged 33, Roger's steward there, also testified that he had been on the visit to enter the premises.

Between 1675 and 1676 the case appeared frequently in the chancery decrees register. Most entries were for process points leading up to a commission of enquiry.[52] In May 1677 the case was heard and was sent for trial at King's Bench.[53] The case summary included Anne and William's continuing assertion that they could see no reason why she should not inherit the properties in full and re-stated the fine conveying them to Wollaston and Roper. The parties were to produce in court all relevant documents, including the copies of the old leases. After the trial they were to return to chancery for any decrees in equity.

The Villiers side won! Their title in the properties was confirmed and Sir Roger was ordered to pay them £80 costs as shown that November.[54] But despite a jury trial Potts argued that there should be a retrial and a stay of execution on the costs order. However, the court said that the £80 costs must be paid and set Potts a two year deadline (from the start of the action) by which to prosecute a retrial, otherwise the finding for the Villiers would stand.[55] From the brief notes it seems that the 30 year term could not be brought up in any future proceedings. This would appear to mean that the codicil and particularly its dubious annotations had been ruled as valid in King's Bench and so Roger was not allowed to challenge this central point in any future action. One wonders how the verdict was arrived at. Two lawyers had sworn the phrase was not in Charles's hand; by implication the court must have thought they were lying.

This clearly left Roger no basis for a new case and despite occasional blusters in the chancery decrees that he still intended to sue and which won him some respite from legal costs, the two year deadline came and went in mid 1680 without the case resurfacing.[56] Despite tensions within the wider family continuing, the Potts London properties had passed irrevocably to the Villiers and there would have been no further challenge to their sale to Wollaston and Roper.

It is interesting that when Sir William Villiers died in early 1712 he was of St Andrew Holborn, although he wished to buried in Brooksby alongside Anne who had died the previous July.[57] Perhaps after all they had retained some of the old Potts property, or maybe the Villiers family had their own property there. Ironically perhaps, he and Anne had no children of their own.[58] Sir William's legacies included £20 to 'my brother Colonel John Drake', Anne Potts's half-brother. He also left £50 to Izakiel Wright, brother to the late Lord Keeper Wright - Sir Nathan Wright, Anne's second cousin.[59] Izakiel was to raise a monument at Brooksby, worth £200, over them with an inscription of his own composition. A rather florid six lines for Sir William's tomb was followed by a brief note about 'Ann ... a Lady of Singular Virtue Piety and Charity'. Her charity, however, had not begun at home.[60]

Chapter 16

A Seaside Convention

With the end of the Cromwellian protectorate and the return of the monarchy, Sir John Potts unexpectedly found himself back in politics. His last few years were spent trying to leave his affairs in good order. All his hopes would be placed in his grandson.

The Restoration and Sir John Potts

By the end of 1659 the tide had turned and following widespread demands, on 21ˢᵗ February 1660 the Long Parliament was recalled, including the secluded members. Not all the original members turned up of course but Sir John, now 68, returned to do his duty. Potts, along with Sir John Palgrave, had received a special pardon under the Great Seal a month or so earlier.[1] Another member to return was the ever-keen Sir John Holland who was soon to be made a deputy lieutenant of Norfolk.

On 22ⁿᵈ February Sir John spent the afternoon in the Inner Court of Wards with Holland, Sir Gilbert Gerard, Crew, Scawen and many others, preparing the first draft of the new qualifications which would need to be met by anyone hoping to stand and be elected for the new parliament. This was urgent business and they had only a few days to argue over the very contentious clauses before presenting it to the House.[2] The next day though, they had to attend the formal election of the Council of State, whose members would run the defences and finances of government between 25ᵗʰ February and 29ᵗʰ May 1660:

> ... these Gentlemen to have the greatest Number of Voices; viz. William Peirpoint, John Crew, Colonel Rosseter, Richard Knightley, Colonel Popham, Colonel Morley, Lord Fairfax, Sir Anthony Ashley Cooper, Sir Gilbert Gerrard, Lord Chief Justice St. John, Lord Commissioner Widdrington, Sir John Evelyn of Wilts, Sir Wm. Waller, Sir Richard Onslow, Sir Wm. Lewis, Colonel Edward Mountague, Colonel Edward Harley, Richard Norton, Arthur Ansley, Denzell Hollys, Sir John Temple, Colonel Geo. Thompson, John Trevor, Sir John Holland, Sir John Potts, Colonel John Birch, Sir Harbottle Grimston, Mr. John Swinfen, Mr. John Weaver, Serjeant Maynard.

Each name was read out and all were agreed. Sir John Potts was one of the Council of State, along with many of his Isle of Wight colleagues, Pierrepont, Grimston and long-standing friends, Sir John Holland and Sir William Lewis. The President was Arthur Annesley, Earl of Anglesey.

The next week the act for calling the new parliament, to start on 25th April, and the qualifications for members were read. More clauses were requested and it was not until 13th March that the committee were ready to put them to the vote. The qualifications were a strange mixture of exclusion of catholics and royalists in the late wars but with mitigating phrases such as: 'unless they have manifested their good Affections to this Parliament'. Every word was carefully chosen (Sir John no doubt in his element) but even so several clauses were rejected and the debate ran late into the evening.[3] Still strongly presbyterian, the house passed some church reforms; two days after the membership debates, on the last day of the session, John sat with friends discussing the augmentations for ministers and the confirmations of such ministers in their livings.

Having drawn up the legal structure by which the new parliament was to be chosen the Long Parliament dissolved itself on 16th March 1660. Did Sir John have any intention to remain an MP? There is nothing to show he was keen to stand for the new Convention parliament (so-called because it was not summoned by a sovereign). Despite the presbyterian moderates' attempts, he would have known that royalists would be elected as MPs. In the meantime he was busy with Council of State business: one of their first proclamations was to order all cavaliers and papists to go out of town on 25th March and not to return to London until 1st May.[4] This was probably meant to prevent any influence on the elections but would have been widely disregarded.

Most of his work at Whitehall involved taking and signing orders for payments: in the two weeks at the end of March and beginning of April his signature appeared on four orders transferring sums totalling around £13,000.[5] He also signed the appointment of Sir Horatio Townsend [sic] as Colonel of the Regiment of Militia Horse in Norfolk on 7th April.[6] Townshend had been busy campaigning for parliament since late February, getting ahead of the action. He was, with Howard, in control of the Norfolk elections and he gained massive personal support as one of the knights of the shire. A little to his surprise, the other seat went to Thomas Lord Richardson of Honingham (who had been intended for one of the boroughs) over Sir William Doyley.[7] Doyley should have been the popular choice since, despite being a royalist, he had scored the highest votes in the earlier 1654 election when ten members were chosen to represent the shire.[8] Potts's stepson John Spelman, who had also been excluded in 1648, sat again for Castle Rising in the Convention. Sir John Holland wrote to Townshend in March saying he would 'not now be willingly left out' but the nominations were pretty well resolved.[9] It would have seemed reasonable, given his age, for Sir John Potts to retire back to a quiet life. However he was to be part of a major change in the running of the ancient corporation of Great Yarmouth.

In April 1660, Sir John Palgrave, Sir John's nephew, consented to stand for Great Yarmouth with regicide Miles Corbett as the borough's representatives to serve in the new parliament due to sit on 25th April. On 12th April, by the normal Yarmouth tradition, they were elected at the meeting of the Corporation assembly. Historically the small group of 12 aldermen and the council claimed the right to vote for the parliamentary 'Burgess' members. This excluded the numerous freemen of Yarmouth from having any say in choosing their members of parliament.[10] Palgrave was made a freeman at the meeting so he could be a valid candidate. Corbett had sat for the borough on numerous occasions and the two names were returned to the sheriff, John Cremer. The minutes gave no hint of a problem except at the end where it was recorded that 'The Bailiffs be desired to forbeare signing and sealing any indenture that may be tendered to them from any of the freemen or others of this Burghe touching or concerning any choice of Burgess for the next parliament other than that indenture for Burgesses which is already signed by the choice of this Assembly'. The indenture had been signed by the 12 aldermen and 32 burgess councillors. Another return was obviously being prepared by the freemen at large who were determined to have a voice in the elections for the first time.

Nothing more is noted in the assembly minutes until 23rd April (two days before parliament was due to sit) when it was agreed that Mr Bailiff William Emperor and Benjamin Bends, town clerk should journey to London about the members of parliament 'to improve their interest about the asserting of the rights liberties and privileges of this Assembly in the Electing of Sir John Palgrave and Myles Corbett esq., Burgesses to sit in the next parliament and that all charges … in this their journey and about retaining counsel and managing of this work shall be allowed'. In parallel, the freemen had sent in the names of Sir John Potts and Sir William Doyley of Shottisham (who then was looking for a seat) as their choice. The contested election had therefore been put up to a parliamentary committee. The Corporation was prepared to hire counsel to put their case and had taken 'all such bookes and records belonging to the Burgh as they shall think fitt which may anyway relate to election of burgesses'. No more was noted in the meetings that followed in May but on 6th June, after some ordinary business, a letter was recorded. Dated Friday 13th May 1660, it was a copy of the report from the committee to the House and read as follows: 'the case upon the double return for the Burrough of Gt Yarmouth … that upon Examination of the fact, the question being whether a select number of Burgesses or the Burgesses at large ought to Elect, the Cttee were of the opinion that the Burgesses at large ought to Elect, And that Sir John Potts kt & bt and Sir William Doyley kt having the greater number of voices are duly elected and ought to sit in this house. Resolved etc That this house doth agree with the Cttee that the said Sir John Potts and Sir Wm Doyley are duly elected and doe sit in this house and that the return be accordingly amended by the Clerk of the Crown, W Jessop Cl of the Commons House of Parliament'.

Without comment, the assembly minutes continued by agreeing 'that Sir John Potts kt & bt and Sir Wm Doyley are made free of this Burrough and that their Burgess letters be given to them accordingly'.[11] This must have been a real blow to the aldermen; never again was the outcome of parliamentary elections to be restricted to their members.

Potts and Palgrave had known and disliked Corbett the 'vindictive doctrinaire lawyer', for years, often trying to reduce the severity of Corbett's actions such as repeatedly standing up for Sir Thomas Knyvett when he was pursued by Corbett and

Beadle.[12] Did they believe that Palgrave would provide the necessary moderating balance? When the issue of the freemen's vote upset the election, did Palgrave persuade his uncle to step in? Potts would have felt it was his duty to champion the rights of the freemen at large. There may even have been a conspiracy between Potts, Doyley and Palgrave to ensure things changed and to unseat Corbett. Doyley was in his mid-50s and had been active in parliament for some years after an unusual youth. He was knighted by Charles I for his gallant behaviour in the service the Lion of the North, Gustav Adolphus of Sweden, the young protector of the protestant faith against the Catholic League. He was also a zealous royalist and supporter of the Restoration. Palgrave and Potts had not stood for Yarmouth before so probably there was an understanding that, whichever way the House committee decided, one of these experienced moderate presbyterians would be elected. Corbett, who never tried to excuse his actions, did not accept the condition of surrender offered by the King. He subsequently fled abroad, was arrested at Delft, tried and executed in April 1662.

Sir John felt far more sympathy for another regicide: his two daughters-in-law, Susan and Anne, were daughters of Sir John Heveningham. Their two brothers William and Arthur had taken opposing sides, Arthur for the King. William had remained in the Rump parliament after the Purge and so was arrested and tried as a regicide when he surrendered in 1660. Sir John Potts supported the hearing of his petition for clemency but he was condemned to death. William's estate had already been under pressure from Arthur who was taken prisoner in 1645. Owning nothing himself but an annual rent charge of £200 on brother William's estate, Arthur had been fined £400. However, William's pleading that he was responsible now for the wife and 6 children of his deceased royalist brother Arthur helped and he was reprieved. His forfeited estates were finally restored to the family but he remained in prison. In 1662 Lady Mary Heveningham, his wife, petitioned unsuccessfully for him to be allowed to be transferred to her home in Heveningham in Suffolk. He remained in confinement until he died 18 years later, in Windsor castle where his brother-in-law Charles Potts, as deputy governor, would have been responsible for his care.

Poor Sir John: no quiet life for him for another year. The elections for the Convention parliament had swept away the republican core, with the restoration of the monarchy top of the agenda. The remaining moderates, including many presbyterians, now saw the royalists take control. Within a month, on 25th May, Charles II entered England. John was one of the deputation that brought the King home.[13]

The parliament was busy with disbanding the army, raising taxes, and creating pardons in order to restore, where possible, a united populace. The Commons Speaker was Sir Harbottle Grimston, with whom Sir John had worked on the Isle of Wight and who, having been imprisoned briefly after Pride's purge, had been in temporary exile. In the Lords, his friend the Earl of Manchester was elected speaker, before the royalist lords arrived in the chamber.

The first session lasted four months and 18 days. Described as a friend of Lord Wharton and a manager in the Convention, Sir John made seven recorded speeches and was named to nine committees.[14]

He sat from 18th May 1660 when the confirmation of his and Doyley's election was recorded. By 22nd May he and Doyley were busy on a committee discussing the bill to void grants of title made over the previous 18 years. At the end of May they met to prepare a bill for excise and customs to improve trade.

It may be that Doyley played a stronger role with their borough, but in late June 1660 John and Sir William were both noted as intending to visit the Orkney Islands on Yarmouth business, to meet the fishing fleet on their return, 'the northern seas being greatly infested by Ostenders'.[15] Competition from foreign (especially Flemish) fishermen was always a major issue for Yarmouth. Whether John managed to avoid the long journey by frigate is not known but on July 31st, Potts was back sitting in the exchequer chamber in committee to consider the bill for settling and restoring ministers in their livings. He was in a group of sixteen, taken from both houses, who went into the City on 14th August to raise a loan of £100,000 'for the Publick service of the Kingdom'. Still working in September, he was added to a committee discussing the accounts of officers of the House (especially the printers and stationer). Before the session was adjourned he had one more task. On 10th September he went to the Lords to ask if they would sit that afternoon 'for that there [would] be Bills of great importance ready for them by Four of Clock' and to remind them about the ministers' bill and that for confirming college leases (which presumably were still to be enacted). He also had to get their consent for an order for issuing a proclamation about the excise. He was obviously effective as all these were achieved that day.

After which Sir John enjoyed a well-deserved two month break! Back to work in the second session, on 10th December he was added to a committee preparing a bill for settling the militia. On 17th November Sir John was in the house listening to the debate about the severity of the crime of William Drake, a citizen and merchant of London. The house 'drew up an Impeachment against him for writing and publishing a dangerous Book entitled, *The Long Parliament Revived*, in which he endeavours to prove that the said Parliament was not yet legally dissolv'd. This rais'd a considerable Noise, but they wanted Time to bring it to a Trial'.[16] Some members were vociferous saying 'that he ought to be severely punished, by being tied up to the gallows, whilst his Book was burning below it; for if he, being a friend, wrote in that manner, what would their enemies do ?'. Sir John Potts, being more moderate, moved only to have him make a public recantation whilst his book was burning. Drake was finally impeached on 4th December.

On the 23rd Sir John spoke in favour of a land tax being given as compensation to the crown for abolition of the court of wards, although this suggestion was not taken up. The committee, of which he was part, was instructed to meet in 'Mr Speaker's chamber', to insert clauses giving the King a part of the excise on beer and ale instead. Those long winter afternoons in committee must have sometimes felt endless as the phrasing of clauses was thrashed out.

At the end of its second session, which had started on 6th November, the King dissolved the Convention parliament on 29th December 1660. The Cavalier Parliament, elected in May 1661, was to be quite a different body with a very strong royalist agenda. Sir John had done his part. He was, after all, nearly 70. The corporation of Yarmouth had more open practices and in January 1661 a minute was recorded in the assembly: [To] 'Sir William Doyley late Burgess in parliament; [we] give hearty thanks for his great care and respect to the Corporation in his letter now read'. Doyley continued as MP for Yarmouth (with William Coventry esq) and was created baronet in 1664. He and Potts had played their part in the modernisation of the politics of Yarmouth.

The final years

John was not active in national politics after 1661, but he still worked in Norfolk at least for another two or three years. He had been nominated for the role of Custos Rotulorum (Keeper of the Rolls) for the county on 26th April 1660 in the place of Hatton Berners esq.[17] At this time the office was still held separately from the more important lord lieutenancy with which it would later combine. Given that shortly after this date his hurried election for Yarmouth was confirmed, Sir John may have declined the honour feeling that he could not undertake yet another public duty. Whatever the reason, Sir Philip Wodehouse the 3rd baronet, the son of his old friend Sir Thomas, was appointed Custos in June 1660. Locally John was a commissioner for assessment for Norfolk (1660 to his death) as was his son John; they were both shown as such in the Mannington rate of 1663, Sir John being assessed at £18, paying £7 13s and his son at £9, paying £3 12s.[18] The collector John Nabbs gent delivered the money into the hands of Sir John Potts on 23rd March 1664. The 72 year-old still took responsibility for the money despite the fact that his son could easily have taken the burden off his father.

In the income tax levy ordered in 1660 for which he was a commissioner, Sir John was not shown at Mannington. His son John paid the £10 (the rate for esquires) and added that his father had paid at London.[19] Sir John was also commissioner for assessment for Yarmouth (September 1660 to death).[20]

Sir John did not however appear in the arrears of subscriptions of knights & gentlemen for repairing Norwich Cathedral of July 1663. Sir John Holland was there with Britiffe and others, John Spelman esq owed £10 and Clement Spelman £5. Perhaps Sir John had already paid.[21]

And what of the old network, his friends from the Long Parliament days? His early supporters Sir Thomas Wodehouse (d1658) and Framlingham Gawdy (d1654) had died, as had other parliamentary colleagues; his nephew by marriage, Simonds D'Ewes died in 1650; his stepson, John Spelman died in 1663 at 56; his nephew and close friend Sir John Palgrave died the year before Potts in 1672. Only Sir John Holland survived. Holland actually gave support to Charles II in Utrecht as soon as one year after Charles I's execution but was still allowed to visit family there! He even met with Cromwell on good terms.[22] The last member of the Long Parliament, Holland was actively still trying to moderate election rows in 1679. He continued as a justice until 1692. Remarkably he lived to his 98th year, dying in 1701.

A grandfather's choice

As always, most of Sir John Potts's time was taken up with helping his family with their financial affairs. At one point his stepson Clement Spelman (involved in one of the wrangles over Willoughby property) named him as a key witness but claimed John was too busy in parliament to attend the enquiry held in Norfolk.[23] His daughters caused him no problems. In October 1660 Sir John was involved in the sale of Wolterton by Richard Houghton to James Scamler (Potts's son-in-law).[24] Son and heir of Robert Houghton, Richard and his wife Helen had lived in the old Wolterton Hall until his father's death in 1657 when he moved to Earlham and set about sorting out his father's considerable debts. Potts had provided a £500 mortgage to the Houghtons in August 1658 secured against Wolterton lands and so was involved in the final transaction conveying the manor, Hall and 220 acres of land, meadow and pasture to Scamler.[25] At this time his £500 was repaid. Daniel Muddiclift of Itteringham was attorney for Potts and Thomas Jackson clerk of Wolterton for Houghton. Anne and James Scamler had a long marriage and were buried at Wolterton in 1681 and 1689 respectively.[26]

John would also have visited his daughter Ursula, Mrs Philip Bedingfield, and his grandchildren at Ditchingham near Bungay, a fine old Hall befitting a girl brought up at Mannington.[27] They had lived there after the death of Philip's father in 1661 and John would have approved of Philip's devoutness.[28] Ursula had a winning way: her father-in-law left her £10 in his will and described her as my 'loving' daughter-in-law. His own daughters and sons were given no such epithets![29] Of Ursula and Philip's eight children, only two sons and one daughter had survived. Philip, the eldest son, was born in 1655. Charles, the other son, five years younger, married Agnes daughter of Sir William Cooke of Broome. Ursula lost her husband in the winter of 1672, her father in 1673, and her brother Sir John junior in 1678.[30] Her son Philip was still a minor when his father died so Ursula held the lands and manors until he came of age. Her husband had also hoped she would encourage the two boys to study divinity. She made her will in September 1673.[31]

When Ursula died early in 1677, her inventory taken in September 1677 by her son Philip, showed her as comfortably off (although still owing some debts left by her husband). A detailed description of the house and goods totalled £789 14s. She had kept a chamber at Intwood, where she may have been living when she died, but in which house is not clear. She may have been companion of Caroline Pickerell who was buried, in Ditchingham, a month before Ursula.[32] Her plate, linen, two beds and £50 would go to her second son Charles. Her daughter Dorothy, her eldest child, had a similar mix of household goods and £150. Among several smaller bequests were money or rings to her brother Charles Potts, Mistress Anne Spilman (her half-brother John's daughter), Mistress Elizabeth Potts, her niece and Roger Potts, her nephew. A few years later, in November 1684, Dorothy married Sir Edmund Doyley bt, of Shottisham, the grandson of Sir John's Yarmouth partner in the 1660 election.

Sir John's male heirs were far more of a problem. Since 1639 and his son's first marriage Sir John had ceded the long-term interest in Mannington to his son John. Sir John had built up debts during the Commonwealth, from his loans, his expenses and the heavy taxation imposed on landowners. The last seven years of Sir John's life were taken up with settling family affairs, ensuring his estates passed on to his son and particularly to his grandson, albeit with some mortgages attached. He made strenuous efforts to repay his debts and leave John and Roger with as little a liability as possible. After he was elected for Great Yarmouth, in 1660 he purchased a modest manorial estate in Clippesby, Repps and Bastwick. This would be a cause of much litigation later.

The following year saw two mortgages raised: there would be more to come. These were taken out by Sir John Potts and his son John. In the first, on 5th June 1661, part of their lands in Irmingland was mortgaged to Richard Catelyn esq of Kirby Cane. A family trustee and elderly brother-in-law of Robert Houghton, Catelyn had been with Sir John in the Long Parliament as member for Norwich until he was unseated in 1645.[33] The second mortgage, for the remaining part of the Irmingland property, followed some 21 days later and continued over many years with subsequent reassignments on several occasions.[34] The Catelyn mortgage was for £750 and seems to have covered the messuage of Richard King and 160 acres. The precise location of the house can only be suggested from the named fields. From the references to Coppings Close and meadows, it probably stood to the east of Elmerdale farm and close to the Itteringham parish boundary.[35] The five year mortgage of 26th June 1661 was with Annabella Hervey daughter of Francis Hervey esq of Weston Favell, Northamptonshire who, a year before, had sold or mortgaged property to Sir John and his sons including Charles.[36] Annabella was lending £600, on the security of the messuage called The White House (Elmerdale farm itself) and rather more fields with it than in the previous descriptions of this part of the overall Irmingland property. These fields totalled 130 acres and had been in the tenure of Erasmus Buck gent and Edmund Bell the elder yeoman, but no current tenant was given. Four years later Roger would inherit these mortgages as the lands formed part of his marriage settlement. He also was to receive all the Mannington estate after his father's death. His inheritance was increased by Sir John three years later, on 6th October 1668, in another settlement on Roger and his wife.[37] This was part of the significant reinforcement of Sir John's property settlements to provide for repayment of his debts, later referred to in various chancery documents.

On 12th December the same year, another mortgage was set up which again was to have a long history. Sir John Potts, his son John and Roger borrowed £200 from Sir John's great-niece Anne Hunt, singlewoman of Norwich. The sum was raised against a total of 140 acres of closes in the occupation of Richard Sexton husbandman.[38] These included Wolterton Close, Johnsons Close, Wolgrave Close, Maxons Close, Gravel Pit Close and others. While no messuage was included, this seems to represent a definable farm unit leased to a single tenant and the lands were largely to the north of Itteringham lying between the Barningham and Wolterton roads, with some to the east of the Wolterton Road. In June 1670 Sir John, John and

Roger also mortgaged Mannington Mere Farm and its buildings and yards, with just four acres of grounds immediately around it, to Christopher Crowe for £500. Each of these mortgages seems to cover a specific tenant farm with its own identifiable rental stream.

Throughout this long period there is a clear impression that his son John, while occasionally being involved in some of these events, lived very much in his father's shadow and the load still fell on Sir John. He clearly saw his grandson Roger, as an emerging man of the world, as the future of Mannington.

Sir John himself was now to find himself repeatedly in court. His involvement with his brother Charles's family, as we have seen, led to his being sued by his niece despite having rescued her and her mother and stepfather, Francis Drake, from imprisonment for debt. On 25th May 1665 Robert Doughty, the justice, took a statement from a young woman complaining about a row with some local women.[39] In passing she mentioned a gentleman 'who came down in his coach to get Sir John Potts arrested' and stayed at the Black Boys in Aylsham. This may be related to an action arising from Drake's debts. William Dalben and William Gardiner (on behalf of the late Nicholas Nicholls gent of London) had won a judgement against Sir John in King's Bench in Easter term 1663. Gardiner pursued him for £1,400 and there had been an enquiry at Mannington in December 1664.[40] Gardiner had had Sir John arrested twice. John claimed this was done deliberately in such a way as to make it difficult for him, as a countryman, to get bail to London for so great a sum of money. They were trying to wear out the 'sickly and aged' Potts by vexatious suits.

Sir John was, by 1665, aged 73, a retired elder statesman who had worked so hard to serve his country, maintain his estate and give his family education and status. He must have wondered why he could not have lived out his last years in peace. Where in Norfolk he was living in the 1660s was not stated but it seems, from chancery references, he visited Mannington only infrequently. Did he come to see the King on his visit to Norfolk in 1671? Most of the population turned out at Norwich but might the 79 year-old Sir John have been invited to Blickling Hall? There the King, with all his entourage, dined with Sir John Hobart and knighted his young son. Sir John, on the other hand, may well have stayed quietly at Roger's home in Ellingham where he probably spent most of his time and where he died, in his 81st year, early in 1673.

By this time he had relatively little left to resolve and his will was brief. It was made in January that year when 'very aged but of perfect memory' and proved in October.[41] Having bequeathed his soul to God he noted that his lands had already been disposed of to his eldest son John Potts esq and his grandchild Roger Potts. He left £100, if it was available after his own debts were paid, to his son Charles; but there was no mention of his son Francis or of any children of Charles or Francis. He said that his personal estate was very small but 'to avoid contention among my children and for the just payment of such monies as by particular promises or my own single security I stand engaged for' he wanted to make a specific bequest to his executor. This was Thomas Newman late of Heydon clerk to whom all money, rents, debts due, arrears, etc were to go for the performance of the will. He gave him a small gratuity of £40. To Newman also, he left all his 'hangings, turkey work, carpets, cushions, bedding, couch stools, velvet cushions, stools, chairs, linen, plate, brass, pewter and other household utensils which I lent to or left at Mannington in the custody of my son John Potts who by my permission has usage of them since the death of his mother my wife about [the feast of] St Michael 1647 to whom I then delivered an inventory of them'.[42] The implication was that Sir John had not lived for any extended period in Mannington after Ursula died. Newman was to pay all Sir John's debts owing by his single bonds or bills under seal. The money would come from the sale of the goods, sums due from his son John, rents of lands which he used called the Halvinge lands (a nice reference to his newly ploughed pasture lands being farmed on a share-cropping basis by his tenant) and what Newman received of other tenants, due since the feast of Our Lady 1666. Sir John died, like his father before him, with unfinished court actions hanging over him despite all his attempts to clear his family's legal backlog.

Sir John left his body in the care of Roger Potts requesting that he be buried at Mannington church: 'done decently but very private without the least funeral expense or pomp near Dame Ursula under the marble stone with an inscription for us both'. For his trouble Roger was to receive an extra £20. So it would be Roger, rather than his son John, who undertook his burial. Sir John was buried at Mannington next to his wife Ursula who had died 26 years earlier. The tomb in Mannington church said 'they died not at one time and could not be buried in the one grave yet desired to be so near as under one cover which is since performed'. It does seem that his son and immediate heir John, living in Mannington, was not to be trusted with this last task.

Chapter 17

A Windsor Knot

Past writers on the Potts family have made little mention of Sir John senior's third son Charles. His note on the Visitation pedigree said only that he was the Deputy Governor of Windsor Castle and died without issue. It did not record his wife but he did in fact marry twice. In his father's will of 1673, he was to have £100 if the money was available from Sir John's personal estate after all his debts were paid. Although the sources are thin, Charles's story appears to unfold as follows.

Charles Potts was Ursula and Sir John's third son and was probably born by the early 1620s. He was not christened in Narborough, unlike his eldest brother. He may have been baptised from his father's house in Norwich but more likely the service was in Mannington, possibly after Sir Christopher Heydon died in 1623.[1] He does not seem to have received university education, nor is there any record of his admission to any of the inns of court. But at this stage of his youth the country was at war and he may even by then have been a soldier. The name Charles Potts is relatively unusual. Some years later, in October 1655, there is an intriguing admission to the Inner Temple of a 'Charles Potts gent of Westminster'. Was this the same Charles? Although the identification is unclear, there is at least a circumstantial case to be made that it is the same man. As we will see, by the 1660s Charles was styled gent (being only a younger son of Sir John) and giving his address as 'of Westminster'. He was paying tax there in 1664.[2] By that time 'Charles Potts gent of Westminster' would be enough to identify him as he had no estate title of his own.[3]

By the early 1650s he was a merchant and may well have decided to get some legal training, perhaps influenced by his uncle Charles and the Wright family. The only other identifiable Charles Potts in London around this time was the Charles, son of Edmund Pott the haberdasher, who died young (see Chapter 15). In the many Potts family deeds, Charles appears only twice. In February 1660, Francis Hervey of Weston Favell entered a fine with Charles Potts, his father Sir John and brother John junior. Charles seemed to be receiving the benefit but, without the rest of the supporting deeds, the details are unclear. It may be another of the mortgages employed by Sir John, to which his sons were party, when sorting out their inheritances. Charles's involvement in this, and in the Fenland action that ran between 1657 and 1660, indicated his presence around London at that time.[4]

Soldier, merchant and adventurer

What is certain is that, later in life after the 1660s, Charles Potts was a career soldier. It has proved difficult to confirm whether he joined the army as a young man at the start of the first Civil War. In 1644 his father was heavily involved in parliamentary duties including the raising of finance from East Anglia. There are some intriguing references in the state papers to a Captain Potts (no first name ever given unfortunately) who just might be Charles. Several entries in June 1644 show that Captains Potts and Draper were selected out of Colonel Norton's regiment and with their men were trusted with the task of escorting a convoy of ammunition and money from Barnet to Sir William Waller. Then they were to remain with Waller rather than return to Norton's regiment which was being sent back to Basingstoke.[5] However, according to Peacock's *Army Lists of the Roundheads and Cavaliers*, no Charles Potts was serving as an officer in 1642.[6] Other references in the state papers show both a parliamentarian and a royalist Potts operating in the Staffordshire area during the early 1640s and a Captain Potts in the Scots army in the mid-forties.[7] A parliamentary report listed many ex-royalists now in the Scots Army which at this point was still parliamentarian in its sympathies. 'Captain Potts's troop' included several men thought to have been previously in the Royalist Army.[8] Was this Charles?[9] Of course, none of these references may relate to him but it is reasonable to believe that the youngest son of this staunch parliamentarian family would have gone off to fight.

Charles, who would not have inherited any lands of his own, was given his father's Adventurer lands in Ireland. Sir John had, as promised, been granted a parcel of lands in return for his loan to parliament which he had subscribed in three lots, each of £200, in 1642, 1643 and 1644.[10] This made him one of the 1,500 or so 'adventurers' who had invested in funding the army to quell the Irish rebellion, but no doubt he felt more like a taxpayer supporting the cost of the army. In July 1653 Sir John Potts was among those who drew lands in East Meath which were 'in the north east quarter' of the Barony of Lune. He may not have acquired more than some tens of acres, probably of grazing land. However, the area in which his lands lay can be identified quite accurately. The old Barony of Lune in the county of Meath covered an area a little to the west of Trim and the river Boyne.[11] The only town of any size was Athboy, in the north of the barony, not far south of the historic abbey town of Kells. The 'north east quadrant' meant that their lands were in the area immediately to the northeast of Athboy, lying next to the Barony of Navan and its lands around Rathmore.

In July 1653, Sir John formally assigned his allocation of £600 worth of lands:

> For the natural affection which I bear unto Charles Potts, merchant,
> one of my sons, and for the better advancement of that noble
> plantation in Ireland by fit persons.

Charles was still listed as the owner in 1659 but he may not have held the land for long. Like most others granted land, Charles probably did not visit his acreage. Assuming they were not lost in the post-Restoration partial re-allocation to the original owners, he probably sold his rights to one of those interested in consolidating large estates out of adventurer lands.[12] John Bligh was one such man and may well have bought the Potts lands. From 1657, Bligh a citizen of London, and later his son Thomas, built a large estate centred on Rathmore founded on adventurer lands and related acquisitions. With the Potts lands lying so close, Bligh would have approached Charles for a deal. Perhaps more important than the land grant itself, the assignment to Charles showed that at this time he was living as a merchant. The timing of the gift from his father was probably triggered by Charles's recent marriage; it was a rare opportunity for Sir John to do something for his younger son.

In about 1653 Charles Potts married Anne, the widow of Samuel Leigh gent of the City of Lincoln who had died in 1651.[13] Anne was the daughter of Thomas Cornwallis esq of the City of Lincoln and her family and the Leighs were already closely connected by marriage. In marrying Samuel, about 1638, she had married her great-uncle's son (although they were not far apart in age).[14] Samuel's grandfather was Sir Edward Leigh of Rushall (d 1617) just to the north of Walsall in Staffordshire. His mother was Dame Ruth Scudamore, widow of Sir Philip Scudamore of Burnham, the second wife of Henry Leigh esq.[15] Samuel had a stepbrother Edward, later an MP, Henry's son by his first wife.[16] Edward Leigh, born in 1603, was a presbyterian, a well-known writer on religious matters and, at least initially, a staunch parliamentarian MP.[17] He would no doubt have been known to Sir John Potts. First elected in 1645, he was, like Potts, purged from parliament in 1648 but he suffered a brief imprisonment in the King's Head in the Strand. During the war, his wife Elizabeth had famously defended the fortified Rushall Hall in 1643 against Prince Rupert's troops. Although the royalists overcame her defence and maintained a garrison there, this was re-taken by Denbigh in 1644 and became again a local parliamentarian stronghold under Edward Leigh, now a colonel. Soldiers of either side would have had the opportunity to meet the members of the senior families in and around Rushall. Did Charles Potts fight in the area? If he was the parliamentary officer Potts known to be in the area at the time, he could have met the Leigh family in this way.[18] If he was there, the experience in garrison warfare could have been useful, after the restoration, for gaining his appointment in the Windsor Castle garrison.

Anne and Samuel had had two sons, Thomas and Samuel Leigh junior who now became Charles Potts's stepsons. Samuel was only about 7 when his mother remarried. Perhaps following his mother's choice - the Potts had always been Cambridge men - Samuel was entered a commoner of Merton College Oxford in Michaelmas term 1660. Although only 15, the following year he wrote a book entitled *Samuelis Primitae or an Essay towards a Metrical Version of the whole Book of Psalms*.[19]

Reflecting his attachment to his stepfather and his puritan upbringing, Samuel dedicated his work to 'Charles Potts esq' his 'father-in-law'. The line engraving of Samuel made by William Fairthorne (c1620-91) used on the frontispiece, depicted his youthfulness.[20] Some apparently considered it a great work for one so young especially given the boy was ill at the time. It was highly praised by Dr Thomas Manton and the Reverend Gabriel Sanger, leading lights in the presbyterian party at that time.[21] However this was the only published work by the young poet and translator. Although he matriculated on 12th December 1661, he left the University without a degree but was admitted to Lincoln's Inn on 23rd April 1663. At this time he would have been about 17, not an unusually early age to study law. After such a promising start, nothing further is known of young Samuel Leigh. He lived at his estate in Boston and may have been the 'Samuel Lee' having children in Lincoln in the 1660s. Despite his early poor health, he was still alive in 1686.

His older brother Thomas was more of a problem to his mother and stepfather. He had married without their knowledge and in June 1664 Thomas lodged a bill of complaint in chancery against them claiming Anne and Charles had hidden his true age from him, a regular chancery ploy.[22] His version of the key dates differed from those in his mother's account by at least two years - 1653 falls midway between them and may be a reasonable assumption of the date of their marriage. Thomas accused Charles and Anne, and his own brother Samuel junior, of conspiring to defraud him of his rights to the property that had been part of his father's holding in the manor of Rushall (not the manor itself) and that they had threatened the tenants there, dissuading them from paying him rent. Before answering his bill in 1666, Charles and Anne (and Samuel junior, then of Lincoln's Inn) counter-sued Thomas and his wife Rachael in 1665.[23] At this time Thomas Leigh gent was of the city of Westminster and may have been living near his mother and stepfather. Charles Potts, in his action, was also given as of the city of Westminster.

In their chancery answer of July 1666 Charles and Anne related that her father, Thomas Cornwallis, had been a trustee for Henry Leigh of Rushall manor in October 1625 when Henry made a settlement on his wife Dame Ruth.[24] The Staffordshire property at issue in the court case had been settled explicitly on Samuel senior after the deaths of Henry and Ruth although the manor itself passed to his half-brother Edward Leigh.[25] The case papers revealed the background to the dispute. Anne had brought to her marriage with Samuel senior a dowry, reportedly of at least £1,500, but no marriage settlement was initially drawn up. During their marriage Samuel intended to settle the Staffordshire premises on her for life and then on their younger son Samuel junior and his heirs. Presumably Thomas was to have whatever property there was in Lincoln and elsewhere. Articles of agreement were drawn up and sent as a brief to one Mr Archer of Gray's Inn (by the time of the 1664-66 action a justice of the Common Pleas). These provided for a life income, from part of the property's annual rental of £250, of £160 a year for Anne and afterwards at a reduced level an annuity for her son Samuel. However, in about 1651, Samuel senior died intestate before the formal documents were finished. Anne was advised that she could take the articles as sufficient evidence of her jointure or dowry rights in the property and on that basis, and as guardian of the 12 or 13 year old Thomas, she received the rents and profits. In about 1653, according to them, Charles and Anne were married and since then had jointly enjoyed the profits. They claimed that Thomas had only reached 21 the year before his bill (ie 1663) and he had pre-empted their giving him an account of his estate by bringing his action so rapidly. They underlined their apparent openness by saying he could always have checked the date in the parish register of where he was born. Considering they lived in London, Thomas would not have found that route particularly easy. In fact, allowing for a bit of licence, Thomas was probably born in 1640 and so came of age three years before his suit.[26]

However, now Charles and Anne had been advised that her claim to a jointure and rights to the Staffordshire property could not be justified on the earlier articles of agreement alone. They went on to complain that Thomas had refused her any dower rights and had turned the tenants in Staffordshire against her, stopping the rental flow. Anne and Charles said that they had had no recompense for Thomas's upbringing and they had proposed that if Thomas paid them £1,500 they would withdraw all rights to the property, drop all claim to dower rights and cancel the entail in the original deed from Henry to Dame Ruth and Samuel senior. Apparently he had initially agreed to this and various deeds between Thomas and Charles had been drawn up and by implication signed, although they may in fact have remained as drafts. Thomas had now changed his mind and refused to make any deal for £1,500 or to recognise any rights of his mother in the property. Anne and Charles blamed Ralph Piggott, (Thomas's wife's father), William Langden (a Leigh kinsman and now lessee), Nicholas Lysett and Edward Leigh for having influenced him. These 'confederates' had brought an eviction notice against Charles and Anne and were intent on depriving them of all rights in the premises. Piggott, in pursuit of personal gain, had married his daughter Rachel to Thomas without a significant dowry and without any consent or even knowledge of Thomas's mother and stepfather.

Samuel junior answered his brother's bill by saying that he agreed with Charles and Anne's answer. He disclaimed all right to the property, except as Thomas's brother and, at that point, his next heir if he died childless. By the summer of 1666, in the action Leigh versus Potts, Charles was under pressure for not delivering a sufficient answer to Thomas Leigh's bill. The action then disappeared from chancery orders. This may well mean that Thomas won by default.

Anne's father Thomas Cornwallis is a known figure in the early history of English settlement in Maryland. In 1634 he had sailed to America as a commissioner of the colony with Leonard Calvert, the governor. As Captain Cornwallis he led the colony's military activities, notably in actions around Kent Island. He became relatively wealthy from milling, tobacco growing and particularly from the fur trade. But he lost all when a protestant Richard Ingle, with a mandate from parliament, started attacking allegedly catholic settlements in St Mary's in 1644-45 and took and plundered Cornwallis's home and estate. Many of Maryland's settlers, having lost most of their goods to Ingle, retreated to Virginia. While most of the Cornwallis family had been catholic, Thomas's father, Sir Charles, was brought up a protestant and there is no evidence that Thomas or his daughters were catholic. It is not known whether his daughters were with him in Maryland, nor precisely when he returned, but the family then lived mostly in Lincoln. One of the other Cornwallis family seats was at Harborne in Staffordshire, barely ten miles from Rushall. Perhaps that had led to the match of Anne with Samuel Leigh. Anne's grandfather, Sir Charles Cornwallis was a knight of the shire for Norfolk in 1604 and had called upon his 'cosen' Sir Christopher Heydon for his support.[27] Cornwallis's third wife, in 1620, was the widow of Bishop Jegon, Bishop of Norwich. Although Sir Charles died at Harborne in 1629 he had been the most active deputy lieutenant in Norfolk between 1620 and 1628. As a justice he had worked closely with the young John Potts, Charles's father, so Anne may have known Charles from childhood.[28]

Might his father-in-law's experience in the Americas have influenced Charles Potts to explore trade opportunities there and in the West Indies? Potts was a merchant around the time of his marriage and three years later there is a reference to a Captain Potts involved in some way in the West Indies. Was this Charles or another Potts family altogether?[29] The clue may lie in the fact that the item refers to Mr Doughty, who was likely to have been William Doughty of Hanworth who spent 11 years or so in trade in the West Indies, living for most of the time in Barbados. There can be no doubt that the Potts and Doughty family knew each other well. Both were involved in Norfolk governance and one of the Doughty family even sat as a local commissioner in one of the Potts chancery cases. A few of William's letters home survive in the Aylsham collection in the Norfolk Record Office.[30] However they date from several years later and none of them contains any reference to this incident or to Potts.

> August 16th 1656: [Received] 265. Robt. Tilghman to Robt. Blackborne. Particulars of certain proceedings he took in the Court at Virginia against Capt. Ruther for bringing certain soldiers there from Jamaica in the *Strong Rowland,* now called the *Virginia Merchant,* Col. Obedience Robins being Judge of the Court, who Tilghman desired to swear and examine Capt. Potts and Mr. Doutye, Col. Scarborough being present. Desires Thos. Price, who has come over with him, may be examined. Endorsed: 'Rec. 12 Aug. 1656.'[31]

Perhaps Potts had, as a merchant, even become a ship owner and possibly ship master. Much later Charles was to write that he had been in royal service for 'upwards of 50 years'. From the late 1660s, after his stay in London, he seems to have become involved with Prince Rupert, now increasingly involved in naval matters, and may have eventually set sail for the West Indies. By the autumn of 1673 Charles Potts formally became Prince Rupert's deputy governor of the garrison at Windsor Castle. In the two years prior to his appointment there are four intriguing references in the state papers to a 'Mr Potts', which could be Charles, working for Prince Rupert in support of his various roles in the navy and as garrison commander of the Tower of London and Windsor Castle.

In September 1671 Charles Modyford wrote from the tower as a prisoner hoping 'not to be detained there by neglect or mistake'. His letter said: 'Mr Potts looked very carefully over every letter and sent me word he had nothing for Lord Arlington but to Lord Sandwich and the Council of Plantations he sent a packet'. The reference to plantations hints at Potts having a link to or good knowledge of the West Indies. In August 1672 Sir James Hayes wrote to the Navy Commissioners, by order of Prince Rupert, directing them to agree with the bearer, Mr Potts, for a vessel of his to carry over the Dutch deputies to Holland, adding that 'his Highness could not send his own order in writing, but that it would be sent tomorrow'. In December 1672 a note of naval and merchant ships at sea included a marginal reference to 'your packets for Jamaica are sent by Mr Potts commander of the Golden Lion' although this may relate to another Captain Potts.[32] This might well have been the *Golden Lion*, a large armed merchantman, which was at the heart of a 'battle' in 1655 off Maryland's coast by the River Severn between puritans and catholics, when Captain Roger Heamans of the *Golden Lion* was persuaded of the appropriateness of using his ship's guns against the catholics.[33]

In August 1673 Prince Rupert wrote to the King from 14 leagues south west of Yarmouth: 'my humble request is that Potts, who now commands in my absence, may have my places at Windsor and Capt Beckman my company of dragoons'. The Prince here was definitely discussing Charles.

Windsor

In September 1673 Charles Potts, the third son of Sir John Potts of Mannington, received his commission as Captain-Lieutenant to his Highness Prince Rupert in his company of foot in the garrison of Windsor Castle.[34] He was directly under the command of Prince Rupert who had been in charge of the Windsor Castle garrison from 1668, when he took over as Governor from Lord Mordaunt. The Prince was governor until his death in 1682 and it seems that Charles Potts lived in Windsor for the rest of his own, much longer, life probably involved in the garrison and administration of the Castle throughout. A letter from Windsor of July 1684 referred to Captain Potts as 'deputy governor of this castle', with whom a consignment of arms had been left for safekeeping.[35]

In keeping with family tradition, Charles Potts 'of Windsor' found himself named in a chancery action in November 1684.[36] Anne Symonds, widow and executrix of Samuel Symonds druggist of London, claimed that Charles Potts still owed her husband's estate £22 or more from a personal bill signed in 1662. After Samuel's death in 1679 she, through the services of one John Bagot gent, had pursued Potts for payment, but he had refused to pay. As so often in these cases, she claimed that he had admitted liability, had offered to pay an instalment but now she had lost the paperwork. Frankly, Charles's answer smacks of the truth. He flatly denied ever being indebted to Symonds. Instead he explained he had used him as a personal banker, lodging £300 with him which he then drew off in small amounts as he needed cash. The bills that Anne had found were simply the receipts he had signed to enable Symonds to record these amounts against the balance he held. At no point had he admitted a liability to pay, but had sent £20 to London in case he did owe money. When no bill was produced his agent had brought the money back to him. No doubt the case would have been readily resolved on production of the note and without it presumably Charles had no liability.

Apart from his Castle position, Charles Potts was one of the local aldermen when in March 1685 a warrant was issued for a new charter for New Windsor in

Berkshire.[37] He was also made one of the five justices of the peace, another of whom was the notoriously harsh Lord Chief Justice Jeffreys (within two months to be elevated to the House of Lords). By April 1685 the Governor of Windsor Castle garrison was Henry, Duke of Norfolk. Charles was his Lieutenant-Governor as well as lieutenant to Henry's own troop of gunners. As number two to a busy man, this again implies that Charles ran the Castle's military activities on a day-to-day basis. In November 1687 Charles was a senior lieutenant in the Earl of Lichfield's Regiment of Foot. By September 1688 he had become a captain in the same regiment. The *Army List* entry notes that Potts 'adhered to James II in the revolution' - a hint at his absolute loyalty to the reigning monarch. Subsequent volumes have no further entries for Charles suggesting that he was not further promoted. It may also imply that he held no formal military commission under William and Mary, having been a staunch supporter of King James. That he considered himself a servant of the crown throughout is clear from a later letter and it is of course possible that he remained in a role of substance at Windsor Castle. He may have been the Captain Potts who appeared as paid two sums of £9 4s in the army accounts of Richard, Earl of Ranelagh, the paymaster general presented in November 1690.[38]

However there was then a long period with no sightings of Charles. He may simply have lived a quiet life in Windsor. Charles Potts was certainly a tax payer in New Windsor in 1691 and again in 1697-98.[39] On the other hand, a letter in the state papers of November 1704 has a passing reference to 'Mr Potts' as the Marshal of the Isle of Wight. Was this another garrison role for Charles? Unfortunately there appear to be no records on the island for this Potts. Charles would however have been about 80 by this time so if the post was his, presumably it was a sinecure.

His first wife Anne had died in 1684 after 30 years of marriage. Charles's agreement to her burial in Rushall may have been influenced by her son Samuel Leigh as a mark of respect for her first husband.[40] After 21 years of being a widower, Charles Potts re-married at a remarkably late stage in his life. On 11th December 1705 Charles Potts of Windsor married Anne Hartwell of Windsor in St Augustine's Church, Watling Street in the City of London. Anne was almost certainly the 'Ann Hartwell daughter of Thomas' baptised in Finchamsted, Berkshire on 10th February 1675. A single woman of thirty she may have been quite content to marry the old soldier!

An old history of Windsor confirms Charles's role there in the years before his death.[41] On 8th November 1714, after the accession of George I, the Duke of Kent was appointed Governor of Windsor Castle. In turn he appointed a number of men to various roles under him, including Charles Potts esq as his Deputy. It is not clear whether Charles's was a new appointment or a re-affirmation of an existing one - some of the other appointments were definitely a continuation of previous service in non-military roles there. Whether his role by then had any military responsibility for the castle's defences is doubtful, but he would have born the burden of the day-to-day management of the fabric of the castle. But in this role Charles Potts appears to have struggled from an early stage of Kent's period of office. On 16th August 1715 the Duke of Kent wrote to Charles:

Sir, I have received your letter and I desire you forthwith to acquaint Mr Peasley that I am well satisfied that he knows he ought not to presume to make any new windows or other alterations in the castle wall belonging to the lodgings in which he dwells without my permission for doing the same; and therefore I do require him immediately after this notice to fill up the breach which he has caused to be made, wherein the new window is now placed, in the same manner that the wall was formerly built, and so as to appear on the outside as before the breach was made. I can by no means allow of your excuse that the servant of the Clerk of Works neglected to forbid Mr Peasley making the window. It was I think your duty to take care that no such alteration be made without my knowledge and approbation, and it must now be your business to see this order obeyed. Kent[42]

In 1717 Richard, Lord (later Viscount) Cobham became Governor and just three years later Charles sent him his resignation, in a letter from Windsor dated 1st June 1720. The wording could be taken to mean that he had been at Windsor for a long time and that for some time the role had not been a military one:

My Lord, I having served the crown of England upwards of fifty years either in the army or being Lt Governor of Windsor Castle am now by age and other infirmities rendered incapable to perform my duty in that post.

Therefore I most humbly beg your lordship's leave to recommend an officer to succeed in that post, who has served the crown of England in the army upwards of thirty years and that is Mr John Olivier who is now a Lieutenant in Major General Evans's Regiment of Dragoons, he having given me sufficient consideration to resign my place to him. And in so doing these shall be forever acknowledged as a singular favour done to one who is My Lord, your Lordship's most humble servant

Charles Potts

Mr Olivier was appointed the very next day. This letter is fascinating as it shows that the post could in effect be sold on by the outgoing holder.

Charles Potts, now nearly 100, did not live much longer. He had made his will in February 1716 as Charles Potts esq 'of New Windsor Berkshire', and he died there in early January 1721.[43] His friend John Harris of Windsor Castle was to act as trustee for all his real estate and goods, to ensure that Charles's wife Anne enjoyed them for her lifetime. His money was to be put out at interest for her. As they had no children, after Anne's death, any money remaining was to pass to Charles Potts the son of Roger Potts. He described Charles as his nephew, but he was of course his great-nephew, and perhaps, given the name, he may have been his godson. Algernon, as the eldest, was the Potts heir and was still alive when the will was made so Charles had been particularly favoured by his great-uncle. Charles junior was also to ensure that Anne should be paid 6% per annum from the value of any money of Charles senior's that he might hold. Small legacies were made to John Harris, Hartwell Black his wife's kinsman and to his own kinswoman Susanna Long (Roger Potts's daughter and the younger Charles's sister). Harris was to be executor and Charles Potts supervisor.

Anne Potts, widow and relict of Charles Potts esq late of New Windsor deceased, made her own will on 20th February 1721.[44] It was proved by her friend Susan Gay widow of Windsor Castle her executrix in April 1727. She left £200 out at interest for life to her sister Mary Black after which the principal was to go to the children of her nephews and nieces on her family's side.[45] The £200 remained unspent by her sister. Mary Black's will was proved in April 1729 and she left small legacies to her six children to be paid in part from the £200 in the hands of Mrs Gay of Windsor Castle.

Charles outlived all his brothers and sisters. His eldest brother, Sir John junior, the heir to Mannington, had led a very different, far less adventurous, life.

PART 3

DECLINE AND FALL

'Sir Charles said to me that he had never a relation but what had disobliged him'

Letter 16th January 1732 Bayfield to Walpole, Wolterton archives

Chapter 18

Sir John Potts 2ⁿᵈ Baronet: Through the Looking Glass

Relatively little is known about the second Sir John (1618-1678). He seems to have lived under the shadow of his father who almost outlived him. Previous writers on the family managed only a few basic biographical facts. Further research has proved that this was indeed a true reflection of John's lack of achievement; he hardly touched the historical record. John remains a shadowy (enigmatic would be too interesting) figure: references to him during his life occurred usually in relation to events surrounding his father and the rest of what is known of him comes from information given after his death.

John was the eldest son of the first Sir John by his second wife Ursula Willoughby/Spelman. He was baptised at Narborough on 28ᵗʰ April 1618, the only one of John and Ursula's children to be baptised there. He had a classic gentleman's education, probably being taught by Paul Amyraut in Itteringham before going to Cambridge where he was admitted to Katherine Hall (later St Catharine's College) in 1634. Venn said he was also admitted to Gray's Inn in October the same year. Perhaps his father was mindful that his own father had been a practising lawyer and his brother Charles was a successful lawyer at Middle Temple. However if John was destined for a career in the law, there is no obvious evidence that he ever practised the law. Maybe he did not take to it. Quite likely, as with many sons of the gentry, he saw studying law as simply the final polishing of a gentleman's education. He seems to have lived in Norfolk all his life but appears to have spent much of his time socialising in Norwich and London.

Marriage to Susan Heveningham

John married twice, first to Susan (or Susanna), the daughter of Sir John Heveningham of Ketteringham Norfolk and his wife Bridget, the daughter of Christopher Paston.[1] They were married on 16ᵗʰ October 1639 in Heveningham in Suffolk, the older family seat, rather than at Susan's family home in Ketteringham. Susan's brother was William Heveningham, the future regicide. One of her sisters, Abigail, married Augustine Pettus, the son of the Mayor of Norwich. Another, Anne, married first Henry Gawdy and then John Spelman, John Potts's half-brother. Susan's father did not live to see her marriage; he was buried in Ketteringham on 17ᵗʰ June 1633.[2]

John and Susan's marriage settlement of 14ᵗʰ October 1639 has survived.[3] As well as showing that she brought a substantial dowry, it is a valuable document for its listing of many of the farms on the Mannington estate. The estate was settled on the married couple and their heirs. This was a tripartite deed, with the parties being: (1) John Potts the elder of Mannington esq, Dame Ursula Lady Spelman his wife and Dame Anne Lady Heydon widow his mother; (2) William Heveningham of Heveningham Suffolk esq and Arthur his brother, and (3) John Potts the younger gent and Susan Heveningham sister of William and Arthur, the sons and daughter of Sir John Heveningham, late of Ketteringham Norfolk, deceased. Susan's portion on her marriage was to be £2,400. The settlement listed in detail the manors and lands of the Potts which would pass to the couple. If they lacked sons, the estate would revert to John's brothers Francis and Charles or to his uncle Charles. The two Dames were each to have an annuity of £200 a year for life. Importantly John and Susan's daughters would have provision for their maintenance until age 18 if necessary and then their marriage portions were specified, effectively using the whole of Susan's portion: at least £2,000 if one daughter; £1,000 each if two; £800 each if three. In Chapter 19 the importance of this clause will become clear.

The detailed specification of the real estate gave a picture of the estate at that time and was used by all subsequent major deeds as the effective start of the title to Mannington. The individual farm and field names are mostly identifiable on the 1595 estate map.[4] The core of the old manorial estate, in some mix of in-hand and tenant farms, was not detailed but simply described as the manors of Mannington, Wolterton and Coldham in Mannington, Itteringham, Wolterton, Calthorpe, Barningham and Oulton. There followed fourteen separately listed parcels of property with their occupiers.[5] Most if not all of these specified lands were separate acquisitions made at various times.

After their marriage where John and Susan lived is not certain but the lack of entries elsewhere for the baptisms of their three children Roger, Elizabeth and Ursula, indicates that they lived in Mannington with Sir John senior and Dame Ursula. Ursula, named after her grandmother and aunt, died unmarried sometime around 1672.[6]

Marriage to Elizabeth Browne

Similarly, it is not known when Susan died or how long John remained a widower. However on 16th July 1661, Sir John settled the majority of a property in Clippesby on his son John Potts esq and his second wife Elizabeth, the daughter of the recently knighted Sir Samuel Browne of Bedfordshire.[7] Browne was cousin to Oliver St John who was a leading player in the House in the 1640s, whose family Sir John Potts could claim kinship with through his grandmother Katherine Leighton. In 1648 Browne had been a Chief Justice of the Common Pleas and he was a highly-regarded lawyer, MP and parliamentary manager during the Civil War.[8] Samuel had worked closely with Sir John Potts both before and during the Isle of Wight negotiations with the King and, as a moderate, had also suffered seclusion in Pride's Purge. In 1649 Browne resigned from all public roles in protest at the King's execution. At the Restoration he was knighted and served again as a judge of Common Pleas. He sat as MP for Bedfordshire in 1660, renewing his acquaintance with Sir John; perhaps the fathers deliberately introduced the couple. Browne gave his daughter a dowry of £2,000 and his will, made in 1667, showed he had paid it in two halves. It

would seem Browne knew John Potts junior already had debts or perhaps Sir John
had warned him to not to pay until the jointure was settled. The will included the
statement 'I often pressed [John Potts] to settle the jointure but until he purchased
Clippesby he did not do so and I would not pay the £2,000 until Elizabeth had a
jointure'.[9] The marriage therefore may have taken place earlier than November 1660
with Sir John having to organise his son into the Clippesby deal in order to release
the money for the settlement. Their marriage was to be childless. Elizabeth outlived
her husband by many years. After his death in 1678, she left Mannington and
went to a house in Norwich which they also appear to have held at this time. Still a
widow, Elizabeth died in 1712 in Highgate in the parish of Hornsey and was buried
at her family seat of Arlesey on 21ˢᵗ July.[10]

Sir John junior remains a rather ill-defined character. A small illustration of his
modest local role survives in a few of his letters to his friend Robert Doughty esq
of Hanworth in 1661.[11] In the summer of 1660, Potts was appointed one of the
commissioners and collectors for the poll tax being raised for disbanding and paying
the army. His father was also named but was away in the House of Commons and
living at Enfield. John, with others, was responsible for bringing in the £402 due
from South Erpingham which he duly handed over to the sheriff, Sir John Cremer,
in late October. The tone of the letters showed a man not quite comfortable in
this role and uncertain about the calculations. Nonetheless he appeared eager to
undertake the collecting and book-keeping correctly. He was travelling regularly
between London and Mannington at this time, perhaps enjoying the new mood
of Restoration society. His wife would have visited her family seat at Arlesey in
Bedfordshire and no doubt her father's house in London. John also appears to have
had the fashionable concern for his health:

> To his much valued friend Robert Doughty esq at his house
> in Hanworth in Norfolk: leave this with Daniell Mudicliff at
> Mannington to be sent with speed
> 27 Mar 1661
>
> Sir
>
> I rec your letter wherein you desire to know what mony I rec and
> what pd the shrieve [sheriff]. The estreates are all gathered except
> that of Aylsham where it is exprest at the bottom what remains
> and where. The sum gathered to my best computation to 402:19:1
> the salary to the collectors and clarks etc 3:7:2 the remaining
> 399:11:11. I pd the shreive for which I have his receipt. I shall by
> gods permission be in Norfolk about a fortnight hence & shall then
> give you further satisfaction in the interim I have sent you this short
> account together with my thanks for your civility to
> your ready friend and servant
>
> Jo Potts

To his much valued friend Robert Doughty esq at his house in
Hanworth
7 Apr 1661

Sir

I had a letter from you while I was in London concerning the Poll
money to which I gave answer & I hope satisfaction but because
my cosyn Houghton left order with my man that I should give you
intimation of my being here if I came into Norfolk I have sent this
bearer to let you know that I am at Mannington and I did intend
to waite on you but by reason of a cold I am unfit to come abroad,
but if either your occasions will give you leisure to receive personal
satisfaction or you signifie your desire in writing, I shall readily shew
my endeavours and remaine

your faithful servant

Jo Potts

I know nothing in arreare but what is mentioned in the estreat of
Aylsham, and for my father I can assure you he have pd according to
his degree at London where he ought to pay as I conceive.

To his honoured friend Robert Doughty esq at his house in Hanworth
Mon 9 Apr 1661

Sir

I cannot but acknowledge your care of your publick kindeness in
particular to my self, which I should willingly have done personally
had I not bin prevented by this unfortunate cold (taken by wet in
my feete as I came). It does confine me to my chamber; the Phisick
is present and will keep me 1 day longer here to prepare me for my
jorny on Thursday about nine of the clock, before which time if
your occasions will permitt you I shall give any further satisfaction,
which possibly I might personally doe: But least [lest] you should
not be able to afford that favour, I have sent you the duplicate of
the estreats which I had, which you may compare with the other, to
rectifie and returne to my man at your best leysure, & keepe which
you please. I had also a letter from my father last night [intimating]
a certificate under three of the commissioners hands and seales, pd
at the Gyle Hall London; and for my self I pd £10 as by the estreat
appeares which is more than duble the purporcion we should have
pd for our estates. I have not the shreives acquittance here, but will

give you a copy of it, the sums I wrot you exactly as I had computed them wherein I trusted not to my owne skill singly & truly to say they fall out just, I should arogate more to my owne skill then is fit for me, but I am not wilfully guilty of any mistakes or neglect, I am sorry for any truble happened either to you or your publick herein, I shall be glad of any opportunity whereby I may approve myself,

yr very faithful friend and servant

Jo Potts

May 9 1660 [sic] To his much valued friend Robert Doughty esq of Hanworth in Norfolk this

Sir

I have herewith sent you the copy of the sheriffs acquittance which I should have done sooner had it come to my hand, yet I suppose it may come seasonably enough seeing it agrees with the intimation I gave you before. If you send up the books before I am down, I shall endeavour to get them received & and if I may be able in anything to serve you here, you shall find me very really, yr friend and servant

Jo Potts

Although he rather peevishly pointed out how much had been paid by Mannington, the letters did not give the impression of a confident landowner in his early forties as might be expected. About this time, Sir John senior settled much of the family property on John and his son Roger. All the pointers are that John was not a particularly worldly man and that Sir John recognised that by placing particular trust in his grandson.

One of the issues that Sir John senior left for his son and grandson to resolve related to the estate that he had bought in Clippesby in 1660. It appears to have been bought simply as a fairly-priced estate that he could use to provide for John junior, his second wife and children. In the event, as problems with the tenant rumbled on, the whole family may have come to regret the day it was acquired. Worse, the Clippesby property was to be at the heart of a major family feud in the 1680s.

The Clippesby estate

Sir John Potts senior purchased a manor and lands in Clippesby and Repps with Bastwick on 10ᵗʰ November 1660 from John Crew esq and Carey his wife of Crewe in Cheshire.[12] The history of the property helps to explain the later court actions. In the sixteenth century Clippesby, together with the manor of Oby, had been held by the Clippesby family of Oby. John Clippesby of Oby esq died in 1598 leaving his wife (Juliana the daughter of Matthew Ellis of Cheshire) a life interest in his estates and specified in his will how his manors should be divided amongst his three daughters as co-heiresses.[13] His wife had for herself a windmill in Clippesby and some lands in Repps with Bastwick, held of the manor of Clippesby. Audrey, born in 1565, was to have the manor of Oby with its lands; Frances, born in 1567, would have Clippesby; and Juliana, born in 1574, was to have the residue in Repps with Bastwick, Martham, Rollesby and elsewhere. Frances seems to have died young or at least unmarried and her share was divided between her sisters.[14] On 20th July 1598, Juliana or Julia, by then apparently a servant of the Countess of Shrewsbury, married Randolph Crew and in 1600 Audrey married Thomas Guybon.[15]

Sir Randolph Crew became a well-known MP and successful lawyer, serving as Chief Justice of the Common Pleas during the reign of James I. He acquired the manor of Crewe in Cheshire, a property which had belonged to Sir Christopher Hatton, and made that his principal country seat. In October 1603, after the early death that summer of Julia her daughter, Juliana Clippesby, widow, settled her lands and tenements in Repps and Bastwick on Clippesby Crew son of Sir Randolph.[16] This split of the Clippesby lands into two parts was to be important later. Sir Randolph remarried to another Julia: Julia Hesketh, née Fasey, the widow of a lawyer. After his death in 1646, Sir Randolph's properties passed to his son, Sir Clippesby Crew, an MP who outlived his father by only three years.[17] The latter's will referred to an April 1647 settlement of the Clippesby estate on Randolph Crew, Clippesby's second son. This Randolph was a known cartographer.[18] When he died of a mugging in Paris in 1657, his estate passed to his elder brother John Crew. No doubt John had little interest in the fairly small Clippesby property so remote from his country seat. John Crew was the cousin of John Crew (or Crewe), MP who had worked with Sir John in the Isle of Wight.

Meanwhile, the Oby part of the Clippesby family properties passed through the Guybon line. On 30th June 1600 in Clippesby, Audrey Clippesby married Thomas Guybon gent, the son of Humphrey Guybon of Stradsett. Humphrey, who died in 1601, was a cousin of the William Guybon of Watlington who was involved in Mannington's affairs. Thomas and Audrey baptised John Guybon, their son and heir, in Oby in 1602 and he went on to marry Katherine the daughter of Francis Mapes of Rollesby. Their eldest surviving son was Clippesby Guybon of Oby gent, born there in February 1630, who married Bridget the daughter of Thomas Blofeld of Sustead in Oby on 5th September 1651.

On 31st July 1656 Clippesby Guybon took two 21 year leases covering the whole Clippesby estate, including the extra lands in Repps with Bastwick, from Sir Randolph Crew.[19] Thus by his ownership of Oby and his leases in Clippesby, Repps and Bastwick, he had recreated the old Clippesby family estate. Chancery papers showed that Guybon paid £230 yearly rent for both leases. The one lease that survives for the Repps with Bastwick part of the estate shows that the manors and lands there, and in Thurne, were leased for 21 years at £120 annual rent. Under this agreement, Crew was to continue to pay taxes and maintain all houses and buildings in good condition; while Guybon was to keep in repair all ditches, drains and fences. This would give Guybon plenty of room to negotiate reductions in his actual net rental payments.

When, in 1660, Sir John Potts purchased Clippesby Hall in Clippesby and Repps with Bastwick from Crew, he acquired with them, as sitting tenant, Clippesby Guybon. Perhaps Sir John's intention had been to own premises near to Yarmouth, where he was MP in 1660. This possible motivation is strengthened by the late 1670s inventory of his son (see below). This included Clippesby and listed a chamber reserved in Clippesby Hall for the use of the lord of the manor, rather than the tenant or farmer. Sir John may have used it as a base when in Yarmouth. Much of the land there was said to be marsh and fen and hard to farm. It is after all on the edge of the Broads and close by the river Thurne. Sir John seems to have been drawn to marshland and fen - his brother's Essex lands, the Bedford Level and now Clippesby. It turned out that Sir John had inherited a bad tenant, one with debt problems who was always slow to pay his rent. The subsequent long saga in chancery has left some depositions that give some helpful insights into the Potts family during the 1660s and later.[20] The debt-related material that involved Sir John Potts junior and his son Roger Potts is covered in a later chapter. Similarly the Clippesby estate became the heart of major chancery actions between Roger Potts and his sister Elizabeth after the death of their father in 1677. Since much of those actions have to do with the next two generations, they will appear later leaving us here to cover the Clippesby story as it relates to Clippesby Guybon.

When Sir John Potts senior had generously made a settlement for John's second marriage, he had given him only part of the Clippesby estate. In his keenness to split his property between his son and his grandson Roger, he had settled on John the Clippesby Hall portion and on Roger the smaller Repps with Bastwick part. During the late 1660s and early 1670s each was therefore responsible for and due their share of the rent from Guybon. Despite the fact that the estate was historically separate and Guybon had held two leases from Randolph Crew, he tried to claim that the estate had not previously been split in this way. He also said that John and Roger squabbled over who was owed what and what expenses or charges Guybon could legitimately charge against each part of his overall lease of the whole estate. This at least may well have been true. No doubt Clippesby Guybon routinely exploited this acrimony between father and son to delay payment. Sir John, John and Roger together pursued Guybon in court for rent arrears and in February 1669 were awarded a judgement for rent arrears of £124 10s (which would seem to have been for the six months to Lady Day for the whole estate). On failure to pay, Roger had even had Guybon arrested.

During 1670 the dispute over rent arrears had worsened to the point where it was agreed to go to arbitration before lawyers John Hobart of Norwich and Robert Doughty of Aylsham, who would review full accounts and give their opinion. In March they found that of £3,500 of rent payable since the start of the Crew leases to Guybon, just £111 10s 9d remained due to John and Roger Potts. Doughty thought this the appropriate figure, but Hobart felt that there was doubt over whether £100 which Guybon claimed to have paid to William Davy (Roger's father-in-law) on 30ᵗʰ March 1667 had in fact been paid. The resolution was for Guybon to make out two bonds: first £150 to cover the definite rent arrears and then a further £100 bond to be held until he proved that he had made the £100 payment to Davy. The bonds were taken out via Augustine Briggs in Norwich. The bonds and all the paperwork regarding the rent dispute would be held by Hobart until the matter was resolved to his full satisfaction. Guybon was to receive a release confirming all rents were paid up to Michaelmas 1670. He was also to continue to enjoy the windmill he had on the estate and should not be penalised for any lands that he had just ploughed, contrary to his lease.

The release was made and the £150 bond was handed over to John Potts, leaving only the £100 matter in contention, which bond stayed with Hobart. Guybon said he paid William Davy the £100 towards the Potts rent and that he had a receipt from Roger some time later. Although Roger agreed that Guybon had gone to Ellingham Hall just days before William Davy died in 1667 and handed over some money, he claimed that only £60 was handed over which related solely to a business transaction relating to an estate in Anmer with which William Davy had been helping Guybon. Davy had refused to do more until he received a payment. Roger had later sent a receipt on the back of a power of attorney which enabled him to act as executor for Davy. That money had never been to the use of the Potts and therefore he said the £100 was still due.

Hobart, from the tenor of his chancery deposition, seemed to side with Roger but was faced with Guybon's witness Mr Dusgate who said he had seen Guybon withdraw £100 in Norwich and had been with him on the visit to Ellingham. He did not say precisely that it was the full amount handed over, nor was he certain that it was for the Potts. Hobart presumably found it too difficult to arbitrate and was unable to persuade Guybon to pay up, resulting in John and Roger going to chancery. During May to September 1671 chancery orders showed that the issue was to be heard by a commission of enquiry.[21] Claim and crossclaim between John Potts junior and Guybon followed in pursuit of the £100. Sir John senior was not directly involved in the complaint and so the action was not affected by his death in 1673. The original arbitrators themselves became defendants against the Potts as the action got more acrimonious. Initial answers were given and the action still could not be resolved. So it went to a commission of enquiry with depositions from all the interested parties and more. In December 1674 Potts was given permission to interview John Hobart as a material witness but by February Potts was found to have jumped the gun and held the commission of enquiry too soon.[22]

In April 1675 the depositions were heard in Norwich. Helen (or Ellen) Gourney, William Davy's wife's sister, of Great Ellingham spinster aged 60, testified that William had told her only £60 had been paid and that it had related to the estate in Anmer and Davy had refused to seal the writings until paid. She had heard that Roger had delivered to Guybon the relevant bond regarding this sum. Roger said much the same. Hobart testified to all the background and importantly added that Francis Dusgate could not confirm that the payment at Ellingham had been to the Potts account. Hobart still held the bond.

As ever in Potts actions, the redoubtable duo of Daniel Muddiclift and Thomas Spurgeon did their bit. Spurgeon said that as early as 1660, just after the purchase of

Clippesby, Sir John senior had settled it on John and Roger. He confirmed that the two of them had become agitated with each other regarding the estate and its rents. Muddiclift added a little more. While Sir John had been living in Enfield, he had assumed that all rent had been paid to John and therefore had not been aware of the extent of the problems with Guybon. When he found out, Sir John had sent for Guybon and threatened to sue him if he did not pay all the amounts due to both John and Roger. Sir John only stopped his action when Guybon came with his accounts to meet him at Muddiclift's house in Itteringham. Presumably, being Sir John, he felt the arrears were not sufficient to justify legal action.

After Sir John senior's death, the legal process continued through 1675 and 1676 in chancery.[23] Three enquiries were held altogether in what was really a rather modest issue. But pride was by now at stake, even as legal costs mounted. In April 1676 at a chancery hearing both parties were found to be intransigent over their claims and the case was ordered to be tried at law at the next Norfolk assizes. After a verdict the parties were to return to chancery for any equity decisions. In November 1676 the chancery clerk recorded that the assizes' verdict had been given in favour of Guybon.[24] Specifically, the receipt on the letter of attorney had weighed against the Potts case. Guybon was discharged, Potts had to pay his own costs and Hobart was to release all the documents that he held to Guybon.

The case was over but relations between John and Roger Potts and Clippesby Guybon remained poor. After John junior's death, another case between Roger Potts and Clippesby Guybon blew up, first sighted in a minor process order in the summer of 1680 and again in process points in early 1681.[25] In April 1682 depositions in Sir Roger's action against Thomas Browne, Clippesby Guybon and John Guybon reveal that at Michaelmas 1673 Guybon had ceased to be the tenant of Clippesby and Sir Roger was questioning the final accounts of that time.[26] Perhaps Roger felt he had lost out over the £100. This time just £50 was at issue and again the case rumbled on for a disproportionate time. Roger's case was that Clippesby Guybon had always been in arrears and that in September 1673 he had owed much more than £70. Sir John junior had said he would accept £50 on account if Guybon could raise it. Guybon on asking where it might be borrowed at interest, had been told by James Fountaine of Salle that Thomas Browne of Aylsham had money available. He hinted that Browne would only lend to Guybon if he had Sir John sign the bond as surety. Fountaine testified in support of Roger as did his Norwich attorney William Payne, gent aged 47. Payne had been cited with Roger in an action by Browne relating to the bond. He believed that with Guybon's name first on the bond it was his and that Potts was only on it as security. Endorsements on the back showed unequivocally that Guybon had paid the interest payments on it to Browne.

Muddiclift, testifying yet again, said there had been a history of rental arrears and that, after the termination of Guybon's lease, he had been repeatedly to Clippesby and Oby to try to recover more than £70 in rent arrears. He had often been told by Sir John junior that the £50 bond was for rent arrears too. Interestingly his statement incidentally confirmed that Roger was not often at Mannington in his youth. Muddiclift said that he had known Sir John junior for 25 years before his death -

that is from about 1652. At that time, with Sir John senior away from Norfolk, Daniel may have arrived to take a major role in looking after the estate. Yet he said he had only known Roger for 16 years or more - from about 1666. During Roger's education at Enfield, Cambridge and at the inns of court, he may have been a rare visitor to Mannington. With his parents perhaps preferring life in Norwich and London, he probably spent most of his vacation times with them or his grandfather in Enfield. Otherwise the estate steward would surely have known him well.

Roger's opposition, however, argued that the bond was in fact a debt of Sir John's. Thomas Browne testified that Sir John junior had borrowed £50 from him and that Guybon was the surety on the bond. Subsequently, in January 1680 and witnessed by Edward Mapes grocer of Norwich, he had assigned the bond to John Guybon. He said that Fountaine was complicit in getting Guybon's name first on the bond rather than Potts, which he had initially started to draft. In May 1682 the case was heard.[27] Sir Miles Cooke was ordered to investigate further whether rent arrears of more than the £50 bond were still outstanding or not. More examination of witnesses followed, but it seems the matter was eventually settled out of court and it did not appear to come back for a final order.[28]

It is entertaining to note that the Guybon brothers ended up fighting in Guybon versus Guybon in 1687.[29] John Guybon, gent of Oby, complained against his brother Clippesby Guybon esq that Clippesby had been indebted to him for £500 in 1682, with a property in Clench Wharton and Tilney used as security for a mortgage. John had recently entered the premises on the default on repayment of interest as well as principal - he had received a court judgement to recover £700. Clippesby moaned that this was hard and un-brotherly behaviour when he was at that time already in prison for debt!

Sir John junior's will

The date of Sir John junior's death has usually been quoted as around 1691. In fact close scrutiny of his grandchildren's baptism entries in Great Ellingham parish registers narrowed down his date of death to late 1677 or 1678. His son Roger became 'Sir Roger' at this time in the entries. Unlike most of the male members of his family, no will for Sir John junior was proved in national or Norfolk courts. This is the more surprising as Sir John was said to have been in the habit of making a new will every time he went travelling. Presumably he believed his health was not robust. Fortunately, the text of his last will was recited in chancery papers and is printed here for the first time. The same source dated his death to early 1678.

The text was used by Elizabeth Potts in her November 1680 bill of complaint to chancery. The action was against her brother and related to the precise contents of the will and a codicil. Sir Roger did not dispute Elizabeth's rendition of the will, except in so far as the will and codicil pertained to Clippesby property and the money bequeathed to Elizabeth. Details of the various actions between brother and sister over this will be covered in the next chapter. She confirmed the rest of the quoted will was accurate.

Elizabeth said that 'in 1677 Sir John Potts her father having a great tenderness and affection for Elizabeth Potts his only daughter … made his last will and annexed a codicil to it in the following words':

29 March 1677

I, Sir John Potts … having had divers sicknesses … mindful of my approaching change which I do daily expect … I commend my soul into the hands of almighty god …

Item … my friends to be kind to my wife and my children to be obedient … especially to my daughter … but in regard to the great debts left upon me by my father besides divers of my own I cannot so fully recompense her as I desired and as she deserves. My children I commit to the goodness and providence of god …

And whereas by four part indenture of 6ᵗʰ October 1668 between 1. Sir John Potts; 2. Me John Potts and my son Roger Potts and Mary his wife; 3. and 4. certain trustees … settling manors and lands and raise and pay £500 apiece (besides maintenance) to my daughters … and power to grant £2,000 and such reasonable interest as I think fit … as I shall declare in my last will … and Ursula now dead so only to raise £500 for Elizabeth … I appoint the £2,000 to be used to increase Elizabeth's portion and pay my debts … £1,000 within 6 months of my decease and £1,000 within a further 12 months after thereafter …

Item. To my dear wife my best coach and my two best coach horses with their apparel this raised by myself and the plate which her mother gave me by will and also her diamond pendant and ring … also the furniture now in my chamber, all but what was left there by my father. Also I give her the bed which she is now working of never yet finished the material being all her own.

Item. To my trusty servant Daniel Muddiclift £5 per annum for life to be paid out of the lease for years bearing the date of 6ᵗʰ October 1668 … if he be dwelling with me at the time of my death or then in my service, willing my children to be kind to him.

Item. To every servant living with me at the time of my death one quarter's wages over and above their yearly wages which shall be then due.

Item. To my daughter Elizabeth all my right and title to my lands manors and rents in Bastwick and Repps expressed and declared to be sold in a deed of 20th April 1669 between Sir John Potts my father and Mr Roger Potts my son.

Item. To the poor of Itringham £5 to be distributed as my executor thinks fit.

Item. My executor to bestow £10 to bind out to apprenticeship some of the children of such as have been labourers for me.

Item. To my grandchild James Potts all my household stuff at Mannington being most of it purchased by myself and my dear wife's provident care and I do will that they shall be continued in the house at Mannington.

Item. I will all my manors messuages and lands in Flegg settled upon my wife for jointure to Elizabeth and her heirs for ever after my wife's decease as also my marsh grounds in Hickling called Longer.

And lastly I give to Elizabeth all the rest of my goods and chattels and money owed me for rents … and otherwise after charges and my debts and legacies are paid …

My body to be laid in the chapel at Mannington by my first wife in whose grave I made provision to that end when she was buried and I would be buried very privately and speedily with as little trouble and charge as is decent.

And I make Elizabeth my daughter sole executrix … desiring that my own single debts may be first paid other debts being my father's proper debts and lands and other securities given for them dated the day and year mentioned herein.

I will also £10 to my godson Daniel Greene which I had before forgotten.

John Potts signed and sealed in the presence of Richard Burrell John Burdwell John Barkham William Trappett

A codicil annexed to my last will: whereas I have appointed the £2,000 … to Elizabeth's portion and payment of my debts … and all my Flegg lands devised in jointure to my wife and to my daughter and her heirs absolutely I do hereby declare … she should only have the said estate as security for her more certain assurance of the payment of the £2,000 which I intend she should have out of my estate … and then my Flegg estate should go to my son Roger to enable him to provide for his younger children … and after my debts and legacies are paid the residue of my personal estate to my son.

Dated 6ᵗʰ February 1678

Supervisors to be my very good friends James Fountayne esq and Mr Edward Britiffe esq of Baconsthorpe.

Witnesses: Thomas Browne, James Scambler junior, Daniel Muddiclift, William Trappett.

James Potts was Roger's first son, but he had died when very young. Daniel Green was family through John's half-sister Barbara Hills. The will showed that most of Sir John senior's household goods had not stayed at Mannington. They probably had been sold, after 1673, by his executor as requested. So Mannington did not contain many long-standing family heirlooms. Otherwise the will seems unremarkable, except for the provisions for daughter Elizabeth which were to keep the lawyers busy for quite some time. His bequest of plate to his wife 'which her mother gave me by will' is a little strange: Elizabeth's father Sir Samuel Browne, around the time of their marriage, had given his daughter and her husband 'some silver plates and other plate which [he had] sent from London [which was] to be in lieu of the plate and linen I should have given them by the will'.³⁰ This may have been at her mother's request but it was clearly to both of them. Browne had extracted a promise that John would ensure Elizabeth would have them if he died first. Little plate was recorded in his inventory (see below) so it may have been sold off or perhaps Elizabeth had kept it firmly in her care. Browne again seemed to lack faith in his son-in-law.

John's request to be buried by his first wife in Mannington chapel seems to provide a good explanation for the mysterious tombstone there which was commented on at some length by Charles Tomes in his 1916 booklet, *Mannington Hall and its Owners*. Tomes described, and made a good rendition of, a sketch made by the antiquary Thomas Martin on his visit to Mannington, probably in June 1733 on the same day he came to Itteringham.³¹ Martin recorded a chest tomb, with an uninscribed slab, set in an arch against the north wall of the chancel and surrounded by heraldic devices carved in the stonework. The arch is now a window and the carvings are no longer there. The broken and re-cut stone of Sir John senior now lies under the window rather than where Martin saw it in the floor of the body of the church. From the drawings it is clear that Edmund Lumner's initials and esquire's helmet (distinctive for its unicorn's head) were at the top of the arch. To the right was the Lumner shield based on three escallops and to the left the Dodge shield of a breast expressing drops of milk. Below these were the Potts and Dodge shields.

Anne Dodge and Edmund Lumner junior were half-siblings from the same mother and some indicative linkage of the Potts to the Lumners was legitimate. However there was no blood tie and using the Lumner and Potts arms in this way was not heraldically correct.

The three shields on the front of the chest tomb were curious. On the right was the Willoughby shield of three water butts for Ursula. The shield on the left was for Sir John senior. It was quartered with Potts and Dodge repeated both top and bottom and left and right. On the central shield the left side repeated this quartering, while the wife's side was blank. Tomes left this as an unsolved puzzle. It may well be, however, that Sir John junior was the perpetrator of the whole of this unfinished piece of work; and that the central shield was to be his. Did he vacillate over whether to include just one or both of his wives' arms on the right hand side? Either would have been permitted and sometimes a husband's shield would indicate both. There is circumstantial evidence that he did not understand his own genealogy. *The Visitations of Norfolk for 1563, 1589 and 1613* does not contain a Potts entry, mentioning them only in that for Dodge. *The Visitation of Norfolk 1664* does show a full Potts entry but it was simply wrong in giving Sir John senior both a father and a grandfather named John.[32] Since in 1664 John junior was firmly ensconced in Mannington it is likely that it was he and not his father who gave this incorrect information to the heralds. It would therefore be quite likely that the same man commissioned heraldic carvings that were at least somewhat misleading in the treatment of the Lumner connection.

In contrast, the arms on Sir John senior's tombstone show a simple but correct version of Potts and Willoughby shields on left and right, with the Potts leopard and the Willoughby owl on the crests. This stone was almost certainly commissioned by Roger as his grandfather had requested in his will. Since Sir John junior requested burial at low cost in his will, Roger presumably took him at his word, not bothering to finish off the odd monument. Indeed he did not have any stone at all engraved for his father and mother.

Sir John Potts junior's Inventory 1678

The same chancery papers included the full inventory of Sir John junior's possessions at Mannington and Clippesby taken very shortly after his death. The inventory was attached to Sir Roger's answer of 21st May 1680 and as this has never been used by other writers on the Hall, it is transcribed here verbatim with format and spelling unchanged. It is of great interest since, apart from the sketch of the south elevation on the 1595 map, previously the only early documentary clues to the scale and nature of the hall were in Margaret Lumner/Paston's 1504 will in which she referred to items in the Great Parlour Chamber, the Great Hall and the Red Chamber above the pantry and buttery. However, that told little about the structure of the building.

An inventory of the goods and chattels of Sir John Potts of
Mannington in the County of Norfolk Baronet deceased viewed and
apprized this 14ᵗʰ day of March 1678

	£	s	d
Imprimis his wearing apparel both woollen and linen	20	0	0
His books	5	10	0
His watch and silver tobacco box	4	0	0

In Sir John's Lodging Chamber

	£	s	d
One posted bedstead 1 feather bed 1 bolster 2 pillows 3 blankets 1 rug 1 counterpane curtains and valens cord and matt 6 chairs 2 stools 1 frametable 1 stand 1 bason frame 1 looking glass a fire shovel and tongs 1 pair of andirons 1 pair of dogs 1 pair of bellows and 1 cabinet the window curtains and rods	13	7	0
The hangings in that chamber and a stove	5	0	0

In the Nursery

	£	s	d
One posted bedstead 1 featherbed 1 bolster and all as it standeth 1 stove 4 chairs 1 stool 1 looking glass 1 pair of andirons 1 pair of dogs fire shovel and tongs 1 pair of bellows 1 bason stand 1 flaskett window curtains and the hangings	6	8	0

In the Kitchin Chamber

	£	s	d
One livery bedstead with a canopy and 2 curtains 1 travis 1 little table 1 chest with iron bars 1 press 1 trunk 2 warming pans	2	12	0

In the Closett there

	£	s	d
One still 6 pewter chamber pots 4 pewter stool pans 2 brass candle sticks several glasses flower pots earthen basons 1 jar and several boxes	2	0	0

In the Maides Chamber

	£	s	d
One posted bedstead with featherbed and all as it standeth 3 empty trunks 1 press 1 stool 2 chests	3	10	0

In the other Maides Chamber

Two livery beds as they now stand and 1 livery
cupboard   3   10   0

In the Purple Chamber

One bed as it standeth 5 chairs 2 stools 3 velvet
cushions 1 other cushion 1 looking glass 9 pictures
1 little table and sattin carpet 1 pair of andirons
1 pair of dogs fire shovel and tongs and window
curtains   22   0   0

In Mrs Potts her Chamber

One bedstead as it standeth 5 chairs 2 stools 2
tables with carpets 1 bason stand and 1 pair of
dogs fire shovel and tongs 1 pair of bellows pair
of snuffers window curtains and hangings and
chimney piece   22   6   0

In the Closett

One table 1 carpet 2 chairs 1 cushion and window
curtains   0   7   0

In the Terrett Chamber

One bed as it standeth   2   0   0

In the Great Parlour Chamber

One bed as it standeth 1 velvet couch 2 velvet
chairs 4 other chairs 2 stools 3 stands 2 tables with
carpets 1 pair of andirons 1 pair of dogs 1 pair
of belows fire shovel and tongs window curtains
1 chimney piece 1 looking glass and 6 pieces of
hangings   45   0   0

In the next Lodging Chamber

One bedstead as it standeth 1 chair 1 stool and
window curtains   2   15   0

In the Red Chamber

One bed as it standeth 1 side board and carpet 2 chairs 1 pair of andirons fire shovel and tongs window curtains and 1 piece of hanging	3	15	0

In the Green Chamber

One bed as it standeth 1 table and carpet 2 chairs 2 stools 1 pair of andirons 1 looking glass and the hangings	3	10	0

In the Upper Little Chamber

One bed as it standeth 1 table and carpet 2 chairs 2 stools 1 pair andirons 1 looking glass and the hangings	2	15	0

In the East Passage Chamber

One bed as it standeth 1 ovall table and one chair	2	5	0

In Mrs Godsalves Chamber

Armour	7	0	0
Wooll	1	0	0
Netts	4	0	0
Beeskeps and lumber there	0	15	0

In Mr Burrells Study

One table with drawers 1 chest of drawers 2 chairs 1 cushion	0	15	0

In Mr Burrells Lodging Chamber

One bed as it standeth one table with drawers 1 side board 1 counter table 4 chairs 1 purr fire shovel and tongs and 1 coal cradle	4	13	0

In the Husbandmans Chamber

Three beds as they stand and one little table	6	5	0

In the Butlers Chamber

One bed as it standeth | 3 | 5 | 0

In the Boyes Chamber

One bed as it standeth | 1 | 0 | 0

In the Storehouse Chamber

Three trunks 2 chests candles woollen cloth and stuffe one glass lanthern 1 brass fire shovel 1 pair of andirons one great carpet 4 great pewter dishes 1 brass mitre 1 lin-- [faint] 1 piece of fustion and much lumber | 29 | 15 | 0

All the lynnen in trunks chests and boxes | 75 | 5 | 0

In the Great Parlour

Two tables 2 carpets 14 Turkey chairs 4 carry chairs 1 pair of andirons

1 pair of dogs fire shovel and tongs 3 window curtains 2 velvet cushions and 2 other cushions | 20 | 0 | 0

In the Little Parlour

One velvet couch 9 cushions 9 chairs 2 tables 2 carpets 1 coal cradle 1 fire iron fire shovel and tongs 1 pair of toasting iron 1 pair of bellows 4 stools window curtains and 11 pictures | 11 | 5 | 0

In the Withdrawing Roome

One table of stone 4 chairs window cyrtains 1 pair of tables with ivory men 4 chairs 1 wicker skreen and 2 pictures | 2 | 5 | 0

In the Great Hall

Three tables 1 settle 2 joint formes 4 stools and 1 pair of doggs | 3 | 0 | 0

In the Pantry

Several pieces of plate as salts tankers spoons forks etc	27	15	0
One napkin press 1 bread byng 1 cupboard 1 table 1 glass case 1 stool 10 knives 1 tray and 1 brass chafing dish	1	9	0

In the Pastryes

Four tables 1 keep 2 stools 1 livery cupboard 1 dizart 2 distills 3 stone mortars 2 pair of brass scales 1 pair of andirons fire shovel and tongs several holland ware 1 basket 3 pots of honey 4 dozen of pewter plates and 4 pewter dishes	10	18	0

In the Kitchin

Sixty nine pieces of pewter	15	18	0
Four spitts 2 dripping pans 1 brass mortar 1 coal cradle 1 fire iron 1 sinder shovel fire shovel and tongs 1 purr 1 Jack 2 hakes 1 pair of dog irons 2 guns 1 table 2 pair of bellows 1 iron back 1 iron peel and 1 coal rake	9	8	0

In the Larrders

One keep 4 meat tubs 1 leading trough 1 kneading trough and 2 frying pans	2	8	0

In the Scullery

Two brass pots 1 iron pot 6 skillets 3 kettles 2 brass stewpans and two gridirons	4	0	0

In the Washouse

One copper 2 hakes 1 brandlett 1 firefork 3 standales 2 killers 1 washing bowl 2 stools 1 dresser and a cloathes basket	2	4	0

In the Boulting Chamber

One boulting mill 8 meal tubs 1 byng 2 hairtems and some feathers	1	17	0

In the Wine Celler

Five dozen bottles of claret	2	5	0
Two dozen and a half of white wine	1	5	0
One dozen and a half of old Rhenish Wine	0	15	0
4 bottles of sack	0	7	0
Mallaga sack	0	15	0
Two great pots of mead	0	10	0
Six pounds of tobacco	1	0	0
80 dozen of bottles	8	0	0
- - - barrels of syder [no amount given]	-	-	-
- - - barrels of beer	-	-	-

In the Brewhouse

One copper 1 mashfatt 1 quilfatt 1 wort tub 2 coolers 2 dales and the rest of beer vessels belonging 1 iron furnace and 1 pair of mault quernes	40	15	0

At the Dyery Manshouse

One copper 1 brass bottle cheese press 4 cheese fatts 3 cheese breadthes 2 standels 1 whay tub 1 barrel churn 2 milk leads 11 killers 9 bowls 2 cheese tables 8 several shelves	5	13	0

In the Granaryes

Thirty combes of rye	12	0	0
Eight combes of wheat	6	8	0
Thirty combes of buck	8	0	0
Twenty combes of nonsuch	8	0	0
One hundred and thirty five combes of barley	54	0	0
Five and twenty combes of white peas	12	0	0

In the Turn Chamber

One turne 1 table vice 2 hand vices several turning tools divers planes several sorts of screws wimbles and abundance of other tools	5	0	0

In the Stables

Twenty horse beasts	76	0	0
The harness for cart horses	4	10	0

In the Coachhouse

One coach and the harness to it	30	0	0
One chariott with the harness to it	10	0	0

In the Yards

Three carts and 1 tumbrill	10	10	0
Three ploughs 5 iron harrows and wooden harrows	4	8	0
One and forty dyery cows	120	0	0
Seven and twenty scotch heifers and three yearlings	52	10	0
Thirteen beasts at the stable sold for	50	0	0
Six swine	3	0	0
The poultry	-	-	-

At John Trappetts

Four killers and one kettle	1	0	0
Nine cows racks	0	15	0

Corn on the Ground

Fifty acres of wheat	200	0	0
One stack and a half of hay	10	0	0
Cows racks and lumber	2	0	0
Dets and ready money	113	8	3

The total valuation of goods for the two properties together was nearly £1,660.

Mannington Hall – the building

The inventory contains many fascinating hints relating to the family members and their lifestyle. Details of those named here are given below. However, the document is most interesting for giving an unique insight into the structure of the main house and its service buildings at this time. Originally, the main house was a fairly simple hall house. The main face was, and is, the west side, now with its pedestrian access over the small drawbridge to the front door. Beyond that door was a cross passage, with rooms to the left behind a structural wall. The passage led to the kitchen and other service buildings. It seems likely that all the services were always in the rear wing and that the north end of the main house contained a parlour or more probably two small rooms. On the right of the passage would have been a screen, probably a simple timber panel divider to minimise draughts from the main door. Behind this non load-bearing screen was the great hall, extending a little more than a third of the length of the west side and traversing from the west back to the east wall of the house. Opinions vary on the construction of the house and in particular the height of the original great hall and when floors were inserted into its upper space. The great hall may originally have been tall and thin, opening right up to the roof, with perhaps a narrow galleried passage at first floor level running along the east wall and allowing movement between the south and north blocks of the upper rooms. However, a better proportioned hall would have been achieved if it was open for a height of two stories with a floor above. The outlines of windows still visible on the outside of the west wall might support such an interpretation. Tomes was strongly of this latter opinion.[33] He argued this from examination of the floor timbers and the marks in the brickwork of the main west wall. Emery on the other hand believes that the great hall had originally been of odd proportions and had reached all the way to the roof, making for complicated access to the rooms on the upper floors at the south and north ends of the main building.[34] He argues, from the structural timbers and window design, that a first floor had been added as early as the sixteenth century, leaving the hall as the main ground floor room with its present ceiling height.

At the southern end of the great hall, behind a thick load-bearing wall, was the great parlour with its chamber above, possibly accessed by stairs in the large turret on the south-west corner. All the status rooms would have had fireplaces, with the flues being built into the very thick east wall. The great hall itself may originally have had a large central fireplace, but the size of the room and the status of the house would perhaps indicate that it was built with a fireplace set into the east wall from the start. Many of these basic characteristics of the house would have survived sixteenth century alterations, albeit with the great hall being reduced in size and floored over. At some point the flimsy cross passage screen was turned into a relatively thin but nonetheless load-bearing wall which included a timber beam along its length at first floor level into which floor timbers could be set.

There was probably always a substantial service range jutting out eastwards from the northern end of the house and stretching to the moat. This would have contained the kitchen, which was frequently placed outside the body of the main house. This range may also originally have been two or three stories high. In the past, it was thought the present dining room block, built on the east wall of the old house, might have been a part of the house from early times. There seems no evidence to support this. Taken together the inventory and estate maps of 1595 and 1742 show that this infilling was not present even as late as the eighteenth century and therefore it must be assumed to be the work of the fourth Earl of Orford in the 1860s.[35]

It seems very likely that the house underwent major improvement in the middle of the sixteenth century. The size and style of many of the windows on the main facades of the old house seem to date from that period. It is likely that the old great hall was floored over, creating extra rooms on the middle floor of the main part of the house and making the whole a more workable space. This modification was probably the work of one of Edmund Lumner's wives, either Rose or Katherine, both of whom lived there for many years. The latter may be likely given she had such a brood of children to house. However Rose was there at the time Edmund made major investments in the estate possibly, in significant part, courtesy of her wealth.

By paying close attention to the evidence for fire places and windows and by following the sequence of the rooms in the inventory one can arrive at a very plausible assessment of the arrangement of the rooms. Although the inventory started upstairs with Sir John's chamber it is rather easier to imagine the house by starting at the bottom and working upwards. The services were probably never in the main house, but if they had originally been in the north end then they were moved in the 1550s to the service wing. The northern end of the house would then have held the withdrawing room and little parlour. They might have both been in the old house, its depth of about 23 feet being just sufficient to accommodate two rooms. If so, the latter would have been at the east side of this space, with the fireplace using the main chimney stack at this end of the house. The room, though small, would have been lit by the big window shown clearly in the north wall, off the centre line of the house, in a 1830s sketch of the Hall. The positioning of this window indeed might imply a wall inside on the centre line - otherwise one would expect a centrally positioned window as on both floors above and on all three floors at the south end. The little parlour was used by Sir John junior as a study or office - where wills and documents were witnessed - and may always have been a place of estate business. A very small withdrawing room would have had the west facing window - a small reception room just inside the front door and without a fire as implied by the lack of fire irons in the inventory. Both these rooms could have been enlarged if part of the cross passage was incorporated into them, but this may have been impractical if there was a load-bearing wall along this side of the passage. Even so, with a need for more or bigger rooms, the passage might have been seen as a waste of space. After all the hall could be used as the route to all the rooms if it had doors in both the front and one back corner (logically the most direct route to the kitchen). An alternative would be that the little parlour had the whole north end and that the withdrawing room was in the kitchen range not in the old house, but this is not wholly convincing. Both these rooms were modestly furnished, so the smaller sizes would seem appropriate. If the withdrawing room had been the first room in the back range it would have been able to have a fire using the back of the stack for the parlour fire but no fire items were shown.

The great hall occupied the centre of the house and was probably by this time already floored over at both first and second floor levels. This is the only way to accommodate all the upper chambers in the inventory. The hall was the dining room for the family, but seems to have been fairly sparsely furnished. Next to the hall was the great parlour, which would have also taken in the large turret room on its south-west corner. Both this room and the hall had fireplaces, probably where they are today. The small turret on the south-east corner may have had a spiral staircase leading to both the upper floors. By 1678 the larger turret was very likely to have been used as room space and no longer incorporated the stairs for which it might originally have been designed.

The first floor contained bedrooms - some quite spacious, but others really rather small and possibly used only for younger members of the family or guests when the house was very full. Sir John's Chamber was at the north-west corner with a main fireplace, a large north window and perhaps two west windows. This room might well have incorporated much of the area directly above the cross passage, which is now a landing. The inventory shows this room and the nursery above having both a fire and a stove in each, logical if they were both rather larger than the present rooms. A second fireplace can be achieved if the flue which now juts out into the stairwell once carried flues for 4 small fireplaces - Sir John's and the nursery, the top floor purple room and the first floor red room. This latter room was probably in the floored-in space over the hall and may have had both of the smaller west facing windows. The red chamber was curtained, but the green room was not (so windowless), although it too had a fire. This could be imagined if the green chamber was effectively a more or less unlit back room/passage with a bed in it and with a small fire using the stack for the main hall flue. It would not have been much of a room but would have provided an extra bed when needed. The great parlour chamber could have been accessed through the green room and may have also connected to the red room. The 'Next Chamber' would have been the first floor large turret room, with a bed in it for the maid of the Lady of the house. The smaller turret would have contained stairs or a closet.

The top floor of the main house would have had the nursery at the north end, probably larger than the room there now, again taking in the landing and having a stove there as well as its main fireplace. A passage along the east wall would have led to the large purple chamber with its two windows and fireplace set in its north wall. The passage stopped at a door into 'Mrs Potts chamber', allowing that large room to have a fireplace and its windows to south and west. The top of the small turret was its 'closet' and the top of the large one was the 'terrett chamber' - an attractive sitting space. The purple chamber and Mrs Potts's chamber may have been rooms for Sir John senior to use after Ursula had died, when he seems to have been only an occasional visitor to Mannington, his son then being in residence. Perhaps the pictures hanging in his rooms were the older family portraits.

All the other rooms in the inventory must have been in the wing running eastwards to the moat and then north along it. For this to be practical, most if not all of this block needed to have three floors by 1678; it may well have done from the 1550s. The top floor might only have extended along the first part of the range (pointing east) - enough to give a room for the cook (kitchen chamber), its closet and two rooms for maids. On the middle floor the sequence in the inventory works well. First would be the upper little chamber - a small room with a fire since a flue could go into the back of the main stack here. One might speculate that in 1504 this was the red chamber above the buttery/pantry, although the conventional view would doubtless be that then the services were located in the main house and so the red chamber would have been what in 1678 was Sir John's Chamber. Next came the east passage chamber, no fire and off the corridor much as it is now. Beyond that was 'Mrs Godsalve's room' full of lumber and then two rooms for Mr Burrell, the rector and chaplain to Sir John junior. One of these had a fire - easily done being above the old kitchen with its large stack going up through the building where it is now. Round the corner in the wing pointing northward would be the three rooms for the men - properly separated from the maids. On the ground floor in this part of the house were the pantry (closest to the dining room, or hall), and the pastries, with one of these having a baking oven using the back of the kitchen range stack. Next was the kitchen - probably a large room exactly where the large fireplaces are now in this wing of the house. Then along the next leg of the building would have been scullery, washroom and boulting house. The cellar was underground - despite the moated setting, the water table must have been sufficiently far down to allow it. In 1740 'the building over the cellar' was pulled down suggesting that it may have been separate.[36] Certainly, from the inventory there must have been more services in stand-alone storehouses further to the north and just inside the moat.

There is nothing to confirm or deny these rear wings being three or two storied. The 1595 map can be interpreted either way. The 1742 map showed only the ground plan with no elevation. However, by 1678 the route of the inventory going straight from Sir John's room to the nursery implied that the staircase at the junction of main house and kitchen wing went all the way up to the top of the house. Indeed the house would have been quite impractical if it had not. This staircase clearly needed to straddle the thick old wall and, at least in part, project outside it, so either there was an extra 'tower' holding the stairs - as was the case by 1830 when the offshot wing had been reduced in height to just the ground floor - or the whole wing had three floors. As a 1550s adaptation of whatever was originally built this seems all very logical. Originally the services block might have been just one or two floors with access to the upper floors reliant on the small turret at the south-east corner. While just about workable for a medieval hall house, the 1550s alterations almost certainly would have included a proper staircase and a three storied range out to the back of the house. Throughout such changes the charm of the west front would have been retained, albeit at the price of the two oddly set windows where the original large hall windows had been.

By 1678 the gatehouse chamber, shown on the 1595 map and mentioned in the Rogers inventory, had gone. It was certainly not shown on the 1742 plan. The small guardhouse near the footbridge that appears to have been present in 1595 was not mentioned in 1678. It may have been derelict, with no contents. However, by 1742 it was depicted with a walled enclosure and may have been a delightful garden enhancement made by Sir Algernon Potts, the 4ᵗʰ baronet.

How did the house evolve after 1678? There would have been little reason for any of the subsequent Potts family members to invest in any substantive structural changes to the house. Sir Roger never lived there. His sons Sir Algernon and Sir Charles both faced financial pressures making it unlikely they would have made more than decorative changes. Neither of them had children to accommodate or any other pressures on space which might have triggered major changes. After 1737, for more than 100 years, the house was simply let as the dwelling house of one of the farms of the Wolterton estate.[37] The accounts show that relatively modest tenants lived there working the farm, rather than senior gentry tenants occupying it for the house. There is no indication through this whole period of any major expenditure at Mannington, other than some remedial work on the gardens and the avenue. There is no indication that the tenants paid a large premium for the hall; indeed for many it may have been a liability. Four surviving water colours of the house, undated but probably 1830s-40s, and a sketch of 1832 all show a badly dilapidated building.[38] The windows on the south side of both upper floors were boarded up, as was the top floor window on the north side. The range that had held services, with rooms above, had become a single story. The impression is that only the northern end and lower floors of the hall were being used. The windows on the west front were essentially the same as today, with the characteristically odd setting of the middle windows on the first floor. Although the 3rd Earl is credited in a later letter with some unspecified work, the house probably stayed in this underused state until the 4th Earl of Orford fundamentally remodelled the house in the 1860s before he took up residence there. This view is reinforced by the description of another watercolour, of 1851, as showing 'most of the beautiful Tudor windows ... blocked up and the whole place [having] an air of neglect and decay'.[39]

The 1678 inhabitants

'Mrs Potts' was presumably Sir John junior's daughter who would have been known as Mistress Elizabeth Potts. Her stepmother Lady Potts would have had the great parlour chamber given the quality and value of its contents.

'Mrs Godsalve' was the unmarried sister of Sir John senior's first wife Barbara Godsalve; two surviving daughters were mentioned in Barbara's mother's will in 1633.[40] Judith Godsalve and her sister Anne, who later married a Mr Ingraham (sometimes Ingram), in 1637 signed a receipt to the executors of Sir Roger Townshend's will for the return of bonds held for them.[41] The girls' brothers, Thomas and Richard Godsalve had agreed, by the bonds, to pay them £40 each and Townshend had been safeguarding their paperwork when he died. Similar assistance had been given to an earlier generation of Godsalve daughters. Barbara's grandfather, Thomas Godsalve had married Townshend's great-aunt Elizabeth, and in his will had made his brother-in-law Roger, joint executor, charging him with ensuring marriages for Thomas's eldest daughters.[42] As we will see, Judith and Anne were also paid annuities for life by the Potts family, no doubt from Sir John senior's sense of obligation towards his first wife's family. Both women, Judith Godsalve, in 1680, and Anne Ingram widow, in 1681, died in Hedenham, leaving only short wills.[43] The inventory of early 1678 showed that Judith had by then left Mannington and her old room had become a lumber room. But whose suit of armour was it? Perhaps Sir John senior wore it at the Musters.

John Trappett was perhaps the husbandman running the home farm and it seems that at this time all the farm buildings refer to those in the farmyard close to the Hall, but outside the moated area. The butler's name has not survived, but it is nice to see that Sir John junior favoured a glass of claret.

More is known about Mr Burrell, the rector of Mannington and Sir John junior's personal chaplain. In 1671 Richard Burrell was presented to the living at Mannington by John Potts junior and as his chaplain lived in the Hall until 1678. During that time Thomas Jackson, rector of Itteringham and Wolterton, died and Burrell had, in addition, been given both parishes in 1674. After Sir John's death, he and Sir Roger did not enjoy the same kind of relationship. Burrell resigned from Mannington, moved out of the Hall and probably lived in the rectory house near Wolterton church. He retained Itteringham and Wolterton until his death around 1720-21. Sir Roger, it appears, presented newly-ordained Michael Batt to the Mannington living. (See Chapter 21 for the later Mannington incumbents.) The parish registers from Burrell's period are a badly written jumble of entries. He may not have been the most scholarly of clerics.

Nonetheless, learning from the Potts family, he was not afraid to go to court to try to increase his income. Although the case was more than 20 years after Sir John junior died, much of the evidence given referred back to his lifetime. In February 1702, as rector of Wolterton, Burrell sued Robert and Elizabeth Greenacre over wood tithes that he thought should be paid to him.[44] The heart of the complaint seems to have been that while some Wolterton people were paying wood tithes, Elizabeth had cut about 360 faggots of hedge wood and had refused to give Burrell his tenth of the wood or any recompense in lieu. Arthur Branthwayt, a noted Norwich lawyer and friend of the Potts, signed the interrogatories as one of the commissioners taking the depositions. This might well imply that Sir Roger was implicitly backing their defence and was therefore critical of Burrell. There is no indication that the Greenacres were anything other than rather modest tenant farmers, who would not have been able to afford an expensive lawyer and London court action. From what was said it seems likely that James Scamler paid for their defence. The depositions give a few more insights into local characters and life here at the time.

Burrell's first witness was his predecessor Thomas Jackson's son Robert Jackson gent of Itteringham aged 68. He had known Burrell throughout his time locally and Elizabeth for 12-15 years, but her husband for only 2 or 3. This implies that Elizabeth was a local girl and we shall see that the events took place while she was a widow from her previous marriage. Jackson said that, during the 20 or so years that his father had been rector of Wolterton, farmers and parishioners had agreed his right to wood tithes but he had commuted the tithes into a cash payment. Kenelm Johnson, an Ingworth butcher aged 63, added that the late James Scamler esq had paid £10 a year to the rector for all his tithes.

Martha Burrell, spinster aged 40 (probably a niece or cousin), had known Burrell for 30 years and had lived with him for about 7. Wolterton residents Thomas Cook, Thomas Whall and the widow Emerson had all paid wood tithes and Richard Lone, a farmer, had made an agreement with Burrell for all his tithes which included reference to wood tithes. But Elizabeth had refused to pay and Martha had heard that James Scamler and other landlords had told their tenants not to pay wood tithes to Burrell. This again implies that Sir Roger Potts may have been against his rector on this issue and that either he or his cousin James Scamler junior paid for the defence.

Two Itteringham men, Thomas Purdy yeoman aged 55 and Edmond Proudfoot carpenter aged 61, could add very little, but Proudfoot confirmed that he had seen topwood cut at the Greenacre's farm. Joseph Reynolds, an Itteringham husbandman aged 28, had also gone to see this wood and said it was not fit for use as timber. Finally William Porter aged 58, Reynolds' father-in-law and also an Itteringham husbandman, who had worked for Burrell, said that wood tithes had only been paid recently and that he had received small amounts of wood from Cook, Whall and Emerson. He had known the two defendants from their infancy. He said that Elizabeth had cut about 25s worth of topwood. Porter had gone with his cart to collect tithe wood, but Elizabeth had told him she was a widow and that her landlord had told her not to pay any wood tithes to Burrell.

The defence questions and depositions made a rather more compelling case that wood was being cut from hedges and small trees to repair the hedges along the highway and between enclosures. As a result everyone, including the rector, benefitted since the land was more productive and so more tithes and herbage could be paid. Wood for hedge repairs was not usually titheable. Elizabeth had cut wood from a hedge bordering her land that ran along the King's Highway and, by the implication of the questions, lay quite close to the Wolterton parish boundary. While she may have occupied the farm adjacent to Mannington Hall and just in Wolterton, it seems more likely that she had a place in Wolterton village, perhaps on the green on its eastern side where the parish boundary with Calthorpe was very close. In those days the highway ran from Itteringham through Wolterton and on to Calthorpe.

Johnson reappeared, now a witness for the defence, and said that he had lived in Wolterton for 20 years, but not during the last 19 and Thomas Fiddy now lived where he had. He repeated that he and other parishioners had not paid wood tithes, only corn and hay. Wood had been cut for building repairs and to make good hedges.

William Greenacre, a labourer of Calthorpe aged 73, was Robert's father. His own father, about 60 years ago, had gone to live in Wolterton in a farm of Sir John Potts senior where William and his father had lived for 8 or 9 years. He had never known of tithe wood being demanded by the rector and said that timber was used for building work. The wood that Elizabeth had cut in 1699 was used for repairing fences that were in poor condition and therefore some topwood had been needed to do the work. The residue was of little value. Philip Greenacre of Holt aged 79, William's brother, echoed the comments about their early tenure of a farm in Wolterton and said that the landlord had specifically let them take 20s of wood each year and that no wood tithes were payable.

Robert Bacon a Banningham yeoman aged 50 had also lived in Wolterton with his father for about 20 years, but not in the last 8 or 9. They had occupied the farm that had been held by William Greenacre and his sons William and Philip. His father had been allowed 40s worth of wood each year by his landlord and no wood tithes were payable; although he remembered his father saying he did pay a small sum to the rector for surplus wood he had sold. He had never heard of anyone paying tithes on hedge wood used for repairs or burnt by the occupier. He thought port or hearth money had been paid to the rector in lieu of wood tithes.

Christopher Mack, a Wolterton husbandman aged 34 and a servant of Elizabeth, said that only recently had Burrell forced some poor tenants to pay wood tithes, without having the right to do so. Again, he said that Scamler had told him not to pay any such demand when he had bought a small parcel of wood from Scamler. Indeed he said that Scamler had told him he would 'save him harmless', another indication that Scamler was supporting the defence. He had been paid by Elizabeth to do the hedge repair work and confirmed that the wood she had cut was only sufficient to do the work and pay him fair wages of 29s 2d. John Tubby, a husbandman of Thwaite aged 25 who had lived with Elizabeth before she married (as a servant no doubt), had helped Mack with the work and confirmed that the underwood and topwood could not easily be separated and so he had carried them all to the yard for firings. The residue had been left in her yard for firings. Frances Dunworth, spinster aged 21, had been living with the defendants as a servant for the last 2 years and confirmed that this wood had all been burnt as firings in their house in Wolterton.

It would seem that Burrell had belatedly tried to change local custom over wood tithes and the action was pursued by both sides as a test case. On the evidence given, Burrell would have lost. However, if Elizabeth had sold some of the wood to pay Mack's wages, Burrell might have had a case for tithes on 29s 2d. But who would take out an exchequer action for 2s 11d?

Clippesby: the inventory

The section of the inventory covering Clippesby is also interesting as it showed that Sir John junior's wife maintained at least one decent chamber and maids' rooms there. Here Lady Potts had a life interest in the rents and profits and perhaps this hints at her making real use of the house even during Sir John's lifetime. Was she keeping a watchful eye on her interest and on the farmer who worked at least part of the estate for Sir John? Several of the rooms in the house seemed to be used more for agricultural purposes than for people! This perhaps depicts what might have become of Mannington Hall during its long period as the house of a tenant farmer after the Potts family died out.

	£	s	d
At Clippesbye			
In the Ladyes Chamber			
One posted bedstead 1 feather bed 1 bolster 3 blankets 1 counterpan 2 pillows 2 pillowbeares 4 curtains 1 head piece to the bed 4 window curtains the chamber hangings 1 little table with a drawer 2 napkins 1 bason stand 2 pewter chamber pots 3 chairs vallens cord and matt	7	10	0
In the Maids Chamber			
One livery bedstead with canopy cord and matt	0	7	0
In the Other Maids Chamber			
One truckle bedstead 1 feather bed 1 bolster 1 blanket 1 coverlet 1 cord and 1 matt	1	15	0
In the Husbandmans Chamber			
Two livery bedsteads 1 featherbed 2 feather bolsters 1 flight bed 1 flight bolster 2 rugs 1 blanket 2 cords and 2 matts	2	0	0
In the Parlor Chamber			
Sixty combes of barley	25	0	0
In the Little Parlor			
One livery bedstead 1 feather bed 1 bolster 3 blankets 1 coverlet 1 cord 1 mat 1 little table 1 chair 1 cushion 1 pair of bellows fire shovel and tongs	2	0	0
In the Great Parlour			
Two tables 2 carpets 12 carry chairs 1 pair of dogs 2 curtain rods and 1 sundial	5	12	0
In the Hall			
One table 1 form 28 sacks and 3 cart ropes	2	8	0

In the Pantry

Six pewter dishes 1 bottom plate 3 trencher plates 1 bason and 2 dozen trenchers	1	13	0

In the Kitchin

One jack and 1 speet	0	10	0
Seven pair of sheets	1	15	0

In the Dyery and Washouse

23 milking bowls 1 salting tray 1 butter keller 7 cheesfatts 3 cheesebreadths 2 churns 1 cheestub 6 shelves 1 cream pot 4 pails 1 pair of cheestongs 1 cheespress and 1 copper	6	10	0

In the Brewhouse

One copper 1 cooler 1 mashfatt 1 guilfatt 1 brandlett 3 beer tubs 1 wort tub 2 standels 1 swill tub 5 iron bars 2 doles 1 jett 1 thead 1 udder and 5 alestools	5	5	0

In the Granaryes

Twenty five combes of rye	10	0	0
Thirteen combes of grey pease	5	4	0
Several sorts of small corn	1	0	0
Hopps	1	18	0

In the Hay Barne

Clover hay meadow hay and fitches	18	10	0

In the Butchers Barne

Forty combes of wheat	30	0	0
Five stacks of hay	10	0	0

In Herney Barne

Sixteen combes of wheat	12	10	0
Sixty combes of barley	25	0	0
Twenty combes of oates	6	0	0

In the Stable

Thirteen horses and mares	31	0	0
The harness for the horses	6	9	0
Three plows as they go	1	16	0
Three pair of harrowes	1	10	0
One screen 1 wyer cive 1 bushell 1 riddle 2 chaffe cieves 3 fanns 6 drag rakes 7 hand rakes 4 long forks 3 short forks 2 muck forks 1 mattock 1 spade and 2 shovels	2	18	0

In the Yards

Twenty cows	60	0	0
Twenty steares	53	10	0
Twenty scotch heifers and 1 bull	42	10	0
Eight scotch fat heifers	41	0	0
Three colts and 1 foal	6	10	0
Three carts with shod wheels	10	10	0
One clod cart and 1 tumbrill	2	0	0
Several bunches of osyers	0	10	0
The wood in the yards	2	0	0
The muck in the yards	25	0	0
Lumber	2	0	0

Corn on the Ground

Eighteen acres of summerlaye wheat	45	0	0
Fifteen acres of other wheat	30	0	0
Ten acres of summerlaye rye	20	0	0
Seven acres of other rye	8	15	0
Eleven acres of fitches	11	0	0
Debts at Clippesby	1	17	0
Ready money there	20	0	0
Errors excepted The Total Sume is	1659	11	3

[signed] William Birresham   [signed] R Potts

The total value at the end of the inventory was of course for Mannington and Clippesby together. A few words used in the inventory may be unfamiliar:

Boulting	Bolt or boult: to sift or pass through bolting cloth. Bolt tun: a great chest fitted with a sieve for sifting flour
Brandlett	Probably a hoop or ring on 3 or 4 legs, with a long handle, for standing pots in
Brass Mitre	Possibly a carpentry tool
Byng	Bin
Dale	Wooden trough pipe or conduit for carrying off liquid
Dole	Probably should be dale
Fitches	Vetches grown for forage
Guilfatt	Gyle vat or tub in which the wort fermented
Hairtem	Tem: a sieve. A sieve made of hair was very fine. For use in brewing
Hake	Adjustable ratched racks or hooks on which the S-hooks hung for pots in front of a fire. Usually in pairs
Keller/Killer	Keeler or killer: a wide shallow wooden bowl used for cooling liquids like milk
Livery bed	Generally for servants, but can be of considerable value. Usually not posted
Livery cupboard	One from which food was served by servants, sometimes also for general storage
Standale/ Standel	An ale stool: X-stand or trestle for barrels
Thead	Tall wicker strainer placed in the mash tub over the hole in the bottom so that the wort may run off clear
Travis	A frame for holding an unruly horse when being shod
Udder	For brewing?
Wimble	Gimble, gimlet, augur for boring holes[45]

So, although his will and inventory provided such extraordinary information, little about Sir John junior himself was revealed. At no point in his life did he engage confidently or visibly in local or national affairs, despite being equipped with an education and contacts that would have enabled him so to do. Was he simply in the shadow of his father? Sir John senior's long life led to his son only enjoying the title for five years. Or was there some weakness in him, either physically or in his character, that led his father to look beyond him to secure the family line? He may simply have been a social dandy who simply lived off his landed income. His portrait (see Chapter 24) depicted a very fashionably dressed man with expensive taste wearing one of his many rings. Although he did nothing to improve their fortunes, he would probably have been appalled by the row that broke out between his two children shortly after his death. His jewels were only a minor bone of contention.

Chapter 19

Potts v Potts: Brotherly Love

Sir Roger and his sister Elizabeth were to spend several years squabbling over the meaning of their father's will and codicil and the precise provisions for her from the Clippesby property. The case itself is at very least entertaining to read; but the court papers also contain a treasure trove of facts about the family and circumstances at Mannington, beyond simply Sir John's will and inventory. What follows is a chronological review of the surviving chancery documents edited down to offer the easiest route through the arguments. There was never any doubt that Elizabeth would be awarded a substantial marriage portion. Thank goodness for Sir Roger's intransigence over the precise terms of it and his worries about the risk of loss of the underlying Clippesby property. Without it, all this information would have not have survived.

In December 1679 Elizabeth Potts complained in chancery against her brother Roger about their father's will and the execution of it. Subsequently Roger sued his sister over elements of the personal estate while the decree from the first action was being implemented. Their bills and answers contain the bulk of the useful information. However, the depositions also add local colour. Here the witness statements have been interspersed with chancery decrees and orders, the latter showing the progress of the case and key judgements on it. As ever, all claims by all parties should be taken with a pinch of salt!

Elizabeth's case was reliant on her father's will and an assessment of his personal estate. In 1661 a family settlement on her father's second marriage had provided for her but only once her stepmother was dead.[1] The settlement on Elizabeth Browne, John Potts junior's second wife, had included £250 a year for life as her dower regardless of any acts of Sir John Potts senior or her husband. While this approximated to the annual rental income from Clippesby, and no doubt the family regarded Clippesby as being used to fund her dowry, she had no specific rights in that estate and it could have been sold without reference to her, as seems to have been the case much later. The same document showed that on the deaths of John and his wife Elizabeth, £1,800 could be paid to their younger sons and daughters if they had not already been advanced in marriage during John's lifetime. The real estate itself, including Clippesby, would pass to Roger as the male heir and would default, if necessary, in age order through any younger sons and then through the daughters. So from this settlement, Roger's sister did not have any right to the property itself. If she had married she would have received her portion. But she did not and so her right to a portion of £1,800 was, according to the letter of the settlement, contingent on both John and Elizabeth being dead (no doubt to protect Elizabeth senior during her lifetime). Elizabeth the stepmother however lived well into the eighteenth century and there would have been a strong argument that the unmarried Elizabeth was not entitled to her portion at the time she sued Roger. Her father's will was the only basis on which she could make a claim for a portion to be paid while Elizabeth senior was still alive. Hence the importance of John's will in the chancery action.

Elizabeth Potts's bill of complaint December 1679

The 'oratrix' or complainant was Elizabeth Potts, sole daughter of Sir John Potts junior deceased, late of Mannington.[2] The basis of her claim was that Sir John senior, her grandfather, on the marriage of John to his first wife Susan Heveningham settled Mannington on John for life and then allowed him to leave £2,500 in his will for his daughters. Her father later became seized of Clippesby, but was in debt for at least £2,000. In his will, made about two years before he died, he left £2,500 to Elizabeth and she was to have the reversion of Clippesby after the death of Dame Elizabeth. She was made executrix. Just before his death in January 1678 he added a codicil confirming the will.

Elizabeth claimed that when their father died Sir Roger immediately went to Mannington and took possession of his real and personal estate and then concealed from Elizabeth documents relating to it, including the will and codicil. Worse, she said Roger claimed that Sir John was jointly bound with him in several obligations to several persons in great sums of money for the debts of Sir John which were still unpaid and that the personal estate would not satisfy them. Elizabeth counterclaimed that these should be regarded as the proper debts of Roger not his father. She said that Roger claimed that Clippesby was to be his under an agreement reached between Roger, his father and Horatio Lord Townshend but no proof of this agreement was shown to her. And he refused to pay her any interest on her unpaid legacy of £2,500.

Indeed she made out that Roger had said the will was void anyway; that Sir John did not make any bequest and if he had, he was not of sound mind. But Elizabeth was adamant that the will was made, was valid and that she should enjoy what was left to her. With most of the witnesses now dead or gone away, she said she could only resort to forcing Roger to tell the truth by this action in chancery.

Sir Roger Potts's answer 21st May 1680: his father's debts

Roger was slow in answering the bill and in getting the will back to Elizabeth and was ordered to do so in chancery first in April and then in June; but he had complied by the end of June by which time his full answer to her complaint was lodged.[3] He agreed that there had been a marriage settlement, but he said the 500 year term interest in Clippesby to ensure the payment of the £2,500 became void by the marriage settlement of Sir John to his second wife Elizabeth. In this second settlement Clippesby was given to Sir John for life and then to his wife for her life entailed to their issue male. And Roger knew of no other Clippesby lands that Sir John held and therefore could have intended for his daughter. The other Potts lands in Repps with Bastwick were conveyed to Roger by his grandfather and were not Sir John junior's to dispose of. Roger said that Sir John died in debt and attached a schedule totalling just over £1,800, asking that it be admitted as evidence.

Debts due and claimed to be due from Sir John Potts [2ⁿᵈ] Baronet at his death for his personal debts for principal money besides interest to several persons besides the general debts and sums mentioned in the agreement set forth in the complainant's bill, viz:

	£	s	d
First to one ___ Worts upon the said Sir John Potts his covenant or bond			
for principal money and which the defendant has paid since his death	400	0	0
And this defendant has paid since his death the interest thereof	36	0	0
To James Scamler esq upon the said Sir JP's own bond for principal money which is not yet repaid	100	0	0
Defendant has paid interest on the above since Sir JP's death	20	0	0
To one Mrs Amy Jackson … Sir JP's own bond principal not repaid	100	0	0
Interest paid by defendant	18	0	0
To Richard Bucke … Sir JP's own bond principal not repaid	20	0	0
Interest paid by defendant	3	12	0
Also the said Sir JP by his own bond stood bound to pay Mrs Godsalve and Mrs Ingram £12 apiece a year for life upon which this defendant hath paid since his death	36	0	0
To John Neale a butcher for a book debt which the defendant paid	32	0	0
William Turner principal … Sir JP's own bond principal not repaid	88	0	0
Interest paid to Turner's executors of £8 4s	8	4	0
And defendant interest more paid	16	11	2

Mr Thomas Browne upon a bond of Sir JP which he entered with one Mr Guybon but this defendant hopeth it may prove the said Guybon's debt though the defendant is sued for it as his father's executor and must pay the same into chancery with interest or as the court will order and the principal being besides interest and charges incurred and to incur	50	0	0
Due from the said Sir JP at his death to this defendant and as he doubteth not to prove	700	0	0
To Mr Nathaniel Browne on Sir JP's bond and this defendant bound with him as his surety and wherein the defendant has paid £50 principal and £3 interest	53	0	0
To James and Daniel Dover on Sir JP's bond and defendant bound with him and which defendant has paid for principal and has paid interest but cannot now remember the certain sum	50	0	0
And Sir JP and the defendant stood bound together to Mrs Jessup for £150 principal and thereof £75 only was Sir JP's personal debt £5 of which he paid in his lifetime for at his death there rested £70 principal which the defendant has since paid and also £4 4s for interest thereof	74	4	0
More claimed by Mr Marke Cockey as a debt due to him above	20	0	0

R Potts (signature)

Roger went on to recite the relevant contents of his father's will made on 25th March 1677:

And I do hereby revoke and make void all other and former wills by me made and whereas by indenture bearing the date 6th October 1668 between Sir John Potts of Mannington Kt & Bt deceased and me Sir John Potts by the name of John Potts esq of the first part; and Roger my son and Mary his wife of the second part; and certain persons named as trustees of the 3rd and 4th parts … concerning the settling of manors … and raising and paying £500 apiece (besides maintenance) to my daughters Ursula and Elizabeth and power given to myself to give £2,000 and interest … by my will …

And for as much as my daughter Ursula is since dead … the £500 due to her ceaseth … I do hereby expressly limit declare and appoint for the maintenance or increasing of my daughter Elizabeth's portion and payment of my debts that the sum of £2,000 with interest at £5% shall be raised over and above the said £500 whereof £1,000 of the £2,000 is to be paid within 6 months of my decease and the other within 12 months after that.

Item. I give to my daughter Elizabeth all my right and title to my lands manors and tenements in Bastwick and Repps expressed and declared to be sold for payment of debts by a declaration bearing date 20th April 1669 between Sir John Potts my father and Mr Roger Potts my son.

Item. I will all my manors lands etc in Flegg settled on my wife in joynture to my daughter Elizabeth Potts and her heirs forever after my wife's decease, as all my lands in Hickling called Longores[?].

And lastly I give to Elizabeth Potts my daughter the rest of my goods chattels money etc … and I make Elizabeth my daughter sole executrix of this my will.

Roger went on to say that Sir John signed this, witnessed by John Bardwell, John Barham and William Trappett. Also he said he had seen a codicil, as mentioned, annexed to the will to the effect that:

Whereas I have … appointed £2,000 (as allowed by the 1668 deed) … for Elizabeth and my debts … and whereas lands etc in Flegg that were conveyed to my wife are to go to Elizabeth I do now hereby declare … that she shall only have the said estate as a security for her better and more certain assurance of the payment of £2,000 to her which I intend she should have out of my estate in full of her marriage portion … and after the £2,000 is paid the interest in Flegg is to go to my son Roger to enable him to provide for his younger children.

Dated 6th February 1678. Also I nominate James Fountaine esq and Mr Edmond Britiffe of Baconsthorpe my very good friends to be supervisors … to assist my executrix.

This was followed by the Mannington and Clippesby inventory covered in Chapter 18.

Roger continued saying that whereas it may be true that his father made such a will, Roger hoped to prove that it was afterwards revoked and not intended to be his last will. Roger had become jointly bound in his father's debts and had wanted better security for their payment than this will afforded him. So Roger and his father agreed to 'refer themselves to the mediation and order of the Right Honourable Horatio Lord Townsend who being pleased to undertake the same on hearing … did make certain proposals that were put in writing … and agreed by John and Roger and were in the words or to the effect following':

> That all differences between Sir John and Roger are agreed and are hereby mutually released and discharged … Roger agrees to pay John's debts and all Clippesby and other lands are to be conveyed to Roger unencumbered … Roger is to pay £900 of debts payable to Mr Hervey, £1,200 to persons to whom they are jointly bound (viz: to Mr Crowe £500, to Mrs Anne Hunt £200, to Mrs Fountaine £400, to Mr Bulwer £100); the sum of £1,000 is to be towards the marriage of Roger's sister Elizabeth and £500 more to John to bequeath … in all the sum of £3,600 to be secured by covenant of Roger as counsel shall advise; that John is to pay all interest due on the debts until Christmas Day next after the agreement; that John is to be barred or bound from the manors conveyed to Roger in his marriage settlement as counsel advises; each are to be bound in £4,000 apiece to meet the agreement and stand by the final determination of Lord Townshend.

Roger said that he and his father were well satisfied with this agreement and that he had since executed the great part of it. Subsequently, John made his will and showed it to Roger and 'offered for him to peruse it but Roger declined to do so relying on his father's assurance … He rested satisfied and his father said he was well satisfied he had so settled all things'. Roger said his sister was well aware of all of this. But Roger said he lived remote from his father and when he came to visit him at Mannington during the sickness from which he died, he heard that Elizabeth or some others in the family were saying that Elizabeth was executrix and that the Clippesby estate was or should be hers. This surprised and amazed Roger since he had not heard his father express any dissatisfaction with the agreement. He suspected his sister 'did design or contrive to supplant him'. Thereupon he sought legal advice, which was that the agreement should hold against any contrivance by Elizabeth. He had not wanted to disturb his father in his weak condition and thought fit rather to have the matters disputed and debated after his death.

Roger's version of events said he had discovered that Elizabeth had burned or destroyed the final will that her father had made after the agreement and had tried to persuade her father to stick to the previous will. When John called for his will, she brought him the old version. On seeing it John was much disturbed and called for his other will. Being informed by Elizabeth that it was not to be found John was much troubled and immediately sent to the gentleman who had made the missing will and who Roger assumed was a witness to it. Impatiently he even sent a second messenger before the first had returned and when the gentleman came John asked him to rewrite the will. But rather than writing a new will, it was arranged to write a codicil but Roger did not know if it had been witnessed by three credible persons. This was imposed on John in his weakness near the approach of his death. Although he understood his father had given an express order to Elizabeth to show Roger the codicil so that he might show it to his counsel and have it altered if it did not reflect the deed of agreement, Roger knew nothing of this until after his father's death

When he saw the concealed codicil, he had spoken to his sister about it saying that the will and codicil would be a great reflection upon the honour and reputation of her and her father. He asked her for the other will which she confessed she had burned. And she then showed him the will and codicil she would use and, apparently contrite, asked Roger to relieve her of the executorship and pay her for her portion whatever Roger thought reasonable. He agreed as long as she gave him an account of all goods or money whatsoever which she had received taken or conveyed away about the time of her father's sickness and before and since his death. Roger suggested they refer the matter to friends and Roger several times came to agreed meetings, but she did not come.

He also believed that 'by the advice and confederacy of others', during John's sickness, she had 'conveyed out of the house goods chattels household stuff money plate linen rings jewels and other goods … and received sums of money or took security for sums of money in her own name belonging to John's estate and would now entangle Roger not only in his father's debts but the securities not being taken out but remaining in the hands of some persons with the contrivance of Elizabeth or some for her … Elizabeth desireth to frustrate the said agreement'. She had tried to conceal parts of the personal estate and leave Roger committed to bonds for which she had taken the money.

He said he had stayed on at Mannington after his father's death and took possession of what he was entitled to. He insisted he knew of nothing that showed Elizabeth was entitled to £2,500. He told her he had taken and disposed of as much of his father's personal estate as he could, and said she had a copy of the attached inventory which, made by her direction, he felt over valued the possessions to the tune of about £300. He denied he ever tried to conceal the true value of the goods. In his view he should enjoy all the Clippesby lands, as the Townshend agreement provided. Roger said he held the will and codicil given to him by his sister and would produce it but during the summer of 1680 Elizabeth played Roger at his own game over the documents and he had to go to chancery in October to get an order to be given a copy of the will.[4]

Elizabeth's second bill of complaint 3rd November 1680

Five months on, Elizabeth Potts, now 'of the City of London', complained that Roger was concealing from her the details of the marriage settlement between their father and his second wife. She did not doubt that the Clippesby lands could raise large sums, as intended, for the portions of any daughters.[5] But she said that at Roger's marriage to Mary Davy there had been a settlement 'in about 1669' of Sir

John senior's manors and lands on Roger and his heirs. This, she claimed, contained provision for Elizabeth's maintenance or portion and £500 apiece was to be paid to Ursula and Elizabeth. Her father was given the power to leave £2,000 in his will. She claimed that her grandfather contracted some debts (which Roger pretended were their father's) and John and Roger had been bound with him as sureties and the premises were liable and encumbered. To clear these some agreement was made between them, by which the manor, messuages, farm, lands and tenements of Repps with Bastwick, a parcel of the freehold estate of Sir John the grandfather and John the son, was to be sold to pay the debts and Elizabeth's portion.

Elizabeth went on to say that a difference arose between Sir John and Roger chiefly in her view 'upon a disgust taken by Roger at his father for the affection he bore Elizabeth and his bounty towards her'. Roger knew that she had always tried to make reconciliation and prevent any misunderstanding between them. She agreed that between making the will and the codicil the disagreement between the two men had been referred to the Right Honourable Lord Townshend. Her bill repeated the same proposal that had resulted but she claimed the agreement was not executed. Her argument was that Roger did not consider himself bound by it and had not sold or mortgaged the lands to enable him to settle the debts. Because he had failed to do so, she argued that the debts became his problem and Sir John's personal estate should not be encumbered with them.

Her version of the deathbed scene was rather different. She said Sir John, as he lay sick, supposing Roger to have laid aside all thoughts of pursuing the Townshend proposal, ordered Elizabeth to fetch his will. He perused the contents and with his own hand wrote the codicil, which Roger knew to be their father's own handwriting, and which was made when he was of sound and perfect mind. She denied burning the right will and keeping the wrong one. Now she blamed Roger for not releasing the papers to her and obstructing probate of the will.

She reckoned the personal estate was worth much more than £2,000 but it had been sold off by Roger and what was left she said she could not find out. Holding all the paperwork Roger was trying to deprive her of her due by claiming Sir John's debts were so great that there was nothing left for her. The whole personal estate should, she claimed, have gone to her and not be 'clogged with any debts whatsoever'. From the lands, the full £2,000 was due to her and Roger should pay it with interest from the time it should have been paid. She wanted a full account of all the personal estate, that described in the inventory and elsewhere, and she claimed damages for Roger's behaviour to her.

Answer by Sir Roger to his sister's second bill May 1681

Not surprisingly, six months later, Roger said that this second bill was designed 'to perplex and vex him and put him to unnecessary charges'. He recited various deeds and settlements and additionally asserted that soon after his marriage his father felled and took away the timber from the jointure lands and that that invalidated the settlement on his wife. A new settlement was made about four years after Roger's marriage and when he had a son living and being about 6th October 1668 not 1669.[6] Originally the intention had been to provide for both the girls but Roger explained (very usefully) that his sister Ursula had died 8 or 9 years since in the lifetime of their father (that is, about 1672-73).

The rest of his answer repeated much of his first but with rather different detail. There had been a will made in March 1676 which had been revoked. Although there had been a difference between him and his father and with Lord Townshend's mediation an agreement had been reached, there was no animosity between them. Roger had indeed accepted himself bound by the agreement and took upon himself the payment of £900 and £1,200 and other debts prior to his father's death early in March 1678. Although the document was not finally engrossed and signed, most of the money was paid and the agreement therefore was executed in his father's lifetime. His father had been satisfied with what Roger had done and said he would change his will. This he did in his own hand and it was signed and witnessed. It bequeathed the manor of Clippesby and all his real and personal estate to Roger and Roger was to pay the debts and pay £1,000 to his sister. Elizabeth, who, when their father was sick, had custody of the keys of the rooms and all the trunks and chests where his father's writings lay, had the opportunity privately to read that will. When she saw that the earlier will was more to her advantage than the latter, she burnt the second will.

He repeated that Sir John when he saw the will was the wrong one, sent for James Scamler esq who had written the correct last will and knew its contents. Although he requested Scamler to rewrite the will, only a codicil was written and added to the old will of before the agreement. Roger was not privy to the contents of the first will (having been happy with his father's assurances at the time) or this codicil until after his father's death. Elizabeth had then given him the will and it was over a year before she asked for it back. Then he confessed he refused, at which she took action in the spiritual court. But Roger had delivered the will to the court of chancery as required and denied he had obstructed probate. He took her giving him the will as her absolute resignation of all interest and that she said Roger should do with her as he pleased as he had said earlier.

In referring to the inventory of the personal estate he added that the goods in the will which were to go to James, Roger's own son, were a part of the inventoried goods. These, and some odd small parcels not in all worth £200, remained after he had paid many of John's debts out of the personal estate as intended by the agreement. He complained again that Elizabeth had removed some of the goods and said he had only been able to raise £800 from those shown on the inventory. Roger denied he had the deeds relating to his grandfather's and father's marriage settlements but only had his own and several other writings relating to their estates. He had taken possession of these estates as advised he was entitled to do. He was now keeping them to defend his right and title and he denied he was trying to defraud Elizabeth of her marriage portion and livelihood. He felt she should be content with the marriage portion of £1,000.

In May 1681 Roger went to chancery seeking permission to proceed for contempt against Elizabeth since she had not answered his cross-bill even though he had answered hers.[7] But Elizabeth countered that he had been slow to answer and that he should pay her costs before being allowed to proceed for contempt. Elizabeth was given an extra term to answer and Roger had to pay her costs resulting from his failure to answer on time. One senses that the tide was going against Roger by this point. Indeed that summer Elizabeth had more favourable judgements on process, while Roger's only hit was his request that she must go into a joint hearing of depositions rather than a separate commission.[8]

Elizabeth Potts's complaints of 12th July and 26th October 1681

The July complaint had much the same content as the previous one. In it she also said that Roger intended to defraud her and was 'confederating' with the three surviving trustees of the marriage settlement - James Fountaine esq, Sir Jacob Astley and Christopher Crowe esq - to get hold of all the deeds and writings to do with his father's and grandfather's marriage settlements and his own and all other deeds relating to the estate. She still claimed she was entitled to the personal estate and monies received from the sale of Repps with Bastwick and to £2,000 not £1,000. In her October complaint she said that the £2,000 was given to the trustees of the settlements in trust for the girls' portions. She repeated the conspiracy allegation and again said that Roger was pretending that his father had contracted debts (which were either his own or their grandfather's). Rather bizarrely in the trustees' answer of October 1681 they declined all knowledge saying: 'it may be true but they do not know that they are made or named trustees in some concerns or settlement between Sir John the grandfather, John his son and Roger the grandson'.

The best local information was given by the witnesses taken at this stage; on each occasion they were asked a set of questions about their knowledge of the parties and what had happened. Because some were appearing for both sides, the enquiries (different questions from each side) were made at the same time and place. It is easy to tell what the questions were by the phrases common to the answers.

Depositions of witnesses October 1681 - first session

The statements, firstly for Roger, were taken at a commission of enquiry on 12th October 1681 at the house of Joyce Bennett commonly called The Three Tuns in the parish of St Stephen Norwich before Thomas Balleston and Francis Wise gents.[9]

Thomas Newman of Baconsthorpe gent, aged 50 and upwards said he had known Elizabeth and Roger for 10 years and knew Sir John senior and Sir John junior for 15 years each before their respective deaths. Sir John junior was in debt and had wanted to borrow money from Newman, with Roger jointly bound with him as security. Roger however said he was already bound for several sums and there were doubts about aspects of his own marriage settlement. Only once these matters were cleared up would he help his father in this way. Newman also testified that in about 1676 Mr Hackshaw, who was married to Miss Annabella Hervey, repeatedly wrote to Sir John for repayment of the money borrowed from her when she was single.

This was £700 principal and accrued interest of £150. Newman approached Roger on Sir John's behalf but Roger said he had debts of his own and children to provide for. The loan was secured against property and he would be at risk if he became bound and his father's claim to raise money on the grand estates proved good. This seems to refer to a known disagreement between father and son over whether Sir John had the right to mortgage the main Mannington manorial estate (as opposed to the purchased additions such as Irmingland) under the settlement from Sir John senior. That Newman was being asked to act as go-between implies that Sir John and Roger were not on full speaking terms.

At this stage their disagreement was taken to Lord Townshend for arbitration. Newman said that Roger had told him he was glad that this resolved matters between him and his father, but he did not know how he would find the amount Townshend had said he should pay. Nevertheless, afterwards Roger had paid £400 to John Man esq and Andrew Fountaine and a further £40 interest on a £400 loan from Fountaine. A £100 bond to Edward Bulwer of Briston was repaid and Roger paid £900 to Mr Hervey. Newman also paid £400 to Mr William Woorts on 13th September 1679 which had been Sir John's debt secured by a mortgage on his Clippesby property as part of the Townshend agreement. And in May 1679 Newman, as one of the executors of William Turner gent, had received payment from Roger of £263 7s, of which £88 was Sir John's debt. He was paying sums for Roger and asked him if the Townshend agreement had been sealed. Roger had told him that Sir Robert Baldock the lawyer was so busy with other matters that it had not yet been put into proper form. Roger also told him that his father had reflected the agreement in his latest will.

Hearing that court action between Roger and Elizabeth was likely, Newman had ridden to see Roger at Mannington to try to persuade him of the inconvenience and scandal that would fall upon the family. He urged arbitration by friends of the family and said that Roger had agreed to Sir Robert Baldock and Sir John Holland. They had been suggested by Elizabeth's friend James Fountaine esq. But subsequently Elizabeth vetoed Holland. Roger said he would work with anyone else chosen by her. Finally Newman recounted that he had owed Roger £50 plus interest and that Sir John asked for the money to be paid to him not Roger. Upon checking, Newman found that Roger was happy to let his father have the money for his pressing needs.

Robert Snell [senior?] of the City of Norwich gent, aged 46, testified very briefly that, on behalf of Elizabeth in May 1681, he had demanded of Roger certain goods and chattels of Sir John's which had been in the inventory. But he did not know what the items were, nor their value.

The statements for Elizabeth were taken next but Thomas Newman, having given his evidence, now sat as one of the commissioners.

Robert Pepper of City of Norwich, Doctor of Law and Chancellor of the Diocese, said simply that, six months after Sir John's death, Roger was in his house in the Cathedral precinct and said that Elizabeth was his father's executor.

Hellen, wife of Richard Houghton of Norwich esq aged 55, explained that she and her husband had owned Wolterton Hall and land in Itteringham, before selling up to James Scamler in 1660. At the end of November or beginning of December 1677 Sir John junior, returning from London, came to her house in Norwich. He told her that he had settled his daughter's fortune and had given her what he could. He had settled it so that her brother should go to her and not she to him (ie Elizabeth would be executrix). Three weeks before Sir John's death he sent for her husband Richard Houghton to accompany him in his sickness, they having been friends from their infancy. Richard went to Mannington and stayed there until his death. When her husband returned after the burial, she asked him what Sir John had done for Elizabeth. He said Sir John had told him he had 'settled this business to his own content and had then lately added a codicil to his will to his great satisfaction and content and that his daughter, out of kindness to her brother, had abated £500 that he would have given her, for he would have given her five and twenty hundred pounds and she would have been contented with £2,000'. Sir John always showed and expressed great love and kindness to his daughter. This evidence suggests, oddly perhaps given the evidence was for her defence, that Elizabeth had agreed to have the lower figure of £2,000.

William Trappett of Blickling, gardener aged 34, was presumably the son of John Trappett the estate husbandman referred to in the inventory. William may also have gardened at Mannington. He said he knew the document shown to him as the last will but did not remember seeing the words written in the margin in four places. But he was well-acquainted with Sir John's handwriting and they were his. He heard Sir John declare this to be his last will and testament in the little parlour at Mannington. John Bardwell and John Barham were also present and he was requested to be a witness. But he went on to say that Sir John was in the habit of making a will every time he went on a considerable journey and he may well have signed another will. He knew the handwriting and the codicil was Sir John's and he saw him seal it. Thomas Brown, James Scamler and Daniel Muddiclift were there and Sir John said he would not have died before doing the codicil for £100 and Elizabeth was very dutiful and kind to her brother.

John Barham of Felbrigg singleman, aged 38, recognised the will but did not remember the marginal writing. However he thought it looked like the will he had witnessed with Richard Burrell, John Bardwell and William Trappett in the little parlour of Mannington. He had not seen any other will.

Richard Houghton of the City of Norwich esq, aged 60 and upward, said that Sir John had sent for him about three weeks before death and he went being his 'ancient friend and familiar acquaintance' and stayed with him at his dwelling house until his death. He soon saw he was a very weak and spent man and he asked him if he had made his will. He said he had and he had added a codicil and given his daughter Elizabeth five and twenty hundred pounds. And she, in kindness, was willing to accept twenty hundred pounds. And while he was there Sir John very often took occasion to show great love and affection to his daughter and he thought she well deserved the same. She was as dutiful a child to him as any man ever had and she was very well-beloved by all who knew her. He saw Sir John call his daughter and ask her go into his closet and find all his earlier wills and burn them and asked

Houghton to go with her to see it done. She and Houghton searched the closet and she found several but Houghton did not remember how many or which she burned. He saw some of the wills which were burnt lying in several places in the closet as loose papers. Before he arrived Elizabeth had picked up two or three others which she said were in the closet 'thrown up and down'. From the Houghton and Trappett evidence, John must have travelled a great deal (or been very nervous) to have so many wills lying about!

Daniell Muddiclift of Itteringham yeoman, aged 60 and upwards, who had been Mannington's estate steward or manager, said that three weeks before his death Sir John ordered Muddiclift, then being his servant, to go or send for James Scamler esq and to ask him to come. Scamler came immediately. Daniel was well-acquainted with Sir John's handwriting and believed the entire codicil concerning Elizabeth, which he had witnessed, was in Sir John's hand. Elizabeth was very dutiful to her father and loving to her brother. Mr Houghton kept Sir John company for some weeks before his death and was looked upon as an old friend. Daniel said Sir John showed kindness to Elizabeth and she was well-beloved by all. Muddiclift's statements for Roger, however, were to be much longer (see below).

Richard Burrell of Wolterton clerk, aged 63, was well-acquainted with Sir John's handwriting and believed the four places in the margin were his writing and he saw him seal it in his little parlour in Mannington when he was requested by Sir John to witness it with John Bardwell, John Barham and William Trappett. He had witnessed other wills of Sir John, but believed that this was the last he witnessed.[10]

Depositions 1681 - session 2

The depositions of witnesses continued on 14th October 1681 at the house of Matthew Denny called The Sign of the Goat in St Gregory Norwich before Thomas Newman, Francis Wise, Thomas Balleston and Thomas Godfrey gents.

Daniel Abell of Mannington butcher, aged 30, had known Roger and Elizabeth for eighteen years and knew both Sir Johns for several years before their deaths. He bought from Roger and Elizabeth's father a number of cattle that he was to pay £260 and upwards for. He paid to Sir John in part the sum of £50 in June 1677, £50 in August, £60 in September and £50 in November. £30 of the last £50 he had paid to Elizabeth and in January 1678 he paid her another £50 and £9 16s in February in final payment.

Daniel Muddiclift of Itteringham said he had known the two Sir Johns for about 30 years before their deaths. This with other evidence showed that he had been in Itteringham and Mannington in service of the Potts since the late 1640s or early 1650s. He and his wife Grace baptised their children at Itteringham from 1652 onwards. Daniel replied fully giving a rounded account of the story as he saw it. For about thirty years before the death of Sir John senior Muddiclift was his servant and agent in his principal affairs. He frequently told Muddiclift that the estate in Clippesby was Roger's and that though Sir John junior occupied it and the stock there was his, he still had to answer for it to Roger. Sir John junior was indebted and often borrowed at interest and Roger was jointly bound in a number of these debts. He cited £100 to Edward Bulwer, £500 to Mr Crowe, £150 to Mr Jessup and £400 to Mr Andrew Fountaine among others. Sir John was obviously in need of cash. Daniel recalled that, four or five years after his [second] marriage, Sir John felled a considerable quantity of timber valued at £150 then growing on farms in Itteringham and 'Elmindale' (the main Irmingland farm, now Elmerdale). He indicated this was before Roger's wife's jointure and so was probably about 1665-66. Sir John felled and sold timber at Mannington worth £5-600 at intervals of some 4 years, some 3 years and some 2 years before his death. Muddiclift did not know the exact amounts but the sales were to one Artis of Beccles, some to one Worthy of Wells, some to Mr Fiddy of Wolterton, some to Parkins of Itteringham and some to Thomas Bell of Oulton.

About 1675 or 1676 Sir John was sued by Mrs Hervey and the others pressed hard for their money to be repaid. Sir John then often told Muddiclift that he 'must take the lead off his house, fell the timber, sell the reversion of Clippesby in Flegg and do all other things he could to raise money for their satisfaction'. Roger no doubt, if he heard of it, would have been appalled. Daniel continued that both Sir John and Elizabeth asked Roger to help his father either to raise money or to be bound with him for the debts but Roger said he was not secured against the danger he was in for his father's debts. And that 'by a second settlement his estate was clogged with powers for Sir John to raise monies and Roger would have nothing left for his wife and children and refused to be bound unless he might be secured'. At this Sir John was very angry and displeased with Roger and continued so for some years. In March 1676 when Sir John was angry with Roger he made a will which Muddiclift believed was the same will which Elizabeth now insisted was the correct one. But at length he did promise to secure Roger by giving him the reversion of his estate in Flegg after the death of Sir John's then Lady, now widow, and that he would refer all matters between him and Roger to the sole determination of The Right Honourable Horatio Lord Townshend. About two months later Sir John declared to Muddiclift that Lord Townshend had settled all the matters between Sir John and Roger and that he was very well satisfied with the arrangements. Sir John often expressed himself well satisfied with Roger 'because he was freed from the vexation & trouble' and he told Muddiclift that he would perform the agreement and fully make it good. Roger had paid £2,200 of his father's debts and he sold (or mortgaged) his estate in Grimston in his father's lifetime and his estate in Bastwick with Repps after his death to raise the money to pay the debts. Sir John was indebted to others at his death: Mr William Woorts £400 (paid 30th September 1679 by Mr Newman as part of the purchase money due to Sir Roger for the estate sold in Bastwick and Repps, the £36 interest for which Muddiclift had paid before that day); to James Scamler £100; to Amy Jackson (wife of Itteringham's rector) £100; to Richard Buck £20; to Mr Nathaniel Browne £50; to James Dover and Daniel Dover £50; to Mr (or Mrs) Jessop £150 some of which Roger had paid or was bound to pay; and another debt to Mr Turner of £100 which Thomas Newman (executor of Turner) had retrieved from Roger. Anne and the Reverend John Jessop were half cousins through Sir John senior's daughter Barbara's marriage to John Hills. He usually arranged for any money owing to Sir John from anyone near Norwich to be paid to Mr Mark Cockey, alderman of Norwich.[11]

After September 1676 Sir John was well pleased with Roger and Muddiclift believed that he soon afterwards made another will, which he showed to James Scamler junior esq and Roger in his closet. When Sir John lay sick, and for many years before that, Roger lived at Ellingham which is 18 miles from Mannington Hall. Elizabeth then, and for many months before, lived constantly with Sir John. She had custody of the keys of closets and other rooms in which Sir John had his writings and 'had opportunity to resort thereto when and as often and in as private way as she pleased'. But Daniel did not know if she found any wills. About 10 days before his death Sir John requested Muddiclift to send for Mr James Scamler junior to come to him urgently - as he put it he 'would not for £500 but speake with him before he died'. Scamler came and, after several hours, Muddiclift was sent for to witness a codicil. Two years after Sir John's death Scamler, in discussion about the will and codicil, said that Roger was 'blaming Mr Scamler'. Scamler said Roger was not acquainted with the will and codicil when his father was alive. Muddiclift heard Mr Scamler say to Roger that Sir John delivered the will and codicil to Elizabeth and ordered her to show it to Roger for his approval. But he believed that Roger did not see it then. Mr Houghton who was with Sir John in his sickness pressed Muddiclift to call in what money was due from creditors for Elizabeth's use, which he did.

Daniel continued his statement, adding a lovely tale. Shortly after Sir John's death Elizabeth asked Roger to take over the executorship and pay her for her portion what he thought fit. She would leave it to him for he was an honest man to all and would be an honest man to her. When Elizabeth gave her mother £20 for mourning without telling Roger, Roger said 'he would go away and leave her, with which Elizabeth seemed so much troubled that she came to Muddiclift with tears in her eyes and told him that her brother so saying to her, troubled her as much as if he had taken a beetle and knocked her on the head and that she did not mistrust him and would never trouble him though she never had a groat'. Presumably she was picturing a small wooden household mallet rather than the heavier type of beetle hammer.

But soon after this Roger did take on the administration of the goods and asked her, he then living 18 miles away, to keep an account of the personal estate that was disposed of and give him an account of it. Muddiclift together with Thomas Spurgeon, at the request of Elizabeth and Roger, appraised the goods and personal estate of Sir John. Elizabeth asked them to set a full price upon them 'for her father's credit', to which they consented believing that no one would thereby have been injured. He now said that they had overvalued the goods by more than £200. The goods willed to James Potts comprised about £400 of the total inventory. James died shortly after Sir John and Roger had letters of administration for him. Muddiclift added that several goods, trunks and boxes were carried in a cart from Mannington to Norwich after the death of Sir John by the order of his Lady and with the consent of Elizabeth. Lady Elizabeth said they were hers. Although this might suggest a Potts house in Norwich, it was probably just the first stage in the carriage of Dame Elizabeth's own goods to London. She was later to die at Hornsey.

After Sir John's death Roger offered to refer all matters between them and Sir Robert Baldock was chosen by Roger and John Norris esq by Elizabeth. But Norris did not come to a meeting and was ineffectual as a referee. Others were appointed, but they too failed to make the meeting even though Roger had gone to the trouble of being there.

Thomas Spurgeon of Matlask gent, aged 51, said that on Roger's marriage to Mary Davy, his father and grandfather had negotiated a settlement with her father William and were satisfied with the marriage portion. In return they assured Davy that the Potts's estate was free of all entanglements. Spurgeon, John Bardwell and Philip Hill (probably another distant relative) had witnessed the settlement at Mannington. He had made the inventory with Muddiclift and said that he thought James's goods were worth £300.

Miles Smyth of East Carleton gent, aged 28, testified that Roger came twice to Norwich to wait upon Elizabeth before any suit commenced between them. Robert Baldock, sergeant at law, was at the second time appointed by Sir Roger as his referee. After waiting some hours for John Norris esq counsel at law, Elizabeth's referee, Sir Roger sent Smyth to find him. He went to Norris's house in Norwich and was told he was out of town. He went back and Roger told him to find his sister and when he found her she told Smyth that Norris was out of town and that she did not know that there was supposed to have been a meeting. This implies she was living in Norwich a year or so after her father's death, presumably before she left for London where she was by November 1680. She never married but lived in St Andrew Holborn with her faithful servant Mary Tarrant. She was buried on 27th February 1722 'from Red Lion Street'. In her will she left £10 and a share in the Lead Mine Adventure to the Holborn girls' charity school.[12]

James Fountaine of Salle esq, aged 40, testified that he had offered to help in the choice of referees. Sir Robert Baldock was not accepted by Elizabeth as he was Roger's counsel. John Norris had attended one meeting, but then Roger's referee did not attend. He knew that Elizabeth was in debt since he had found a friend who would lend her £50. He believed she only had 22 guineas that her father had given her and no other estate. Perhaps he was a soft touch?

John Frost of Great Ellingham gent, aged 35, was Roger's steward at Great Ellingham. He said that Sir John junior was normally indebted and often took money at interest. He had frequently wanted Roger to be bound with him, which he did for £900 to Mr Hackshaw and £500 to Mr Crowe. Five years ago Hackshaw arrested Sir John for the £900 debt. In September 1676 Roger paid £960 and he heard that Mr Crowe sued for the £500. Then Roger refused to be further bound with his father. Sir John promised Roger that he would be recompensed by the reversion of Lady Potts's property in Clippesby and other towns in Flegg hundred after her death. Everything was referred to Lord Townshend in or about October 1676. Sir Robert Baldock, at the request of Sir John, attended the Townshend meeting and drew up the documentation. Both were well pleased and Elizabeth told Frost she was 'exceedingly pleased and rejoiced at the agreement'. The agreement was that Roger would bear the cost of the £900 paid to Mr Hackshaw and the £500 to Mr Crowe. He would also cover £200 and interest to Mrs Hunt and £400 plus interest to Andrew Fountaine.

Elizabeth tried to get in what was due to her father before his death and had several sums from John Reeve, a quaker to whom Sir John usually sold his crops of corn. Finally Frost asserted that John Barham, coachman to Sir John, at the time of his death carried away upon his horse one chest or box in the evening when it was beginning to be dark. Frost said to him 'you need not be thus private in carrying anything, for if they be yours, or of right belonging to you or any other, you need not carry them so obscurely. Sir Roger would not be against carrying them away in the daytime'. Barham told him he had been ordered to carry them away, but what was in them he did not know; and nor did Frost.

The last of the witnesses were two of the creditors. James Dover of the City of Norwich merchant, aged 40, said that Sir John had owed him £50 plus interest and Roger was bound as surety with him. A year ago he received from Sir John £50 and £3 interest and the previous interest had also been paid. Nathaniel Browne of the City of Norwich gent, age 35, said that in 1669 John Potts esq was indebted to him for £50 principal. Needing his money, he assigned the bond to Elizabeth Cockey and Roger had since settled the debt.

Depositions 1681 - session 3

The depositions were adjourned to 19th October and those for Elizabeth were held at the house of John Seman commonly called The Rose in Conisford in the parish of St Peter Parmentergate Norwich before the same three commissioners.

James Scamler the younger of Wolterton, aged 40 and upwards, gave evidence about the will-making. In his last sickness and about a month before he died, Sir John had sent for him by Muddiclift or some other person. He went to Mannington where Sir John said he intended to make some alteration in his will and had sent for Scamler to advise him. Sir John ordered Elizabeth to fetch his will to him from his closet and she went to the closet. On receiving a will from her he asked Elizabeth if there were any other wills in the closet but she said there were none. Sir John told her to go and search again to be sure no other will was left.

Sir John gave the will to Scamler who was asked to read the will to his daughter, which he began to do when they were interrupted by Lady Elizabeth coming into Sir John's chamber. Sir John asked them to finish reading it in another room. They came back afterwards and discussed altering the will by a codicil and Scamler wrote the codicil on the back of the will.

He said he saw Sir John write, with his own hand, the codicil now produced on the back of the will and dated 6th February 1678. Sir John 'declared great satisfaction and gave God thanks that he had enabled him to write' and called Thomas Browne, Daniel Muddiclift and William Trappett as witnesses. Five or six days after he made the codicil, Sir John asked Scamler to write the three lines and two words on the back of the will beginning 'I do also nominate …' and ending 'execution thereof' to which Sir John subscribed his name.

The same day James was examined for the other side.[13]

James Scamler, now answering for Roger, said that he never saw the Townshend agreement but Sir John and Roger had often spoken about it. Relating to the agreement, John Norris esq was drawing up writings and Scamler saw his draft lease and release. Sir Robert Baldock, however, having drawn up the first agreement, would not use any other counsel's writings. His need to hurry down to London, though, had stopped him from completing the work. Sir John had said that as the document could not be finished, he would make his will to secure performance of the agreement. When asked by Sir John to 'write over the will' Scamler refused but said it would be better to add a codicil. He drafted it but did not write in his own hand as he thought Sir John's hand would be better. He did not know that Roger was unacquainted with this will until after Sir John's death.

Again, in November 1681, Elizabeth had chancery process orders in her favour against Roger over his delaying tactics.[14]

Complaint of Sir Roger of 16th May 1682

Two and a half years after the action started, Roger went on the offensive.[15] He referred to the suits against him by his sister Elizabeth which had been heard on Saturday 19th December 1681. It was then ordered and directed that he should pay her £2,000 for her portion, 'viz: £1,000 persuant to the Lord Townshend agreement with interest since it was due by the agreement to be paid, £500 to be paid off at £50 pa in persuance of the settlement of 6th October 1668 and £500 out of the personal estate of Sir John Potts'. All this was to be subject to Sir John Hoskins of the court of chancery taking the accounts of the personal estate as far as it extended after debts and funeral charges. Elizabeth was to convey over and release to Roger all her right title and interest in the real and personal estate of Sir John or as Sir John Hoskins directed them.

This seemed clear, but in February Elizabeth had to go to chancery for an order chasing Roger to pay the first £1,500 of the award, which he was required to do without further delay.[16] However, Roger won confirmation that he would have the reversion of the properties once these first payments were made. He had pushed this point because he had argued that he did not have ready money to pay the award and would have to mortgage the premises. To do so he would have needed to demonstrate good title.

Roger said that in obedience to the order, about 3rd March, he paid £1,500 to Elizabeth in discharge of the £1,000 and £500 that were immediately to be paid. He said he was entitled to the residue of the personal estate after he paid her the further £500 due and now wanted an account from her of all the details. He still claimed she had had access to it all and the ability to conceal part of it which she carried away and embezzled. By Roger's account, his father did not have much money or bonds owing to him but did have considerable 'goods of husbandry and household' and in particular had a pearl necklace worth £120. He then itemised other jewellery worth £170 or thereabouts which had not appeared in the inventory:

A ring set with a ruby and two small diamonds
Eight other rings all set with 7 diamonds apiece
One other single stoned diamond ring rose cut
One other ring called a Turkys
One other ring called a Ruby Dublett
One other ring called a Green Dublett
One small amythyst
One large amythyst
One bastard amythyst
Two christalls
Two mourning rings
Five cornelian rings

Sir John obviously had a liking for finery. There were also, Roger said, several gold guineas and other pieces of gold to a very great value. His father never admitted to having money as he owed so much but he would keep £1,000 by him. Also he had sold timber to the value of £700. Roger said that Elizabeth knew about all this and should declare to the court what she knew and 'whether she or others with her knowledge did not carry and convey away from John's house in Mannington or elsewhere part of his personal estate other than what she has previously attached as a schedule'. She should declare what she had done with any money and whether she ever gave any account to Sir John in his lifetime. Roger demanded a full inventory of all the jewellery, rings, plate and household stuff, their values and what had become of them. Then, he said, the debts might be paid and the decree of chancery complied with.

Elizabeth's answer of 22ⁿᵈ June 1682

Elizabeth referred back to the May 1680 complaints and answers and said that, at that time, she had agreed that the personal estate belonged to Roger as long as he paid her £2,000. She said she did not take any money out of the house in bags or in any other ways. She had not embezzled any part of her father's estate, 'nor ever wronged or injured her father in the worth of one farthing nor consented to the carrying away of his money and goods … nor connived with any other in doing so … save only that some small gratuities were given to the servants of her father and others that watched with him in his sickness, not all to the value of £10'.

She insisted she could not give any particulars of the personal estate other than as set forth in the inventory but she gave an account of all the monies she had received from Roger in a schedule attached to her answer. Roger, she said, had the whole personal estate.

A schedule of monies received of the complainant and his wife or his order

	£	s	d
For a dust coate	0	17	0
Paid to the Pole [poll tax?] for me	0	1	0
Paid for my watch mending	0	9	0
Paid for a pair of gloves	0	2	0
Received at London June 15th	1	0	0
Received at London June 22nd	2	10	0
Received at London	1	0	0
Received after at London	0	5	0
My sister [-in-law] paid for a coife	0	3	0
Received July	0	5	0
Received September 2nd	1	10	0
Received October 15th	0	10	0
Received November 7th	1	0	0
Received of my sister [in-law] November 28th	2	0	0
Received of my brother December 13th	1	0	0
Received of Daniel Muddiclift January 16th	20	0	0
My sister [-in-law] had of me at Bury as I came from London with them	0	18	0
Received of my brother 1st April	4	0	0
Total is	35	14	0

S Clerke [the chancery clerk for this action]

The accounts suggest Elizabeth was spending considerable time with her brother and his wife and that her immediate needs were being met. She was now pushing for the last £500 that she was due, as a part of the £2,000 awarded her, out of the personal estate. The referral to Sir John Hoskins to take the account had annoyed her and she felt she should not have to suffer such a vexatious suit. Although not part of her father's personal estate, she agreed she had received the sums in the attached schedule which she was prepared to allow into the account of the court, even though not obliged to do so.

As to the jewels specified in Roger's bill, she confessed that she had a necklace of small pearls with a bracelet made up with four pearls mixed with some 'aggatts' given her by her father when she was young, which she generally wore; and out of some of them so given she gave part of them to the complainant's daughter to make a necklace. This would have been Susan, Roger's only surviving daughter. Elizabeth also claimed three diamond rings were given her by her father in his sickness. The ruby ring, set with two small diamonds she recalled her father gave to Mrs Fountaine who received it from Elizabeth in Roger's presence and with his consent. She had even shown Roger the three diamond rings and asked if she should inventory them but he had replied that, as her father had given her them, she need not include them. All which pearls and diamond rings, whereof two were set with seven diamond stones apiece, and one single rose cut diamond ring and a ruby ring with two small diamonds she was ready to show but she believed they were not worth £10 in total. (One of the diamond rings she later left to her niece Susan.) She denied knowing of any other jewels whatsoever, save only one mourning ring which she gave to Roger and some small gews of little value given her by her father when she was very young. Those and her usual attire and decent apparel were again all not worth £10.

On the other hand, she drew attention to Roger having a pair of organs, worth more than all the rings and jewels, which she had been given by her grandfather. She had not thought fit to trouble her brother for them previously but hoped they might now be considered since he was so vexatious and troublesome in matters of such mean value and small moment. She also denied she ever had one piece of old gold from her father, except twenty guineas that he gave her for her own use without account. She did not know of any papers or writings of her father except what she left in her brother's custody in the house when he took possession. She said Roger, not John, had cut down about £500 worth of timber belonging to John and he should be accountable to the estate for it. She asked the court to dismiss the complaint.

In July 1682 Roger was chased once more for not providing details of their father's personal estate to Sir John Hoskins for the assessment of what had been available to pay the further £500 to Elizabeth.[17] Through the autumn and winter problems continued, with yet more costs incurred in the retaking of depositions and accusations of delaying on either side.[18]

Depositions - February 1683

In an attempt to clarify the debts that needed to be paid (and therefore see what was left) more statements of witnesses were taken at the house of John Younges being a common inn in Oulton on 1st February 1683 before Edward Earle, Peter Wilson and Thomas Balleston.[19] Different debts came to light.

James Scamler the elder of Wolterton, aged 73, said he had known Roger and Elizabeth for 30 years and their father for 40 years or more. On 14th June 1676 he saw Sir John sign and seal an obligation to the use of 'Anne Flowerdew widow of Hawstead Essex'. Sir John was bound for the personal sum of £200 for the payment of £103 on the following 15th December. As the sum was unpaid at his death, Roger, as executor, on 6th October 1680, paid £20 as part of the interest due. So five years of interest and the £100 principal remained due. Scamler had heard that Roger had been threatened with being sued, as executor, because he 'meddled with the personal estate of his father for some debts due'. Although he did not know whether that was true, he believed that Roger by 'intermeddling' had made himself liable for his father's debts.

Robert Jackson of Itteringham gent, aged 49, as the son of the rector, had known the family for thirty years. At the time of Sir John's death he owed £100 to Amy Jackson as executrix to Thomas Jackson, clerk deceased, by a bond of 24th March 1673. Interest of 6% a year had been paid by Sir John until his death and since then Roger had paid Amy £24 interest (to 1681) and £10 as part of the principal, but the rest was still due. Since Roger had 'intermeddled' he had become liable for the debt.

John Tyrrell of Mannington singleman, aged 22, had known Roger and Elizabeth for ten years and Sir John, before his death, for five. As Roger's servant Tyrell had paid £3 17s, owed by Sir John, to Andrew Hayes of Norwich, apothecary, for physic prepared for Sir John. He had heard that Roger was threatened but did not know by whom.

John Bardwell of Itteringham grocer, aged 40, had known Roger and Elizabeth for eighteen years and Sir John for fourteen years before his death. Sir John had owed him £17 which Roger had since paid. Interestingly, this is early evidence of a shop in Itteringham; Bardwell had probably arrived in the village in 1665 or thereabouts.[20]

The depositions continued for yet another session on 6th February at the house of Thomas Jessop being yet another common inn in Oulton.

William Wiggott of Tuttington gent, aged 29, said that six years ago he met Anne Jessup, now his wife. Before that time, £150 was lent by John Jessup, Anne's uncle, to Sir John with a bond for repaying with interest. Wiggott explained this was part of the portion of his wife. Anne received £10 from Sir John before her marriage and she had interest from Sir John and since his death Wiggott had received £140 and one year's interest on the bond. He had heard that Roger had become liable for Sir John's debts. Anne was Sir John Potts junior's great-niece, orphaned as a baby.

Daniel Muddiclift was back giving testimony again and said that he knew there were several debts due at the time of Sir John's death. It was clear that Muddiclift had been closely involved in the family's accounts, even paying out of his own money. Following the Townshend agreement, for eighteen months, Sir John received £300 revenues and profits from the manors and lands in Clippesby but despite this the debts were substantial. One debt was to Richard Buck for £20 and half a year's interest and another to Muddiclift for £5 by a bill. Also there was due by covenant £12 per annum to two people whose surname were Godsalve (one of these since 'intermarried with one Ingram deceased') and during their lives Roger paid the £12 a year as executor for four years. The Godsalve sisters had both died during Roger and Elizabeth's suit. Sir John owed £31 12s 2d to John Neale of Reepham, butcher, which Roger had paid, and he had been bound to Mr Crowe, now of Bilney, by a mortgage owing £15 for interest on £500, which interest Roger had paid. Roger had also paid John Bardwell of Itteringham £17 owed by his father. Thomas Browne, now of Aylsham had sued Roger as executor for his £50 which had also been paid. The bond to Mr Jessup for £150 had involved Sir John and Muddiclift. Of this £140 had been paid. He had thought it was Sir John's debt, but now believed that half of it was Roger's. Roger had paid £6 or £12 interest for £200 owed by bond by Sir John to Mrs Anne Hunt (since Anne Palgrave). Roger had been sued and threatened with being sued over the debts.

Daniel went on to say that Elizabeth, soon after her father's death, took possession of part of the personal estate and sold part of it - particularly most of Sir John's wearing apparel which was valued at £20 in the inventory. She also gave Sir John's watch to Mr Richard Burrell, which might at first have cost £5 or £6 but was valued in the inventory at £3. Lady Potts, Sir John's widow, shortly after his death and with the consent of Elizabeth, took possession of the coach, harness, horses and furniture of the chamber (worth £58 in the inventory). Roger spent £50 on funeral and mourning expenses. This was modest, in keeping with his father's will and no doubt Roger's wishes.

Muddiclift finally clarified Sir John's timber sales. Since 1667 or 1668 he had felled £150 worth from Roger's estate at Mannington (ie Roger's Irmingland farm) and he cut another £850 worth on the estate in which he had a life interest (ie the main Mannington estate), making £1,000 in all.

After all these depositions (and, no doubt, accompanying beers) the action returned to London. Sir John Hoskins made his report, but unfortunately it has not survived either in the bills and answers or in the decree books. However, both Elizabeth and Roger then had a bout of arguing for exceptions to the report and further debates about the adequacy of answers.[21]

Elizabeth's further answer 11th May 1683 and the end of the business

In further response to Roger's bill of complaint and to the report of Sir John Hoskyns dated 12th March 1683 Elizabeth maintained that she seldom or never had the keys to her father's trunks and chests containing his personal estate as her stepmother, being housekeeper, had them. But the keys of his study, where his writings or money lay, he kept himself and in his sickness and for about a month before he died, when he was not able to go there himself, he sometimes gave Elizabeth the keys to fetch a book or such writing as he had occasion for. Otherwise she never had any key other than when he asked her to carry or fetch something.[22]

She also denied that in her father's sickness any rings, jewellery, ready money, plate, linen or goods whatsoever of her father were taken away by anyone to her knowledge. Of her father's possessions she remembered only a watch which her father commanded her before several witnesses to give to the chaplain in his house. This she did. She knew nothing of Sir John having made a declaration of his having £1,000 or any monies at all by him. She could not remember having made any such statement herself and if she had, it was 'only idle in her so to do' as there were no grounds for saying it. Similarly she did not remember having sent for any tenants, debtors or others for money. Had she done so, it was by the command and order of her father and for his sole use. That was all she had to say!

In July 1683 there was a major hearing in chancery to consider the exceptions.[23] Elizabeth claimed that Hoskins had not included £500 payable by Lord Townshend and £350 paid by Sir John Potts to Mr 'Bagshawe' [Hackshaw] on behalf of Roger. It was decreed that both should have been included with interest and Hackshaw was ordered to attend court to give evidence. Her third item was disallowed and her fourth regarding Roger paying costs was only allowed to the extent that Roger had money in the personal estate to pay the £500 bequest and not otherwise.

Roger in his turn claimed items that Hoskins had disallowed: £58 for a coach and horses and a chamber for his mother, £3 to Mr Burrell, £15 to the poor. He was granted £34 of this since he had already been allowed £200 in the report for overvaluation of goods in the inventory. He waived his second claim. His third was that he should have been allowed the goods left in the will to his own son James and which were worth £400. Again because of the valuation adjustment, he was allowed this claim but only to the tune of £300. His other six claims were all deemed insufficient to be allowed!

Hoskins had calculated the whole of the personal estate of Sir John and both Elizabeth and Roger were after a share of what remained after Sir John's debts were paid. This would not be unreasonable as both for a time had acted as executors and thus residuary legatees. As executor named in the will, Elizabeth had the strongest claim to any residual balance as long as she could win her assertion that Roger had had the whole personal estate and she had not siphoned off any of it. In any event another big total was now at issue.

In July, Hackshaw was examined and the court confirmed that the £350 should have been included.[24] During the summer Roger asked for more time to obtain bills for the payment of the money he was ordered to pay into court and through the autumn he continued to argue about what should be paid.[25] However, at another major hearing in December 1683 the court again became decisive.[26] In July, Roger had been ordered to pay £1,177 into court. Roger lost his argument that the £350 paid to Hackshaw should not be treated as part of Sir John's estate and he was ordered to pay the £1,177 to Elizabeth immediately. Hoskins was to compute the interest due on this amount given the delay in payment. Indeed the decree recorded that Roger's paperwork regarding the claim was such as to make his claim vexatious and so Elizabeth was also awarded costs since December 1682. However, her appeal against his earlier exceptions to the judgement was not allowed.

Further machinations continued over several months. Roger, grasping at straws, tried to suggest that the absence of his full title from his copy of Hoskins' report invalidated it.[27] Nonetheless in June 1684 the order was made absolute and Roger had to pay the £1,177 in chancery, a further £135 ordered against him, plus costs and interest - perhaps close to £1,500 in all.[28] Even then he delayed payment and Elizabeth was back in chancery as late as March 1685 when she had an order allowing her to proceed via the sheriff of Norfolk for recovery of the debt.[29] The record went silent; nearly seven years after their father's death, Roger paid up.

The precise sum paid remains unclear given the brevity of the decree notes and the lack of Hoskins's two reports, but after all these years Elizabeth had achieved an initial interim payment of £1,500 and a further £1,500 or so from her brother relating to the personal estate, which was a very fair result from the wording of her father's will. She would have been able to live comfortably in London off the interest of her capital. Roger had achieved the reversion of all the Clippesby property, again a fair result given the obvious intent of the will and other settlements.

All-in-all Roger's record in chancery actions was not good. He had effectively lost to Guybon, Villiers and now his sister. Only the lawyers really won! It is not surprising that Sir Roger did not participate in any other major chancery actions.

Chapter 20

Sir Roger Potts: Bottom of the Poll

Sir Roger's life is far better documented than that of his father. Apart from the details found in his suits with Elizabeth, his sister, other sources show he was much more active in Norfolk affairs, including standing unsuccessfully for parliament in 1689. Having spent little time at Mannington he had scant affection for it and lived a comfortable life as a country squire at Great Elllingham. Having rowed with his father and sister in his middle age, he had a poor relationship with his own sons towards the end of his life.

Roger was born to Sir John Potts junior and his wife Susan Heveningham in about 1643.[1] He was educated at Enfield School in the parish where his grandfather lived and spent much of the 1650s. Roger was obviously a favoured grandchild, as was evident from the wording of Sir John senior's will. For many years Sir John took care of his education and maintenance not only at school but also at Cambridge and the inns of court. He gave him an 'exhibition' of £100 a year on condition that he accounted for his expenditure to Sir John. His grandfather also paid for Roger to be admitted to a chamber in Inner Temple, where for a while Roger lived. In Chapter 19, chancery depositions revealed that Roger had not been in Mannington at all during his teenage years.[2] His higher education clearly befitted a future heir but his attendance sequence was rather odd. This may be explained by the passing reference in one of his later chancery depositions that he had wanted to travel as a young man. Inner Temple admissions showed Roger Potts gent of Mannington admitted on 20th November 1660.[3] This may have been a formality to ensure a place. At seventeen, in January 1661, he was admitted to Caius College Cambridge.[4] After university, he was admitted to Middle Temple (his late great-uncle Charles's inn) in 1669.[5] Perhaps in the mid-1660s he had returned to Inner Temple, but it is also possible that he may have taken time off to travel as he had intended. In 1662 his grandfather and father settled on him certain land in Irmingland and Itteringham of the annual value of £100-120. This was to encourage Roger in his studies and to 'make proof how he could manage that small beginning of an estate'. Ever since he had managed this farm (now called Elmerdale farm), making leases on it and receiving rents. Sir Roger remained attached to this property in later mortgage and debt affairs.

Marriage and property

On 1st February 1665, William Davy of Great Ellingham settled a portion of £1,500 on his only daughter and heiress, Mary, for her marriage to Roger Potts. Davy came from an old Norfolk family from the Gunthorpe and Ingoldisthorpe area.[6] His father Henry, who had died in 1595, had been sheriff and an alderman of Norwich; William's mother was Elizabeth the daughter of Richard Webb of Ixworth, in Suffolk. William himself was married to Margaret Gurney; a London lawyer with a busy practice, he acted as executor in several of her family's wills and was also very active in the affairs of his cousin Elizabeth Gawdy's family.[7] No doubt Sir John Potts senior would have known the Gurneys well when he lived in West Barsham with his first wife Barbara and, through them, the Davy family. Given Sir John's interest in his grandson, it is likely he enabled Roger's introduction to Mary Davy.

Roger's tripartite marriage settlement, between Sir John Potts senior and John Potts junior, William Davy and Anthony Webb gent of London, and the young couple, was similar to John's 1639 marriage settlement in that the Mannington estate and all its manors and lands would pass to them after his father's life interest.[8] One difference was that now some of the lands were already mortgaged. The next day, on the Feast of the Purification of the Virgin Mary, in Great Ellingham church, Roger and Mary were married. Anthony Webb, a silkman and mercer of London was not only a relation but also the partner of Mary's uncle, Henry Davy, a Merchant Taylor. A surviving letter of 1664 showed that William Davy had promised a friend who was in need of money to pay some rent for him in London.[9] To enact the transaction, he would write to his cousins Robert and Thomas Webb in London to ask them to transfer the money. The Webb house in Fleet Street would have been full of financial and legal papers and, as related in Chapter 15, was used as a safe place for many Potts documents - before it burnt down in the Great Fire a year after Roger's marriage.

Mary's mother, Margaret, was the youngest sister of Edward Gurney whose will was proved in February 1642, naming as his executors his wife Frances, William Davy his brother-in-law and 'Ellen' Gurney.[10] Margaret's nephew Henry inherited the main seat of West Barsham and other lands, but died married yet without children in about 1660.[11] When he died, Henry Gurney left the family seat at West Barsham to his wife (the unnamed daughter of William Adams of Middle Temple); his executors, however, again including William Davy, were empowered to sell the properties to pay his debts. Henry Gurney was also in the process of negotiating to sell a property at Great Ellingham to William's brother Henry Davy junior. When Henry Davy made his will in March 1659 it was quite explicit that he intended to acquire Great Ellingham to add to his houses in London and Norwich where he had been born.[12] At some point before 1666 Henry Davy died, but his will was not proved until the same day as his brother's. His various legatees included Anthony and Elizabeth Webb (she was also a cousin) and their children. William Davy was made sole executor and was the residuary legatee after all debts, charges and other legacies were paid. This was how Great Ellingham came to William Davy and then to Roger Potts.

Mary's father made his will in May 1666 and was buried on 1st April 1667; her mother already having died, Mary had to administer the will that July.[13] Mary was to deal not only with her father's debts but also those of her uncle Henry, as William had not had time to execute fully his brother's will prior to his own death. William asked to be buried near his wife and his brother in Great Ellingham church. After debts and charges had been paid the balance of the estate was in fact left not solely to Mary, but equally to her, William's wife's sister Helen Gurney and William's grandchild James, the son of Mary and Roger Potts. Provision was also made for Anne, the daughter of William and Henry's sister Anne Heigham, and small bequests to Gawdy and other cousins. These included Anne Spelman the daughter of John Spelman of Narborough deceased, Roger's cousin.

In October 1668 Roger and Mary secured a second settlement as Sir John senior continued to ensure his property was clearly bestowed on his heirs.[14] Written 18 months after William Davy's death, the deed reflected Mary's status as his heir. In exchange for her £1,500 dowry she received rights in the Mannington estate. The two settlements were written in very similar terms. One or two fields were now named more precisely and one tenant had changed. However, for the first time the deed specifically itemised three more farms. Fenton's messuage and Saxthorpe New Closes in Mannington and Saxthorpe totalled 50 acres and were occupied by William Hill (he was probably related to the Hill who had married Barbara Potts). Mannington Mere and several named closes near Mossymere and across the Little Barningham boundary of Mannington parish totalled 220 acres and were occupied by William Ryall. The third farm contained most of the closes between the Barningham and Wolterton roads in Itteringham, and closes in Wolterton. It comprised about 149 acres in the occupation of Richard Sexton. Sexton's land was 'to be by him tilled and sowen to halfes'. This is the only specific reference (reinforced in Sir John senior's will) to the practice of crop sharing, rather than rental payments, that has been found in the Mannington estate. While the wording is potentially ambiguous, it suggests that the whole farm had until now been pasture and that Sexton was to plough it up. Once its arable productivity was established a fair monetary rent would be agreed.

It seems unlikely that all three were three new farms; the first two were clearly marked farmsteads on the 1595 Mannington map. But the pattern of naming only parts of the estate in these marriage settlements was purposeful, usually differentiating non-manorial land. Later in the century all the farm units were typically recited in key documents, so at this stage the intention seems to have been to facilitate some sort of division of rents between John junior and Roger as well as enabling mortgages with clear title. Although the precise nature of Sir John senior's approach to sorting out his debts has not survived, it is known that Mannington Mere farm was part of the arrangements. Sir John senior and Roger first mortgaged the farm in 1670; in 1676 Roger and Christopher Crowe came to some further agreement, presumably to pay the outstanding interest. In 1676 the mortgage was assigned to Sir Robert Baldock of Tacolneston in trust solely to the use of Roger and his heirs (but not his father), with the £500 principal having been paid to Crowe by Roger. At least this piece of the estate was firmly back in the family.[15]

Roger also had to handle the consequence of one of the 1661 mortgages his father and grandfather had raised. In 1676 Annabella Hervey, who had lent £600 on White House Farm in Irmingland, married John Hackshaw, a senior London councillor and member of the Skinners' Company. Annabella sued Sir John Potts junior, Roger Potts and James Scamler (who had been her trustee in 1661) in chancery.[16] Only the bill of complaint survives. The terms had been for £750 to be repaid on 26th June

1666, this being principal and accumulated interest. But by 1676 only a modest amount of interest had been paid, despite repeated requests for the full amount. Roger had held the premises and had been taking the rents even before his grandfather's death. In 1673 he had paid some of the interest, leaving the debt at £750 which would be treated as principal. But nothing had been paid since and the Hackshaws were seeking redress. They knew that Sir John senior had made provision for his debts to be paid off, but the Potts were now claiming that there was a prior settlement of the premises which invalidated the mortgage. Justice was clearly on the side of the Hackshaws.

The Hervey/Hackshaw mortgage was restarted at £1,000 principal on 18th October 1676 when the messuage and 221 acres of lands were mortgaged by Roger Potts to John Hervey of Ickworth Suffolk esq His Majesty's Treasurer and Receiver General as trustee for Thomas Hervey gent of London and William Masemore of Middle Temple.[17] Presumably Sir John junior and Roger had paid off the other 1661(Catelyn) mortgage before or soon after Sir John senior's death in 1673 but had not been able to pay off all his debts and needed a continuation of a mortgage on the Irmingland estate.[18]

Home and children

After her father's death, Mary and Roger were to make Ellingham their home. There is no indication that they ever lived in Mannington, which was probably intermittently rented out after his father's death. Roger kept a chamber (probably the suite his grandfather also used) and possessions there, presumably for his occasional visits on estate business. Mannington was certainly rented out to Oliver Le Neve esq and his family between 1690 and 1692.[19] Various letters from his brother Peter Le Neve and others were addressed to him at Mannington. Oliver and his wife Anne Gawdy lived there prior to moving back to a family home at Great Witchingham. They had married some time before 1687 when a daughter Anne was baptised at Witchingham. A son Francis was also baptised and buried there in February 1689 and their first son Oliver was buried in August the same year. Of their nine children, Isabella was baptised at Mannington in May 1690, their third son, John (Jackie) at Little Barningham in August 1691 and Francis ('4th son') at Mannington in August 1692.[20] In July 1692 Mary Browne wrote from Saxthorpe to 'Madam Le Neave' at Mannington, clearly in response to an enquiry from her about a suitable wet nurse and suggesting the wife of Christopher Brettingham of Hempstead.[21] Letters from traders in London continued to be addressed to the Le Neves at Mannington in 1693. However, by November 1692 they had already moved into Witchingham and in 1693 Erasmus Earle wrote to them there saying that he seldom saw them now that they had moved out of Mannington. Anne had a little girl Elizabeth in 1694 who died a year later. A last daughter Henrietta who was born in early February 1696 may have led to her mother's death, as 31 year old Anne was buried on the 20th. Little Francis died aged five the following spring. The following year Oliver reluctantly fought a duel, on Cawston Heath, unfortunately (and unexpectedly) killing Sir Henry Hobart of Blickling, and had to flee abroad for a year or two.

Roger and Mary were also unlucky with their young children as the parish register of Great Ellingham shows. Their first son James was baptised on 16th February 1666. Chancery papers show that Sir John junior in early 1678 had bequeathed goods in Mannington to Roger's son and heir James. James seems to have died at some point between 1678 and 1682. Great Ellingham burial entries for 1677 to 1706 have not survived, but chancery materials show that he died not long after Sir John junior and certainly before the end of the Potts v Potts case in 1683. There was apparently a long gap before their son Philip was baptised on 20th March 1671 but it may be that at least one other child, John, was recorded elsewhere. Philip was to become the eldest son and heir, but died unmarried in 1698 aged 27. Blomefield's recital of the verse inscription on his Great Ellingham tombstone showed that the family held Philip in great affection, describing him as a friend to all. The inscription on his marble stone 'in Juventa languidus Morbo grave' might be taken to imply that he had been weakened as a boy by illness and this might explain the lack of a formal education. There is no sign of Philip attending university. It was Algernon, not his elder brother Philip, who received the gentleman's education at Cambridge and the inns of court.

Algernon, who was in due course to become the heir, was baptised on 12th March 1673. The use of the name is unusual: all the other sons had Potts family first names, implying that Roger had a strong sense of family history, probably imbued in him by his grandfather. Five years before, Sir John's friend Lord Algernon Percy, the Earl of Northumberland had died and his grandson Algernon Seymour had been baptised in 1670. Maybe Sir John suggested the name or perhaps Mary thought it sounded fashionable, not aware of its original French meaning -'with moustaches'. Two months after the baby's christening, the register recorded that Sir John Potts senior died on 14th May 1673 indicating that he died at Roger's house. He had probably lived with him for some months before his death and, possibly, for some years. This arrangement would help to explain why Sir John in his will asked for Roger to undertake his burial at Mannington. Roger's little son, John, named for his grandfather, was buried on 24th February 1674. Their daughter Mary was born on 15th September, baptised on 22nd September 1674 and buried on 25th June 1676. Another son Charles was born on 13th January and baptised on 20th January 1676. The last child recorded, Anne, was born on 6th February and baptised on 14th February 1678. It seems that she too must have died as an infant since there is no mention of her after this. The baptism of Susan, the only girl to survive, has not been discovered but the registers are patchy.[22] The surviving parts of the registers hold no other family entries until Sir Roger's burial there on 3rd November 1711.

Dame Mary Potts's death, given as 1701 by the Visitation entry for the Davy family, also has not been verified. Unfortunately, no gravestone was noted by Blomefield for her in Great Ellingham and the surviving registers lack the years around 1701. The 'Lady Potts' charity in Itteringham shows that she was alive in 1700. Organised and partly funded by the Robins family of Itteringham, this was the purchase of a field and large gravel pit the annual net revenues of which were to be doled out to poor widows of the parish. Described in the 1832 *Report of the*

Charity Commissioners on Norfolk Charities, it appears from the then surviving overseers' book that Thomas and Richard Robins bought two acres of land in Broomhill from Sir Roger Potts in about March 1700.[23] Thomas Robins funded the initial purchase price of £18, but £10 of this was then to be raised by the overseers and Lady Potts would contribute the £8 balance. Itteringham's inhabitants would take the gravel for the highways and the 8s annual rent paid by Henry Smith for the 2 acres would be divided equally between 8 widows of Itteringham. The purchase being from Sir Roger implies that the 'Lady Potts' involved was his wife Mary, not his stepmother Elizabeth who would also have used the title Lady Potts.

Dame Elizabeth, however, was most likely to have been the 'Lady Potts' who paid 4s in the pound 'aid' in 1693-94 on behalf of Francis S Pemberton in St Pancras, Kentish Town Middlesex.[24] Given the family animosity around the time of Sir John junior's death, it is highly unlikely that Lady Elizabeth would have supported the Itteringham charity.

Legal practice

Roger had studied the law when in the chambers his grandfather had bought for him. Although he may not have been a practising lawyer for very long, he used his knowledge in family matters. As well as his appearances in the many family actions, a number of chancery actions survive which include Roger in his role as trustee in a will or other transaction. In 1672-73 Roger was involved in a rather straightforward dispute with Clement Spelman over quitrents and fines in the manor of Carbonells in Rockland dating back to 1645 to 1663.[25] At the time William Davy had leased this small estate from Sir Richard Berney, lord of the manor there. Another family example saw Roger as the last surviving trustee of a 1675 deed involving his cousin Sir William Heveningham and William's daughter and sole heir Abigail, who married Henry Heron esq of Cressey Hall Lincolnshire.[26] In early 1707 as the last trustee still alive he participated in a conveyance and mortgage of the Ketteringham home of the Heveninghams.

Another typical action was by Gardiner Hewitt esq against Roger and others.[27] Hewitt was a 'booksmith' or bookseller of Norfolk and the son of Sir William Hewitt deceased and his wife Dame Ursula who had remarried to Sir Robert Baldock of Tacolneston (Roger's attorney in the Potts v Potts case who failed to engross the Townshend agreement). The action related to various clauses in Hewitt's will and a bond for their performance by Baldock, which had been lodged with Roger in about 1670. Now, in 1677, the will had still not been performed, Baldock would not respond and Roger would not enter the bond into suit. Worse, he was said to be confederating with Gardiner's brothers and sisters. Roger was only caught up at the margins of this family action between Baldock and the Hewitts which rumbled on until 1682.[28]

During the 1680s Sir Roger was one of the commissioners at an enquiry held in Norwich regarding payments for a free school in Aylsham originally endowed by Nicholas Norgate alderman of Norwich as a letter reported at the time, which is summarised here:

> There is a free school in the town of Aylsham: £160 was given by Mr Nicholas Norgate Alderman of Norwich to the school and land worth £10 pa. In 1650 Captain Osborn, owner of the land charged with the annuity, with the consent of the inhabitants of Aylsham, gave £200 to Major Robert Doughty of Aylsham to settle the £10 annuity on the mills of Aylsham and Doughty made a deed of feoffment to trustees and it was paid for 34 years by Doughty and his son Captain Robert Doughty. In 1683 Miles Baispool gent of Aylsham bought the mills. He saw the deeds and in July 1684 (with Capt Robert Doughty) paid £5 to the school-master for half a year's salary for the period ending Christmas 1683 and promised to pay the remainder after the assizes and to pay it in future. But, after this, he had denied the payment of the annuity and arrears. Having got one of Doughty's deeds in his hands, when requested to re-deliver it, he said he had mislaid it somewhere. But since then he denied having the deed and still refused to pay the annuity. At a chancery enquiry for charitable uses taken in Norwich before Sir Roger Potts bt, Ralph Hare esq, Isaak Preston, Edmund Themelthorpe, William [Old?] & Francis Repps esq, the substance of the aforesaid was found by jurors and after that a decree was made by four of the commissioners for the payment of arrears and for the time to come. But Baispool put an exception against this decree into chancery and endeavoured by dilatory proceedings to tire out the prosecutor. The request was for a speedy end to this vexatious suit.[29]

In April 1688 Sir Roger Potts was a defendant in chancery in connection with his role as a trustee for the related D'Ewes family.[30] The action, 'Dewes versus Dewes', is not particularly exciting or revealing but it does show the importance of contacts in managing a family's legal and financial affairs. A £4,000 portion from a marriage settlement had not been invested immediately in a mortgage or other security as the trustees were supposed to do. The plaintiffs represented the younger daughters of the bridegroom's father, to whom the proceeds would pass, and wanted a return on the money. The defendants seemed to be concerned that they would expose themselves to being sued if they picked poor investments. The decree required the investment to be made, but also indemnified the defendants from all costs, damages or hazards in the management of the trust. Subsequently a mortgage for £3,500 on a property in Lincolnshire was approved by the court as a suitable investment for the bulk of the funds.

Sir Roger, with two others, was trustee for Dame Priscilla D'Ewes, the widow of Sir Willoughby D'Ewes. Sir Willoughby was named after his mother, Elizabeth Willoughby, the daughter of Sir Henry Willoughby, Roger's great-uncle. Sir Willoughby and Dame Priscilla's eldest son, Sir Simonds D'Ewes junior, married De La Reviere Jermyn, daughter of Thomas Lord Jermyn in the summer of 1687. Her father's dowry payment was to pass straight through at their marriages to Priscilla and Elizabeth D'Ewes, the under-age sisters of Sir Simonds and his younger brother Willoughby. Sir Roger Potts was acting as trustee for his young cousins.

Another chancery suit in 1688-89 saw Sir Roger again involved as a defending trustee, this time in George Smith's action against Nicholas Wilton.[31] Wilton and his wife Thomasine held a number of manors and properties in Wilby, Berkhall, Hargham, Quidenham and elsewhere in Norfolk and Suffolk. Debts had mounted to the extent that repayment might jeopardise the settlement on his three young daughters, by then under the guardianship of Thomas Holland esq. Quite why they had a guardian while their parents were both alive was not made clear. Sir Roger had been a trustee in an earlier marriage settlement that had set up the total of £4,000 for portions for the girls. Wilton owed large sums to Mrs Dorothy Walpole, Alderman Guybon of Norwich, Philip Harbord and others, including Sir Robert Baldock, Roger's own lawyer. Some property had been sold to Smith, but the whole estate was encumbered with the £4,000 settlement so Sir Roger could not release his trustee interest in any of the property. Wilton said that the lands sold would pay off much of his debt and he still had sufficient property to support the remaining mortgages and pay the portions for the girls. The action showed how complicated affairs could get if a whole estate became encumbered with debts. At least at this stage the Potts family debt problems had largely been managed by mortgages on the separately held parts of their estate.

Political life

Roger did his duty attending the assizes and in local government. He was first placed on the Commission of the Peace for Norfolk in July 1673 and he remained a justice of the peace until his death.[32] Although by an act of 1673 anyone holding public office had to show a certificate proving he regularly took the sacrament, Sir Roger's certificate (from the vicar and church wardens of Great Ellingham) was dated 1689, the date of the next commission.[33] He like many others found attendance on the sheriff at the assizes very expensive and in 1675 he signed a long proposition for reducing the costs (and improving the behaviour) of the sheriff. The 40 signatories agreed that should any of them become sheriff their livery would be plain grey worsted camblet with moderate trimmings and that none of them would take more than 40 servants to the assizes (but no less than 20). The cost of the assize dinners was also given a budget. It was being suggested that the gentry split attendance at the winter and summer assizes between them (Roger was down for the summer). That way their expenses would be greatly reduced.[34] In 1688 Sir Roger and family, including Lady D'Ewes's family, attended the August meeting in

Norwich as reported by 'M' Chamberlain (either Martha or Mary, the half-sisters of William Windham of Felbrigg) in a letter to her brother. Although the assizes were unremarkable and the High Sheriff, Thomas Seaman, 'pitiful', the evenings were full of dancing and gossiping until 3 in the morning. Sir Roger 'inquired much where Lady M was to settle'. Elizabeth, the widowed Lady Maidstone, was Windham's full sister and was looking for a home for her and her two children. Windham was keen to avoid their living at Felbrigg and preferred to reside in Twickenham with his wife. His sister teased Sir Roger by saying the widow was hoping to settle with him. Roger replied that was news to him and Lady Potts made it clear that 'it would not be very agreable' to her![35]

Roger and others were tax commissioners for Norfolk in February 1696 instructed to raise 3s in the £ for the King.[36] By September 1698 Roger was a deputy lord lieutenant and spent much of that month at Norwich Castle with his colleagues who included Sir Henry Hobart, Sir Francis Guybon, Sir Jacob Astley and Robert Walpole. They were there to assist the Duke of Norfolk with the latest contentious oath which many were refusing to swear. The following year they were calling upon their militia in response to a threat of French invasion. In March 1696 Sir Roger headed the group meeting at the castle to arrange for militia troops to assist in disarming Norfolk papists, as ordered by the government. It is to be hoped that he remembered his grandfather's caution in moving too swiftly in such matters, as this order was rescinded six days later! In 1698 and 1699 he was commissioned by special writ to swear in firstly Robert Candell and then the splendidly named Wormley Hethersett as justices for Thetford.[37]

It is clear that Sir Roger had political ambitions. A reply to a letter of his of 1682 from a Mr Robert Long (presumably of Reymerston) showed Potts had tried to use Lord Townshend's name to provoke political indiscretions from Long. He failed; the letter is a masterpiece of polite non-committal.[38] *The History of the House of Commons* notes that Sir Roger stood as a Whig in 1689 but came bottom of the Norfolk poll and did not stand again. Nevertheless he remained active throughout his life as a campaigner for others. In October 1688 Sir Roger was, with Sir Francis Guybon and Sir Henry Holland, one of the principal promoters of an appeal to King James II for a free parliament.[39] Initially the Duke of Norfolk was not keen to be involved, but on 1st December he led a 300-strong column of knights and gentlemen and made a declaration in Norwich. This all came too late to influence James - the Prince of Orange was already on his way to England and King James's reign was all but over.

Humphrey Prideaux, the Dean of Norwich and friend of his son Algernon, reported in one of his letters of 27th November 1693 that:

> Whenever there is a new parliament, the knights of the shire for Norfolk will be Sir Henry Hobart and Sir Roger Potts, and for Suffolk Sir Samuel Bernardiston and Sir Jarvis Elways all stiffe Republicarians; but I hope most of the burroughs will provide better[40]

Roger was still a Whig at this point, but Prideaux was wrong about him standing. However, as with many in this age, Sir Roger changed political affiliation. Although he had accepted a commission in the lieutenancy and militia from Charles, 2nd Viscount Townshend in May 1701 and was said to 'rejoice at his Lordship having been appointed Lord Lieutenant', he was soon disillusioned.[41] By May 1702, when Robert Walpole was assessing the opposition in the various Norfolk seats that he might stand for, Sir Roger was seen as a 'violent Tory' and firmly one of the Tory camp led by Roger's friend Sir Jacob Astley, Colonel Harbord and others.[42] Another letter of 1702 showed Sir Roger Potts to have been active in the discussions by the knights of the shire about who should be asked to stand for the county seats.[43] The key county figure of the time was, of course, the new lord lieutenant, Viscount Townshend. His brother Roger Townshend and Sir John Holland were the sitting Whig MPs. The Townshends were plotting to try to get Holland (with whom they had various disagreements) to stand down at the next election and for fresh candidates to unite the somewhat split Whig vote. To that end Townshend wrote to tender his resignation hoping that Holland would do the same. But in a stormy meeting Sir Roger Potts and others encouraged Sir John Holland to stand again, which in due course he did. Those seeking Holland to stand may have done so as much to confound the Townshend plan as anything. The result was that Sir John Holland headed the poll, but his Whig running mate was defeated by the Tory Sir Jacob Astley. As Townshend, and indeed Robert Walpole, had feared the county vote was split. While Sir Roger Potts's role in all this may have been modest, it cannot have endeared him to the senior Whigs in Norfolk and may have been part of the process by which Roger evolved from Whig to Tory.

The country was rife with anti-papist feeling and informers were keen to make trouble. A man called John Woodcock wrote to the Lord Keeper, Sir Nathan Wright, from Norwich Castle in November 1701 saying he would give evidence against a Mr Blackbourn, 'a papist in Norfolk' who 'said on Jan 15 that they were all rebels that stood to maintaining the King William's laws and that he would as freely shoot him as a mad dog. On July 6 he said he would willingly kill him. I informed a justice who desired me to hold my tongue; and because I could not, he hath cast me in prison. I beseech you to send to the county gaol and you shall have oath made by me and one more'. Sir Roger wrote to the Secretary of State explaining that Woodcock was not a good character and it was agreed to warn the assize judge about him. It may well be that Roger was the justice Woodcock complained of but his story rings less true when it appears he in fact was imprisoned for debt![44]

At the height of concerns about papist plots Sir Nicholas L'Estrange, Sir Robert Yallup and Sir Christopher Calthorpe refused to take the oath of allegiance. Prideaux described Yallup as 'the greatest knave in nature' but the other two as 'very honest gentlemen'. By late April Yallup and Calthorpe chose to remain in custody rather than sign. Prideaux thought that Yallup still hoped the plot would succeed but that Calthorpe was simply a mild and honest man misguided in his belief that he should not sign as a matter of conscience. The latter should, he believed, therefore have been let out of prison. In June Prideaux wrote a long letter on the Calthorpe case.

Calthorpe some years past had defeated Sir John Hobart in one of the elections for the county. Now his son Sir Henry Hobart (Sir Roger's Whig running mate in 1689), apparently out of malice, was pursuing Calthorpe. Prideaux clearly did not like Hobart and wrote that he should concentrate on paying off his debts, for which he was renowned, rather than prosecuting his neighbours. Calthorpe was not a papist and yet many who were had simply avoided attending the assizes when the oaths were taken and were still left un-pursued. Despite the discomfort, Calthorpe had complied with everything he was required to do as an objector to the oath.

Writing with news of the assizes in August 1696, Prideaux turned again to the Calthorpe case and reported that Sir Roger Potts was one of those concerned against him and had tried to persuade a gentleman to write to Calthorpe to give himself up again as a prisoner at the assizes. Apparently Hobart was intent on trying to take up the case in parliament. However, Sir John Treby, Chief Justice of the Common Pleas, ruled at the assizes that in effect Calthorpe's commitment was illegal. Calthorpe and L'Estrange were discharged based on the timings of their refusals to take the oaths relative to an act of pardon. Even so the issue rumbled on, which Prideaux thought was shameful.

The few clues to Sir Roger's character all seem to point to a rather bombastic and at times aggressive man. A portrait, not yet traced, was said by Tomes on seeing it in 1910 to show 'not the long thin face of the other [Potts] portraits but a stout man of middle age who looks to have been a bon vivant'. Perhaps a polite description of a rather red-faced country squire? While his politics shifted over time, it is unlikely that moderate men such as Prideaux would ever have taken to him. His reputation in Norwich would not have been helped by the fact that Algernon, his eldest surviving son, was for extended periods not on speaking terms with his father. While both were committed Tories by the early 1700s, they may have not seen eye to eye on political matters, with Algernon being a more thoughtful character. While Algernon did not stand for parliament, he was at least politically active behind the scenes by the last years of his father's life. Although very little has been written about him, Algernon turns out to have been an interesting and attractive character.

Chapter 21

Algernon Potts: Politics and Religion Do Mix

Algernon Potts (1673-1716), the 4th baronet, only held Mannington for a few years and past writers have written little about him. He turns out to have been an interesting, quintessentially eighteenth-century man. Married to a wealthy widow, Algernon was a part of Norwich's intellectual, literary and political set, based in and around the Cathedral precinct. A city couple, he and his wife Frances moved to the country in 1711 after he inherited Mannington where they began to recreate their tasteful lifestyle. Whatever big plans they might have had for the house and grounds will never be known; within six years they were to die there only a few days apart.

Algernon, born in 1673, was Sir Roger's fourth son but his eldest brothers James and John died before Algernon was ten. Philip, the next eldest surviving son was probably too sickly to attend university and Algernon therefore received the better education. After attending Bury Grammar School - and perhaps in expectation of Philip's early death (he died at 27 in 1698) - Algernon was admitted to Magdalen College, Cambridge in 1690.[1] In July 1693 he entered Lincoln's Inn and Sir Roger may have had hopes that Algernon would pursue a legal career.

In April 1694, just before Algernon was due to go down to London, he accompanied his father at various meetings to do with the 1684 will and estate of Augustine Briggs senior, alderman of Norwich and twice MP for Norwich.[2] The action, which related this and was brought in 1700 by Sir Roger against Augustine Briggs junior, an alderman of Norwich until James II's purge of 1688, is otherwise of minor interest. Roger was involved in a very long-running and still unfinished set of executorship accounts dating back to 1684. Fed up with Augustine junior's errors and intransigence over money due to him, Roger finally took Briggs to court. The depositions by Ralph Hare of Hargham, Robert Day and John Frost (Roger's steward at Ellingham) show that the Briggs family had effectively operated as a retail bank for Potts. Large sums of cash went through their books. In April 1694, for example, Algernon had taken a bag containing £40 in coin to Briggs junior and had from him for part of it a bill for £20 usable down in London where he was shortly to go. Other deposition references, including Algernon's own, show him to have been helping his father in the rather difficult negotiations over the Briggs accounts.

Marriage and money

There is however no indication that Algernon practised law for any length of time. It is likely that he spent a few years at Lincoln's Inn and came to live in Norwich from the late 1690s. Algernon married a woman thirteen years older than him, Frances Calibut, originally from Saham Toney.[3] Frances was the second wife and widow of Thomas Crane a successful merchant of Norwich who had died about 1st June 1700 leaving her childless but very wealthy.[4] In his will, proved within a month of his death, as well as a life interest in various Saham Toney and other estates, Crane left her outright his house in St Peter Hungate, other houses in Norwich and houses in Gately and Colkirk. He also left her his half of her family property that she had brought at their marriage. The daughter of Richard Calibut, she had inherited land from her father and her brother Philip in Saham Toney, Ovington and Threxton.[5] She and Algernon married in Norwich at St Michael at Plea on 30th October 1700. Sir Roger Potts did not approve of this 'hasty' marriage. He no doubt thought it risked being childless and so boded ill for the continuation of the family line. If so, he was right. Frances, by then aged 40, bore Algernon no children.

Before, and in the early years of, his marriage it is not clear how Algernon spent his time. He does not seem to have been in trade of any sort. There is no sign of any active involvement in the Ellingham, Mannington or Clippesby estates and he had no landed estate of his own. At this time, he seems to have played no part in local or national politics. Although gradually he could be found in minor local government roles, the references were few and far between. 'A. Potts' in June 1712 was named as one of the commissioners in Norfolk for executing the act of 1709 for recruiting for Her Majesty's service. However, with Henry Davy, John Knyvett and T [Thornhaugh] Gurdon, he complained that the men who had volunteered and completed their three years were being whipped and forced to stay on despite the act.[6] On looking more closely however, Algernon was in fact very engaged in the issues of the day, but as a scholar and a writer, the occupations of a gentleman of leisure.

Despite Frances's money, chancery papers show that Algernon, like many of the upper classes of the day, was not quick to pay debts and meet obligations.[7] A month after her husband died, an action was started in chancery by the attorney-general on behalf of the mayor of Norwich and various citizens. Thomas Crane and his friend Dr Peter Parham had been executors of the will of Richard Ireland clerk, who had left various charitable and other legacies totalling over £1,000. Crane had been slow to pay these out and had been taken to chancery where an order was made against him in 1698. The 1700 complaint was that all the money had still not been paid. Frances, as his executor, and subsequently Algernon as her husband were taken to task for the remaining sums. Their first answer to the complaint in February 1701 was a masterpiece of: 'we are strangers to the original action' and have 'nothing to answer to' in the complaint. They even asserted that Crane did not leave enough money to pay his own debts and that Frances had only his personal plate. They denied liability and said it should be up to Parham to pay if anything was due. A month later they submitted an answer to an amended complaint. They were still 'strangers' to the original proceedings and believed that Ireland had not left sufficient assets to cover his bequests. However they now admitted to having sufficient assets to pay the still unadministered sums on the original chancery schedule, although they insisted Crane had already paid most of these. Presumably eventually they paid up as no chancery orders have been found.

A fascinating find appears in the next chancery action started in November 1700 in which Frances and Thomas Crane's three nieces took Frances and Algernon to court over legacies that they had been expecting to receive from Crane.[8] Also on the side of the defence was Thomas Shuckforth, Crane's eldest nephew who by his uncle's will would ultimately inherit all his landed property after Frances's life interest.[9] William and Frances Shuckforth had three boys and three girls, Crane's only nieces and nephews. The girls, two of them by now married and acting with their husbands, said that they had been promised legacies of £50 apiece by the will of their grandmother Joan Crane, Thomas Crane's mother and the widow of Thomas senior, who had been Saham's rector and was buried there on 4th February 1662. When of age they had not pursued their uncle, as Joan's executor, for payment as they said he was a wealthy merchant and the money would produce a good return invested with him. They also were given to believe that he would leave them large legacies in his own will, particularly since he had no children of his own and had been very close to the Shuckforth family.

However, they were misinformed. Thomas's will left the residue of his personal estate to Frances, from which she should have £200. In consultation with Dr Parham and Crane's 'brother Burton', she was to divide the rest between their friends and family as they decided. The girls claimed he had left a massive personal estate. Algernon and Frances refuted this and also denied any ability or reason to pay legacies originating in Joan's estate. They refused to pay any further money to the girls. After the death of one of the girls, the other two, Mary Duffield (with husband John) and Ann Shuckforth restarted the action. In their answers in 1701 and 1702 Algernon and Frances's argument became clear. They said Thomas Crane had found that Joan had died with significant debts which had left no money for any legacies. Indeed he had paid her debts and taken nothing for himself except a silver tankard and plate, which Frances now had. His own estate had been very modest after his trade debts had been honoured. The chancery action also revolved around cash or monies owing to Crane. Algernon said he had examined the books of William Browne, a London merchant and Crane's 'factor'. Details followed about money sent to Crane and payments to various Norwich weavers, for funeral costs and so on. The net result was, according to Algernon, that there was no residual personal estate for Frances to distribute under the clause in the will. That might have been the end of the matter but the nieces threatened them with imprisonment in the Fleet and the process rumbled on through the summer with Algernon consistently taking exception to the plaintiffs' arguments.[10] A master's report was made in July, implicitly in Duffield's favour, and Algernon obviously disagreed with him. The matter was to be heard next term. But the tenor of the orders was that Algernon was fighting a losing battle and the final decree was likely to go against him when the court reconvened for Michaelmas term. As there were no further decrees an out of court settlement probably ended the matter. Whatever the girls received, Crane's obligations were over as far as the Potts were concerned. Frances left them nothing in her own will.

Thomas Crane's merchant house

Fortuitously, the full inventory of Crane's possessions, taken shortly after his death and lodged in chancery for this suit, has survived. Most of the value of the total of £463 lay in £338 of trade goods. Cash, bonds and bills were not included. The possessions in the inventory are of little interest (the most valuable item being a clock and case at £8) but the description of the rooms confirmed that Frances and Thomas Crane had lived in a very substantial merchant house in Norwich.

The rooms in the order they were inventoried were: Little Parlour, Great Parlour, Hall, Warehouse, Packing Room, Closet, Kitchen, Larder, Small Beer Cellar, Brewhouse, Pantry, Mill House (with a malt mill in it), Best Beer Cellar, Stable, Old Chamber over the Kitchen, Maids' Chamber over the Kitchen, Little Parlour Chamber, Gallery, Great Parlour Chamber, Little Gray Chamber, Maids' Chamber, Mens' Chamber, Study, Garrett and a garden. From a reference in St Peter Hungate parish records, Thomas Crane was known to have lived in the same house in St Peter Hungate parish for 40 years, which was then bought in 1702 by Henry Youngs, a Norwich hosier.[11] A recent chance find of the deeds of sale has enabled the house to be located precisely and revealed that Youngs paid Algernon and Frances £420 for it in August 1702.[12] Also selling the property with Algernon and Frances were Francis Longe esq of Spixworth, probably their lawyer, and Robert Wright esq of Downham Suffolk, possibly the husband of one of Crane's sisters.

The deeds gave detailed abuttals of the house, garden and extra tenement naming the current and earlier occupants for the neighbouring houses. FR Beecheno in his article on St Peter Hungate said that the Crane house had previously been owned by Thomas Harman (given as Herman in the deeds) having been purchased in 1637 by his father Richard Harman, two years before he was mayor of Norwich.[13] Sir John Potts senior, who worked closely with Harman in the 1640s, would have known this house well. The deeds show that the house was on the boundary of St Peter Hungate parish and St Simon and St Jude, and that on its south side the property abutted Princes Inn Lane, now Waggon and Horses Lane.[14] To the east and partly to the north it abutted the house that had been owned by Sir John Pettus. Sir John was alderman, mayor and sheriff of Norwich as well as sheriff of Norfolk. Both his sons were knighted and Sir Thomas was sheriff in 1632. The Pettus House is known to have been at what is now 41-43 Elm Hill and a fragment of this galleried house remains.[15] From these deeds, the inventory and Beecheno's map, it is clear that the Crane house, now the site of 39 Elm Hill, was of similar design to its next door neighbour. The overseers' accounts for St Peter Hungate show that Crane and Mordecai Hewett were the senior citizens and two wealthiest inhabitants of the parish, reinforcing the belief that Crane lived in a very similar high status house to Pettus.[16] The deeds described it as having a garden and an additional tenement, probably on the other side of its Elm Hill frontage. The 1696 Thomas Cleer map of Norwich shows this area with several gardens behind these Elm Hill properties just as the abuttals suggest.[17] Frances's house therefore was a very short stroll away from the Erpingham Gate entrance to The Cathedral Close.

Life in Cathedral Close

Algernon now lived the life of a leisured gentleman in Norwich with a significant involvement in the political, ecclesiastical and intellectual life of the city. The 1702 deeds show that Algernon and Frances were already at that time living in The Close, a very fashionable part of Norwich. From the speed of his marriage to Frances after Crane's death, the Cranes must have been part of Algernon's social circle, implying that Algernon was living in The Close or nearby, well before 1700. Given the relationship with his father, there is little likelihood that he lived at Great Ellingham before his marriage to Frances. After their marriage, Algernon and Frances lived in at least two different rented houses in The Close.

The Dean of Norwich, Humphrey Prideaux, entered in his diary on 24th December 1701 that he had 'sealed a lease to Mr Potts'.[18] A valuation of the rents in The Close of 16th April 1703, used to work out tax charges for each house, showed Algernon Potts esq as the inhabitant of Dr Littell's house. Littell was one of the prebendaries whose houses were in various places around the precinct and it is unclear which of these Algernon used. However, Algernon may previously have rented another house in the Close. Certainly he had already featured in Prideaux's diaries, if only a few days earlier in December 1701, regarding timber sales from the Dean and Chapter's woods in Gately and Colkirk. Algernon had inherited, via Frances, Thomas Crane's lease of ten acres of coppice woods in Gately. He had wanted to buy timber from the Dean and Chapter but complained that their valuation was too high, particularly since the last lot felled had sold at a lower price. He also disagreed with the Dean over the taxable value of the copse.

At some point between 1703 and 1708, Algernon and Frances moved out of Dr Littell's house and became under-tenants of the large house still standing immediately inside the Erpingham Gate and now known as Number 71. Although he was not directly a tenant of the Dean and Chapter, who owned all the property within the precinct, he was cited as the under-tenant of Anne Burleigh widow of Sandringham in the renewal of her lease in 1709. This gave a definite location and from the Cathedral lease books, Humphrey Prideaux's diaries, the Dean and Chapter act books and the 1649 parliamentary survey of the Dean and Chapter properties in and around Norwich it is now possible to give an account of this house.[19]

Before about 1620 Sir William Denny, Recorder of Norwich, had lived in a house on the same site facing Almary Green to the east, with Tombland and later the precinct wall to the west, the gatehouse and the way leading to the west door of the Cathedral Church north and the orchard leased to Sir William to the south. However, this became dilapidated after he moved across the green to a new house.[20] In December 1626, following the expiry of Denny's lease of his old house, Dr John Hassall agreed to take it down and rebuild it as a prebendary's house initially for himself and then for the use of other prebendaries after his 14 year lease term. He was given 12 months to do the rebuilding and was allocated £15 for the workmanship and timber from Eaton Wood for it. However, he clearly never started on the project as within months he had been promoted. By mid-1628 he was installed as Dean and no longer needed this accommodation. In March 1628 he was discharged of his obligation to do the rebuilding. In April Denny surrendered his lease of the orchard and in May 1628 the prebendary Fulk Roberts was given permission to dismantle and rebuild the house with a budget of £40. This act book entry shows clearly that the old house was still standing in 1628. During 1628-29 the new house was built and in April 1629 the prebendaries John Spendlove and Nicholas Howlett reviewed the expenditure. By April 1630 it was occupied by John Spendlove the elder, who with Roberts was heavily involved in the Dean and Chapter's finances and building management. Hassall, Roberts and Spendlove had all been installed as prebendaries during 1615 and 1616 and were the dominant players in the act books of the 1620s.

Spendlove was to live in the house for many years and was certainly there when in 1649 the surveyors for parliament described the house and its 'true' value:

> A new house of stone and brick built in part upon the wall of
> the Close on the west side of the Almary Green and abutting on
> Sir William Denny's orchard and stables on the south within the
> Close; containing 3 stories and 4 rooms in each storey with a small
> court before the door and a woodyard and garden adjacent. All
> encompassed and divided with a stone wall and containing about ½
> a rood [1/8th of an acre] of ground.

In due course the stables became the prebendaries' but the orchard was absorbed into the property. While the rent in 1649 was only 20d the surveyors said it was worth £10 11s 8d per year. A lease to Spendlove of 1644 was declared void under the parliamentary act and the precise circumstances of the property and the players involved are unclear from the cessation of the chapter minutes in 1649 until after the Restoration. The Dean and Chapter properties were all sequestered and presumably let out to others. Hassall lived out his life in North Creake until his death there in 1654. Fulk Roberts as the senior prebendary was allowed £35 a year from his vicarage of Trowse. Spendlove was only allowed 2s 6d per week by the sequestrators and lived out the Commonwealth period in great poverty. After the Restoration, he regained his prebend and presumably reoccupied his house but was imprisoned for debt where he spent most of his time until his death in 1666.

In 1666 the property presumably passed directly to William Burleigh esq the next tenant visible in the lease books; but unfortunately his first lease of it has not survived. A minor entry in the lease books shows Burleigh was already involved in Dean and Chapter property during 1660-67, although whether in a major role for the Dean and Chapter or just in the house in the precinct is unclear. William Burleigh certainly had the property by 1676 when he is believed to have added the present main staircase and adjoining room, perhaps to make a grander house as The Close was becoming gentrified and largely secularised.[21] He was granted a lease renewal in 1680 when the property was described as being late of John Spendlove. Burleigh, whose memorial inscription is in the Cathedral, was of Litcham and

Cambridge and educated at Gray's Inn.[22] He was factor and advisor to the Dean and Chapter and steward to the court and manors of the Dean and Chapter. He ran all their properties, quite possibly from immediately after the Restoration, and no doubt had the pick of the available houses in The Close. His first wife Mary Sayer predeceased him in 1679. He obviously married again before his death in April 1683 aged 55. Anne, his widow, must have been much younger than him; she was still alive in 1723, with her son-in-law, James Hoste esq then her under-tenant. In 1694 Anne was granted a fourteen year lease renewal (within an overall forty year lease) and instead of the standard £30 renewal fine she only had to pay £16 in consideration for how much her husband had done for the Cathedral. However, she was required to create a new staircase to two rooms which were part of her property but were above the prebendaries' stables abutting the western end of her garden. These rooms were called The Garden House and she had to create a way to them from her own property rather than through the stable yard.

At this time the property was let by Anne to John Coates. John Coates of Norwich wrote his will and died in the summer of 1695.[23] Among his other bequests was a small amount for 'the poor belonging to The Close of Norwich' - not all the occupants were grand and there was a prison inside The Close. As he left no immediate family other than his brother and married sister, at this point the lease for the house may well have become available. By 1703 Anne's tenant was Francis Longe esq. Described as of Spixworth, Longe lived in The Close and was the friend of Algernon and Frances who helped them sell the Crane house. He acted as a coroner and JP for the Cathedral - the Dean and Chapter had the right to hold their own courts on Cathedral and precinct matters.

However, Anne Burleigh kept a strong involvement in the house and may well have lived in it herself from time to time. Prideaux's diaries showed that in June 1701 she and the Dean and Chapter were at odds over her desire to create a new coach access route into the back yard of the property. To create it she wanted to make a hole in the garden wall and a new coach way across the Green. The Dean wrote that this was a trespass, but she considered that there was nothing in her lease to prevent it. Prideaux suggested arbitration by a lawyer for either side. He proposed Arthur Branthwayt esq of Norwich, for the Cathedral. Branthwayt was the heir (in 1710) to the family's Hethel estate but was a practising Norwich lawyer and for more than 30 years was the steward for the Cathedral - effectively Burleigh's successor.[24] Branthwayt also had a house in The Close, although in 1703 it was let to a Mrs Newell. Anne first refused the idea of arbitration, then accepted it and then without waiting for such a meeting just knocked a hole through the wall anyway and set up her new gates.

The Dean and Chapter were determined to protect their rights against her encroachment on the Upper Green, no doubt particularly since she had so 'rudely and passionately' refused their offer of arbitration. By December 1701 Anne had married her daughter to James Hoste esq and her house in The Close had been part of the marriage settlement on James. Prideaux wrote that Mrs Burleigh 'expressed a great deal of pride and passion and could never be brought to listen to any reason herein expecting that we should yield up our rights to gratify her humour and pride and being exceedingly angry' that they would not. Hoste was of 'a much better temper and soon saw the justice of our cause' and agreed to a token 6d annual rental for the encroachment and the action was over.

In October 1708 Hoste applied for the lease to be renewed and it seemed that the 1694 requirement to create a new way to The Garden House rooms had still not been met. Prideaux wrote that two of the prebendaries were still inconvenienced by the route through the stables. In March 1709 Prideaux noted that Mrs Burleigh had been offered a reduced entry fine if she agreed to the new way. He added that she could easily have done this 'through her summer house in her garden'. This indicated that she had both the two upstairs rooms called The Garden House and a summer house in the garden. Presumably the summer house was a ground floor room set against the back wall of the stables and from which a staircase could easily have been built up to the two rooms. She still refused to create the new way.

By this time Algernon was the under-tenant. In 1709 Anne Burleigh was still only paying an annual rent of 16s 10d for the whole property plus responsibility for repairs. Of this, 3s was in lieu of three fat hens showing how long the memory of the ancient rents survived. What Algernon paid Anne is not recorded, but it was unlikely to be more than the sum of £20 rent Longe had paid in 1703. Algernon was certainly held in high regard by the Dean and Chapter. In November 1708, at the end of the seven years of his lease of the Gately and Colkirk underwoods, he was granted a new lease for 21 years at the same annual rent as before. Instead of the appropriate entry fine of £35 he was only charged £25 'which was done out of respect to Mr Potts who is our neighbour and very civil person'. It was rare for discounts to be given except to someone who had repeatedly been of service to the Cathedral. A year later Algernon complained that he had also been promised first refusal on timber sold from Gately but that this had not happened at a recent sale. Prideaux disliked the principle of such a commitment but conceded that at the next sale the timber would go to Algernon as long as he matched the highest competing bid. In November 1711 it was noted that the Dean and Chapter had previously agreed to waive all tax on the woods for the lives of 'Sir Algernon and his lady' - another sign of their warmth towards him. By 1711 he had assigned his lease of the woods on to Mr Warner of North Lenham and it was noted that the tax rebate should not apply to Warner.

Family correspondence shows that Algernon and Frances were still leasing the house in 1711. They would have enjoyed a life of civilised leisure. They had a large, albeit not truly grand, house and fair-sized garden in the former orchard with a small garden house plus a summer house in one of the most favourable spots in Norwich. Among the families that were tenants in The Close around this time were several families that have featured or will appear in the family's story - Hobart, Townshend, Astley, Guybon, Branthwayt, Gurdon and Wrench. Algernon was living off Frances's own income and perhaps an allowance from his father. As might be expected he also built up a number of debts although they were not crippling. No doubt he assumed in due course these could be dealt with when he came into his inheritance of all Sir Roger's estates at Ellingham, Mannington and Clippesby.

Algernon, book worm and gardener

Algernon seems to have been a man of literary tastes. He was probably the major contributor to the Potts library in Mannington. When this was later sold off in 1737, it was quite naturally then described as the library of Sir Charles, the last baronet.[25] Dr Clive Wilkins-Jones of the Norfolk and Norwich Millennium Library has analysed some of the titles of the 405 works listed in the sale catalogue but with only the titles to work on, could not conclusively identify the creators of the library.[26] Most of the books could have been bought over quite a span of years, even back into the relatively early seventeenth century, particularly since many had gone through multiple editions. He felt it most likely that members of the family added to the collection over the years and that it was thus a family heirloom. A few titles were definitely first published after Algernon's death and could only have been bought by Sir Charles or Dame Mary. Further research has shown that Sir Charles was one of a long list of subscribers to a 1727 edition, translated by John Maxwell, of Richard Cumberland's 1672 *A Treatise of the Laws of Nature.*[27] The several books on heraldry in the catalogue have proved hard to date. Although they may have dated back to Sir John Potts junior's work on his tombstone or heraldry may have interested Algernon, it is quite likely that these belonged to Sir Charles and Dame Mary, bought to help them build the case that she should be acknowledged as being part of the Smith family and entitled to bear the old Torbock arms (see Family Notes 13). The bulk of the library was that of a serious household. There were works on the arts and poetry, on music and dance, a few plays, but few other works of fiction. Someone was interested in different aspects of mathematics and in particular in surveying. These may again have been Algernon's but might they have come from an earlier generation? The 1640s portrait of Francis Potts showed him with compasses and a plan - a military surveyor or architect perhaps?

Further consideration, however, points to the books being largely Algernon's collection. Sir John senior had asked for his household goods to be sold to pay his debts and that was done, as shown by his son's will. Any books in his personal possession at his death would presumably have been kept by Roger and would probably have stayed at Ellingham. Sir John junior had only a small number of books in the inventory of his effects totalling some £5 in value, which does not seem to indicate a library of any size. In the early 1650s Sir Edward Dering noted book purchases in his accounts which implied that major works (eg Machiavelli, and Sir Francis Bacon's *Natural History*) might cost 6s 6d each, with lesser unnamed works often costing a shilling each.[28] As a general guide many books would cost 1s or 2s each, with pamphlets appreciably less and major works going for 5s or 6s - or even more depending on the page count and binding.[29] So, Sir John's £5 worth was perhaps a collection of 30 or so volumes if assuming a bias to more serious works. Since his inventory tended to inflate the value of his goods, to enhance his reputation, it is unlikely that the valuers would have used an average as low as 1s per book. If they had this would put an upper limit on his collection of 100 books. It seems more probable that his was not a significant library but rather a modest set of old favourites and religious texts. Roger, of course, did not live at Mannington and there is no indication that he had a large library, nor any concern for books whether at Mannington or Ellingham.

However, Algernon lived a cultured life in Norwich before moving into Mannington. In 1707 he is known to have donated a fine copy of André Tacquet's *Opera Mathematica* (1668) to Norwich City Library where it remains.[30] There is no doubt that he was a well-read man. In a letter of 1710, he said he was keen to keep the books and goods in Mannington as heirlooms, which showed that he had inherited at least some older books there.[31] Further analysis of the publication dates of about half of the 1737 list has shown that the large majority of these were published in the period 1690 to 1716. Even those that had been published earlier were frequently reprinted and the editions in the library may well have been ones that came from this period when Algernon was at his most active. As so few of the books were first published after 1716, it is inconceivable that Sir Charles had a major hand in the library's creation. Unfortunately, no-one in the family seems to have used book plates and after the sale there have been no sightings of any volumes that can be said to be from the Potts library.

In considering Algernon as a man of gentlemanly pursuits, it is worth noting that one of the books in the Potts library was *The Art of Pruning Fruit Trees*, which must have been the translation into English in 1685 of the French book by Nicolas Venette.[32] Also in the library were Samuel Strangehope's *The Compleat Gardener* (probably the 1696 edition) and an English edition (probably of 1703) of Henrik van Oosten's *The Dutch Gardener or the Compleat Florist*. No other member of the family is likely to have needed to buy such works, yet Algernon had fruit trees in his garden in The Close and he may have made a pleasant garden there. It is also possible that when he came to Mannington in 1711 he and Frances made improvements to a garden potentially in disarray after many years with, at best, short lease tenants in the Hall.

Hawkes's 1742 estate map of Mannington clearly showed the old guardhouse near the footbridge into the garden on the west of the house. This was now a feature, at the southern end, of an enclosed section of ground, creating a walled and quite private garden that could not be seen from across the moat and in particular from the farmyard.[33] Sir Algernon and Frances may well have built the walled garden and used the rear of the guardhouse as a shady summer house, perhaps to replicate the shelter that they had been used to at the bottom of the garden in The Close.

The map also showed tree planting far more extensive than that in 1595. The avenue of trees to the west of the house and other avenue walks were in fine condition and apparently made up of mature trees (see Plate 7).[34] From a particular of the estate in 1737, immediately prior to its sale to Horatio Walpole, it is known that between 10 and 15 acres around the hall, including 'the Long walks', were not let with the tenant farms.[35] The dating of this reference contradicts the belief that Walpole, who delighted in trees and planted widely at Wolterton, was responsible for those at Mannington. While his accounts before 1742 included entries for planting at Mannington - additions to the Avenue and new planting at Mossymere - these areas were clearly designated by notably smaller tree symbols by Hawkes.[36] In addition to these pleasure grounds, the map showed there were four other areas of managed avenue walks: in the pastures for some distance up the main avenue (beside the road towards Mere farm); in the fields to the west of the Hall; along the beck in the area of Lady's Wood; and possibly in 'Dovehouse orchard' on the other side of the lake from the Hall. Further fields surrounding the Hall were heavily timbered, described as 'park' and no doubt created attractive land in which to stroll. Walpole extended the park concept inherited from the Potts.

Unfortunately there is no evidence of which generation first laid out the park and who planted the long walks. The land near to Mannington Hall was traditionally used for sheep pasture; Sir John senior may well have set aside a large acreage to be sheep closes but with substantial timber planting as a long-term investment, creating a parkland setting. 'Avenues' were made popular by John Evelyn through his book *Sylva* which was published in 1664 and re-printed three times by 1706. Perhaps Sir John junior, always keen on the latest fashions, redesigned the planting to create long rows in the 1670s. By the early eighteenth century this would have resulted in mature parkland with fine walks. It is most unlikely that the landscaping would have been created by his son, Roger Potts, who was an absentee landlord for thirty years. The 1710 rental described the house as having 40 acres of gardens and orchards and 50 acres of park not let out to the tenant farms. By 1716 timber on the estate was described as mature suggesting Algernon was not the planter although he may have actively managed the woodlands. The last owner before 1737, Charles, had money problems and had to fell timber, perhaps from the main woodlands (although he did replant with saplings). At some point before 1737 the unlet parkland had been greatly reduced in size leaving fewer than 20 acres around the Hall, although no doubt the timbered closes would still have created an attractive setting for the Hall and gardens.

Algernon's circle: church and politics

For more serious reflection, well over half the books in the library covered religious matters, classical and modern history, morals and philosophy. Algernon was closely connected to and involved with the well-known clergymen and scholars Simon Ockley (perhaps best known for his 1708 *The History of the Saracens*) and Humphrey Prideaux, the Dean of the Cathedral. He would also have known the clergyman and antiquarian Dr Thomas Tanner very well. There were multiple connections. Potts and Ockley were childhood friends. Potts, Prideaux and Tanner all lived in The Close at the same time. Potts and Prideaux were both patrons of Ockley and Prideaux had encouraged Ockley in his Arabic studies for which he was to be most famous. Another of Ockley's patrons was Robert Harley who was chief minister from 1710 to 1714. Algernon corresponded with him on political matters. Prideaux was rector of Saham Toney from 1686 to 1694 and may even have married Frances and Thomas Crane there in the mid 1680s. Prideaux's son Edmund in 1717 married Hannah the daughter of Sir Benjamin Wrench, which family as we shall see was at the heart of Algernon's social circle and who had a house in The Close.[37] As Prideaux's diaries show, he put his son Edmund in as steward to the Cathedral on the death in 1717 of Arthur Branthwayt.

On 8th March 1705 Sir Roger Potts wrote to Dr Tanner, then Chancellor of Norwich Diocese, enquiring after his son's health.[38] This rather sad short letter indicated that Roger and Algernon were probably not then on speaking terms. Algernon may not have had robust health - there were ten medical books in the library.

There is no debate about Algernon's relationship with Simon Ockley who was of a Great Ellingham family, although born in Devon.[39] Ockley (1629-1720) was an orientalist and the son of Thomas 'Okely' of Great Ellingham, Norfolk, and his wife, Thomazin. Although he came from a gentleman's family, he struggled against poverty throughout his career and relied on his patrons for aid. The first of these, Algernon Potts, befriended him as a boy, and perhaps obtained his admission as a sizar to Queens' College, Cambridge, in February 1694. He took his BA in 1698, and already showed considerable linguistic talent. Around 1700, Ockley was appointed to a Hebrew lectureship worth £10 annually. The importance he attached to this early support was made clear in the dedication 'To Sir Algernon Potts of Mannington in Norfolk' in Ockley's *An Account of South-West Barbary,* based on the life of a christian slave, published in 1713.[40] Ockley described himself as 'Chaplain to the most Hon Earl of Oxford & Mortimer, Ld High Treasurer of Great Britain' and the lengthy dedication included this opening section covering his relationship with Algernon and Robert Harley, Earl of Oxford:

> Sir, Be pleased to pardon me, if I presume to do myself the Honour of prefixing your name to this little Book, out of a grateful sense which I retain of the favours received from your vertuous & worthy family from my Infancy, & more particularly the personal respect which I owe to you. You were pleased, overlooking generously the Inequality of our respective circumstances, to Honour me with your friendship when I was very young. And there is no Person that is acquainted with the Sweetness of your temper, sincerity of principle, both with regard to church & state & many other excellent qualifications with which you are plentifully endowed ... [Ockley continued about not having been able to keep up his relationships] ... Now since Providence has been pleased to favour me at last with the Protection of a most Illustrious & magnificent Patron, who is no less an able Judge than a liberal encourager of all polite learning; I begin to take Breath a little ... [4 ½ pages later] ...
>
> Sir your most obliged, Humble servant

Rather oddly, there does not seem to have been a copy of this work in the Potts library by 1737, even though there were the other famous works by Ockley and Prideaux. Perhaps the dedicated volume was kept by the Long family with the family portraits as an heirloom.

Sir Algernon's letter of thanks to the Reverend Simon Ockley, 'Arabick Professor of Cambridge', has survived in the British Library:

From Sir Algernon Potts March 9th 1712/13

Dear Sir

I had the favour of a letter from you some 2 months since, the book you mentioned came not to me till very lately (it being sent to Mrs Oliver who having no notice of it had like to have sold it) I return you my hearty thanks not only for the present itself which, as all things you do are, is very valuable but more particularly for the Honour you have done me in Setting my name before it, which yet I am not vain enough to value my self upon, being sensible that whatever Honour the Patron receives from a Dedication (were he ten times more deserving than myself) is not only owing to but as in Justice done, returns to its Author as Dr Garth says on the inimitable Mr Prior [quotes a short poem]

what therefore enhances your present to me is not so much transmitting my name with your own to those who shall read the performance, as your free & generous owning that Frendship between us which as it took root in our Infancy, will, I hope, grow up with us & last as long at least as this life if not to the end of duration itself. I most heartily rejoice at your good Fortune in having so good a Patron of all virtue & learning as the Hon'ble the Ld Treasurer is so well-known to be & I cannot but hope this Nation in particular & the learned world in general will in time be sensible of a particular advantage from his kindness to you, in the meantime tho' your avocation be great & your application to things of moment much greater, yet you must, I'm sure, have some unbending hours in which you will think of me among others; there is none, I dare be confident, can more highly value a correspondence with you then will always,

your most Faithfull Friend & most humble Servant

A. Potts[41]

This is in a small book of letters to Ockley from 1699 to 1718, including letters from Humphrey Prideaux of Norwich in 1700 and 1717 and also letters from friends in Oxford. In 1717 Ockley needed money following his imprisonment for debt in Cambridge Castle.[42] In May 1717 Ockley wrote from the Castle to his most important patron, Robert Harley, to say that his previous letter had been hasty and that his debts were £340 not £200. He hoped Harley would assist.[43] After Ockley died, his widow Martha wrote to Harley relying 'on his clemency' to her and her daughters.[44]

Humphrey Prideaux was another key figure in Algernon's life in Norwich.[45] Born in 1648, he was to spend most of his adult life as a senior clergyman and scholar living in The Close in Norwich. He first arrived in Norwich as a prebendary in August 1681 and from the outset he was responsible for rebuilding the Cathedral's library. However he also maintained his academic life in Oxford where he achieved his Doctor of Divinity in 1686. Prideaux then announced his intention to leave to get married to Bridget Bockenham of Helmingham in Suffolk, who brought with her a substantial dowry. They moved to Norfolk and, in 1686, Prideaux took up the rectory of Saham Toney where he was an assiduous and resident rector until 1694, when he returned to Norwich. Throughout this period he apparently retained a home in The Close where he had to keep most of his books given the modest accomodation in Saham Toney. While in Saham Toney he became a close friend of both Sir Edward Atkins (Lord Chief Baron of the Exchequer) and the 90 year old Sir John Holland, the old friend of Sir John Potts senior. No doubt Sir John Holland's essentially moderate views coincided closely with Prideaux's own. On returning to Norwich, Prideaux took up his role as a prebendary of the Dean and Chapter and in this role he became the treasurer for the Cathedral. He was responsible for most of the business and property affairs of the Cathedral and would have worked closely with Thomas Tanner when he arrived in Norwich in 1698 as chaplain to Bishop Moore. Tanner was to be made Chancellor in 1701, a commissary to the Dean and Chapter in 1703 and archdeacon of Norfolk in 1721. He spent much of his time in Norwich before eventually being made Bishop of St Asaph. In 1702 Prideaux was made Dean and continued to serve in that capacity until his death in 1724. He was a strong contender to be made Bishop of Norwich in 1707 but ruled himself out because of his age.

He was clearly well-regarded as both as a cleric and as an administrator, with a highly developed sense of ethics as shown by various occasions when his views were sought by the bishops in the House of Lords over proposed legislation. But he was also a busy and fairly prolific scholar and author. He was interested in many aspects of church history and had a particular fascination with Arabic history. He was known for his 1697 book on the life of Mahomet. While he drew on many sources for his Arabic history, he is not thought to have been an Arabic speaker himself. He is however credited with actively encouraging Simon Ockley to learn the language to add to his mastery of Hebrew, Latin, Greek and various European languages.

As with other clergyman of the time he did not resist mixing religion and politics. In 1688 he preached two brave anti-popery sermons in Norwich. Equally bravely he shut the precinct gates against a large and violent mob intent on pillaging the home of one of his fellow prebendaries who was known to have papist sympathies. In 1689 he swore the contentious oaths of allegiance to William and Mary, rejecting all papal and foreign jurisdictions. In 1690 he published, anonymously, *A Letter to a Friend Relating to the Present Convocation at Westminster* although his authorship became known. In 1691 he engaged with the bishops on potential legislation relating to plural benefices and clandestine marriages. He suggested a compromise allowing plural benefices at a local level and argued successfully that the controls (through licences/banns) on clandestine marriages were sufficient not to need additional and more swingeing legislation against them.

Whigs, Tories and obedience: the 1710 election

From the 'revolution' of 1688 onwards there was a continuing debate about whether it was spiritually and legally appropriate for people to have blind obedience to their masters, or whether a bad ruler could be ejected by his people. This debate continued in a very visible way right through to the elections of 1710 when Benjamin Hoadly, then Bishop of Bangor and later Bishop of Winchester, became perhaps the country's best known clergyman for his active campaigning. He believed that the Whig perspective, that rulers were not inviolate, was legitimate. Prideaux is known to have been a supporter of the Whigs in the run up to the 1710 election and thus may have agreed with this idea to some extent, but as a moderate man he was certainly not in favour of this intellectual stance being allowed to create a licence for general civil disobedience and disorder. In 1710, in Norwich, Prideaux published his book *Of the Original Right of Tithes*. The 1836 edition of his book described his moderate stance thus:

> In party matters ... he always showed himself firmly attached to the interest of the Protestant cause and the principles of the revolution; but without joining in with the violence of parties, or promoting those factions and divisions which prevailed both in the church and state during the greater part of his life. He was concerned that the historic lay appropriation of tithes had been wrong. But his writing and preaching at this time was interrupted for two years by severe pain from a kidney stone. This was subsequently successfully operated on, but between 1709 and 1712 or so it seems that he did little and even stood down from his rectory in Trowse because of his inability to preach.

At around this time Simon Ockley was making good progress in his career. In 1711 he was appointed, probably through Harley's sponsorship, to the Sir Thomas Adams chair of Arabic, which he held until his death in 1720. Ockley had hoped to succeed as professor much earlier, and his disappointment seems to have led to an estrangement from the fellows of Queens' College, as a result of which he lost preferment to a living in their gift. When he at last obtained the chair, his annual income was increased by £40. He probably undertook little teaching as the subject of Arabic studies in eighteenth century universities was in decline. Having published his 1713 'pot-boiler', which showed his abilities in translation of Arabic, Ockley was briefly employed by the government in 1714 to translate correspondence from the ruler of Morocco, Mawlay Ismail with whom England had commercial links. However, Harley's fall from power in July 1714 lost Ockley his most influential patron, and he had no further employment under government.[46]

Robert Harley, or Lord Oxford as he became, led the government between 1710 and 1714. In the 1690s Harley had effectively been the leader of the Whigs and the chief opponent of the crown in parliament.[47] However by 1701 he was responsible for negotiating the preparations for the Hanoverian succession and became the speaker of the House and a clear supporter of the crown. By 1703 he had become a close adviser of Queen Anne, negotiating between her and the leaders of both the Whig and Tory parties. Throughout this time he involved himself with members of both parties. He fell from power in 1708 and then at least partly allied himself to the Tory cause. In 1710 he returned to power as Chancellor of the Exchequer, but his overtures to various Whigs were rebuffed and he was forced to turn more extensively than he wished to the Tories. Later that year parliament was dissolved and at the election Harley came back into power, but with far more Tory members than he had hoped for. He had wished to maintain a balance with a good number of Whig MPs both generally, and in his administration as chief minister - technically he was Chancellor of the Exchequer and Commissioner of the Treasury, but at the time he was often referred to as premier or prime minister.[48] Soon the Whig Robert Walpole was dismissed as Secretary of the Navy as a sop to the 'October Club' of back bench Tories. In 1711 Harley was responsible for the launch of The South Sea Company and its involvement in the national debt. In this year he was made Lord Treasurer and raised to the peerage as Earl of Oxford. In the 1713 election the Tories won with an even bigger majority than in 1710. Yet by 1714 Harley, for various reasons, contemplated resigning. In fact he was dismissed that July by the Queen. But on her death the following month he took his place on the Privy Council and led the process that guaranteed the succession passing to the House of Hanover, despite all the Jacobite pressure of the time. However, he was not supported by King George and lost all his offices and faced impeachment for allegedly supporting the Jacobite cause. The charges were never brought to trial and were formally dropped in 1717, thus acquitting him of the charge.

Throughout his political career Harley was known for clouding issues and keeping options open. He often made completely impenetrable statements in pursuit of this guarded approach. He was not the Jacobite that some thought and that a number of Tories were or became. He was clearly a man with essentially moderate opinions and, while around 1710 he was strongly aligned with the Tories, he cannot be said to have lost all his earlier Whig tendencies. Indeed it can be argued that the Whigs had become more radical, atheistic and republican in intent over the years, whereas the Tories had evolved into a party of principles much closer to Harley's underlying belief in limited taxation, altruistic public service, cultivation of the wealth of the nation and personal liberties. While later a high church man, in 1710 he still had many presbyterian clergymen friends and maintained a moderate stance in relation to dissenters. During 1710 and 1711 Harley constantly hedged and thwarted high church Tory schemes in parliament.[49]

All this makes it hard to interpret the precise implications of some correspondence between Harley and Sir Algernon Potts. An undated contemporaneous copy by Harley himself of an extract of a letter from 'Alganoun Potts' has survived in a bundle of papers generally dating from 1703-09.[50] From its content it might well date from early to mid-1710 and it clearly shows Potts as one of Harley's wide network of correspondents on the ground that gave him a close feel for the mood of the nation in the run up to the election in October that year. More than this, it clearly shows Algernon as an active member of the Tory group in Norfolk.

A Copey of part of a letter from Sr Alganoun Potts to me

Dr Sr

Steward Barney haveing acquainted you and Mr Gurdon with the transactions of the Norwich Mob I shall say nothing of that but must beg leave to tell you the Gent. att our Club last Satterday were very Voluntious & think that the honest Gent. of this Cuntry who has been so instrumentall with great industry & expence to serve her Majs & the Govt. att the last Election are very much dejected thay are not countinanced by the presant Ministry for their faithfull services haveing labored with great Uneasyness & long oppretion under the late Ministry & the Presant Ld Lieut: and are every day more & more exasperated to have a person so obnoctious to the Governt and under such a sensure of Parliament left stil to Lord it over them Sir Ed Bacon of Gillingham swares he will not stir nor spend a shilling next Election & the generality of the Gent. in our intrest sayes the same if thay have not spedyly a new Ld Lieut: thinking it absolutly necessary to have the Comms. settled some time before the Election come on else will be of little or no effect or att least render the Election very difficult. Some of our friends of note you know are going off so far from us att least as to give us no assistance (to say no worse) for no other reson but that our intrest is not incorraged as thay fully expected.

You know the proseeding of Mr Presson [?Preston] against Mr Bever so need not say any more of that but if he & two or three of the gang be not turned out we must expect a deal of troble but our Knights I suppose will prevaile with the Keeper for that so need not have trobled you with it   Nor had I now with this but att the request of our Club who would force me to write this to desire you would presse the Lord Tresur' to give us a new Lord Lieut else depend upon it the County & Norwich will be lost & Ferrier vowes he will not stand for Yarmouth, if so Ld Townshd will gett in his Brother.

Therefore we beg you will re[newe] yr influences with Ld Tresur' & we doubt not sucksesse if you are as pressing with him as you are active here

when I here you are come down I will wayte on you at Beck hall etc

The rest is private businesse

The reference to the 'transactions of the Norwich mob' seems to date the letter. He was probably referring to the widespread, large and often unruly public demonstrations that occurred during the trial of Henry Sacheverell and greeted his effective acquittal in the Commons in March 1710. For example, Abigail Harley in London wrote to Edward Harley in Oxford on 2nd March 1710 to tell him that Sacheverell's mob had pulled down Mr Burgess's meeting house (ie, a dissenters' meeting house) in Lincoln's Inn Fields adding: 'This is methinks an odd way of defending passive obedience and non-resistance'.[51] A few days later, her next letter forecast that the Sacheverell business would break the Whigs.

'Steward Barney' was Richard Berney of Langley, the attorney and steward of Norwich who won one of the two Norwich seats on the Tory ticket in October 1710. He was the son of John Berney of Westwick, who was in turn the youngest son of Sir Richard Berney baronet, the son of Sir Thomas of Reedham.[52] Richard the MP was steward of Norwich from 1703 to 1727, when he was made Recorder. His great-grandmother was Julyan, daughter of Sir Thomas Gawdy of Redenhall. He married Mary the daughter of Augustine Briggs, Mayor of Norwich in 1695-96. The other winning Tory in Norwich in 1710 was Robert Bene of Frettenham and Norwich, a brewer who successfully ran the Norwich business founded by his father Thomas. He was sheriff in 1694-95, an alderman by 1708 and was elected mayor in May 1710 on a strong Tory platform. While mayor he was elected to parliament in October 1710 and remained in the Commons, like Berney, until 1715.

Gurdon was Thornhaugh Gurdon esq (1663–1733) who was at this time a trustee for the Potts family. A Cambridge-educated antiquary, he was also Receiver-General of Norfolk and so involved in tax gathering and political affairs.[53] Though of Letton, he apparently lived much of the time in Norwich where he published books on the history of Norwich Castle and on the 'High Court of Parliament'. He was another of Algernon's scholarly group living in or near The Close. In May 1711 Colonel Horace Walpole (uncle of the emerging Whig leader Robert Walpole and his brother Horatio who would later acquire Wolterton and Mannington) wrote to Robert Harley urging, at the instruction of Sir John Wodehouse and eight other Norfolk MPs, the post of general receiver of taxes for the county should be granted to Gurdon.[54] This letter shows that Gurdon had the support of the triumphant Tory group and that Horace had worked hard for the Tory cause at the election.

The reference in Algernon's letter to 'our club' referred to a local group of Tories - Norwich was renowned then and later for its many political groups bound to each other and to action by oaths of association. It is quite likely that this group was based on the community living in The Close. Their complaint, voiced by Algernon for the group as a whole, is not wholly clear. Obviously they disliked Townshend intensely and pressed for his removal; but quite why they expected more recognition for their efforts and patience from an essentially Whig ministry is not explained. Perhaps an implicit message was that Algernon wanted Harley himself to write encouraging and appreciative words to the Norwich Tories.

Sir Edmund Bacon of Gillingham was the sitting MP for Thetford, successfully returned there in 1710. The 'obnoxious' lord lieutenant was Charles, Second

Viscount Townshend, who served from 1701 to 1713.[55] So, despite this attempt, Potts and his friends failed to unseat him. Charles's brother the Honourable Roger Townshend was elected as a Whig to one of the Norfolk seats in 1701 and again in 1705.[56] In 1708 Ashe Windham, Lord Townshend's man, took over the seat for the Whigs. By 1709-10 and certainly in the run-up to the October 1710 election there was widespread argument around the country about replacing lords lieutenant and other officials to try to influence local opinion in the forthcoming election.[57] Potts obviously saw Lord Townshend as a threat to the Tory campaign. Townshend was causing Bacon and many of the county gentry to waver in their views and more particularly to hesitate from investing heavily in active campaigning. Potts was right to be concerned about turnout and funding as, even though across the country the Tories won many seats, in Norwich and Norfolk the number of votes cast only just gave them victory.

'Mr Presson' was the ubiquitous Jacob Preston esq of Norwich and London, a merchant and man of affairs, heavily involved with the Potts family. 'Bever' has proved elusive. Might he have been the London stationer, bookseller and publisher Thomas Bever?[58] More likely here Beevor was the intended name. Perhaps, Preston had launched an action against one of the family of William Beevor, rector of South Walsham. William, a few years later, was involved in a minor matter in the exchequer; his eldest son John was a barrister of Furnival's Inn active also in Norfolk and his second son Thomas was a Norwich grocer who much later was certainly politically active.[59] It is likely that this was a local legal matter and the knights of the shire managed to get it withdrawn through a direct appeal to the Lord Keeper of the Great Seal, who until September 1710 was William Cowper, 1st Earl Cowper.

Cowper was a Whig, but in 1709 and 1710 he was known for taking a stand with the Tories against Whig views on demands for peace in the war with France and against some of the intentions of the Duke of Marlborough. He presided over Sacheverell's trial and presumably had a significant part to play in his very light sentence. Harley and the Queen tried to persuade him to stay in his role in the run up to the 1710 election but he resigned that September since so many of his friends were no longer in government. He would have been seen by both Potts and Harley as a fair man and likely to intervene in an unfair case if sound argument was made to him by two knights of the shire. His role would have enabled him to do so effectively. 'Our knights' would probably have been the two Tory knights of the shire - Sir John Wodehouse and Sir Jacob Astley - who defeated the Whig incumbents (Sir John Holland and Ashe Windham) in the 1710 election. Sir Jacob was never a rampant high church Tory during his long parliamentary career; but rather an essentially moderate one who even was persuaded by Robert Walpole to switch to the Whig party cause in 1714.[60] In 1710 Jacob Preston of St Mary Norwich voted for the Whig candidates; presumably Algernon saw Preston as the bad guy on this occasion.[61] Of course, the issue may have been entirely non-political in nature.

Ferrier was Major Richard Ferrier MP for Great Yarmouth who won there as a Tory in the elections of 1708 (when he topped the poll), 1710 (when described by Tanner as a 'very sensible candidate') and 1713. He voted against the impeachment of Sacheverell. The head of a wealthy merchant family he was active in parliament particularly on trade matters. He married Ellen the daughter of Robert Long of Reymerston - a family that often appeared close to the Potts. His fellow Tory MP throughout this period in Great Yarmouth was George England to whom he was related by marriage. England was married to Alice the daughter of John Jermy of Bayfield. Jermy, often described as of Norwich, was very definitely closely involved in Potts family affairs.

At the end of the letter, Algernon wrote that he would attend Harley when he was next at Beck Hall. This was Beck Hall in Billingford between Bawdeswell and North Elmham, not far from Norwich. This property belonged to Thomas Coke, later Earl of Leicester. His father had died in 1707 and in 1710 Thomas was still only 13 years old so his estates were being looked after by guardians. His grandmother was Lady Anne Osborne, daughter of the Duke of Leeds, who after Robert Coke's death remarried the Colonel Horace (or Horatio) Walpole above, but had no children by him. As Lady Anne Walpole she brought up both Isabella Le Neve and Dorothy - Dolly to her friends - Walpole, sister of Robert Walpole, later Prime Minister.[62] The beautiful Dorothy became the second wife of Charles Viscount Townshend. Lady Anne lived in Beck Hall and we assume this was a regular meeting place for members of the Walpole and Townshend families and others involved in both political and literary matters. Harley was presumably a regular visitor. Algernon may have met Harley through this Norfolk connection.

Algernon, the writer

Algernon also has a possible claim as a pamphlet writer.[63] To support this, a little background follows on the senior churchmen of the time and their predilection for arguing in print.

As we have seen, Benjamin Hoadly had by 1710 become a national figure for his repeatedly expressed views on the appropriateness of resistance against bad rulers or 'magistrates'.[64] In 1710 he published *The Original and Institution of Civil Government, discuss'd*, an important statement of his views and an answer to the previous year's famous sermon by the Tory high church Bishop Francis Atterbury supporting passive obedience. As Anthony Page has written:

> Hoadly argued that the 'public good' was superior to the sovereign's right to rule, and that the people were justified in resisting a king who went against their communal interests. While Tories labelled such a view as republican, this mainstream defence of the Glorious Revolution envisaged popular intervention only in times of constitutional crisis. Yet in acknowledging that the people were the ultimate source of political authority, the mainstream Whigs established a political context that fostered the development of radical interpretations of the constitution.[65]

At this time Atterbury, Dean of Carlisle, was a senior church figure, a leading voice in Convocation and another of the heavily politically involved churchmen of his day.[66] Although not made a Bishop until 1713 as Bishop of Rochester, he enjoyed the status and access to key players as if he was of such rank. From the early 1700s he had been Archdeacon of Exeter under his friend Sir Jonathan Trelawny, the Bishop there until 1706 when he was promoted to Winchester.[67] Trelawny had been followed as Bishop of Exeter by Offspring Blackall. One of his sermons had triggered an avalanche of pamphlets.

The exchange of pamphlets published in London has been summarised:

> On Tuesday 8 March 1709 Offspring Blackall, Bishop of Exeter, preached a sermon before the Queen on the anniversary of her succession. In it he maintained that rulers were 'ministers of God' and none on earth had the right to question or resist them. The sermon was published with the title The Divine Institution of Magistracy (London: H.Hills, 1709) and provoked a leading low church divine, Benjamin Hoadley, rector of St Peter le Poer in London, to publish Some considerations humbly offered to the Right Reverend the Lord Bishop of Exeter (1709) in which he claimed that 'the gospel of Jesus Christ hath not utterly deprived man of the right of self-defence'. The Bishop reacted with his The Lord Bishop of Exeter's answer to Mr. Hoadley's letter (1709). Hoadley offered An humble reply to the Right Reverend the Lord Bishop of Exeter's answer (1709), an anonymous 'student at Oxford' produced A submissive answer to Mr. Hoadley's humble reply (1709). A Student of the Temple joined issue with such titles as The best answer ever was made, (London, J.Morphew, 1709), A better answer than the best answer ever was made, A modest reply to the unanswerable answer and so on, to a total of at least seventeen items.[68]

Atterbury was thought to have been heavily involved in the defence of Henry Sacheverell at his impeachment trial early in 1710 in the House of Commons.[69] Sacheverell had made vociferous sermons supporting the passive obedience line. So inflammatory were they that he was impeached for potentially inciting sedition against the crown. He was found guilty at his trial and sentenced to three years of not preaching sermons - seen as a very modest penalty for such an apparently serious charge.[70] Harley initially was reluctant to support him in the House but eventually did lead the church defence of Sacheverell in debate. It seems likely that Harley gradually became aware of the opportunity to manipulate the huge public support for Sacheverell against the Whigs.

For some years Atterbury had been in Harley's immediate circle, but when sent in September 1710 by other high church Tories to urge Harley to more rapid action on the Tory agenda he was rebuffed by Harley. Even so, in December Harley recommended him as Dean of Christ Church. But Atterbury's advocacy of the high church proposed reforms made little headway against Harley's prevarications during the 1710-11 session. Atterbury went on to move away from Harley politically and ultimately became a known and committed Jacobite.

Hoadly led the charge against Sacheverell, Atterbury and Blackall. A long-standing sympathiser with dissenters and moderate non-conformists, Hoadly nevertheless was a clear supporter of the validity of the bishops in the church constitution. He explicitly campaigned during the election for the Whigs, who were inherently supporters of his low church views against the aggressively monarchist views of high church Tories. He believed in conditional obedience, rather than the high church argument for non-resistance and passive obedience at all times. He argued that the revolution that had brought William and Mary to England had been legitimate. But many saw his stance as a dangerous generic support to rebellion and unjustified disobedience.

Where did Humphrey Prideaux stand on all of this? He and his clerical colleagues are known to have been strong supporters in December 1703 of another brewer Thomas Blofield who was successfully voted in as Tory candidate in Norwich, along with fellow Tory Robert Davy.[71] However, by May 1708 Prideaux had become an active campaigner among his clergy colleagues for the Whig Waller Bacon. He remained a moderate Whig through the events of 1710. Was Algernon stirred by his reading to take up the pen and join the fray? Dr Wilkins-Jones has suggested that Potts may have been the author of the pamphlet *Faith and Obedience: or a Letter to Mr Hoadley, Occasioned by his Doctrine of Resistance, and Dispute with the Bishop of Exeter*, printed by Henry Crossgrove of Norwich for Mrs Oliver in 1711.[72]

Mrs William Oliver - the Mrs Oliver referred to in Algernon's letter of thanks to Ockley - was a well-known Norwich bookseller. Crossgrove, the publisher, book seller and launcher of *The Norwich Gazette* was actively engaged in local politics on the opposite side of the political divide from the other major bookseller, publisher and newspaperman William Chase.[73] Both stood repeatedly at this time for Norwich Corporation and Crossgrove was a committed Tory and seen as a Jacobite in his tendencies. He would have been happy to print a book on the obedience issue which supported the Tory high church position.

The pamphlet in question, with most of its 65 or so pages written as a letter, was published anonymously, signed only by 'AP'. The dedication of the pamphlet is worth quoting in full:

> To the Reader.
>
> Christian Reader,
>
> The following letter was wrote last winter, while the doctrine of resistance rid triumphant, and that of obeying for the sake of god and his Christ lay bleeding at her feet, well nigh sentenc'd and condemn'd by authority and power to be made her sacrifice; at which time being at leisure, I thought myself concern'd to try what

I could say in defence of so distress'd a duty. And finding it chiefly oppress'd by one whose office was rather to have cherish'd and maintain'd it, I was led to some expressions which may possibly seem harsh, and which I assure thee, since the patrons of resistance have so widely mist their aim, should never for me have seen the light, did I not find the poison of that tenet so generally spread, and so epidemically infectious still, as to need a present antidote; for which reason only, till some more effectual remedy be prepar'd, I have ventur'd to present thee with this. If it pleases god that anything here said should either convince thee of, or confirm thee in thy duty, to his holy name be praise.

Farewel.

The writer was affronted at Hoadly's interpretation of St Paul's words in the gospels being falsely presented and twisted to support the case for resistance when a governor or magistrate was thought to be acting against the public good. 'AP' believed that Her Majesty was the minister of god and that other 'magistrates' of all kinds drew their power from her. It could not be argued that the supreme magistrate drew his power from the people while all the other ministers drew their power from god. So the 'excellent precept of obedience' was the 'duty of every christian'.

The writer went on to analyse and criticise Hoadly's past sermons. In particular he thought that Hoadly had mis-interpreted Romans XIII which had also been the subject of other sermons, especially one by Gilbert Burnet (by now Bishop of Salisbury) that had been delivered in Covent Garden in 1674 and subsequently published. AP 'consulted several pieces of divinity I had by me'. It is clear that he had read several books and sermons by Hoadly as well as referring to writers of ancient Rome and even Hobbs - he came close to suggesting Hoadly must be an atheist, but tempered this jibe by saying that he did not think he could be. He also addressed the implication that the Glorious Revolution could be used to support the idea of selective resistance. Since the King had abdicated before any uprising took place, there was no act of resistance. William of Orange had 'too small an army to conquer us' and anyway had the 'justice of the cause' on his side. It was therefore entirely wrong to use the Revolution as an argument that it would be legitimate to dethrone Anne if she acted against the perceived good of the public.

The long letter ended: 'Your Friend, A.P. Norwich Dec 1 1709'.

There can be no doubt that Prideaux would have been very supportive of the stance taken in the pamphlet. It was a calm and reasoned refutation of Hoadly's interpretation of the gospels and their content on obedience to god's ministers. Moderate men of either political persuasion would no doubt have approved of it. At no point was the writer bombastic, even though he apologised for what might be perceived as the severe tone of the work.

Was Algernon AP? The evidence is compelling. Algernon's letter to Harley shows he was politically engaged at the time and supported the Tory cause which the pamphlet so clearly espoused. His academic and legal background would have given him the ability to construct a complex argument and deliver it in an articulate manner. His constant exposure to Prideaux, Tanner, Ockley and others would have made him keen to converse regularly on these intense and topical matters. Examining the 1710 poll lists for Norwich produces no other candidates for an 'AP' of reasonable status in the community. Anthony Parker, a glover, voted Tory and Anthony Parmenter an alderman voted Whig. The former is unlikely to have been a writer and the latter is ruled out by his Whig affiliation. At the county level, there are no other obvious contenders for the initials AP except Augustine Palgrave who died aged 81 in Barningham in March 1711 and for whom there is no evidence of any political activity at that late stage of his life.

What other support is there for Algernon being 'AP'? The general style of the pamphlet was that of an educated and logical man arguing from a widely read background. It was not heavily based on the biblical quotes that one might expect from the writing of a clergyman at that time. The specific sermons referred to in the text were not listed by name in the 1737 sale catalogue, but the Mannington library had dozens of sermons and similar books and pamphlets and some unnamed 'sermons'. There was a copy of Hobbs's *Leviathan*. There can be no question but that this collection of religious, philosophical, political and historical works would have given Algernon the wherewithal to write *Faith and Obedience*. But were the Mannington books definitely his? The 1737 sale catalogue did not claim to contain all the titles, but presumably it covered those that were well-known and still at least somewhat current. The collection of 405 books listed was very varied, with works on virtually every factual subject. Just over 130 relate to religion and the debates of the time, in which religion and politics were intermixed. Of these, only two or three seem to have been first printed after Algernon's death and all might well have had earlier editions. Unfortunately the sale list gave no publication or edition dates. A noticeable number of the religious books came from the few years between Sir Roger's and Algernon's deaths. Most came from the period from the mid 1690s to about 1715. Of the earlier works, all were classics and had gone through many editions. Even if a few of these books came from earlier generations, the religious collection as a whole had to be Algernon's. There were many volumes on ancient Greek and Roman history and society. Several of Norfolk-born Roger L'Estrange's translations of classics, including his Aesop's fables, first published in 1692, were in the collection. L'Estrange was an outspoken Tory and for many years was licensor and surveyor of the press, so controlling what was published. He had retired to concentrate on translating and publishing his own works and died in 1704.

The analysis of the possible publication dates of the 80 or so more modern history and philosophy books produces a similar pattern although the history books are harder to date with certainty. The dates of the books on how to be a justice of the peace and on public speaking also look to fit best with Algernon. By April 1711 Algernon (at the same time as his father) was a justice of the peace and it would be in character for him to have researched not only what the role entailed but also to try to improve his ability to speak well in public.[74] He was not on the previous commission list for 1709, so it seems that 1710-11 was when he really stepped up to taking on his responsibilities as the next head of the family.[75] Or, was Algernon contemplating becoming a political candidate, or writing speeches behind the scenes for others?

Further circumstantial support for Algernon being 'AP' comes from another pamphlet published in 1713 for sale in London and Norwich and entitled *Passive Obedience Establish'd and Resistance Confuted*.[76] Published anonymously, its dedication showed it to be by a 'Gentleman of the City of Norwich' and it was signed 'AB'. The parallel style to 'AP' earlier was probably intentional. This may well have been written by his friend Arthur Branthwayt. It contained a dedication that could well be interpreted as being to Potts and Prideaux. 'AB' declared that when anything potentially destructive to church or state happened, people should defend against such attacks and not stay silent on the issues. He dedicated this, his first book, to the 'judicious and ingenious examiner' who had 'detected and repulsed' the assaults of a 'faction against monarchy and episcopacy'. His final words of dedication were:

> That the Reverend Doctor may never be afraid to preach, nor you
> to write, such useful and necessary truths; that Her present Majesty
> may long live in health, peace and prosperity, and ever encourage
> such worthy patriots of their country.

The choice of title, the content of the work and the anonymous authorship all argue that AB dedicated his book to AP - to Algernon Potts - with a subsidiary dedication to Prideaux. Although of course other clerics could be meant, Prideaux was by far the most well-known locally as a writer and particularly assiduous preacher.

In his booklet AB explicitly did not try to take either a Whig or Tory, or a high or low church stance. He wanted to set out a learned review of the arguments for and against the proposition that kings only held their position through the supreme power of the people. He argued that this was a false proposition and contrary to scripture, reason, the laws of the land and the constitution of the country. The argument for the supremacy of the people would lead to the sins of impiety, perjury and treason. The King was the anointed representative of God.

> ... my whole design and labour, which was nothing else but to
> settle publick peace and good by obedience to authority (which is
> now endeavour'd to be destroy'd by some busy and intermeddling
> incendiaries) ...

In the 94 pages of the main pamphlet AB set out a learned and disciplined set of proofs of each of these planks of his argument. The whole has the feel of a lawyer setting out his case and the long section of extracts from statutes going back to medieval times would have required at least some familiarity with the law to marshal and summarise these facts so effectively. Arthur Branthwayt, as a lawyer, steward for the Cathedral and one of The Close set, would have been well-equipped to write such a work. The 1710 Poll Book contains no other AB contenders in Norwich, nor can we find any other reasonable contender in the county. However, Branthwayt voted Whig in 1710. He failed to be elected in 1714-15 as MP for Castle Rising.[77] But the pamphlet quite explicitly stated, and was written accordingly, that the issue was not a party political matter, but one that affected the safety of the nation as a whole. It is very notable in Prideaux's diary that he recorded Branthwayt's death in 1717 with a long and quite atypical summary of his life and good works for the Dean and Chapter. No other individual had received such a lengthy and emotional entry.

So, the conclusion is that Algernon and Branthwayt wrote the two pamphlets and were supported in the background by Prideaux, Tanner and others. These were the tangible products of a highly engaged wider scholarly group centred on The Close. The issues they addressed were at the top of the political agenda of the time, but were as much matters of religious conscience and personal philosophy.

The later years and untimely demise

Algernon's interest in ecclesiastical matters was reflected in local parish matters. An interesting document has survived that showed Sir Algernon was granted, by Erasmus Earle esq of Heydon, the next void turn of the advowsons of Salle and Cawston rectories.[78] Earle had given the next turns to Algernon, but wanted to will the rectories thereafter to Pembroke Hall Cambridge and so drew up a trust deed involving Sir Ralph Hare of Stow Bardolph to ensure that both his wishes would be met, even if he died before Algernon's turns. Nothing in the deed indicated a financial transaction with Algernon; it looked like a favour to a friend, perhaps in return for a favour done. It does however firmly place Algernon's circle of friends among the senior gentry of the county. The grant was contingent on Algernon putting in Thomas Browne MA. The son of Thomas Browne of Norwich (the cleric and master of Pembroke College Cambridge from 1694 to his death in 1706), young Thomas was ordained as a deacon in London in 1713 and as a priest in Norwich in July 1714.[79] He duly became Cawston's rector in 1721 and Salle's in 1734, holding them until his death in 1747. Both parishes were of reasonable size and would certainly have offered a better income than Mannington, even if it had been vacant.

After Burrell's resignation from Mannington in 1678, Michael Batt had held the living. With Sir Roger being absent and few residents, it is likely that Batt also was non-resident and the church ceased to be used for much of the next thirty years.[80] Batt also held the much larger parish of Chelmsford from 1696 where he died in 1706. In Mannington, he was replaced by Thomas Bond (possibly the same as the rector of Little Ellingham) who in turn resigned in 1710. It seems likely that Algernon was content with his father's last choice of rector, presented that year. The young Roger Coleman, who had become a priest in 1704, may have been related to Francis Coleman, gent of Bramfield, Suffolk. Francis was in the middle of purchasing Roger's Great Ellingham estate when the latter died the following year. As the next chapter will show, Algernon came into the Mannington estate after the negotiation of a family settlement with his father in 1710, not long before Sir Roger's death in

1711 at the age of 70. If his father had presented a rector (whether deliberately or not) that his son did not care for, Algernon might have been able to remove him when he came to live there. Coleman, however, remained the holder of the living throughout Algernon's time. Nevertheless, Thomas Browne appears to have been Algernon's 'minister' - probably his private chaplain - in 1714 around the time of his ordination. This was also the likely time of the restoration of Mannington church and the renewed holding of divine service there with which Algernon has been credited.[81] Whether Browne stayed on with Algernon and then served his brother Sir Charles before entering Cawston in 1721 is not known. Coleman resigned Mannington in 1726 and Sir Charles presented Benjamin Knight.[82]

Unlike his father, Algernon did not live to a ripe old age. Both he and Dame Frances died in November 1716; she succumbed first, on Wednesday 21st and he exactly a week later, on Wednesday 28th. Both were buried, on the two Fridays, forty-eight hours after their deaths, in Mannington.[83] The two of them dying at the same time, with neither being particularly old, implies they may have contracted an infectious disease, perhaps smallpox which was endemic at this time. Indeed, Algernon had written to Dr Tanner from Mannington on 22nd December 1714 about the death from smallpox of one of his tenants:

> Sir
>
> I have lost one of my principal tenants John Bond of Wolterton to the smallpox and his widow is in great concern how to get letters of administration, being not able to go into Norwich having at this time her own aged father children and 2 servants sick in her house of the same distemper. Sir, the Will will be brought you some time this week by one of the appraisers off the goods, Mr [.hi.a.er]* of Matlask and if you will please by him (if such a thing be at anytime done) to send the oath which the widow should [take] with a power to Mr Browne my minister to administer the same it shall be owned an obligation to
>
> yr most humble servant
>
> Ae Potts
>
> My wife joyns with me in most humble service to yourself & lady
>
> My tenant has left his widow well to pay & I believe you will meet with no troble about her administering[84]
>
> [* Almost certainly Richard Whitaker of the tanning family in Matlask and in 1725 High Sheriff]

By good fortune, in an apparently entirely unrelated group of documents, an unsigned draft of Frances's will has survived.[85] Dated 23rd November 1700 and made with Algernon's express consent, she left her real and personal estate to Algernon, with the Calibut family lands (rather than the Crane lands) after his death to pass to her nephew John Repps gent. Repps was the son of Francis Repps of Mattishall whose first wife was Frances's sister Lucy Calibut. Lucy had died aged 23 in 1681 and Francis Repps died in 1692. Frances deliberately referred to the Shuckforth girls' chancery action and asserted that her first husband had meant her to have all his personal estate without any dispute about the residue. She therefore gave all her personal estate (by implication including her first husband's personal estate) to Algernon; from this he was to pay a number of £20 or £25 bequests to members of her family.[86]

Frances's property in Saham Toney, as we shall see, had become an issue between Algernon and his father. Thomas Crane had willed outright to Frances and her heirs all those lands which had been hers before their marriage. In the large majority of his own family's Saham Toney lands, he had left her only a life interest after which, if he and Frances had no children, they were to pass to Crane's nephew Thomas Shuckforth.[87] As a result, the value of the whole farm, when selling up, would be much less than if she had owned it all outright. The scale of the property was given in *The Norwich Gazette* of 10th May 1707.[88] A letting notice from Algernon described the Saham Toney farm as 100 acres of arable, 50 of pasture with further mowing ground and meadows and a malting office, available from Michaelmas that year. Sir Roger thought that it should be sold to pay some of Algernon's debts and believed that Algernon had agreed to this. However, it seems that Roger had not grasped the legal situation in Saham Toney. While in a letter Roger did refer to 'jointure land', showing that he knew part of the farm was only Frances's for life, he appeared not to know that her own Calibut family lands were already substantially mortgaged.[89] In March 1706, Algernon and Frances had mortgaged the manor of Woodhouse in Ovington and a messuage and lands in Saham Toney to Elizabeth Coulson, widow of Thorpe next Norwich, for £450 plus interest. As the deed also recited a debt of £576 to John Repps of Mattishall, presumably the mortgage was to provide for a substantial repayment to Frances's nephew. A Robert Wright was also involved who seems likely to be family too, given his involvement in the 1702 house sale and a further Wright reference in her will. This arrangement remained in place until October 1711 when the mortgage, by then for £500 including rolled-up interest, was assigned to John Mason of Necton esq.

Algernon made his, very short, will the day before his death, on 27th November 1716 when he was 'weak and infirm'. Three men witnessed the will: Thornhaugh Gurdon (his antiquarian friend from The Close), Matthew Long his brother-in-law, and George Jenney. Frances had been given his real estate in a prior settlement document which provided for Charles Potts to inherit after her death. Algernon simply left all his personal estate to his executor James Norris, the Norwich mercer to pay his debts as soon as he conveniently could.[90] Norris was to 'make the best he can' of Algernon's goods for the benefit of his creditors. If Charles purchased some of his brother's belongings, such as his library, that would account for its survival.

Algernon's life had been very different from his father's and their relationship was not close. His father's debts had created problems for the next generation and their solution had resulted in the family settlement of 1710. His 'sweet-tempered character' had been sorely tried.

Chapter 22

1710: No Big Deal

By the late seventeenth century and into the first decade of the eighteenth Sir Roger Potts had become heavily indebted. A substantial number of mortgages on Mannington and other property were taken out and regularly re-assigned. These would not be particularly unusual and worthy of comment were it not for the survival among the Walpole papers of a rather strange family settlement. By good fortune a folder of letters has also survived and the two sources together give a remarkable insight into family relationships and the management of their financial affairs. Ironically Sir Roger appears to have himself become everything that he was critical of his father about in the late 1670s. Although Tomes in his booklet Mannington Hall and its Owners *used a few very short extracts from the letters, here they are quoted at length for the first time. The letters have been presented as they were written, with undated ones placed where from their content seemed most appropriate. These extracts include the barest minimum addition of punctuation to help make sense of the meaning.*[1] *Sir Roger Potts, particularly, was of the old school and little punctuation interrupted his long streams of consciousness. A few letters have not been reproduced because their content is repetitive and with no more substance than, usually, yet another rant by Roger at his eldest son Algernon's perceived behaviour. To add interpretative detail to the names and events mentioned in the letters, background information on family relationships and affairs is given letter by letter where it helps to explain the content or the stage in the family negotiation process.*

The settlement was dated 3rd October 1710.[2] One might normally expect to see family settlements that convey property, via trustees, to the use of the father for life (with provision for his wife outliving him) and then passing to his eldest son. Before inheriting on his father's death there might be some provision of an annuity or rental stream for the son, or perhaps some part of the overall family estates would be given immediately to him, his wife and their heirs. This Potts deed is unusual, although no doubt not unique, because all the family estates passed immediately to the son, with an annuity being then paid to the father for his life.

The four parties were: Sir Roger Potts of Mannington; Algernon Potts his son of Norwich; Thornhaugh Gurdon esq of Norwich and Jacob Preston of Beeston St Lawrence (family trustees and as such the owners of the property in law); Clement Hyrne of Haveringland and Robert Britiffe esq of Norwich (Roger's executors). The primary requirement in the settlement was that the Potts estates of Great Ellingham, Clippesby and Mannington should be used to pay the debts of Sir Roger and Algernon listed in the attached schedule. Once the debts were settled, Algernon would get the residue of the estates and would receive the remaining rents and profits for life, whereas Sir Roger would receive only a fixed annuity of £240 per annum paid quarterly.

The schedule showed 16 creditors with a total of £10,990 owing to them - a very large sum:

Executors of Israel Long Esq	£3,000
John Marcon gent	£200
Mr Wallis	£2,300
Mrs Fownes or her assigns	£1,200
Mr James Harrison	£1,000
Mrs Hare	£1,000
Mr Isaac Jermy	£1,000
Mrs Newman	£350
Mr Ives	£200
Mr Rogers	£200
Executors of Roger Howman	£50
Elizabeth Curtis	£100
Mrs Jecks	£100
John Pierce	£50
Mr Thomas Bond	£40
To be paid to Sir Roger Potts	£200

The Britiffe letters

The story of this rather unusual arrangement unfolded in the letters from members of the family to Robert Britiffe, the well-connected lawyer and MP who looked after the family's major legal affairs. Other letters, between family members, also had legal content and thus had ended up with Britiffe.[3] The correspondence showed the emotion and negotiation within the family that went on before the agreement was reached and indeed afterwards. Sir Roger and Algernon both built up debts although the majority of these were clearly Sir Roger's. They seem to have been equally guilty of bad behaviour towards each other. Charles, the younger brother, initially comes across as the concerned good guy only involved at the margin but the reader may be the judge when all the known facts have been presented.

The correspondence started somewhat innocuously, but from the beginning it was all about family debts. On 28th February 1710 Charles Potts wrote from Fleet Street to Robert Britiffe seeking Britiffe's help in getting payment from his father:

> … I am very desirous of having all accounts between my father
> and me stated and settled every quarter or as often as may be with
> conveniency, persuant to which I have here inclosed sent you a
> particular of his account from the last bill and the vouchers. If he

> objects against any error I am ready to mend or satisfy, not knowing of any error. And if I have any vouchers that were not herebefore delivered up I am ready at any time to search for them. …

Charles was a woollen draper and Merchant Taylor in London. When Sir Roger Potts wrote to his son, at an earlier period, asking him to make enquiries of Peter Le Neve at the Heralds' Office regarding Hickling sewers, Charles was at the Sign of the Naked Boy in Fleet Street.[4] Fleet Street may have been both Charles's home and his business premises, but the close proximity of Naked Boy Court to the Fleet prison makes it most likely that this was his place of business only.[5] By 1710 Charles clearly obtained goods for his father and brother. The implication here was that his father rarely paid his bills. It also introduced the underlying theme of Britiffe as a go-between for family members when direct communication did not seem to have any effect.

Fortunately for him, Charles was somewhat remote from the extent, severity and urgency of his father's indebtedness. By chance, a letter to his sister Susan has survived in another collection.[6] Susan had married Matthew Long, the son of the wealthy Israel Long esq of Dunston Hall near Norwich. Her widowed mother-in-law, Mrs Sarah Long, was executor for Israel Long and, as such, being owed £3,000, she headed the list of Potts' creditors.[7]

On 27 May 1710 Charles wrote in quite emotional terms to 'Dear Sister' Susan at Dunston to say that he was surprised to have just heard that her mother-in-law and her attorney Mr [John] Carter of Norwich had taken out a writ in the court of common pleas against Sir Roger for the £3,000. He asked Susan to use her best efforts to stop the proceedings and asked for twelve months to be allowed to try to sort out debt repayment. He was sure that their father would, by then, have sold Mannington which he really believed he intended to do. He argued that the estate would be worth more if it had all its liberties and freedoms intact. Fortunately Susan's draft reply was written on the letter too. She wrote that Mr Long (her husband) and another friend of Sir Roger had already used their best efforts to avoid a further prosecution. As for time, their father would be 'treated respectfully' provided he gave satisfaction regarding the title for the mortgage to ensure that it was on a sound foundation. She said that Britiffe would be in London soon and promised to 'satisfy you in every way'. Susan ended by assuring Charles that her husband joined with her in doing everything they could to make things easy for Sir Roger.

The reference to a mortgage seemed odd, since there is no sign in the Potts mortgage deeds that there was any Long involvement at this stage. It looked as though this was an unsecured loan and that the writ had been issued to make the debt more pressing and formal. But this interpretation turned out to be too kind to Sir Roger. The truth is that the £3,000 was the sum he had promised to pay as Susan's portion on her marriage to Matthew Long in December 1702.[8] It was obviously never paid.[9] No doubt Sarah Long knew all about Susan's father's long-running chancery actions against his sister in the early 1680s and judged that starting legal proceedings was the only way to force Sir Roger to pay the long overdue marriage portion. By the Trinity term 1710 and, well into the main story, Sarah Long got her way with a final concord giving her and Robert Britiffe rights to the manors and estates of Great Ellingham and Clippesby.[10] Britiffe also acted for the Long family.

Sir Roger's offer to sell

From its content, the next letter appears to be very early in the sequence and was quite probably triggered by the Long writ.[11] Undated, Sir Roger Potts wrote to Robert Britiffe giving his basic pitch for the solution to his and his son's debt problems:

> Sir, I have often thought of the whole concern of my family and am come to the resolution that a deed be made to settle Mannington, Ellingham and Clippesby in Clement Hyrne esq and Jacob Preston esq to empower them to sell so much of the whole will pay the debts in the first place, then to stand seized of the remainder or make a settlement to me for life and to my son Algernon for life and to his heirs male of his body and for want of such, to my son Charles and to make Algernon's wife a rent charge out of it if she survives him and me.
>
> And for this satisfaction for selling off her estate I will make a lease for my life of so much of Mannington rents as to make a true recompense to them in payment for what they part with. Though I have nothing of which might have been towards my debts yet I am willing to do kindly by them.
>
> This I hope will be sufficient instruction if not let me have what you want for I desire to finish with what speed you please this and that for which [I] long satisfaction. I am
>
> Your faithful.
>
> Roger Potts

The postscript to a letter of 7th June 1710 from Sir Roger to Britiffe made clear that discussions about a major family settlement were by then under way but that Algernon's first response was not acceptable:

> My son's offer at having Clippesby and Ellingham settled by the same deed on him which I think is perfect nonsense for me to divest myself of my estates and still stand bound for the debts upon them, besides I never proposed settling Ellingham.

A further undated letter from Sir Roger to Britiffe commented on Algernon's next response to his father's initial settlement proposal. The amicable and positive tone seemed to fit the early stages of the process, but might alternatively have come in a brief cessation of hostilities around August:

> Sir, the proposal my son makes is that Ellingham and Clippesby should be sold and that his wife will also sell hers to make Mannington clear of all debts to be settled upon him as a family estate with a jointure to his wife. Now I think it may be necessary for her to have a fine passed this term to put that estate in a condition to be sold, for till she doth pass it by a fine she can make no title. This I thought necessary to hint to you so that you may please to advise my son in it. …

Sir Roger intimated that a fine would be needed to establish sufficiently clear title in Frances's Saham Toney lands for them to be sold - somewhat superfluous advice to give a lawyer.

> 10ᵗʰ June 1710 Sir Roger Potts to Robert Britiffe:
>
> Sir, my son Algernon when with me told me that you could help me to chapman* for my off farms at Mannington. If it be so, I desire you will please to think of it and put that of Armingland off for me or help me to 1200 upon it by a transfer of the mortgage now upon it. The present tenant is an able man and payeth £120 per annum rent for it.
>
> Mr Tayler, my son thinks, may be a chapman for the whole; he being desirous to marry his grandson and wants a seat. If so, I beg you will please to assist my son in tempting him to lay hold.
>
> I shall be glad to know what my son says to my letter. I hope to send to you on Monday that Charles Halford is returned with success.
>
> I am your humble servant.
>
> *Chapman here is being used as a verb for to deal in or trade: a delightful bye gone age without Estate Agents to sell property!

Armingland was one of the variants used for Irmingland, adjacent to Mannington and Itteringham. The specific farm, then known as The White House, is readily identifiable from abuttals as the land around what is now Elmerdale Farm on the Aylsham to Holt Road. Although immediately abutting the main estate it was of sufficient size and of convenient location to separate off from the core estate. Roger's grandfather had given him this farm as a young man to learn estate management and he still looked after it. The property had been the subject of a series of mortgages but, with its own separate deeds, the current mortgage did not encumber the manorial estate itself. The farm could be sold if the mortgage could be re-assigned, although in fact it remained in the estate to 1737 and beyond.

Charles Halford has yet to be identified but was obviously a go-between. 'Mr Tayler' may be of the Taylor family of Norwich and Attleborough, briefly covered by Walter Rye in *Norfolk Families*. Thomas Taylor, a baker of Attleborough, in 1713 sold a messuage and land in Great Ellingham, which at least shows that the family were interested in some way in land in Ellingham.[12]

> 15th June 1710 Sir Roger Potts to Robert Britiffe:
>
> Sir, I received a letter from my son this day with great pleasure and satisfaction and desire you will please to hasten the deed for corroboration of Mrs Long's security and the remainder of both Ellingham and Clippesby in trustees hands, such as you and my son shall name, to be sold for the payment of debts upon them and to raise money for the payment of other my debts and also for my son's debts which he saith are £1000. I hope to get a purchaser for Ellingham presently and at your return from London we shall advise further with you. …

Sir Roger was anxious to get the Sarah Long security resolved; no doubt he was being pressed by the whole family in support of Sarah. Subsequent comments in the letters reveal that she was most assiduous in chasing for the money.

> 23rd June 1710 Algernon Potts to Robert Britiffe:
>
> Sir, since we parted I have proposed to my father that I should have £2000 allowed me out of the two estates; one out of Ellingham as soon as sold and the other out of Clippesby when the whole £5000 be paid. Which finding him averse to it, I desire no deed be drawn till you come down or hear further from me.

Algernon was actively but unsuccessfully trying to push his father to agree to settle more of the money on him sooner. In an undated letter, from about this time, Algernon proposed to Britiffe that the settlement should provide for the money from the sale of the estate to be vested in trustees and to go first to paying debts, then to interest payments and then to an annuity for his father with the residue to himself. If he died there should be a provision for his wife for her life and the rest to go to his father and heirs. If his father died before him then the estate should pass to Algernon after debts were paid. Also he said, his father may bequeath £500 to Charles if he so desired. He saw this as the 'fairest for all'. Algernon, still hopeful of changing Roger's mind, suggested leaving the sum to be paid him out of Ellingham blank rather than the £1,000, since his father and he had yet to agree it.

Sir Roger was at least now willing to sell Ellingham as he discussed with Britiffe on the 21st July 1710 having a 'particular' or property description of Ellingham drawn up. The following month, on 19th August, Roger updated Britiffe on his negotiations. His 'cousin Bedingfield' thought Ellingham was too big for him so Roger was also dealing with Mr de Grey. He agreed he could raise £100 to pay interest overdue to Mrs Long but he had new worries that Algernon had found his own debts greater than Sir Roger had imagined. He also added that he thought the Irmingland farm must be sold to pay his own debts.

Cousin Bedingfield was Charles, the second son of Philip Bedingfield of Ditchingham husband of Sir Roger's aunt Ursula Potts. His father had been a trustee for the first Sir John Potts. Thomas de Grey esquire of Merton was the current head of that long-standing family, which for at least 150 years had owned the small manor of Bury or Berry Hall in Great Ellingham. They had been friends of the Potts family since marrying into their neighbours and relatives the Palgraves of Barningham. The de Greys were targeted because they might have been interested in turning their Ellingham estate into a more substantial one.

Sir Roger's dire straits were shown by his inability (or unwillingness) up to then to find £100 for an interest payment and Algernon now admitted to more than £1,000 of debts. The precise amount was not given but around £1,000 was not a particularly unusual amount for a gentleman to owe, especially an heir apparent. If Roger thought the sale of Irmingland would solve even his immediate problems he was off the mark. The farm was only 200 or so acres and was already encumbered with a £1,200 mortgage.

A few days later on 25th August, Sir Roger wrote to Britiffe, referring to a letter sent that morning by hand of Dr Howman, his physician, regarding instructions for the deed of settlement. He sought £24 to pay Mr Lomb. This was 'interest money for part of the estate I sold his father which I had … I am to pay it as long as my mother liveth'. The Lomb reference remains unclear, but recurred on 12th September when it appeared that this was an obligation to one of his stepmother's circle.[13]

However the following day, the 26th, Sir Roger Potts told Britiffe he was in too poor a state of health to commit to a meeting. He had taken a dose that Dr Howman gave him which he thought might ease him. He finished 'I am so desirous to have Mrs Long satisfied your way of doing it'.

A batch of the letters and notes from September 1710 all had to do with drafting the settlement. An undated 'particular of the Mannington Estate in Mannington, Itteringham, Wolterton, Little Barningham, Saxthorpe and elsewhere' included a rental list and annual valuation of the estate:

Matthew Digby (now somebody else I know not who)	£105
Thomas Blogg	£42
Richard Hill	£90
Thomas Dewin	£120
Robert Jackson	£53
Robert Rose	£37
John Leake a mill with 2 tenements	£35:10/-
John Bond	£94
William Empson	£90
Edward Plane with a lime kiln	£31:10/-
John Empson all land	£4:10/-
	£711:10/-

Besides days works of thatchers dawbers and ditching work at the tenants charges by covenants in all their leases which cost some owners at least £50 a year

The Mansion House with outhouses garden orchards meadows waters and dovehouse about 40 acres
The park by computation 50 acres
Groves and underwoods 20 acres
The osier ground which has been let for £10 per annum
In all £88:10/-
Total £800:00:00

The particular is most useful as it gives a good basis for the likely annual value of the estate when it later came to be sold to Walpole, and therefore the multiple of the rental stream that he paid for it. Also, it showed that at this time the house and its substantial park were routinely being let as an entity separate from farmland if the opportunity arose. The rent, assuming the osier ground went to a local tradesman, was about £78 a year. Later letters showed that the house was in a poor state of repair and it was probably empty at this time. Indeed with so little acreage attached, the rent must have seemed relatively high. Over the years there would have been an intermittent string of short-lease gentry tenants, with the owners throughout retaining a couple of locked rooms probably on the top floor.

Sir Roger's letter of 1ˢᵗ September 1710 to Britiffe, apart from being full of carping and bluster, stressed that the annuity being proposed for him was far too low. His next few letters - he wrote to Britiffe at least twice a week - noted that negotiations were continuing with Mr de Grey and on 8ᵗʰ September, that he had written to Algernon with a schedule of his debts but now feared the last item of £150 to clear loose debts would not be sufficient and needed that to be £200. This was altered in the final schedule. After another letter on the 10ᵗʰ, with yet more bluster, Sir Roger wrote on 12ᵗʰ September regarding drafting the deed. He confirmed various items including £500 on his own death to go to his son Charles and the interest on the debts to be paid out of Mannington rents and from the sale of the estates. His own annuity he said was to be £60 quarterly although he noted that £200 plus Ellingham rents would:

> barely pay my loose debts and maintain me till Christmas that I am
> to receive my first quarterly payment of sixty pounds a quarter and
> then am to begin the world again anew and then expect to be secure
> from the claim of any creditor in this for principal or interest else
> why do I part with my estate to my son for if I must go to a gaol
> at last I had better do so now and save you the trouble of making
> writings … I mean nothing but plain and honest and if my son will
> insist upon unreasonable in circumstances I can't help it.
>
> I consent to let alone the annuity of £10 to Betty Pierce and as to
> the £20 to Mr Lomb and £10 to Mr Spurgeon I own I did agree
> to allow my son during my lady's life and whether you think fit to
> mention it in the deed or that I do it by my writing you shall advise
> to allow it my son out of my annuity during her life but they must
> be secured by deed.
>
> Now I must take leave to add that I believe you never knew any
> father yield so easily and willingly to strife himself to satisfy a son all
> circumstances considered …

His flow of anxious thoughts and allusions to gaol were indicative of how difficult the family discussions must have been, despite his belief that he was yielding so 'easily'.

Ten days later on 22ⁿᵈ September 1710 a meeting was being proposed which from an undated letter from Algernon to Britiffe was to be on 2ⁿᵈ October to be followed by the signing on the 4ᵗʰ:

> Sir, I understand you are writing to Sir Roger. I could wish you
> would desire him to consider against tomorrow what annuity he will
> be contented with and to get a schedule of his debts ready that I may
> bring them to you tomorrow night, that no stop may be put on the

execution of the deed on the day proposed viz 4th inst. You know best what argument to use to hasten him and to induce him to be contented with £200 per annum, which the more I think of appears every hour to me the more extraordinary annuity considering all circumstances chances and hazards.

Even at this late stage Algernon was pressing for the lower annuity. Right might have been on his side, but he failed. The day before the preparatory meeting Sir Roger sent his excuses to Britiffe:

Sir, I have got cold with riding about upon the service of our approaching election to that degree that I fear I shall not be in a condition to come to you tomorrow as I intended. …

The concerns over his future had not prevented Sir Roger's continuing interest and activities in the political sphere. However, in an undated long letter from Sir Roger to Britiffe, he agreed to the settlement which was signed on the 3rd. Sir Roger noted that he had sent the schedule of debts; he was 'pleased to hear that Mr de Grey will purchase part of Ellingham' and he would send to his 'cousin Charles Bedingfield that we may agree as speedily as may be' [ie, the estate being reduced to a suitable size for Bedingfield to purchase the balance] 'but then I shall not have a house to hide my head in and my estate out of my power'. He said he 'must have a power to recover rents in arrears' and to 'know when I shall be quit of all concerns of paying interest or debts and that my annuity of £60 per quarter shall begin and I be at ease'. He wanted to add in a £10 annuity to his servant Elizabeth, wife of John Pearce, and a power to charge £500 upon the estate to pay his son Charles Potts and 'others I may be obliged to'. He was willing for Mr Lomb and Thomas Spurgeon's £30 annuities to be paid out of his £60/quarter 'for my lady's life'. His son, he said, had agreed to him having the Michaelmas rents of Ellingham and Mannington and for his first payment to begin at Christmas.

The reference to John and Elizabeth Pearce is interesting. John, his coachman, was on the debt schedule and was owed £50. These two servants obviously stuck by Sir Roger, but perhaps they had no choice given the money owing to them. As we have seen Thomas Spurgeon gent of Wickmere/Aldborough had been a long-standing servant and aide to Sir John senior. He died without wife or issue in 1727.[14] These requirements to pay Lomb and Spurgeon had obviously been placed on Roger by his father or grandfather. 'My Lady' was Dame Elizabeth, Sir Roger's stepmother, still alive at this date.

These letters effectively summarised several of the terms of the final settlement. All three estates were committed to be sold to pay off debts. Algernon was due the residue. Sir Roger had his £240 a year starting at Christmas 1710. He was allowed to bequeath Charles £500 and did. Spurgeon was to receive just £10 a year after the death of Dame Elizabeth Potts of the City of London, widow (but from the estates, not from Sir Roger's annuity). The Pearce £10 annuity fell by the wayside, although the £50 debt was later paid.

The aftermath

The 69 year old Sir Roger was now to leave his home and was not happy.

14th October 1710 Sir Roger Potts to Robert Britiffe:

Sir, I was so mauled with my journey to Norwich that I could not stay to see you though I am very much in pain till I talk with you of my affairs. For I think the articles are short of what they should contain and some other matters I have to speak to, but my grief is I do not see my son take care to raise money. And as to his farm at Saham I had discourse with Mr Muston since I saw you and he tells me his client hath taken a particular account of the number of acres and finds that the whole is let at ten shillings the acre and to take out a great part of the land which is now ploughed and hath formerly been pasture and is jointure. What will remain at plough grown to that farm is not worth above 4s an acre so that he saith seriously to me he thinks his client bids a full price and more than any other man will give for it, the houses and fences being indeed very ruinous.

I am at a great stand and have put out two servants and making preparation to flit. My son offer me to board with him but I told him before I would not live at Norwich. …

[PS] I beg all the writings may remain in your hand till I speak to you.

Horse and stable door come to mind - after all the deed was signed. Algernon, with plenty of room in his large house, presumably was simply being polite in offering a Norwich home to his father and probably well knew he would refuse. The John Muston mentioned was of Watton. He was involved in arrangements relating to Frances's property in Saham and elsewhere and in 1716 took over from Thomas Wright esq a mortgage on the property in Wodehouse in Ovington.[15]

Roger, regretting the settlement already, continued to moan about Algernon's behaviour and motives.

20th October 1710 Sir Roger Potts to Robert Britiffe:

Sir, I have not yet recovered the cold I got at our election and besides that to see my countrymen mad; and, which is nearest to [me], my son so bigoted as to neglect me and his main concern of taking to manage the estate he hath so eagerly grasped at hath raised my contemplation of what is past and made me very melancholy. The main point of which is that you have contrary to my order given him a power to destroy all the timber and to let down the houses or sell them off the estate, which you and I hope he will not do; yet if he should I find a guilt beginning to prick me that I should leave it so much in his power. I do not know when I shall go to Mannington but have sent again. Pray let me know which day next week you will be at home and if possible I will see you and discourse further.

I am your most humble servant.

A small flicker of concern for his son, however, was shown in Roger's wish that he should not be weighed down by debt as he himself had been.

27th October 1710 at Mannington Sir Roger Potts to Robert Britiffe at his house in St Giles Norwich:

Sir, I find the inventorying the goods here of more difficulty than I thought of and value too, but nothing we can do will avail us without sale of lands. I wish you would please to speak to Mr Branthwayt it may be he incline Mr Grey to deal for Ellingham and it may be you may if you try to incline my son to sell Saham Tony estate for anything will help him to make speedy payment of interest will make him easy else he will find calls so thick upon him as will weary him to death as I know by too much experience.

I am your most humble servant.

[PS] I hope to be at Norwich on Thursday next. I go home tomorrow but dare not venture by Norwich.

Arthur Branthwayt we have already met in Algernon's circle. He also acted formally as trustee for the de Greys in their Ellingham property.[16] He was well-connected to the Potts family. He leased a messuage and 31 acres in Repps with Bastwick (part of the Clippesby estate) from Dame Elizabeth Potts in 1699.[17] One of his sisters, Julian, had married Mundeford Spelman of Narborough - a cousin of the Potts, being the grandson of Dame Ursula whose second husband had been Sir John Potts senior. Branthwayt also witnessed the 1705 will of Roger Howman who featured on the list of Sir Roger's creditors.

However Sir Roger soon reverted to blaming his son for everything.

31st December 1710 Sir Roger Potts to Robert Britiffe:

Sir, I am strangely alarmed by receiving two very sharp dunns one from Mr Wallis the other from Mrs Long by a letter from Mr Snowden by which I perceive my son intends nothing less than to have me die in a gaol for I told him that Mr Wallis would be sharp if he did not pay him or apply to him which he might do by his brother Charles who is acquainted with him. And as to Mrs Long I doubted not but he would at least have applied to but Sir you may now see to what a state I am plagued by trusting him who takes no care of me nor of his own interest all the consolation I have left is that my writings are safe in your hand which I expect you will please to keep till you find some way to secure me better than I am yet.

I intend to be at Norwich … to consult Doctor Howman for some infirmities of my body …

Although no longer responsible for his debts, it was not surprising to find Sir Roger was still in the firing line. Mr Wallis was the second largest creditor, owed £2,300. From 1698, Anne Wallis of Bethnal Green in Stepney London, widow, had provided a mortgage on Mannington.[18] Sir Roger had clearly not honoured his commitments to her in the past and in 1710 James Wallis her grandson, now the mortgage holder, was not inclined to trust Sir Roger. In 1703, after Anne Wallis's death, her executors William Coatsworth esq and Thomas Clark merchant had sued Sir Roger in chancery for the principal sum of £2,000 and interest for the full period since 1698.[19] It seems that Potts claimed variously that there was no such mortgage; the money was never lent; if it was he never received it; or it was repaid in Anne Wallis's lifetime. He refused to repay or to give up his title deeds, saying of the latter that Mannington had other charges on it that were antecedent and that there was a complicating entail on the property, in which he had only a life interest, which would mean the mortgage would not stand up. All of this was clearly nonsense since a valid mortgage deed did exist and Anne Wallis had, in fact, simply taken the assignment of a mortgage started with Samuel Danvers in 1693. By 1708 James Wallis gent of London, grandson of James Wallis merchant of London deceased, had the Mannington mortgage and retained it throughout this period. Presumably the court action forced Sir Roger to pay his arrears of interest and he would have known that Wallis would thereafter always be quick to demand his money and would have no hesitation in further recourse to the law. Mr Snowden was Samuel Snowden, clerk of Newton Flotman near Dunston, who had been an executor of the Susan Potts and Matthew Long marriage settlement of 1702.

Sir Roger's health had not improved and he was quick to mention any problems in his letters, still two or three a week, to Britiffe. On 9th January 1711 he reported that he 'was taken on a sudden with an extreme pain in my chest last night'. At that time the negotiations with de Grey regarding Ellingham were still continuing but on the 14th Roger said they were talking to de Grey and Mr Coleman. In the end, the de Grey/Bedingfield axis did not purchase Great Ellingham. Roger was still complaining of creditors still pursuing him for debts when they should now seek his son for payment. Another letter with the same moan also added that his son had undervalued goods at Mannington by £300. However Roger graciously said that he wanted no money for them.

On 21st January 1711 he sent another update in which he said he had shown the estate to Mr Coleman; he had had a letter from Mrs Fownes to say that she would this term enter upon Irmingland if she 'had not from me some account to prevent it'; and that he hoped to hear that his son had signed the bond. These are the first mentions of Mr Coleman. This was almost certainly the Francis Coleman that Blomefield reported bought Great Ellingham from Potts.

Three days later on the 24th, Algernon Potts wrote to Britiffe following up the settlement. He mentioned he was dealing with Mr Barker, presumably the William Barker, worsted weaver of Edgefield, who in 1724 cropped up in the assignment of security on £2,300 borrowed by Sir Charles Potts.[20]

The January weather had obviously been severe. Algernon asked Britiffe to get his father to send him an inventory of goods at Mannington and to send him the keys to the house, 'that I may see what damage this weather has done or is like to do there which by some information I have had I may fear will be great'. He also referred to goods that were locked up there and offered to pay his father for them and the books, which he noted had not been used for 20 years or more. He hoped his father would not remove them as 'I had much rather they should remain an heirloom in the family' and he was prepared to give security that they would be treated in that way.

That Sir Roger still had possessions locked up at Mannington to prevent Algernon getting at them reflects the lack of trust within the family. Algernon's comment on the books showed that the Hall had not been regularly occupied for a long time, certainly not occupied by the Potts for many years. From the inventory of Sir John junior it was clear that there was not a large collection of books left there at his death. Most probably there was a modest number of old unused books which Algernon was keen to keep and add to his own collection. The comment supports the view that the book collection sold in 1737 was largely Algernon's.

As the spring of 1711 advanced, Sir Roger was still missing meetings with Britiffe in the middle of March through illness but was keen to off-load his complaints about his son's behaviour. He was not too ill to remind Britiffe on the 19th that William Empson had arrears of rent of £168 or thereabouts owing and to ensure that one of his creditors (to whom he owed £200) did not appear on the schedule of debts. Empson was a Mannington estate tenant and Sir Roger was chasing last year's arrears still due to him. What he expected to be done about the mystery creditor that was not on the schedule (only his additional 'loose debts of £200' appeared there) goodness knows at this late stage.

Sir Roger's next letter showed that negotiations were going ahead with Mr Coleman for Ellingham although he resented Algernon's interference. 30th March 1711 Sir Roger Potts to Robert Britiffe:

> Sir, I received yours by Mr Coleman and (though my son's folly hath lessened the price I am sure he would have given if he had left me to have treated him or would have consulted me before as I had often desired) I am pleased it is done. And now Sir, I must take care that the money may be rightly applied, that is to the satisfying

the creditors mentioned in the deed and particularly those who have only my bond or note for their security; and the two hundred pounds mentioned as my loan debts, for which sum I pay six per cent interest and the party will take it at a very short warning. You know Sir, that it was upon his own offer to sell his wife's estate that I consented to the settlement you have had the trouble to make. But so it is that upon my mentioning to him the sale of that his wife, with a french assurance, huffed me and he did little less. And [he] hath taken no manner of care not so much as by sending writing or speaking to me of the condition in a civil manner to have some patience or anything that I could ever understand.

So that I must depend upon you to take so much care of me that I may be safe and to have some shelter against suits which may fall upon me. For if I should be clapped into a gaol I fear they who should in all reason and conscience secure me from it would be first to make sport at it.

This and Empson's arrears I recommend to you. I am to meet Mr Coleman at Norwich Tuesday come seven night; in the meantime I shall be glad to hear from you. I am

Your affectionate humble servant.

Roger's motivation to resolve his debts clearly stemmed in part from his real fear of the ignominy and discomfort of being imprisoned for debt. The main settlement even included a clause explicitly indemnifying him against imprisonment for non-payment of the scheduled debts. His daughter-in-law Frances had obviously upset him with her 'french' ways (presumably he thought her affected).

1st April 1711 Sir Roger Potts to Robert Britiffe:

I received your kind letter thankfully last night and searched for the counterpart of Mrs Fownes mortgage but I have none of it. It was a mortgage to Mr John Harvy and by my Lord Harvy confirmed to Mr Nailer and from him to Mr Fownes. The [substance] of this will and the two last were done by Mr Gibson the scrivener in Loathbury who is the acquaintance I know; and I send this early that you may please to send him for them or order whom you please to give you account of them. The charge you must and shall be allowed.

The reference confirmed that the Irmingland mortgage in which Mrs Fownes had an interest, had passed through various hands: John Hervey, executor of Sir Thomas Hervey; Francis Naylor of Staple Inn; George Naylor of Lincoln's Inn and through to Joseph Fownes gent of Deptford in Kent, deceased by 1711.[21] 'Mrs Fownes or her assigns' was the third largest creditor in the schedule at £1,200 and Elizabeth Fownes was the joint executor of her husband's will proved in 1709.[22]

Four days later Charles Potts who was helping, where he could, with affairs in London, wrote to Britiffe regarding the mortgage. Mrs Fownes and Mr John Harrison, clerk of the exchequer, of Deptford (Fownes's nephew and joint executor) were seeking repayment of the whole of the £1,200 at 5½ percent due 29th May, but 'they don't care how soon the money is paid'. Charles wanted clarification from Britiffe as to whether he and Mrs Fownes's son-in-law and agent Mr Ellis should send the original documents to Norfolk by special messenger or whether they should be scrutinised and attested to by a lawyer in London.

The lack of the original mortgage deed caused Charles to write on 21st April to 'Dear Brother' Algernon at his house in The Close in Norwich. They clearly had to find the deed to satisfy a 'client of Mr Britiffe' who would not trust Britiffe to draw up an abstract of title without it. Charles, in writing to Robert Britiffe about the matter in May, said that 'Mrs Fownes's agent is no lawyer but a pitch and tar wholesale man and understands no more that way than myself'. By September 1711 the paper work had been resolved and this mortgage had been re-assigned to Mr John Morse, merchant of Norwich.[23]

Algernon now agreed to put in writing what his father wanted him to do but the old man had been upsetting another 'old gent'.

> 8th May 1711 Sir Roger Potts to Robert Britiffe:
>
> Sir, my son now saith he is willing to seal such a bond for my security against all my personal allegations and for conserving the goods in Mannington as you were pleased yesterday to mention. I tell him if I may see the draft of the condition of such a bond and can approve it I will send it to you to be executed. And as soon as you will please to send me word that it is sealed and in your hand he shall have all the keys of Mannington and the goods therein.
>
> I was this morning with Mr Knights and after some very foolish shifts and that he forced me to some harsh words. He at last came to promise he would join and help his daughter to make an end with me and pay me all my money as soon as you have drawn the writings. I will send to Thomas Spurgeon to send you those writings he hath in his hand as to the title. Most nay all but two little fields which is to be conveyed to Knights being bought of Mr Ramsey by my grandfather and by him conveyed to me. I beg sir you will please to keep the old gent to this, which I perceive is very easy for you to do in which you will very much oblige.
>
> Your most humble servant.

The transaction referred to is hard to pin down precisely, but had to do with the sale of some land of the Mannington estate in Little Barningham to the Knight family, owners of other land there. Another Walpole deed, of 1720, conveyed the manor of Stafford Barningham to John Gurney the younger worsted weaver of Norwich. This manor was sold or mortgaged by Frances Knight of Norwich Cathedral precincts, the widow of John Knight gent deceased of the same place and their eldest son John.[24] The Knights were Algernon's close neighbours.

Mr Ramsey was John Dix Ramsey of Wickmere whose large estate, passed down from William Dix at the end of the 16th century, had parcels of land in the surrounding villages. It seems likely that the two little fields were those in an exchange of an acre or so each of Wolterton land between Sir John Potts and John Dix Ramsey of February 1666.[25] The exchange was interesting for the mutual enfranchisement of each other's previously copyhold cottages in the other's estates, turning them explicitly into freehold properties and indicating that the copyholds had previously been brought back into manorial control.

The 8th May letter also showed Thomas Spurgeon in a position of trust with family papers. As a young man he had been a 'servant' of Sir John Potts senior and probably the Mannington estate steward, looking after it while Sir John was away. Later a yeoman of Matlask, he was by this stage of Wickmere and no doubt the family were committed to paying him what was effectively a pension. He presumably also looked after the Norfolk interests of Dame Elizabeth as part of this arrangement.

Two days later however Sir Roger was having another go at his son in his letter to Britiffe.

10th May 1711, at Haveringland Sir Roger Potts to Robert Britiffe:

Sir, I received yours and am willing and desirous to have all matters fixed as you mention. And because my son expressed such haste I came hither now and have on Saturday last put up in a chest some of those goods I did not intend to leave to my son; others, and a good many I think he shall not need to have and think it highly reasonable I should make money of them. And so I intend to do but shall not make him wait till I do dispose them but trust him with them till a proper time so as I have left the key in the door to my chamber for his present use and have only the keys of the other rooms which shall be delivered as soon as he pleaseth. For I stayed here on Friday last from there because Mr Hirne told me he expected my son here on Monday. I waited upon you at Norwich when he thought fit to be out of town though I doubt not you had given him to understand I had sent you word I waited [but he did not] come so that the delay hath been by his own fault. He never would come to me to consult anything but now he seemeth to think it my duty to attend him.

I have business of several sorts which require my going to Ellingham today so can't come to you at Norwich till Whitsun week which is the time Mr Coleman hath appointed me to meet him. But my son may carry his hasty spouse thither as soon as he please I having lent him the keys and the goods for her entertainment but expect to have them delivered to me again if he doth not give me security to leave them in the house and also to secure me against personal debts and obligations.

I do not see that the condition of the bond you sent me doth reach any further than to secure that the goods shall be suffered to remain in the house till the time of his death and that, this notwithstanding, she may then imbezzle them which is the main point I desire to be secured against.

I can say no more at present but which I shall always that

I am your very humble servant.

Clement Hyrne of Haveringland was clearly a friend and his house conveniently *en route* from Mannington to Ellingham. Sir Roger thought Frances to be in too much haste to occupy Mannington even though this was seven months after the settlement was signed. The issue over possessions still rumbled on and he did not trust her with the family heirlooms should Algernon die first.

At least the brothers were on speaking terms; on 31st May Charles Potts sent to his 'Dear brother' a short note regarding getting lace for him and about the abstract from 'his cousin Grey'. James Grey of Wolterton was the nephew and heir of James Scamler the younger whose father, James Scamler the elder, had married Anne one of the daughters of Sir John Potts senior by his marriage to Barbara Godsalve. The meaning of the reference to an abstract is unfortunately unclear. In due course Grey's sisters, as his heiresses, were to sell Wolterton to Horatio Walpole.

Sir Roger was still very perturbed about his finances despite some brightness on the horizon.

22nd June 1711 Sir Roger Potts to Robert Britiffe:

Sir, Mr Colman [sic] came and paid me £200 and hath promised me to put some more into your hand. I beg you will keep it till I may have some satisfaction that my son doth not intend to spend all he can get and leave the debts unpaid. I am at present very ill and in great disorder of mind about my affairs my dependance is wholly upon you so rest

Your humble servant.

This was presumably a goodwill payment ahead of the completion of the purchase of the Ellingham estate.

In a letter of 30th June to Britiffe relating to the mortgage business Charles Potts revealed the fascinating detail that he had recently been married in secret. Unfortunately he did not say why this had been necessary but that he would explain all to Britiffe when he next saw him. However, the news had got out to his family via the restless curiosity of Mr Preston. Charles said he had known the lady for some time and his cousin James Grey had recently met and approved of her. He added: [he] 'does pronounce me happy. I hope he may be right though it has been some time in hand'. Mr Preston was no doubt Jacob Preston the family friend and trustee who will reappear in the next chapter.

Meanwhile his father was still certain Algernon was about to blow all the sale money.

> 10th July 1711 Sir Roger Potts to Robert Britiffe:
>
> Sir, my son hath used me so basely in several respects as almost to craze me. Now I want health to come to you and meet my other trustees to have a full discourse of matters and to take care the money my estate's sold for may be employed to the payment of my debts; which was the end for which it was sold and not that he should take the money and employ it to other uses to fulfil his own pride and luxury.
>
> I desire you to let my friend in Briston see the writings and consult what to advise me to do that the money may not be imbezzled and no debts paid. I am not in a condition of health to travel but hope may by the Assizes kiss your hand at Norwich.
>
> I am your most faithful friend and servant.

'My friend in Briston' is unexplained. The Britiffes themselves had land in the Briston area but this seems an unlikely way to refer to them. Augustine Earle esq had land in Briston but was resident in Heydon. Most likely his 'friend' was Sir Jacob Astley of Melton Constable and Briston. The long-lived Sir Jacob had been executor for Sir Roger's marriage settlement in 1668 and was still alive in 1711. At a guess, perhaps Sir Jacob was also the friend who had anonymously lent £200.

Now Algernon was suffering with a cold as he explained in a letter written to Britiffe from Mannington on 17th August 1711. He could not come to Norwich to see Mr Coleman - 'I am taken with such a cold and pain in my neck as I fear the riding will not agree with [me]' - so he asked if Britiffe or Mr James Norris could receive the money Mr Coleman had to pay. He arranged to see Britiffe the next week regarding the removal of Mrs Fownes's mortgage which he understood, by his brother, Mr Webb had done with and approved the title, 'his opinion I have writ for and hope to have it by tomorrow's post'. James Norris, mercer of Norwich, was later sole executor of Algernon's will and presumably here was acting for Algernon in the sale of Ellingham.

The following week Charles Potts while writing to Britiffe regarding speaking to executors of a will and getting a deed copied and attested, said he had been summoned to his sick father:

> … At the urgent command of my father and he being much indisposed I shall set out on Monday morning if not tomorrow for Ellingham with my wife. But my stay will be short and indeed [I] could ill spare time to come at all but was loath to displease.

Good old Charles! This was probably the last time he saw his father. There are no more letters from Sir Roger who presumably now was sinking fast. Algernon was splitting his time between his two homes in Mannington and Norwich. His letter of 26th September to Britiffe asked about progress regarding Mr Coleman suggesting that the Ellingham conveyance was still being finalised. He wrote from Mannington that he would not be coming to town before Monday 'having several workmen about me here which I am not willing to leave before unless you think it needful'. The implication was that he was repairing Mannington Hall and was close to taking up residence there.

Peace at last

Sir Roger Potts died on 14th October 1711.[26] It is not clear whether this letter was sent from Mannington or Ellingham but Algernon had obviously been unable to get to Norwich, presumably because of his father's death.

> 18th October 1711 Sir Algernon Potts to Robert Britiffe:
>
> Dear Sir, Yours I received. I am sorry that Mrs Colson is in so great haste. She had certainly had her money this day, had I not been obliged on this occasion to forbid the gentleman who was to pay it coming to Norwich, knowing I must have disappointed him if he had. Whether I can possibly get him to Town so soon as Saturday now I very much question but will try if I can. Otherwise if you can let her have so much money out of what you have in hand of Mr Colemans I engage to set it right again next week when we come together. In the meantime I rest
>
> your assured friend
>
> and humble servant
>
> A Potts

[PS] My servant Daniel is now in Norwich if you please to send me answer by him this night whether what I propose concerning Mr Colemans money may not do. It may save me a great deal of trouble, tomorrow being the funeral.

'Mrs Colson' was the widow Elizabeth Coulson who in 1706 had provided Algernon and Frances with a mortgage on the Saham Toney farm. Algernon's letter was dated four days before the deed which assigned the mortgage to John Mason esq of Necton, by which he paid £500 to Mrs Coulson. It would seem that Algernon had built up interest arrears and she was keen to see some return on her loan and indeed the return of principal.

The reference to the funeral being on the 19th is odd. Roger's burial at Great Ellingham was registered on 3rd November, so perhaps Algernon was referring to a prior funeral service before the interment itself. Sir Roger's will, made in December 1710, had requested burial there near his dear wife with the least charge and the utmost privacy.[27] He left the estates (as in the settlement) remaindered to Algernon and his male heirs only but if Algernon had no son, the estate should go to Charles. However if Charles also had no son, then Charles's heirs would inherit, thus snubbing Algernon and Frances even on his deathbed by ensuring that her relatives would have no stake in the estate. He left the £500 as allowed to Charles, who was also made executor and was reminded that all the debts in the schedule should be paid. And finally he left 'to my trusty good servant Elizabeth, wife of John Peirse my coachman £50' desiring she would buy an annuity with it.

Algernon and Charles

No letters survive from October 1711 until the summer of 1712 when Algernon was at Mannington, apparently resting his leg.

7th July 1712 Sir Algernon Potts to Robert Britiffe from Mannington:

Sir, I depend on you for a bill to Mr Marcon of sixty-five or seventy pounds which I beg you'll return him this night for the interest due to Mr Harrison. I could get no bill under 14 days after date so must be content to pay the longer interest above unless you can help me in such an exigence. If you can I beg you you'll let Mr Cook know it by this messenger. He depends on you already I find for the £170 you mentioned but I told him he could have but one £100 for I had bespoke the rest. I am taking physic for my leg or would have waited on you this day myself.

John Marcon esq of Norwich was the son of the John Marcon merchant of Norwich who was owed £200 in the 1710 schedule. The sum had arisen from the assignment in 1702 of a small Potts mortgage from Richard Robins of Itteringham to John Marcon the elder, secured on 140 acres of Mannington estate fields in Wolterton and Itteringham.[28] The original £200 had been loaned by Anne Hunt the great-niece of Sir John Potts senior in December 1668; she had married Nathaniel Palgrave clerk of Letheringsett the same year and in 1691 Susan Fiske, widow, had taken it over. She in turn had assigned the mortgage in 1699 to Robins. The mortgage appeared still to exist in 1733, with John Marcon junior's widow Rebecca Marcon involved in an assignment. Presumably no-one had ever pressed for repayment of such a relatively small sum. Like Algernon, the Marcons lived in the Cathedral Close in Norwich. John senior had died in May 1711.[29] His son married Rebecca the eldest daughter of Dr Benjamin Wrench, later Sir Benjamin, a notable Norwich citizen. John Marcon junior died without issue in 1723, leaving his wife a wealthy woman with interests in his substantial estates in Norwich, Edgefield near Mannington, Forncett St Peter, Horstead and elsewhere.[30] She subsequently married Harbord Harbord esq of Gunton. As joint executors she and her father would have taken on John Marcon's debts due and owing and indeed Sir Benjamin held a mortgage on Mannington in 1737 as we shall see. Rebecca, twice widowed, died in Aylsham in 1753.[31]

Affairs between Algernon and his brother now started to become strained. Charles had been buying some of his father's belongings from the estate. In early December 1712 Charles wrote to Britiffe regarding money owed to him by his brother. He hoped that Britiffe would pay him out of the rents of the tenants at Michaelmas as business was bad:

> … the goods that are agreed for amount to £62:3/9d the whole
> [being] £90:6/9d. I entreat you to do me the favour to press him
> up to the £62:3/9d for I really and truly want it … for I never had
> money come in so dull before and I have lately advanced a sum as to
> the parcel of old family pictures which are charged at £15. I am not
> so pressing to sell them at all but am willing they should go along
> with the rest of the pictures and furniture at Mannington provided
> my brother will give me a particular of them all together and
> security that they all shall go along with the family as he must. …

Charles was concerned his brother might not look after the heirlooms as promised to their father. Not only that but now he was seeking help from Britiffe regarding his brother's debts!

The fallout was immediate. He wrote to Britiffe on 20th December acknowledging receipt of a payment for £40 drawn on a Mr Ganning from Sir Algernon. He asked Britiffe to thank his brother as he could not bring himself to write to him:

> 'I received also from him such a chiding angry letter as I never
> received from any person in my life and for no other reason but
> because I used pressing arguments for my own and upon my word
> for no reason in the world but pure want of it. … When I have

paused a little I will answer my brother's letter as I am unwilling to do [so] in the same style and therefore will wait a little before I write.'

Charles also wanted the 'about £30' due to him from Britiffe from Mrs Knight's tenants. He seemed genuinely surprised by the vehemence of Algernon's response.

Payment of debts

Here the Britiffe letters stopped. A few more points can be made about the names on the debt schedule not so far covered. James Harrison appears to have been a relative (perhaps the son) of the John Harrison, goldsmith of St Paul's Covent Garden, who in March 1709 took over a £1,000 mortgage on two Mannington farms - Fenton's on the Saxthorpe side and Mere Farm on the Barningham side of the estate.[32] In June 1712 this mortgage was assigned to Mr Thomas Cooke esq of Norwich and remained in place until paid off by Horatio Walpole.[33]

The Isaac Jermy of Bayfield debt also related to one of Sir Roger's mortgages. As early as 1685 Jermy had provided £1,000 secured on Clippesby.[34] Mrs Alice Newman was the second wife of Thomas Newman of Baconsthorpe (who had died by 1710) and the stepmother of Charles's first wife, Elizabeth Newman. Alice was the daughter of Robert Jermy of Bayfield. Rebecca Wrench/Marcon/Harbord's sister Mary had married John Jermy of Bayfield - showing how substantially all these families were interconnected by marriage.[35]

Mrs Jecks was presumably the wife of Thomas Jecks yeoman 'then the younger' of Carleton Rode who had made a £200 personal loan to Sir Roger and Algernon Potts in 1700 and which in 1712 Sir Algernon extended to £300 as a secured loan, which he repaid in 1714.[36]

The Ives debt was another long standing small mortgage. On 16th July 1701 Sir Roger had committed to a £200 mortgage with Anne Bulwer, widow of Buxton. The property mortgaged was his messuage and 60 acres in Little Barningham then in the occupation of Edward Plane.[37] In 1706 after her death her executor assigned the mortgage to Edmond Locke gent of Norwich. In February 1708 he in turn assigned it to Thomas Ives, a grocer of Watton who appeared in the 1710 schedule. Thomas Ives may have been related to the Clement Ives who was a tenant of the Mannington estate in the late seventeenth century or even Jeremiah Ives the alderman of Norwich.[38]

Mr Roger's debt was probably a personal loan from a Norwich gentleman. He may have been of the family who held various city offices in the first half of the eighteenth century. Thomas Bond, who was only owed £40, was most likely the incumbent of Mannington, put in by Sir Roger in 1706. He resigned in 1710 so he may well have been paid off. The last creditor - Elizabeth Curtis - has not been identified. It is possible that a couple of these small debts were in fact Algernon's.

The sale of Ellingham took its time to reach completion. Eventually in September 1712 it was sold to Francis Coleman gent of Bramfield in Suffolk for £4,310.[39] The deed detailed how the money was to be shared out. £1,050 was paid to Alice Hare to pay in full her mortgage and interest. Alice Hare spinster and Ralph Hare esq of Hargham had provided £1,000 in 1697 secured on the Great Ellingham estate and Ralph had died in 1709.[40] Sarah Long received £2,200 as part of the £3,000 principal owing to her. The deed also specified that the £800 balance was to remain secured on Clippesby. Ten other mortgage or bond holders (all those on the schedule other than Messrs Marcon and Bond) each received what appears to be one year's interest of 5% on their loan. One received payment in full - rather decently they paid John Pearce the coachman his £55.

Clippesby was agreed to be sold for £3,500 to George England esq of Great Yarmouth in December 1713.[41] Roger's stepmother Dame Elizabeth, who had had an income for life since 1661, had died in July 1712 thereby removing any possible impediment to achieving a full price. The lease and release went through in early June 1714 and Algernon's absolute surrender from Clippesby manor lands a few days later.[42] At long last in April 1716 there was evidence that Sir Algernon and Frances finally sold her Calibut and Crane interests in Saham Toney. The two of them surrendered manorial lands to Thomas Wright esq of East Harling, who by July had conveyed them on in trust.[43] The mortgage sequence already referred to shows that on 12th April John Mason's executors - Frances his widow and Richard his son - assigned the mortgage to Charles Wright of Kilverstone esq who paid just over £541 principal and overdue interest on behalf of Thomas Wright of East Harling. Three days previously Thomas Wright conveyed the property in trust to John Muston gent of Watton. This deed showed that Wright had agreed with Algernon to buy from him the freehold and inheritance of the property for £800 out of which the money due to John Mason would be paid. The property then remained in Thomas Wright's family, surfacing again in the 1730 jointure arrangements for his second son Robert Wright esq of Middle Temple and his wife Catherine Wyche.[44] The £800 sale price makes clear that there had not been any significant unmortgaged value in this property in 1710.

So by mid-1716 Sir Algernon had cleared his father's and some of his own debts. In so doing all other properties had gone. He and Frances may have decided not to retain their rented Norwich house. They had Mannington, clearly seen as the prestige seat where they made their home and spent time and money on improvements. In July 1715, Sir Algernon made a jointure for life of the estate to Frances.[45] But neither of them lived to enjoy it for long. As we have seen, both died in November 1716. Dying suddenly, there was a modest amount of debt outstanding which remained unpaid for another 20 years. The final resolution was not to be reached until after the deaths of Sir Charles and Dame Mary Potts in 1732 and 1737 respectively.

Chapter 23

Sir Charles Potts: The Bubble Bursts

In November 1716 after the death of his childless brother Algernon, Charles inherited the baronetcy. Twice married, but leaving no children, Sir Charles was to be the last of the male line of the Potts family when he died in 1732. Like most of his forebears he too was no stranger to the courts, particularly as a result of his involvement in the South Sea Bubble. Contrary to popular opinion, he did not lose everything and his widow lived on in Mannington, resisting the temptation to sell to Horatio Walpole of Wolterton, until her death in 1737.

Charles Potts had been born at Great Ellingham in January 1676, the youngest of Sir Roger's four sons. He may have been named for his great-uncle Charles of whose will he was later supervisor and beneficiary. As a younger son, he did not receive a university education or study the law but became apprenticed to John Wright of the Merchant Taylors' Company. He was admitted as a freeman of the City of London on 7th February 1700 and operated as a woollen draper from premises at The Sign of the Naked Boy in Fleet Street. Once established, Charles married Elizabeth Newman, the daughter of Thomas Newman of Baconsthorpe, on 22nd June 1701 at St Luke Chelsea. Elizabeth, who may have been a childhood friend, died childless at Charles's house in Kensington on 2nd September 1706 aged just 21.[1]

Dame Mary Potts

Perhaps Charles had experienced parental criticism or meddling on his first marriage, although this seems unlikely given the past supportive role the Newman family had played as trustees. Whatever the reason, when he remarried five years later he did so in secret. On 30th June 1711 he told Robert Britiffe that the news had been leaked to his family through the determined curiosity of Jacob Preston. Charles had known his new wife, Mary Smith, for some time and his cousin James Grey approved of her. Why was Charles so concerned about the news getting out? One possibility is that Mary was from a relatively modest trade family and he may have believed his family would think he had married below his station.

An explanation for Preston's interest was hinted at in a letter of 1717 in which Charles wrote to Dr Thomas Tanner, then archdeacon of Norfolk (a friend of Algernon and well-known antiquarian), regarding a Mannington tenant and payment of tithes.[2] In a footnote he referred to Tanner's wife as his 'old acquaintance'. Tanner's second wife Frances was Jacob Preston senior's daughter.[3] His first wife, Rose the daughter of Bishop Moore of Norwich, had died in March 1708. After a few years, probably in about 1713 he had married Frances, although the exact date and place is unknown. A note in Prideaux's diaries for September

1713 recorded that 'Mrs' Frances Preston had lately married Dr Tanner and after an absence of some years living in St George Tombland had moved back into The Close. This shows that the Preston and Potts families had lived for a long time in close proximity in Norwich and fuels the possibility of an earlier relationship between Charles and Frances.[4] Perhaps she had been an old flame rather than just an acquaintance of Charles. Had Jacob Preston hoped at some point they would marry? Maybe this was why Preston junior had been so curious to discover who Charles had chosen to marry in 1711, when his own sister (then 33) was still unmarried.

Lydia, Sir Charles's mother-in-law

Who was Mary Smith, the second wife of Sir Charles Potts? Her background is somewhat mysterious. The antiquarian the Reverend James Bulwer asserted, albeit without giving a source, that her father was Thomas Smith a merchant, as did Burke's *Extinct and Dormant Peerage*.[5] Fortunately Mary's mother, Lydia, can be identified as she lived long enough to see her daughter become Lady Potts. A widow, she had moved in with them by December 1720 (when she made her will) and died at Mannington nearly ten years later. She had married again after Mary's father had died so gave her name as Lydia Norman alias Smith. She left everything to 'my loving and only child Dame Mary Potts'.[6] As this was at the height of Sir Charles's problems with the South Sea Bubble, Lydia deliberately and explicitly prevented her 'worthy son-in-law' (who was to have a ring) or his creditors from accessing the money. Her good friend the lawyer Edward Parre of Doctors Commons was to be her executor and trustee for Mary. However Lydia outlived him and Mary was granted administration of her mother's will in 1730.[7] Lydia's reference to her only child does not preclude the possibility of another child already having died. As we will see, Dame Mary had a niece, Catherine, who was her heir in law in 1737. Catherine was the wife of John Turner of Great Burstead Essex and his will of 1763 showed their eldest son as Smith Turner, very strong evidence that his wife was a Smith girl.[8] Lydia must have had a son who married and had at least one daughter but who had died before 1720.

Despite the extraordinary frequency of Thomas Smith as a name at this time, a possible identification has been made for Lydia's marriage to Thomas Smith. A marriage licence was applied for on 29th May 1669 by Thomas Smith aged about 29, bachelor of St Margaret Westminster and Lydia Underhill aged about 27, spinster of St Clement Danes Westminster. The licence allowed them to wed in either St Andrew Holborn or the Chapel of Gray's Inn.[9] As the St Andrew's register shows no such marriage, they presumably chose Gray's Inn Chapel although the register for that particular period has not survived.[10] If so, this may later have been the venue for the quiet marriage around 1710 or 1711 of Sir Charles and Dame Mary which has not yet been found elsewhere, despite a thorough search of Fleet prison marriages and a number of parishes known at the time for clandestine weddings.[11] With her mother still alive, it would have been an easy choice for Mary to want to marry there too. The Smiths may well have stayed in Westminster where there was a William

Smith baptised in St Margaret's church in March 1670 to a Thomas and Lydia.[12] He seems likely to have been Mary's brother but sadly no more of Thomas and Lydia's children appear in St Margaret's register.[13]

Lydia may have moved elsewhere and given birth to her daughter after her husband's death but no baptism for Mary has yet been discovered. Two 'Mr Thomas Smith' burial entries, in 1671 and 1673 respectively, were recorded at St Margaret's church. Was one of these two gentlemen Thomas the merchant? Perhaps they were father and son. The first was 'from London', dying elsewhere and being brought back to a family vault in the 'North Chapel'. Or were they related to Sir Thomas Smith of Hatherton Cheshire who seems to have had links to St Margaret's Westminster? Sir Thomas died in 1622 having had 22 children - plenty of scope for younger sons and descendants in trade. But he brings in the most intriguing and frustrating part of Mary Smith's story. Sir Charles Potts's tombstone at Mannington, no doubt erected by Mary herself, still lies in the ruined Mannington chapel. Various writers, including Tomes, using the antiquarian Thomas Martin's 1730s notebook as their source, commented that the gravestone included Sir Charles Potts's arms on the left and the Torbock arms based on an eagle's leg on the right for his wife.[14] The arms of the old family of Torbock of Torbock in Lancashire (often given as Tarbock or Tarbuck) descended in the main line of the family until well into the seventeenth century.[15] They were also used as the basis of the arms of Torbock alias Smith, or vice versa, by Richard Torbock alias Smith of Newcastle-under-Lyme and his descendants.[16] Published Visitation records for Lancashire and Cheshire in the seventeenth century are vague on the family's spread but it would seem that Dame Mary Potts was descended from Richard. Perhaps Sir Charles used the books on heraldry in the Mannington library to help him make the case for her entitlement to the arms. The linkage of Dame Mary back to the Smith alias Torbock family of Newcastle is now very difficult to prove. Sir Thomas Smith of Hatherton was distantly related to the Smiths of Newcastle-under-Lyme but bore very different arms from the Torbocks thus ruling out a family relationship. See Family Notes 13 for more details on both the Torbock and the Smith alias Torbock lines and for the problem of disentangling these 'wrong' Smiths of Newcastle from the Smith alias Torbock family also of Newcastle.

Lydia's own Underhill origins remain a mystery. One possible baptism, although about three years or so too early - unless she lied about her age to her first husband - was on 23rd December 1637 of 'Liddia Undrill' to Henry and Marie at Burbage, Leicestershire.[17] Lydia's second husband, Mr Norman has been tentatively identified as one combination of names does seem to fit the facts. On 15th May 1683, Harebred Norman married Lydia Smith in St Martin in the Fields.[18] The distinctive family name of Harebred is a Yorkshire speciality and a Harebred Norman was baptised on 12th April 1655 to his father Thomas Norman in Monk Fryston, Yorkshire (a few miles to the north-east of Pontefract).[19] At a guess Harebred came to London in trade of some sort and met Lydia. There had been various Normans in St Martin in the Fields but whether that was Lydia's original home, and if the Normans there were related to the Yorkshire ones, is conjecture.[20] Perhaps Harebred, so much younger than Lydia, might have been an apprentice or servant of her husband who went on to marry the widow and they continued in business together? A Thomas Underhill, Merchant Taylor, was admitted freeman of London in 1623. Could he have been an uncle of Lydia? This raises the question of whether the Merchant Taylors, Sir Charles Potts's company, was the common denominator in all this. Frustratingly, Dame Mary's exact identity must remain uncertain.

The South Sea Bubble

Tomes and others have written that 'tradition has it' that the Potts family was ruined by the South Sea Bubble. Tradition, in this case, was wrong. Sir Charles did indeed trade very heavily in South Sea Company stock, but appeared to have sold most of his holding at prices sufficient to avoid catastrophic losses. Like many others at the time, he also refused to complete some contracts. As the stock plunged in value, particularly in September 1720, he avoided paying out money committed perhaps only a few days earlier at high market prices. His will, made at the time of the collapse, specifically required his executor not to pay his South Sea contracts. It was probably this reference that caused later writers to assume bankruptcy for the family. It is now clear, from a complicated case in chancery that dogged him for several years, that although he stonewalled over a deal, it did not represent bankruptcy. When Mannington, his only major asset, was eventually sold there was plenty of equity left in the property and Sir Charles had only added a manageable amount to the family's long term mortgage and personal debts. He was neither bankrupted nor even apparently substantially impoverished by the collapse of the bubble. But the details of his involvement bring to life an episode which resonates today in the years after the 'dot.com' share price bubble of the turn of the twenty-first century and subsequent banking crises.

Sir Charles traded very actively in South Sea Company stock in the summer and autumn of 1720.[21] The surviving chancery suits were an action by Thomas Brand, Goldsmith of Lombard Street London, in 1722 against Potts and Potts's counterclaim in 1723. They contain very different views of the circumstances of certain stock trades in mid-summer 1720 at the height of the bubble. The information contained in these lengthy, detailed and combative documents allowed some analysis of the extent of Charles's trading and cumulative losses. Potts claimed to have sold all his stock by Christmas 1720 by when the South Sea share price had collapsed and shares had become more or less unsaleable. As no other chancery action against Potts was taken out, it does seem Potts had indeed sold all his stock and that the only contracts he refused to honour were the ones in the Brand case. If he had other unfulfilled contracts, imperfect paperwork probably prevented anyone from seeking redress against him. That he was adamant on this refusal to honour the Brand contracts is clear: the issue remained as a clause in his will and re-emerged after the death of Sir Charles and Dame Mary.[22]

The South Sea Bubble arose from an attempt to engineer a new approach to reducing the national debt. Much has been written about the events of 1720-21 and a brief reminder is all that is necessary here.[23] The South Sea Company was enabled to underwrite the national debt and from March 1720 intense speculation in its stock took off. The directors of the company realised that while the stock kept rising a pyramid selling scheme could make its early participants very wealthy. Those running the operation and involved in jobbing or selling stock were aware of what they were doing. Recent analysis has shown that the market in part-paid subscription shares (about 10% of the stock issued), despite the complexity of valuing such shares as options or warrants, was highly efficient and behaved much as a market in such instruments would today with all the benefits of huge computing power and a very sophisticated understanding of how stock market arbitrage works.[24]

Between April and August four tranches of subscription shares were launched and one major tranche of fully paid stock, all additional to the large number of original shares already issued. The new launches were specifically hyped up and offered at higher prices than the current market price, in an attempt to produce a renewed upward surge in prices. For the first few issues this worked. The Company also launched schemes to transfer government annuities into South Sea stock and to enable stock holders to borrow money against the security of stock registered with the Company. Incentives to buy stock came from the underlying greed of all buyers hoping for an easy gain. This was accompanied by a cynical flooding of the economy with cash to ensure people felt they had enough access to money to trade in stock. Confidence grew when shares paid a 10% stock dividend in June 1720 so investors thought they saw an immediate return on their investment. The arrangements for borrowing against stock also included warrant-like incentives for access to more stock.

The market price for stock reached a short plateau in May of £400 per single £100 nominal value share (from here on referred to as a market price of 400). By mid-June the price had surged to another mini plateau of 800 and within days, before the end of June, had briefly touched its peak of 1,100. From here it settled at about 900 for two months. The Company had to close its stock register between 22nd June and 22nd August. This meant that very little volume was transacted as nobody outside the Company could register their ownership of shares and thus receive the 10% 'mid-summer' stock dividend and be certain that their transaction would be honoured.

In the last days of August the market price started to turn down from around 900 to around 800. Many sold out at this point and made enormous fortunes from their stock. But the optimism in London was that the stock would rise again and people rumoured that they had heard it would rise to 1,200 or even 1,500. Wrong! The price fell remorselessly in the first week or so of September to about 500. During the later part of the month it settled for a while at around 300. During October and November further falls took the price down to 200 or even lower. Throughout the April to December period the stock also showed high price volatility on a daily basis within this general pattern of rise, plateau and fall.

How did Sir Charles do in all of this? The chancery papers included a detailed schedule from him of his opening holding of capital stock and all his transactions (volume only and not prices, unfortunately) from 24th June to 24th December 1720. Or at least those transactions that he was prepared, in court, to accept as legitimate. This showed that he opened with 4,750 stock plus a further 475 shares from the summer dividend. By the end of the year he was left with just 10. The following is an assessment of what this might imply for his gains and losses from share dealing. However, this must necessarily be merely a hypothesis since what mix of share types at what purchase prices made up his opening holding is unknown.

At an average market price of about 900 at the end of June, Sir Charles's 5,225 shares were worth about £47,000 if he could have sold them all at that price. It must have been an anxious two months waiting for the register to re-open in the hope of starting to realise a gain. (To put the sum in context, at an inflated multiple of its underlying rental stream, the Mannington estate sold for £20,000 in 1737.) There is no sign that Sir Charles was particularly wealthy from his merchanting activities and he held no other significant assets. He stood to make a huge gain from a successful sale, but he was speculating heavily and dangerously.

What had his stock cost him? A few trades were described in the chancery papers which, with a few sensible assumptions, can offer a rough estimate. He bought parcels in early to mid-May when market prices were at 400 or a little less and that was probably when he started trading. There is nothing in the chancery materials to indicate that he held any part-paid subscription shares at this time (the two big issues were in April). He borrowed £2,800 from the Company against 700 shares, which he probably re-invested at about 400 or just under. He also bought parcels of stock at 765 and probably 905 to 1,000.

During this time, as he later admitted in court, he had mortgaged his estate for £2,400 to underwrite his trading. But most of the trading would have been done on promissory notes rather than cash payments. The action against him by Thomas Brand was about that very point. Brand said that in August Potts had a 'very good opinion of the rising condition of the stock' and that he had had good information that it would far exceed the then price of 900. Brand advised against a purchase since the price was already well above the real value of the stock but was convinced by Potts to buy 500 shares, half for each of them. He did so, he said, on 13th August from a Mr Tutt at 905, that day's market price. The stock was to be transferred into Potts's name on 22nd August, the next available transfer day (when the register re-opened). Brand was 'ready at the books' at the South Sea Company that day, but he said Potts failed to turn up at the books to receive the transfer of stock. However, no promissory note was written between them until Brand requested one on or around the 7th September when the stock transfer between them apparently took place. He said the note recorded a commitment by Potts to pay a price of 905 for 250 of stock.

In due course, Sir Charles refused to accept the resulting debt of £2,262 as an honest transaction and in particular claimed that Brand had withheld the stock from him until well into September. The note therefore according to Potts, from its date, was a different forward contract to buy that was unfulfilled and also at a price that was way above the prevailing proper market price for that stage in September. It had not been registered under the provisions of the act of parliament in 1721 and therefore was void. He argued that if it had related to an earlier transaction that too would have been void under these later rules since more than six days had elapsed between purchase and receipt of stock. Since the date and market price seemed at odds, he challenged Brand to prove what stock he had bought from whom on what day at what price.

The best estimate is that Potts had paid an average price of between 650 and 750 for his total holding. At the lower level he sat on a potential gain of £16,000 and at 750 a gain of about £11,000. In these estimates of his gains and losses, a conservative estimate of 750 has been used which may slightly overstate both his potential total gain and his possible cumulative loss by the end of the year.

With the re-opening of the registers the price began to fall and, despite the optimism of men like Sir Charles, it never bounced back. He must have still been hopeful, since he made purchases of nearly 1,900 shares in late August. But even so, by the end of the month, he had become a net seller of stock and his holding was down to 4,065 shares including bonus shares (which were fully tradable). From the pattern of his daily transactions and market price movements we estimate that by the end of the month he held shares worth just over £31,000 and profit-taking had probably allowed him to reduce his exposure to about £14,000. In other words, if the market had collapsed to nil at that point and he never sold another share, his cumulative losses would have been about £14,000. He would have been forced to mortgage Mannington to the hilt to avoid bankruptcy at that level of indebtedness. Sir Charles was not one of the most astute investors in the bubble. He did not sell out at the peak and stay out of the market as some did. He could not resist buying again in mid-September, despite the further significant price falls. It appears his maximum exposure to cumulative loss rose again to more than £16,000 (putting the whole value of his estate on the line). But by October he became a more determined seller, when the totally optimistic retained all or much of their share holding in the vain hope of a price rise. As a result Sir Charles reduced his cumulative exposure to under £9,000 by mid-October and by selling virtually all his stock by the end of the year it seems likely that he ended up with a loss of about £5,000 overall.

This might have been reduced yet further had he managed effectively the gain to be made on bonus shares bought during the summer (assuming he had acquired the first 475 bonus shares at nil consideration and sold them at full market price). Ignoring his bargains that included obvious summer dividend shares where buying and selling volume was matched within a day or so, there were some trades where he appeared to acquire parcels of 10% dividend stock which were probably still being bought at the market price times the net, not the gross, number of shares. He would then have sold them later at full value. If so, he may have reduced his indebtedness by a further £1,000 or so.

The table opposite shows Sir Charles's trades in 1720 in South Sea capital stock (each of £100 nominal value), with his opening balance on 24th June of 5,225 including 475 bonus shares.

	Purchases	Sales	Net holding
22nd Aug	550	550	5,225
26th Aug	550	330	5,445
26th Aug		1,100	4,345
26th Aug		100	4,245
26th Aug		100	4,145
29th Aug	110	300	3,955
29th Aug	50	30	3,975
29th Aug	110	10	4,075
29th Aug		10	4,065
29th Aug		550	3,515
31st Aug	550		4,065
14th Sep	330		4,395
19th Sep	100		4,495
21st Sep		100	4,395
21st Sep		100	4,295
21st Sep		160	4,135
21st Sep		50	4,085
21st Sep		100	3,985
21st Sep		50	3,935
23st Sep		25	3,910
26th Sep		25	3,885
30th Sep		1,000	2,885
30th Sep		815	2,070
14th Oct		160	1,910
14th Oct		500	1,410
17th Oct		1,000	410
9th Nov		200	210
9th Dec		200	10
Unsold 24th December		10	
Total	7,575	7,575	

Sir Charles Potts's South Sea trades in 1720

Interestingly the estimated loss of £5,000 roughly coincides with a statement he made to chancery that his dealings with Brand alone had netted him a loss of £4,999 or more. It is doubtful that Brand was his only intermediary for all his dealings but as an indication of the fact that he had made a net loss (the sympathy line of defence) and as an approximation of the extent of his losses it may well be about right.

Would he have actually paid out such a sum? He defended the case resolutely against Brand and seems to have avoided paying up. Several chancery decrees were made during the protracted proceedings.[25] Sir Charles argued that the promissory note was a concoction and, since ultimately Brand could not produce evidence of whom he had bought the shares from and at what precise price, there was nothing to say what sum should be paid to Brand, even if a genuine transaction had taken place. The last court order for Brand to produce documents was in December 1725.[26] No further decrees have been found and it seems Potts won by default, but the action technically may have remained open until one or other of them died. Brand seems to have been involved in many suits; with so much interlocking paperwork, he may well have been unable to disentangle his affairs and prove fair dealing. At worst, he may indeed have tried to con Sir Charles into paying an arguably unfair price for stock that was from his own holding and not bought at the market price of the time.

In his chancery submissions Potts cited the act of parliament providing for registering disputed South Sea trades by 1st November 1721. He said that Brand had not used this option for the contract at issue between them (and indeed two other trades between them for a total of 1,000 shares made at or near peak prices) and so he did not have to recognise any of these trades as legitimate. In particular the act provided that for trades before 29th September 1721, where the recipient had not received the actual stock within 6 days, the contract would be deemed void. Potts asserted that a significant part of his trading with Brand fell into this category, as Brand had withheld the stock from May trades until late August and the alleged August transaction until September.

Potts may well have used this option to mitigate any losses on trades with other parties. He would not have been vulnerable to it being used by others against him if he had registered his own sales and passed on certificates at the right time in the autumn of 1720. It seems likely that Sir Charles was smart enough, as a merchant by background, to deal correctly with the paperwork to minimise personal risk. It may even be that it was only through this sharpness that he avoided very substantial losses. At this time, there was bubble-like speculation in a number of other companies and Potts may also have gambled in some of these shares too. The key was to get out of the stock before the price collapsed completely and the stock became unsaleable and, even if belatedly, the pattern of his trades showed he realised that.[27]

In the end, Sir Charles found legal (even if to a modern eye not wholly ethical) means to wriggle out of his loan from the Company and from various specific trades committed to with Brand and probably others at or near the peak of the market. Nobody else seems to have pursued him in the courts. Anyone who had been slow to convey stock before the forced halt to registration during the summer would have been open to later refusal to pay by purchasers. In the rough and tumble of trading during the price collapse many more would have failed to ensure the paperwork was meticulously kept. Many would not have realised the importance of registering disputed trades by the deadline, relying as Brand did on having a promissory note in hand. In 1721 the pursuit of instalment payments on the subscription shares was formally halted, so if Potts held any of these 'contracts' he would probably have emerged without significant losses on them. He probably lost of the order of £4,000 to £5,000 and he and Dame Mary may have had to tighten their belts for a few years while they paid back debts using Mannington's rental income stream and, possibly, timber sales. This was neither bankruptcy nor severe impoverishment. The spectre of being forced to pay some or all of these contracts may have hung heavily over him, but as time passed it would have become clear that he had escaped more lightly than some.

Sir Charles at Mannington

Sometime after 1716 and before 1720 Sir Charles, Dame Mary and her mother moved from London to live in Mannington. By 1720 he was a justice of the peace for Norfolk.[28] The estate still had various mortgages on it but in 1720 he made a settlement of Mannington on Dame Mary his wife for her life after his death.[29] A mirror image of his brother's earlier arrangement for Frances, it was drafted in the same style and with the same recitals. At the same time Charles made his will which is a *tour de force* of recitals of past family affairs and deeds.[30] Apart from leaving Mary the estate and residue as his heir, he made bequests of £500 each to four people. Three of them were London friends who had been major mortgage and unsecured lenders to Sir Charles - Robert Bull woollen draper of Fleet Street, Edward Parre gent of Doctors Commons and Thomas Vaughan gent of Inner Temple.[31] Indeed Robert Bull was a trustee in the will of Charles's first wife Elizabeth in 1706.[32] Quite probably one or all of these three had provided finance to him during the South Sea Bubble and the legacies may well have been made at the time as thank you statements. We do not know if he had any unresolved contracts involving them directly, but the sums at £500 might well have been loans for parcels of stock as this was a commonly used transaction size. Indeed he might well have promised to repay his friends via his will to defer payment and avoid law suits from them.

He also left £500 to Catherine, Dame Mary's niece. Perhaps he had also borrowed from Catherine's husband John Turner. Immediately after these significant sums came the final bequest of a derisory £5 apiece to his sister Susan Long and her husband and children for mourning. The Longs had not received anything in Sir Roger's, Sir Algernon's or Sir Charles's wills. At the rational level one can say that was because there had been a £3,000 marriage settlement to Susan and Matthew. But at the emotional level it is hard not to believe that the small bequests by Sir Charles, particularly contrasted with the generous sum to Dame Mary's niece, were meant as a deliberate snub.

Walpole's arrival and Sir Charles's death

Although Sir Charles and Dame Mary had retained a place in London, they seemed to have lived at Mannington for much of their time. When the Hall was sold after both had died, they left extensive furnishings, books, musical instruments and household goods. Despite their active use of the house, they found themselves under constant pressure to sell to a land-hungry neighbour. Horatio Walpole had purchased the old Scamler estate of Wolterton in December 1722 and was busy building his fine house there.[33] Keen to enlarge his property, Walpole kept up a long-running campaign to buy Mannington from Sir Charles and after his death from Dame Mary.

One cluster of letters in the Wolterton archive dates from just before Sir Charles's death until two years or so after it. How long before 1731 Walpole had been trying is not clear but he may have wanted Mannington from the very beginning. The letters also show that Sir Charles had fallen out completely with the long-standing family attorney Robert Britiffe as well as with all his surviving relations - the Long family.[34] The most revealing perhaps were those from Thomas Cooke of Norwich, who had a mortgage outstanding on Mannington and clearly was trusted by Sir Charles and Lady Potts as well as Walpole. Two letters were from J Bennett of Aylsham who, from the educated hand and wording, was probably a local lawyer.

The first letter, from Thomas Bayfield, Walpole's estate steward, indicated that Sir Charles had been thinking of selling Mannington if the price was right. There was no hint that he was upset at Bayfield doing a valuation and suggesting a price.

> Antingham 3rd October 1731 Thomas Bayfield to Horatio Walpole:

> ... I have been with Sir Charles Potts and have taken a view of his estate and have given him my judgement of the value of every estate as near as I could both by view and the best information I could get of the former tenants; but find he thinks and say that I under value his estate very much and talk in that wild manner that he did to Your Honour when at Wolterton and that he can let it for a good deal more. I will by the next post give Your Honour a particular of every estate as I have stated them but had not time without losing this post. ...

Walpole seemed to let the matter rest for a few months, a delay that proved to be too late.

> Antingham 16th January 1732 Bayfield to Walpole:

> ... I never see Sir Charles Potts since I took the survey of his estate nor never shall see him again. I received Your Honour's on Thursday and he died on Friday morning about four o'clock. He was at Mr Paston on Thursday night as they say and very merry and come

home and went to bed very well and was taken ill about 3 in the morning and died within an hour with stopidges, which they say he was very much troubled with. Tis said that he had a will by him and have given all that he can to his Lady, the estate and all as persons say; which I am apt to believe for he said to me that he had never a relation but what had disobliged him and he would as soon give it to me as them. ...

Mr Paston was presumably his neighbour Edward Paston of Barningham Hall. Sir Charles probably died from a final stroke or heart attack. He was only 56. Bayfield's letter also confirms that Sir Charles was not well-disposed to his Long family relations. His small bequest to them in his will seems to have been deliberate; that it was taken by all as an insult was confirmed from another few fragments of correspondence in the papers of the Long family of Dunston.[35]

On 15th January 1732 Edward Howman, a doctor in Norwich who was related to the Longs, wrote to Mrs Susan Long now at Sampson's Hall, Kersey, Suffolk. The essence of the letter was to tell her that her brother 'Sir Charles Potts died yesterday morning very suddenly of an apoplectic fit', dying in his chair at Mannington after getting up. He echoed that Charles had been at the Pastons, but had a slightly different version of the timings:

> it seems he had been a day or two before at an entertainment at Mr Paston's and drank pretty plentifully tho' I don't hear to excess. He arose very well yesterday morning and died in his chair. As to other particulars, how he has left affairs I can hear nothing.

Howman's father Roger, also a wealthy doctor, had been a trustee for the Long family - in particular in Susan's own 1702 marriage settlement - and his executors had featured as a small creditor on the 1710 schedule of debts. Quite possibly Edward was doctor to the Long family as he or one of his brothers clearly had been to Sir Roger. However he seemed not to know of Sir Charles having some sort of heart condition prior to this final attack.[36]

Edward's closeness to the Long family was shown by his direct language in his next letter of 21st January. He related that Sir Charles had 'settled everything in the strongest manner' on her ladyship and had only left the Longs £5 apiece for mourning. He reported that her ladyship said she had no relations left in the world and 'insinuates that civil treatment may produce a suitable return [implying a past lack of civility] ... Mr Long [Susan's son Israel] will send compliments of condolence'. Howman urged Susan to do the same adding 'her dear ladyship seems to expect compliments of condolence'. Apparently the funeral was to be on the following Sunday or Tuesday and escutcheons were to be made in town 'and a hearse and coaches hired of Mr Bateman, but these last have been countermanded'. Howman also suggested that Susan should look at Sir Roger's will and the settlement made upon Sir Algernon. She should apply to Mr Britiffe as to how Sir Charles, as merely a tenant for life, could give the estate away to his wife. Obviously anxious to help he added a postscript saying he had already spoken to Britiffe who promised to look into the terms of the old settlement.

The affairs of any substantial family were publicly talked about and no doubt Norwich was abuzz with gossip about the will and its perceived family slight. Britiffe wrote to Susan on 29th January to say he had written to Lady Potts 'in favour of your family' but had yet to look at the settlement papers. Meanwhile Israel had written to his mother on 16th January, having been acquainted of Charles's death by his uncle Carter, with all the same information about Sir Charles's death and his will. His version agreed with Bayfield's as to timing - out on Thursday night and dead Friday morning. He was unable to tell his mother anything about the will and financial matters, being an 'utter stranger to the affairs of the family, as you very well know'. In another undated letter he said that Lady Potts 'felt kindly' towards Susan as her only relative - transparently not the whole truth.

At that time the Long family camp fell silent. No doubt they discovered that Sir Roger's will had made Charles the residuary heir in the event of no male issue from Algernon and that Charles was perfectly within his rights to leave everything to his wife. The ungenerous manner of the £5 token bequests suggests he still harboured a grudge against his sister and the Long family, either for the original writ against Sir Roger or perhaps for their treatment of his wife. He had certainly died with an action against his sister in chancery unfinished. The Longs may have been hoping that by being 'civil' to Mary she might drop the case.

Did the rest of the world note Sir Charles's passing? A month after he died, a one-line entry in the *Gentleman's Magazine* recorded his death but his name and seat were misspelt: 'Sir Charles Pott [sic] of Maningham [sic] in Norfolk Bt'.[37]

Negotiations to buy Mannington

Walpole did not let the grass grow under his feet and pushed for Dame Mary's response to his offer to buy Mannington. In an undated part of a letter, J Bennett of Aylsham wrote to Horatio:

> Sir Charles was interred but on Monday so [I] can't as yet hear whether her Ladyship (to whom it seems he has devised the fee of the whole estate) is inclined to sell at present or not. One Feazer a tenant in Plumpstead Hall is concerned in the letting and setting the farms for her. But I'm informed that Mr Jacob Preston of Beeston is the person who gave the directions about the funeral and by whose advice her Ladyship proceeds in her affairs. The estate, if to be sold, is certainly a fine tract of land lying entire with a good quantity of fine young timber, though when Sir Algernon died there was a good deal of timber of full growth. As soon as I can inform myself more particularly [I] shall disclose the same to you, as I am
>
> Your most humble servant, J Bennett

The Prestons of Beeston St Lawrence had been involved over a long period as occasional Potts family trustees, in particular in the 1710 family settlement. The older Jacob Preston JP had died in 1683 aged 70 and being a near contemporary of Sir John Potts junior (1618-1677) he may well have been a friend. Of his children, Sir Isaac was a barrister and Jacob junior, referred to here, was born in 1674 and died in 1753. Despite his indiscretion at the start of their marriage, he clearly had become a close friend of Sir Charles and Dame Mary, and may have seen himself as their financial adviser. The reference to fine young timber supports the view that Charles may have cut a quantity of trees to pay some of his debts.

Thomas Cooke may well have been another local adviser for Potts on financial matters and from his ability to see Lady Potts so soon after Sir Charles's death, he must also have been a friend. His letters were so beautifully written and with such a delightful turn of phrase they have been quoted here in full.

Norwich 22nd January 1732 Thomas Cooke to Horatio Walpole:

Sir, I had the honour of your letter last post and I shall proceed in the manner you are pleased to prescribe me. There are various reports as to the disposal that Sir Charles Potts has made of his estate but I can give credit to none of them. I verily believe from some passages in the conversation I have had formerly with Sir Charles (too long to mention here) that he has given all he could to My Lady. But as I am not absolutely certain of this I think it will be the best way for me to wait upon My Lady in a little time when I imagine she will in some measure be recovered from the surprise that the sudden death of Sir Charles must have given her and then I shall inform myself from her own mouth of all the particulars you mention. And as soon as I have made this visit I shall give you a full account of everything. I have the better pretence to go over to Mannington as part of the estate is mortgaged to me and there is now near to two years' interest due to me upon that mortgage.

I can only repeat what I have said and which you Sir may depend upon that if on this occasion I can be serviceable to you I shall be ready to do it in the most effectual manner I am able. You will do me that right as to be persuaded of this trouble and of my being always

Your most obedient and humble servant

Aylsham 31st January 1732 J Bennett to The Honourable John Fowle esq at the Excise Office London (one of Walpole's men):

Sir, since my last [I] have made it my business to know if Mannington is to be sold or not and my information produces a negative. I've asked Mr Preston himself, his answer is that Her Ladyship has no occasion to part from it, that the whole is given to her, and that he knows she'll not dispose thereof. If ought otherwise occurs the same shall be communicated to you by your ever humble servant

Thomas Cooke's second letter seemed also to refer to Jacob Preston.

Norwich 23rd February 1732 Cooke to Walpole:

... It fell out a little unluckily that as I went over very early last Thursday to Mannington (before the post came here) I did not receive your letter till after my return from thence late in the evening which indeed I wish had come to my hands before I made this second visit. There is lately at My Lady's desire a gentlewoman come from London, a relation or friend of hers, and they have already I believe agreed to go to town in about a month or six weeks time. And till then I dare say My Lady will come to no determination as to what she is to do about the estate, tho' she now talks of various things she can do as cutting down a good quantity of timber or selling part of [the] estate which lies at the greatest distance and keeping the house and the best part of the rest that lies about it. But these seem to be loose and sudden thoughts without any certain resolution or foundation. My own opinion is that as she has had and is like to have so much trouble with the tenants, and as some of the farms are now fallen and more will soon fall into her own hands, she will be in a little time tired out with the vexations and expense of her country affairs which I believe will be a strong inducement for her to part with the whole estate and a good round sum of money paid down and a considerable annuity for her for her life (which last she seems fond of) will also be prevailing reasons with her to do it. And upon these terms I am persuaded she will, and perhaps in long time neither, be not only willing but even glad to dispose of it.

The gentleman you point at in your letters is the same who told My Lady that some persons who proposed to Sir Charles to buy his estate did it at your desire and request. This same gent I know was much acquainted with Sir Charles but if I knew anything of Sir Charles' mind he had no such great influence over him nor perhaps with her neither. She without doubt is well-pleased to hear him magnify the estate beyond its true value. The person without all doubt that My Lady will be chiefly guided by in the conduct of her affairs is her lawyer at London who I know lives in the Temple but his name I have forgot. Yet if you desire to know it [I] can inform myself and of the very place where he lives in such manner that nobody shall know I do it at your command or upon your account.

Sir Charles told me formerly that several of the neighbouring gentlemen had proposed to him to buy his estate and he named Lord Harbord, Mr Harbord, Mr Warner and Mr Britiffe; but I imagine Sir Charles did not believe they did this by your direction because I have heard him say more than once he was informed that Mr Britiffe had a mind to purchase this estate for one of My Lord Hobart's sons I think it was the youngest who as he was his grandson was also his godson and bore his name. When I say Mr Britiffe had offered to buy this estate I should tell you it was only what had been spoken of when Sir Charles and he met together accidentally in visiting; for all correspondence had been at an end between them for some years past, Sir Charles having had the greatest animosity imaginable against Mr Britiffe on account of some ill treatment he said he had received at his hand and which Sir Charles made no scruple to speak of on all occasions with the utmost resentment. So that in my opinion Sir Charles would never have treated with Mr Britiffe about the sale of his estate upon any terms whatsoever, but notwithstanding this Mr Britiffe has I know sent My Lady since Sir Charles' death a letter of condolence with offers of his service which was a compliment I believe she did not expect from him for the reasons before mentioned. If this letter was only as a bare compliment I am not able to say, for My Lady only told me of it but did not show it me. But unless Mr Britiffe in that letter said anything to her about purchasing the estate I'd adventure to assert that nobody else has hitherto done it, for My Lady has often repeated it that she had not admitted of any visits but from myself and that gentleman you mention in your last to me who was at the funeral and stayed that night at Mannington and has been again to wait upon My Lady as I understand since the visit I so lately made her.

I have now Sir wrote at large in several particulars because I thought it possible that some of these hints might be of use to you in your pursuit of this affair and if it should so prove I have my end and aim which was to contribute whatever small assistance I was able to afford towards bringing about anything that you desired to have done or that might add to your content and satisfaction. Be pleased to believe that I am ever with a constant inviolable attachment and respect

Your most obedient and humble servant

PS Mr Britiffe I am told sets out for London tomorrow morning. I presume you will not think it proper to acquaint him with anything here written and the rather when I tell you I have had no acquaintance nor business with him now for above two years past

Perhaps the lady from London was Dame Mary's niece Catherine Turner. The identity of her London lawyer is not known. The gentleman who visited Lady Potts may have been Preston, or Lawrence Charters of whom more shortly. It is interesting to see that Potts and Cooke had fallen out or at least stopped dealing with Britiffe.

Britiffe, Dame Mary and Walpole's court actions

Sir Charles's issue with Robert Britiffe dated from an action Charles brought against his sister Susan Long, the family trustees Thornhaugh Gurdon, Jacob Preston and their lawyer Britiffe, over the money in a side deal to the 1710 settlement. Although the papers of the time do not survive, Dame Mary was allowed to continue the actions in 1732.[38] Apart from brief entries in the decrees, all that has survived of this is Britiffe's answer of June 1733 to the bill of complaint of Dame Mary Potts and John Turner and Catherine his wife. His rather guarded answer was grounded in the family settlement of 1710 in which arrangement alone he and Clement Hyrne (now dead) were executors for the trustees Gurdon and Preston and the Potts family.

Britiffe said that he was not sure that he had been involved in the other document cited in the bill. Indeed he rather thought he had not. His short and rather cryptic reply referred to an alleged arrangement whereby Algernon and Charles agreed that Algernon's considerable debts to Charles would be addressed by allowing Charles in future to will £1,000 in return for immediately paying £600 of Algernon's other debts. Apparently this agreement was made in a document of June 1714. The bill of complaint must have said that this sum was to be raised by Hyrne and Britiffe as trustees although Britiffe seemed to be denying that he had any involvement in the deal. It was not, he said, part of the 1710 settlement and so he had no obligation to find the money to honour it. However, Britiffe's answer is hard to interpret without seeing the complaint. He also said that the £1,000 was regarding a legacy or grant in a private side deal (again, not in the formal 1710 settlement, albeit possibly made at the same time) from Roger to Algernon. This would fit perfectly with the repeated mention in the letters of Roger and Algernon negotiating over £1,000 apparently related to Algernon's interest in Ellingham. Britiffe described this side deal as an agreement that if Algernon had a daughter he should receive £1,000 for her portion. But if he did not, the money and interest at 5% would come to Algernon himself. With no child, Algernon would have believed the deal would deliver him the money. Britiffe said Algernon assigned this bequest or grant to Charles. Again, it was not part of the formal 1710 settlement and so Britiffe had no liability in the matter. While the details are not wholly clear it is evident that Charles thought he was due £1,000 (probably plus interest) which Britiffe, as family executor, had refused to pay and which Algernon certainly did not have when he died. This would have been sufficient to cause the falling out. Prompted by his will, Dame Mary, after Charles's death, had one more try at getting money from Britiffe. It is doubtful if she succeeded.

Horatio Walpole himself had also had a run-in with Britiffe during a lengthy series of chancery actions relating to Walpole's purchase from the Spelman family of all their estates including the manors and houses in Wickmere, Calthorpe and Wolterton. Only the answer, probably in the winter of 1728-29, of Robert Britiffe esq of Norwich, one of the defendants in a bill of complaint by the Honourable Horatio Walpole, survived.[39] Britiffe, acting as the Walpole family lawyer, confirmed that articles had been made on 7th July 1724 between Edward Spelman alias Yallop esq (also a defendant in this bill) and himself (for and on behalf of Walpole) as set out in the bill. Britiffe had heard that on 31st October 1724 Spelman had taken a mortgage for £5,373, advanced by Walpole, until an absolute purchase of the premises could be completed. The money was Walpole's and Britiffe's name had only been used in trust and he had been indemnified, saved harmless and paid his costs. He denied any unlawful combination and said he had nothing else to answer to. Spelman had enormous debts and was entangled with the Naish family. The £5,373 cash advance was used to pay off some of the Naish indebtedness, but then Spelman struggled with the Naish family to get an account of what more he owed them. The sale to Walpole became mired in all this and, no doubt, Walpole blamed Britiffe in part for allowing him to become so embroiled and exposed.[40] Sorting out the problems took many years before Walpole finally got the estates. Cooke would have understood why Walpole was very wary of Britiffe's potential involvement in the Mannington situation.

The next letter in the negotiations introduced one Captain Charters.

Antingham 28th September 1732 Thomas Bayfield to Walpole:

I received Your Honour's with order to pay Captain Charters what money he had occasion for. I had let him have five guineas before ... and five guineas since ... and I took his note for the whole and he would not take any more. ...

A small bundle of letters from Mary Walpole writing from their London home in Whitehall to her husband Horatio, while he was away in the Low Countries in 1734, have three main themes running through them.[41] Mary was very upset at Horatio's absence and missed him keenly, as did their children. She was clearly much involved in mobilising support for him at the imminent election, particularly since he was not going to be able to be back in the country to campaign for himself. Also, almost all the letters carried some reference to Lady Potts and most of these mentioned 'Charters' in the same context. It would seem that Horatio's campaign to persuade Dame Mary Potts to sell Mannington to him continued.

Cockpit 16th April 1734:

My Dearest Dear,

...[PS] I have not heard nor seen Charters since you went. I intend to go and see Lady Potts toward the end of this week when the bustle is a little over in the City; for the mob made sad work last Thursday and My Lord Mayor narrowly escaped with his life as is said, though I believe they talk more than it really was.

Charters was (Captain) Lawrence Charters esq of St Margaret Middlesex and Gentleman of the Horse to the Right Honourable Horatio Walpole, Coffer to His Majesty's Household.[42] With no wife or children of his own, he made significant bequests to Horatio and his children when he made his will in September 1732. His personal items such as a snuff box given him by the Prince of Ansbach, a watch, swords, pistols and spurs were all of or decorated with silver, gold and diamonds - an image of a former military man of conspicuous display. It is also clear that he had a room of his own in Wolterton Hall with his own furniture, plate and tea service in it. He must be taken to be a friend of and fixer for Horatio rather than merely a servant. Charters had obviously become a very close friend of Lady Potts and, in Walpole's mind, perhaps able to influence her to sell Mannington. A bit of a charmer perhaps although the charm was not directed at Mary Walpole, nor did it work on her as her next letters revealed:

> Cockpit 23rd April 1734:
>
> ... I forgot to tell you in my last [19th April] that I had been to see Lady Potts and found her at home. I stayed and drank tea with her but nothing passed but in the common way. She never mentioned a word of Charters and I have heard nothing of him since you went. ... I have no dislike to have them to dinner any more than I think it something out of the way to ask a man that has taken no notice of me at all since I have been alone. ...
>
> Cockpit 3rd May 1734:
>
> ... Lady Potts is just gone and for my part I don't understand her. She talk much of Mr Cook's inviting her to the elections at Norwich but she says she shan't go till they are over; and the talk of clothes [she] said she should never wear nothing but black or grey except she alters her condition. She has sold her chambers at the Temple, as she says, for I hardly think there is a word of truth in anything she says. As for Charters I never seen him since you left England. I hear he goes to the elections by those that have met him. ...

Reading between the lines, one might interpret the reference to Lady Potts and her mourning black as implying that a marriage to Charters was deemed a possibility which would change her condition. The previous letter certainly implied they might be invited together to dine at the Walpoles. When Mary Walpole wrote again on 14th May she referred to sending a letter to Charters (clearly in London) and getting a message back saying that he would be going to Norwich for the election. Again she said she had not seen him since Horatio left and considered him 'a very unaccountable man as ever I heard of in my life'. And in a PS she wrote: 'I have been this afternoon to see Lady Potts who says she goes out of town a Friday sevennight. She is to dine with me next Friday'. However she found her prey hard to pin down.

Cockpit 21st May 1734:

> ... I was to see Lady Potts this afternoon but she was not at [home];
> her man said that she goes out of town tomorrow. As to Charters,
> I received yesterday by the post a letter directed for him which I
> found by the outside came from Norwich. I sent it to his lodgings to
> know if he was in town. They said that he went to the election but
> they expected him in two or three days. I think there is nothing to
> be depended upon in either of these two people. ...

Charters remains a rather elusive character - just as Mary Walpole found him. The implication in the letters is that he had the ability to influence Lady Potts. From the references to him going to Norwich for the election, it might seem that he was a Norwich or Norfolk property owner going there to vote, but he does not appear in the 1734 and 1735 voter lists. Perhaps more likely he went to Norwich to drum up support for Walpole and his sole residence in Norfolk was his room at Wolterton Hall. He died the following year in the autumn of 1735. There is no indication that Dame Mary ever 'changed her condition'.

Death of Dame Mary

Dame Mary Potts outlived Sir Charles by just a few years, dying at Mannington in February 1737. Despite being a substantial property holder she died intestate: the deeds relating to the sale of the Mannington estate to Horatio Walpole esq in April 1737 show that she had made no provision for the disposal of her estate.[43] The estate was sold by Sir Charles Potts's 'heir at law' Israel Long of Dunston esq and Dame Mary's 'heir at law' and niece Catherine, the wife of John Turner of Great Burstead Essex.

Walpole moved quickly. By 25th February a signed agreement was reached to sell him the Mannington estate for £20,000 (£20,029 by the time a little interest had been added). Particulars showing the rent, by farm, have survived from 1710 and 1737 (see Chapter 22).[44] Both show similar annual income totals: £787-800 if the hall and its gardens were included and £720-760 if not. Notes enclosed with the deeds of 1737 show the estimated annual rental stream, after taxes, of £492. Even allowing for taxes and no rent for the Hall and park, this looks somewhat low although it may reflect the difficulties of finding tenants alluded to in Cooke's February 1732 letter. Whatever the precise annual rental stream, Walpole paid a remarkably high multiple, showing how keen he was to get this estate, contiguous with his Wolterton lands. Perhaps the sum indicated that he believed the properties and rents could be improved, but later tenants' accounts showed that he did not get much above £750 gross for many years. The agreement to sell was confirmed in chancery on 3rd of March. This action confirmed the intention to pay and discharge the debts of Sir Algernon Potts and the mortgages on the estate. No doubt the main reason for the chancery action was to provide Walpole with some measure of protection for undiscovered Potts debts that might later emerge and apparently be chargeable against the estate.

Susan's daughter Mary Long by now was Algernon's administratrix and was to receive £900 from the sale to pay her uncle Algernon's non-mortgage debts. Perhaps she was behind the advertisement in *The Norwich Mercury* of Saturday 19th March 1737:

> The unsatisfied creditors of Sir Algernon Potts, late of Mannington, Bart are desired to bring in an account of their several demands to Mr Palmer, at Mr Riches's house at Little Barningham near Aylsham, in order to their being paid off.[45]

This might be interpreted as a worthy attempt by her, 20 years after his death, to find any remaining smaller local creditors rather than the bigger and well-known ones in Norwich. However, the use of the house of a tenant of Walpole perhaps indicates that it was him again trying to ensure no local debts still survived that he might later feel obliged to pay.

In a letter surviving with the deeds Mary Long wrote to Walpole on 17th April from Sampson's Hall, Kersey, Suffolk:

> My sisters and I have executed the conveyance of Mannington Estate to your Excellence and I have signed the receipt on the back of the deed for the sum of £900 made payable to me, which money I desire your excellence will please to pay to my brother Long to be applied by him towards the discharge of the unsatisfied debts of our Uncle Sir Algernon Potts.

The letter itself was receipted on the reverse by Israel Long on the 20th April: 'received £900 from Horatio Walpole'.[46]

Catherine and John Turner were to receive £460 and then the residue was to be split equally in two between them and Israel Long. Of this £460, £210 was to pay off the old Robins/Marcon mortgage. From notes in Walpole's own hand with the deeds it seems likely that the other £250 was money that Algernon owed the Turners themselves but which was not included in the £900 of debts. The Turners were to indemnify Long against the South Sea contracts of Sir Charles which he had specified in his will were not to be honoured after his death.

Interestingly there was also with the deeds a letter of 19th April from Peter Leheup advising Walpole:

> Sir, I have perused this draught of a conveyance; and the only objection that occurs to me, is that there may be some debts of Sir Algernon or Sir Charles Potts affecting the estate not yet discovered, and you have no indemnity against them, which I think you should have had by bond from Long and Turner at least. That there are

debts is possible, because in Sir Charles Potts's will, he mentions South Sea Contracts which he requires his heirs not to comply with, and it does not appear how the £900 to be paid to Mary Long takes in all the debts of Sir Algernon.

There is no sign of Walpole taking this advice from his brother-in-law (Leheup had married Elizabeth Lombard the sister of Mary Lombard, Walpole's wife). He simply retained £5,047 to pay off the three outstanding mortgages, which he did later in the year. £2,696 was paid to Mary Barker (daughter and executrix of William Barker gent of Edgefield) paying off what had been the Wallis mortgage. £1,068 went to Thomas Cooke esq of Norwich for what had been the Hyde/Harrison mortgage. £1,283 was paid to Sir Benjamin Wrench for a relatively recent £1,200 mortgage for which there was no back history recited in the documents.

This last may have been a residual sum still outstanding on the mortgage of his estate that Sir Charles recounted in chancery that he had taken out in May 1720 to fund a £2,410 purchase of South Sea stock. In late March 1721 Sir Charles had a mortgage for £3,000 with Edward Parre of Doctors Commons, which they assigned to Thomas Vaughan of Inner Temple.[47] This was most likely the South Sea debt, subsequently partly repaid and later transferred to Sir Benjamin. Of Charles's debts at the time of Dame Mary's death, only this £1,200 mortgage may have been connected with his South Sea trading. If Sir Charles did sustain some £4,000 to £5,000 of trading losses in 1720, it would seem that over the ensuing years he had coped with the consequences without recourse to extensive mortgaging of Mannington.

Finally, after all these charges, Walpole paid £6,811 each to Catherine Turner and Israel Long, demonstrating very clearly that considerable equity was left in the Mannington estate. John Turner esq died in 1763 and left his mansion house in Billericay and lands in Great Burstead to Catherine for life. These and his lands in Canvey Island and Prittlewell in due course would pass to his eldest son Smith Turner.[48] There is a suggestion that John Turner had been either living on the estate or at least keeping a close eye on things around the time of Dame Mary's death. A rental naming the tenants, dated March 1737, a month after she died, showed that 'Mr Turner' had a large farm at Mossymere 'in his own use'.

The end of the Potts family at Mannington

It remained only to sort out the family's personal effects, most of which clearly the Longs had no interest in keeping - so much for many of the 'family heirlooms'. The *Norwich Mercury* carried a detailed advertisement for the sale on Saturday 23rd July 1737:

> At Mannington Hall, near Aylsham, on Wednesday next, will be exposed to sale, the household goods late Lady Potts's, with variety of pictures and tapestry, and a complete sett of brewing utensils, the

copper holding about seven barrels, and mash-vat new, with two
leaden pumps, and a malt mill; several musical instruments, viz. an
organ, 2 spinnets, virginalls, 2 violins, and 4 flutes; with musical
books for various instruments; and also a library of books: Likewise
a large quantity of Tarras* for free-stone-masons and builders. For
further information enquire of Mr George Steygould, or Mr William
Perkins in Norwich. NB there's a turret-clock with a large bell to
be sold; likewise two coaches and harnesses, one old, the other the
little the worse for use, with side glasses, and a whole front glass, and
several pair of wheels, one pair never us'd. The musical instruments,
etc, and library, are to be seen or sold the day before the publick sale.

* Tarras: an old form of terrace and in this context presumably a
quantity of terrazzo polished cement and marble chip floor mosaic.
Perhaps from a re-flooring project never completed.

It would seem that the books were snapped up in a job lot by William Chase
the bookseller of Cockey Lane Norwich who advertised every week in *The Norwich
Mercury* of which he was the publisher. As already discussed, Chase printed a
'Catalogue of a valuable collection of books in most faculties; most of which were
bought out of the study of the late Sir Charles Potts Bart at Mannington Hall'.[49]
These were 'to be sold cheap … in a sale beginning Tuesday August 9th and to
continue all the Assize-week'. The catalogue listed 405 books - a varied collection of
works ranging from the academic to household matters and medical tips.

As shown in Chapter 21, most of this library was probably accumulated by
Algernon. However a few books were first published during Sir Charles's last twenty
years in Mannington and one or two only in the five years after his death. A volume
of *Statutes at Large* was given as volume '6' which covered 1722-1734. As this seems
an odd purchase for Dame Mary to have made, perhaps this was a printing error for
volume '5'. That volume spanned the South Sea Bubble years and would have been a
useful source for Sir Charles in quoting the various acts used in his defence in chancery.
A small number of books on health and medicine seem likely to have been Algernon's,
including perhaps Strother on *Fevers* from the year of his death in 1716. However, two
volumes appear to have been first published in 1726-27 and may provide clues to Sir
Charles's health: in 1726 Sir Richard Blackmore's work on *Gout and Rheumatism* and
in 1727 Nicholas Robinson's *A New Method of Treating Consumptions*.

Dame Mary probably bought *Cases of Impotency and Virginity*, apparently
published in 1732, after Sir Charles's death. This book, covering a 1727 case in the
Canterbury Court of Arches between Catherine Weld alias Aston and her husband
Edward Weld, was no doubt a sensation at the time. The midwives declaring
Mrs Weld a virgin were not believed by the court, which preferred to believe the
husband's doctors who said he was not impotent.[50] On a more genteel note, it seems
that Dame Mary played music since she had all six volumes of *Musical Miscellany*,
published between 1734 and 1736. These English and Scottish songs for the violin,

flute and harpsichord of course do not prove whether the musical instruments were hers or whether, like so much at Mannington, they had originally belonged to Algernon and Frances. The organ, however, may have been that promised by Sir John Potts senior to Elizabeth, as argued over in the case between her and Roger. It may have passed first to her aunt, Ursula Bedingfield, as noted in her inventory, before Elizabeth made her claim for it.[51]

And what of the estate? The 1737 rental gave the occupier of the farm 'in the Hall yard' as George Copland, implying a small farmhouse stood in the yard. After the sale to Walpole, Copland's farm was increased in acreage to include the 14 acres around the Hall and other fields probably previously in the Mossymere farm. The lands must have been significant as his rent jumped from £95 to £151, of which £25 was for the Hall, gardens and 14 acres. Copland had moved up in the world and was now living in the Hall which was to continue to be used as the farmhouse of tenant farmers for many years.

So, after 250 years, the Mannington Potts line and the baronetcy died out and all their estates and heirlooms except for a few portraits were sold (see Chapter 24). After all the courtroom squabbles, the anguish of the 1710 settlement and the turbulent period of the South Sea Bubble, Roger, Algernon and Charles had not consumed all the family's hard-won resources; Mannington Hall was intact and sound enough to stand largely unchanged for the next hundred years. In the end, the Potts family was not let down by reckless generations but by its genes.

Chapter 24

Postscript: Have You Got the Picture?

Some 250 years or more after this story started the male Potts line died out with Sir Charles Potts, the 5th baronet. The Long family kept the bloodline going a little longer - but with many girls and very few boys in the various parts of the family even they did not manage to last beyond the end of the eighteenth century. Charles's sister Susan married Matthew Long of Dunston and had by him three daughters (Susan, Mary and Sarah all of whom died unmarried) and one son Israel. See Family Notes 10 for sources and further details. Israel married Elizabeth Corrance in 1725 and had four children who died in infancy and a daughter Elizabeth who died unmarried in 1757. Israel died two years later leaving his estate to Ozias Churchman, the only grandson of one of his aunts Judith Long who had married Henry Davy of Mangreen. One of their three daughters, Anne Davy, married William Churchman of Illington and Mangreen and Ozias was their only son. However, in a legal action the will was overturned and Israel was deemed to have died intestate. Eventually his sister Sarah, the last of the Long family with any Potts blood, inherited Dunston Hall and all its contents, having survived many years more than her two sisters.

In her will, made in 1791 and proved in 1797, Sarah made provision for her brother's wife, who was still alive; but the bulk of the estate was given to the son of Ozias's sister Anna Churchman who had married Robert Cowan Kellett. Their son Robert Churchman Long/Kellett, clerk, and his descendants held Dunston Hall until the late 1950s when the estate was sold. Why does this matter? Sarah's gift of the whole Long family estate was contingent on three things, or the bequest would be void. First, she requested that all household goods, pictures and furniture in her capital messuage and buildings and gardens of Dunston Hall were to be deemed as heirlooms and as far as the law allowed should be enjoyed by the person in possession of the house. Second, a schedule or inventory was to be taken after her death. Finally, the recipient was to use the surname of Long only and to quarter the Long arms to those of the Kellett family. The Kelletts did indeed change their name to Long, preserving Kellett through the generations as a Christian name, and they also received a grant of alteration to their arms to include the Long arms.

Sir Roger, Algernon and Charles Potts before her had also wished the family pictures to survive as heirlooms so when, in 1909, Prince Duleep Singh visited Dunston Hall as part of his research on paintings in Norfolk houses he found a cluster of Potts portraits as well as many of the Long family.[1] The owner, the Reverend EK Long, was at the time having some of them restored by Boswells. Some of the pictures gave a definite age of the sitter but the Prince attributed ages to others based on dress and style. The Potts portraits had been painted over a period about 30 years. First Sir John Potts senior's mother, Dame Anne Heydon, if the Prince's estimated age of 50 is correct, would have been painted in about 1617 or 1618, when Sir Christopher Heydon was still alive (see Plate 1). However as she lived to be 75 and the portrait could easily reflect a lady in her early 60s, the dating may be between 1618 and say, 1634. Sir John Potts himself was painted at age 62, as given on the painting, which dates the sitting to 1654 and during his time at Enfield. The portrait is initialled CDN, which Duleep Singh took to be Cornelius de Neve, a well-known Flemish portrait artist of this period almost the same age as Sir John (see Plate 2 and cover). In 1651 De Neve had painted Nicholas Fiske, who had just achieved publication for a work by Sir John's guardian, Sir Christopher Heydon.

For the picture of Sir John's wife, Dame Ursula Potts, again the Prince estimated an age of 50. Ursula was born in 1584 which if 50 is correct would make her portrait date from around 1634. As she lived until 1647, it could easily be a few years later (see Plate 2). Of their children's portraits only that of Francis had a definite age, 18, given on the picture (see Plate 3). Francis, as noted in Chapter 10, was painted somewhat differently from his brothers, probably around 1638 to 1640. Duleep Singh guessed an age of 25 for Sir John Potts junior, who is known to have been born in April 1618 making his painting date from around 1643 (see Plate 4). The artist is thought to be Sebastian Bourdon (1616-1671) which is interesting as he has not been particularly noted for visiting and painting in England in the 1640s. Bourdon was in Europe 1634-1637, working on a commission in Paris in 1643, helped found the French Royal Academy in 1648 and was court painter to Queen Cristina of Sweden from 1652.

The estimated age for the youngest brother, Charles Potts, was 22 and while we do not know his birth year, a 1643 date for the painting is quite reasonable. Unfortunately we have not found a photograph of Charles's portrait or the original. Duleep Singh noted another portrait that might have been the daughter Ursula, but his identification was hesitant. However there is some facial similarity between Ursula and her brother John. Given that, and the kiss-curl they both sport, it seems a reasonable suggestion (see Plate 4). This would mean that all the offspring of John and Ursula (but not their older children by other spouses) had been painted. It is quite possible that, following Sir John's elevation to the baronetcy in 1641, his wife and three of the children all had their portraits painted sometime around 1641-1643. Did Bourdon visit Mannington?

Francis was known to be travelling and may have had his portrait made abroad before he died. There is nothing about the detail to suggest a posthumous image. It has been suggested that the work is in the style of Adrian Hanneman of The Hague (1601-1671). Hanneman painted a fellow painter Cornelius Janssen or Johnson and his family (when Hanneman was hoping to marry into the family). Janssen painted Dame Ursula's nephew and neighbour Sir John Palgrave. Made nervous by the civil war Janssen returned to Holland in 1643 but he painted Sir William Campion in 1648. Palgrave's picture may date to that time or before 1643. Earlier in his career Janssen is also said to have painted Sir Edward Dering in 1626 as well as Sir Henry Spelman, Sir Edward Coke and Sir George Villiers. De Neve is also said to have painted Villiers (1627).

An indication of the cost of portraits and frames in this period can be found in the accounts for 1648-52 of Sir Edward Dering, a royalist who had estates in Kent and a house in London.[2] Since he employed Cornelius de Neve at the same time as Sir John this is a particularly relevant source. He made two payments to Le Neve for his wife's portrait in late 1648 and early 1649 totalling just over £6. He also bought from him a picture of the King (£2) and spent 6s on 'a new frame to my grandmother'. In 1650 and 1651 he paid Lely £5 for his own picture and £10 for a larger portrait of his wife and the same for another larger picture of Mrs Montague. Another frame for the wife's picture apparently cost £4.

Duleep Singh described a final Potts portrait of a woman estimated to be 28 in about 1700 which he thought might depict either Susan Long, Sir Roger Potts's daughter or his wife Dame Mary. The more likely is Susan, who was born around 1678 or later. She could have been painted at around the time of her marriage to Matthew Long in 1702 when she was about 24 or so. Her portrait would then have remained in the Long family rather than hanging at Ellingham in her father's house.

The plate in Ketton-Cremer's *Norfolk in the Civil War* showed that the portrait of the first Sir John Potts was known to be in private hands in the 1960s. That gave us hope for the fate of the other family portraits. The portraits all survived until at least 1959, up to when Sarah Long's wish had been met. But that year, after the death of EF Long, his brother and heir the Reverend WN Long made arrangements to sell the pictures and other contents of Dunston Hall.[3] Correspondence showed that Mr Hawcroft of The Castle Museum and Christies, the auctioneers, examined the pictures and concluded that they were worth little - more in fact for the frames than for the pictures themselves. A small number of Long portraits were kept by the family, but presumably by then the Potts family connection was not so well-known or not thought to be important. Those portraits were sold and dispersed.

Fortunately a local collector, the late Bryan Hall, who was fascinated by Norfolk history and an acclaimed expert on its families, did recognise their importance and on 17th June 1959 he purchased at least five of them: Sir John senior, Dame Anne Heydon his mother, Lady Ursula his wife, and their sons Sir John junior and Francis Potts. Whether he bought more of them we do not know. In 2004 Bryan had a major sale of his massive collection of antiques and some of the pictures were illustrated in the catalogue by Bonhams of Ipswich. With the help of Bonhams we were able to trace two of the paintings straight away, Francis and Sir John junior. Francis was still in his home county and Sir John junior fortunately had been cleaned and photographed by the expert owner before being sold on to a new home in the Midlands. What of Bryan's other three? He was not only widely respected for his knowledge but also loved for his generosity. Through the kindness of his partner we found the portrait of Sir John senior had been left in his will to the current owner of Mannington Hall - right on our doorstep. Bonhams also helped us track down Bryan's own annotated copy of Duleep Singh's published two-volume work on the portraits, which had been purchased by another local resident. Tucked inside, was some correspondence which led us to the new home of Dame Anne Heydon - again a gift by Bryan to a local connection.

One to go! From the correspondence we had also learnt that Bryan had showed the picture of Lady Ursula to an American art historian in 1962 who had taken a photograph of her. In 1965 he received a request for permission to use the photograph in an article she was writing. With great excitement we contacted both the museum she worked for and the relevant journal in America. Sadly not only did she not use Ursula's image in the final article but the museum had no record of the photograph. Then we discovered that in 1909 Duleep Singh had made photographs of some of the portraits as he visited the houses! The volume in which they were pasted is now cared for at the Duleep Singh collection in Thetford. With great trepidation and special gloves, we opened the book and were delighted to find an ageing faded snapshot of Ursula! It was obviously not good enough for the Prince to use in his own published work and so we have only this reference shot to use in this book (Plate 2). The painting was not listed in the 2004 catalogue and was not left in Bryan's will. At some point between 1965 and 2004 he may have given Ursula (Willoughby/Spelman/Potts) to a loving home. Where is she now? Does anyone recognise her?

Of finding the others, those not bought by Bryan in 1959 and not photographed by the Prince, we have little hope. If anyone reading this knowingly holds Charles Potts we would love to hear from you.

Roger Potts the 4th baronet also had a portrait made but as he lived at Ellingham it did not descend with the rest of the family portraits. Tomes, on seeing it in 1910, when it was in the possession of Mrs Tyrell of Thetford, commented that the picture was in a bad state of preservation. Roger, he said, did not show 'the long thin face of the other [Potts] portraits but a stout man of middle age who looks to have been a bon vivant'. Mrs Tyrell (probably Sarah Rebeckah widow of George) lived at The Wilderness, White Hart Street, Thetford until at least 1922 when she would have been in her 80s. Are there any of her descendants still around who might know Sir Roger's whereabouts?

Family Notes 1: Apott and Potts

The Potts name probably emerged independently in a number of places. In addition to Cheshire, families named Potts can be found fairly early on in Bedfordshire, Yorkshire, the North East and at least one Thomas Potte in Suffolk, to say nothing of Blomefield's reference to a thirteenth century Potts in Itteringham. (TNA Catalogue references – eg, C 1/5/68 and C 1/16/363 & 365) There is no continuity of the Potts name in Itteringham, so that link has proved just an odd coincidence. The other counties are of course possible sources of the family, but none seems to have an obvious lineage much earlier than that found in Cheshire. By the middle of the sixteenth century the Potts name was fairly common and can be found in London and elsewhere around the country. Reaney gave Pott or Potts as derived from either Philpott, a medieval diminutive of Philip, or from someone who lived by a hole or pit or who came from a manor named after a hole in the ground. He has nothing particularly helpful to offer on the origin of the Apott or At Pott surname. (PH Reaney *The Origin of English Surnames*, echoed by P Hanks and F Hodges *A Dictionary of Surnames*)

Cheshire: Pott Shrigley sources

A copy of the May 1393 court roll of the 'Hallemot' of the Forest of Macclesfield (effectively the local manorial court) showed that Thomas de Potte had daughters Elena and Margaret and another daughter Emma married to John the son of John Togod of Pott Shrigley. Emma and John were admitted to Thomas's lands in Pott Shrigley. Another surrender and admission of January 1412 showed Agnes daughter of John Togode come into a messuage and field called Pottesfield lately occupied by John de Potte in Pott Shrigley. This property was probably named for this family but Earwaker cited a deed of 1432 which showed that Pott Hall was definitely owned by another family.

In April 1505 Richard Downes of Overton and John Pot of Pot were involved together in an entry fine. (A little later, the appearance of James and a John Apott in Cambridgeshire - Sawston and Pampisford respectively - or in London, shows that the John of Pampisford was not the same as John of Pott Shrigley.) In June 1528 a letter of attorney warranted to surrender to the court a long list of lands including 'a certain parcel of land with houses standing on it, with a croft etc, in the town of Pott Shrigley once called Pot Hall and now Pot Kechyn' rent 1d pa ... and a croft called le lees in the town of Pott Shrigley lately held by John Pot of Pot together with lands and tenements between le Colcloghe' and the highway called le Rakes, lately held by the aforesaid John and sometime by James Pot his brother, rent 8d pa'.

In July 1539 one of the parties in a deed with Roger Downes esq was John Potte yeoman of Cheshire. In May and June 1545 court roll extracts showed Elizabeth the widow of Nicholas Pott and in the same deed references to John Pott of Dunge, in Kettleshulme just to the east of Pott Shrigley, and a messuage held by Thomas Pott in Hurdsfield, which lies between Pott Shrigley and Macclesfield. The court rolls for January and June 1551 showed three different John Potts alive at this time: John Pott of Pott, of Dunge and of Harrop. Harrop Brook runs through Pott Shrigley, so all three of these men and their families were living in close proximity. Other references show John Pott of Dunge during the 1550s and in July 1571 a list, probably of tenants, included John Pott, Widow Pott and Renold Pott. There is then a gap in Potts entries until a court roll of December 1588 which showed Francis Pott of Pott gent involved in a surrender with Sir Peter Legh, Edmund Jodrell gent and Edward Sutton gent. The jurors included Roger Pott and the surrender had a remainder to Francis Pott junior and his younger brother Roger, the sons of Francis senior. (Cheshire and Chester Archives and Local Studies Service, DDS/109, 111, 179, 204, 207-209, 227, 233, 285, 484)

Cheshire: the Potts tree

The evolution of the Potts clan in Cheshire is hard to work out with precision, particularly with incomplete local parish register survival, even though there are many entries for the family in the Prestbury registers. (It is possible that further work on surviving manorial and other documents in Cheshire and a detailed exploration of Lichfield Consistory and York Prerogative wills might yield further information on the family. Extensive Duchy of Lancaster records for Macclesfield in TNA might also help.) The 1558 Prestbury churchwarden's accounts show at that time there were at least four different Potts families locally: John Potte of Dunge in Kettleshulme, Thomas Potte of Hurdsfield, Roger Potte of Pott Shrigley and Lawrence Pott the elder of Rainow. All must have been closely related to be involved together in matters relating to Prestbury church. John Potte of Dunge died in 1563. (*Cheshire Life* vol 31 Number 6 June 1965, p 41)

The most likely, albeit incomplete, family tree for the Cheshire Potts therefore may be as follows. The family was anciently of Pott Shrigley and the heads of the family were John Pott of Pott Shrigley a land holder around 1412 and then John one of the stewards of the Hallmot court of the Forest of Macclesfield by 1450. He had three sons: John of Pott Shrigley, probably his heir, Roger probably of Dunge and James of Sawston. From James the Mannington Potts descended. John seems to have stayed in Pott Shrigley and may have died in the 1520s. His son and heir was John the yeoman. He was the John Pott of Pott Shrigley alive in the early 1550s. His son Roger Pott was given in the 1613 Cheshire Visitation as the head of the family in Pott Shrigley. Roger's son and heir Francis died in 1596 leaving Francis as his heir and a second Roger of Norton. (TNA, PCC will 1596, PROB 11/87) The Visitation showed his third son as Edmund, who became the London haberdasher (although Francis's will only referred to other sons Thomas and John not shown in the Visitation pedigree, implying that they had already died).

Roger, alive in the 1490s, seems to have produced the Dunge line. Probably his eldest son was Roger and a younger son was the John Apott of Pampisford - John was such a pervasive family name that it is likely to have been used by Roger senior for one of his sons. The Cheshire Visitation of 1613 showed a Roger married Anne Sutton of Rushton Spencer (later and possibly then this family were stewards of the Earls of Derby lords of Macclesfield). This Roger, junior, had son and heir John of Dunge married to Bridget Jodrell and Francis of Macclesfield married to Anne Jodrell. John was alive in the 1550s and had sons John and Leonard and daughters Grace and Bridget. Leonard remained in Dunge.

Cambridgeshire

There is no sign in the, albeit patchy, surviving manorial records for Sawston and adjacent villages that Apotts were resident there before James and his wife Alice. Similarly, there is no reference to any Apott or Potts in early deeds and leases for Pampisford. (Cambridge Record Office, box 488; Cambridge University Library, QC 17/26-40; QC 55/1-86) References later to family members in Babraham and Pampisford (where there is still a Potts marsh) imply that the family's origins may have been in the former. However fifteenth century document survival for Babraham is poor and no early references to the name have been spotted. There seem to be no other very early wills to help in Cambridgeshire and, throughout, the Babraham line seems to have left few wills. The one hint that the family might have had Cambridgeshire connections comes from a 1375-77 reference to the wife of a John Pot who briefly held a life interest from her previous husband in the Loveday family lands in Great Wilbraham. (British History Online, *A History of the County of Cambridge and the Isle of Ely, vol 10,* 2002) There is no indication of their retention by Pot and nothing to indicate where he came from. With so few early sightings of the name, even in our review of a significant number of abuttals and witness/feoffee lists, we believe that any early Potts are coincidental and that the Cheshire family was the source of all the Apotts in Sawston, Babraham and Pampisford.

After 1543 the only Sawston court book entries for Potts relate to Thomas Potto and his family. For example, in October 1544 Thomas Potto, a butcher and yeoman in Sawston, surrendered Dobde's messuage and 10 acres of land to his wife Johann Campion for her life. This shows the family ties between the Potts and Campion families - there were two generations of Joan in the line of William Campion, grocer of London for example who might have married Potto (see Family Notes 3). Thomas was the elder of two brothers. He was in Sawston by 1534 when he achieved the first of several court book entries for misdemeanours. The exact relationship to the main Potts line is not clear, but a branch of the family flourished in Babraham and Pampisford as can be seen from a number of wills and administrations. (CRO, Ely CC wills VC10:144; VC11:60; VC 14:135; etc) Thomas and his brother were probably sons of John and Jane Apott of Pampisford. Thomas Potto died in 1554 leaving a will in which he referred to his brother William Potte or Pottes of Bradfield in Essex, where another Potts family flourished. (CRO, Ely CC will, 1554, VC 12:148) Thomas Potto's son Richard was a farmer and tanner in Sawston. (CRO, Ely CC will 1567 VC 15:98) Richard's brothers William, the eldest of the three, and Edward also farmed in Sawston. Another brother John had died between 1554 and 1567. Later in the sixteenth century the families of William and Edward moved to Cambridge and elsewhere in the county, retaining the Potto spelling, and the Potts family had no further direct connection with Sawston. None of these wills mentioned members of the main line of the family, which suggests they were cousins from the Babraham line and by the mid-century effectively not involved with the London Apotts.

While James Apott/Potts of London was active in the property market so was his cousin John Apott or Potts of Babraham. The *Survey of London vol 27* refers to a 1537 grant of land in the precinct of St Mary Spital the Priory site to one Stephen Vaughan, which included a tenement with an adjacent fenced garden leased to John Apott. We believe this was John Apott of Babraham, James's cousin. A royal grant of July 1531 showed John Apott as a trustee for Dalham manor and advowson. (*LPFD Henry VIII vol 5*) Dalham, a manor just in Suffolk to the east of Newmarket with lands in adjacent Moulton, was the seat of the Stuteville family. A number of TNA documents show that John Apott had property and commercial activities in London as well as property in Cambridge and just over into Suffolk at Cavenham and Moulton. During 1538-44 John a Pottes held a lease on the parsonage of Cavenham in Suffolk. (TNA, C 1/963/24) A royal grant was made in October 1542 to John Apott of Moulton Suffolk of a tenement in the close of the Hospital of St Mary without Bishopsgate in London. (*L PFD Henry VII vol 1*) In December 1548 a patent roll entry referred to John Apottes and his tenure in Isleham and Fordham Cambs, part of the holding of the chantry of Isleham. (*CPR Edward 6*). That same year there was a reference to a William Pottes in Chyche in Essex (St Osyth) - probably, since it is not far distant, the same as the William Pottes of Bradfield Essex the brother of Thomas Potto the butcher of Sawston. In August 1552 John Apott was one of the people in Babraham to whom the church goods were given for safekeeping in the inventory of church goods that year. He was also a signatory to the return. (Hertfordshire Archives and Local Studies)

John Pottes yeoman of Babraham appears to have leased a messuage called The Sign of the Holy Lamb in St Benet in the City of London to Walter Stone in January 1561 for 16 years. At some point during 1558-79 a chancery action was taken out by Stone over the bond held as surety for the rent being paid. (TNA, C 3/164/9) During the same period John Pottes of Babraham lent £150 to the widow of Edward Moreton, a London grocer, in return for leases on her property in Bucklersbury. (TNA, C 3/142/32)

John Potts was also involved in other actions relating to Cambridgeshire properties. In May 1547 John Pot yeoman of Babraham had trouble from Alan Chapman gent of Babraham, who had dispossessed him of his lands at Huntingdon Hills leased for many years from John Huntingdon esq of Sawston. He sued Chapman in the court of requests to try to retrieve the lands. (TNA, REQ 2/15/21) In an undated pre-1547 Star Chamber suit he and Edward Wood asserted that Henry Carlton had perjured himself in a chancery suit by Alan Chapman against the plaintiffs relating to the Manor of Bruisyard and Montpelliers in Babraham to which Potts and Wood believed they had perfect title. (TNA, STAC 4/5/14 and STAC 2/24/171) Many more items from the 1550s and 1560s show that this was an acrimonious suit involving several generations of the Chapman family and indeed Sir Philip Paris (one of the Chapmans at one time had been going to marry a Jane Paris). (TNA,

STAC 4/17/19; STAC 5/P40/28; STAC 4/W1/19; STAC 7/19/22; WARD 7/10/83; C 1/1344/16; C 43/5/7; C 3/47/39; C 142/107/6; C 142/141/49; C 1/903/2-3; C 1/1344/17; C 1/1417/7; C 1/1479/47-49; SP 46/190/63) An action of 1575 showed that Alan Chapman gent of London held the manor, indicating that John Potts had probably ultimately lost out on full possession. (TNA, REQ 2/117/24) However, perhaps the actions had always been about holding on to a parcel of lands within the manor. On 1st October 1575 a licence was granted to John Pott the elder, Agnes his wife and John Pott the younger to alienate named lands in Babraham then in the tenure of John Pott (which one not stated, but probably the elder), a parcel of the manor of Bruisyard there. (*CPR Elizabeth I vol 6 1572-75*) Another Patent Roll entry mentioned John Pott in Bruisyard manor in January 1577. (*CPR Elizabeth I vol 7 1575-78*) John Potts of Babraham did not leave a will.

In 1587 John Pott the elder gent of Wilburton near Ely and John Pott his son sued John Atkinson and Isabel his wife over complicated transactions involving horses bought a few years earlier from Richard Pott of Westminster and involving Richard's brother Leonard and Leonard's daughter Elizabeth. (TNA, C 2/Eliz/P16/32) The Atkinsons were administrators for Leonard. Richard had died in 1582 as his will showed. (TNA, PCC will 1582, PROB 11/64) His legacies included one to John the son of his brother Leonard, so perhaps this was John the elder of Wilburton. By this date Leonard was a name used by some of the Cheshire Potts and it is possible that this action involved distant Cheshire cousins, or perhaps these were younger sons of the Babraham family as the Cambridge and London locations might imply.

London

In London there is no significant body of earlier references to an Apott family and in particular no surviving will. However, there are a couple of hints that there may have been a Potts family here. Two undated fragments from a chancery action survive from the late fifteenth or just possibly early sixteenth century covering parts of a London action of William Sefoule against William Crosby brewer and William Pott or William Poule clerk, regarding a modest debt linked to John Grove. (TNA, C 4/139/102 and C 4/5/54) The spellings of all the names are very strange in the piece in which the clerk is spelt Poule, so probably the second document, giving 'Pott', represents the correct spelling. But this is not positive evidence of a Pott family in London and there are references around the country to two or three clerical William Powles or Poules. (TNA, C 1/553/12, C 1/600/10, C 1/151/103) However, exploring these names led to the will of Sir John Crosby alderman and grocer of London made in 1472 and proved in 1476. (TNA, PCC will 1476, PROB 11/6) In this long will there is a legacy of the very decent sum of £10 to Elizabeth Potte the wife of __ Lyndesee late grocer of London now deceased. This seems likely to have been the William Lyndsey citizen and grocer involved in a debt at the Staple of Westminster in 1463. (TNA, C 241/248/22) The grocery connections hint at the main family. But was Elizabeth born a Potte or now remarried to one? If there was a Potte family, was it from Cheshire or elsewhere?

Further afield

The possibility of a German Potts family comes from the orders granted at Heidelberg Castle on 18th October 1423 to John Pott and two other citizens of Cologne by Louis III, Count Palatine of the Rhine. (TNA, E 30/1584) The three were empowered to collect on his behalf 500 marks due for repayment by that Michaelmas by Henry VI of England. Louis's first wife had been Blanche Plantagenet the daughter of Henry IV and no doubt there was regular contact between the two courts. Presumably these three Cologne men were merchants regularly visiting London. Another source shows a passing reference to a medieval Cologne Burgess named Gerwin Pot. (MM Poston, *Medieval Trade and Finance*, Cambridge University Press, 1973. An undated footnote reference on p 75 to Pot's 'negotiator' Johan Peldan, from the context is probably late fourteenth century or early fifteenth.) However, there is no reason to believe these Pots were linked to the Cheshire family.

Another family called Pot were traders between London and Scotland and the Low Countries for much of the fifteenth century. They were probably of Dutch origin rather than British. Various references to them survive in Dr HJ Smit, *Bronnen Tot de Geschiedenis van den Handel met Engeland Schotland en Ierland, 1150-1485*. Dr Pat Reynolds and Roland Desnerck have kindly translated for us the account book entries which indicate that they were probably local men from North Holland rather than English merchants resident in Rotterdam or Utrecht. However the readings are ambivalent and there is an outside chance that they were English mercers. Most of the notes seem to involve aspects of the wool trade, although one early entry showed more general trading. On 10th Sept 1400 at Westminster, a royal order was made to the collectors of the customs in London and the keepers of the passage there, to suffer John Pot of Utrecht to ship 4 horses called 'aumblers' which are now in the port of London in a ship of Gouda (van der Gowe in Holland) and take them to any parts he shall please, any command of the king notwithstanding; provided before his departure he pays the customs subsidies etc thereon due and takes with him no letters or aught else to the prejudice of the King or the realm. (Smit, as given, 2 vols, Martinus Nijhoff, 1928, entry 768; Cal. Close Rolls Henry IV, 1399-1402, p 167) Other entries showed a Peter Pot in 1409 and brothers Wouter and Jacob Pot active in the 1440s to the 1460s. In addition to their involvement in trade it is possible that Jacob was a minor gold dealer. They are probably irrelevant to the history of the English Potts family and the established use of Pot rather than Apott seems to rule them out as a source of the mysterious Londoner William Aputt in the 1490s.

Sussex and William Aputt

The other most interesting and concentrated medieval use of the name linked with a place-name was in Sussex. By the fourteenth century Sompting manor held a 60 acre estate in West Grinstead called 'La Potte', presumably what later became Pothill Farm. (British History Online, TP Hudson, *A History of the County of Sussex, vol 6 Part 2,*

1986) An encroachment onto Pot Common was challenged in the 1530s. At nearby Shermanbury one of the early houses called Potts Farm has been dated to the seventeenth century, but is among a cluster some of which are medieval in origin. (TP Hudson, *vol 6 Part 3*, 1987) In 1221 a Richard de la Potte was active in Sussex and in 1296 Margaret atte Potte lived in West Grinstead. (PH Reaney and R Middlewood, *A Dictionary of English Surnames ...* , 1991; J Glover, *Place Names of Sussex*, 1975) Chancery documents from 1417-18 show the existence then of the manor of Potte in Sussex. (TNA, C 44/25/8 & 9) A manor of Pott was held for much of the fifteenth century by the Tauk or Tawke family and from their other holdings this seems likely to have been near Chichester but might have been the West Grinstead place. (*Cal.of Inquisitions Miscellaneous, 1399-1422, vol 7*, HMSO, 1968; *Cal.of IPMs, Henry VII*, vol 3) The Sussex subsidy rolls show a Robert atte Potte in 1327 and a William atte Potte in 1332 among others with Pot based names. (*Sussex Record Society vol X* of 1910 cited in RE Lewis and SM Kuhn, *Middle English Dictionary*, 1983) However, there is no obvious reason to connect this 'atte Potte' family to the Cheshire Apotts.

William Aputt, the grocer of London, may have come from Cheshire or may be linked to the Dutch and German families, or the Sussex ones. With no early Potts admissions as London freemen, might this imply a settled 'stranger' family that took some time to become accepted as local? Perhaps William Aputt operated as a retail grocer and had not yet reached the status of a successful wholesaler which would have enabled him to become a member of the Grocers' Company and through that a freeman of the city of London. On balance though, it seems likely William Aputt was in fact another brother of James Apott, the earliest certain progenitor of the Mannington Potts.

Bedfordshire

A comment is needed on the Potts family of Chalgrave in Bedfordshire. By the middle of the sixteenth century they were an established family in their county and from then on had various sons educated at the inns of court. It would seem that this family had no connections whatsoever to the Cheshire clan. Their name arose from the places called Potton and Pottsgrave in Bedfordshire in a parallel development of the surname. They did not adopt the Potts arms. No doubt if there had been a linkage they would have been quick to adopt the arms since a Thomas Potts of Chalgrave was at Lincoln's Inn just ten years or so ahead of John Potts esq of Mannington. John's son, later Sir John of Mannington went to Emmanuel College at the same time as John, son of Nicholas Potts of Chalgrave. The latter went on to Gray's Inn and writers have confused him with Sir John, who did not attend any inn.

Family Notes 2: Bathurst, Clampard and Vavasour

Another chancery action involving a family challenge to a will, falls outside the main story, but showed that Edward Dodge's nieces after his death were unhappy enough at Robert Bathurst's apparent inheritance of all Dodge's lands to pursue him in chancery. (TNA, C 2/Eliz/H17/57) It may well have been linked to his refusal to hand over John Potts's writings to Anne his widow. The Heydons were of course Sir Christopher and Dame Anne who had married in May 1598 and the Vavasours were Sir Thomas and Dame Mary the widow of Peter Houghton - the two wives being the daughters of John Dodge of Mannington. Robert Bathurst was Edward Dodge's nephew by his sister Mary and John Bathurst of Horsmonden, Kent. Mary, after Robert's father died, remarried to Francis Clampard gent, but was herself dead by the time of this action. However, she had sons Edward and Francis Clampard. Edward the elder was therefore Edward Dodge's second nephew and involved in helping Robert with the execution of his will.

Dodge lands in Gloucestershire and Kent

The Heydons and Vavasours started their action with a recital that Nicholas Raynton and George Raynton, late citizens and haberdashers of London deceased had possessed the manor of Lechlade in Gloucestershire, with its 40 messuages, 16 cottages and 17 tofts, the rectory and so on. For those interested in further local detail, Dodge's Gloucestershire IPM contains a long description of the Lechlade manor transactions, not repeated here. (TNA, C 142/253/71) The Rayntons were bound with John Payne goldsmith of London via a statute of the staple in £8,000 to William Gilborne and Thomas Rigges in November 1580. The Rayntons later conveyed the manor to Bennett Bartholomew and John Weaver. In December 1588 these two and Nicholas Raynton sold it to Edward Dodge and Peter Houghton jointly, but with an encumbrance still on the property.

The manor was then worth £800 per year. Because of the past mortgages and encumbrances Edward and Peter were advised not to own it in their own names but through trustees - Raynold or Reginald Nicholas esq and Francis Clampard gent. But Dodge and Houghton ran it as their own estate and kept courts there and issued leases in their own names, until in May 1593 (about the time he became alderman) Peter Houghton released his right and title to Dodge and his heirs. An item survives in the papers of the attorney-general Sir John Popham (1581-92) which seems to be a draft of letters patent for this transaction. (TNA, PRO 30/34/10)

The Dodge nieces said that Edmund Dodge in his will had devised two parts of the manor to Robert Bathurst and the third part to descend to Anne and Mary. They claimed that they were due £400 a year as their share and that Nicholas and Clampard were now wrong to prevent them enjoying their rights in the manor.

Bathurst and Clampard answered that while the estate in 1588 had been worth about £800 a year or less, it had been encumbered in August 1587 with a £100 annual payment to Thomas Rigges, relating to the past debts, which still had some

70 years to run. The reversion of the manor itself was held by Nicholas Raynton, Weaver and Bartholomew. When Dodge and Houghton acquired the manor from these three they also bought out the encumbrance but left it in place to their uses so that they could bequeath this money differentially from the estate itself. They said that Dodge paid Houghton £5,800 for his share. This was a little low for a normal multiple of half the estate's net revenues but not necessarily untruthful for a transaction within the family. Reginald Nicholas and Francis Clampard were left with possession of the extent or encumbrance only as trustees for Dodge.

They continued that while Nicholas and Clampard were seized with the extent, Dodge was seized with Lechlade and one capital messuage called 'Compelieng' other messuages and lands in Wrotham, Leybourne and elsewhere in Kent to the clear yearly value of £240; and lands and woods in or near the forest of Wichewood in Oxfordshire. Dodge then became indebted to various persons and fell sick at his house in Lechlade. Bathurst said that on 18th December 1597 Dodge, without any help or advice to guide him, wrote his will in his own hand. Bathurst went on to quote extensively from the will and asserted that there was no provision for rights to Lechlade to be divided. It all went to him after Dodge's considerable debts had been paid off.

The action produced a number of chancery orders during its twists and turns. In the Michaelmas term of 1598 it seems that the arbitration had failed. (TNA, C 33/95 and 33/96) The plaintiffs, the Heydons and Vavasours, had heavy-hitting lawyers on their side, with the solicitor-general as one of their counsel. The attorney-general had also been present at the arbitration meeting that had failed - presumably Coke harboured no hard feelings towards John Potts's widow. The plaintiffs now had to agree who would be acceptable to hear the case. A year later it was reported that the commission of enquiry to value the premises and the 'extent' had been a fiasco, with one of the three commissioners leaving at the outset as he did not know the people or situation. (TNA, C 33/97) The other two then abandoned the hearing, even though two would have been sufficient to proceed. So the claim to a third of Lechlade manor had to wait for the process to restart.

It would seem that Robert Bathurst, the sole executor, faithfully reflected Edward Dodge's will which had been made on 18th December 1597and proved on 13th January 1598. (TNA, PCC will 1598, PROB 11/91) To his niece the Lady Vavasour he left his houses and lands in Wrotham and Leybourne and elsewhere in Kent and then to her male heirs on condition that she paid £50 a year to her sister Anne (then Potts). If Mary had no male heirs (she only had daughters by her first husband) then the bequest would switch round and Anne's male heirs would pay Mary's heirs the £50 annuity. All his houses and lands in Lechlade he left to his nephews Robert Bathurst and Edward Clampard, who were charged with first paying in full his debts of about £6,000. Edward was to have £100 a year for himself and from the remainder they were to pay, over the next 10 years, a total of £440 to their brother Francis Clampard. Dodge's niece Helinge and her husband Henry Helinge were to have certain specified smaller farms and houses in Lechlade. His niece Raynton, ('then and now the wife of William Raynton', according to Bathurst) was to have an annuity of

£40 and his Spencer niece (the wife of James Spencer) was to have the same. £100 was to go to the poor. All his other lands in Gloucestershire and Oxfordshire were to go to Robert Bathurst, contingent on paying the legacies. Minor provisions for tithes and rabbit warrens went with the relevant lands. His niece the Lady Scudamore was to have his best diamond and Sir James Scudamore his best horse.

Of these nieces, three were definitely daughters of Francis Clampard gent of Wrotham, the second husband of Mary, Dodge's sister. (d 1614, PCC will) Mary Clampard married William Raynton, son of Nicholas Raynton of Great Barrington Gloucestershire. (d 1597, PCC will) The Raynton (or Rainton) connection is interesting given the later story of Sir John Potts in Enfield. Elizabeth married Henry Heylyn (or sometimes Helinge) gent of Burford Oxfordshire. (d 1622, PCC will) He seems to have been the brother of Peter Heling the St Peter Cornhill London grocer, who served as alderman at exactly the same time as Peter Houghton, who mentioned Henry in his will. (TNA, PCC will 1602, PROB 11/99) Another unnamed Clampard daughter married James Spencer.

Sir James Scudamore of Holme Lacy in Herefordshire, had married Mary Houghton elder daughter of Peter and Mary Houghton on 21st March 1597, but she died in August 1598. In 1599 Sir James remarried to Mary the daughter of Sir Thomas Throckmorton of Gloucestershire and the widow of Sir Thomas Baskervile. Sir James and his father were well-placed at court and renowned in particular for Sir James's prowess at the tilt. As James excelled in breeding and training war horses, Dodge's bequest to him of his best horse was most appropriate.

Finally Edward Dodge's will defined a default sequence for Lechlade and his Oxfordshire lands in the absence of male heirs, demonstrating the relative age of his key nephews and nieces: Bathurst to Edward Clampard to Francis Clampard to Mary Vavasour to Anne Potts.

Bathurst in his chancery answer also described certain rents and fee farm payments that were charged on the estate and a £25 fee farm granted by Dodge to Richard Bancroft Doctor of Divinity and 'now Bishop of London'. These would have to be paid from the £100 extent on the estate, as was originally intended. He was absolutely clear and resolute that Dodge had never intended Lechlade or Oxfordshire lands to go to his Dodge nieces.

The answer of Raynold Nicholas focused on further detail of a particular taken to establish Lechlade's annual value when the estate was sold to Dodge and Houghton. He argued for £764 not £800 and confirmed that the extent was held by him and Clampard only as trustees. It had not yet been assigned to anyone else. He sought the court's help in being removed from his involvement in the matter.

The Heydons and Vavasours stuck to their guns and re-asserted their case. But Bathurst simply stated that the will was clear and the extent was his as executor to dispose of in pursuit of Dodge's intentions. A full hearing was recorded in the summer of 1600. (TNA, C 33/98) Edward Dodge's co-heirs, as Anne and Mary were referred to, stated that Bathurst as executor had had plenty of money from the estate to pay all the debts, charges and legacies. The disagreement over the 'extent' continued. The matter was ordered to go to trial and in the meantime Bathurst should continue to enjoy his full possession of the estate. To prepare his defence Bathurst was allowed to question the two knights as to whether they had taken any improper actions to overthrow his title to the estate, as long as he gave them notice first of the questions. There seemed to be no further chancery orders, but with the will standing it looks as though Bathurst would have won. Certainly he lived on at Lechlade and was sheriff of Gloucestershire in 1611. He died in 1623 as 'of Lechlade', leaving a son and heir Edward who, a staunch royalist, was made a knight and baronet in 1643. (TNA, PCC will 1623, PROB 11/142)

Sir Thomas Vavasour

Sir Thomas Vavasour of Copmanthorpe in Yorkshire and Skellingthorpe in Lincolnshire by 1598 had married Mary Dodge/Houghton. Intriguingly in one reference she is said to have been the daughter of John Dodge 'of Copes', presumably what is now Copes Farm in Frinsted Kent. (*HofC, 1558-1603;* marriage is not recorded in Frinsted registers) This is the only indication that John Dodge may have retained property in Kent, rather than being full time in Mannington. However, as yet, no documentary evidence for when he was in Copes has been found. Thomas was the son and heir of Henry Vavasour of Copmanthorpe and Margaret daughter of Sir Henry Knyvett of Wiltshire. During Elizabeth's reign he was active as a soldier, particularly under the command of the Earl of Leicester. He is known to have carried letters from him to the Queen and earned her respect as well as Leicester's. He was a gentleman pensioner from 1586 to 1603. This would have brought him into contact with Francis Flower, while his soldiering would have connected him to Sir Thomas Leighton. He was a member of parliament for Wootton Bassett and then Malmesbury in the three parliaments up to and including 1589. From 1589 onwards his career was at court.

He is also known as the brother of Anne Vavasour who in 1581, while a Lady of the Bedchamber, gave birth to an illegitimate child of Sir Edward de Vere the Earl of Oxford. Vavasour is known to have challenged de Vere to a duel which it seems did not take place.

In addition to being granted a lucrative Port of London office he was Knight Marshal of the Household for James 1, which would have brought him into close contact with Sir Richard Wigmore. If we are right that Sir Richard had grown up at Mannington, they were kinsmen by marriage, Wigmore having the same mother as Vavasour's wife. (*SPD James I,1603-10*) Sir Thomas Vavasour made his will in October 1620 and it was proved in November that year. (TNA, PCC will 1620, PROB 11/136) There was no indication that Mary was still alive. His heir was Charles his eldest son. Substantial property and monetary legacies were left for the portions of his younger children William, Mary and Anne. The elder son became Sir Charles Vavasour and died in 1644. His brother, Sir William was a royalist soldier and after 1645 spent much of his career abroad until his death in 1659.

Family Notes 3: Campion

Campions in Sawston, Cambridgeshire

A William and Margaret Campion appear in Sawston manorial accounts for 1391-94 with a Richard and Robert Campion in 1454 and Robert in 1461. Here, given the subsequent recurrence of the names, they will be called Richard 1 and Robert 1. The later widespread use of the surname around southern Cambridgeshire is probably evidence of two brothers being active in the middle of the fifteenth century. We do not know when Richard 1 died, but assume he had a son Richard 2 who was alive in 1507 as a witness to James Apott's will. A later will made in 1539 also referred to Richard's children, reinforcing the view that this was a son of the 1454 Richard not the same man. Robert Campion the elder of Sawston died in 1486 leaving a will in which he named his three sons - Robert 2, Edmund 1 and Thomas 1. (CRO, Ely Consistory Court will of 1486, VC 3:73. It is also worth noting that the wills for two William Campyons, father and son, from Icklingham and Bury St Edmund's do not seem related to this family - Sudbury Wills 1452, 129 Baldwyne, R2/9/129 and 1482, 333 Hawlee, R2/2/333)

Robert 1 left a tenement and four acres or so of lands to his wife Alice, together with a dozen silver spoons, wheat, malt and 'half an ounce of saffron lying in the fields of Sawston near a place called Dale'. To his sons Robert and Thomas he left two further five acre parcels of land. Edmund as a cleric was not left land, but he was an executor with his two brothers. Thomas 1 died in 1502 leaving a will in which he asked to be buried in Sawston. (CRO, Ely Consistory Court will 1502, VC 4:155) He left legacies to his wife Emma and their three daughters Alice, Joan and Christian. He had three sons. The eldest, Thomas 2, was a left a tenement called Dykes and lands including a meadow called Dales Yard which he would have after Emma's death. However, Thomas 2 was a successful merchant taylor in London and did not return to Sawston. The second son William was left land in Sawston and nothing more is known about him. He may well have died childless, or have produced some of the unexplained Campions in villages not far from Sawston such as Whittlesford and Middleton. He must have been of a younger generation than William the grocer senior. The third son Robert 3 was a baker in London as given in the will. He went on to have a daughter Joan who married a man called Watson and was alive in 1539. Robert 3 seems not to have left other children or a will. Thomas 2 started what was later to be the Leighton line of the family and much of that pedigree can be found in the Harleian Society volume on the Visitation of Essex. He died in 1539 and his detailed will reinforced his strong sense of connection to Sawston and to his nephews and cousins. (TNA, PCC will 1539, PROB 11/27) His son William carried on the line with sons Henry, Thomas and William, before his death in 1576 as William Campion of Hertford. His elder daughter Christian died unmarried, but Margaret married William Blackwell who was town clerk of London from about 1539 to 1570. (TNA, PCC will 1576 William Campion, PROB 11/58; and Blackwell wills TNA, PCC will 1570 William Blackwell, PROB 11/52 and Margaret Blackwell 1586, PROB 11/69) The Blackwells in 1544 bought Campions Manor in Epping from Helena the widow of Edward Campion (d 1539) the last of a line that had lived in the parish from at least the early fourteenth century. Edward and Helena had been living in London. (L Campion, *The Family of Edmund Campion*, The Research Publishing Co,1975; British History Online; *Victoria County History of Essex, vol 5*) It is quite conceivable that the Sawston Campions originally came from a younger son of this family, although this has not been proved.

Of Thomas 1's daughters, Alice cannot be traced any further. Indeed she was not even on the Leighton pedigree, so she might have died relatively young and unmarried. However, it is also possible, that she married John the brother of James Apott the grocer. Christian married Henry East of Holywell with Needingworth in the County of Huntingdon and had a daughter. Joan married John Thirlby the town clerk of Cambridge (d 1539) and had two sons named Thomas, one of whom was born about 1500. He became in turn the Bishop of Norwich and then of Westminster and Ely among other roles including many years of royal service as a diplomat. The *ODNB* in its piece on Bishop Thomas Thirlby incorrectly says Joan Campion was the daughter of William Campion of London. Thirlby was among the bishops who would not accept the church reforms of the early years of Elizabeth's reign and so was removed from office and spent his last years in prison in the Tower and Lambeth Palace, where he died in August 1570. As a committed catholic he was involved in the education of one of the Walpole family and no doubt would have known Edmund Campion the Jesuit martyr. Further notes about him and his link to the Walpoles are in Augustus Jessopp's book on Henry Walpole the Jesuit, *One Generation of a Norfolk House*, 3rd edition 1913. Before his arrest Thirlby conveyed his house in London to Margaret and William Blackwell. William Walpole of Harpley married their youngest daughter. Thomas Campion 1 also left small legacies to his nephews Robert 3 the grocer and Edmund 2.

Thomas 1's brother Robert 2 clearly lived in Sawston and had a substantial family there before dying in about 1512. His death is deduced from manorial court documents that show his eldest son Edmund 2 appearing from that date onwards. Robert 2 left no will and his family has been constructed from the wills of others. His wife was probably named Agnes. Edmund 2 inherited the family tenements and lands and at his death in 1544 described himself as a yeoman of Sawston.

Campion Grocers

Edmund's brother Christopher was a London mercer and brothers Walter and Robert were grocers, a Walter Campion being admitted in 1527. Christopher left a London Archdeaconry Court will in 1572 and with his wife had a son Christopher and three daughters. Walter's will appears to have been lost, but he is thought to have had children. Robert 3 the grocer died in1517. (TNA, PCC will 1517, PROB 11/18) His will is particularly helpful for family relationships, in addition to naming Dorothy his wife and William his son. Robert is interesting since he must be the Robert Campion apprenticed to William Campion 1 in 1494. This clearly connects the two sides of the Sawston Campion clan. Two sisters completed Robert 2's family: the unmarried Philippa and the unnamed girl married to John Dale.

Edmund 2 seems to have married twice, having sons John and William by his first wife and Robert, Edmund, Christopher and Aleyn by his second wife Joan. These four were very young when he died. The case is compelling that the young Edmund went on to become the Jesuit who was martyred in London in 1581.

It would seem that William 1 the grocer came from the Richard 1 line rather than the Robert 1 side of the family - he was certainly not in Robert 1's will. Presumably there were again three brothers here - Richard 2, William 1 and John 1. Richard 2 was in Sawston to witness the Apott will in 1507 and his children were referred to by William 1's second wife in her will of 1539. This implies that they were probably Londoners by that stage. A John Campion was apprenticed to a grocer in 1469 and was probably a brother of William 1. Another John was admitted as a freeman grocer in 1494 and was probably the son of John 1. Yet another was admitted in 1527. None of the three Johns appear to have left wills and no more is known. While we have assumed they were father, son and grandson, it is possible that the middle one was a son of Richard 2. It is of course possible, although less likely, that all the Johns in fact came from the Epping family which is known to have had a senior member named John in the late fifteenth century (although he has not been linked to the Grocers' Company). A John Campion held courts at Campions in 1490 and 1524 and was succeeded by the Edward Campion who sold out in 1544.

That leaves William 1. The first certain reference to the Campions as grocers in London is the 1467 start of the apprenticeship of William Campion 1 under Richard Lee. (Guildhall Lib, Grocers' Company Admission books and court records) Campion must have switched masters as he was admitted a member in 1474-75 under John Colman. William joined the trade just at the time that Aleyn or Alan Lumner was at his peak in taking on apprentices and no doubt he would have been well-aware of the Lumners. William was to have a string of his own apprentices between 1480 and 1505. In 1497 and 1505 he was one of the Wardens of the Company and he was Master in 1524-25. One of his apprentices who started in 1494 was his nephew Robert Campion 3 who died in 1517.

William 1 died in 1531, leaving a widow Anne who was probably his second wife since when she died she listed his children, making clear they were not hers. (TNA, PCC will 1531, PROB 11/24) Anne died in 1540 and her will is one of the sources of references to the unnamed children of Richard 2, perhaps implying that some or all of them too were in London. (TNA, PCC will 1540, PROB 11/28) Interestingly, when she made her will in 1539, she had an apprentice of her own showing that she was carrying on the business. William 1 had a son William 2 and daughters Martha (married to Edward Murrell) and Joan (married to John Devin). William 2 was also a member of the Company of Grocers but died well before his father leaving a widow Margery and a daughter Joan, the latter mentioned in Anne's will. William 2 left Margery his lease of The Falcon and of the house he lived in. (Guildhall Lib, London Commissary Court will 1519, 9171/9/f. 140) Martha and Joan had children, with William Devin becoming a grocer.

Campions of Goudhurst, Kent and East Sussex

Some have assumed that Henry Campion mercer and brewer of London (mentioned in Stow, d 1588) and his MP son William Campion of Goudhurst might also have been related to the Sawston clan, but there is no reliable evidence for any such link. (L Campion; Stowe's *Survey of London*; *ODNB*; *HofC*; TNA, PCC will 1588 Henry Campion, PROB 11/73; TNA, PCC will 1599 Margaret Campion widow of Henry and daughter of William Cordell of Long Melford Suffolk, PROB 11/94; TNA, PCC will 1616 William Campion of Goudhurst, PROB 11/127) Indeed, materials held by the East Sussex Record Office show that Henry the mercer and brewer was the son of Thomas Campion the second son of Edward Campion of Campion's Hall Essex. Thomas's elder brother Edward junior was next in line in Essex and his son John was of Essex but also had property in Monmouthshire and had only one daughter. Edward junior seems likely to have been the Edward Campion who sold Campion's in 1544. So Thomas and his son Henry continued this branch of the Campions in the south-east. Henry's son William continued the family line and is known for his purchase of Combwell Manor in Goudhurst, Kent. (East Sussex Record Office Catalogue of Danny manuscripts and items DAN/6 - E Green, *Pedigree of the Family of Campion of Essex, Kent and Sussex*, 1907 reprint from *Miscellanea Genealogica et Heraldica*; - and DAN/1 - a 9-generation pedigree of 1640; Comber, *Sussex Genealogies*)

William the MP died in 1616 and was succeeded by Sir William, sheriff of Kent in 1628 who died in 1640 leaving a widow Dame Elizabeth. (TNA, PCC will of 1616 William Campion, PROB 11/127; East Sussex Record Office, DAN/14; TNA, PCC will 1640 Sir William Campion, PROB 11/142) He in turn was succeeded by the royalist soldier Sir William Campion who died in battle at Colchester in 1648. (Copy of May 1648 will in Danny papers - DAN/170; TNA, PCC will 1648 of Sir Henry Campion brother of Sir William, PROB 11/205; PCC will made May 1648 but not proved until 1657 of Sir William, PROB 11/269) By his wife Grace Parker, daughter of Sir Thomas, he left a young son and heir William Campion esq born in 1640 and a second son Edward. When Grace remarried, Dame Elizabeth became executrix of her son's will and obviously looked after the young William and Edward.

In the eighteenth century the Campions of Goudhurst acquired by marriage Danny Park, Hurstpierpoint, Sussex. Deeds from this line of the family from the second half of the sixteenth century included references to Christopher Campion and his wife Agnes, without giving any clues to relationship. Presumably this was one of the two London mercers of that name from the Sawston line. Perhaps the Essex and Sawston based branches of the family at least felt some affinity even though there is no proof of a common ancestor.

The well-known poet and musician Thomas Campion, a son of a John Campion but otherwise of obscure origin, seems to be unrelated to the Sawston clan, despite speculation to the contrary by Leslie Campion. (L Campion; *ODNB*) The East Sussex Record Office materials solve the origins of Henry the brewer and his family but show no room in that family for the poet. It is just possible that the poet was the son of Henry's cousin John, the last Campion of Essex. Another possible father would be the third John the grocer from the Sawston family. The Campion surname was by no means unusual and unrelated families are entirely possible.

assumed father CAMPION with two sons

Richard CAMPION 1 assume 3 sons and 1 daughter

Alice

Robert CAMPION 1 of Sawston will 1486

Richard CAMPION 2 of Sawston? fl 1508

children fl 1539

William CAMPION 2 grocer will 1519

Margery

Joan CAMPION

William CAMPION 1 grocer will 1531

first WIFE

Anne will 1540

Edward MURRELL

Martha CAMPION

William MURRELL

Edward MURRELL

John DEVIN

Joan CAMPION

William DEVIN grocer

Benet DEVIN

John CAMPION 1 grocer

John CAMPION 2 grocer son here or of Richard 2?

John CAMPION 3 grocer son here?

James APOTT of Sawston will 1508

assume Alice CAMPION daughter here

James APOTT

John APOTT

daughters Elizabeth, Jane, Joan

Family of Richard Campion 1

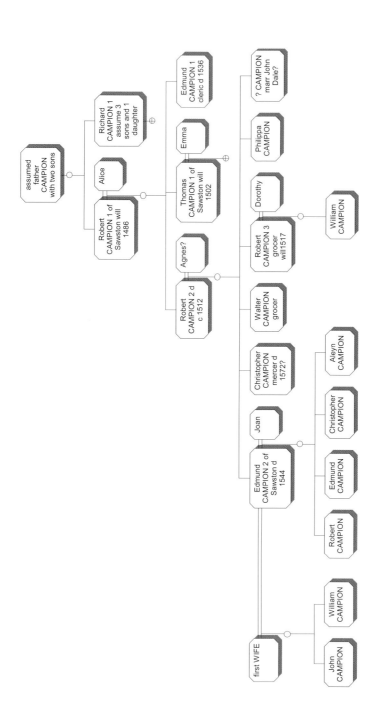

Family of the senior line of Campions of Sawston

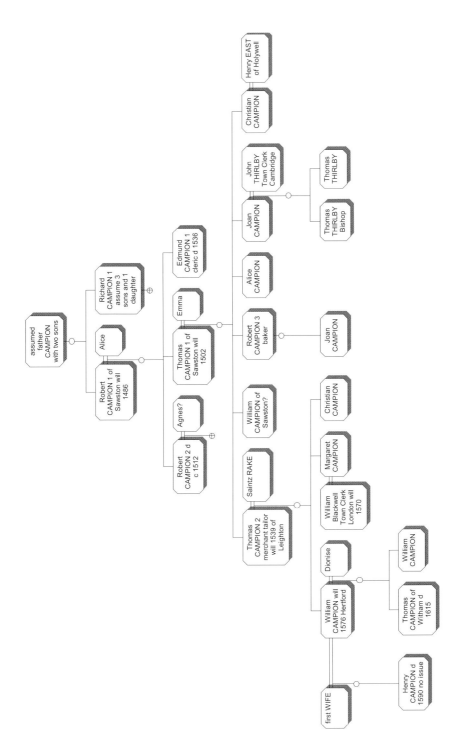

Family of Thomas Campion 1

Family Notes 4: Cooke of Little Barningham

Richard Cooke, identified in the Star Chamber action in Chapter 5, had three sons and at least one daughter. His 1541 will listed his wife Margaret, eldest son William and other children Thomas, Richard 2 and Alice. (NRO, ANW 1536-45 will, 155 Athowe) Thomas, the youngest, had sons Richard and Roger, both of Sheringham. William died in 1576, leaving a will which showed that he had had two wives and one daughter by each with subsequent marriages into the Barker and Empson families. (NRO, NCC 1576 will, 130 Cawston) With no son, presumably his brother Richard 2 became his main heir as the Star Chamber materials indicate.

Richard Cooke 2, who died intestate about 1588, had two sons Thomas and William. Thomas, the elder, became an affluent weaver/merchant/wool chapman and it seems that his younger brother operated as yeoman farmer of their lands.

Thomas Cooke married Maud (sometimes given as Matilda) Wright on 15th June 1566 in Little Barningham and he was buried there on 25th February 1591. In a long, complicated and interesting will containing details of some Little Barningham properties, Thomas left a life interest to Maud and subsequent passage of his real estate between his brother William's sons Thomas and Richard 3. (NRO, NCC will 1590, 674 Flack) Maud had no surviving children and William's sons inherited. William Cooke had married Susanna Wright (perhaps Maud's sister) on 30th July 1573, and they had sons Richard 3 in 1576 and Thomas in 1586 as well as six daughters. William was buried in 1608, leaving a will. (NRO, ANW will 1608, will 4/3) His son Richard 3 stayed in Little Barningham and had a family there. Thomas went to Cambridge and became a well-known cleric, preacher and author. (Venn) He was, after his mother's life interest, heir to lands that his father had bought of Richard 2. Thomas does not appear to have had children. In this way the Cookes' Little Barningham property largely passed in due course to his brother Richard's heirs.

Richard Cooke 3 and his wife Amy had several daughters and at least two sons: Richard born in 1616 and Edward in 1619. Edward became a weaver in Norwich and featured in a Walpole deed regarding lands in Little Barningham. (NRO, WAL 1609/3, 292x3) This included an abstract showing a very complicated route of the lands to Edward via the Shipdham family and others, including Spelmans and Sir John Potts. From Edward the lands passed in the 1650s to John Crome baker of Norwich.

Another later Walpole deed hinted at a marriage relationship between Daniel Muddiclift the Mannington steward and the Cooke family. (NRO, WAL 11, 268x4) This was a small transaction in October 1658 regarding land in Little Barningham in which Edward Cooke of Norwich worsted weaver bought a small piece of arable land in Marlpit Furlong in Little Barningham for Daniel Muddiclift yeoman of Itteringham and his heirs. Why? Was Daniel's wife Grace a Cooke girl?

Cooke also received 3 pieces of land in Little Barningham from Sir John Potts and John Potts esq, showing the Cooke family were still in some way present there. Cooke surrendered the land at Le Chase Close ('once William Cooke's') and at Heckham Close ('once Richard Mountney's') in November 1674 to William Bacon (the court steward presumably) to the use of John Crome senior of St John

Maddermarket baker and his heirs. (NRO, WAL 14, 268x4) Again, was a marriage connection possible between Cooke and Crome? Muddiclift was one of the witnesses with Thomas Jackson the Itteringham rector. In May 1684 John Crome surrendered the land to the use of his will. At this time Thomas Page received the surrender, implying that he was the Potts court steward at the time.

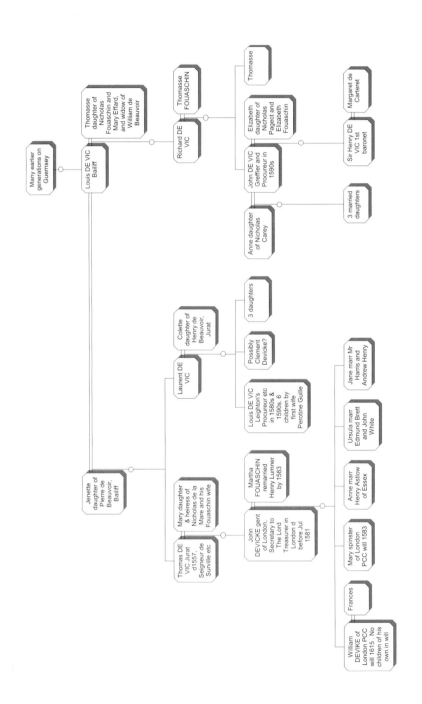

De Vic Family Tree

John de Vic

Martha Lumner's first husband John Devicke (usual in London, or de Vic on Guernsey) has an entry in the *History of the House of Commons, 1509-1558* by virtue of being MP for Portsmouth just once in November 1554. He was born by 1533 and dead by 1581 and had both Jersey and Guernsey links. The son of Thomas de Vic, a Guernsey Jurat from 1520 to just before his death in 1557, his mother was Mary daughter and heiress of Nicholas de la Mare. Through her the de Vics inherited the Seigneury of Surville on Jersey and a large estate at St Sampson on Guernsey. According to *The House of Commons*, John married not Martha but Elizabeth the daughter of Thomas Fasshyn [Fouaschin on Guernsey] of Southampton. For three generations the families of de Vic and Fouaschin had intermarried. John Devicke was Thomas Fasshin's first cousin. Thomas Fasshin, merchant of Southampton, left an undated PCC will proved on 28th April 1558. (TNA, PCC will 1558, PROB 11/40) He asked to be buried in St Michael Southampton by his first wife Elizabeth Bacar [Baker] and asked for a tomb to be built in the chancel near the high altar giving details of his work as a merchant and with a picture of him with his children behind their mothers his two wives. He left money to Winchester Cathedral and all the parish churches of Guernsey. To his current wife Elizabeth Carter he left £300 among other bequests, including his lease of the King's Arms in Cheapside London. He obviously had considerable property in Southampton and Guernsey and to a lesser extent in London. He advised his children never to have anything to do with one of his brothers-in-law, Thomas Carter (the other was unnamed), who had had him arrested in his bed in Guildford as if he were a vagabond over a sum of money due to Elizabeth! It has to be said that this would not make for good family relations.

His two sons, Thomas ('my eldest') and Walter, were to have his real estate. Walter would get houses in Bull St Southampton and the manor of 'Samares' and a windmill purchased of George 'Samares' (no doubt George Sausmarez of Guernsey who died without issue in 1551 as seigneur or lord of the manor of Sausmarez). Thomas was to have his manors and lordships (fiefs/seigneuries) of Anneville, Le Comte, Carteret, Beuval, Robert Devicke and others. If his sons had no heirs the default would be to Nicholas Samares and John Samares for the Guernsey and Southampton property for their lives split 50:50 between them. Subsequently the property would default to the mayor and city of Southampton forever. His sons were to be executors. The 'Fashin' family, as it became, was covered by the Hampshire Visitation which showed Thomas (son of Nicholas Fashin gentleman usher to Henry VII) married to Elizabeth daughter of Walter Baker of Southampton. There was no mention of the second wife. Wrongly, the pedigree showed Walter as the first son, but with no further details - presumably he died unmarried. Thomas the son was also of Southampton and married Alice Huttofte of Southampton and had a large clutch of children by her, the eldest son being George (IGI has a 1608 marriage for him in Hampshire). George probably supplied the details to the herald. *(The Visitations of Hampshire and the Isle of Wight, 1530, 1575 and 1622-34*, Harleian Society vol 64, 1913)

In his will Thomas also named five daughters. Four were to have £100 at marriage: Margery, Jane, Agnes and Margaret. There was no Martha, although one of the two Ms might of course have been an original mis-transcription when the will register was made. His daughter Elizabeth was clearly just about to get married to John Devicke. Fasshin left John £100 on their wedding day and then five marks a year until he had received a further £20. He also committed to making good his promise to pay for their wedding dinner and 'double raiment' to Elizabeth.

So there is a bit of a puzzle! The only evidence for John Devicke marrying Elizabeth Fasshin/Fouaschin would seem to be her father's will and certainly this was the only source cited by *The House of Commons*. Yet the Visitations showed the daughter Elizabeth married to James Jefferes of Chilworth (her sisters were shown as Jane = __ Beaumys and Agnes = __ Simpson of London. There was no mention of Margery and Margaret, let alone a Martha marrying a Devicke).

Presumably the wedding of Elizabeth Fasshin and John Devicke did not take place. Chancery submissions and her own daughter's will prove that Devicke's widow was definitely Martha and that she married Henry Lumner (not Lumley as in the *House of Commons* entry). She was thought to be the daughter of Thomas Fouaschin according to the pedigree by EF Carey, but nothing corroborates this. (Edith F Carey, *An Eminent Guernseyman, Sir Henry De Vic*, Guernsey Society of Natural Science and Local Research, vol 6, 1911) The Visitation reference seems to rule out the possibility that Devicke married two sisters, first Elizabeth and then Martha. And there was no Martha in the will of the man supposed to be her father. The best assumption therefore seems to be that, despite the incentive, the marriage to Elizabeth did not happen and that Martha was from another branch of the Fouaschin family.

John Devicke and Martha had several children who lived in London. The only son, William, was probably the youngest, born in 1572 and married in 1613. (Carey and IGI) His sister Mary made her will in 1582 which was proved at PCC in 1583. She described herself as spinster and was presumably an adult although her mother Martha was still alive. Mary must have been at least 10 years older than her brother. Rather sadly she was leaving her mother the wedding ring that she had given her (presumably her first, as she was now Mrs Lumner). Perhaps she'd had the gift as the eldest daughter but knew she was not going to have the chance to use it. From her will and William's of 1615 (also PCC) it is clear there were three other sisters, all married by 1615, Anne (Astlow), Ursula (Brett) and Jane (Harris). Carey had Jane married to Andrew Henry and both may be correct. However Carey wrongly had Clement Devicke as William's brother. Mary's will made clear that Clement was her 'cousin', with a wife named Elizabeth. He witnessed the will and was young William's proxy during his minority. He was probably a son of one of John Devicke's uncles Laurent or Richard but which branch of the family he fitted into remains unclear.

John Devicke died before 1581 but where and in what circumstances is not known. No will has been located.

Family Notes 6: Ralph Dodge

Ralph Dodge seems to have been a distant cousin of John Dodge from Cheshire. He was a Cambridge educated man and was ordained priest at Norwich on 7th April 1590. (From JA Venn *Alumni*: Matriculated from King's Michaelmas 1583. Of Cheshire. BA from St Catherine's 1585-86; MA from Queen's 1589. There are no other Dodge entries in Venn.)

His first living was as the vicar of Marham. Blomefield wrote that he was presented as rector of Marsham [sic] by the Queen in 1590 but in fact Marham was a vicarage not a rectory at that time. He held Marham until he died at the end of 1610. While Venn and Blomefield have Dodge as rector of Mannington from 1589, in fact the Bishops' registers show him not formally presented there until 19th July 1592 by Sir William Heydon, Sir Christopher's father. This date seems more likely being after his ordination. It may be that Dodge was being lined up as successor to his predecessor Robert Green who had been presented there in 1577. Dodge may even have been assisting in Mannington since Green seems to have held multiple rectories - eg Irmingland also in 1577. The Heydons had the Mannington presentation rights for some time before this from their Saxthorpe lordship and indeed at no time, back to about 1300, had the lord of Mannington presented to the Mannington rectory. So John Dodge did not present Ralph, although he must have had considerable influence in the appointment.

The Star Chamber action showed that Ralph Dodge was present in Mannington in the summer of 1589. Why was he at Mannington while studying in Norwich for his ordination if not related to the Mannington Dodges in some way? Fortunately the clue lay in his will made in 1610 at Marham. (NRO, ANF will 193 made November 1610 and proved February 1611). Since we know that Sir Christopher had an interest in having his own chaplains at Mannington after his 1598 marriage to Anne Potts it seems quite possible that Dodge was actually resident in Marham while holding both livings, although he may not have enjoyed all the financial benefits. He gave his copyhold lands and tenements held of the manor of Oldhall and Westacre in Marham to his eldest son John Dodge when 21. These two manors in Marham had been held by the Spelmans of Narborough since the mid sixteenth century or earlier. This is probably just an odd coincidence since he arrived in Marham many years before the Potts/Spelman connection. Quite possibly John's godfather was John Dodge of Mannington.

Other direct family in his will included Mary his wife, Francis his second son and Ralph's brother 'Ottywell Dodge'. Mary's father was Philip Wattson of Fincham. A reference to a bond to be lodged with Henry Bedingfield implies some linkage to that family - was Bedingfield influential in appointments in Marham? If both Ralph's sons died, Mary had a life interest and then all his property should pass to William Dodge the son of Robert Dodge. The Harleian Society *Cheshire Pedigrees of 1613* showed the family of Dodge in Stockport claiming a line there back at least to the time of Richard II. The head of the family in 1613 was Robert Dodge whose wife was Dionisia Barber from Derbyshire and they had sons William (the heir, age 13) and George and 3 daughters. Robert's pedigree unfortunately showed no siblings, but his will cited his brother Ottiwell (see Chapter 5 *fn*124). Ralph's will tallies with the Cheshire family and since John Dodge of Mannington had no male heir, Robert and his son William were, by 1610, the main line of the family. So it is highly likely that Ralph and Ottiwell were younger brothers of Robert Dodge of Stockport. The Visitation also showed an Oliver Dodge of Stockport then married to Elizabeth Randall of Offerton and with three children. Oliver was probably another brother of Robert.

Dodge retained Mannington where the next rector, according to the Bishop's register, was Samuel Wycks (the family name also is spelt Weeks and Wix) presented by Sir Christopher Heydon in March 1611, after Dodge's death.

Entertainingly Ralph's will also left to his son John the £20 'which Sir Christopher Heydon and his Lady doth owe unto me for the tithes of Mannington these 13 or 14 years last past' - a foretaste of Sir Christopher's indebtedness. The beginning of the period referred to, 1598, coincided with the death of John Potts esq and the marriage of Anne Potts to Sir Christopher. Heydon had his own personal chaplain, William Bredon, so Dodge, living at Marham, may have been superfluous at the Hall. Whatever Dodge's legal rights as the rector, Heydon would have seen no reason to pay him tithes for little work done in the parish.

Whatever the precise arrangements, it would seem that Mannington, despite being a parish church, was still in the ruinous state described in 1552. An entry in the Itteringham register around this time shows Mannington servants being registered by Itteringham's rector, again just possibly implying that the chapel did not have a regularly present rector and that events there may have been limited to the Lord's family. On 22nd June 1600 James Lobley married Anne Wright in Itteringham, both servants of Sir Christopher Heydon of Mannington. On the other hand the Wrights may simply have been an Itteringham family.

Family Notes 7: Godsalve

The Godsalves were a well-connected family established in St Stephen Norwich and Buckenham Ferry for many generations. Thomas Godsalve had been registrar of the Norwich Consistory Court in the early years of the sixteenth century. (NRO, NCC will 1544, 275 Mingaye) He had greater ambitions for his son John whom, through links with Thomas Cromwell, he was able to place in royal service, as a clerk of the privy council and later comptroller of the Mint. John and his father were even painted by Holbein in 1528 when Thomas was 47 although as minor landowners they were lower status than Holbein's normal subjects. Sir John, who was knighted under Edward VI, was also said to operate as a mercer, although no trace of him has been found in any livery company records. (*ODNB*; TNA, PCC will 1558, PROB 11/40) Sir John's eldest son William died without issue probably in 1561. (NRO, NCC administration 1560-1563, fo 161) His second son and heir Thomas 1, of Buckenham Hall and Norwich, added to the family estates in Norfolk and may also have been involved in trade, since his son and grandson certainly retained an active involvement in trade as well as their landed interests.

Thomas Godsalve's six children

The will of Thomas 1, made and proved in 1588, referred to his wife Elizabeth and more sons and daughters than shown by *The Visitations of Norfolk*. (NRO, NCC will 1588, 304 Holmes) Elizabeth was the daughter of Richard Townshend and she was buried on 10th September 1602 in Buckenham Ferry. (NRO, Archdeacon's Transcript; NRO, NCC administration 1589-1605, fo 290) Bishop Redman's presentments for 1597 show that she had not received communion for many years - she was a catholic recusant like some other members of the Townshend family at this time. The executors were Thomas's wife, her brother and Richard Godfrey, the lawyer and senior servant of the Earl of Arundel.

While the Visitation showed 3 sons and 3 daughters, Thomas's will showed five sons Thomas 2, John, Henry and Christopher possibly in age order, as well as his eldest son Roger born c 1568. His daughters, given as Eleanor, Elizabeth and Anne in the Visitation, he named as Elizabeth, Anne, Mary and Suzanne. The will showed that Thomas held seven or eight manors and other lands, including tenure of Caistor St Edmund near Norwich. He also had plate handed down from his grandfather and great-grandfather, with which he urged his eldest son to be careful.

Of the sons, Roger, as seen in Chapter 9, married Barbara the daughter of Richard Cutts esq of Debden Essex and their daughter Barbara married John Potts, later Sir John. The story of his siblings and their families is summarised here. Of Henry nothing is known for certain. Venn showed Henry, brother of Roger Godsalve following him to Gonville and Caius College in 1596, but assumed that he died young. Certainly he does not appear in the inns of court, unlike his brother who went to Gray's Inn in 1588. However, a Thomas son of Henry Godsalve was baptised 29th October 1609 in Fenton Lincolnshire. (IGI) This may be an entirely unrelated family, although Blomefield believed that Roger's second son Thomas had Lincolnshire connections and was married to Bridget daughter of Cyprian Godfrey of Gainsborough. (IGI certainly shows the baptism in Gainsborough of Bridget in May 1597 to Cyprian and Margaret Godfrey) Of Roger's last two brothers, John also left no obvious trail, but he may well have been the John Godsalve buried in Itteringham on 9th August 1648, having been living locally under the aegis of Sir John Potts. No other John Godsalve on the family tree would fit the bill and we know that to his death Sir John certainly retained some responsibility for other members of his first wife's family, Barbara's two sisters.

Christopher was most probably the Christopher Godsalve recited in a 1650 chancery defence by his three sons Roger (the eldest and heir), Charles of Martham Norfolk and John a linen draper of London. (TNA, C 5/13/93) This related to a disagreement about a loan and bond of 1626 from which Charles Osborne gent of Kirby Norfolk said £16 was still owing. The Osborne family of Kirby Bedon were part of the Godsalve family network in villages to the south of Norwich. This action showed that Christopher had died before 1650 and had been of Barton, Norfolk (having briefly been arrested and imprisoned in Norwich over the debt). His son Roger would be the Roger Godsalve of St Stephen Norwich who in 1661, left his estate to his wife Elizabeth, with small legacies to his nephew Charles Godsalve (presumably son of Charles of Martham) and the children of his brother-in-law John Spendlove clerk of Martham. (NRO, NCC will 1661, 308 and 588 Tennant) His wife Elizabeth died in 1667. (NRO, ANW administration 1660-1667, fo 137) His sister Elizabeth married Spendlove on 1st August 1643 in St Mary in the Marsh Norwich. (IGI) The young Charles married in St Gregory Norwich in 1673 and died in 1685. (IGI; NRO, NCC, administration 1673-1688, fo 178) John the linen draper was probably the John married to Anne who had sons Charles and Christopher baptised in St Michael Cornhill London in 1647 and 1648. (IGI)

Eleanor's name was corrected by the 1664 *Visitation of Norfolk* to Mary (although Blomefield persisted with Eleanor). Mary married Thomas Ward of Postwick, whose son Thomas was of Bixley. Thomas senior died in 1610-11 and Thomas junior in 1632. (TNA, PCC will 1611 of Thomas Warde, PROB 11/117; NRO, NCC will 1632, 128 Morse) This family is probably of relevance in that stemming from this marriage, Thomas Ward senior and junior were later involved as trustees in the Godsalve property debacle. (Cambridge University Library, Department of Manuscripts and University Archives, 33/9-14)

Finally, Roger's elusive brother Thomas Godsalve 2 may have been involved in trade in London. We have found no trace of him but believe that it was his son Thomas 3 who made a PCC will in December 1684 which was proved in April 1687. (TNA, PCC will 1687, PROB 11/387) He referred to two aunts - Dye or Day and Elizabeth Adesworth who had lands in Hascombe Gloucestershire - who were almost certainly two of the other daughters of Thomas 1 of Buckenham Hall. Although Thomas 3 would seem to have been the son of Thomas 2, no evidence for his birth nor that of his brother Christopher and sister Dorcas has been found. Dorcas a spinster of Great Tower Hill left a PCC will made in 1683 and proved in 1684, with her brother Thomas as executor and with a bequest to John the son of her brother Christopher. (TNA, PCC will 1684, PROB 11/376) The 1687 will showed that Thomas 3 was married to Rebecca but had no children. He was a wealthy mariner (presumably a merchant not admitted to one of the major trading companies) of Tower Hill London. His main bequests were to the under-age children of his brother Christopher - John, Thomas, Anne and Elizabeth. The IGI shows that a Christopher Godsalve and his wife Elizabeth baptised children with these names in St Olave Hart Street London between 1672 and 1683. The will is most interesting for the clauses in which Thomas 3 left rings to his nephews. John was to have £400 and a seal ring with the Godsalve arms cut in a cornelian. Thomas 4 was to have £500 (perhaps a favoured godson?), 12 acres in Hascombe and a ring with the Godsalve arms in a garnet. He said this ring 'had been enjoyed by several Thomases before and was the only thing left by a Thomas Godsalve a bachelor who died in Norwich' ... 'who had as I have been very well-informed about £800 a year [in] land'. The 'bachelor' may have been an error, but this seems to have been the childless second son, later heir, of our Roger. As the head of the family by the mid-1620s he would have had the family seals which perhaps dated back to his great-great-grandfather Thomas. Presumably at his death (or perhaps that of his younger brother Richard) his uncle Thomas 2 inherited the rings and from him they went to his son Thomas 3 the will writer of 1684/87. Or they may even have gone direct to his first cousin through some non-family intermediary who was not able to give Thomas the full story. Certainly the rings had been held by many 'Thomases' and may have included the one shown in the Holbein portrait.

Clearly Rebecca had some difficulty over dealing with her husband Godsalve's will after her remarriage in 1689 to a William George esq of Cirencester. (Gloucestershire Archives, P86/1 CH 1/7) Their marriage settlement included provisions relating to Thomas's debts and legacies as well as his Kent lands. As Rebecca petitioned parliament over the legacies to Christopher's children, presumably there was not enough money left to pay them. (Parliamentary Archives, HL/PO/JO/10/1/435/432 and 10/3/184/26)

Family Notes 8: Hertfordshire families - Mynne and Kettell

Mistress Frances Kettle or Kettell was the head servant of John and Philip Potts's mother Katherine at Eltham at the time of the two men's deaths in 1598. A gentlewoman, she was the granddaughter of Thomas Kettell gent and his wife Jane, daughter and heiress of Philip Bitterley esq of Kings Langley. Their son and heir, John Kettell gent of Kings Langley married Katherine Mynne in Hertingfordbury near Hertford on 25th February 1550. (Hertfordshire Record Office, contemporaneous Hertingfordbury parish register extracts - the register does not survive)

Katherine Mynne was one of the daughters of John Mynne of Hertingfordbury (who died in 1543) - a major family in Hertfordshire that had come from London and the Epsom area and which had another major branch in Norfolk, including one member in Wolterton and Itteringham for a time. Katherine's younger sister Anne married Richard Boteler esq of Stapleford, Herts (14th July 1571) and her sister Susan married John Darnall (8th July 1562). (Hertingfordbury parish register extracts. John Darnall gent was also of Hertingfordbury as identified by his 1605 PCC will, PROB 11/106) Richard was the youngest and favourite brother of Katherine Potts/Doddes/Flower who no doubt was pleased to take his wife's unmarried niece, Frances Kettell, into her household, especially as the young woman's mother and sister had both died. Katherine may well have known the Kettells through her second husband as William Doddes had links with Kings Langley and may have come from there. Frances's father John Kettell married again, on 11th September 1582 in Kings Langley, to Barbara Villiers. It is possible that she came from the family later to be of Brooksby who are linked to the Potts story in the seventeenth century. In John's will made in 1585, Barbara's uncles were apparently named as Richard Butler and John Darnall gent making her a relative, probably a niece, of his first wife. (TNA, PCC will 1588, PROB 11/72) Unfortunately the link has not yet been made. For example, George or Andrew Mynne, Katherine's brothers, could be candidates for Barbara's father, but there is no mention of a daughter Barbara in George's 1581 PCC will (PROB 11/63) and nothing is known of Andrew, who is only identified from his father's will. (TNA, PCC will first proved in 1543 of John Mynne PROB 11/29) Perhaps John Mynne had another daughter; in his 1543 will the girls were young and unnamed. (TNA, PCC will 1543, PROB 11/29) He had been a merchant of St Botulph without Aldersgate in London and around 1540 had purchased lands in Hertingfordbury and elsewhere in Hertford from John Butler [Boteler] of the exchequer. His second son and heir was George Mynne and George's will was witnessed by his brother-in-law Richard Butler. (TNA, PCC will 1581, PROB 11/63)

Frances Kettell had four brothers, one of whom, George, died in Kings Langley in 1593. The others were Ralph and Christopher and her eldest brother John. (TNA, PCC will 1593, PROB 11/81) In the 1614 will of Richard Boteler there is a reference to 'Katherine' Kettell , a niece to his wife Anne. As Frances's sister Katherine Ketell had died it is not clear to whom this refers. She may have been a great-niece, a daughter of one of Frances Kettell's brothers, Christopher or John. (TNA, PCC will 1614, PROB 11/123)

Ralph Kettell of Kings Langley, the third son of John Kettell and born in about 1563, was to become rector of Garsington in Oxfordshire and for 44 years the much praised President of Trinity College Oxford, until his death in about 1643. He was married at least twice but had no surviving children of his own (a daughter Mary was born and died in 1606). After the death of his first wife in 1623 he married the widow of Edward Villiers esq of Northants, the mother of two daughters. The elder, Elizabeth had been married at 14 to the 'frugal' George Bathurst whose fifth son Ralph was Kettell's godson and successor at Trinity. We suspect that this Villiers was related in some way to his father's second wife. (British History Online; *History of the County of Oxfordshire Volume 3*; Clare Hopkins, *Trinity: 450 Years of an Oxford College Community*)

This close knit collection of Hertfordshire families, linked by marriage, is a classic example of a family network; in this case one which, with the related Coningsby and Doddes components, completely dominated the senior circles of the county for the last two or three decades of the century. It would have been surprising if John Potts had not done a volume of legal work for his mother's family network.

Family Notes 9: Sir Christopher Heydon's Children

William Heydon Sept 1585-1627

Sir Christopher's eldest son William, born in September 1585, was sent to Caius College at 12. On 19th December 1597, Christopher wrote:

> To my very good friend Mr Fletcher, fellow of Caius College, Cambridge
>
> Mr Fletcher, I determine after Christmas, to send my son to you ... I pray you provide him, a chamber & a good bed, likewise all the furniture, which at my coming thither I will pay for. As for linen, he shall bring sufficient for his use with him.

William was admitted as a fellow-commoner on 7th February 1598. Like most of his family he soon fell into debt. In 1601 on 10th November (at the end of Sir Christopher's *annus terribilis*) his father had to write a letter paying the boy's debts so he could return to his tutor. William was still there, behaving badly, in the summer of 1603.

He was destined to be a soldier and by 25 he was a junior paymaster with Prince Henry but was rarely paid - in 1612 he claimed £8,000 in back pay. By 1616 he was serving under Sir Horace de Vere, as a Captain, in the Low Countries and was knighted in 1620. He succeeded to the position of Gentleman Usher of the Privy Chamber in 1625 and then in 1626 to the important post of Lieutenant of the Ordnance at the Tower. As this meant he had to undertake the day-to-day work of organising the supplies for war, he returned to England, getting a captaincy of his company in the Netherlands for his younger brother Miles. Batten says William inherited the income from Cley and Blakeney lands in 1626 on the death of his idiot great-uncle. However the 1626 inquisition is not 'post mortem'; it appears to confirm there was no change in Christopher's state of mind and noted that his annuities were in arrears. William was named as heir following Sir Christopher's death in 1623. He would then be responsible for paying the annuities and may not have been doing so. He was still owed £1,300 by the Crown for the Palatine expedition.

Sadly his rise was to end with his appointment, in February 1627, as Lt-General of the Artillery for the expedition to La Rochelle later that year. In July, at the Isle of Rhé, he was carried into the sea by a mob of soldiers in flight and drowned. (For a full account see Mason's *History of Norfolk*, Vol 2. p.119: this is a rare volume occasionally bound in with volume 1.) He never married.

[Taken largely from Barbara Batten's unpublished thesis *The Heyday of the Heydons*, c1960]

John Heydon 1588-1653

John, born June 1588, appears to have been fighting from a young age. He was in the service of Henry Howard, Earl of Northampton, with the rank of Captain and he was Keeper of the stores at Sandown Castle. He was left £100 by the earl in his will in 1614. Could this suggest that the young man had done some honour in his service? Perhaps he had sustained a wound? It seems most likely that this is the John (not his uncle Sir John) whose left hand is now in Norwich Museum. He certainly kept company with duellists: in September 1613 he travelled to Antwerp with his friend Edward Sackville, Earl of Dorset to be his second in a duel which was to end in the death of Lord Bruce of Kinross. Sackville lost his little finger but we have no account of a duel for John. (*Notes on Duels and Duelling*, Lorenzo Sabine, Boston, 1855) In February 1615 Sir Dudley Carleton received a letter from his friend John Chamberlain revelling in the story that at the wedding of Jane Drummond to the Earl of Roxborough, 'young Heydon with one hand' quarrelled with the Earl of Essex and upset the feast (and therefore the Queen). Heydon was sent to the Fleet to cool off and lost favour at court. (*Gents Mag* 1853 p 481-488; Philip Gawdy also wrote of the incident) It is very unlikely that Sir Christopher's brother Sir John would not have been described as Sir. Nor would he have been called 'young'. (Sir John would have been at least in his late-40s by then!) The hand in question was severed diagonally right across which perhaps suggests a heavy sword wound in battle rather than a duel. Henry Howard, the Earl of Northampton would not have rewarded a duellist: while he firmly believed in the code of honour and understood why men fought, he helped King James in his campaign to stop duels. (Markku Peltonen, *The Duel in early Modern England*, 2006) It is particularly interesting that it was the younger John's daughter, Mirabel Lomax, who left the hand to her son when she died at Eye in Suffolk in 1702. It then found its way, apparently, to Canterbury Museum and is now in the Fitch Room at Norwich Castle. Could John the nephew's story have been confused later with the 1600 duel of his uncle? (See Chapter 9)

John's life was as curious a mixture as his father's had been. By July 1616 he was in the service of Edward Lord Zouche, warden of the Cinque Ports when Sir Christopher asked John to get leave of absence to come to see him. (CSPD 1616) In 1623 he had a position of paymaster (like his brother-in-law William Godson to whom his half-sister Anne was married) with Lord Charles Stanhope, Master of the Posts. ('The humble petition of John Heydon and Wm Godson gentlemen November 23rd ', *Packhorse Waggon and Post* , Jn Crofts, 1967; APC has William Godsell (sic) imprisoned November 23rd 1621 - to be taken from New Prison Middx to Bridewell London - committed by Sir Lewis Lewknor. He was freed 2nd January 1622 as William 'Godson') He was in the Low Countries in 1627 when his brother William was killed but raced home to ensure he secured the place of Lieutenant of the Ordnance. He claimed William had made him his deputy when absent and later said he was recalled by the King 'in compassion for his irreparable loss'. (CSPD 1630 p 436) Once in post, he discovered that there was deeply entrenched corruption in the Tower and his determination to stamp this out made him unpopular. He spent seven years clearing William's name and rooting out the problem. (CSPD re Ordnance accounts 1630-31) He turned out to be a brilliant organiser and planner; the supplies were increased and he soon had the full support of the King. Living in the Minories (at Heydon House) he had collected ship-money for the King in Middlesex. He was knighted in 1629. In 1642 he realised he would have no alternative but to support the king and he left London on 4th August 1642 to organise the ammunition at York; in late 1642 he was with the army and went to Oxford as Lt-General of the Artillery. He was Commander of the King's Artillery Train and on the King's Privy Council. However when Oxford surrendered, Fairfax allowed him to leave and live quietly at his house (although sequestered). Was this by the influence of Sir John Potts?

There is no evidence that John Heydon maintained any other links with his Norfolk relatives. His first patron Howard was pro-catholic and once he had sided with the King he would not have been welcome in north Norfolk. As his father's heir, he was still the target for those with claims on Baconsthorpe. In 1642 John Smith of Ingatestone, Essex pursued him for an unpaid annuity and Heydon had a grant of annulment from the King for the arrears of the annuity. (Letters Patent Chas 1 1642-46) In 1643 he was declared a delinquent and his estates were sequestered. The inventory of his goods taken in July 1643 (BL Add Ms 28191D) only came to £37 of which £5 13s was for his 63 books. Batten suggests that this was his Minories household but it is assumed by others to be Baconsthorpe. (EAA 102 *Baconsthorpe Castle*) Baconsthorpe had been compounded early on and was let out by the committee at £80 in 1646. (Batten refs SP23 G205 pp 779,781,785 and Cal Cttee for Compounding Vol 1, p92, 114; Cal Proc of Adv of Money p1310 pt III) He discharged the sequestration by a compounding payment of £294. In September 1651 at the committee for advancement of money, Sir John Haydon [sic], of London, appeared in a list of those against whom no proceedings were taken and was assessed on £100.

John was not lucky in his private life either. He married late (when nearly 40) in December 1628 to Mary Phillips, the half-sister of Christopher Gardner of Surrey. John had known Christopher's cousin Sir William Gardiner at the Minories. (Although cousins, the surname spelling differed as shown) They had a daughter in February 1630 but she died young. He acquired an estate near Croydon Surrey and had more surviving children, Anne, Charles (who we meet at Baconsthorpe later but who died without issue), William, Cory and Mirabel (who married Laurence Lomax). His wife and he had split by 1650 when he was living at Addington. (For the 1650 case between Gardner and John over his wife's estate see Batten Chap XIV and TNA, C 10/4/98.) By 1652 he was living near Heston in Middlesex and he died in October 1653.

He was remembered not only for his military genius and perhaps his hand, but also for his mathematical scholarship. He had been awarded LLD at Oxford on December 20th 1642 by the King. He is also credited with some writings and may well be the 'cousin John Heydon' acknowledged by Henry Hexham in his 1642-43 edition of *The Three Principles of the Art Military*. His son William died in 1689 the last Heydon male heir.

Miles Heydon 1589-post 1626

Miles, born July 1589, is not well-documented, apart from his baptism in Saxlingham and his admission to Inner Temple in 1610. He was granted the administration of his father's goods in 1623 suggesting he was then available in Norfolk. The last heard of him was in 1626 when he took a captaincy in the Netherlands from his eldest brother, William.

Thomas, Henry and Nathaniel Heydon

Nothing more is known about Thomas than his baptism at Saxlingham in January 1591. He may have died young. The only source for Henry and Nathaniel is Blomefield. Batten describes Henry as the third son but there is insufficient time between John and Miles's baptisms. She noted that a Henry Heydon was admitted pensioner of St John's College Cambridge in 1609 which would be consistent with a baptism around 1592-3 (just before Mirabel's death) but the Heydon name was not unique to the Norfolk family. (Venn has Henry Matric pensioner Easter 1609)

Frances Heydon

Frances could be the child of either wife of Sir Christopher but was most likely to have been born to Mirabel. (Blomefield suggested she was the third daughter of Sir John Heydon, Christopher's son but the dates could not work) However the known five Saxlingham baptisms of Mirabel's babies do not include a Frances. They run from 1585 to January 1591 (5 in 6 years) and she died in July 1593 (possibly in another birth). Blomefield said there were two more sons. Given she was 22 ½ in 1593 it is unlikely she was bearing children much before 1585 (aged 14). However the Sharrington registers, the parish where Christopher and Mirabel were living, do not survive so it is possible that one or two baptisms could have taken place there, rather than waiting for a service at the family church. If one of the boys (or even twins if there were two other sons) had been born in spring 1592, Frances could have been a live birth in the summer her mother died. The events could of course have been reversed, with Frances arriving earlier than the boy(s).

What is known is that Frances Heydon married Henry Draper 'of Bromley, Kent'. Henry was the son of Nicholas Draper gent deceased when, in 1605 aged 16, he was admitted to Caius College, at that time a magnet for young men of Norfolk and Suffolk. (Venn, *Gonville and Caius College Biographical Dictionary*; A year after Henry went up (his surety was Mr Browne), John and Edward Duke were admitted. Born in Worlingham, Suffolk, they had been at school in Hedenham Norfolk. Their surety was also Mr Browne. John was later to marry a daughter of Sir Thomas Rous.) Interestingly he had been sent to school at Lynn, Norfolk, under Mr Mann and Mr Squire. Perhaps there was a link with the Drapers of Norfolk? Henry's father Nicholas was also described as 'of Bromley Kent' but in 1596 was resident in Walbroke Ward in the city. (1595 list of non-Londoners resident in the city - British History Online. Nicholas may have been the protestant witness at court mentioned in 1567. He was also probably the head juryman at the inquest taken at Deptford Strand on the body of Christopher Marlowe the playwright in 1593)

Henry left Caius in 1612. Venn then matched him with a Henry Draper ordained at London about 1623-4 who he thought went on to be rector of Worlingham in Suffolk until his death in 1657 but that must be another man. How long he and Frances were married is not known nor when Henry died, but Frances was described as Draper's widow by March 1625 when she remarried.

The London marriage licence of that date was for Frances, then of Great St Bartholomew and Philip Vincent gent aged 24. (Guildhall Lib, JL Chester, *London Marriage Licences, 1521-1869*, 1887) That it is the same Frances was revealed in the life story written by Vincent later in his life. He said he married 'the daughter of Sir Christopher Heydon, the famous astrologer'. (Collections of the Massachusetts Historical Society, Series 4 Vol 1 1852, p88) Philip Vincent, son of Richard Vincent, was baptised at Coningsborough, Yorks on November 23rd 1600. He was a Peterhouse student, obtained his MA and was ordained. After their marriage he had the rectory of Stoke D'Abernon in Surrey (from Sir Francis Vincent - not related). His story gave the dates of his tenure as from 1625 until he resigned the living on 16th August 1629. The parish register for Stoke D'Abernon confirmed that he was rector there at the right time. (SHC, STKDAB microfilm) Francis, then described as 'onely son of Philip Vincent Rector of the Church' was buried at Stoke on 9th February 1626, having presumably been baptised in London. John, son of Philip Vincent, was baptised on June 16th 1628 and according to Vincent also died young. By 1631 the rector of Stoke was named as Thomas Neesham which confirmed the resignation date.

Vincent said their third child, Henry, was born in London on 20th December 1629. His baptism entry in St Andrew Holborn register for 13th January 1630 added they were living at 'Wineboults house in Cursitor Alley, Chancery Lane'. Frances, herself, Vincent recalled sadly, died on 30th November 1630 and was buried in the church of 'St Andrew London'. Her St Andrew Holborn register entry was in fact dated 21st November 1630 'out of John Scott's house in Baldwins Court, Grays Inn Lane'.

Distraught, Vincent took to a life of wandering and enterprise, sailing to Guiana about 1632 and by 1636 had settled in New England.

568

Family Notes 10: Long of Dunston

We are indebted to Una Long for her detailed contribution to the 1979 introduction to the Long of Dunston catalogue in the NRO. To these notes we have added further information. Israel Long senior in 1662 married his cousin Sarah Long, daughter of Matthew Long, Israel's uncle. Of their sons, nothing is known of Israel who presumably died young, Robert died in 1668 and Thomas in 1706. Matthew, born in 1663, was therefore the only son and heir when his father died in 1709. Four of Israel's daughters survived. Mary died unmarried in 1718 aged 55. Sarah married first John Carter the Norwich lawyer mentioned in Chapter 10 and secondly Robert Miller of Norwich, apparently leaving no issue by either husband. Alice married John Davy of Dunston and their eldest child Sarah was mentioned in Israel's will made in 1703. (NRO, NCC 1709 will 259 Famme) Judith married Henry Davy of Mangreen and her three daughters were again mentioned by Israel. Of these Anne was to become particularly important to Itteringham and indeed the Potts story. She married William Churchman of Illington and Mangreen. Their unmarried daughter Mary Churchman was to inherit, from a friend John Framingham, one of the large farms in Itteringham not within the Mannington estate (now known as Hill Farm).

Sarah Long outlived her husband by 10 years or more and was to prove a determined executrix of his will. In her will made in 1716 and proved during 1719-20 she left legacies to her daughters Mary Long, Sarah Carter, Alice Davy and to the daughters of her deceased daughter Judith Davy. (NRO, ANF 1719-20, will 125/616) Her main heir and executor was her son Matthew and she asked her friend Samuel Snowden of Newton Flotman to assist him as supervisor.

As noted in Chapter 10, Matthew had married Susan Potts the only surviving daughter of Sir Roger Potts in 1702, when £3,000 was settled on Susan by her father Sir Roger Potts. They had one son and heir Israel and three unmarried daughters: Mary who died in 1757, Susan who died in 1766 and the last of the line, Sarah, who died in 1797 - more of her shortly. Sir Roger's sister Elizabeth kept up with her niece's family and on her death in 1722 some of the jewels that had belonged to her father, Sir John Potts junior, reappeared. Her 'diamond ring with 7 stones' she left to her niece Susan Long and her 'locket with turkey stones to be made into 2 rings one for her husband [Matthew] and one for her son'. Susan's daughter Susan was to have Elizabeth's Japan work trunk 'and all the work in it and little pictures in it'; the other two daughters [Mary and Sarah] were given her worked screen and worked picture. All three girls received a share each in the Lead Mine Adventure.

Matthew died in August 1724 after a fall from his horse leaving substantial bequests to his wife and daughters. (NRO, DUN (C) 59/8, NCC 1725, will 414 Gregson) Israel was to inherit all the real estate in Newton Flotman (where most of the Dunston estate lay) and Norwich. Susan his wife was to be executrix assisted by the ubiquitous Robert Britiffe esq (she was buried in Dunston in January 1735). Young Israel married Elizabeth Corrance in 1725 and had four children that died in infancy and one surviving daughter Elizabeth who died unmarried in 1757 at the age of 27.

Israel, who separated from his wife in 1749, died in 1759 leaving his estate in a will to Ozias Churchman, the son of William Churchman and Anne Davy and, as the sole grandson of Judith Long, by the 1750s, the only male alive in all the various Long family lines. However, in a legal action the will was overturned and Israel was deemed to have died intestate. Eventually his sister Sarah inherited Dunston and all its contents, having lived many years longer than her sisters.

William Churchman's will, made in 1769 and proved in February 1770, is interesting for its references to the debts of Robert Cowan Kellett who had married his daughter Anna. (NRO, DUN (B) 110, 497x4) Having given Kellett a marriage portion of £3,000, Kellett had borrowed a further £5,100 from his father-in-law, which Churchman knew from the state of his affairs would not be repaid. Churchman assigned the debt to Anna. Mary, his spinster daughter, had a balancing sum of £8,100 worth of assets and Mangreen Hall and other local property. The residue was divided between the two women.

In her will made in 1791 and proved in 1797, Sarah Long, the last of the family with any Potts blood, made provision for her brother's wife - formally given as 'Mrs Long' - who was still alive. (NRO Original ANF will of 1797, not included in the microfilmed register but available as an original document) Among several others, she also made a bequest to Mary Churchman, one of the sisters of Ozias. The second sister Alice had died in 1773. But the bulk of the estate was given to the son of Ozias's sister Anna Churchman who had married Robert Cowan Kellett. Robert Churchman Kellett, clerk, became Robert Churchman Kellett Long and his descendants held Dunston Hall until the late 1950s, when the estate, house and contents were finally sold.

This inheritance was reinforced by Mary Churchman when she died in 1803. (TNA, PCC will 1803, PROB 11/1390) She left Mangreen Hall to Anna Kellett and then to Anna's son who by then was known as Robert Churchman Long. Incidentally she left to her old friend Mary Moxon widow her messuage and lands in Itteringham for life and then they were to pass to Mary Long the younger daughter of RC Long. Not until the sale of this small estate in the 1820s did the Potts and Longs finally lose their material links with Itteringham. Only the portraits remained (see Chapter 24).

Family Notes 11: William Potts and Potts of Eltham

William Potts of Eltham may have been a cousin of John and Philip. He was probably from the Babraham line of the Potts clan - perhaps a younger son or more likely grandson of the John Potts senior of Babraham and London active in the 1550s. The Eltham parish register shows that William Potts baptised three children in Eltham: Mary in January 1595 (but buried in March that year), Frances in January 1596 and William in March 1599. After that there is no further sign of him and his family in Eltham. Armed with these register entries we have been able to discount the small number of surviving wills in the London area and Kent that might otherwise have been considered to be of this William Potts. It is just possible that he might have been the Mr Potts who lived in St Ethelburgh and from whose house in August 1605 a James Vandenpoole was buried in St Helen Bishopsgate. (Guildhall Lib, St Helen's parish register) A London Consistory Court administration of September 1613 for William Potte of St Ethelburgh next Bishopsgate merely said that his widow was Isabella. (Guildhall Lib, X19/5, 140 Crompton)

Beyond that tentative identification nothing more has been found about William Potts. It seems likely that with the death of the senior members of the family, William Potts moved out of Eltham - perhaps to London. A detailed survey of Eltham manor of July 1605 contained no references to any Potts or Flower people or property. Nor for that matter did it mention the Cottons, later of Eltham and friends of the Potts family. (TNA, E 164/44)

Assuming William Potts was a cousin, it raises the intriguing question of whether he produced a long line of Potts that ultimately returned to Eltham. Although there are no Potts entries in the Eltham registers from after the late 1590s until the 1790s, a John Pott was buried there in 1801 in his 89th year. Among his sons, he produced an affluent London merchant Robert Pott whose 1824 burial is commemorated by a tablet on the wall in Eltham church. If this line of Potts had by chance been connected to William Potts of Eltham, then ultimately they might technically have been in line to inherit the Mannington estate in 1737 and the Walpole family might never have acquired it!

Family Notes 12: Stubbes

Edmund Stubbes was active as a lawyer in Norfolk in the 1590s. His brother Francis married the sister of Edward (later Sir Edward) Coke the Queen's attorney-general who prosecuted John Potts so aggressively. Potts worked as an arbitrator with Richard Stubbes to try to resolve John Dodge's dispute with the Cooke family. Who were the Stubbes? The *ODNB* provided some of the answers but was uncertain on the early history of the family and did not cover Richard. Here is a little more detail. Throughout, we have used Stubbes which was how Edmund signed his name but the name was often seen as Stubbe or variations on it.

The family in Scottow descended from Robert through William and his wife Margaret, the relict of Roger Taylor. (D Gurney, *The Record of the House of Gournay*; Harleian Society Visitations of Norfolk and Suffolk and Norris manuscript notes on various family pedigrees now in the NRO in the Rye MSS Collection) She died in 1464. Their son John married 'Hawicia' a daughter of Roger Taylor (presumably by a previous wife). John senior of Scottow died in 1488 (TNA, PCC will 1488, PROB 11/8) and Hawicia in 1505. (NRO, NCC will 1505, 126-7 Ryxe) At her death they had five sons, Robert, Edmund, Edward, John and Walter and one daughter, Margaret, still living. Margaret had three sons and one daughter by her Tanne [Tanner?] husband. Nothing seems to be known about Robert and since he was not mentioned in his eldest brother's will in 1514 he probably died unmarried before then. Edmund, Edward and John all featured in Walter's will. (TNA, PCC will 1514, PROB 11/18) Edmund was rector of St Michael Coslany in Norwich and Master of Gonville Hall Cambridge. (Venn, *Alumni*) He was an executor of the will of Anne Drury (widow of Roger Drury and previously wife of John Palgrave) of Norwich made in 1501 and proved in 1503. (Palmer & Tucker, *Palgrave Family Memorials*) Dying without issue the same year as his eldest brother, he bequeathed his property in St Botolph Norwich to Walter, who in turn left it to his own son Edmund, presumably a godson. (TNA, PCC will Edmund Stubbes 1514, PROB 11/17) Edward and Alice (probably née Belamy) had Christopher and three daughters. (TNA, PCC will Edward Stubbes 1532, PROB 11/24)

That left Walter and John and their families. John remained in Scottow and married Alice the daughter of Hamond Clopton of Cheston in Suffolk. He died in 1525 leaving a will made in August 1525 and proved the following February. (NRO, NCC will 1525, 148-152 Groundesburgh. This will has been indexed as 'Stulb' since that and several other versions of 'Stubbes' are included in the text of the register version of the will) John had sons Andrew, the heir, Edmund and four daughters, although only Andrew, Dorothy and Faith were mentioned in his will. He also had nephews Walter and John and niece Margaret Stubbes. Andrew married Alice the daughter and co-heiress of John Richers of Bungay where they lived. Their daughter Anne married Francis Guybon son and heir of Anthony Guybon of Suffolk. Andrew's son Richard became Richard Stubbes esq of Edgefield and later Sedgeford. In Irstead on 25th September 1561, as Richard Stubbes gent of Baconsthorpe, he married the sixteen year old Elizabeth daughter of Anthony Gurney of Ellingham by his second wife Elizabeth Tyrell. She seems to have died without bearing him children as it is believed that both his daughters were by his second wife Anne Gooding (or Golding) daughter of Richard Gooding esq of Boston, who was the widow of John L'Estrange esq the third son of Sir Nicholas. It was this marriage and the interest in west Norfolk property that took him to live in Sedgeford, where he died in 1620. His daughters and their husbands were left property in his will. (TNA, PCC will 1620, PROB 11/135) Dionise married Sir William Yelverton bt of Rougham, the lawyer. Alice married Sir Hamon L'Estrange and through this much of the property returned to the L'Estrange family. However, one small manor was left by Richard to his beloved cousin Edmund Stubbes of Trinity Hall Cambridge, which reference confirmed that Richard was indeed related to the other Stubbes. Richard also left manors and lands to Francis Guybon gent, by then also of Sedgeford, his nephew.

Back to Walter and the main line of the family. He seems to have been the first of the family to favour Buxton, where he held a small manor, over Scottow. However, he was obviously a well-travelled man. He asked to be buried in the chapel of Gonville Hall if he died in Cambridge. From his bequests, he obviously had strong links to the churches of St Andrew Holborn, Scottow and St Margaret Norwich. His wife Audrey was left her jointure lands in Roughton and Alby. He also had lands in Felmingham, Wickmere and Wolterton and surrounding towns as well as the family lands in Scottow. From his and her wills we know that they had four children, Margaret, Edmund, John and Walter junior. (NRO, NCC will of Audrey Stubbes 1539, 271-3 Godsalve; TNA, PCC will Walter Stubbe 1514, Prob 11/18) Margaret, joint executrix of her mother's will, married William Bishop of Marsham. At first we thought he might have been related to or the same man as the William Bishop gent of Marsham who was married to Margaret Lumner (he died in 1545 and she in 1566 with no mention in their wills of anything to do with the Stubbes family but with clear references to Margaret's brother Edmund Lumner of Mannington). However, Audrey's will made the latter William Bishop gent a supervisor and Jane Whittle's research into Hevingham and Marsham makes clear that there was also a probably unrelated William Bishop worsted weaver here at the time, who was probably Margaret Stubbes's husband. (Jane Whittle, *The Development of Agrarian Capitalism, Land and Labour in Norfolk 1440-1580*, Oxford Historical Monographs, 2000)

Margaret's brother Edmund seems to have died young and without issue between 1514 and 1525. Walter junior of Buxton died apparently unmarried in 1528 leaving his place in Horstead, other lands and his leases of the mills in Buxton to his mother or his brother John after her death. (NRO, NCC will 1528, 104-6 Palgrave) John, the eldest son of Walter senior, and his wife Eleanor had three sons and four daughters (one of whom, Alice, married Thomas Cartwright a religious writer of the time). George Horseman esq of Booton in his 1558 will left his Booton and Witchingham lands entailed to his four sons and if they had no heirs, to his friend John Stubbes of Buxton and his sons John junior, Edmund and Francis. (NRO, NCC will 1559, 211 Goldingham) This showed the Stubbes boys to be listed in age order. John senior's will is fascinating for the detailed provisions he made to encourage all three sons to study both divinity and the law. (NRO, NCC will 1562, 258 Cowlles) He had himself been admitted to Lincoln's Inn in 1534 and was a practising lawyer in Norfolk. All three seem to have done as asked with stints at Cambridge and at the London inns. John and Eleanor's daughters were each left a good dowry of 200 marks as long as Eleanor approved of their marriages. Clement Paston esq was to be one of the supervisors.

The eldest son, John Stubbes junior, admitted to Lincoln's Inn in 1562, is covered in the *ODNB* for his religious writings and for having his hand cut off for daring to criticise Queen Elizabeth's putative French marriage. Thereafter he signed himself as 'scava', short for 'the left handed', and the will with this signature and explicit protestations of loyalty to the Queen firmly identify him as the John Stubbes of Thelveton Norfolk who died in 1590. (TNA, PCC will 1590, PROB 11/75) He left a wife Anne and a 'son in law' Francis Sharnbourne, her son by a previous marriage, but no children of his own. He had lands in Buxton, Frettenham, Horstead, Stratton (presumably Strawless) and Hainford, as well as his manor of Thelveton. His mother 'Ele' was still alive when he made the will in 1589 and he left her his great bible. Perhaps she lived with him? There may be documents surviving in the TNA relating to a dispute over Thelveton.

His brother Edmund, the local lawyer, married Mary but seems to have had no children before he died in 1614 as Edmund Stubbe esq of Lincoln's Inn. (TNA, PCC will 1614, PROB 11/123) He was admitted to Lincoln's Inn in 1575, just three years ahead of John Potts and presumably they would have known each other well from 1578 onwards and particularly after John Potts married his Norfolk bride in 1584. In his will, in addition to bequests to Humphrey Guybon esq and his wife Elizabeth, his niece Anne Crumwell, and his maid servant Audrey Bacon, he referred to his nephew John.

John senior's third son Francis carried on the family line by his children with Anne the sister of Sir Edward Coke. Most were baptised in Scottow in the 1580s and 1590s. Coke and Stubbes had known each other at Cambridge. (*ODNB*) Anne was also known for her writing on religious matters. Their eldest son was John and his uncle Edmund's will referred to the suit that John had brought against him. Edmund had been encouraged by the boy's other uncle Sir Edward Coke to resolve the dispute amicably, but despite his own olive branch his nephew persevered in the action. (TNA, STAC 8/140/27; STAC 8/271/26; STAC 8/271/27)

Francis's second son Edmund junior (presumably his uncle was godfather) seems to have been altogether more family oriented. It was he who was left the bequest of a manor from his cousin Richard Stubbes of Sedgeford. Edmund studied at Trinity and achieved BA, MA and BD by 1631. In addition to his legal career, he also continued the family tradition, inherited from his uncle Edmund a previous incumbent, of being the rector of Huntingfield in Suffolk until his death in 1659. This living was in the gift of Sir Edward Coke who held a country seat in the parish and from 1614 owned the manor.

So the Stubbes family were lawyers through and through, but tempered with a strong religious streak. Based in Scottow and Buxton and of a similar social status to the Lumners and Dodges, they would have known our families well and there is sufficient evidence from the Potts chancery and Star Chamber materials to show that Edmund Stubbes did legal work for them. Richard Stubbes as MP for Thetford in the 1589 parliament would also have known John Potts well.

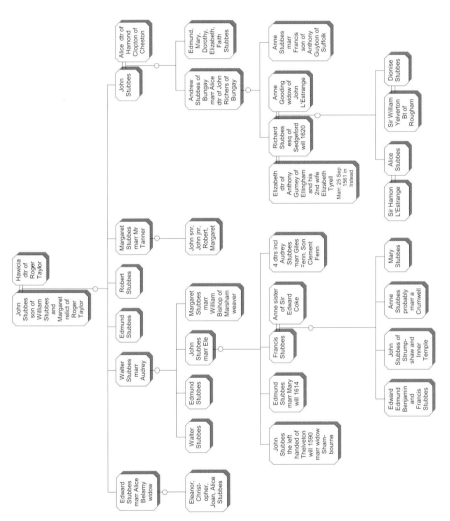

Stubbes Family Tree

Family Notes 13: Torbock of Torbock and Smith alias Torbock

The Torbock family was dominant in Torbock, Lancashire for many generations as shown by the Lancashire Visitations. Although the name of place and family gradually evolved into Tarbock and Tarbuck, here we have stayed with Torbock. In 1611, the last significant family member, Sir Edward Torbock, sold the manor to pay off debts. Through his sons Edward and George the family continued in the area for some generations. However there is nothing to indicate that Dame Mary Potts drew her descent from the children of Sir Edward, but rather from a younger branch of the family in the previous century. Nonetheless the main line of the Torbocks was active and influential in the Merchant Taylors' Company and we believe that they might have sponsored Mary's father or grandfather to become a merchant. For this reason they are included here.

Torbocks in London

Three Torbocks were Merchant Taylor freemen of the City of London. (Guildhall Lib Register of Merchant Taylor Freemen) First, Sir Edward Torbock, the head of the family and knighted in 1606, was presented freeman on the occasion of the Company's banquet for King James on 16th July 1607. He died in prison for debt in 1617. The will of Dame Clemence Torbock, Sir Edward's second wife, has survived but provides no clues to help with how the Smiths came to argue successfully to take over the Torbock arms. (Guildhall Lib, MS 9052/9 original London Archdeaconry Court will 1638. This shows only that she was a Potley by birth)

Second, Robert 'Torback', apprentice of John Morris, was admitted on 16th January 1572. This date would imply he was born in the late 1540s, which would make him probably of the same generation as Sir Edward's father also Edward. (British History Online, *Victoria History of the County of Lancaster, vol 3*, 1907. Assuming Robert and Edward senior were brothers, their father Thomas died in 1554 when his IPM showed William his eldest son to be 28. William died just a few years later leaving two very young daughters. The manor was entailed in the male line and passed to the next eldest brother Edward. Edward esq had another son Thomas.) The will of this Robert Torbock citizen of London and Merchant Taylor has survived, which shows that he later married his original boss's daughter or at least one of the family. (TNA, PCC will 1610, PROB 11/115) His first wife was buried in St Andrew Undershaft, their home parish where he also wished to be buried. His second wife Julian Morris was to be one of his executors. Robert seems to have had no children. He left legacies to the two daughters of the deceased Robert Torbock late of Northwich (about halfway between Newcastle and Tarbock). Was this Robert a son of the Thomas mentioned above? He also left legacies to his kinsmen Peter and George Torbock and George's sister Alice and her children. John Morris, clearly the unmarried junior John Morris, was to have Robert's house and much of the contents. Other Morrises were mentioned including William, who was also a Merchant Taylor of London. The Morris family occurs very often in the Merchant Taylors' freemen record. Might there have been a linkage through one of them to the Smiths?

576

Third, a Thomas Torbock was admitted freeman of London in 1626 as apprentice of Ralf Honyworth. Was he perhaps a son of Thomas the brother of Sir Edward?

The Torbock name continued in London for a century. In 1730 Mary Torbock spinster of St Andrew Holborn made her will, albeit mentioning no others of that name in it, nor with any Potts reference. (TNA, PCC will 1733, PROB 11/658)

Smith alias Torbock

The Smith als Torbock arms are cited in books as being used variously in Lancashire, Staffordshire and Yorkshire in that order of frequency. But these are usually undated references and may not be relevant to Dame Mary's claim. PW Phillimore's *Shropshire Parish Registers* refers to a Jane Smith als Torbock and a John Smith als Torbock but these may be of a later generation. For the Smith als Torbock story we have to go back to the early sixteenth century.

The Staffordshire Visitation of 1583 set out the origins of the Smith branch of the Torbock family. (HS Grazebrook, *The Heraldic Visitation of Staffordshire of 1583*, 1883) The main family in Torbock, later Tarbock, descended from Sir William Torbock of Torbock. His third son Richard Torbock of Torbock moved from Lancashire to Newcastle-under-Lyme in Staffordshire and became known as Richard Smith, 'by accident' as the Visitation noted. His son and heir was John Smith als Torbock whose 1561 will named a brother Ralph and a Thomas Smith Bailiff of Newcastle who may have been another brother. By this date it is very hard to tell apart the als Torbock Smiths from the other Smith family in Newcastle. Both from time to time held the post of mayor and alderman and other town roles. The other Smiths were the grander and better known and in due course were significantly involved in the iron foundry business. The John Smith als Torbock had two daughters, Anne and Eleanor, and two sons. Richard, the eldest was mayor and, like his father and brother John, briefly the MP for the burgesses of Newcastle. (*HofC 1509-58, Volume 3*) Richard died without issue in 1581 and John, married to Margaret Pickman, became head of the family. He seems to have died by 1583 when the Visitation showed his son Ralph as head of the family with two brothers John and Edward already having died. Ralph explicitly gave himself as Ralph Smith gent of Newcastle, alias Torbock and bore a version of the Torbock arms.

The Visitations showed a daughter of one of the John Smiths als Torbock married into the substantial Terrick family of nearby Clayton Griffith. The Newcastle town records for 1599 showed that Ralph Smith of Clayton Griffith was bound over to keep the peace in a dispute with a Newcastle trader. (T Pape, *Newcastle Under Lyme in Tudor and Early Stuart Times*, Manchester University Press, 1938) This may have been our Ralph, some years after his last mayoral stint, perhaps in his later years living with his sister. Again this might hint at Ralph not having surviving children.

Although this much is reasonably certain, we have not found the link from Ralph to Dame Mary Potts. Later Staffordshire Visitations do not show the Smith als Torbock family at all. (Ed HS Grazebrook, *The Heraldic Visitations of Staffordshire, 1614 and 1663-64*, 1885) This implies that Ralph had no surviving children, or that the whole family moved away perhaps to London. However, the various seventeenth century London Visitations do not include a Smith bearing the distinctive Torbock arms. While Newcastle parish registers have survived they show for the period 1585 to 1606 children being baptised to four different Smiths: Ralph (probably but not necessarily ours), Humphrey, Robert and John. Some of these might be the other Smith family, but might equally be issue of the younger sons of the original Richard Smith als Torbock. Both Smith families used the name Thomas from time to time, although it was particularly dominant in the other Smith family. A Thomas Smith gent was mentioned in town records taking his oath as a burgess in 1623 and it is just possible that he was Ralph's son. He played no active role in the town, but certainly owned property there. Another Thomas Smith was admitted to the Assembly in 1644. Were these the father and son we are looking for, or members of the other Smith family? The Smiths that remained in Newcastle until the end of the seventeenth century seem to be from this other Smith family as indicated by their pedigree and one or two PCC wills. (TNA, PCC will 1695 of Thomas Smith gent of Newcastle-under-Lyme, PROB 11/424; an exhaustive search of all PCC wills with relevant names and geographies from before 1600 to after 1700; extensive searching of the IGI database. The Smith als Torbock line did not feature in any of the versions of Burke's Peerage or Landed Gentry or similar books.)

Unless further research into Lichfield and York wills provides clues not yet found, at this stage Dame Mary's descent from these Newcastle-under-Lyme lines has not been proven. Probably at some point, perhaps around 1600, part of the family moved to London and became involved in trade. There may have been a couple of generations of Thomas Smith - Mary's father and grandfather. Unfortunately by the middle of the seventeenth century there were several Thomas Smiths in London and Westminster and no will has shown the connection. Presumably Dame Mary's mother Lydia had heard enough details about the family from Mary's father before he died, to establish the connection.

Family Notes 14: Wigmore

John Wigmore of Lucton who died in 1546 was the son of John senior and Agnes Stevenson. (The reference to his wife comes from *The Norfolk Visitation of 1613*, which showed John and Agnes of Herefordshire as the parents of Robert Wigmore of Roughton.) It seems that John junior had four brothers and two sisters although his 1546 IPM, concerned only with the inheritance of his son Richard, did not recite other family members. (TNA, C 142/173/101) He certainly had a brother Thomas whose own minor lands locally passed to his nephew Richard of Lucton as shown by his IPM of 1579. (TNA, C 142/186/7) This Thomas and Richard the mercer of London were the brothers in the will of William Wigmore gent of Shobdon who died in 1540. (TNA, PCC will 1540, PROB 11/28)

William married Alice the daughter of Richard Warnecombe and they produced an only child Thomas, the MP. William died shortly afterwards and his will is quite helpful. In 1540 he only leased Shobdon manor and encouraged his wife and father-in-law to purchase the manor and lands. It seems they did as it passed down William's family. This implies that he was probably only fairly recently in the manor and there had been no prior Wigmore there before him. He can also be found involved in receiving a dissolution grant with John Scudamore esq of Wilton of the Blackfriars' monastery in Hereford. Perhaps Shobdon was held by Scudamore with Wigmore having an option to buy. (*The Hereford Guide*, 1808. It is also worth pointing out that this John was probably the grandfather of Sir John Scudamore, c1542-1623. Sir John, while a teenager, was a ward of Sir James Croft and married first a daughter of Sir James. This girl was almost certainly the daughter of Alice Warnecombe/Wigmore who had remarried to Sir James Croft after Wigmore's death. He inherited his grandfather's substantial lands, which consolidated his position as head of the third Herefordshire family after the Crofts and Coningsbys. The Wigmores came a little way behind in the batting order and arguably only held onto that through their Croft and Scudamore connections as we shall see. Sir John sat frequently in parliament from 1571 to 1597. See *History of The House Of Commons* reference and link to Croft shortly. Dansey family PCC wills of 1557 and 1568 also link together the Wigmores, Scudamores and Monningtons. A local Herefordshire will particularly shows Thomas Wigmore resident locally in 1568 - Edward Hopwood of Pembridge will of that year summarised on the Wills of Herefordshire website)

William Wigmore's will inferred that his brother Thomas was nearby in Herefordshire, which would match the lands held by Thomas in the 1579 IPM. Despite holding Shobdon, William himself in fact wanted to be buried in St Michael Wood Street London. The London connection was reinforced by the reference to his brother Richard holding money for him that was to be paid to someone in or near Ludgate. This looks like Richard the London mercer and perhaps he and his brother were in trade together. William left equally to Richard and Thomas his letters patent of the receivership and customership of Abergavenny.

William left his land to his wife and son, but in case they died the default went to his elder brother Richard, then his brother Thomas and then to his two unmarried sisters Sybil and Eleanor. His brother 'Roger' was mentioned in the will but was specifically not included in the default sequence for the lands. This might well imply that he was a cleric or a comfortably-off man. Either Roger was an original transcription error for Robert, or Roger may have adopted the name Robert. Robert Wigmore was certainly from the Herefordshire family as proved by his arms but he lived and died in Norfolk where he worked for Bishop Nix of Norwich. He does not fit easily into the clan other than here and if his life was spent in a religious environment he would be unlikely to appear in a default sequence.

The main Lucton line passed through John junior's only child Richard by his first wife Eleanor daughter of Sir Thomas Cornwall. (He seems to have had no children by his second wife Mary the daughter of Sir John Longdon). His eldest son Richard died in 1580, leaving his son Richard junior as heir. (TNA, PCC will 1580, PROB 11/62) Richard junior died childless the next year, shortly after his marriage to Anne Monnington daughter of Richard. (TNA, C 142/194/4) Anne's mother Katherine was a daughter of John Scudamore esq of Holme Lacy. The Lucton estate passed to Richard junior's brother William, leaving other siblings Edmond, John, Thomas, Sybil and Mary in reserve. William married Anne Throckmorton and had as their eldest son John, a priest, whose son Robert inherited. These last two generations were particularly noted as catholics, with well-known jesuits in their ranks of whom two changed their surname to Campion out of respect for the martyr. (*ODNB*) In 1652 the estate was sequestered at Robert's expense.

The Shobdon line was arguably more politically savvy and probably not as strongly religious. After his death in 1540, William's heir was his very young son Thomas. He grew up as a ward of Sir James Croft who had married his mother Alice and who was mother of Croft's children. In due course Thomas Wigmore esq of Shobdon sat in parliament several times alongside his half-brother Edward Croft, most notably for Leominster thanks to his stepfather's patronage. (*ODNB*; *HofC 1558-1603, Volume 3*. Edward Croft married a Norfolk girl, Anne the daughter of Thomas Browne of Attleborough) The line continued through his son Warnecombe by Thomas's wife Mary Evans. After the death of the grand old politician Sir James in 1590, Thomas disappeared from the public eye. He left no will, but had died deeply in debt a few months before October 1599 when his son was involved in a chancery action regarding his father's debts and his inheritance of the mortgaged Shobdon manor. (TNA, C 2/Eliz/B16/37)

Family Notes 15: Willoughby and Hawe

Hawe

The Hawe (later consistently Hawes) family was originally from Bassingham near Aldborough (no distance from Mannington), but by the mid-sixteenth century were in Fordham and Hilgay in the fenlands. The Hawes had, in 1544, obtained property in Hilgay and Southery from Robert Hogan esq who had been granted the Priory of Modney after its dissolution.

James Hawe had married Anne, the daughter of Clement Harward of Aldborough and Bassingham (part of the same family that Emmanuel Callard later had trouble with). James Hawe esq of Fordham made his will in 1554 naming his heir as Henry Hawe of Hilgay esq. (TNA, PCC will 1554, PROB 11/37; *Visitation of Norfolk 1613;* Suff RO HD 1538/53) Henry married Ursula Holditch daughter of Robert Holditch esq from Ranworth, bringing the Ursula name into the family. (Holditch has several variant spellings.) Their only daughter and main heir was Frances Hawe who married John Willoughby, the son of George. George, of nearby Wiggenhall, was a younger son of the Willoughby family whose seat was in Risley in Derbyshire (see below). John and Frances's daughter, Ursula Willoughby, was to marry first, Sir Clement Spelman of Narborough and second, John Potts of Mannington. Blomefield quotes from a wall monument in Hilgay All Saints church that Henry Hawe died on 31st September 1592 and Ursula his wife on 8th December 1594 - they had been married for 44 years. Henry Hawe's will made in 1588 and proved in 1592 shows that he made rather complex arrangements for his real estate ensuring that his daughter and son-in-law, John and Frances, should make provision for his brother's son James. (NRO, NCC will 1592, 238 Appleyarde).

To his nephew James he left his capital messuage of Modney with all its buildings and lands in Modney field and Hilgay field and elsewhere. However, this was only until John Willoughby purchased the property or provided James an alternative suitable house to live in and an annual income of £20. In any event the property was entailed to John and Frances and their male heirs and only in default of boys would it revert to James. Further provisions were included to prevent James thwarting the intent of the bequest or creating waste on the property. For the immediate seven years after his death the Willoughbys were to have Modney anyway, paying James £20 a year. His aim was clearly that Modney should go to the Willoughbys and James should get a home and £20 a year. The other main Hawe estate in Hilgay, the manor of Downhall, was to go to John and Frances in trust for their son Henry (or his brother Francis if he died), provided that they used the profits for Henry's education until he was 21. Henry Hawe's other lands in Hilgay went to his widow for life and then to John and Frances. Since John's inheritance of Risley seemed at this time remote, he and Frances were living in Hilgay or Southery or nearby. Indeed they probably did live for a time in the capital messuage at Modney. Their children were baptised in Hilgay. Henry Hawe's inventory, taken by James Hawe gent on 1st November 1592 depicted a small hall house with the usual rambling service rooms.

(NRO, DN/INV9/176) In his goods, valued at £804, he had napery, silver and gilt plate for use in the dining chamber and linens for the 'gesse' chamber; a small armoury included a set of pistols.

Willoughby family

At much the same time that Frances Hawe's father Henry died, her husband John's uncle Michael Willoughby, the head of the family at Risley, Derbyshire, also died. Michael and Katherine Willoughby had no children. In his will proved in May 1592 Michael left his extensive lands to Katherine and after her death to Henry Hawe as trustee to the use of Michael's brother George for his life. (TNA, PCC will 1592, PROB 11/79; Derbyshire Record Office D4898/1/73, 40 Harrington. Richard Stubbes notary public was present when the will was proved in London - no doubt Richard Stubbes of Sedgeford acting for his near neighbours and showing again the connection of the Stubbes family to so many of the main characters.) After that it would all pass to George's son John Willoughby and Frances his wife and their heirs. John Willoughby and Katherine were to be his executors. Katherine's will proved in May 1594 made no change to the entail on the estates. (TNA, PCC will 1594, PROB 11/83) She made provision for the chapel that she and her husband had recently had built just across the road in Risley, including money for teaching children for free. She left legacies for Michael's brothers and sister. Katherine's 'very good nephew' John Willoughby was one of her executors and, of course, was to be the main inheritor of the Risley estate. Ursula, one of John Willoughby's daughters and later wife of Sir John Potts, was particularly favoured with the gift of two silver cups, two fine tablecloths and two cupboard cloths. Katherine was 'a woman of very goodlie & charitable disposition ... having good score of wealth and habilitie and no children of her own'. She had taken in and brought up a girl called Anne who later, when married, ended up in court against John concerning a horse and woman's saddle. (TNA, REQ 2/283/48)

Some light can be shed on why Michael might have made John his heir rather than one of his own brothers George, Raphael and Baptist. Repeatedly in the late 1590s George and Raphael and his wife Elizabeth, all of Wiggenhall St Mary Magdalen, were listed as popish recusants in certificates and returns to the Archdeacon of Norfolk. (NRO, DN/DIS 9/1a) While this showed a significant catholic strand in the Willoughby family, no doubt Michael and Katherine were mainstream protestant as shown by building the chapel in Risley. It is most unlikely in this period that it would have been for catholic services.

After leaving Hilgay, John Willoughby and Frances had no desire to retain their fen lands. In 1602 they sold to William Guybon gent of Watlington various fen grounds in Hilgay and Southery including those called Spanish Delfe, South Fenne, Depe Middles, Overseton and Netherseton (alias Oversetells and Nethersettells) and Twytlebiche all of which had been owned by Henry Hawe. (Derbyshire Record Office, D156M/E3/12) This transaction showed that Guybon could reclaim £10 if he was ever lawfully evicted from Overseton and Netherseton, indicating even then the riskiness of fenland ownership in the early seventeenth century.

582

On 14th April 1605 James Hawe gent of Hilgay (the nephew) granted and gave his interest in a property to Frances Hawe his daughter and sole heir for her advancement in marriage. (DRO, D5054/9/2/8) This deed cited an earlier one of 10th May 1603 in which John Willoughby of Risley and Henry, his son and heir, had leased to James the manor or lordship of neighbouring Southery. The package had included a foldcourse, the capital messuage called Modney (now Modney Hall) where James lived, a cottage called Modney Coate and fenland on the west side of the river Great Ouse (to which Modney was immediately adjacent on the east bank). The witnesses included John Constable. If Frances married is not known.

On 21st November 1614 Sir Henry Willoughby of Risley (Ursula's brother) and George Mellor, one of his servants, conveyed a parcel of Hilgay and Southery lands in trust to John Constable gent, another of Sir Henry's servants. (DRO, D5054/9/2/1) The property was to be for the use of Sir Henry and Dame Elizabeth and their male heirs and in default of any boys the property would pass after their death to Henry's brother Francis Willoughby esq and his son or sons, if any. At this time three distinct elements were described. First a cottage or tenement called Modney Coate in Hilgay, named after the old priory of Modney. This cottage had six acres of land in Hilgay and was in the occupation of one Cuttinge. Perhaps more important it also held 1,200 acres of fenland across on the western side of the river Great Ouse. Second was a messuage and 41 acres of land, meadow and pasture in Hilgay and Southery. Third was another much smaller parcel of 20 acres of fen ground in the occupation of Edmond Skipwith esq. On the same day another deed reinforced the transaction as it related specifically to Modney Coate and the large parcel of fenland, by permitting Constable to secure a common recovery, but still to the use of Sir Henry. (DRO, D5054/9/2/11 and DRO, D5054/9/2/3 being the recovery) Sir Henry obviously kept up links with his home parish of Hilgay after taking up residence at Risley. He presented his chaplain Phineas Fletcher as rector of Hilgay in 1621. Sir Henry died in 1649, unfortunately leaving no sons but four daughters on whom he had doted. By his first wife, Elizabeth Knollys whom Henry married about 1603, he had daughters Anne, born around 1605, and Mary possibly born in 1614. By his second wife Lettice Darcy (daughter of Sir Francis) whom he married about 1621, he had daughters Catherine and Elizabeth the youngest. (Most of the facts on the Willoughby family and their relations come from Burke's *Extinct and Dormant Baronetcies* with some additions from Visitation records, wills and chancery papers.)

Anne Willoughby's first husband, in 1639, was Sir Thomas Aston bt by whom she had daughters Magdalen and Mary as well as their son Willoughby Aston. Sir Thomas Aston was most famous for his campaign to maintain the established church and he published *A Remonstrance against Presbytery* in 1641. A royalist, he died in battle in 1646. (J Maltby, *Prayer Book and People in Elizabethan & Early Stuart England* CUP, 2000) Anne then married Anchitel (or Anchetil) Grey, MP for Derbyshire, the son of Henry Grey, 1st Earl of Stamford. By him, she had a daughter Elizabeth, to whom the Risley seat passed in 1702 after the death of her father who had lived there for many years.

Mary Willoughby married Sir Henry Griffith, created baronet in 1627, of Burton Agnes in Yorkshire. Her son, Sir Henry, married Margaret Wortley but had no children and the baronetcy became extinct. His sister Frances Griffith became sole heiress and married Sir Matthew Boynton bt and produced an heir who continued a long line of Boyntons.

Catherine Willoughby married first Sir James Bellingham bt of Hilsington, a lawyer and MP and the son of the first baronet Sir Henry and his wife Dorothy Boynton. They had no children. Catherine then married George Purefoy esq, the son of George Purefoy (whose second wife was a daughter of Sir Francis Darcy) of Wadley in Bucks. Catherine and George had Henry, who was to become the 1st Baronet Purefoy in 1662, but he died in the 1680s without issue and the title became extinct.

Elizabeth Willoughby (as seen in Chapter 11) married first, in 1642, the very much older Sir Simonds D'Ewes bt of Stow Hall Suffolk, the parliamentary colleague of her uncle Sir John Potts. Their son Sir Willoughby D'Ewes and Dame Priscilla his wife (daughter of Francis Clinton of Stourton Lincolnshire) had an heir, Sir Simonds D'Ewes, and other children. After 1650 Elizabeth married again to Sir John Wray of Glentworth in Lincolnshire. They had no children. When Elizabeth died, Sir John Wray married Sarah, daughter of Sir John Evelyn of West Dean Wiltshire, by whom he had his only daughter and heir Elizabeth Wray.

After Sir John Wray's death Sarah married again twice: first to Thomas, Viscount Fanshaw and then to Sir George Saunderson, 5th Viscount Castleton, from a Saxby, Lincolnshire family. She had no children by them, but her daughter Elizabeth Wray married Nicholas Saunderson, George's heir apparent by his first wife Grace. Elizabeth and Nicholas had a son Wray, but both Wray and Nicholas died before Sir George and the title passed to the son of James, Sir George's second son.

Between these four daughters, their husbands and children, Sir Henry Willoughby's family property was ultimately divided. His landed property had been settled before he made his last will in October 1653. (TNA, PCC will 1654, PROB 11/240) He died the following March and was buried with his ancestors in their chapel in the parish church of Wilne, in which parish Risley lay. Monetary bequests were made to his grandson Sir Willoughby Aston and his granddaughters Magdalen and Mary Aston. He also gave plate to his grandson Sir Willoughby D'Ewes. He bequeathed the sword given him by his 'son' Purefoy to a Mr Roberts.

Clement Spelman caught in the Aston firing line

Sir Henry's brother Francis Willoughby had made his will in early 1652 and Clement Spelman, his sister Ursula's lawyer son, was executor. In October 1663 Mary Aston, Henry's granddaughter and still a minor, sued Clement Spelman of Middle Temple through an action brought by her guardian the Honourable Anchitel Grey esq of Risley. (TNA, C 6/167/1) Mary claimed that her great-uncle Francis left £1,000 to her and her sister Magdalen. She had turned 17 that May and so claimed her legacy was now due. Spelman was accused of concealing the will and withholding the legacies with intent to defraud.

Clement Spelman put up a spirited lawyer's defence. First he pointed out that her natural mother, Dame Anne Aston, now the wife of 'Ansatiell' Grey, being still alive was properly her guardian not her stepfather. He also said that it was true that the £1,000 had been left for Mary at age 17 or marriage but that Francis had died without leaving enough to pay his substantial debts and legacies. Several other people had threatened to sue Spelman for their money and he had to satisfy debts before he could pay out any legacies. He would only pay the two legacies if Grey would agree to be bound to save Spelman harmless from Francis's creditors. Clement Spelman went on to list various substantial debts owing to members of the family - Palgraves, Spelmans and others. It is clear that the total was well in excess of £5,000. Rather endearingly, Spelman said that he had already paid Magdalen her £1,000 at his own personal cost. This was because 'he held her in high affection and intended to marry her if god appointed ... he resolved to pay even if it was to his own purse rather than there be any suit between Dame Magdalen and himself'. Whether in the end there was any money to pay Mary we do not know. Magdalen in fact married Sir Robert Burdett of Derbyshire and so presumably Clement lost his £1,000!

In November 1664 Mary's brother, Sir Willoughby Aston bt of Madeley Manor Staffordshire, took up the attack on Clement Spelman over family inheritance. (TNA, C 6/169/7. Willoughby was to become a major figure in post-Restoration Cheshire politics.) He claimed that his father Sir Thomas before his death in September 1645 had lands in Cheshire worth £300 a year. He stated that he was then only two and Clement Spelman pretended to take care of the estate. Now aged twenty-one he sought a full account of the rents and profits, but Spelman had refused to give him this and indeed any information on the tenants.

Clement answered from Narborough in January 1665 that Willoughby had in fact been five when his father died and he had turned twenty-one about three years ago. He also said that Sir Thomas had a life interest only in these lands and conveyed them to Dame Anne (Willoughby) as her jointure. In March 1648 Dame Anne had bargained and sold them to Sir Henry Willoughby, John and Clement Spelman in trust, with the rents to go to Dame Anne for the education of young Willoughby Aston. The other two trustees were now dead, but Clement had paid out the rents as he should. Since Dame Anne was not part of the action, he saw no reason to give out information to Sir Willoughby and said he could not be held accountable for any actions by Sir Henry during his time as the lead trustee. (TNA C 33/223 & 224)

Sir Willoughby did not give up and that June he was back in chancery with a similar action also involving his mother and her second husband, Anchitel Grey, as complainants. (TNA, C 6/75/11) Spelman now said that during the recent war the lands had been sequestered and during that time he had been asked by Sir Henry to go to Chester and enter the lands, which he had done. But Sir Thomas Aston's brother John got possession of the lands by a pretended deed of trust from Sir Thomas. This had led to chancery suits between the daughters of Dame Anne Aston and John Aston. After John's death, Thomas and Maud Parsons had obtained the premises, but with much travelling and associated costs, Spelman had prevented them from keeping the lands. He had spent much more on all this than he had ever received from the lands.

In parallel to his defence against Sir Willoughby Aston, Clement Spelman was by 1664 defending against Anchitel Grey esq, the guardian of the young Mary Aston. (TNA, C 33/223) In Easter term 1665 the case was summarised in chancery orders. As executor of Francis Willoughby's will, Clement Spelman was being pursued by various people for sums totalling about £5,000. The legacy of £1,000 to Mary Aston was just one part of the problem and there was insufficient money in the personal estate to pay it as bequeathed. However, there were other assets and it appears that the action had effectively come to chancery to win permission for Clement to pay the sum out of these other assets ahead of any other legacies. This the court ordered should be done and Mary Aston was also to be granted costs and damages in lieu of interest between her seventeenth birthday on 12th May 1663, when she legally came into the legacy, and the date of the chancery order.

However, by that summer it seems that Mary Aston refused Clement's attempt to pay her the £1,000. She would only accept it if costs and damages were added (perhaps she had been taking lessons in foot stamping from orphan Annie Potts!). These had been judged at about £26 and about £100 respectively. But Clement now argued that he had insufficient sums in the estate to pay the extra £126. His claim was obviously at least reasonably credible. It was ordered that he should pay the £1,000 and that a commission could be set up to enquire into the plaintiff's assertion that there really were funds available to pay the £126. The case did not reappear in chancery orders - presumably a settlement was reached.

Too many daughters and too many marriages!

Appendix 1: Thwaite

John Lumner the grocer was heavily involved in chancery actions regarding Thwaite manor in Norfolk. At some point during 1544-51 he acted against Miles Hubbard (Hobart) esq over a claim on Thwaite, showing that the London Lumners were still very much connected to their Norfolk roots. (TNA, C 1/1242/49-52) His father's cousin Margaret Lumner had brought the manor to her marriage to Heydon from her first marriage to Richard Browne. Blomefield wrote that the manor of Thwaite was conveyed in 1519 by Henry Heydon and Margaret his wife to Thomas Astley (Margaret's cousin - her aunt Margaret had married Astley's father Thomas Astley). This was probably a trustee conveyance at or not long after their marriage. Certainly by the 1522 subsidy list Henry Heydon esq, a Lincoln's Inn lawyer, was the main landholder in Thwaite. Lumner claimed that in about 1530 or 1532 the manor of Thwaite, through trustees, was conveyed to Henry Heydon esq and Margaret his wife, with the reversion after both had died being to Henry Lumner his father for life and then to himself and his heirs. (TNA, STAC 2/25/188) The manor was held by the trustees until February 1536 when Henry Heydon and Margaret were seized of it and she subsequently held it by right of survivorship (implying that Heydon died at that point). Margaret then remarried, to Henry Crouch (also Crich, Critch, Cruche, etc) gent and, through the two of them and Sir Edward Boughton of Kent, the deeds had been retained and had come into the hands of Miles Hubbard esq. John Lumner believed he was entitled to enter the premises and hold the manor but Hubbard had blocked this by an action for trespass. So Lumner now sought access to the writings to resolve the matter.

Hubbard replied that he agreed with Lumner's account of the early circumstances but that Henry Lumner had bargained and sold the manor (the date and other detail has been torn away) to Sir Edward Boughton. He concurred that in February 1536 Margaret alone was seized but the reversion was now to Sir Edward and his heirs. She married Henry 'Crytche' (the scribes were obviously having difficulty settling on a version of this name) and in 1540-41 Sir Edward sold the manor to this Henry and his heirs. As a result John Lumner no longer had any rights to the manor.

John Lumner replied by repeating that he was to have the manor through the named trustees or 'cognisees' after Margaret Heydon and Henry Lumner's life interests. He said that Hubbard had expelled him from the manor and taken possession by force of arms. He said that while his father had borrowed from Sir Edward Boughton, the manor had never been bargained and sold to him. One Harry Cowlie had pursued Henry Lumner for his wares and merchandise in lieu of his debts. Pretending that it would protect his Thwaite manor, Sir Edward had attempted to defraud Henry Lumner by persuading him to hand over by deed of gift all his property and to take sanctuary in Westminster while he dealt with Henry's creditors. Henry trusted Sir Edward and made the indenture but to the use of himself and his heirs not to Sir Edward's use. Boughton made no great haste to settle Henry's debts, which Henry could have done himself since his goods and chattels were then worth above £2,000. Henry stayed in London and did not go into sanctuary and then asked Boughton to return the indenture of gift, but he was refused. Instead Boughton proposed keeping the papers, Henry would have possession of his lands but Boughton would continue to act for him over his debts through a letter of attorney from Henry. John insisted no deed of bargain and sale was made and no money was paid by Boughton to Henry Lumner for Thwaite.

Miles Hubbard replied to this that it was all simply not true and that his first reply stood. (Miles was the second son of Sir James Hobart of Hales Hall and was of Plumstead near Norwich. He married Ellen daughter of John Blennerhassett of Frenze. Their eldest son, Thomas Hobart of Plumstead married Audrey Hare of Beeston and fathered the famous lawyer, judge and builder of Blickling Hall Sir Henry Hobart. Miles's younger son was John Hobart of Thwaite who married and had children by Anne daughter of Sir Philip Tilney of Suffolk.)

In 1544 Henry Crouch settled Thwaite on Miles Hobart esq of Little Plumstead and it continued in the Hobart and Kemp families for several generations, before it came to the Walpole family. The Lumners did not manage to make good their claim to Thwaite but their arms along with those of Heydon remained in the window of Thwaite church.

Appendix 2: Decoding the Sixteenth Century Mannington Estate Map

This is reprinted from a longer article published in The Annual No 17, *NAHRG, 2008. The original article contained further information on the mapmaker George Sawer and his family. The version here is without the illustrations referred to but see Plates 5 and 6 for the map and some other extracts. This article was published prior to the completion of our research for this book and in some respects our knowledge has progressed further. A second article is planned for publication in* The Annual *in 2009 dealing with the places and field names on the map.*

For over a century it has been thought that the oldest surviving map of the Mannington manorial estate in North Norfolk dates from 1565. This map is privately held by Lord and Lady Walpole, who kindly allowed us access to it to produce this article [i]. The inks are very faded and the best way to view much of the content is from the published works mentioned below and the black and white photographs taken in 1970 now held in the Norfolk Archive Centre [ii]. The latter include features, such as the layout of the buildings at Mannington Hall, which are now more or less impossible to make out with accuracy. This article and a subsequent one on the field information are designed to place all the features of the map which by using computer enhancement and documentary research are now accessible, in the public domain [iii].

The map is confidently dated as being drawn up in 1565 in RJW Purdy's 1901 article on *Mannington Hall* [iv] and Charles Tomes's booklet on *Mannington Hall and its Owners* [v] Indeed Purdy reproduces part of the map and shows *1565*, in an apparently old handwriting style, boldly positioned on a close not far from the site of Mannington Hall. Later articles have continued to quote this date [vi]. However, detailed examination of the original map shows this dating to be wrong and the positioning of the date on the reproduction of the map to be superimposed. This article sets the record straight on the date and explores in more detail what else can be learnt about the origins of the map. The next article will cover some of the landscape and field features that can be found on this map - not an easy task since some of the detail is now illegible and no field book survives to explain field usage or many of the code letters used on the map to denote users of strips and closes.

On the original map, the field in which Purdy positioned the date of 1565 has no such annotation. In common with other hedged closes belonging to the manor it is numbered and named with no other information on it - in this case: *30 The Sheeps Pasture alls* [alias] *Sheeps Cours*. The only date legible anywhere on the map is in one of the two large but only partially legible text boxes on its left hand side. In the upper of these two boxes are 19 lines of text, badly faded in parts, which appear to describe the purpose of drawing the map and the local sources used to produce the details of field allocations. The final line is badly faded, but it clearly ends *by me, Geo Sawer*. On the fifth line from the bottom one can read *the 25th day of July of 1595*. At a quick look it is possible to mistake a 9 for a 6 but with the help of digital photography, we can be sure that the date here is 1595. When the image is blown up, the down-stroke of a 9 becomes reasonably obvious and the absence of the upstroke of a 6 is clear.

The Map

The map is on a single membrane of parchment measuring 115 x 71 cm. While there are some stitch marks on the edges there is nothing about the layout or coverage to indicate whether there was another section on a second membrane. That the manor had some lands in Little Barningham, as we know from the court rolls of the time, means there could have been another section of the estate survey covering the part of Little Barningham off the top of the map. However, the large majority of the manor's holdings are on this single extant parchment.

The Mannington parish boundary is clearly delineated by a wide green colour wash. The partial parish boundaries of Itteringham, Wolterton and Wickmere can also be made out in paler colour washes. These match the modern boundaries, although Mannington is now united with Itteringham parish. Only land in the western part of Wolterton parish had been acquired by the estate in the 1540s, so the map does not extend across as far as Wolterton village and the eastern side of the parish. There is a compass drawn on the hill to the west of Mannington Hall. The top of the map is approximately north-north-west, not north - worth remembering when trying to match up to a modern map. From the features that can be compared on a modern map it seems as though the survey work of George Sawer was precise and accurate.

The map sets out the closes controlled by the manor, edging them in green and black, with many delightful little drawings of gates showing that these boundaries were hedged. These closes are nearly all named and most are numbered, although we cannot tell whether they were tenanted or part of the home farm. Various other notable features are also included and the complex network of roads, tracks and sheep drove ways can be made out. In addition and apparently in the same hand/ink we can make out drawings of quite a number of houses. Attached to many of these are names which relate to contemporary, or former, owners or tenants, all of which fit with what we know of late sixteenth century residents from the Itteringham parish register, wills and Mannington court roll entries (although from the sixteenth century the latter only survive from 1525 to 1567 and then nothing until one court of 1595) [vii]. As an example, on the eastern edge of the map, is shown *Mr Houghton's* house. In the 1580s Wolterton House and much of the surrounding land was held by Thomas Armiger. In 1592 he sold the capital messuage and surrounding acreage to Gregory Houghton, Alderman of the City of Norwich [viii]. This lends support to the 1595 dating of the map.

In addition to the text of the original map, there is another slightly different but still early hand which annotated the map in a brighter and now more orangey ink. This adds some further information particularly on the Saxthorpe side of the manor, although much of the annotation is illegible even under digital magnification. The date of these annotations is not given and is unclear from the content, but from the names deciphered and our knowledge of the evolution of the estate we believe it probably dates from the 1620s or 1630s. Unfortunately the three text panels on the map are only partially legible. These include a thin key-lined box on the

590

bottom right hand edge of the map containing what seems to be one line of writing from which nothing at all can now be deciphered. Just above it there is a measure showing 'a scale of perches' in 10 single divisions and then in tens from 0 to 50. The close juxtaposition of scale and key might imply the attribution, denoting date and surveyor, was in this corner.

John Potts - the Commissioner of the Map

Who might have commissioned it? We know that John Potts, a London lawyer, married into the Dodge family who were the holders of Mannington after the extended period of Lumner ownership [ix]. Potts purchased Mannington in 1584, rather than gaining it by inheritance. But initially he did not take up residence. His wife Anne's parents, Katherine and John Dodge, were still alive and living in Mannington Hall: one of Katherine's previous husbands had been a Lumner and she had a life interest in the estate. This is made clear by John Potts's will made in November 1593, in which he described himself as of Itteringham and referred to his leases by which 'father and mother Dodge' have the occupation of Mannington. By December 1597 when he added a codicil he was of Mannington and he died a few days later [x].

Why does this matter? Intriguingly, the map's field numbering starts not with the fields immediately around Mannington Hall but rather with those around the next most substantial house on the whole map which is at the location of the present 'Old Rectory' near Itteringham parish church. The implication is that the map was commissioned by John Potts, the owner of the estate, and that in deference to him the field numbering begins around a house of importance to him at the time rather than the manorial estate centre. The suggestion that Potts was living in this Itteringham house is strengthened by the fact that neither Mannington Hall nor this house are named on the map. To the map maker it would be self-evident to whom these two houses belonged, removing the need for naming them.

Careful scrutiny of the very faded drawing of the site of what is now the 'Old Rectory' yields a little more information. The site was mapped as one rectangular enclosure set within another - possibly both being attractively fenced or walled, but not enclosed with the markings used for field hedges. The house in the centre of the site would seem to have had an enclosed garden and/or a courtyard to the south, separated yards to the north and possibly farm buildings on the northern perimeter. A smaller building on the south-east corner of the site was probably a cottage for a retainer and matches the location of a cottage that was present there as late as the nineteenth century enclosure and tithe maps. An old water mill ('Kirk mill') on the stream now called The Cut sat close to the site's south-western corner. A path and bridge across The Cut are evident, as is an entrance to the house and its courtyard from the lane on the east side of the site. The drawing of the house is unfortunately too faint to tell its size and shape, but it seems to have been substantially taller and longer than the drawings of cottages and houses elsewhere on the map. It seems to be oriented with its main facade roughly south facing and as long as the garden/

courtyard in front of it. Whatever the precise layout and house design, there can be no doubt that this was a high status substantial home in an attractive meadow setting and larger than all the other houses illustrated except Mannington Hall.

The scale of this whole site would possibly explain the volume of finds made by Davison just to the north of Itteringham village and in the fields adjacent to this site, which caused him to wonder if the village had once been larger and had become partially deserted [xi]. The site warrants further archaeological investigation. So, we can be sure that the map shows the Mannington estate in 1595 and that John Potts commissioned it. But why?

Why was the Map Made?

Such an expensive undertaking, as this would certainly have been, must have arisen from significant need for the survey to be made. John Potts was involved in a number of legal actions after his purchase of Mannington and at first we thought it likely that the map was drawn to help him illustrate matters concerning the estate in a law suit [xii]. Also he held his first manor court as Lord of the Manor in May 1595 and although this shows no direct evidence of disputes, it would appear no court had been held for over 12 years which could easily have led to problems [xiii].

But when we started work on the map, we could only focus on what we could glean from the map itself. The two text boxes on the left hand side of the map seemed likely to give us good clues to why it was commissioned. However, infuriatingly, many hours of scrutiny left us with only part of each box deciphered. Local manor names, feast days, names of local people providing information and the date in 1595 being that of a court held that day were legible, but the whole meaning was still unclear. Elizabeth and Paul Rutledge helped hugely with their interpretation that this was probably something to do with winter sheep grazing rights, but we could only hold this as a hypothesis. And then we had a stroke of remarkable luck. While working through estate papers for Wolterton in the eighteenth century we came across a letter to Horatio Walpole from Richard Ness, the estate steward [xiv]. Walpole had built the new Wolterton Hall, created a substantial park and gardens around it and was resolutely buying up lands in the area to create a large agricultural estate. He had already acquired the Mannington Estate after the death of the last of the Potts line in 1737.

The letter is very typical of Ness letters to Walpole and is written in his wonderfully neat handwriting. It is transcribed here as faithfully as possible to show his less than modern spelling and punctuation.

31 January 1749/50 To my master about the bounds of his manor at Mannington
Hon.^d Sir/ Woolterton Jany ye 31.th 1749/50

I have rec.^d yours of the 27.th, we have had so little rains or snows since your Hon.^r left the country, that there is at present but little water in the new pond, but I am under no apprehension but it will hold water, and answer the end designed when the rains and snows falls

Since my last I examined an old survey taken in 1595 intitled as under

A plate of the Manors of Mannington, Woolterton, and Itteringham, lying in the Towns, and fields of Mannington, Saxthorpe, Barningham parva, Woolterton, Wickmere, and Itteringham, with the Liberties of Shack for the sheep of the Lord of the said Manors, in the fields and grounds of Mannington, and Saxthorpe, from the feast of Saint Michael the Archangel untill the feast of Saint Gregory; And in the fields and grounds of Mannington and Barningham parva, from the feast day of Saint Michael aforesaid, untill the feast of Saint Matthias the Apostle; And in the fields and grounds of Woolterton, and Itteringham, from the feast of Saint Michael aforesaid, untill the Annunciation of the Blessed Virgin Mary, as the limits and bounds of the said several shakes are noted in the red lines in this plate in the several townships aforesaid, taken of the information of Edm.^d Barns, Wm Larwood, James Jamlin, Thos Graver, and Wm Sutton, at the court holden for the said Manors the 25.th day of July 1595, and the said Thos Graver and Wm Sutton were sworn, and upon their oath did declare, that within all the aforesaid noted limits they have known the sheep of the Lord of the aforesaid Manors to be kept as aforesaid, by the space of twenty years past, by me Geo: Sawer

Memorandum that whereas divers of the field lands mentioned in this plate are noted with certain letters, Viz M for lands belonging to the Manors of Mannington, Woolterton, and Itteringham, Note also that where there is Ys, any other letter joined: M it is to answer a table of the several contents of the lands so noted, Also BC signifieth the lands of the Manor of Coldhams in Barningham, EC the lands of Sir Edwd Clerk K.^t. D the lands of Wm Dix Esqr P the lands of John Payne Gent: L: the lands of Chris: Langdon Gent: J the lands of Wm Jarvise EB the lands of Edm.^d Barns Y the lands of Thos Youngs

From which I think may be inferred that all those fields and lands contained in this plate, your Hon^r has the Royalty of, and are within and contained in those Manors; and this land in which the trees grew, appear to be within the precinthe of your Hon^r Manor of Mannington

There is sent by the coach one Turky and Chine, one Hare, one Cock Pheasant Two Braces of Partridges

I am your Hon^{rs} Obed^t Servt
Richard Ness

The Field book or Table of Contents are not in my custody

His interest in the 1595 map was related to some current issue about timber rights. The map shows the wooded areas of the manor quite clearly. So in 1749 it was clearly being used to resolve a local dispute.

As best we can tell from what is still legible on the map, Ness has reproduced exactly what was there, at least as he read it. However he has altered some of the spelling and punctuation - for example the second time shack appears he renders it as *shake*, whereas *shak* is clear on the map itself. However, there are two small points at which we think a different reading is called for. He records Sir Edwd Clerk Kt as one of the land owners. This was a misreading by him for *Sr Edward Cleer [Clere] Knight* who is clearly shown on one field in Itteringham and who we know held 100 acres or so of Itteringham at this time – he was a close neighbour, being in Blickling [xv]. Also he gives James Jamlin as one of the informants. We believe this is his version of Gambling, shown as such on some of the strips close to the centre of Itteringham. The other names are all recognised local figures. The Payne family had been a substantial one in Itteringham for more than 50 years. Jervis or Jarvis's house is shown on the map in Itteringham village. Graver is another Itteringham resident of the time and subsequently. Larwood held the Bintry Farm area of Itteringham and land in Saxthorpe. Dix was a major force in Wickmere and Calthorpe. Barnes was another Wickmere farmer of some scale. Sutton was a Little Barningham family. Young we do not yet know, but from the incidence of Ys in just a small number of strips on the Wickmere boundary he probably was a resident of Wickmere. In our next article we will describe further these people and the lands they held.

The three areas outlined in red, referred to in the text, are visible on the map once one knows what to look for. Unfortunately the colour has faded and it is hard to distinguish from the colouring of some of the paths and roads. We have reproduced the sheep shack boundaries on a photograph of the map. The main red line runs all the way round the large open field stripped area; sometimes following close hedges; sometimes pathways and on the Barningham and Wickmere boundaries it also follows the parish boundary markings. It comes surprisingly deeply into Itteringham village, right down almost to the site of the village shop today, and this probably implies that at least during the late autumn and winter there would have been a gate across the road here. It runs on towards Wolterton along the boundary of the adjacent manor. On the fainter Saxthorpe side of the map one can also make out sections of what seems to be a red line edging three Mannington manor closes (two in Mannington parish and one in Saxthorpe) and taking in a relatively modest amount of open field area inside the Saxthorpe parish boundary in the field of Saxthorpe. This area is quite restricted and does not stretch as far north as Little Barningham parish.

The third red line, taking in Mannington manor lands in Little Barningham, is not fully discernible, but there is certainly a section running along the field boundary immediately to the north of Mere Farm, around two sides of *The Brome Hill* field and on into Barningham. The northern limit of this area, partly in Mannington and partly in Little Barningham, is not clear. It may either have run, as we have depicted, right along the upper frayed edge of the map or, as we have said, there might have been another small section of map attached to the main one.

So there may have been multiple purposes in surveying the manor and producing this map:

- To record the lands of the manor of Mannington at a relatively early point in the ownership of a new Lord of the Manor and at a time when he faced some legal issues

- To show the areas that had been made into closes

- To clarify the ownership and occupation of all the strips in the large open field stretching from the Barningham parish boundary through half of Wolterton parish and down into Itteringham, particularly since a number of strip owners or users were from outside the manor itself

- To record the agreement of local major farmers (some of whom may have been estate tenants) that Mannington manor had winter rights of grazing and dunging their sheep on the whole of the main open field area and in small sections of Saxthorpe and Little Barningham also.

Was the map needed particularly because there had been local disagreement or dissent over field boundaries and/or sheep grazing rights? It is unfortunate that the record of the July 1595 court referred to has not survived.

However, on the map there is a reference, near the Wickmere boundary, to Dix having strips in the manor *inuistly*, hinting at some dispute. Similarly on a close, on the Wickmere parish boundary but clearly within Mannington manor, is written *Mr Dyx inuistly so*. The wealthy merchant and landowner Mr William Dix, resident in his substantial mansion at Wickmere Hall, was also the trustee/manager of the Duke of Norfolk's estates 16. Perhaps he was not satisfied with his lot and was known for illegal sorties across the boundary and encroachment onto Mannington land. This may have been just one of the issues at the time relating to the administration of the manor, which John Dodge had run for many years without a single court.

Our thanks for enabling this piece of research go to Lord and Lady Walpole who allowed us access to the original map and indeed contributed to deciphering and interpreting it. They enthusiastically supported our research into their estate papers at Wolterton, where Elizabeth Rutledge as Archivist has been most generous with her time and knowledge in helping us to make the most of what this map can reveal. Our thanks also go to Jonathan Neville for his excellent photographs, without which we would have struggled to decipher much of the content of the text on the map.

© *Maggie and William Vaughan-Lewis*

10 Dec 2007

References

i   Wolterton archives 10/25

ii   NRO Accn. Walpole 19.11.1970

iii   Vaughan-Lewis, W & M History of the Potts family, work in progress

iv   Purdy R J W 'Mannington Hall' Norfolk Archaeology XIV 1901 pp 321-8

v   Tomes C S Mannington Hall and its Owners, Norwich 1916

vi   Davison, Alan, Norfolk Archaeology Vol XLII pt 2 1995.

vii   NRO, NCR 24 Shelf e; Wolterton archives 2/25

viii   NRO, WAL 608/8, 276x5.

ix   Tomes op cit; Blomefield F History of Norfolk.

x   TNA, PCC 1598 will, PROB 11/91.

xi   Davison, op.cit

xii   Vaughan-Lewis, work in progress

xiii Wolterton archives 2/25 m9 .The earlier courts have been copied up, perhaps at Potts instruction

xiv   Wolterton archives 8/43,

xv   NRO, MC 3/28.

xvi   NRS Volume LXIV Bacon papers Vol IV; Blomefield.

Notes to Chapter 1

1. TNA, PCC will 1508, PROB 11/16
2. Francis Blomefield, *An Essay towards a Topographical History of Norfolk*, 11 vols, 1805 (hereafter Blom)
3. Harleian Society Vol 1, *The Visitation of London 1633, 1634 & 1635*, 1880. The other Visitations consulted were *1568, 1569-90*, Harleian vols 109-110 and *1687*, Harleian Society new series 16. (hereafter *London Visitation*)
4. TNA, PCC will 1504, PROB 11/14
5. Downes Papers in the Cheshire and Chester Archives and Local Studies Service (hereafter Cheshire). An excellent calendar is available online via the A2A website.
6. These paragraphs are drawn from Blom on Raynham and Ingoldisthorpe and TF Teversham, *A History of the Village of Sawston, Part 2*, 1947.
7. Downes papers; Geoffrey's will; Lady Joan's PCC will; and a number of books that cover aspects of Geoffrey and Lady Joan, including: C Harper-Bill, *Religious Belief and Ecclesiastical Careers in Late Medieval England*, 1991; *The Plumpton Letters and Papers*, The Plumpton Family and JW Kirby, Camden Society and Royal Historical Society, 1996; F Madden, *Collecteana Topographica et Genealogica*, 1843; J Biancalana, *The Fee Tail and the Common Recovery in Medieval England, 1176-1502*, 2001
8. TNA, C 241/113
9. Cheshire, DDS/481, a letter written from London in the early 1490s
10. Cheshire, DDS/483
11. The will was published in full in *The Cheshire Sheaf, First Series, ii (1880-82)*, pp 46-8 and 51-2.
12. He received his MA from Jesus College Cambridge in 1515-16. JA Venn, *Alumni*
13. Cheshire, DDS/206, which in 1545 provided for Roger Downes's nine daughters and their marriage portions, with Master Geoffrey Downes, DD, Chancellor of the Cathedral of York, in a trustee role. This Geoffrey was probably Roger's uncle and one of the many brothers of Robert the head of the family who died rather young in 1520.
14. Cheshire, DDS/167
15. John P Earwaker, *East Cheshire: Past and Present; or a history of the Hundred of Macclesfield in the County Palatine of Chester*, 1877
16. TNA, PCC will 1494, PROB 11/10
17. Cheshire, DDS/127
18. Cheshire, DDS/139 and 140
19. Cheshire, DDS/149 and 150
20. Cheshire, DDS/162
21. Cheshire, DDS/161
22. Cheshire, DDS/549
23. TNA, C 1/209/24
24. Teversham; L Campion, *The Family of Edmund Campion*, 1975
25. The chancery action was by John Apott of Sawston, husbandman and son of James Apott, against James Apott of London over the detention of deeds relating to land in Sawston claimed by the defendant, a bastard son of James TNA, C 1/462/17.
26. TNA, C 4/98/49
27. TNA, PCC will 1508, PROB 11/16
28. TNA, PCC will 1501, PROB 11/12

29. CRO, Ely Consistory Court will 1525, VC 8:100
30. CRO, box 488 early manorial documents
31. Guildhall Lib, Ms 11592 Grocers' Company Apprentice and Freemen Admissions
32. Guildhall Lib, Ms 11571/3
33. TNA, C 1/417/30
34. TNA, STAC 2 18/236 & /237
35. TNA, STAC 2 18/237
36. TNA, C 1/1520/2
37. TNA, C 1/1016/93-7
38. TNA, C 1/972/18
39. TNA, C 1/991/53-4
40. TNA, C 1/1206/54
41. TNA, C 4/67/68, an undated item
42. TNA, REQ 2/18/35
43. TNA, C 1/972/18
44. TNA, C 1/880/33
45. Guildhall Lib, London Record Society, *Two Tudor Subsidy assessment rolls for the City of London: 1541 and 1582*, 1993
46. *CPR* Edward VI
47. TNA, REQ 2/17/8
48. British History Online, *Victoria County History of Bedfordshire Volume 3*
49. Guildhall Lib, Ms 11588/1; 1556 is the first year for which these records survive.
50. TNA, PROB 10/32 will 95, among a group of original wills that may not have been proved.
51. TNA, SC 12/28/3; SC 12/31/12; SC 12/8/29; SC 6/Henviii/1587
52. This roll also showed a John Pott in Albury near Bishop's Stortford - was he the Babraham man?
53. TNA, E 179/121/176; T Robson, *The British Herald*, 1830; W Brigg, *Hertfordshire Genealogist and Antiquarian, Volumes 1-3*, 1895-99; D Jones-Baker, *Hertfordshire in History: Papers Presented to Lionel Munby*, 2004
54. TNA, PCC wills: 1553 Thomas Wygg of Mentmore Bucks, PROB 11/36 and 1585 Robert Wigg grocer of London, PROB 11/68
55. *London Visitation* shows two generations of Arthur Holte in London from the late fifteenth century.
56. TNA, PCC will 1572, PROB 11/54 John Parker senior's personal estate went to his wife Anne, as his executrix, and two of his children John and Anne Parker. His elder daughter Margaret had already had £200 given to her husband Robert Phillipson on their marriage. He mentioned his three brothers Thomas, Hugh and Rauf Parker, his sister Alice Croket and children of his sister Margaret Browne. Alice and her son Thomas lived rent free in a house that John leased of Mr Alderman Offley. His apprentice at this time was a William Ebden – coincidentally another Sawston name - and he mentioned his cousin Doctor Ebden. This was the overseer of his will Mr John Ebden, Doctor of Divinity. He mentioned another cousin Ellen Clere. His maid servant was Margaret Bydell, probably the Margaret Bedall of the earlier Apott will. His express wish was that his wife would keep herself single to look after his children and he said that as a result he had 'given to her more liberally of my lands', which went to her for life and then to his son and his heirs. He may have already left property to Anne by deed as the only

property left to her in the will was his 'mill commonly called the windmill with the hill whereupon the mill stands and 40 foot of assize compass about said the mill … lying in a certain field called London Field in the parish of Stebnnhythe [Stepney] Middlesex'. Elevated postmills to the north and east of the city can be seen drawn on the Agas map of London dated to the 1560s. To his daughter Anne he left his messuage called The Peacock in Bridge Street in St Leonard in East Cheap.

57. The spelling Paris is used throughout for Parris, Parys, Pareez, etc.
58. TNA, PCC will 1505, PROB 11/14
59. TNA, PCC will 1520, PROB 11/19
60. The other daughter Anne married William Mordaunt of Hempstead just over the boundary in Essex.
61. TNA, PCC will 1517, PROB 11/18
62. TNA, PCC will 1520 of William Parys, PROB 11/19
63. TNA, PCC will 1559, PROB 11/42A
64. *The Visitations of Cambridgeshire 1575 and 1619,* Harleian Society vol 41, 1897; *Miscellanea Genealogica et Heraldica 5th series volume 2*
65. There had been a Paris family in London - eg, the 1485 will of John Paris pewterer of London TNA, PCC will 1485, PROB 11/7. He was of St Botolph beside Billingsgate and also had a 'great tenement The Swan' in Holborn and lands in Kent. His father was William. His wife and daughter were both Agnes. There was no male heir. There are also PCC wills in 1517 of a John Paris of London, leather seller and in 1550 of a Thomas Paris, gent of London; but neither seems to provide a link to Margaret. TNA, PCC will 1517, PROB 11/18 and PCC will 1550, PROB 11/33
66. TNA, PCC will 1518, PROB 11/19
67. John Burke, *Extinct and Dormant Baronetcies of England,* 1964 (1844)
68. Blom described him as a 'Visitor of Abbies' at the dissolution and there was a Paris property in Norfolk at Pudding Norton.
69. G Townsend, *The Acts and Monuments of John Foxe, vol 6,* 1838
70. TNA, PCC will 1558, PROB 11/40

Notes to Chapter 2

1. An Alice Pott was baptised at St Clement Eastcheap on 2nd August 1551. Although Alice was Roger's grandmother's name, this would be too close to Elizabeth's baptism to be Roger's child.
2. The Pardon Roll of January 1 Elizabeth [1559] included: Roger Apott of London alias of Lyons Inne in the parish of St Clement Danes without the bars of the New Temple London alias citizen and grocer of London. *CPR* Elizabeth I vol 1 1558-60
3. TNA, PCC will 1561, PROB 11/44
4. In his 1540 will he left her his whole estate for the maintenance of the free school. TNA, PCC will 1540, PROB 11/28. The wealthy grocer's widow, Avice remarried Sir Anthony Knevet, Gentleman Waiter of the King's Private Chamber. Knevet made Avice his executrix and left her his personal estate and everything she had from her previous husband so that she could continue to perform Gibson's will. He also indemnified her from his own debts. TNA, PCC will 1548, PROB 11/32. At her death she left the school in the care of the Coopers' Company. John Stow, *A Survey of London 1598*; Liza Picard, *Elizabeth's London,* 2003

5. D Jones-Baker, *Hertfordshire in History: Papers Presented to Lionel Munby*, 2004
6. TNA, PCC will 1567, PROB 11/49
7. Mistakenly Harleian Society, *The Visitations of Hertfordshire 1572 and 1634,* vol 22, 1886, says she was the daughter of Sir Ralph Boteler of Woodhall in Watton-at-Stone Hertfordshire by his wife Katherine Kilpeck. Nothing is known of this Sir Ralph who does not feature in the obvious local histories, seems not have added to the family estates and left no will. This appears to be a reference to a much earlier generation, but it is often cited as her and her siblings' father.
8. Huntingdon Record Office, Archdeaconry of Huntingdon will vol 8 page 52
9. A family bible gives 14 children up to November 1534; the *Visitations of Hertfordshire* has 19 but excludes Katherine.
10. TNA, PCC will 1554 of John Gale gent, PROB 11/37, wife Elizabeth and 'brother' William Butler as overseer
11. Katherine Boteler, being a younger daughter of the first Sir Philip, was only a few years older than her nephew Sir Philip who was head of the family after Katherine's eldest brother died. He and Katherine had their children at much the same time. His son, also Sir Philip, died in 1592, predeceasing his father by 14 years.
12. TNA, PCC will 1576, PROB 11/58
13. TNA, C 142/149/71
14. Various TNA documents and *London Visitation*
15. TNA, PCC will 1554, PROB 11/37
16. TNA, C 1/1297/26-28
17. *Victoria County History of Hertfordshire,* 1907-1937
18. WJ Hardy, *A Calendar to the Feet of Fines for London and Middlesex, vol 2,* 1893
19. *CPR Elizabeth I* vol 2 1560-63
20. TNA, C 1/1297/26-28
21. TNA, PCC will 1557, PROB 11/25
22. TNA, PROB 2/311C
23. Hertfordshire Record Office, *The Hertfordshire Genealogist, vol 3*; *Calendar of Feet of Fines* as above
24. *Calendar of Feet of Fines* as above
25. In March 1574 a William Doddes was one of 24 governors given a grant to found a grammar school in Barnett, Herts. *CPR Elizabeth I* vol 6 1572-75. At this time he was styled as citizen of London; which, if this was our man (which might not be so), would match with him having then lived in Islington and probably having a London trade background.
26. TNA, PCC will 1577, PROB 11/59
27. Guildhall Lib, Lincoln's Inn *The records of the Honorable Society of Lincoln's Inn: the Black Books,* vols 1-4, 1897-2001
28. Harleian Society, *A Collection of miscellaneous grants, crests ... and exemplifications of arms, Pts 1-2* vols 76-77, 1925 -26
29. T Robinson, *The British Herald or Cabinet of Armorial Bearings,* 1830; MA Lower *The Curiosities of Heraldry,* 1845; G Seton, *The Law and Practice of Heraldry in Scotland,* 1863
30. BL, Add Ms 14295 f.31 & Harley Ms 1359 f.98b. Further BL sources: Guil 68; Add Ms 12474 f.51b and 4966 f.63 have not been checked.

31. Blom refers to a William Potts in Itteringham in 1274 who, while he may have been a local man of some substance, was not a knight and was almost uncertainly unrelated.

32. G Rice, *Transcript of Sussex Wills, vol 3*, Sussex Record Society 1938

33. KA Fowler, *Medieval Mercenaries*, Blackwell, 2001; EJ Mickel, J Nelson, GM Myers, *The Old French Crusade Cycle*; websites for the Louvre, Chateau de la Rochepot, French and German Wikipedia on the Pot family, the Order of the Golden Fleece, the Order du Saint-Esprit, etc; various mid-nineteenth century translated editions of Enguerrand de Monstrelet's *The Chronicles of England, France and Spain* on Google Books

34. *The State of England Anno Dom,1600* by Thomas Wilson, State Papers Domestic PRO (ed F J Fisher) as printed in *1603 A Turning Point in British History,* Christopher Lee 2003, p.55. Also Lee p.56-7: In 1603 more than a thousand young men went to Oxford and Cambridge … There was a third university, the Inns of Court, which provided the lawyers but was also where young men were sent to learn a little law in order to manage the family estates ... there was considerable debate about the laws of inheritance ... Sir Francis Bacon wrote that laws were confusing and obscure and thus landowners were often worried about the process of passing on the family estate. ... Wilson in 1600 recorded 1 marquess, 19 earls, 2 viscounts, 39 barons, 500 knights and 16,000 gentlemen. If we take our definition of a gentleman as someone with an estate of say 300 acres we should add to it a further definition: gentleman was a recognisable title for someone who did not have to labour.

Notes to Chapter 3

1. *LPFD Henry VIII* vol 19

2. *LPFD Henry VIII* vol 21

3. Agas map as printed in *The A-Z of Elizabethan London,* Prockter and Taylor, London Topographical Society No 122, 1979

4. E Williams, *Early Holborn and the Legal Quarter of London*, 1927

5. TNA, SC 6/henviii/2396 and /2400. 'PRO' references to the 1500 and earlier rental rolls are all cited in E Williams, *Early Holborn.*

6. *Miscellanea Genealogica et Heraldica 5th series vol 2*

7. TNA, REQ 2 1/71   Around April 1524, Thomas Perpoynte, citizen and draper of London, took action against Thomas Edwards, citizen and grocer, over the debts and lands of John Nanseglos the elder, TNA, C 1/556/24. Nanseglos had, for £200, mortgaged his Redfans property to Henry Daker another London draper and owed £290 to Thomas Edwards covered by a statute of the Staple of Westminster. Edwards had now exercised the statute, called in the debt and had claimed Redfans, the Holborn property and land in Northamptonshire so that he could enjoy their annual rents until his £290 was paid off - which would take some 13 years. The bill of complaint to chancery showed that Perpoynte believed he had done a complex deal with Edwards whereby he had paid off Daker and arranged that Edwards would receive title to the Holborn lands and some cash in return for cancelling the debt from Nanseglos. This would then leave Perpoynte holding all Nanseglos's debts, effectively charged against the remaining Essex and Northants properties. But Edwards had reneged on the deal. Later Perpoynte paid off Edwards and at the peak it appeared that Nanseglos owed him over £1,100 by Perpoynte's reckoning. At one point during this period, Nanseglos had even been put in prison for non-payment of a debt.

8. TNA, C 1/660/8 and /11; SC 6/Elizi/3368; C1/55/1 and /4; C 1/1509/9; C 241/278/10 and /94; C 241/283/31; C 131/106/1 and /35; REQ 2/5/30; REQ 2/1/71
9. E Williams, *Early Holborn*
10. TNA, PCC will 1545 John Romyng, fletcher PROB 11/30; PCC will 1566 Richard Cliffe gent, PROB 11/48; C 142/146/62&63; C142/155/148; C 142/201/136; C 142/203/18; C 3/39/79
11. WJ Hardy and W Page, *Feet of Fines for London and Middlesex vol 2*, 1893
12. TNA, PCC will 1523, PROB 11/21
13. TNA, PCC will 1523, PROB 11/21
14. TNA, C 142/116, 142/95, C 1/796/32, C 1/670/204, C 1/670/17, REQ 2/8/278; TNA, PCC will 1546 of William Rest, PROB 11/31
15. TNA, C142/149/71. The enquiry was slow to happen, being commissioned on 5th June 1567 and re-commissioned to enquire better into his property in October 1570 - *CPR Elizabeth I* vols 4 and 5.
16. TNA, C142/158/6
17. TNA, C142/256/40
18. TNA, C142/262/101
19. Mark Eccles, *Christopher Marlowe in London*, Harvard University Press, 1934
20. Guildhall Lib, Ms 4248
21. *HofC; ODNB*
22. *ODNB*; John Stow, *A Survey of London written in the year 1598,* ed Antonia Fraser, 2005
23. TNA, C 142/190/4
24. TNA, PCC will 1579, PROB 11/61
25. TNA, PCC will 1575, PROB 11/57
26. Margaret was the daughter of _ Bostock of Newington, Surrey. Douglas Richardson, Kimball G. Everingham, David Faris, *Plantagenet Ancestry: A Study in Colonial and Medieval Families*, 2004
27. TNA, PCC will 1588, PROB 11/72
28. TNA, C 24/201
29. TNA, PCC will 1584, PROB11/67
30. TNA, C 3/214/62
31. TNA, C 33/77
32. TNA, C 33/78
33. TNA, C 33/80
34. TNA, REQ 2/276/33
35. WJ Hardy and W Page, *Feet of Fines* as above
36. TNA, PCC will 1559, PROB 11/42B
37. And see Peter Whitfield's excellent 2006 book *London: a Life in Maps* for other references to this area in the sixteenth century.
38. Websites of AIM25 and St Bartholomew's Hospital
39. Mark Eccles, *Christopher Marlowe*; 1598 Subsidy Roll
40. *A Descriptive Catalogue of Ancient Deeds in the PRO, vol 6,* 1890
41. TNA, C 2 Eliz/L10/60
42. TNA, C 33/90
43. TNA, PCC will 1586, PROB 11/69
44. TNA, C 33/102
45. TNA, C 33/104

46. John's IPM: ... and of and in five messuages in St Botolph without Busshopgate London ... and that the five messuages in St Botolph were held of the Queen freely and not in chief and value £3 pa. Katherine's IPM echoed this: ... and in five messuages in St Botolph extra Bishopsgate, London ... five messuages in St Botolph held of the Queen in free and common socage and not in chief value £3 pa.

Notes to Chapter 4

1. C Tomes, *Mannington Hall and its Owners,* 1916
2. The chancery and exchequer versions of the Mannington IPM of 1558 differed in their descriptions of the relationship between the various members of the Sharrington line who were included as potential inheritors of Mannington in default of male heirs.
3. Vaughan-Lewis*, Lordship and Landscape* working title in progress, 2008
4. Some sources in error give his father as married to Maud Fewell.
5. NRO, Norwich City Court Roll 16, NCR Case 1, m6 dorse
6. She had remarried to John Hore esq of Childerley, Cambs after Sir Robert's death in about 1426. Her brief will mentioned no individuals other than Lumner and his co-executor John Rowith. TNA, PCC will 1436, PROB 11/3; C 1/9/179; E 326/303
7. J Gairdner, *The Paston Letters*, 1987 microprint edition; N Davis, *The Paston Letters and Papers of the Fifteenth Century, Part 1*; R Barber, *The Pastons: A Family in the Wars of the Roses*, 2004; C Richmond, *The Paston Family in the Fifteenth Century* 3 vols1990-2002
8. TNA, C 139/141/4
9. He may have held the office of Bailiff at Thetford in 1471, at that time a Crown appointment of high status held for life. Hamon Le Strange, *Norfolk Official Lists from the earliest times to the present day,* 1890
10. Gairdner as above; [1460] April 6, vol 3, 208 'Sir, further, I am in building a poor house. I trust God that ye shall take your lodging therein here after when you come to your lordshipps on tho partes. And I durste be so bold on your mastership to ask of you 12 copill of oken sparris, I wold heartily pray you not to have them, but ther they may be for bore beste and that is at a yard of yours in Saxthorpe, called barkers. I have ash but no oak, but little now comyth the felling thereof etc.'
11. Considerable work has been done by many authors to produce comprehensive lists of licences to crenellate. The most accessible and comprehensive summary of this work sits on the website The Gatehouse compiled by Philip Davis. This shows no entry for Mannington in the source documents such as the Charter Rolls and Patent Rolls and no evidence of any secondary source hinting at a licence.
12. MI brass in Itteringham church
13. NRO, NCC will 1483, 139 Caston
14. See footnote 36 in Chapter 5
15. NRO, NCC will 1504, 128/9 Rixe
16. NRO, NCC will 1494, 202-5 Wolman. Thomas Brigges left small bequests to two monks - Henry Brigges and Nicholas Lumner. We assume the former was a brother (Thomas died without issue making a brother Edward his heir) and that Nicholas was perhaps a brother of William Lumner senior. Nicholas did not feature in Margaret's will. Again, these Lumners were absent from the later default sequence showing that they produced no heirs.
17. The name has a variety of forms including Winborough. The Norfolk village is now spelt Whinburgh.

18. Critically, Thomas Langdon's father, also Thomas (married to Margaret Davy), died in 1506-07 and left a will implying that his children Thomas and Elizabeth were under age. NRO, NCC will 1506-07. However, Margaret Lumner's daughter Anne must have been born in the 1450s or 1460s (the 1470s at the very latest), which would have made her a full generation older than her alleged husband Thomas Langdon junior. On the other hand, William Lumner junior had his children in the 1490s making for a perfect match with a young Thomas Langdon born around that time also. Anne Lumner married the young Thomas Langdon, the second largest landholder and farmer in Wolterton after the Moore family. The elder Thomas Langdon had been the Secretary to Lord Scales and is thought by some to have been the first of the family to come to Norfolk. JJ Muskett, *Suffolk Manorial Families*, 1900; Suffolk Record Office (Ipswich), HD 1538153, Clarencieux Cooke's notes for his Heraldic Visitation of Norfolk. However, *Norfolk Genealogy* vol 22 gave his grandfather as the Secretary and argued for Wolterton origins for the family - we disagree with the first point and tend to agree with the second. The Heydons, Langdons, Brigges and Lumners all knew each other well from legal and administrative service to the largest land-holding families of Norfolk such as the Dukes of Norfolk and Suffolk and those close to them (Anthony Woodville, Earl Rivers became Lord Scales and effectively took over the large and powerful affinity group of the Dukes of Suffolk). Thomas Langdon senior seems to have been active as a Lumner family trustee around the turn of the century and this supports the belief that he, not an earlier Langdon, was the Secretary to Scales.

19. Edward or Everard Brigges married and had children by Cecily daughter of Edmund Moore of Wolterton. Cecily was mentioned in Anne Boleyn's 1510 will.

20. It is also worth noting that Brigges made detailed bequests to all the Lumner children and there was no additional unmarried Anne Lumner amongst them. The only puzzle is the Joan Lumner, who from the size of her legacy was an unmarried girl receiving a promise of a marriage portion. While possibly an unmarried daughter of William and Margaret, it seems quite likely that this was the young Joan daughter of Thomas and Anne who in time would marry Henry Dawbney of Sharrington. Margaret's will made no mention of a Joan, but then she did not do grandchildren.

21. We have found no other reference to a James Lumner and the wills of Aleyn and Thomas in London specifically preclude either of them having a son of that name. There is no indication that another Lumner brother left any children.

22. NRO, NRS 2624, 12C2

23. Jane Whittle, *The Development of Agrarian Capitalism: Land and Labour in Norfolk, 1440-1580*, 2000

24. NRO, NCC 1500 will of Thomas Astley esq, 221-2 Cage; note on Thomas Astley from *IPM Henry VIII vol 2*: Thomas was son and heir of John Astley esq and married Margery, daughter of William Lumner. She died before Thomas and he died 8th November 1500. They had as their son and heir Thomas 'the elder' aged 26 in November 1501.

25. *CPR Henry IV* vol 4; JE Thorold Rogers, *Oxford City Documents 1268-1665*, Oxford Historical Society vol 18, 1891; *HofC, 1386-1421* entries for John Spencer, John Wynter, John Wodehouse and John Tyrell

26. Guildhall Lib, Ms 11592A. The early rendering of his name suggested he was related to Roger Limmoa gent of St Michael Bassishaw London who left a Commissary Court of London will in October 1470 naming his wife Alice and daughter Anne. Guildhall Lib, Ms 9171/6, 1470, register 6 fo 62. However, no evidence was found to connect them.

27. TNA, PCC will 1491, PROB 11/8, catalogued in error as Aleyn Lounds or Lomms

28. Guildhall Lib, *Calendar of Letter-Books of the City of London vol K: Edward IV and Henry VII*

29. *IPM Henry VIII* vol 2

30. TNA, PCC will 1492, PROB 11/9, Elizabeth Lomnor widow

31. TNA, C 1/209/24

32. *Acts of Court of the Mercers' Company 1453-1527*, Cambridge University Press, 1936. Interestingly it is clear that a Cambrai lawn merchant, Reyner Lomner, was operating in London in the 1470s. He was involved in a long series of court actions in about 1474, notable for the high costs incurred in pursuing a debtor in the Mayor's court, King's Bench and Common Pleas. There is no indication that he was related - a rare parallel development of the surname from the same Luminour root seems likely. P Tucker, *Law Courts and Lawyers in the City of London, 1300-1550*, 2007

33. J Gairdner, *The Paston Letters*, 1987 microprint edition; N Davis, *The Paston Letters and Papers of the Fifteenth Century, Part 1*; R Barber, *The Pastons: A Family in the Wars of the Roses*, 2004

34. *ODNB*; will reproduced in full in S Bentley, *Excerpta Historica*, 1831

35. *CPR Henry VII* vol 2 1494-1509

36. TNA, PCC will 1492, PROB 11/9, catalogued in error as Lynnis

37. Guildhall Lib, *Calendar of Letter-Books of the City of London, vol L: Edward IV and Henry VII*

38. Guildhall Lib, Ms 11592A. As 'Lumner', Henry had his own apprentice, Jerard Ledar, admitted in 1517. To be admitted five years after Henry perhaps Ledar had started his apprenticeship with someone else. However, the 1512 admission falls just at the end of a known 5 year problem period for recording admissions and Henry Lumner may have been admitted several years earlier. If so, this would also reduce the apparent disparity in age between him and his brother. We can find no earlier Henry Lumner as a member of a senior merchant company and cannot explain this Henry Lumner except as the son of Thomas the mercer. Henry the grocer was in the later family default sequence and in the logical place in that sequence to be the younger brother of Thomas of Sharrington.

39. Guildhall Lib, Ms 23489

40. *LPFD* vol 16

41. *LPFD* vol 15

42. *LPFD* vol 3

43. TNA, C 1/845/46-47

44. TNA, C 241 283/2, C 241 283/11, C 1 563/21, C 1 735/16, C 1 840/40

45. *LPFD*, vol 12

46. *LPFD* vol 11

47. The 'elder' Thomas Astley, son of Thomas Astley and Margery Lumner, had married first Anne Boughton from Lawford Warwickshire (W Betham, *The Baronetage of England*, 1802). By her, Astley had his son and heir John. Confusingly he also had another son John by his second wife Anne Wood, so the precise identity of the John Astley above has to be assumed. The younger John seems likely. Anne Wood from East Barsham was the sister of Lady Elizabeth wife of Sir James Boleyn and her son John Astley of Maidstone was to become Master and Treasurer of the Jewel Office to Queen Elizabeth and Chief Gentleman of the Privy Chamber. This John Astley was also a Member of Parliament several times, including the 1589 session. ODNB. His son Sir John Astley was to become Master of the Revels. GF Beltz, *Review of the Chandos Peerage Case*, 1834; John Chambers, *A General History of the County of Norfolk etc*, Norwich 1829

48. TNA, C 1/947/33-35. As far as we can tell this Boughton was not from Warwickshire (where a man of the same name can be found), but from Burwash Court in Plumstead next to Woolwich, where he also held Woolwich manor. TNA, PCC will 1550 of Sir Edward Boughton of Woolwich, PROB 11/33; WH Ireland, *England's Topographer ... History of the County of Kent*, 1830; T Wotton et al, *The Baronetage of England*; A Collins, *The English Baronetage*; D Lysons, *The Environs of London vol 4*, 1796. One of his descendants is believed to have sold the Woolwich manor in 1555 and by 1575 it was held by Sir Christopher Heydon, but the precise details of the sale are vague. Boughton's sons and executors were Nicholas and Henry - TNA, C 147/364. His will showed that he had three other sons and three daughters and that Nicholas was named for Sir Edward's father. The will contained no reference to Warwickshire. Burwash Court, previously held by Thomas Grene esq, was acquired during the reign of Henry VIII by Sir Edward Boughton. The mechanism to acquire Plumstead would seem to have been a 1538-39 exchange of some of Boughton's other Kent lands with the crown, in whose hands Plumstead was at that time. E Hasted, *The History and Topographical Survey of the County of Kent, vol 9*, 1800. There is some speculation that the Boughtons had been trustees in a deed relating to the manor of Woolwich in the 1460s or 1470s, but this is so vague that we cannot be certain that they were ever anciently of Kent. It is not clear when they bought Woolwich manor which was still in other people's hands at the turn of the century. Sir Edward has not been connected to the Warwickshire Boughton family, but it is at least possible that he was a younger son of that family (in which Edward featured very regularly as a first name). A link to the Anne Boughton married to Thomas Astley is therefore possible but by no means certain.

49. William Roche was in office in 1540.

50. TNA, C 1/1242/49-52

51. LPFD, vol 20. The reference may have been to the John de Blase who left a PCC will in 1583, PROB 11/65; a Blase Saunders was Warden of the Grocers in 1573.

52. In fact two wills survive, both proved in the PCC. The earlier one, TNA, PCC will 1508, PROB 11/16 contained many original transcription errors and seems to have been re-proved in 1515 in PROB 11/17. The second one is the same will but with spelling made clearer.

53. TNA, REQ 2/3/40

54. Confused? For those interested in the tenure of Thwaite manor the actions make entertaining reading TNA, C 1/735/15, C 1/961/67, C 1/970/69, C 1/1210/63, C 4/43/5, C 147/364, REQ 2/3/388, REQ 2/3/40.

55. *Monty Python's Flying Circus*, BBC Television

56. *LPFD* vol 15

57. Blase Saunders was admitted to the Company of Grocers in 1541, having been an apprentice of William Butler. This made Saunders a contemporary of James and Roger Apott in the Company and he would have been well-known to them. This is another indication of early links between the Potts and the Lumner/Dodge families. As well as helping Katherine Wigmore as overseer, he was mentioned in Edmund Lumner's 1558 IPM. He left a will in 1581 as Grocer and Merchant of the Staple. TNA, PCC will 1581, PROB 11/63

58. NRO, 1494 NCC will Wolman 202-5

59. TNA, IPM of 1542 in E 150/642/5 and C 142/ 66/52 - there are minor differences between the two versions but these do not confuse the key information contained. It is

noteworthy that at no point do these IPMs refer to Thomas as Margaret's son - in fact no relationship was stated. Perhaps the officials found it all too difficult to describe her relationship to Thomas as his aunt through her first of three husbands.

60. NRO, NCC 1479 will, 49, 5A Caston

61. Sir John Heydon of Baconsthorpe died in 1479 having been married to Eleanor Wynter daughter of Edward Wynter of Winter Barningham. Sir John's will mostly contained religious and charitable bequests. His son Henry, later Sir Henry Heydon, was an executor and there was a mention of Lady Boleyn (presumably the mother of Anne, who was daughter of Sir Geoffrey and Dame Anne Boleyn of Blickling and wife of Sir Henry Heydon according to the Visitation). Also there was a passing reference to Ed Moor (possibly Edmund Moore of Wolterton) being 'consanguinei mei'. But otherwise the will provides no help on the detailed structure of the Heydon family at the time. The Visitations and Blomefield do not add anything material so Sir Henry Heydon's siblings are uncertain, even though much more is known about his children and subsequent generations. Our suggestion is as follows: Heydon lands were settled on Thomas Lumner senior of Sharrington in 1499-1500 implying that his mother was a Heydon and therefore a daughter of Sir John and sister of Sir Henry. Aleyne Fenner in his article in NAHRG's *The Annual* Number 13 2004 on the Hobart family of Hales Hall showed that Sir Walter Hobart c1477-1538 married first Elizabeth Heydon and second Anne Ratcliffe; the latter in 1510 or 1511. This would make it quite possible that Elizabeth, who probably died in childbirth in about 1507, was the daughter of Sir John Heydon d1479. The Visitation has this Elizabeth as a daughter of Sir Henry Heydon, but there was no mention of her in either Sir Henry's 1503-04 will or in that of his wife Dame Anne (née Boleyn) in 1510. So another daughter might well have existed without leaving any documentary record; but spotting other children of Sir John Heydon has proved impossible to date. The linkage between the Lumners, Brigges, Boleyns and Heydons can also be seen in a clause in Thomas Brigges's long will of 1494. NRO, NCC will 1494, 202-55 Wolman. He gave his wife Margaret a life interest in his manor of Frettenham. Afterwards she paid a life annuity to John Skering there, who seems with his wife Margaret (probably a Bardolf), to have been the previous owner. After Margaret Brigges's death the manor would remainder to Sir Henry Heydon and his heirs providing that the Heydons paid 200 marks to his executors and 200 marks to William Lumner of Mannington. However, Frettenham manor seems to have passed by fine in 1500 from Margaret and Edmund Paston to Sir Robert Clere and Sir Robert Drury, probably as family trustees for Sir William Boleyn of Blickling. Clere had married Boleyn's daughter Anne. Sir Robert Drury of Hawstead was the heavy hitting lawyer and Privy Councillor to Henry VII whose first wife was Anne the daughter of Sir William Calthorpe. Drury's involvement reinforces our belief that the Lumners and Calthorpes were intermarried by this period. In his will made and proved in October and November 1505, Sir William left his manor of Frettenham to his son (Sir) James Boleyn provided that he paid to William Lumner the money as set out in Thomas Brigges's will. TNA, PCC will 1505, PROB 11/14. Presumably the Pastons and Sir Henry Heydon, in a complex deal, had conveyed the manor directly to Sir William, who was brother of Sir Henry's wife Anne Boleyn. William Lumner's rights to the 200 marks had been warranted in the fine. Blomefield. This may have happened at the same time as the fine recited by the Lumner of Sharrington IPM. Perhaps, not implausibly, the Frettenham and Sharrington deals were interlinked between the Lumners, Brigges, Heydons and Boleyns?

62. NRO, Rye MS 17

63. For example, TNA, C 1/557/35 and 557/36

64. Harleian Society, *The Register Book of St Dionis Backchurch*, Registers vol 3,1878

65. *CPR 25 Elizabeth*; TNA, C 66/1224 mm 12-13

66. TNA, PCC administration 1563

67. TNA, C 3/109/54

68. TNA, C 22/670/44

69. NRO, ANW will 1509-19, will 348

70. NRO index cards for Sharrington

71. HB Walters, *Inventories of Norfolk Church Goods 1552*, NA, vol 28 part 3, 1941

72. NRO, NCC 1559 will, 50 Colman

73. TNA, C 3/116/62, dating from 1558-79

74. NRO, DN/DEP part 5 1550-51

75. In 1529 - NRS, Rev ED Stone, *Consistory Court Depositions, Norwich 1499-1530*, vol 10, 1938

76. *A Descriptive Catalogue of Ancient Deeds in the PRO,* vol 1, 1890

77. 28th January 1516 TNA, E 210/1061. Detailed abuttals and occupants were given and would be of interest to those living in the hamlet now called Southgate on the northern side of Cawston parish. Itteringham too had a way called 'Seagate Way' shown on the Mannington map of 1595 heading north out of the village and both were either the 'way towards the sea' or a ditched way. Wolterton archives 10/25

78. Given as aged 11 in the 1542 IPM

79. TNA, PCC will 1531, PROB 11/24

80. TNA, PCC will 1552, PROB 11/35

81. TNA, REQ 2/198/13

82. NRO, NCC 1593 Administration A126; NCC Inventory 10/283

83. There is an interesting snippet in a deed of August 1591 which referred to lands called Mayes and Bodhams in Gunthorpe which Geoffrey Myghte had from William and Edmund Lumner and which he was then conveying to his brother Thomas and others (*A Descriptive Catalogue of Ancient Deeds in the PRO, vol 6*). This reference to the undated prior purchase was presumably to William of Sharrington and Edmund his son and heir.

84. NRO, NCC 1604 Administration A237; Syderstone parish register shows the burial of a Henry Lumner on 10th April 1600, perhaps a son of Robert Lumner. North Creake shows the baptism of Elizabeth daughter of Robert Lumner gent on 19th August 1599.

85. Some or all of Robert's Sharrington lands were sold to Sir Thomas Hunt, but from later deed references it would seem that these did not add up to either a complete manor or a particularly substantial landholding. NRO, WHT 1/1/1-3 and 1/3/1-10

86. NRO NCC 1597 Administration A188

87. NRO, NCC Admon 1605-26 fo 154 and NCC Inventory of 1613-14, DN/INV/26/217

88. Wolterton archives 10/25

89. Thomas is mentioned in passing in a 1643 deed that recited an earlier Houghton family marriage settlement showing he had once held lands in Earlham as son and heir of William Lominer gent, who could only have been William of Sharrington. NRO, WAL 608/13, 276x4

90. JJ Muskett, in his major 1900 work on *Suffolk Manorial Families*, showed Elizabeth the daughter of Hamon L'Estrange esq of Gressenhall and Hunstanton to have married an unspecified Lumner. Researchers of the L'Estranges, presumably using old family papers,

show Elizabeth buried in Elsing church on 9th October 1573 (sic), by which date she was married to a Lumner. JR Mayer, *Extraneus, A Social and Literary Chronicle of the Families Strange ...*, 1986. However, the Elsing parish register shows 'Elizabeth Lestrange daughter of Hamonde L'Estrange esq was buried 9th October 1572'. While she might have been betrothed she was probably not married and the registers in the L'Estrange places of Elsing, Gressenhall and Hunstanton contain no references at all to any Lumners. There is no evidence of another Elizabeth. Her siblings were mostly baptised between 1560 and 1574, indicating that if she had been betrothed she was one of the eldest children and can only have been 'married' for a very short time when she died, presumably aged about 14 or not much more. There are two candidates for a Lumner boy of marriageable age at the time. The first would be William, the second son of Edmund of Mannington. He does not appear to have survived to adulthood. The alternative is young Edmund of Sharrington, who as the heir apparent of this family would have been a more suitable match for a senior daughter of the L'Estrange family. No other Lumner would fit the bill (unless his brother Robert was twice married, but this seems very unlikely). Perhaps the old L'Estrange work was simply wrong. In that the court materials hinted at some uncertainty over whether Edmund Lumner of Sharrington was definitely dead, perhaps he too was lost at sea.

Notes to Chapter 5

1. Her first husband was probably related to Robert Whynberg who wrote to Sir John Paston describing his extensive travels to Kent and in Norfolk on estate steward business including attempts to collect rents in contention with a Mr Lovell. Gairdner ed. *The Paston Letters*, 1987 vol 5 p244-5. The letter has an incomplete regnal year and could be either shortly after 1474 or 1500. The reference to Lovell suggests the earlier date. Elizabeth's father would have known and worked with Whynberg. A later Whinborough married Amy Boleyn sister-in-law of Thomas Payne of Itteringham, the Blickling steward.
2. NRO, NCC administration 1558, no 36
3. NRO, ANW will 1570-72, no 210
4. Writ in *CPR Edward IV* vol 22, Part 2; NRO, Rye MSS 4691/60, Z3F; TNA, C 1/57/79 & 80 and C 1/63/208 and C 1/63/209
5. TNA, C 1/220/42
6. *LPFD* vol 1; Sir Philip Calthorpe had a house in Norwich close to the Cathedral in St Martin at Palace Gates, which had previously been Sir Thomas Erpingham's. Henry Harrod, *Gleanings Among the Castles and Convents of Norwich*, 1857. Two Drurys - William and John - were among the feoffees in an indenture of 14th August 1529 spotted by Harrod in the Norwich Corporation Records. The Romehall property in the lease was abutalled to Sir Philip's house. There can be little doubt that this was a long standing home for Sir Philip.
7. Sir Philip Calthorpe was referred to in the 1522 subsidy roll for Erpingham which showed the two main land holders as Richard Pye and Sir Philip Calthorpe; the latter not resident in Norfolk, 'being with the lady princes'. During the early 1520s, as a temporary measure, Sir Philip and his wife Jane looked after the household of the future Queen Mary, Henry VIII's eldest daughter by Katherine of Aragon. *ODNB* entry for Queen Mary.

8. TNA, E 101/61/16
9. 1522 subsidy list, TNA E101/61/16
10. Mannington court roll, NRO, NCR 24 Shelf e
11. TNA, PCC will 1495, PROB 11/10
12. TNA, C 131/250/1
13. She was there as Abbess of the Nuns Minoresses in 1497 as Margaret Calthorpe - British History Online, *Victoria County History of Suffolk vol 2*
14. By his first wife Mary, sister of Sir William Say, the Visitation and other sources show he had son and heir Philip, Dorothy a nun and Elizabeth who died young. By his second wife Jane, daughter of John Blennerhassett esq of Frenze, he had Henry, Thomas married to Alice L'Estrange, Katherine married to Anthony Heveningham and Anne married to Henry Ratcliffe Earl of Sussex.
15. TNA, E 635/1 & /2, IPM
16. TNA, E 326/996
17. Sir Philip Calthorpe junior married Amata or Anne the daughter of Sir William Boleyn of Blickling and thus aunt to Queen Anne Boleyn. Queen Anne Boleyn was the daughter of Sir Thomas Boleyn the second son of Sir William of Blickling. ODNB, Blomefield, etc. They had a sole daughter and heiress Elizabeth (whose third husband was Sir Drue Drury). Sir Philip junior died in 1552 by which time Anne was dead. TNA, PCC will 1552, PROB 11/35. While this shows that the Calthorpes would have known the Lumners as neighbours of the Boleyns it does not shed any light on the elder Sir Philip or the identity of Margery Lumner.
18. TNA, 1535 IPM
19. NRO, NCC will 1545, 223-5 Whitefoot
20. NRO, DS603 352x3, Easter 29 Hy VIII Final concord refers to the gift.
21. NRO, ANW will 1565-69, will 100, Margaret Bishop widow
22. *LPFD* vol 5
23. *LPFD* vols 19 and 21
24. *LPFD* vol 19
25. *CPR Edward VI*; Lewis's *Topographical Dictionary of England*, 1848
26. To be covered in detail in work in progress, Itteringham Lands and Lordship
27. NRO, WAL 608/1-2, 276x4
28. M & W Vaughan-Lewis, *Landscape and field names in 16th century Mannington and Itteringham*, forthcoming article in NAHRG, *The Annual*, 2009
29. *CPR Philip and Mary* 1553-54; original deed being now TNA, E 210/9968
30. *CPR Philip and Mary*
31. *LPFD* vol 8
32. *LPFD* vol 9
33. *LPFD* vol 15
34. *LPFD* vol 17
35. *LPFD* vol 21
36. Tantalisingly, while exploring the Spring family, we came upon the will of one John Lymmor fuller and clothworker of Lavenham. TNA, PCC will 1529, PROB 11/23. His surname might well be yet another variation on the theme of Lumner. Might he have been the John Lumner draper son of William and Margaret, or related to him? His wife had predeceased him and he appeared to have no children. From his charitable bequests he also had strong links to nearby Stanstead. The house where he lived was to be sold by his executors. Another house in Lavenham 'toward the common between

Maister Springe on one side and Gent of Bury on the other was to be kept in repair for the majority of John Lymmor the younger, son of his kinsman John Lymmor the elder (perhaps of Stanstead?). The latter had a total of seven children under 20. The 1480 will of Thomas Lymnor of Bury again hints strongly at a Lumner or Lyminour origin but his will, and indeed that of John Lymmer of Lavenham in 1538, give no clues to the origins of this family group. Peculiar Court of Bury St Edmunds, 1480 will, Hawlee fo 298; Archdeaconry of Sudbury, 1538 will, Poope 131 and original will W 1/4/111

37. TNA, PCC wills 1486, PROB 11/7 and 1510, PROB 11/16; Harleian Society *The Visitation of Suffolk 1561*, new series vol 2, 1981; JJ Howard The *Visitation of Suffolk of 1561 with Additions*, 1866; *ODNB*. Lavenham church retains many carvings of the Spring arms on its stone and woodwork, matched only by those of the de Vere family - the Earls of Oxford who were lords of the manor and into which family the Springs were married through Thomas 3's niece marrying Aubrey de Vere, the second son of the 15th Earl of Oxford.

38. TNA, IPM of 1523, C 142/40/13. Bridget was his only child born to Alice Appleton his second wife although she had two other daughters by her first husband as Alice May - Alice who married Richard Fulmerston and Margaret who married William Rysby. Robert had a clutch of sons and daughters to carry on the family in Lavenham. TNA, PCC will 1549, PROB 11/32. In 1514 Robert's brother John married Dorothy the daughter of Sir William Waldegrave. He was to become Sir John Spring of Hitcham and Cockfield, Sir John 1549 and Dorothy 1564 both left PCC wills.

39. Erneley, the son of Sir John Erneley the Lord Chief Justice of the Common Pleas, was executor of Bridget's mother's will in 1538. TNA, PCC will 1538 Alice Spring, PROB 11/27. William Erneley died in 1546 leaving his wife Bridget and three sons. TNA, PCC will 1546, PROB 11/31. She remarried to Sir Henry Husse.

40. TNA C142/40/13, 1523

41. Interestingly the Visitation did not show Guybon's second wife Rose, nor his daughter Anne; The Visitation updates of the seventeenth century clearly had no Lumner family members alive to help ensure the record of their existence and intermarriage with various middle level Norfolk families. Rose's mother was named Anne which adds marginally to the view that Rose was the mother of Anne Guybon. Neither of the wills of Thomas Guybon senior or junior contained any mention of Thomas's daughter Anne who was to marry William Lumner of Sharrington. Thomas Guybon the son died in 1570, leaving children William, Humphrey and Beatrix (married to William Gresham the son and heir of Sir John Gresham of London) by his first two wives. TNA, PCC will 1570, PROB 11/5. William, the eldest son, reappears in legal actions concerning Mannington. The Visitation showed Thomas the son as having four wives, with the last being Agnes Clarke yet his will referred to his last and living wife as Anne - perhaps an example of the frequent interchangeability of these names.

42. Alternatively, Robert Clarke may simply have received Bintry temporarily as trustee for Lumner in an unknown transaction. Soon afterwards the manor was in the hands of the Larwood family of Itteringham.

43. TNA, PCC will 1531, PROB 11/24

44. Inventory of Church goods 1552, *NA*, vol 27, 1941, pp 406-7. Itteringham, in comparison, had in 1552 a proper complement of church goods being looked after by the churchwardens John Dowtie and John Cootes and rector James Mason who was to be deprived of his living in 1554.

45. Mannington court roll as above

46. TNA, C 1/1001/18-23. This related to an agreement between Rose's first husband Thomas Guybon and a William Hall involving a £14 bond, which Rose and Edmund were now claiming had not been paid.

47. It is unlikely that she was born to Edmund's second wife as she would have been no more than 12 at marriage.

48. TNA, PCC 1552 will Rose Lumner, PROB 11/35

49. *LPFD* vol 19

50. TNA, PCC will 1540, PROB 11/28

51. Harleian Society, *The Visitation of Herefordshire, 1634,* new series vol 15

52. TNA, PCC will 1553, PROB 11/36. Richard Lee was the eldest son and heir of Thomas Lee of Langley in Shropshire, just to the north of Ludlow. Harleian Society, *Visitation of Shropshire 1623*, vol 28. After the death of John Leighton, his widow Joyce remarried Richard Lee thus making Lee Katherine's stepfather or 'father in law' TNA, C 1/827/31.

53. About another half dozen Saunders family members were admitted to the Grocers between the 1530s and 1570s.

54. TNA, PCC will 1558 Edmund 'Lonmer' of Mannington, PROB11/ 41

55. JA Venn, *Alumni*

56. IGI (uncorroborated) has the 1576 marriage of Joan Throckmorton (the daughter of John Throckmorton and Margaret Puttenham) to a Richard Wigmore of Feckenham. In fact this was the Throckmorton's parish not that of the Wigmores. This would make Joan a daughter of Sir John and sister of Sir Francis. By this date Feckenham was the manor of Sir Francis Throckmorton executed for treason in 1583. The marriage raises the possibility that it was our Richard, although the name was also used by the Herefordshire Wigmore families. However, the Richard Wigmore of Hereford around this time was of Lucton and the pedigree shows him to have married Anne Monnington and shows no link in that generation to the Throckmortons even though there was a marriage link between the two families later. *Visitation Herefordshire, 1634*

57. TNA, SP 12/108/61

58. Gilbert Burnet, *Bishop Burnet's History of his Own Time*, 1850

59. Ed W Holl, *The Analyst: A Quarterly Journal, vol 7*, 1837

60. Virginia F Stern, *Sir Stephen Powle of Court and Country: Memorabilia of a Government*, 1992; *ODNB*

61. Devereux Papers, box V, 76, 77 at Longleat

62. Salisbury, Cecil Papers XIV, XVI at Hatfield House

63. *CSPD James I* 1603-10

64. *CSPD James 1* 1611-1618

65. J Lingard, *A History of England*, 1840

66. *CSPCAWI Addenda* 1618

67. US Historical Documents Archive and other online references

68. Sir Thomas married Mistress Mary Wigmore on 16th November 1609 in Twickenham. London Metropolitan Archives, DR017/A/01/002

69. The sum might be interpreted by applying the twenty times annual profits applied to land valuations, particularly since no doubt the money was to flow from the Bettes lands in Irmingland and Oulton. By this stage in his middle years Dodge might have counted on another twenty years of life and thus the jointure would have been worth the perfectly respectable sum of £800 or so which might well have been settled on an elder daughter of a country gentleman. Bettes's 'bet' that Dodge would have less than twenty years paid off, but only by a couple of years

70. Blom lists them, but we have not found his source and the Visitation record of the Bettes family shows only the main male line.

71. TNA, PCC will 1621, PROB 11/137

72. Tanner 68.5r. Possibly Michael was a relation, although he might simply have preached as a well-known cleric. He is described as from a genteel Somerset family, but the vagueness about his origins could well mean that was an error for Herefordshire. Anthony á Wood, *Athenae Oxonienses, vol 2, (1967)*; J Foster, *Alumni Oxonienses*, 1892. He was born about 1588, graduated from Oriel Oxford (BA 1608, MA 1611), became rector of Thorseway near Caistor in Lincolnshire and was renowned for his zealous sermons, several of which were published between 1619 and 1641. He might have been one of the twelve children of William Wigmore of Lucton and the Catholic Anne Throckmorton, six others of whom were nuns or Jesuits (*ODNB* entries for some of William and Anne's children). What was the link to the Wigmores of Stamford Lincolnshire who bore the arms of the Herefordshire family in the seventeenth century? Daniel Wigmore, a wool merchant, was several times mayor of Stamford in the 1660s and involved in the river widening there. He accounts for the use of the arms and by his two wives had a number of children. However, the Lincolnshire Pedigrees only went one generation back to his father Richard Wigmore of the Isle of Ely married to Bridget Newman of Norfolk. Harleian Society, *Lincolnshire Pedigrees*, vol 52, 1904. We cannot be certain how Daniel fitted into the Herefordshire family. Another Daniel Wigmore had been ordained in 1602 and went on to become Archdeacon of Ely before his death in 1646. He had acquired the manor of Little Shelford in Cambridgeshire and installed a kinsman Gilbert Wigmore as Rector in 1641. Gilbert's son Daniel was born in Shelford in 1645 (IGI) but seems not to have survived long enough to be recognised by the Pedigree writers. Gilbert also bore the Herefordshire family arms, but his parentage is not known. These Wigmores clearly originated in Herefordshire and presumably they too may have been, or stemmed from, children of William and Anne of Lucton.

73. Tanner 76. 6v

74. TNA, PROB 6/14B/160

75. NRO, NCC Administration Robert Bettes 1558, no.36; NRO, ANW will Elizabeth Bettes 1570-72, 210. John married at least twice. His son and heir Henry was in fact the second son by his first wife, who was either Anne or Bridget Coote daughters of Christopher Coote of Blo Norton. *Visitations of Norfolk* seems to show both having married Bettes and this may in fact be the case. While the Bettes pedigree shows Anne as the mother of John's first three children, the Coote pedigree has both married to Bettes and one of his early children was named Bridget. Assuming he was married to Anne, this supports the view that he would have had a daughter named Anne, who might have married Richard Wigmore. The eldest son, as shown by Heydon and Irmingland register dates, was Thomas born six years before Henry in 1563. However, he seems to have died before Henry.

76. NRO, NAS 1/2/6/Irmingland

77. The main Bettes family seems to have died out or moved away from Norfolk after this. With relatively few family wills, they are not a well-researched family. Both John and his son Henry may have died in Oulton intestate but as no administrations for them have been found they may have died elsewhere. Margaret died in 1615 in London and did leave a will as Margaret Betts widow of 'St Barkins'(All Hallows, Barking) in the City of London. TNA, PCC will 1615, PROB 11/26; and a sentence of 1619, PROB 11/133.

Her Oulton and Denver connections were identified; as were her deceased husband John and brothers Robert and (Sir) Edmond Gawsell. She was living in London, presumably since one of her married daughters was there and another daughter had been buried nearby, but asked that her chests and contents be brought to London, which implies she still had a strong presence in Norfolk. Her sister the widowed Bridget Hall was made executrix. She asked that Bridget be allowed to live with her son-in-law John Penkethman husband of Helyn Bettes, with whom she perhaps was already living.

78. NRO, NCC Administration 1591, no.59

79. NRO, NCC will 1600, 183 Force/OW 95. Her daughter Margaret had married Thomas Archer of a long-standing Salhouse family in Salhouse on 15th April 1591, just days after her father's administration had been granted. Their daughter had been baptised there on 3rd March 1594.

80. NRO, NCC Administration 1588-1605, no.273

81. Unfortunately, since few Bettes wills have survived, we have not been able to prove the connection absolutely although the circumstantial case is very strong. In particular, John Bettes senior appears not to have left a will and, apart from a fleeting reference to a bond of a John Bettes in Baconsthorpe in 1605 there is no definite indication that he remained in Norfolk. NRO, MS 11967, 30A2. Indeed this bond may well refer to Grace's son. Equally, there is no remaining sign of Henry – the family just seems to have evaporated locally after nearly two centuries of ownership of Irmingland's manors. However, the case for Grace's marriage to William Bettes is a very strong one and it is hard to explain the 1585 arms in any other way that fits the available facts. The most serious contender for another interpretation comes from the other branch of the Herefordshire Wigmores in Norfolk around this time. Shown as such in the Visitation, they can also be identified as Herefordshire Wigmores from their 1586 grant of arms in Norfolk, again using the three greyhounds courant device. Robert Wigmore of Roughton had been a servant or employee of Bishop Nix of Norwich and in his 1571 will he asked to be buried near him in Norwich Cathedral. NRO, NCC will 1571, 394 Brygge. The Bishop had died in 1535 and we assume that Robert had continued a career in Norfolk closely connected to the See or the clergy more broadly. While leaving his will as of Norwich, he was generally thought of as of Roughton, where his daughter Anne married Thomas Robyns on 10th January 1564. Two of his sons were mentioned in his will and Robert lived locally. For example in the 1590s he was of Stody and cropped up in Chancery and other actions with the Cooke family of Little Barningham who also had legal disputes with the Dodges of Mannington. In a Norwich City court deposition in September 1575 Robert described himself as 'gent of Stody aged 38 or thereabouts'. NRO, Norwich City Records, Case 12 shelf a (2). Being born in about 1537 would imply that his father was some years older than our Richard the mercer, but of the same generation. From the Visitation pedigree there is nothing to link Robert or his brothers John and Bartholomew or his sisters Anne and Joan to the Bettes family. John, the heir, married Anne Berney of Gunton and had a daughter Elizabeth married in Roughton in 1592 to John Godvale. Bartholomew, a ship's captain, had at least one son by 1571, but little more is known. Bartholomew Wigmore was the captain of *The Nightingale of Ipswich* laden in Portugal and attacked and pillaged by the French in July 1585. *CSPF Elizabeth* 1586-88 vol 21 part 1. The other sister Joan married Thomas Heyward of North Elmham. Although it is interesting to see this further connection of the Herefordshire Wigmores to Norfolk, there is nothing to link any of them to the Bettes family.

82. *CPR Philip and Mary* 1554-55
83. Similar versions of the IPM in TNA, E 150/652/24 and C 142/115/17
84. NRO, Norwich City Records Interrogatories and Depositions 1561-67, Case 12 Shelf a (1) c
85. TNA, PCC will 1562, PROB 11/45
86. TNA, SC 2 192/26
87. TNA, C 3/206/17 and C 2/Eliz/C18/41
88. TNA, PCC will 1561, PROB 11/44
89. British History Online, RG Lang, *Two Tudor Subsidy Rolls for the City of London*, 1993
90. TNA, C 1/704/17
91. At around this time he had leased it on to one Thomas Jurdon on a one year at a time lease, which he had now called in after just one year. Jurdon challenged such unfair behaviour since he had spent money on improving the buildings and now could not get a return on his investment or any recompense for it.
92. TNA, E 211/166; EA Webb, 'The monastic buildings: Monastic close, fair ground, gardens and grave-yard', British History Online *The Records of St. Bartholomew's Priory [and] St. Bartholomew the Great, West Smithfield: vol 2* (1921), pp. 181-195
93. WJ Hardy, *A Calendar to the Feet of Fines for London and Middlesex, vol 2*, 1893
94. TNA, PCC will 1544, PROB 11/30
95. This would have been the old church of St Mary on the south side of The Strand which was demolished in 1549 by Protector Somerset to make way for Somerset House. It was only replaced in 1714 by the James Gibbs designed current church of St Mary le Strand.
96. TNA, C/1/662/2. A little earlier he had been involved in chancery as an executor of the will of Isabel the widow/wife of Thomas Rothewoode, a London girdler. TNA, PCC will of Isabel Rothewoode 1528, PROB 11/22; TNA, C/1/565/15 and C/1/582/69
97. Erna Auerbach, *Vincent Volpe, the King's Painter*, Burlington Magazine, 1950, vol 92, Nos 562-573, pp 222-227. Also resident there was John Brown the haberdasher and wealthy senior court painter who died in 1532. *ODNB*; WAD Englefield, *The Painter-Stainers' Company*, 1923; A Borg, *The History of the Worshipful Company of Painters, Otherwise Painter-Stainers*, 2005. Brown had joined the Haberdashers to become eligible to be made an alderman, since the Painter-Stainers' Company was not of sufficient status to support the appointment. It is believed that Richard Callard had married one of his daughters from his first wife and the shared name of Alice supports this. In his will Brown made Richard Callard and Edmond Lee goldsmith his overseers. TNA, PCC will 1532, PROB 11/24. Lee was referred to as his cousin and Lee and Callard and their wives were to have mourning gowns. The implication was that these were his daughters and their husbands. His second wife Anne and his two underage daughters Elizabeth and Isabel were of course the major beneficiaries of the will. Richard Callard was also given his best 'pryminer' [primer]. Callard was also a key participant in the 1532 conveyance by Brown of his London house to the Painter-Stainers for their use as a livery hall. Brown was a Warden of the Company of Painters and Stainers and possibly its Master.
98. From our perspective it is interesting to wonder whether one of these, John Bettes the elder, was related to the local Bettes family. Certainly the *ODNB* and other authors know nothing of his background and our family was very active in trade in London at this time. In any event as a painter enjoying commissions from court he would have been known to the Callards. A possible attribution to Bettes of a portrait of Sir John Godsalve provides a tenuous Norfolk link.

99. British History Online, 'Islington: Other estates', *A History of the County of Middlesex: vol 8: Islington and Stoke Newington parishes* (1985), pp. 57-69

100. She was called Agnes in Sir John's own will - TNA, PCC will Sir John Clerke 1539, PROB 11/27. Past authors have seemed to use these first names interchangeably as this example proves. There is no doubt about the identification. Her legacy was restricted to the 200 marks that Richard had committed to in a prior bond - a sixteenth century pre-nup restricting her rights to his lands and other property. As Sir John Clerke's third wife she had also been married before to Nicholas Pynchon one of the sheriffs of London and a butcher who died in 1533. Henry F Waters, *Genealogical Gleanings in England*, 1901, p 845. We are indebted to Nancy Briggs for her April 2005 entry on the Brass of the Month website of The Monumental Brass Society commemorating Sir John Clerk and his splendid tomb in Thame Oxfordshire: 'Clerk of North Weston manor was the third son of William Clerk of Willoughby, Warwickshire. As the inscription on his brass records, he 'toke louys of Orleans duk of longueville … prisoner at ye Jorney of Bomy by Terouane', better known as the Battle of the Spurs, on 16 August 1513. Clerk, who was knighted for this exploit, died on 5 April 1539. Shortly before his death, he rebuilt the 14th century manor house of the Quartermain family. Clerk was married three times, firstly to Jane Lee, a member of a prominent Buckinghamshire family; she died in 1516 and was buried at Quarrendon. The church is in ruins, but her gravestone was seen by Lancaster Herald in 1611; it is possibly to be identified with the indent of a lady with three shields, *c*.1510, known from a dabbing in the Ashmolean Museum. His second wife, Elizabeth Ashby, died on 5 February 1533/4 and was buried at Blakesley, Northants. Three shields survive from the monument erected by their son, Ambrose. Elizabeth was also the mother of Clerk's son and heir, Nicholas. Clerk's third wife was Agnes, widow of Nicholas Pynchon, sheriff of London, who owned property in Writtle, Essex'.

101. Between 1544 and 1551 a chancery action showed John Callard being accused of detention of deeds relating to the property of Henry Upcotte deceased of 'Monkokehampton', not far south of Great Torrington. TNA, C 1/1142/88. Unfortunately, badly torn, it no longer carries any information as to where Callard was from, but he may have been brother John. Another badly damaged and undated scrap from the first half of the sixteenth century mentioned that John Callard had at one time been seized of a property now at issue and which would seem now to be the tenement of Thomas Maye in Torrington. TNA, C 4/25/113. A Callard Farm property a mile or so to the south west of Burrington village near Barnstaple in north Devon there today still marks the spot. Ordnance Survey; www.streetmap.co.uk; Google Earth. The Visitation shows that the family of Callard of Callard was descended through a repeated mix of Richards and Johns. Harleian Society, *The Visitation of Devon 1620*, vol 6. By the middle of the sixteenth century the head of the family was John Callard, married to Elizabeth the daughter and heir of William Southcott of Chudleigh. Unfortunately siblings in the early generations were not recorded and no Devon wills have survived to help with identification of all family members. However, we believe he was Richard's brother and overseer. John's eldest son and heir was Thomas who married Margery Moone of Ashe in Surrey and who went on to have children, including one named Richard. Thomas had two brothers named John, and one called Ralph. We assume one of the Johns died young and the other was John Callard of Mannington. Ralph was probably the Ralph Callard of Menver in the Cornish Visitation *The Visitation of Cornwall 1620*, Harleian Society, vol 9. There were four named and married sisters; one of whom, Anne, married William Dawes gent of Cornwall.

616

102. *ODNB*

103. The arms were distinctively Spanish: Gyronny of six pieces, or and sable; on each division or, a Moor's head couped sable. These arms of the Callards of Callard in Devon are also found in Norfolk according to heraldry sources. T Robson, *The British Herald or Cabinet of Armorial Bearings*, 1830 and other heraldry books on Google Books. We assume that Emmanuel used them. The only other arms-bearing Callard or Collard family of this era was in Kent. They were unrelated and had entirely different arms, so they can be ignored.

104. *CSPF Edward VI* 1861

105. *ODNB*

106. When Robert Underwood died in March 1588 he left Margery his manors, houses and lands for life and after her they were all to pass to his eldest son James. NRO, NCC will 1588, 205 Homes. He asked her to look after James as if he was her own child. Thomas and Katherine may also have been from his first marriage.

107. TNA, C 33/67. Only the orders from the early stages survive but the action was described in follow-on actions TNA, C 3/206/17 and C 2/Eliz/C18/41.

108. Blom described the tenure of Booton manor as having come from Robert a younger son of Robert Harward of Aldborough. His eldest son Thomas died and so John succeeded to the property. He married Bridget the daughter of Christopher Perne of West Barsham and from him it came to his son Robert (the one in these suits). This Robert died without issue and the estate passed to his sister Elizabeth and through her marriage to Thomas Claxton of Great Levermere in Suffolk and so to their heirs. Blom made no mention of Callard's claim to part of the estate.

109. TNA, C 33/67

110. TNA, C 33/68

111. TNA, C 33/74

112. TNA, C 33/69

113. TNA, C 33/73 and C 33/74

114. TNA, C 33/75 and C 33/76

115. TNA, C 33/77 and C 33/78

116. TNA, REQ 2/117/23

117. TNA, REQ 2/131/1

118. TNA, REQ 2/193/3 undated. For Cromer pier see also *Stiffkey papers*, Camden Society 3rd series, vol 26

119. Folger Shakespeare Library, L.d 703, L.d. 704; fully transcribed in Morgan, Key and Taylor *The Papers of Nathaniel Bacon of Stiffkey IV*, NRS vol 64, 2000 (hereafter *Bacon Papers IV*)

120. TNA, STAC 8/91/4 and E 133/145/1

121. NRO, ANF 1607-09 will 153

122. Harleian Society, *A Visitation of the County of Kent 1663-68*, vol 54, 1906

123. Harleian Society, *Grantees of Arms*, vol 66, 1915

124. J Barnard and G Vernon in their introduction - *Theologo-historicus, or, The True Life of the Most Reverend and Learned Divine* - to an 1849 edition of Dr Peter Heylyn's *Ecclesia Restaurata*. Heylyn was an early seventeenth century cleric whose grandmother, by her second marriage to Francis Clampard, was Mary the sister of Edward and John Dodge. This might explain the vagueness of the Kent Visitation and the difficulty of finding any early evidence for the Dodges in the county. The Kent Dodges' arms were based

distinctively on a breast expressing drops of milk and this was the device used by the Cheshire family certainly by the 1613 Visitation. Harleian Society, *Pedigrees Made at the Visitation of Cheshire, 1613*, vol 59; Thomas Robson, *The British Herald ...*, 1830. It seems to date back to an original grant in 34 Edward I to Peter Dodge for bravery in the battles of Berwick and Dunbar. However, various commentators on the internet believe that the document containing this original grant may in fact have been a later fabrication used to support input to a Visitation, such as the Cheshire one of 1613. It seems more likely that, if it was a fake, it was used to support John Dodge's grant of 1546. Halliday Hill House in the Foggbrook area of Offerton a little to the south-east of Stockport is generally recognised to have been the family seat and is now a listed building. Dodge mayors of Stockport included various Williams between 1433 and 1486, Olivers in 1500 and 1571 and Robert in 1592. This Robert was head of the family at the 1613 Cheshire Visitation, which showed him married to Dionisia Barber daughter of Nicholas Barber of Alsop in Derbyshire, with son and heir William aged 13 and second son George, plus three daughters. Robert's father was George married to Joan Owldon of Brinnington in Cheshire; his grandfather was William and his great grandfather was Robert Dodge of Stockport. This early Robert was probably, by counting the generations, a brother of the Richard Dodge of Wrotham who started the Kent line and since the family was anciently of Stockport Robert was presumably then the head of the family. The 1613 Robert Dodge seems to have had several brothers. Oliver and Ottiwell were both producing children baptised in St Mary's Stockport in the 1590s (IGI). Robert, Oliver and Ottiwell all feature in various ways in Cheshire wills from the late 1580s to the early 1600s (internet extracts). Ottiwell was repeatedly mentioned in Robert's will, made and proved in 1625, as well as being one of the witnesses. The proved copy of this will is available as a digital image on the internet (www.dodgefamily.org, although it does not state from which probate court). Although by 1625 Robert styled himself simply as yeoman of Bosden (probably Bosden Farm next to Offerton), the identification is certain on several counts. His eldest son and main heir was William and his second son George, matching the Visitation entry. George was left a messuage in Stockport and reference was made to a document written the day before the will in which Robert's main properties had been settled on William with a requirement to provide for the 'younger children' - presumably the three daughters in the Visitation. George was also left a 'garden stead' in Castle Hill Stockport and a 'doale or hole' in a 'mean field' in Stockport. Was this what is now the huge gravel pit immediately beside Halliday Hill House and the Farm? (Google Earth) The will made as executors his 'friends' John and Laurence Barber of Alsop in Derbyshire, presumably Dionise's brothers. A third executor was another friend Edward Warren – presumably Edward Warren esq the head of the family at Poynton Hall just to the south of Stockport. The Warrens had the manors of Poynton and Stockport and the presentation rights to the rectory of St Mary Stockport among their substantial assets. Cheshire Record Office, DVE 2401/20. No doubt Robert Dodge was a man of some influence in the area, even if he was styled neither esq nor gent. Similarly his grandfather William Dodge was only described as 'husbandman of Offerton' in his 1575 will proved by the Rural Dean of Macclesfield. A copy survives in Cheshire RO, DVE 2401/2/8.

125. Documents in the John Rylands Library, Manchester University show connections between the Dodges, Jodrells, Hulmes and Shalcrosses, all names with Potts connections. See in particular RYCH/251.

126. TNA, C 2/Eliz/H17/57 and TNA, PCC will 1597, PROB 11/91 made 18th December

127. We assume Compelieng was the same as Comp Farm today which sits in Wrotham Heath, between Wrotham and Leybourne. A derivation from Comp and Ling would fit a heathland location. The area around here was obviously a major area of heathland and immediately to the south is Comp Hill Wrotham and Great Comp and Little Comp villages. Comp is said to be derived from camp or fortification; but another interpretation might be from campo, a field. British History Online. There is also still a Dodge Farm at Smarden quite some miles away to the south east, but no other link has been found to this village.

128. *LPFD* this letter is in the addenda vols: R Hutchinson, *The Last days of Henry VIII*, 2005 p154

129. Perhaps she was the sister of the John Carleton whose will of 1541, although not mentioning any sisters, gives his mother as Elizabeth. TNA, PCC will 1541, PROB 11/28

130. Taken from online sources quoting from one of the contemporary accounts by John Proctor. Was John Dodge the Groom Purveyor of His Majesty's Carriage who on 1st January 1546 sued John Jenyns the Warden of the Butchers' Company? TNA, REQ 2/7/9. This action was about disputed grazing rights in a pasture in 'Rederyff' (Rotherhithe) that led to a violent quarrel between a John Doge and Jenyns's servant. Doge/Dodge felt aggrieved that as a junior member of the same company, he had no recourse in the normal courts because of the warden's influence. However, John Doge the butcher left a will in 1555 showing that he had brothers William and Roger and no children of his own. TNA, PCC will 1555, PROB 11/37. He does not appear to connect into the main Dodge family, unless he came from a much earlier offshoot. John Dodge of Wrotham also appeared in a chancery action of 1556-58 which involved withholding from Thomas Cooper documents relating to property in Charing in Kent. TNA, C 1/1419/64. Dodge (presumably John senior) denied all knowledge and there is nothing more in the badly damaged bill and his answer to identify him further. By an odd coincidence an undated scrap of an answer by Henry Lumner to a chancery action has survived also involving a Thomas Cooper. TNA, C 4/97/1. The action related to plate and other items probably in Thomas's will. Which of the three Henry Lumners this was is not clear. Thomas was possibly the father of Elizabeth Lumner and she may have had a sister named Anne Thorp. The probability is that Elizabeth was Henry Lumner's wife. Might the Lumner and Dodge families have known each other in mid-century; or was this just a co-incidence with a common name?

131. TNA, C 1/406/11

132. TNA, C 1050/31-33

133. TNA, E 210/10123

134. TNA, C 3/52/3. The action itself is of little importance, being a disagreement over a £60 loan made by Wigmore to Harry Parry clerk, allegedly in return for a lease of the prebend of Brownes Wood in Middlesex.

135. NRO, WAL 608/5, 276x4

136. TNA, REQ 2/ 86/2

137. *CSPD* 1547-80

138. TNA, SC 2/192/26

139. The surviving court rolls will appear in future work, but for now it is worth recording that the rolls at the TNA were in fact late sixteenth century copies and seem to have been made for the Heckham Heath issue and enquiry and related actions between the Cookes and Dodge.

140. The clerk made an error: Cooke and Coote were separate families.

141. TNA, E 134/32Eliz/Trin9

142. Elizabeth Coote was the widow first of John Stanley and then the widow and executrix of Christopher Coote gent of Testerton who left all his goods to her in his nuncupative will proved in July 1587. NRO, NCC will 1587, 86 Holmes. This Christopher Coote gent would seem to be the second son of Christopher Coote esq of Blo Norton as shown in the Visitation and Elizabeth was presumably his second wife as the Visitation shows his wife as Barbara. Assuming this he was the brother of Anne Coote/Fermour who had married John Bettes.

143. Cooke should be Coote as before and Roades was probably also an error for the Francis Reade gent of Aylsham whose will was proved in April 1598. NRO, ANW will 1597-98, 405 Lincoln; TNA, C 2/Eliz/D12/34 undated but after Feb 1591

144. We have found no trace of this in civil law materials and assume it was a common law action. Similarly John Curson remains an unidentified mystery man whose interest in Coldham is unclear. He may be of the Belaugh/Billingford family.

145. TNA, REQ 2/163/30 and /31

146. The detail of these actions is far too great for this volume but in a future work we will explore the insights they generate about the environment in and around Mannington manor.

147. NRO, NCC will 1590, Flack 674. Richard was apparently, according to previous writers, unrelated to Edmund Stubbes the local lawyer and cleric and brother-in-law of the famous lawyer Edward Coke. Blom and others had him marrying the widow of John L'Estrange (d 1582) and thus coming into the manor of Sedgeford, where he had presumably moved to not so long before the Requests action. Blom; Burke *Extinct and Dormant Baronetcies*, WC Ewing, *Norfolk Lists*, 1837; and other Google Books entries. He was, like John Potts, a member in the 1588-89 parliament when he sat for Thetford as Richard Stubbes esq of Sedgeford. One of his daughters Dionise married Sir William Yelverton (later the first Baronet) in 1586-87. By his will Stubbes left the rents of Runton and Sedgeford to the Yelvertons and mentioned that other lands had already been conveyed to his daughter Alice and her husband Sir Hamond Le Strange to the use of the Yelverton sons Sir Henry and William. TNA, PCC will 1620, PROB 11/135. These dates make clear that Stubbes's daughters must have been by a prior marriage not noted by Blom or others and we wonder if he had married an Edgefield girl or even a Cooke? He also bequeathed a Runton manor to his cousin Edmund Stubbes of Trinity College Cambridge, who was the son of Francis Stubbes and nephew of Edmund Stubbes our local lawyer. JA Venn, *Alumni*. This links him definitely to our Edmund the lawyer.

148. TNA, 35 Elizabeth (1592-1593) STAC 5/C80/32

149. TNA, STAC 5/Y2/7

150. NRO, NCC Administration book and Rougham parish register

151. TNA, C 3/280/56. 1604 Heydon answer in action v Jane

152. TNA, C2/Eliz/B3/44

153. TNA, PCC will 1587, PROB 11/71

154. Glasgow University Special Collections, GB 0247 MS Hunter 5 (S.1.5) 27, 7 recto col. a: *De Illustrium Virorum et Foeminarum Casibus. Anglice* John Lydgate's translation of Boccacio's *Fall of Princes* (incomplete). Probably published in the 1470s. The university website carries some beautiful images of pages from the book.

155. Quoted from in F Madden et al, *Collecteana Topographica et Genealogica*, 1840
156. Marginal note against Lumner PCC will. In January 1630 Lumner's daughter Elizabeth, by then wife of Walter Pauncefoot, was granted administration to deal with everything left unadministered by Jane Lumner. NRO, NCC 1629 Administration in PRCC 2/1/2
157. TNA, DL 4/31/30
158. NRO, Bishops Registers DN/REG, 226 & 228
159. In Augustus Jessopp's book on the Jesuit Henry Walpole - *One Generation of a Norfolk House*, 3rd edition. 1913 - he wrote that Jane became Edward's housekeeper; but that was an error. The recusant certificates and returns do not show the two in the same parish. The housekeeper reference may have been a misinterpretation of the notes that showed some heads of household as keepers of a house - ie the whole household was catholic. Edward in 1595 was listed in Wolferton where he 'keepeth a small house'. Similar wording was used to describe Jane that year in Brandon Parva, indicating that she was head of the household.
160. NRO, DN/DIS/9/1a
161. This John Drury is likely to have been one of the Aylsham family and a close relation of Stephen Drury there. However, JJ Muskett (usually comprehensive and brilliant on the Drury families) was vague about how they fitted into the major lines of the Drury clan. An earlier 1605 certificate is said to have showed Jane as in Runhall, but this is likely to be an editorial slip for Rushall where she was shown in a number of previous returns. ed TF Barton, *The Registrum Vagum of Anthony Harison*, NRS vol 32, 1963. John Drury was perhaps a relation but within a couple of years he had dropped off the returns. An infuriating entry of 1611 listed Jane's Catholic household in Hainford, including her named servants, with her daughters shown as 'Mary Lumner gen als Everard wife of Nich Everard' and her sister in parallel style married to the same man! Later Hainford entries showed Nicholas Everard present at one point but there were no further entries for the daughters that would explain whether both were married or just one. However as later Elizabeth was married to Pauncefoot, it must be Mary married to Everard. It is quite possible that she may have died shortly after her marriage to Everard since she was not listed in 1615 when Nicholas Everard gent was again on the list at Hainford.

Notes to Chapter 6

1. Harleian Society, *The Visitation of Shropshire,* vol 29
2. Ed Simon Adams, *Household Accounts and Disbursement Books of Robert Dudley, Earl of Leicester*, Royal Historical Society, Camden 5th Series vol 6, CUP, 1995
3. *ODNB*. We are particularly grateful to Dr Darryl Ogier, Island Archivist, not only for his *ODNB* entry for Leighton, but also for his most helpful response to enquiries about the Wigmores, Lumners and de Vics. We would have known far less about the context of their roles on the island without his extracts from island sources and dialogue by email on some of the puzzles regarding family relationships. However, the final interpretation and speculation, where we have been forced into it, is our own.
4. The relationship seems not to be precisely as given in the *ODNB*. Leighton and Robert Dudley shared a common ancestor, John Sutton 4th Baron Dudley, but were not of the same generation. John Burke *A General and Heraldic Dictionary of the Peerages of England ...* , 1831. John Sutton's eldest son was Sir Edmund Sutton and he was followed by John and then Edward Sutton the 6th Baron Dudley who was father of Joyce the mother of

Thomas Leighton. The 4th Baron's second son was John who took the surname Dudley and whose eldest son Edmund was executed in about 1510. His son John Dudley married Jane Guildford and they had among their children Henry, Robert Earl of Leicester, Ambrose Earl of Warwick and Guildford who married Lady Jane Grey and lost his head over her.

5. Blount was later to have a central role in Essex's revolt and would have been well-known to Sir Christopher Heydon. Adams as above.

6. *ODNB*

7. *ODNB*

8. *CPR Elizabeth I* vol 7 1575-78

9. TNA, REQ 2/34/59

10. Sir John was a young son of Sir George Throckmorton.

11. Leighton's uncle, John the 7th Baron Dudley, had as his heir Edward whose daughter was Anne. TNA, PCC will 1586 of Edward Sutton Lord Dudley, PROB 11/69. Dame Anne Throckmorton remarried to Thomas Wilmer, a lawyer in London and heir to his father's estate in Starton, Northamptonshire. TNA, PCC will 1581 of Thomas Wylmer gent, PROB 11/63. Also: *ODNB*; *Northamptonshire Visitation*; *Shropshire Visitation*; *Burke's Peerages*, 1831; and other Google Books and website sources

12. *CPR Elizabeth I* vol 5 1569-72

13. Leighton's Lieutenants were Thomas Compton, Thomas Wigmore from 1580, George Paulet from 1591, Edward Lord Zouche (his daughter-in-law's father) from 1600, his son Thomas Leighton esq in 1604 and Peter Carey from 1605. The Bailiffs were again Thomas Compton, William de Beauvoir from 1571, Thomas Wigmore from October 1581, and Louis de Vic from 1588.

14. *CPR Elizabeth I* vol 6 1572-75 and vol 7 1575-78

15. The Priaulx Library, Guernsey, St Peter Port register

16. Anon (ed), *Actes des États de L'Île de Guernsey 1605 à 1651*, Guernsey, nd, p 357

17. The Earl of Leicester's accounts for November 1587 included an embarkation list of his considerable household when he was returning from his time as Governor-general of the Netherlands. Named among the 'Gard of the shott' was Edmund Lumner. As Edmund of Mannington had died before July 1587, this is probably his cousin Edmund of Sharrington of whom little else is known. Adams as above

18. From Dr DL Ogier: JH Le Patourel (ed), *The Building of Castle Cornet Guernsey: 1 Documents Relating to the Tudor Reconstruction*, Guernsey, 1958, pp 61,64. Although mis-transcribed in the printed account as 'Sumner', nineteenth century transcriptions of the same documents at the Island Archives in fact render the name correctly with an initial 'L'.

19. Guernsey Island Archives, Historical Documents v. f.9

20. Island Archives, Historical Documents v. f.12

21. SHC, LM/COR/3/335

22. Edith F Carey, *An Eminent Guernseyman, Sir Henry de Vic*, Guernsey Society of Natural Science and Local Research, vol 6, 1911

23. Island Archives, Historical Documents v. ff.16-18, f.39 and f.123

24. TNA, C 1/1214/22

25. For example, TNA, E 211/628 and C 1/147/94

26. *CSPD Addenda* 1566-79

27. *HofC*

28. Adams as above
29. TNA, PCC will proved July 1583 of Mary Devicke of All Hallows the Great, PROB 11/65
30. Island Archives, *Biographical Papers I*, ff. 5-6
31. Clement had married Elizabeth Nodham in November 1562 in St Gregory by St Paul's in London. IGI He may have been a brother of Louis or perhaps John de Vic of Guernsey. Mary also left legacies to John Vawse fishmonger and his wife Joan.
32. TNA, PCC will 1615, PROB 11/125. William had no children by his wife Frances Hanchett whom he had married in 1613 and left his estate to her and his three married sisters - Anne Atslowe (?), Jane Harris and Ursula Brett. IGI
33. There are no such baptismal records on Guernsey and as yet none has been found in London registers.
34. Edith F Carey, *An Eminent Guernseyman: Sir Henry de Vic,* Transactions of the Société Guernsiase, 1911; HJ Rose, *A New General Biographical Dictionary*, 1857; J Gorton, *A General Biographical Dictionary*, 1833. Carey's guess at the relationship to Sir Thomas Edmunds is a puzzle. Carey noted that William de Vic and Edmunds wrote to each other in the 1590s as 'loving brothers'. She assumed a close relationship, with a sister or half sister of William having married Edmunds. Her speculation that a Lumner daughter married him seems a bit of a stretch and another interpretation is possible. If there had been a Lumner daughter (and no baptismal evidence has been found) she could only have been barely of marriageable age by the mid-1590s. She would have to have been older than that to fit Carey's theory. The nature of Mary's 1583 will is such that if she then had a half-sister, she would have mentioned her in her legacies but she did not. Carey also thought William had a brother, which seems to stem from a misunderstanding of who Clement Devicke was - his cousin not his brother. There is no evidence that William had a brother. His own and his sister's wills taken together preclude that and show the same three sisters alive in both 1583 and 1615. So there could not have been another full sister who was the first wife of Edmunds by the mid-1590s. Carey's letter references and her additional reference to a 1596 attempt to sell plate to Edmunds can best be explained as the 'brother' offering plate for sale to Edmunds being the husband of one of William's three married sisters - with 'brother' being used as was normal for brother-in-law. We have not explored the families of the sisters' husbands Brett, Astlow and Harris/Henry to see if any one of them might have had a sister who was the mysterious first wife of Edmunds.
35. TNA, C 3/213/38 and 39
36. TNA, C 33/70
37. *APC* 1579-80
38. *CSPD Addenda* 1566-79
39. *APC* 1579-80
40. *CSPD Addenda* 1566-79
41. *CSPD Addenda* 1580-1603. 25th January 1581 (although this looks from the content more like 1580 or earlier). G Beauvoir junior and Guillaume (ie William) Beauvoir to Sir Thomas Leighton Governor of Guernsey at London. Notifying and warning him of matters in Guernsey ... letters have been sent to Mr Wigmore your lieutenant and the Bailiff and Jurats ... regarding the costs of certain people ... Bailiff and Jurats prevented your lieutenant, myself, Nicholas Carey and John Delacourt as assistants from collecting

the charges ... letters and people are coming to the Privy Council ... . Same day: Names of Commissioners appointed for Guernsey matters: Norton of London; Thomas Fashion of Southampton alias Seigneur d'Anneville; John de Vic senior of Guernsey; John Andrew of Guernsey alias Seigneur de Saumares [the Seigneurs were old Island titles. 24th May 1580 Privy Council to Sir Thomas to send the Bailiff and James Guyle to the Privy Council to answer the complaint of Nicholas Carey - *APC* 1580-81. 25th July 1580 Council to Sir Thomas to say they have heard Carey versus the Bailiff and found the Bailiff to have acted too harshly in imprisoning and fining Carey for his words against Guile. The imprisonment was sufficient and the fine of £120 should be repaid or mitigated, which Leighton was to sort out with the Jurats - *APC* 1580-81

42. 28th August 1580 the Privy Council papers included a very long section relating to all the various complaints by the islanders, most of which related in one way or another to taxation. Many were found in favour of Leighton, a few for the islanders and some were referred back to the Jurats to resolve points of detail. *APC* 1580-81

43. *APC* 1580-81

44. 1st November 1580 letter from Privy Council to Sir Thomas regarding complaint by Peter Carey against his brothers John Carey and William Beauvoir regarding a long running suit for recovery of certain lands of the inheritance of their father wrongfully held from them by their brother Nicholas Carey; which now being recovered by Peter, John and William were refusing to pay their part of the £80 costs incurred. Leighton to sort out who should pay what. *APC 1580-81*. 31st March 1581 Privy Council note to Thomas Wigmore Lieutenant to Sir Thomas Leighton regarding the non-attendance at Council of John Carey in his inheritance dispute with his brother Peter, who had been in attendance for some time at significant cost. APC 1581-82

45. *CSPD Addenda* 1580-1603

46. 10th October 1581 Sir Thomas to Walsingham urging, on this occasion, the Council to support the cause of the ministers of Guernsey who were complaining that the people of the island were refusing to pay them their full due in tithes. *CSPD Addenda* 1580-1603

47. May 1582 note *CSPD Addenda* 1580-1603. 17th June 1582 Sir Thomas wrote to Walsingham asking him to consider Louis de Vic's request for some recompense for the costs of his three visits to Council in defence of Her Majesty's rights. On this visit he was being sent with the requested abstract of Guernsey laws and customs. De Vic understood the island well. *CSPD Addenda* 1580-1603. De Vic, as Procureur of the Queen, had written that month regarding being allowed his attendance charges over the last 14 months.

48. *APC* 1581-82

49. *CSPD Addenda* 1580-1603

50. Further petitions and notes were recorded in September 1582 *CSPD Addenda* 1580-1603

51. Also annexed was a note touching Beauvais [Beauvoir and Beauvais seem to be interchangeable] and Baudoin in answer of the discourse presented to the Bishop of Winchester. 'Articles by Louis de Vic against Baudoin and William Beauvais. That the divine service, such as used in England, has been rejected by their means, the gates of the churches in the island closed and the pastors silenced. Answer: this is a calumny against the ministers, who have not introduced themselves into the churches, but being called by the government, and charged to keep the same order throughout, have been preaching and instructing the people, administering sacraments, etc. Baudoin and Beauvais had no power to act as they were accused, nor would the people have endorsed it, the churches have always been open on Sundays, for preaching prayer and sacraments. That William

Beauvais took the office of Bailiff on the decease of Thomas Compton, and he and his associates took the authority of Dean. Answer: this is a calumny, but at the Governor's order they did punish dissolute dames, drunkenness, etc, and this gave rise to it. That Beauvais, magistrate, and Baudoin, minister, said it were better never to have prayers or reading in the church than to use the English service. Answer: they would never presume to alter the form of service without permission of the Governor and consent of the elders of the church, and this imputation is of malice'.

52. Note of October 1583 on customs due to the Crown showed Louis de Vic as Her Majesty's Procureur, Sir Thomas Leighton Governor, Thomas Wigmore Bailiff and 10 of the Jurats William Beauvoir, Jean Blondel, Nic de Saumarez, Nic de Mesurier, Nic Carey, Jean De la Court, Thos Blondel, Edouard Le Fevre, André Henry, Jean André. *CSPD Addenda, 1580-1603.* Louis de Vic was also Procureur in 1584.

53. *CSPD 1547-80.* It is not clear when Nicholas Carey took over being Lieutenant-Governor from Wigmore. They both are described as Lieutenant around the mid-1580s but in 1588 Carey seems to have been Leighton's lieutenant.

54. *APC 1586-87*

55. Tanner 78.127

56. *CSPD Addenda, 1580-1603*

57. *CSPD 1581-90*

58. 1589 subsidy roll showed him assessed at £40. Harleian Society vols 109-110

59. *Extracts from original Ms re Norwich Corporation: Musters etc,* NA1846,: '1588 Payd to George Fenner 22 April for gilt cup weighing 38 oz and half at 5s 5d an oz which was given to Sir Thomas Leighton kt Gen' of her Maj forces for his favours to the City; Item ... to Tho Armyger, Sir Williams Heydon's clerk, for a reward in writing as letter touching the soldiers (Yarmouth); Item ... to Richard Scottow, for a gallon of sack, 3s 4d and a gallon of clarett wine 2s 4d given to Sir Thomas Leighton the first night he supped at Mr Pecks; Item for boathire when [the accountant] went to deliver letters to the Counsil and twice to speake with Sir Thomas Leighton; Item for passage and repassage by water twice to Greenwich to speak with hym for powder and for the great ordnance'; Entry for the armourer and his men repairing & fitting armour, day and night in April 1588 'when Sir Thomas was here'. Thomas Armiger was almost certainly the same man who sold Wolterton to Gregory Houghton about this time.

60. *APC* 1588

61. *APC* 1589-90

62. *CSPD Addenda* 1580-1603

63. *APC* 1591-1597

64. *CSPD* 1595-97

65. *APC* 1597-98

66. *List of Records in the Greffe,* Guernsey iii, p 90

67. Thomas of Guernsey's father Richard (d 1553) had been the younger brother of the MP's father William Wigmore (d 1540).

68. The implication was that Thomas Wigmore had died - although the wording 'late of Guernsey' was ambiguous. Presumably on Thomas's death Leighton had recovered one half of the grant (which Thomas had probably not mortgaged) and now was buying back the other half to regain full control. If Thomas of Guernsey had still been alive in 1596 any document of this kind would certainly have been drafted to include him actively in the guarantee of peaceable enjoyment to Sir Thomas Leighton. It did not.

69. Sir Thomas had two daughters: Anne who married Sir John St John 1st Baronet of Lydiard Tregoze in Wiltshire and Elizabeth who married Sherrington Talbot esq of Salwarp in Worcestershire and Lacock in Wiltshire. Some books show the sisters as daughters of Thomas Leighton esq rather than his sisters. However, the best researched works show them to be Sir Thomas's daughters. Generationally this fits their husbands' dates well. Sir John St John was a cousin of the St Johns Barons of Bletsoe in Bedfordshire, from a fifteenth century common ancestor. Anne married St John, not Elizabeth as some works have it. Elizabeth's husband was the son of John Talbot of Salwarp and Olive, the daughter of Sir Henry Sherrington of Lacock.

Notes to Chapter 7

1. The 1589 subsidy roll showed: Francis Flower in lands and fees £20 in St Sepulchre parish in Farringdon Without ward as a stranger or non-resident. Harleian Society, *vols 109 and 110*. He was also shown in St Andrew's Holborn. Both these entries seem likely to refer to his assessment based on Katherine's property - she was not assessed in her own right.

2. Although he is not now thought to have had children and his will made no reference to any, Francis Flower was believed by nineteenth century writers to have had a son George who became a successful soldier in Ireland where he lived from about 1600 to sometime after 1627. *A Biographical Peerage of Ireland*, 1817. George was knighted for his services. In time this branch of the Flower family became the Viscounts Ashbrook. We have not been able to confirm whether this is accurate or whether this George fitted into some other branch of the Flower family.

3. *HofC*; the name of Katherine's father is given as Rafe Butler in error for Sir Philip.

4. William Camden, schoolmaster antiquarian and author of *Britannia*, in his notebook penned a few punning lines on the death of Flower. We do not know if they ever saw the light of day. BL, Add 36294 f.29

5. E Williams, *Holborn*

6. TNA, C 2/Eliz/D10/56

7. Eric St John Brooks, *Sir Christopher Hatton Queen Elizabeth's Favourite*, 1946 and *Encyclopaedia Britannica*, 1910

8. Philip Sidney, *The Poems of Sir Philip Sidney*, 1962

9. Harris Nicolas, *Memoirs of the Life and Times of Sir Christopher Hatton*, 1847

10. A 1590 plan of Eltham Palace shows 'My Lord Chancellor's Lodgings' at this spot. TNA, MPF 1/228

11. In 1588 the robed senior heads from Oxford assembled in his rooms before presenting Hatton with the Chancellorship. Brooks as above

12. Cheshire Record Office, DCR/3/24/3

13. *CPR Elizabeth I* vol 8 1578-8; Centre for Buckinghamshire Studies, D-C/1/266

14. Buckinghamshire, D-C/1/266

15. Northamptonshire Record Office, FH600

16. Brooks, as above, p 280

17. East Sussex Record Office, SAS-CO/1/1124-1141 In December 1588 Robert, son and heir of John Bathurst deceased and grandson of Robert, was involved with Dodge in what seems to have been a deed placing these Bathurst family lands in trust for Robert. John Bathurst of Horsmonden Kent had married Edward Dodge's sister Mary and their

son Robert was to become the heir of the childless Edward Dodge. After John's death Mary married Francis Clampard of Wrotham. These names and details were recited in TNA, C/2/Eliz/417/57. The 1596 recovery involved his relatives Robert Clampard clothier of East Peckham and Francis Clampard gent of Wrotham.

18. Burke and other nineteenth century writers gave him as one of the Houghtons of Houghton Tower Lancashire, but his father was of London and Peter and his brother were born in London. J Burke, *A General and Heraldic Dictionary of the Peerage and Baronetage ... ,* 1832. Presumably his father was a younger son of the main line of the Lancashire family. John Stow in his 1598 *Survey of London* noted that both Peter Houghton and his father Thomas were buried in St Michael Cornhill. Peter bore the same arms as the Houghton Tower family (sable three bars argent - crest a bull pass argent) Thomas Robson, *The British Herald or Cabinet of Armorial Bearings of the Nobility and Gentry ... ,* 1830 The heralds who organised his funeral represented Lancaster and Chester and one of his daughters was described as of Houghton Tower Lancashire in later pedigree records of the Bedingfields in Norfolk. While Peter did not leave a will, his brother did. Thomas Houghton the younger citizen and haberdasher of London, TNA, PCC will made December 1572 and proved July 1573, PROB 11/55. He left money to his father Thomas the elder and to his brother Peter Houghton, with smaller amounts to his two sisters Jane wife of William Phillipps and Elizabeth wife of Nicholas Stevens. *The London Visitation of 1568* showed William Phillips of London gent, one of the Queen's 'Costomers for the Wool', married to Johann daughter of Thomas Houghton. The residue of Peter's brother's estate, after this total of £40, went to his wife Avys and his children (unspecified) when 21. Avys was to be executor, with the four men as supervisors who were to have four black gowns. Then at the end of the will, added in March 1573, he said that he had withdrawn the money for the four men but left them the gowns. He said that the reason for the withdrawal was written in his book of remembrance - perhaps he had suffered a trading loss of some scale?

19. *CPR Elizabeth I* vol 3 1563-66

20. This could be the delayed admission of the father or the normal admission of the son. We suspect the latter and that he subsequently shifted to become a haberdasher - not unusual among members of the senior merchant companies.

21. *The Visitation of Lancashire, 1567*, Chetham Society, 1871. However, the early pedigree does not show the London branch of the family and is vague on siblings of this Sir Richard and earlier generations. Sir Richard had four sons. After his death in the late 1550s his heir Thomas Houghton esq built the grand Houghton Tower in Lancashire, finishing it in 1565. Bede Camm, *Forgotten Shrines: An Account of some Old Catholic Halls and Families*, 2003 However, as a catholic recusant, about five years later he fled to the continent and died there still in exile in 1580. In 1580-81 the catholic Edmund Campion is known to have visited Houghton Tower on his Lancashire travels. The Lancashire Houghtons continued to have catholic tendencies even if most of them outwardly conformed. Thomas was dispossessed of his estates which passed to his childless brother Alexander, who in his 1581 will left them to his younger brother Thomas Houghton esq of Brynescoules (third son of Sir Richard by his second wife). GJ Piccope, *Lancashire and Cheshire Wills and Inventories*, 1860. The son of this Thomas was Sir Richard Houghton who was made baronet by James I in 1611.

22. Guildhall Lib, Grocery Company Admissions Book and notes therein from the Court Minutes as before

23. Various references in State Papers Domestic series, online TNA catalogue
24. *CPR Elizabeth I* vol 9 1580-82
25. TNA, E 211/111
26. TNA, E 211/175
27. *A Catalogue of the Lansdowne Manuscripts in the British Museum*, section 37, number 93
    Other references to him and wine include TNA, E 134/40 eliz/hil 5
28. *Manuscripts of the Marquess of Bath preserved at Longleat vol V 1533-1659*, HMC vol 58, page 88
29. *CPR* vol 8
30. A Beaven, *The Aldermen of the City of London 1908 and 1913* in 2 vols
31. One or two minor documents in the TNA attest to Houghton's involvement in constraining the activities of other merchants, pursuing debts owed and indeed becoming liable himself for a fine on a writ of habeas corpus. TNA, SP 46/20/fo 5,5d; TNA, SP 46/18/fo 225; TNA, SP 46/40/fo 1
32. Wrotham parish register
33. The Norfolk Houghtons were from a long established Gunthorpe family. Gregory and Robert were younger brothers of John. Gregory bought Wolterton Hall in the 1580s and his family continued in Wolterton and Itteringham until 1660. Robert was Sir Robert Houghton of Ranworth, a high-profile lawyer.
34. F Madden et al, *Collectanea Topographica et Genealogica*, pp 292-3
35. I Atherton, *Ambition and Failure in Stuart England ...* , 1999
36. SHC, P7/1/1 Original register is damp damaged, but examined under U-V light shows Elizabeth Hawt[..] ; W Betham, *The Baronetage of England*, 1802; Burke's *Peerage and Baronetage*
37. Blom
38. The Charity Commissioners report on *The Endowed Charities of London* of 1829 still showed this £400 in a list of bequests by grocers.
39. TNA, PCC Admon 1597, PROB 6
40. TNA, REQ 2/280/56, REQ 2/39/55 and REQ 2/46/10
41. Lambeth Palace Library, Carew Manuscripts, MS 615
42. JE Neale, *Elizabeth I and Her Parliaments, vol 2, 1584-1601*
43. *HofC*
44. Katherine Gawdy's eldest half brother died just before his father in 1566 and the second half brother Thomas became a Judge on The King's Bench and died in 1588. Her third brother born Thomas but confirmed as Francis Gawdy, later Sir Francis the Lord Chief Justice of Common Pleas, married Elizabeth Coningsby in Redenhall in 1563. Blom, *ODNB*, Burke's Extinct Baronetcies, *Norfolk Pedigrees Part 5*, Norfolk Genealogy vol 22
45. *ODNB*; E Foss, *The Judges of England, Volume 5*, 1857; Google Books
46. NRO, NCC will 1600, 25 Force
47. TNA, LR1/41, Office of the Auditors of Land Revenue, vol1 for 1583-1603
48. *HofC*
49. TNA, E 179/152/493. His £5 in land was followed by Robert Kempe gent and Richard Marshall both at £4.
50. The Dynnes seem relatively absent from the Heydon parish register after about 1590 despite having owned the dominant manor and having built its very fine house. Henry Dynne esq built the house in 1582 but died in London and was buried in Heydon on 30th December 1586. His stepmother Beatrix was buried in Heydon in January 1590

and her will was proved in February 1591. NRO, NCC will 1589, 293 Flack. Perhaps most of Henry's many children remained in London, although a Thomas Dynne had children baptised in Heydon in 1593 and 1594. Alice Dynne was married there in 1592 and William Dynne gent was buried there in July 1594. Blom wrote that Dynne's manor and lands were sold by 1588 to William Colfer senior who settled it then on William junior and Richard Colfer; and after this it came to Robert Kemp esq who was buried in Heydon in 1616. Nothing has been found to confirm this. Perhaps the relatively modest Colfer family were related to the Kemps by marriage and Blom had seen a marriage settlement. A court of requests action of 1594 showed that Henry Dynne's son William Dynne gent of Sharrington was then actively trying to sell a messuage and lands in Heydon and elsewhere to an unnamed Kemp. TNA, REQ 2/196/105. His half-uncle had a lease of the undescribed lands which was complicating the sale. Presumably this was a minor property that the Kemps were trying to buy to consolidate their holding. Robert Kemp's daughter Elizabeth was baptised in Heydon in October 1595 and his son Robert in December 1596.

51. Stinton was later home to Sir John Spelman the royalist.

52. NRO, NRS 23319, Z95 and NRS 27299/18-21, 385x7. Buggin was also mentioned in a recital in a deed of 1633 as having had a stake in some Irmingland lands, TNA, WARD 2/321/118/1

53. NRO, MC 341/1 and 341/2, 706x4A

54. TNA, C 142/374/107

55. NRO, WAL 608/5, 276x4

56. Wolterton archives 20/4/9A, 68. He included an additional note in which the round brackets are the writer's:
   Notes of writings left at Norwich June 12th 1721:
   Exemplification of the estates at the request of John Potts esquire
   Inrolment of a recovery for Mr Potts of the manors of Mannington. Hilary Term 27 Elizabeth [Jan-Feb 1585 and presumably the surviving item above]
   Indenture of bargain and sale between John Dodge and John Potts esquires of the estates in Mannington (NB this is a marriage contract)
   Five several fines of Dodge and Lumner (Memorandum: June 12th 1721 then delivered the said fines to Potts)
   Seven old parchment writings relating not all to the estate tied up together (Memorandum: at the same time delivered of the old writings)
   Memorandum: This is a schedule of Sir Charles Potts's writings … left in Mr Jermy's hands and since returned to Sir Charles when he and Lady Potts were at my house 2nd June 1727

57. TNA, C 142/256/40. The first part reads: And they say that before John Potts died: Edmund Lumnor esq was [at the time of] Mary 1 [1553-54] seised of the manors of Mannington and Wolterton and in 10 messuages, 1 watermill, 1000 acres land, 100 meadow, 50 pasture, 100 woods, 50 furze and bruar and liberty of a fold-course, with appurtenances in Mannington, Wolterton, Saxthorpe, Little Barningham, Itteringham, Oulton, Blickling, Corpusty, Aylsham and Ingworth and the advowson of Itteringham church and half the advowson of Wolterton church; and in Hilary Philip & Mary 1&2 [Jan-Feb 1555] a fine was levied between John Southcote and Blasimer [Blase] Saunders plt and Edmund and wife Katherine Lumnor, and William, John, Henry and John Lumnor def. [ie, 2 Johns], [property] to use of Edmund and Katherine and their male

heirs [in default of whom] first William, on death to John, to Henry, to John, to Henry son of last mentioned John or the heirs of Edmund. And Edmund was seised in his demesne and fee, and Katherine was seised in her demesne and fee for her life [and by] 13 Feb 1555 Edmund and Katherine had produced heir Edmund. And Edmund the father and Katherine were seised and after 19th August Philip & Mary 5&6 [1558] the said Edmund Lumnor the father died thus seised of such estate and Katherine survived him and held it by right of joint tenant in survivorship for her life, remaindered to her son Edmund.

58. TNA, STAC 5/A48/26; TNA, STAC 5/A47/12

59. Other writers have misinterpreted the evidence and said he paid £3,000. Jane Lumner tried using the same mis-information in her action later.

60. Itteringham's rector, Edward Atwood may have been too ill. He died in May 1585. Weeks was also of Baconsthorpe; Mannington's living was in the gift of the Heydon family so Weeks may have been a natural choice to cover.

61. Wolterton archives 10/25; M & W Vaughan-Lewis, *Decoding a Sixteenth Century estate map of Mannington,* The Annual No 17 2008, NAHRG. A second NAHRG article is planned for 2009 covering place and field names on the map and a number of ideas about the evolution of the landscape in and around the Mannington estate. This map showed this house in Itteringham as a focal point of the field numbering system, not Mannington Hall itself as one might have expected. This indicated that the Potts residence was here and not Mannington. The drawing of the house is now very faint but it is clearly depicted as sitting in a much larger and more complex site than all the other houses on the map bar Mannington Hall.

62. Nathaniel Bacon letter May 1591: *Bacon Papers III*, NRS vol 53, 1988

63. Wolterton archives 2/25

64. Vaughan-Lewis article as above

65. TNA, C 33/84

66. TNA, C 33/87 and 33/88

67. TNA, C 33/91

68. TNA, C 33/91 and 33/92

69. TNA, STAC 5/A55/20

70. AMW Stirling, *Coke of Norfolk and his Friends, volume1*; AD Boyer, *Sir Edward Coke and the Elizabethan Age*; CW James, *Chief Justice Coke,* 1929

71. *ODNB*

72. In his 1562 will John left bequests for John, Edmund and Francis to study divinity and then the law. NRO, NCC will 1562, 258 Cowlles. John was to become a noted writer on religious and other matters, for which he lost his right hand over a tract criticising the prospective royal French marriage, even though he protested to his death his loyalty to the Queen. *ODNB*

73. TNA, PCC will 1590 John Stubbe gent of Thelveton, PROB 11/75; PCC will 1614 Edmund Stubbe, PROB 11/123; PCC will 1620 Richard Stubb of Sedgeford, PROB 11/135. This nephew was John Stubbes of Inner Temple and Strumpshaw, son of Francis. There was a quite acrimonious action involving various members of the Stubbes and related Fenn families, with alleged forgery of documents relating to property in Strumpshaw. TNA, STAC 8, 140/26 and 140/27; STAC 8/ 271/26 and 271/27

74. TNA, C 33/92

75. NRO, ANW 1590-92 will 281 made October 1591 and proved December 1591. Bequests went to sons Richard and William and one daughter that had been married to

John Woolsey and another to a Plaford of Northrepps. The will was to be supervised by John Dodge esq.

76. TNA, STAC 5/A48/26; TNA, STAC 5/A47/12

77. Interestingly at this time Love's had a sufficiently large hall in which to hold the 1594 enquiry and had in the past been the home of Richard Larwood of the family who had bought Bintry manor and farm just across the road in about 1540.

78. The ownership of Love's and its reintegration into the estate by John Potts's son in the 1620s and more detail on the complexities of Nowers manor will be covered in a future book on lands and lordships.

79. TNA, C2/Eliz/L11/46

Notes to Chapter 8

1. Eltham parish register held at Eltham Church and viewable by appointment

2. TNA, PCC will 1597, PROB 11/89. To our reading of the will it was not made ten years earlier as has been suggested in his *HofC* entry.

3. TNA, PCC will 1597, PROB 11/91

4. The Stubbes assumption matters. Edmund 'Stoble' or 'Stuble' appeared in the will not only as signatory to the codicil, but he was also mentioned in the will as a trustee with other Norfolk friends and family in Potts's acquisition of land from Bettes and in the codicil as a recipient of a ring in a short list of friends and family. We have found no evidence of the existence of anyone called Stoble/Stuble at this time. Edmund Stubbes was a London lawyer and involved in legal matters to do with Mannington, including a family will. Also a Stubbes family lived in Eltham at this time. It seems likely that that all these references are to the same man - Edmund Stubbes the lawyer - and that he was a friend of John Potts and a near neighbour both in Norfolk and possibly also in Kent.

5. TNA, C142/256/40

6. NRO, DS 603, 352x3 has Blomefield and others' notes on Irmingland.

7. In 1598 John Bettes and his wife Margaret sold their remaining property to Thomas Catlyn (later Catelyn) of Lakenham near Norwich. A fine that year also showed them, with their son and heir Henry Bettes and Anne Potts widow and others involved, confirming the property to Catlyn. Perhaps the purchase of a part of these two manors, without any old deeds providing title, was seen by John Potts as slightly risky and in need of reinforcing documentation. Presumably Anne was in the 1598 fine on the same basis, but this time effectively quitclaiming any interest to Catlyn. Within a few years the manors had been sold on to Nathaniel Bacon and Henry Hobart at which time Heydon and Potts agreed with Hobart to enjoy the lands they each had despite lack of clear title. NRO, NRS 8552, 21C1

8. This site, not too far from the old site of St Andrew's church, may have been the ancient site of the Whitefoot manor, a suggestion also made at the time by Nathaniel Bacon who bought Catlyn's Irmingland lands. Bacon needed to establish where the ancient manors had been as no comprehensive deeds or records had survived. A September 1608 memorandum noted that 'Mr Pottes hath a white house and a dove house and suggest that Whitefooteshall may lie in the lands purchased there'. The implication of the note was that Bacon assumed Hastings manor was at the Corpusty end of Irmingland where he built his grand hall. NRO RAY (6) 65-66 Sep 16 1608 in *Bacon Papers V* forthcoming NRS volume.

9.   NRO, NAS 1/1/5/41; and 5189 in forthcoming *Bacon Papers V.*
10. TNA, PCC will 1598, PROB 11/91
11. TNA, PCC will 1599, PROB 11/93; John Potts IPM 'And that Katherine late wife of Roger Potts received all the issues and profits from the messuages in Purpool lane in St Andrews and in St Botolph and St Sepulchre from the death of John Potts to 22nd December 41 Elizabeth on which day she died and after which Christopher Heydon receives the issues and profits'.
12. Hertfordshire Record Office, contemporaneous transcripts of certain parish register entries for the major families only. The registers are lost and it would seem only those with names like Boteler and Mynne were extracted by the transcriber.
13. John Potts IPM 'And they say that Katherine (recently wife of John Dodge) received the issues and profits of the manors of Mannington and Wolterton (as in the fine) [from 20th December 1597] to 11th December 41 Elizabeth [1598] on which day she died, and after which Christopher Heydon, who had married Anne late wife of John Potts, received the issues and profits'.
14. NRO, NCC 1598 Administration number 219
15. NRO, NCC 1598 inventory, DN/INV 15/158
16. PCC wills; Norfolk and Suffolk Visitations; JJ Muskett; Burke and other sources
17. Frances was his daughter by his second wife Katherine Finch, not his first who had been a Calthorpe.
18. In the May 1598 action he was given as of the age of 8 or 9; to fit in between the known baptisms of siblings he must have been born between about December 1589 and April 1590.
19. John Potts IPM: 'And that John Potts is the son and heir of John Potts deceased and is aged 7 years. And that the said Sir Christopher Heydon did seize as his ward John Potts the son after the death of John Potts the father, before the death of Katherine (lately wife of Edmund Lumnor, the father) and of Katherine (lately wife of Roger Potts) and in his hands took him, And that Anne late wife of John Potts, from the death of John Potts during her widowhood, and Christopher Heydon, after his marriage to her, receive issues and profits for all the other premises mentioned'.
20. St Andrew Holborn parish register: 'Mistress Ann Potes'
21. NRO, NCC 1598 will, 52 Adams
22. TNA, C3/284/60
23. His IPM as Edward Dodge of Lechlade is TNA, C 142/253/71 and as Edward Dodge of Kent is TNA, C 142/255/140. Dodge asked to be buried in whichever parish church was closest to where he died - Wrotham or Lechlade. TNA, PCC will 1598, PROB 11/91
24. These ages are probably about a year out; Anne's MI gives her dying in 1642 at 75 so born c 1567-68, Mary was older so born c 1565-66.
25. TNA, C 3/280/56
26. TNA, C 33/103
27. TNA, C 33/104
28. NRO, ANW 1604 Administration A237

Notes to Chapter 9

1. K-C, *Civil War*, p 108
2. *Baconsthorpe Castle Excavations and Finds 1951-1972*, East Anglian Archaeology 102
3. CW James, *Chief Justice Coke,*1929
4. NRO, NRS 8578, 21C1
5. *Baconsthorpe Castle* as above; TNA STAC 5/H8/21
6. BL, Eg 2713 f.190, Gawdy papers Vol 1
7. Barbara Batten, *The Heyday of the Heydons,* c 1960. Typed thesis. An excellent work which sadly remains unpublished.
8. *Bacon Papers II*, NRS vol 49 p214, 216
9. *Bacon Papers III*, NRS vol 53 p 123
10. TNA, STAC 5/H8/21
11. TNA, PCC 1594, PROB 11/84
12. Batten says he was a 'faithfull friend'.
13. *ODNB*; Batten
14. Batten
15. C142/428/105
16. Anna Beer, *Bess,* 2004
17. Tanner 76.7
18. Mansfield is also variously given as Maunsell or Mansell within the same documents.
19. Beer, as above p106
20. 44/60 in *Hatfield House, Cecil papers*, HMC Report Vol VI
21. Calendar Salisbury Mss ix p24
22. *APC* 1598
23. *Gents Mag* Vol XXXIX, 1853
24. A Hassell Smith, *County and Court: Government and Politics in Norfolk, 1558-1603,* 1974
25. John Chamberlain letter to Dudley Carleton dated 10 Oct 1600, Google books *Letters of John Chamberlain*
26. *APC* p731, for 26 Oct 1600, mentions only Sir Christopher Heydon and Frances Clere esq attending council.
27. Hassell Smith says the Christopher Heydon /Townshend challenge happened at the previous summer assizes, before John's duel.
28. HMC Report, *Gawdy family papers*
29. *APC* Jan 1600/1 p89, 95
30. Hassell Smith as above
31. BL, Eg 2722 f.81. This is undated but see Hassell Smith *County and Government*; an incorrect date is given in HMC Report *Gawdy papers*, of 1588-89. As he is at Mannington, the letter can only date from after 1597.
32. Hassell Smith as above
33. Folger L.d 241
34. APC Feb 1600/1 p486
35. TNA, E 178/1487
36. Batten
37. *APC* p487
38. Rates 1601-2 *Stiffkey Papers* ,Camden Society, vol 26; *Bacon Papers Vol IV*, NRS 64, 2000
39. *Bacon papers vol IV*

40. BL, Eg 2714 ff. 239,416, 446
41. Batten; *Gents Mag* 1853, says there was a story that he was faced with an order from chancery in February 1614 for the Sheriff to raise the county and throw Sir Christopher out by force.
42. Blom in his Baconsthorpe entry referred to the children by Mirabel as 'Sir William, Sir John, Henry, Nathaniel, *etc* and by Anne, a son Thomas and four daughters'. Other writers have generally echoed Blom, leaving some confusion as to the total number of children, to whom they were born and their names. Hewitt *North and South Erpingham* p39 says eight children were shown on Mirabel's tomb. Mannington and early Baconsthorpe registers do not survive. Thomas was a son of Mirabel but the names of Henry and Nathaniel have not been found elsewhere than in Blom to date: of the four daughters that Heydon and Anne were said to have had together we have found mention only of Martha. Batten adds Anne and Frances. However Anne was in fact Anne's last child by Potts, baptised in Jan 1598 and Frances was probably one of Mirabel's. Batten does not take Anne Potts's previous children into account.
43. *ODNB*
44. *APC* 1601 p149
45. *Bacon Papers IV*
46. *APC* March 1600/1 p 194
47. Quoted in NRO, DS 603, 352x3
48. Tanner 74.192
49. Duleep Singh suggested her age was 50 but dated the portrait by style to c1635, when she would have been in her late 60s.
50. *ODNB*
51. Batten Chap 7; J Chambers, *General History of the County of Norfolk*, 1829
52. Tanner 75.317 1609, thanking her.
53. Blom, 1582 settlement
54. At this time the meaning of nativities was astrological forecasts of someone's life.
55. *House of Gurney* as before; *Lives of Eminent Antiquaries Elias Ashmole and Wm Lilly*, 1774
56. *ODNB*; Heydon's book was published in facsimile in 1977 by De Cepo Press
57. Wood, *Atheniae Oxonienses* vol 1
58. For an entertaining summary of this work, see *The Retrospective Review*, J R Smith 1853 p 264; Batten is also excellent on Heydon's works.
59. *Astrologomania or the madness of Astrologers*, reproduced in facsimile, 1968, De Cepo Press
60. Tanner 75.247. The Lady Montague may be Magdalene Montague late wife of Rt Hon Anthony Ld Viscount Montague of Medhurst, Sussex. Her will was proved April 1608. Pyhrra daughter of Epimetheus was also known as Ephimedis but here Ephemeris (pl. Ephemerides) is more likely, being a daily notation of the stars for astrological readings.
61. *ODNB*
62. Bertram Schofield, *The Knyvett Letters (1620-1644)*, 1949, pp 19-22
63. Both Knyvett and Simonds D'Ewes had £40 a year and found it too little. Schofield and Wilfred R Preest, *Inns of court under Elizabeth and the Early Stuarts*, 1972
64. *Baconsthorpe Castle* as above. See also Rose, *NA* 38, 336-343,1984, *NA* 40, 93-100, 1987
65. On 22nd June 1600 James Lobley married Anne Wright in Itteringham, both servants of Sir Christopher Heydon of Mannington.
66. Batten
67. *APC* 1st March 1600/1

68. Tanner 75.350 - five letters 1610-1628; *ODNB*

69. Why Sir Nathaniel Bacon's hospitality should be a jest is not known.

70. Tanner 74.192

71. Jak Bettes may be John Bettes, perhaps related to the local Oulton family.

72. Was the Stationers' Company grip on publishing such as to make it expensive to register each printing? Heydon is not listed in Stationers' Company records.

73. JA Venn, *Alumni*; Ketton-Cremer was also in error by saying 'he was a member of Gray's Inn before he retired to Norfolk': Potts was active in Norfolk in the 1620s and 30s.

74. MF Keeler, *Long Parliament*, 1954 pp 312-3

75. Tanner 283.170

76. London Metropolitan Archives DRO17/A/01/002; Burke's *Gentry*, under Sir Robert Barker, wrongly gave Mary being daughter & sole heiress of Edward Wigmore of Twickenham esq and marrying 2ndly Edward Barker.

77. *Correspondence of Lady Katherine Paston, 1603-1627*, NRS14,1941

78. Tanner 74.192

79. The first edition of the *History of the House of Commons* entry for John Potts in error says that his first wife was Anne the daughter of one Mebwoke. This is a misreading of an unrelated Dagenham marriage to a Thomas Potts.

80. There is no hint of this marriage in a letter of 23rd October from Heydon to Bacon which concerns some deeds Bacon is trying to track down and which he hoped Heydon or Mr Potts held. Folger L.d 348

81. Elizabeth was the eldest but died aged 13 weeks in 1583 buried at Aveley, Essex; *Visitation of Suffolk 1613*, DS Collection Thetford Lib. Other sources say Jane died unmarried.

82. BL, Add 41140 f. 75 An accurate copy will be published in the forthcoming *Bacon Papers V*, NRS

83. 1605 BL, Stowe 150 f.200; 1617, Stowe 150 f.230; Add Ms 41140 f.100

84. BL, Stowe 150 f.224

85. It is just possible that Barbara, or more likely an earlier Godsalve girl, served at court. Her grandfather was said to be a godson of Queen Mary.

86. Only one reference has been found to Roger Godsalve als Godsall in CUL, Buxton 40/102

87. NRO, HMN 7/314 f.265

88. Vaughan-Lewis, work in progress 2009

89. NRO, T/NS1/20

90. NRO, T/NS1/26

91. TNA, STAC 8/180/13

92. TNA, STAC 8/181/28

93. *House of Gurney* as before; some sources give Willoughbia as being Ursula, his second wife's child - probably confused by her surname being Willoughby. It might be that a Willoughby was her godmother. Willoughbia or Willoughbria was a popular name at this time - Willobia was also used by Sir Austin Palgrave for his son, buried Feb 1619 North Barningham although this may well reflect his wife's maiden name; three other usages occur in Itteringham in the 1620s and 1640s including W Potts's marriage to John Ward. Her sister Anne Potts's daughter Willoughbie by James Scam(b)ler was buried in January 1649 at St Stephen Norwich.

94. John was described as of West Barsham in a deed of December 1615 although in 1614 he was of Buckenham Ferry. They may have lived in both places.

95. *Registrum Vagum*, NRS vol 33 p 298
96. Folger L.d 307
97. *The Chorography of Norfolk*, ed Christabel Hood, 1938, Jarrolds; Blom wrongly gives Sir John.
98. Venn, *Caius*; *Peerage*
99. Charles Green, *Herring-nets and Beatsters*, NA,1969, p 419
100. Tobias Gentleman, London, 1614, quoted in Wikipedia
101. Theo Rabb, *Enterprise and empire....1575-1630*, 1999; *CSPC*, James 1
102. Folger L.d 306
103. HMC 11th Report App IV *Mss of Marquess Townshend*; other instances - 1632 Thomas Godsalve of Gorleston NRO, BRA 926/76; 1624 Thomas esq appeared in a Privy Council complaint about his violating the privileges of Yarmouth - he should have used Gorleston for his coal cargo. APC
104. NRO, NAS 1/1/ 5/14
105. Folger L.d 480
106. Folger L.d 305
107. Dorothy died shortly after her sister c1635 and Sir Thomas died in 1636. Their son was a royalist imprisoned in 1643. *ODNB*
108. NRO, NCC will 1588 304 Holmes
109. TNA E 178/5538
110. Suffolk Record Office (Ipswich) 1C/AA1/69/42 will
111. NRO, MC 2409/16/6
112. Hilgay parish registers
113. NRO, Henry Hawe NCC 1592 will 238 Apleyarde
114. Ursula may have known Spelman through a distant link through the Athowe and Cobbe families - *Bacon Paper s IV* p212. Hilgay, where she grew up is not far from Wiggenhall and Narborough. Her uncle George Willoughby lived in Wiggenhall St Magdalen.
115. Austin's mother Urith was the daughter of William Saunders of Ewell: the Saunders family were briefly involved with the Potts Holborn property.
116. Deed which mentions both in 1599 regarding land in Little Barningham, NRO, DS 603, 352x3.
117. Tanner 74.192, and Tanner 283.170

Notes to Chapter 10

1. TNA, PCC, PROB 6/11 f.77
2. Tanner 289.130 John Potts esq £22 (margin £20), cf with Sir Charles Cornwallis £20 Aylsham, John Dix esq Wickmere £22.
3. HMC 11th Report App IV *Marquis of Townshend* p21
4. He died in 1680 and should not be confused with Clement Spelman, a distant cousin and a royalist, who died in 1679.
5. Katherine married Lougher in May 1629 and could have had a child before her death. John Lougher succeeded his father at Letheringsett and was later presented to Baconsthorpe by Katherine's brother-in-law, William Crowe, in 1661. After ejection, he was the congregational minister of Alby and Repps. From her memorial verse in Mannington chapel it seems the name was pronounced 'Lower'.

6. NRO, RYE Ms 54 vol 1
7. Harleian Society, *The Visitation of Essex, 1634*, vol 13, 1878
8. Robert Palgrave senior, d1596, of N Barningham and Antingham had a daughter Frances born December 1582 and alive in 1594.
9. Although given as 'of Parndon Essex', it is possible that Edmund's family also lived in Eye, Suffolk as that church has a monument to Mary relict of Edward [sic] Sadler of Parndon, Essex (died 1661 aged 94). Unfortunately there are no Sadler burial register entries in Eye.
10. TNA, E 44/338 and 44/339. Conveyance by Rose Clitheroe of Salle, widow of Lambert Clitheroe and their yeoman son Thomas also of Salle, to Charles Potts esq of Middle Temple.
11. TNA, C5/41/26
12. NRO, WAL 213,216, 218
13. M & W Vaughan-Lewis, *Decoding the Sixteenth Century Mannington Estate Map* as before for details
14. M & W Vaughan-Lewis work in progress 2009
15. *Inventory of Church goods 1552*, NA, vol 27, 1941, pp 406-7
16. Anne's memorial in Wolterton, now lost, is reputed to have given her age at death as 76, in May 1681. This would make her birth 1605, four years before her parents' marriage and her father aged only 14. A more likely date would be 1610.
17. NRO, NAS 1/1/5/51
18. TNA, C 2/Chas1/S36/69
19. NRO, WAL 144/3, 290x3
20. BL, Add 27967 f.87 and *Notebook of Robert Doughty* NRS vol 54, 1991
21. The name is given as Hills in Cockthorpe and Hill or Hills in Wood Dalling and Itteringham.
22. TNA, PCC PROB 11/155 proved February 1629. Incidentally Edmund's will was overseen by Sir Thomas Hyrne of Haveringland and the ubiquitous but shadowy John Smith of Arminghall the son of Dame Agnes Clere.
23. A brief story is told of the courting couple, reported by Dorothy Gurney: 'Mr Hill that married Mr Potts his daughter, when he was Suter to his wife, she was fumbling of some tune with her fingers upon the Table; Lady, says he, I durst lay a wager I could tell you what you play. I dubt it says she, so she tryed it againe. Now tell me what I play: why I thinke you play the Foole says he; which complement much vext her and put her extremely out. H F Lippincott, *Merry Passages & Jeasts: A Ms Jestbook of Sir Nicholas Le Strange*, 1974 p234
24. TNA, PCC will 1662 PROB 11/311
25. In Felmingham church (under a fitted carpet) there is a 1694 memorial near the altar to Barbara Hills but this could also be the wife of Francis Hills of Itteringham.
26. NRO, 1690 ANW will 55/75
27. John Hill's will was made in May 1662 when Jessup may have been failing; Blom gives the memorial tablet to Anne as 1659 Old Style
28. TNA, C10/81/36
29. NRO, NCC 1642 will, 2 Barker
30. *Michaelmas 1664 Hearth Tax assessment,* Norfolk Genealogy vol 15, for Brooke only gave George Ward gent 12 hearths and John Ward gent 5 hearths.
31. TNA, C10/81/36

32. Wolterton archives, 19/34, 64L: also abstract NRO, WAL 2A, 268x4
33. *Visitation of Suffolk 1664*
34. Suffolk Hearth Tax showed 9 hearths against 10 hearths for Thomas Pumfield.
35. TNA, C10/81/36
36. TNA, E134/11Wm3/East26
37. HW Saunders, *Stiffkey Papers 1580-1620, Camden 3rd Series, 26 p39.* Letter from Barker
38. HMC 11th Report App IV *Marquis of Townshend* p21, and Mason p251
39. *HofC* gives earlier ie 1620-1648, 1656- death. GL Owens, *Norfolk 1620-1641,* unpublished thesis 1970, gives an earlier start year, 1619–death.
40. The records of the court of Norfolk Quarter Sessions have only some bundles surviving from 1629 to the 1640s; the order books survive only after 1650 and the clerk rarely wrote in the names of the justices present at the sessions. Later John did appear at the Norwich Castle session on 14th April 1640 with Miles Hobart, John Holland and others but not at the other locations where lists survive. John Spelman was a regular at the Lynn sessions. NRO, C/S1/6
41. NRO, WHT 7/2
42. J Pound, *Tudor and Stuart Norwich,* 1988
43. Tanner 69. 105; and cf Sir John Doddridge, Folg L.d 132,1617
44. NRO, QS bundle 27
45. NRO, Ms 12195b
46. Tanner 243.18. Sir Charles Cornwallis, as a friend of the Earl of Northampton, was predominant in the Norfolk lieutenancy in the 1620's. He had also been a close friend of Sir John Hobart.
47. Tanner 243.28, 33, 37, 43. Unfortunately very faint and illegible in parts.
48. Rye, W *State papers Chas 1 re musters etc,* Norfolk & Norwich Arch Society, 1907
49. Rye W as above
50. Tanner 69.196; the cousinship Thomas Derham (later Sir Thomas d 1645) claimed was through his sister Anne who married Roger Pratt (his second wife). Pratt's brother Francis married Temperance Moundeford daughter of Bridget Spelman of Narborough. Pratt's sisters married two Gawsell brothers. Susan's son was Gregory Gawsell of Watlington. Susan's daughter Anne Gawsell married Thomas Boteler a Hereford cousin of John Potts. Edmund Moundeford was Temperance Pratt's nephew.
51. Mason p263. He described him as Sir John which he was not at this time.
52. NRO, MC152/9-11
53. Rye as above
54. NRO, COL/13/22
55. Bell v Bell 1630, NRO, Ms 12195b
56. Ch. 218 in *Calendar of Charter and rolls preserved in the Bodleian Library,* p191
57. *CSPD* vol 183 p492
58. TNA, E44/340 1637
59. Sir Robert and Mary had their first child at Swannington nine months later and their son Robert in 1584.
60. Blom vol 2; M Sayer, Norfolk Genealogy Vol 4
61. NRO, NAS 1/1/12/Hickling/10-17
62. For an excellent Jermy family history see website *The Jermys of Gunton (1)*
63. Sir Henry Sidney's widow was Jane Jermy, daughter of Francis Jermy of Suffolk. Her husband had died in 1612 and was buried in Walsingham. Letheringsett manor was

conveyed to John Jermy of Gunton from Sir Henry Sidney before 1612. John Jermy esq presented Thomas Lougher to Letheringsett in 1629. The Letheringsett living stayed in the family. Lougher married Frances Potts; Sir John Palgrave's son, Nathaniel, married the daughter of Edward Worsley the rector in 1662, and was himself rector in 1674 presented by Robert Jermy.

64. *ODNB* and Hassell Smith

65. Duleep Singh for some reason suggests 22 as his age despite the inscription.

66. NRO, DUN (C) 64, 65, 66. Dr Jones of Kings College

67. William Paston's aunt was first wife of Sir Thomas Holland who had been so grateful to John Potts in 1619.

68. TNA, Italian typewritten calendar of *State Papers Foreign Sicily and Naples*; Evelyn, ed Maynard Smith, *John Evelyn in Naples 1645*, 1914. There are a number of other Francis Potts. A London Court of Hustings entry for Francis Potts is much later, probably 1669. London Metropolitan Archives, CLA/023/PL/02/027, and many other references on A2A make it likely that this Francis was from the Cheshire family.

69. Tanner 64.145

70. *ODNB*

71. HCJ vol 2

72. Sir Robert Cotton's library held a copy of a seditious tract by Sir Robert Dudley. Sir Robert and other owners of the tract were brought before the Star Chamber. He was briefly imprisoned, but his library was permanently denied him from that point on. Sir Simonds wrote: 'When I went several times to visit and comfort him in the year 1630 he would tell me they had broken his heart that had locked up his library from him'. T Mortimer, *The British Plutarch*, 1791 Before he died in 1631 Sir Robert requested Sir Henry Spelman to tell the Lord Privy Seal and Council that their lengthy detaining of his books from him without any reason had been the cause of his mortal malady.

73. Were these Cottons linked to Sir John Cotton of Landwade, with his links to Sir John Potts? Sir Robert Cotton (1571-1631) was the son of Thomas Cotton of Denton Hall in Connington Huntingdonshire and was succeeded as second Baronet by his son Thomas (1594-1662), whose only son was young John (1621-1702). Their family was not directly related to the Cottons of Landwade, at least for many generations, although both families frequently served locally as sheriffs during the sixteenth century and would have known each other well. J Burke, *Extinct and Dormant Baronetcies*, 1841. However, they did not bear the same or similar arms. T Robson, *The British Herald*, 1830. Nonetheless, it is interesting to note that they were descended from an earlier Thomas who had married Joan the daughter of John Paris esq of Linton. It seems highly likely that they were distant kin of the Potts through this connection, whether or not they all knew it.

74. British History Online, *State Papers of John Thurloe* vol 5, 1656-57

75. The Fontanelle cemetery was opened in 1656 for plague victims. Before that the dead were buried in a variety of tufo caves and church ossaries. Inf: Biblioteca Nazionale di Napoli.

76. Burke's *Extinct Baronetcies* confused Francis and his uncle Charles, making Francis the father of Anne. This may have been the source for the tentative symbol on the published version of the pedigree.

77. NRO, WAL 1148, 286x4

78. NRO, Rye Ms 54 Vol 1

79. Charles Potts was listed as a tenant in 1635 and 1638.

80. TNA, PCC will 1645, PROB 11/195; *Visitation of Norfolk, 1664*

81. The William Nabbes of Bampton in Oxfordshire who left a will in 1691 - TNA, PCC will 1691, PROB 11/403 - is thought to have been a relative and as a mercer may give a clue to the family's wealth. Another mercer Simon Nabb (not Mabb as catalogued) left a will in 1660 which cannot be directly linked to our Nabbs but did mention a Sussex cousin named Edward - TNA, PCC will 1660, PROB 11/298. A John Nabbs was living in Dalling in 1622. NRO, WHT 7/2.

82. John Nabbs was later to take on the old Hastings manor in Hindringham where he died in 1666. TNA, PCC will 1666, PROB 11/320. John had a younger brother Edward.

83. J Warren was taught by him before 1627. Venn, *Caius*

84. This single surviving entry from the lost register appears in *Heirugia Anglicana*, ed The Ecclesiological Late Cambridge Camden Society in 1848 quoting from the weekly paper the *English Churchman*, No 148 Oct 30 1845.

85. Parish register; *ODNB* wrongly gives the name as Christopher.

86. Venn, *Caius*; NRO, NAS 1/1/14 (i)

87. In 1633 Mannington's next incumbent Edmund Deye was presented by Thomas Hacon at Potts's grant. He resigned and was replaced in 1634 by John Money, later an independent at Wymondham.

88. *ODNB*

89. KO Kupperman *Providence islands 1630-1641*, CUP,1993, p259

90. HCJ vol 2

91. NRO, Guestwick register 28th Mar 1641/2

92. BL, Add 15903 f.59; Robert Ashton, *Counter Revolution 1646-48*, c1994 reference not confirmed

93. On 16th May 1654 he was instituted (patron Sir Henry Mildmay) to Wanstead church in Essex. *Essex Arch Soc* 1900 p284 Lambeth ms. There is some confusion between which Christopher Amyraut held other livings, some say Paul's father, others including *ODNB* say his son. Venn gave Christopher 'Amirald' of Norfolk admitted to Jesus April 1649. He attained BA in 1653 as Amiraut. Christopher had Hindringham in 1653. If this was Paul's son, another of that name must have been born after the Wolterton 1633 burial of Christopher. Kupperman says Christopher is ancient when ejected from Mundesley but Calamy says this is Paul; a Christopher Amyrault was ejected from New Buckenham in 1662 , was then at Baconsthorpe and died at Southrepps. Three of his children, including Rebekah 1691, were buried at Sidestrand. Hood, and NA

94. K-C, *Civil War*, p72, 81 and see Wren impeachment papers 1641; Case was described as 'cur' in 1631 in Itteringham.

95. There is no record of Anne having any children. Case remarried in 1637 to widow Ann Booth and her son the Irish judge Robert Booth married Mary Potts of the unrelated Chalgrave family.

96. Tanner 71.98

97. Jan 1634, Feb 1637 *Notes & Queries*, Feb 1633 *Knyvett Letters* as before. Lent assizes moved from Thetford in 1833.

98. BL, Eg 2713 f. 86

99. BL, Eg 2713 f. 87

100. Fully printed in *Knyvett Letters* p 84

Notes to Chapter 11

1. Most of the letters are from the Tanner collection, held on microfilm in the Millennium Library Norwich; some originals have been checked at the Bodleian Library for clarity and extra information.
2. Tanner 67.176, Printed in K-C, *Civil War*, p 109
3. Tanner 67.178 printed in K-C p110
4. Tanner 67.189 printed in K-C p111
5. Clive Holmes, *The Eastern Association in the Civil War*, 1974
6. HMC Report on *Gawdy family Mss*,1885, p176
7. Probably Ursula's uncle, *Bacon papers IV* p212 footnote
8. *Journal of Sir Simonds D'Ewes for the Long Parliament* vol 1, Yale, 1923
9. CV Wedgwood, *The Kings Peace*, 1964
10. All quotes from House of Commons Journal, courtesy of British History Online
11. Holmes, as above, misses this date and therefore suggests Norfolk was slow to petition.
12. D'Ewes, as above, marginal note 'Noe great moment'; Franklin was later hounded by Cromwell's men and died while escaping. K-C
13. BL, Harl. 6395; WJ Thom, *Anecdotes and Traditions,* Camden Old series vol 5, 1839 p 79 No 134
14. J Adamson, *The Noble Revolt: the overthrow of Charles I*, 2007
15. This is Tanner 66.65, as quoted KC p122; wrongly cited as 66.15 by Adamson as above.
16. *HofC*, 1660-1690
17. K-C, *Civil War*
18. Wedgwood as above
19. Thomas Knyvett was unusual in managing to avoid this expense; *Knyvett Letters* as before
20. Tanner 64.185
21. HCJ for 26th March 1642 gives 'forty thousand' not 4000 meeting on Blackheath.
22. Tanner 114.101
23. *Knyvett letters* p104-5
24. Tanner 63.32 not printed in K-C; poor condition. Possibly Augustine Holl of Norwich.
25. The reference suggests a full house at Mannington: Ursula, his wife, perhaps his brother Charles and a half-sister, who might be Martha (Heydon) Crowe. It could also be Judith Godsalve, the sister of his first wife who lived at Mannington at some time. Alternatively it could be a greeting for his Willoughby in-laws. His own sisters were all dead.
26. Tanner 63.43
27. Gregory Gawsell of Watlington (later High Sheriff in 1649) was related to both families and to Derham.
28. Tanner 63.51
29. Tanner 63.98
30. Simonds D'Ewes diary, BL, Harl. 163 f.293v
31. BL, Harl. 164 f 257v
32. Tanner 63.119
33. Holmes says Holland's diplomatic illnesses were proverbial in the House.
34. Tanner 63.121. Part printed in K-C. The use of country versus county has been mentioned by others. K-C deliberately changed country to county. *Civil War* p368. It could be of note given the determination of Potts and Holland to keep Norfolk's peace as

their first priority. However, the original of this letter shows that Holland used country not county as K-C printed. The meaning of country, of course, at this time would still suggest to the reader the local region, rather than the nation.

35. Tanner 63.116

36. Tanner 63.125; it is not clear to whom he referred as his cousin, perhaps, very loosely, Martha Heydon. His aunt Agnes Crane married John's guardian's grandfather. Sir Robert was married first to Dorothy Hobart then to Susan Alington.

37. Elizabeth was born 29th June 1628 Suffolk Record Office, 21327/2

38. Anne Wynn and Lettice Willoughby were the daughters of Sir Francis Darcy of Isleworth.

39. BL, Harl. 384 f.251

40. *CSPD*

41. BL, Harl. 383 f.206

42. Tanner 63.126 part printed in K-C

43. Tanner 63.117 part printed; K-C p146

44. Tanner 63.117

45. HLJ, vol 5

46. BL Harl. 386 f.233

47. John Walter, *Understanding Popular Violence in the English Revolution: The Colchester Plunderers*, CUP, 1999

48. HCJ, 17 August 1642

49. Tanner 63.130

50. HLJ, vol 5 26 July, 1 August

51. *ODNB*

52. Tanner 62. 132

53. Tanner 63.134 printed without alterations in K-C p148

54. Blackwood; K-C

55. BL, Harl. 386 f.234

56. BL, Harl. 384 f.246

57. Wynn later returned to the House and joined Potts on a committee in June 1648. He was secluded in the Purge that year.

58. Robert Ashton, *Counter-Revolution 2nd Civil War 1646-8*, c1994

Notes to Chapter 12

1. Full details of these first meetings are given in K-C, *Civil War*, pp149-150

2. Tanner 64.7-10; the section relating to Sir William Denny is printed in full K-C p177-8 but referenced as 64.33

3. Tanner 64.25 printed K-C p155

4. Tanner 64.30

5. Tanner 64.30, 32,122

6. Tanner 64.88 printed in K-C

7. Tanner 64.70 printed K-C p155; HCJ vol 2

8. K-C; Heyward, an early friend of John Selden, died at Reepham in 1658.

9. Tanner 69.194

10. Tanner 64.96 reverse

11. Tanner 64.84

12. Tanner 64.88
13. K-C, *Forty Norfolk Essays*
14. Tanner 64.91
15. It is just possible, given that Manchester did not call him Sir John, that the wrong John Spelman - ie Potts's stepson - had been disarmed but given that Sir John Potts was so involved in the original order that can hardly be true.
16. Tanner 64.93
17. Gawsell was related to the Spelmans through the Pratt and Moundeford families; Gregory's sister Anne had married Thomas Boteler of Watton-at-Stone, a Potts cousin.
18. Tanner 64.94 The recipient is unknown and was probably leasing a house. Hindringham was a Dean and Chapter manor, held by the Hastings and Hunt families. No new names appear in the court roll for 1642-1645, NRO, CHC 135482.
19. BL, Harl. 384 f.182
20. Tanner 64.97
21. Tanner 64.95,96
22. Tanner 64.102, 103, 104
23. Tanner 64.101
24. Mason, as quoted in K-C p166
25. HCJ vol 2
26. Tanner 64.106
27. HCJ vol 2; HLJ vol 5. John Potts was confirmed as DL for City of Norwich 3rd January 1643.
28. NRO, Assent book DN/Sub/1/1
29. Denzil Holles was certainly fiery but his portrait does not fit the description; similarly Oliver St John's portrait is not helpful despite his having 'a dark and clouded countenance' (Clarendon) and a fifteenth century ancestor described as a stout black man (*Burke's Baronetage*); William Strode was certainly called by D'Ewes a 'fiery spirit' and was one of 5 members impeached in 1642 but he seems an unlikely correspondent for Potts.
30. Tanner 64.111
31. Tanner 64.114, 115
32. Tanner 60. 376, wrongly indexed in Tanner's Codex as 1646
33. TNA, Sir George Strode PCC will 1663, PROB 11/311
34. BL, Harl.164 f.294v
35. Holmes as before
36. NRO, AYL 198
37. Tanner 64.118 reverse
38. Tanner 64.116
39. Tanner 64.118
40. Tanner 64.123
41. Tanner 64.126
42. Tanner 64.122
43. Tanner 64.124
44. Tanner 64.64.122, 124, 125
45. NRO, AYL 198
46. K-C p154
47. Tanner 64.145

48. the date stone gives 1642; Vaughan-Lewis work in progress on Houghton family.

49. K-C, *Forty Essays* p 19-21; Tanner 64.145-6

50. NRO, AYL 198

51. This happened in N Erpingham. NRO, AYL; Holmes as before.

52. BL, Harl. 384 f.183

53. BL, Harl. 386 f. 236

54. Tanner 62.352 showed a smaller sum, possibly £18, from Berney received by Cromwell on 19th March.

55. Mostly printed in K-C; also in full in Carlyle, *Letters and Speeches of Oliver Cromwell*, vol II

56. Carlyle gives the original as saying Mr F Cory but others have Thomas. Francis Cory the Recorder who had assisted the mayor, was replaced in 1644. There was an earlier Thomas who was Mayor and another who later was an alderman.

57. K-C says Kemp and Sir William Doyley were in Holland.

58. *Knyvett Letters* p110

59. Mullinger, *St John's College, Cambridge* pp 126-7

60. HCJ vol 3

61. The Covenant read in full: I A. B. in Humility and Reverence of the Divine Majesty, declare my hearty Sorrow for my own Sins, and the Sins of this Nation, which have deserv'd the Calamities and Judgments that now lie upon it; and my true Intention is, by God's Grace, to endeavour the Amendment of my own Ways: And I do further, in the Presence of Almighty God, declare, vow, and covenant, that, in order to the Security and Preservation of the true Reformed Protestant Religion, and Liberty of the Subject, I will not consent to the laying down of Arms, so long as the Papists, now in open War against the Parliament, shall, by Force of Arms, be protected from the Justice thereof; and that I do abhor and detest the said wicked and treacherous Design lately discovered; and that I never gave, or will give, my Assent to the Execution thereof; but will, according to my Power and Vocation, oppose and resist the same, and all other of the like Nature: And, in case any other like Design shall hereafter come to my Knowledge, I will make such timely Discovery, as I shall conceive may best conduce to the preventing thereof: And whereas I do, in my Conscience, believe, that the Forces raised by the Two Houses of Parliament are raised and continued for their just Defence, and for the Defence of the true Protestant Religion, and Liberty of the Subject, against the Forces raised by the King; that I will, according to my Power and Vocation, assist the Forces raised and continued by both Houses of Parliament, against the Forces raised by the King without their Consent; and will likewise assist all other Persons that shall take this Oath, in what they shall do in pursuance thereof; and will not, directly or indirectly, adhere unto, nor shall willingly assist, the Forces raised by the King without the Consent of both Houses of Parliament: And this Vow and Covenant I make in the Presence of Almighty God, the Searcher of all Hearts, with a true Intention to perform the same, as I shall answer at the Great Day, when the Secrets of all Hearts shall be disclosed. HCJ Vol 3

62. Mason

63. K-C

64. *Knyvett Letters*; Holmes as before

65. Mason

66. *Knyvett Letters* p129

67. NRO, BOI 42/23. Robert de Grey and his mother were party to the marriage settlement of Palgrave and his second wife Anne Gascoigne, née de Grey, in 1634. Robert died in early 1645. NRO, NCC will 1645, Burlye 21

68. Holmes as before

69. K-C has some errors regarding the different Miles Hobarts; see website article '*Miles and Miles of Hobarts*'.

70. Antonia Fraser, *Cromwell*, 2004 p 130

71. K-C, *Three Generations*

72. K-C p198

73. Edward Astley married Elizabeth the Dutch-born daughter of Sir Jacob Astley; he was knighted Dec 1641 and died in 1654 while High Sheriff; for his letters see K-C *Three Generations*

74. For some idea of the cost of the troops £5,049 9s 4d was paid in December to 'Col Sir Jo Palgrave, his Lt Col Sir Edw Astely and to Serjeant Major Calthorp and two other Capts of his regiment': £5,990 16s 8d was paid to 'Col Sir Miles Hobart & Captaynes & others of his regiment'. Accompts of part of Disbursements of County of Norfolk Paid to army, 12ᵗʰ December 1643, Tanner 62.445

75. BL, Eg 2643 f.19

76. NRO, AYL 198

77. NRO, AYL 198, £1,000 = 2 months' weekly assessment

78. Mason

79. See NRO, MC 557/2 for supportive letter from Association colonels to Manchester in 1643.

80. Tanner 62.273

81. HCJ vol 3: 1643

82. BL, Harl. 165 ff.190-1; Holmes p191

83. HCJ vol 3

84. *Calendar of the Committee for Compounding*, HMSO

85. *Calendar of the Committee for Advance of Money*, HMSO

86. *Baconsthorpe Castle*, as before, p4

87. BL, Add Ms 28191D; Batten as before

88. Batten; *Baconsthorpe Castle*; TNA C10/88/24

89. Tanner 62.431

90. Tanner 62.489

91. Tanner 62 423-424

92. Tanner 62.471

93. Tanner 62.543; others give this as 5ᵗʰ February but the date is in the fold of the paper

94. *Knyvett Letters* introduction

Notes to Chapter 13

1. K-C, *Norfolk Portraits*, p25

2. Tanner 61.14

3. Tanner 62.426

4. K-C, *Civil War*

5. Cpt John Jubbes in Sir Miles Hobart's regiment who may have become Lt Col Jn Jubbes of the Purge at Army Council November 1647. See K-C, *A Note on Thomas Windham* in NA vol 32 pp50-52

6. Quoted in C Wedgwood, *The Trial of Charles I*, 1964
7. K-C, *Norfolk Gallery* p31; Bishop Joseph Hall *Account of His Sufferings* p lxiii
8. Christobel M Hood, *Sequestered Loyalists and Bartholomew Sufferers*, 1922
9. *Knyvett Letters* as before
10. Beadle got his just deserts in December 1644; he fell out with Corbett over delays in presenting his accounts; he was arrested and lost his position. *Knyvett Letters*
11. Tanner 69.208
12. HCJ vol 3
13. HCJ vol 3: 31 October 1644
14. Exchequer documents show Cory paid over £1,500 in assessments between April and October 1643, the largest payments recorded. Between November and March 1644 the Norfolk loan had reached £8,920 and he received £111 10s interest! This suggests he had raised all the necessary money. TNA, SP28/350/4. He was to pay in over £9,000 between June 1648 and 1649. SP 28/350/2.
15. HCJ vol 3
16. The Bedingfields were a major catholic family and Sir Henry had been abroad in Flanders for some time, having been named by the House in early 1643.
17. Alison Plowden, *In a Free Republic*, 2006
18. HCJ vol 4
19. John Selden, K-C *Civil War* p219. Selden was a lawyer and a member of the Westminster Assembly.
20. HLJ vol 7 19 March 1645
21. Suffolk Record Office, HD 36/A/2138
22. NRO, MC129/1
23. HCJ vol 4: 1 July 1645
24. HCJ vol 4: 9 July 1645
25. Tanner 60.178
25. Tanner 60.178
26. John Adamson, *The employments of Robert Scawen* in *Soldiers, Writers and Statesmen of the English Revolution* by Woolrich, Gentles etc, 1998, CUP
27. Tanner 60.214
28. Tanner 57.269
29. BL, Harl. 384 f.259
30. Tanner 57.284
31. Tanner 57.348
32. Jurkowski, Smith and Crook, *Lay Taxes in England and Wales*, PRO, 1998
33. BL, Harl. 384 f.261
34. Valentine's name is usually given as Walton but he writes Wauton.
35. NRO, MC129/2
36. HCJ vol 4: 14th and 16th March 1646
37. Tanner 59.453, printed in Henry Cary, *Memorials of the Great Civil War 1646-52*, vols 1-2, 1842
38. HCJ vol 4: 17 September 1646
39. NRO, MC129/3. For catalogue entry 'Tandy' read Gawdy; the Bacons are brothers but were sons of Edward Bacon.
40. NRO, PD 439/1 parish register flyleaf
41. Tanner 58A. 8
42. House of Lords Record Office: HL/PO/JO/10/1/230

43. Mason, p307, gives wrongly as J Petts
44. William was presumably related to Thomas Newman whose family were gents of Hunworth and area. Thomas Newman of Baconsthorpe was later executor to John Potts's will.
45. HCJ vol 5: 28 May 1647
46. Tanner 58A.116; printed in Cary vol 1, as above
47. Tanner 58A.127
48. Tanner 58A 129
49. Tanner 58.335
50. *The Vindication of the Character and Conduct of Sir William Waller knt by himself*, printed Debrett 1793
51. BL, Harl. 283 f. 216
52. NRO, AYL 190/4
53. Tanner 58.606. Jacob used kinsman and cousin in letters to Potts but the relationship is not clear. There was a distant link through Sir Drue Drury.
54. Tanner 58.606
55. Tanner 57(1).21
56. The estimated numbers vary: a note in the Corporation papers suggests 500-600 rose but dates it to 1647. NA, 1846
57. HCJ volume 5
58. Robert Ashton, *Counter- Revolution 2ⁿᵈ Civil War 1646-48*, 1994
59. *ODNB*
60. Tanner 57.273
61. *A Descriptive Catalogue of the Etched Work of Wenceslaus Hollar*, 1982. p235
62. The following extracts are from Tanner 57. 293, 294, 300, 310, 382; *CSPD* 1648; and the HMC *Report of the Portland Welbeck Mss.*
63. Tanner 57.294 Signed by Pierrepont, Thomas Wenman, J Potts, Browne, Grimston, Bulkely, Crewe &1 other
64. Tanner 57.300 Signed by J Potts etc with Denzil Holles who did not sign the first report.
65. Tanner 57.313
66. Tanner 57.315
67. Tanner 57.293
68. *ODNB*
69. *ODNB*
70. Tanner 57.345
71. Tanner 57.359. The Cressett family of Shropshire, Edward and sons Edward and Richard, were royalists; this may be Edward Cressett, a commissioner for removing obstructions to church land sales, c1647-49. Edward Cressett was MP in Middx 1657. Thanks to Dr Stephen Roberts for this suggestion.
72. Tanner 57. 369. There were two Sir John Evelyn MPs, uncle and nephew, at this time and Potts had worked with both the Surrey and the Wiltshire man; from the language about the Scots this was probably the younger Evelyn.
73. Tanner 57.371. The signature is difficult and in Cary p37, this is printed in error as a letter from Mr J Francis. Tanner's Codex notes that the signature of this letter and that of 57.382 are similar which is true. However the latter is the son on the Isle of Wight. He could not have been in both places. Sir Thomas Pelham married as his third wife, Margaret Vane daughter of Sir Henry Vane senior. This is probably their son Nicholas Pelham, whose birth is given as c1650 in *HofC* vol 1690-1715.

74. Tanner 57.385 Doddridge was MP for Basingstoke; see HCJ 24 October 1648
75. HCJ as above
76. Tanner 57.395
77. *CSPD* 6th Nov 1648

Notes to Chapter 14

1. HCJ: 14 March 1649. No-one could travel without government permission.
2. Potts is not on the 1646 list of DLs or JPs. Tanner 96.133
3. *HofC*
4. NRO, CS1/17
5. *Norfolk Quarter Sessions Order Book 1650-1656*, vol 26, NRS,1955
6. *HofC*; he is on a list of Justices for the year 1657 TNA, C193/13/6 but does not appear in the volume placing names on the commissions between 1651 and 1658 TNA, C231/6.
7. NRO, MC 482/2
8. NRO, MC2409/62/5; MC482/1; K-C, *40 Essays*
9. NRO, AYL documents give 1649 but K-C *40 Essays* says 1650 which is supported by the Holt burial register entry for Mr. William Hobart son of James, on January 4 1650/1.
10. Mason
11. NA 1846, *Extracts from Corporation Mss* as before
12. NRO, MC 482/1-4; Hood 1922 as before
13. Thanks to Ellie Betts for first drawing our attention to this case.
14. K-C, *Forty Norfolk Essays*
15. NRO, NAS 1/1/14/Edgefield/(i)-(n). This must be Sir John, not his son. The reference to 'my sons boy' must be to a servant of John Potts esq; Roger would have been only 10 or 11.
16. Letter 1608, BL, Add 41140
17. TNA, C5/39/17 refers to 'my house at Enfield'.
18. The manor house went between 1665 and 1670 to the then master of Enfield School, Robert Uvedale who set up a boarding academy there. Birkett Marshal, *History of Enfield School,* 1958. Thomas's mother Prudence was daughter of Henry Boteler esq but this seems to be a different line of Botelers from that of John's grandmother.
19. Venn, *Caius*
20. TNA, C9/31/43
21. Tomes, *Mannington Hall ,* as before, p17
22. See footnote 84 for Chapter 10 for last suggested date that registers were seen.
23. TNA, PCC will 1649, PROB 11/208
24. TNA, C 10/12/66
25. London Metropolitan Archives, DRO/004/AO1/001-5
26. David Pam, *The Story of Enfield Chase*, The Enfield Preservation Society, 1984; TNA, DL 44/1216
27. HLJ, volume 11 : 4th June 1660
28. TNA, DL 4/111/28, 44/1216, 43/7/8, 9/12, 5/37, 41/190, 41/622, 28/78/17
29. TNA, C 6/139/209 and C 22/690/39
30. From Google Books: Samuel Wells, *The History of the Drainage of the Great Level of the Fens Called the Bedford Level*, vol 1 publ 1830

31. Minutes recited in Wells as above
32. TNA C 33/210, 212
33. TNA, C 6/139/209
34. TNA, C 33/232
35. TNA, C 22/336/26
36. TNA, C 33/233
37. Derbyshire Record Office, D5054/9/2/2
38. On the reverse was noted that on 16th October 1682 this deed had been used in interrogatories and depositions in an action between Maria 'Alston' (one of Sir Henry's grand-daughters and heirs) and Nicholas Sanderson. These are TNA Aston v Sanderson C22/583/44 and Sanderson v Aston C22/704/9.
39. DRO, D5054/9/2/5
40. DRO, D5054/9/2/4
41. On the reverse also is noted that the deed was shown to William Graver (one of the witnesses) on 9th April 1684 as part of Maria Aston's defence against Sanderson. Graver and Thomas Gawen also had been shown it on 30th April 1660. If correct this date shows that this had been a very long drawn out action. This seems likely to be the case - there are three Aston v Spelman chancery items from 1663-65 at the TNA, C 6/167/1; C 6/169/7; C 6/75/11
42. DRO, D5054/9/2/7
43. DRO, D5054/9/2/10
44. The deed would be of great interest to west Norfolk historians as it contains a schedule of the tenants and their rents and terms of years still to come. DRO, D5054/9/2/6
45. DRO, D5054/9/2/6
46. TNA, C 22/704/9 and C 22/583/44

Notes to Chapter 15

1. *Visitation of London, 1633-35*; *Visitation of London 1687*, as before; *The Visitations of Cheshire 1613 and 1663* as before; WH Rylands, *Some Cheshire Heraldic Documents from the Ashmolean*, Transactions of the Historical Society of Lancashire and Cheshire Volume 62, 1911

2. Edmund Pott was in St Lawrence Jewry in 1638 - tithe documents at Lambeth Palace. The only other 'Mr Potts' in this London-wide survey, of St Andrew in the Wardrobe, paid a very modest rent and does not appear to be one of the relevant family. Assuming this, no member of any relevant Potts families was shown as a London resident that year - British History Online *The Inhabitants of London in 1638*, TC Dale, 1931. Edmund was involved in a 1646 deed in Lancashire as a trade creditor of John Crombeck who was conveying a lease. Lancashire Record Office, DDG 18/25; Cheshire Archives, P 38/1 refers to a Pott Shrigley baptism of Edmund Pott in about 1640. A lease of 1653 of various of Lord Brereton's manors and lands in Chester to Edmund Pott showing Edmund's children as Edmund, Sarah and Joseph TNA, E 214/734. Evidently there was a MI for Edmund Pott in Islington's old church, British History Online, D Lysons, *The Environs of London*, vol 3, 1795. He was recorded as having died in 1650 as Edmund Pott gent, with a first wife Sarah Thompson daughter of Anthony Thompson of Cambridge and a second wife Jane daughter of Joseph Lane gent. The marriage to Sarah was at St Sepulchre Cambridge

on 3rd May 1631. Their children (Edmund and Sarah) were baptised in St Lawrence Jewry. Edmund's will as a citizen and haberdasher of London was made and proved in 1650. TNA, PCC will 1650, PROB 11/212. His wife Jane was the primary beneficiary of his property in St Lawrence Jewry and elsewhere. His son Joseph, by Jane, received other property and children Edmund and Sarah £100 pa for life and a £1,000 dowry for Sara. He also left legacies to his sister Brereton and the children of his brother Roger Pott. A reference to a debt due from Ralph Smith of Leek also connects him to the Smith family of Newcastle-under-Lyme. See Family Notes 13 Torbock. The younger Edmund moved to Bury St Edmunds where he had a family with his heir William becoming a London fishmonger; his brother Joseph became a mercer and died overseas about 1680 without having children.

3. TNA, C 6/101/74 and C 6/148/85
4. Also covered by the mortgage were Howell lands in Sussex (the college or chapel of Bosham and various lands with it) which he had from the Dean and Chapter of Chichester. The lease on the Bosham chapel property had itself already been the subject of action between the Howells and the Dean and Chapter, resulting in a long lease renewal to Howell. *Sussex Archaeological Collections...*, Sussex Archaeological Society, 1856 Google Books. This account made no mention of the mortgage.
5. The action was still rumbling on in 1668 between the Milways and Dame Sarah Howell and others, TNA, C 6/186/76
6. Folger Library, Ld 479
7. NRO, KIM 3/9/3
8. TNA C 231/6 f234; Essex Archives Online, ASS 35/94/1
9. Drake married first Elizabeth daughter of Sir Alexander Denton and second Dorothy daughter of Sir William Spring of Pakenham Hall, Suffolk. The place of his marriage to Susan Potts has not yet been located.
10. The Drake family lived at Burwood, Surrey, and held Bishop's manor in Esher, together with the manor of Walton Rectory. SHC, 442/-. Richard Drake of Esher, married to Ursula Stafford, died in 1603 leaving as son and heir Francis. Francis married Joan Tothill (sometimes Tottel) one of the two daughters of William Tothill, a lawyer and steward to Francis Bacon. Tothill acquired Shardeloes manor near Amersham, Bucks, in 1595 and after his death in 1626 this manor passed to Sir William Drake the eldest son of Francis and Joan. Joan herself had died in 1625 and her sister Catherine Tothill renounced her half of the manor to Sir William in 1632.
11. Sir William left his Amersham properties to his nephew, also Sir William Drake, the son and heir of Francis Drake. PCC will 1669 Prob 11/330. The nephew also became MP for Amersham and died in 1690 leaving a son and heir by his wife Elizabeth daughter of Sir William Montague.
12. Sir William Drake of Sharveloes Bucks, TNA, PCC will 1669, PROB11/330
13. TNA, C 22/1011/1
14. TNA, C 217/ 71/1
15. TNA, C 5/35/58
16. TNA, C 22/1011/1
17. TNA, C 9/31/43
18. Vaughan-Lewis: work in progress on Itteringham and Mannington manors and lands.
19. TNA, C 5/41/26 and C 5/39/17
20. Nathan Wright had bought the manor of Cranham from the Petre family for £6,100 in 1647. British History Online

21. TNA, C 6/177/26
22. TNA, PCC will 1653, PROB 11/231
23. Essex Record Office, D/DHt/T210/1 In December 1630 Giles Fleming acquired a 60-year lease of the manor of Southall in Rainham through Nathan Wright and others as trustees. In May 1632 the premises were settled in his will on his younger son Edmund to ensure that when 21 he would receive a portion of £800. Even after that milestone in September 1642, Edmund only received £360 and in March 1650 he, through the trustees, conveyed part of the premises in a £200 mortgage to Nathan Wright with Charles Potts as Nathan's trustee. The mortgage was still unpaid in early 1655 when it fell to Sir John Potts to sort out. Wright and Edmund Fleming each received rather less than they had committed when the lease, now with a reduced term of years, was sold on to Anthony Taylor. Sir John had no financial stake. The deed, however, shows the considerable work that must have been involved in resolving a lawyer's estate, including his trustee commitments.
24. After the death of his wife Anne, their son Benjamin, who became a baronet in 1660, would inherit the London house and the Essex properties Ockendon manor and Cranham Hall and manor. He left his personal estate in thirds. One went to his wife. One went to Benjamin and Frances and Jane his unmarried daughters. The final third he divided into various legacies. Susan, Mary and Alice were to have £2,000 each. Wright made other bequests to the Skinners' Company, his married sisters and his brother Ezeckiell and his sons. Ezeckiell was made an overseer alongside Edward Herris of Lincoln's Inn, one of Nathan's cousins, with William Herris also of Lincoln's Inn asked to help them and the executors who were to be Nathan's three sons-in-law and Benjamin once he came of age. TNA, PCC will 1658, PROB 11/274
25. Francis Drake had four sons Richard, Nathan, John and William alive in 1667 - in Sir William Drake's PCC will 1669. Nathan and John were probably both by Susan; William was the eldest and inherited his uncle's estate and seat in parliament.
26. The usual stated mileage between Norfolk and London, used in other actions.
27. TNA C 33/230
28. TNA, C 6/178/29 and C 6/177/27
29. TNA, C 6/178/29
30. TNA, C 6/177/27
31. NRO, WHT 1/254/2/2
32. TNA, C 33/230
33. *Marriage Licences at the Faculty Office of the Archbishop of Canterbury at London, 1543-1869*, 1886
34. TNA C 33/230
35. TNA, C 6/182/86
36. TNA, C 10/153/71; TNA C 33/233
37. TNA, C 33/235
38. TNA, C 33/237
39. TNA, C 33/239
40. TNA, C 33/241
41. TNA, C 22/1011/1
42. TNA, C 10 163/51
43. TNA, C 10/175/75
44. TNA, C 10/180/47 and C 10/179/41 and others in C 10
45. TNA, C 6/50/68

46. TNA, C 5/540/43, C 5/571/33 and C 22/415/17
47. TNA, C 5/540/43
48. William Villiers was the grandson of Sir William Villiers and his wife Rebecca Roper, daughter of Robert Roper esq. of Heanor Derbyshire. They were distantly related to the Ropers of Kent. Rebecca remarried to Francis Cave of Ingarsby (a royalist d 646). Her daughter Elizabeth Cave married, about 1660, William Wollaston esq of Shenton Leics. REC Waters, *Genealogical Memoirs of the Extinct family of Chester of Chicheley*, 1878 ; Rebecca's uncle Thomas Roper's eldest son was Col. Samuel Roper (d1658), lawyer, antiquary, Calvinist and Treasurer to the Earl of Denbigh's army. The Thomas Roper mentioned in the action was probably Samuel's second son, born 1641. He was an antiquary like his father. His brother Samuel (1634-78) was of Lincoln's Inn. W Dugdale, *Visitation of Derbyshire 1662-64*. It may be possible to trace the London properties through Roper or Wollaston.
49. TNA, C 5/571/33
50. TNA, PCC will 1653, PROB 11/231
51. TNA, C 22/415/17
52. TNA, C 33/244, C 33/246 and C 33/248
53. TNA, C 33/248 f. 498
54. TNA, C 33/250 f. 94
55. TNA, C 33/250 ff. 278, 481, 544 and C 33/252 f.602
56. TNA, C 33/256 ff.58, 71, 352, 413
57. TNA, PCC will 1712, PROB 11/526
58. Sir William Villiers, sometime MP, died in February 1712 aged 67; his wife Anne Potts died 31 July 1711 and had been buried in Brooksby, the old family seat in Leicestershire. He had sold his manor of Brooksby to Anne's cousin Sir Nathan Wright the Lord Keeper of the Seal. Villiers had been King James II's Master of the Horse, a lucrative royal household appointment. He was the only son and heir of George Villiers (d1682) and had a sister Penelope whose daughters received most of his possessions. George had been the only son of Sir William Villiers (made Knight and Baronet in 1619 and died in 1629), who had been the eldest son and heir of Sir George and was the half brother of George Villiers the favourite of James I. With Sir William Villiers MP, the baronetcy became extinct. Sources: British History Online, various Google Books entries and nineteenth century volumes covering extinct baronetcies
59. The more famous Sir Nathan Wright, Lord Keeper of the Seal, was Nathan's nephew. Susan's father, Nathan, had been one of four brothers, sons of the Reverend Robert Wright of Dennington Suffolk, himself the second son of John Wright from near Hornchurch and a Gray's Inn lawyer. Nathan's brother Euseby married three times but died without issue. Sir Benjamin Wright of Dennington, also a London merchant, died in Spain having only had one daughter. Brother Ezekiel was rector of Thurcaston and lived until 1691. His eldest son was the celebrated lawyer Sir Nathan Wright and the younger son was another Izakiel or Ezekiel, who was asked to arrange the memorial to William and Anne Villiers. Sources: British History Online, various Google Books entries and nineteenth century volumes covering extinct baronetcies.
60. Thanks to M Britton, churchwarden of St Michael's and All Saints Church, Brooksby, Leicestershire

Notes to Chapter 16

1. Mason p326
2. HCJ vol 7: 22 February 1660
3. HCJ vol 7: 13 March 1660
4. *Rugg's Diurnal 1659-1661*, Royal Hist Soc Camden 3rd series vol 91,1961
5. BL, Add 4197
6. NRO, BL/T/2/1
7. Transactions of American Philosophical Society vol 55 Pt 2, 1965
8. Doyley 2501 votes, Hobart was next with 2152, Prof R Temple, *A 1654 Protectorate Parliamentary Election Return*, in Cromwelliana Series II No 3, 2006
9. Tanner 239.196b
10. NRO, Y/C19/7
11. Rather loose residency requirements were agreed in 1620, 'such as be freemen & inhabitants of the Town', NRO, Y/C 19/5 p228. Sir John was not resident; Doyley certainly had an estate in Yarmouth later.
12. K-C, *Forty Norfolk Essays*, p38
13. Brunton & Pennington, *Members of the Long Parliament*, 1954
14. *HofC*
15. *CPSD* Chas II 1660-61 June 25-30
16. HCJ
17. TNA C 231/6 f.462 apparently in place of Hatton Berners: it is not clear when or if Hatton Berners was Custos. He died in April 1667 at Wiggenhall St Mary.
18. NRO, AYL 193/4,5; AYL 306; HMC *Report on Lothian Mss* gives the entries differently, at £15/£6 and £8 64s
19. NRO, AYL 202
20. *HofC*
21. Tanner 134.202. Unfortunately the accounts of subscribers have not survived.
22. *Journal of Simonds D'Ewes diary* as before
23. TNA C 33/214
24. NRO, WAL 144/3, 290x3
25. NRO, WAL 1441/1 and 1441/2, 290x3. This eastern part of Wolterton was described as 'the scite of the manor of Wolterton als Woulterton'; the western part of the parish, was in the Mannington estate and called 'the manor of Wolterton'.
26. NRO, Rye Ms 52, Wolterton memorial inscriptions
27. The hall was later rebuilt in 1727
28. *Visitation* and NRO, NCC will 1661, 295
29. NRO, NCC will 1661, Tennant 299
30. NRO, NCC will 1673, 492 Alden
31. NRO, NCC will 1677, 271 Wiseman
32. Intwood Hall belonged to Miles Hobart of the Blickling family. Miles of Intwood died in 1671. He had married Frances Peyton (after she was widowed from an earlier Sir Philip Bedingfield). Frances died in 1631 but had the main Hobart line including John who died in 1683. In the early 1680s the Hamond family seem to be the main residents in the parish. (NRO, NRS 16391 gives, in 1681, witnesses for Intwood cum Keswick as Robert Hamond Roger Hamond Wm Howard Francis Eagle Henry Boyes). However Ursula's husband was also related to the Pickerells. Henry Pickerell of Intwood and Frances were buried in Ditchingham in 1679.

33. NRO, WAL 328, 272x6
34. NRO, WAL 327/1 -11, 272x5
35. Coppings Beck was the old name for the rivulet that flows from Oulton Spa to the Bure, for some of its course marking the Irmingland/Itteringham parish boundary.
36. TNA, CP/25/2/583. The Bedingfields may have provided the link to the Herveys; Francis Hervey was the brother or nephew of Stephen Hervey whose son Martin Hervey married Rebecca Strode. Their daughter Elizabeth married Sir Robert Bedingfield, brother of Sir Henry. She was buried at Ditchingham in 1688. Francis's father (or grandfather) was Francis Hervey sergeant at law who died in 1643.
37. NRO, WAL 1166/2, 287x1
38. NRO, WAL 622, 276x5
39. *The Notebook of Robert Doughty 1662-1665* , NRS vol 54, 1989 p55
40. TNA, C 9/31/43
41. NRO, NCC will 1673, 504 Alden
42. This inventory has not survived

Notes to Chapter 17

1. Or just possibly West Barsham where his father had lived with his first wife. No registers for either parish survive from this period.
2. British History Online, Taxation Act lists
3. He is described as of Westminster in a 1664-65 act granting a royal aid. *Statutes of the Realm, vol 5* In 1661 and 1672 royal aid lists however he does not appear – just Sir John and his son John. He could have been a soldier, become a merchant, then gone to Inner Temple, and then returned to the army.
4. TNA, CP/25/2/583/1659/60HIL
5. TNA, *CSPD* vol 19
6. Edward Peacock, *Army Lists of the Roundheads and Cavaliers*, 1863
7. TNA, *CSPD* vol 21; TNA, *Calendar of Proceedings of the Committee for the Advance of Money 29 July 1650:* Captain John Potts of Wolverhampton, a Popish recusant, was taken in Dudley castle.
8. HLJ vol 8: 2 June 1646; HLJ: vol 8: 1645-1647 pp. 343-351
9. An intriguing reference survives in the *CSPD – Commonwealth* vol 3 with a 20 August 1652 reference in the Council of State's daily proceedings to: 'the petition of Frances [sic] Pottes referred to the Irish and Scotch Committee'. This could be Captain Potts but the petition is not on the microfilm of SP18/24 nor in the draft order book SP25/31.
10. TNA, *CSP Ireland* 1647-60 and *Addenda* 1625-60
11. Trim Heritage Centre, map of the baronies of Meath
12. Trim Heritage Centre, booklets by Noel E French on *Athboy* and *Navan*
13. The date for Charles and Anne's marriage has been taken from evidence in a later dispute. TNA, C 10/114/61
14. Thomas Cornwallis (c 1605-76) of Lincoln was the youngest son of the noted diplomat Sir Charles Cornwallis (d 1629) of Brome Hall in Suffolk and Harborne in Staffordshire. Sir Charles was in turn the third son of Sir Thomas Cornwallis of Brome in Suffolk. Harleian Society, *Visitation of Lincolnshire,* vol 50; *Suffolk Visitation of 1561.* Sir Charles of Beeston was Ambassador to Spain from 1603 to 1609 and then Treasurer

of the Household of Henry Prince of Wales. He became DL of Norfolk at the age of 63. Thomas married Anne the daughter and heir of Samuel Bevercotes of Ordsall Nottinghamshire. Anne's mother was Maude the daughter of Sir Edward Leigh of Rushall (d 1617), and the sister of Henry Leigh. This line of the Cornwallis family then descended through Thomas and Anne's son Bevercotes Cornwallis, baptised in 1620 in St Margaret's Lincoln. His elder sister, apparently born in 1612, was Anne who married first Samuel Leigh, her cousin (her great uncle's son but of much the same age as her since Samuel came from Henry's second marriage).

15. Dame Ruth was one of the daughters of Griffith Hampden esq (d 1591), of Great Hampden Buckinghamshire, by Anne Cave. Some give her father as Sir Edward Hampden (d 1628 PCC will) but Griffith's will of 1592 TNA PROB 11/79 shows Ruth was his daughter. Ruth's eldest brother William married Sir Henry Cromwell's daughter Elizabeth, the aunt of Oliver Cromwell. Their eldest son and heir was John Hampden, Pym's great parliamentarian supporter with whom John Potts worked in the House. Through her sister Anne, married to Robert Waller, Ruth was distantly related to the Botelers of Watton-at-Stone, Potts's grandmother's family. Ruth married three times: in 1588 to Edward Oglethorpe esq (d after 1597); then to Sir Philip Scudamore; in 1616 she married Henry Leigh in Isleworth. She died aged 73 in 1649. REC Waters, *Genealogical Memoirs of the Extinct family of Chester of Chicheley*, 1878 and *Gents Mag* 1828.

16. Another son Richard had died between 1625 and 1632.

17. *ODNB*

18. Web hits but no first name

19. Published London 1661; Anthony Wood's *Athenae Oxon*, as before, vol 4 pp 478-9; Pishey Thompson, *The History and Antiquities of Boston*, 1856 and *ODNB*. Samuel junior is usually described as of Boston, Lincolnshire. His father Samuel senior is sometimes of Rushall - his father's seat - of Boston or of Lincoln. Thompson says Samuel junior was admitted to Oxford at 25 which is obviously in error.

20. The engravings are held by the National Portrait Gallery and give his age as 15 in 1661.

21. Manton, rector of St Paul Covent Garden, had preached for the Long Parliament and would have known Samuel's uncle Edward Leigh and Sir John Potts.

22. TNA, C 10/114/61

23. TNA, C 10/77/96; TNA, C 33/224 and C 33/226

24. TNA Catalogue and Google Books hits

25. By Henry's will made in 1632. TNA, PCC will 1639, PROB 11/180. Samuel received minor legacies in the will which was witnessed by Ruth Scudamore and of which Thomas Cornwallis, Henry's 'friend' was one of the overseers with son Edward as executor. A second deed relating to the premises in 1639 between Dame Ruth and Edward was no doubt a reinforcement of the 1625 settlement after Henry's death.

26. Thomas was probably the 'Thomas son of Samuel Lee and Anne' baptised in St Margaret in the Close Lincoln on 19th May 1640.

27. Folger L.d 241

28. Sir Charles is given as of Beeston Norfolk in *Visitation of Suffolk* and paid £20 for lands at Aylsham in 1621 Subsidy. Tanner 289.130

29. Possibly one of the unrelated Potts who settled in America in the seventeenth century.

30. NRO, Aylsham collection

31. British History Online, *CSPCAWI: Addenda* 1656, vol 9 pp. 105-116

32. There was also a Captain Thomas Potts of the Golden Hind of London named in the CSPCAWI at this time.
33. Various Google Books references including E McK Avery, *A History of the United States and its People from the Earliest Records* and CC Hall, *Narratives of Early Maryland 1633-84*
34. Charles Dalton, *English Army Lists and Commission Registers 1661-1714*, 1892
35. *CSPD*
36. TNA, C 9/102/29, C 33/264, C 33/268
37. *CSPD*
38. *HCJ vol 10*: 1688-1693, pp. 514-519
39. British History Online, Taxation Act lists. There is no entry for a Charles Potts as a taxpayer in Westminster, in 1691 or later.
40. MI in Rushall
41. RR Tighe and JE Davis, *Annals of Windsor vol 2*, 1853
42. The source for this was given as 'in a ms vol of copies and extracts in possession of Mr Secker'. We have not been able to trace this volume to see whether there was any further mention of Charles.
43. TNA, PCC will 1721, PROB 11/581 proved in August; buried 12th January St John New Windsor
44. TNA, PCC will 1727, PROB 11/615
45. Anne's sister married William Black at Bray on 8th February 1676; the legatees included various Blacks, a Serle and a Pilkington.

Notes to Chapter 18

1. Susan was baptised in Ketteringham on 14th October 1621.
2. NRO, parish register and NCC will 1633, 198 Tucke
3. NRO, WAL 374, 273x2 and another copy in WAL 1148, 286x4
4. Vaughan-Lewis, NAHRG article as before
5. All free and charterhold lands and some copyhold lands now occupied by Edmund Bell together containing 221 acres in Irmingland, leased for 10 years to Edmund and William Bell on 25th May 1639. In addition to the 221 acres another farm is then described including The White House messuage, a close called Little Elmingdale and the site of the former old chapel of Irmingland. These together were the purchases from the Bettes family by John Potts in the 1590s; The long meadow of 9 acres in Irmingland and Oulton leased in March 1632 for 20 years to Christopher Buck gent; The messuage called Loves – occupation not given; King's meadow in Itteringham; 50 acres of land in Itteringham purchased of John Smith esq; 3 closes of meadow and pasture in Itteringham called Shoppe Close, Bromehill and Long Meadow in the occupation of [Mary] King widow; The messuage and yards, orchards, etc in Itteringham being 5 roods occupied by Edmond Clarke which John Potts had purchased of John Crome; Mickle Mill in Itteringham [the main 'large' water mill] with all its water courses and flood gates had been leased to Thomas Leman in September 1634 for 10 years. With the mill went the adjacent close and house on it called Birchams and meadows around the site totalling 16 ¼ acres. Leman also had the 2 acre meadow purchased of Robert Houghton and 5 pieces of land in Itteringham field totalling 7 acres; The messuage and farmhouse known as Diers with its 76 acres of land meadow and pasture was occupied by John Jollye, who also had the 1 acre

pightle of pasture immediately to the south of the church; Thomas Jackson, [Itteringham's rector but probably living in Wolterton where he was also rector], occupied 33 acres of closes, lands, meadow and pasture in the centre of Itteringham; Thomas Skinner occupied the messuage land and pasture called Gravers Close in Itteringham; Thomas Barvil had parcels of open field land in Itteringham totalling 9 acres. By a 7 year lease started 12th August 1636 John Hardiman had the messuage, barns, stable and orchards that used to be at the eastern limit of Itteringham and quite close to Wolterton Hall. The farm had land meadow and pasture totalling 115 acres mostly in various closes on the Wolterton side of the parish around the farmstead. Hardiman also had much of Sweetingtree Close and Mickle Meadow Hirne; William Larwood had 21 acres in Saxthorpe, including a meadow named Betts. The nature, location and history of these separate lands will be covered in Vaughan-Lewis, *Itteringham Landscape and Lordship* work in progress.

6. See Chapter 19. The loss of the Mannington registers has meant nothing can be proven but the chancery actions have provided many new dates.

7. NRO, NRS 1867 and 1868, 11A4

8. *Visitations*; J Haydn, *The Book of Dignities*, 1851; *ODNB*

9. TNA, PCC will proved May 1668, PROB 11/327

10. Elizabeth appears to have been born before her father settled in Arlesey (one of Samuel's sons was baptised there in 1638) and she did not marry from there: *The parish register of Arlesey*, Bedfordshire County Council 1984. Earlier editions of the printed transcript for Arlesey give Dame Elizabeth *Petts* but this has been amended from 2008.

11. NRO, AYL 193/4(2)

12. NRO, NRS 1864, 11x4 and NRS 1865, in which the property is described in full detail.

13. TNA, PCC 1598 will, PROB 11/91

14. *Visitations* and the evidence of all the lands being vested in either Audrey or Julia.

15. *Visitations*, *ODNB* and Oby parish register

16. NRO, EVL 267, 458x3

17. TNA, PCC will 1646, PROB 11/196 and PCC will 1649, PROB 11/207

18. *ODNB*

19. NRO, EVL 282, 458x3 and TNA, C 22/815/9

20. TNA, C 10/165/84, C10/170/83, C 10/165/43, C10/106/149, C 22/815/9, C 22/815/6

21. TNA, C 33/238 ff. 441, 455, 568

22. TNA, C 33/244 ff. 133, 275, 314

23. TNA, C 33/246 ff. 12, 78,100,105,145, 251, 254, 291, 456, 515, 661, 667

24. TNA, C 33/248 f. 193

25. TNA, C 33/254 f. 529; and C 33/256 ff. 72,191 and 343

26. TNA, C 22/815/6

27. TNA, C 33/258 f. 477

28. TNA, C 33/260 f. 266

29. TNA, C 9/123/10

30. TNA, PCC will 1668, PROB 11/327

31. Martin's notebooks have survived in Walter Rye's papers NRO, Rye MS 17/1-4.

32. Indeed by creating two Johns where there should only be one, it showed John Potts married to his own mother and by her being his own father!

33. CS Tomes, *Mannington Hall and its Owners,* 1916

34. A Emery, *Greater Medieval Houses of England and Wales, 1300-1500,* 1996

35. Close scrutiny of both the maps and their drawings of the site does not support an infilling block. In 1742 it was definitely not there and it is hard to explain why it would have been by then demolished if it had been there in 1678. The water colour sketches of Mannington made in the 1830s also showed no wing in this site at the back of the house. The older map is of course very faint, but it is hard to say that there is anything shown other than the kitchen range to the east of the old house's main block. Tomes's view of the 1595 map was definitely that there was no such infilling block - he was only concerned with the height of the kitchen range. Purdy had said three floors for that, but Tomes thought it looked like two only. We tend to think Purdy was right.

36. Wolterton archives 3/3/1

37. This can be shown from the estate accounts held in the Wolterton archives.

38. Watercolours painted by the Rev James Bulwer; sketch probably by Robert Blake Humfrey, all in private hands.

39. Article by Bryan Hall published May 1951. The watercolour by WN Mileham of Aylsham was in his possession at the time but its whereabouts are unknown.

40. Suffolk RO, Archdeaconry of Suffolk IC/AA1/69/42

41. NRO, BRA 926/76, 372x 9

42. NRO, NCC will of 1588, 304 Homes

43. NRO, ANF will 1680, 137/152 and ANF will 1681, 87/165

44. TNA, E 134/1Anne/East1

45. David Yaxley, *A Researcher's Glossary*

Notes to Chapter 19

1. NRO, NRS 1867, 11A4

2. TNA, C 10/199/55

3. TNA, C 33/254 ff. 286,385 and 533

4. TNA, C 33/254 f. 578

5. TNA, C 10/212/71

6. This is then recited at length and apparently accurately, for date and contents, by comparison with the copy that survives in the Walpole papers. NRO, WAL 1166/2-3, 287x1. The original settlement of 1st February 1664 is NRO, WAL 376 273x2.

7. TNA, C 33/256 f. 410

8. TNA, C 33/256 ff. 416,482,562 and 576

9. TNA, C 22/815/7

10. This shows Burrell was a very old man when he died around 1721. Burrell's appalling hand-writing records Itteringham baptisms to 1717, marriages to 1714 and burials to 1718. He may have become ill and incapacitated sometime before his death. Nothing is recorded then until 1721, when a new rector John Rush was appointed.

11. Mark Cockey had been listed in the debts as owed more than £20, presumably as part of the transactions he handled for Sir John. Cockey was the presbyterian alderman chosen by the dissenters group to stand for parliamentary election against William Paston when alderman Augustine Briggs refused. Cockey lost. His opponents called him 'Dutch and Scottish' Cockey. Evans, *17th Century Norwich,* 1979 p 258.

12. TNA, PCC will 1722, PROB 11/584

13. TNA, C 22/815/7, second part

14. TNA, C 33/258 ff. 10, 48, 63 and 99
15. TNA, C 10/220/66
16. TNA, C 33/258 ff. 175,194 and 278
17. TNA, C 33/258 f. 561
18. TNA C 33/260 ff. 64, 88,143,147,157 and 294
19. TNA, C 22/816/13
20. In a future work we will show that there is good reason to believe the shop was on the same or much the same site as it occupies today, subsequently passing through the Robins, Fish and Sims families before coming to the Fairheads of recent memory.
21. TNA, C 33/ 260 ff. 308,314,436,455,527,580 and 582
22. TNA, C 10/212/72
23. TNA, C 33/260 f. 748
24. TNA, C 33/260 f. 638
25. TNA, C 33/260 ff. 639,686,709; C 33/262 f. 24,78 and 89
26. TNA, C 33/262 f. 138
27. TNA, C 33/262 ff. 154,445 and 538
28. TNA, C 33/262 f. 665
29. TNA, C 33/264 ff. 101 and 139

Notes to Chapter 20

1. His age was given as 41 in 1682 - TNA, C 22/815/6 - but 17 in January 1661 by Venn, *Caius*
2. TNA, C 22/815/6
3. www.innertemple.org.uk
4. Venn, *Caius*
5. Venn, *Caius*
6. Daniel Gurney, *The Record of the House of Gournay*, Supplement 1858, Thow Kilyan. We have used this modern spelling of the name which was often given as Gournay or Gourney at the time.
7. Gurney; JA Venn, *Alumni* has him born in St Peter Mancroft, admitted to Caius College Cambridge in 1613 aged 16 where he gained both a BA and MA by 1621 and was admitted to Gray's Inn in 1630. The unexplained gap may imply a period of legal training at another Inn before transferring to Gray's Inn.
8. NRO, WAL 375, 273x2
9. Daniel Gurney as above
10. TNA, PCC will 1642, PROB 11/188
11. TNA, PCC will proved February 1661 but not dated when made, PROB 11/303
12. TNA, PCC will 1667, PROB 11/324
13. TNA, PCC will 1667, PROB 11/324
14. NRO, WAL 1166/2, 287x1
15. NRO, WAL 1136, 286x2, badly damaged
16. TNA, C 10/486/90
17. NRO, WAL 329, 272x6
18. The 221 acres were said to be now occupied by Richard Sexton which previously were Richard King and formerly Edmund Bell. The White House and its 31 acres and meadow had also been in the occupation of William Bell. Another version of this deed,

NRO, WAL 327/2, apparently in error, gave the Richard Sexton lands as purchased by the first Sir John Potts of Nicholas Bell; in fact it would appear this large part of Irmingland land was in the original Betts purchase. Probably the mortgage drafter confused the small exchange of lands by bargain and sale between Potts and the Bells in 1637, for the purchase by Potts of all the lands in which they were his tenants. NRO, WAL 348, 273x1, WAL 349, 273x1 and WAL 350, 273x1. In fairness, by 1742 the Irmingland farm totalled 310 acres, so from time to time small amounts of land had been added to the 260-280 acres that John Potts had originally bought from the Bettes in the 1590s. 1742 estate map, Wolterton archives 10/26. Maybe some of the additional land had been held by members of the Bell family, but evidence of these infilling purchases has not been found – not uncommon for many small purchases by the estate.

19. NRO, MC 845/1-20, 798x7; NRO, MC 44/20, 500x1; Walter Rye, *Calendar of Oliver Le Neve's Letters*, 1895

20. Although the Mannington register is lost fortunately the baptisms were noted in the Gt Witchingham register.

21. *Eynsford Families*, Norfolk Genealogy vol 4 1972, says that John was buried aged 6 but that must be an error. 'Poor Jackie', who had learning difficulties, lived until the age of 20 and died in London in 1711. Rye as above

22. It is possible that Anne's entry is that of Susan. The child may have been called Susanna and become known as Susan later.

23. The overseers' book is now lost. It is possible that the Rev. Robert Walpole, the Itteringham rector, kept some of the parish records at Marylebone, London, where he also held a larger parish.

24. British History Online

25. TNA, E 134/24Chas2/East22 and E 134/25Chas2/East14

26. NRO, MC 70/9, 542x1

27. TNA, C 10/195/21

28. TNA, C 10/199/12 and C 22/765/36

29. Tanner 137.144

30. Wolterton archives, 19/35

31. TNA, C 6/271/102

32. TNA, C 231/7; NRO, C/Sda 1/1, 1/3, 1/4, 1/6 and 1/7

33. NRO, C/Scb 1/2/1/10

34. HMC *Report on Mss of the Marquess of Lothian* 1905. The printed summary is ambiguous as to whether the servant numbers were for the sheriff or the gentlemen attending.

35. Ketton-Cremer, *Assize Week in Norwich in 1688*, NA vol 24 (1932) pp 14-17; K-C *Felbrigg*

36. Mason

37. TNA, C 231/8

38. NRO, MC 1601/101, 862x8

39. Mason

40. Ed. EM Thompson, *Letters of Humphrey Prideaux to John Ellis, 1674-1722*, Camden Soc New Series vol 15. Prideaux also wrote at great length about a celebrated local case that involved Sir Roger.

41. HMC *Report of the Mss of Marquess Townshend*, 1887; *CSPD* Mar 1701 p249

42. JH Plumb, *Sir Robert Walpole The Making of a Statesman*, The Cresset Press, 1956

43. D Hayton, *A Note on the Norfolk Election of 1702*, NA, vol Part 3, 1980, pp 320-323. Letter preserved in Cambridge University Library in the Marquess of Cholmondeley (Houghton) manuscripts, Correspondence 214. The letter, of 7th May 1702, was from Sir Charles Turner to his brother-in-law Robert Walpole.

44. *CSPD* Wm III 1701 pp457-575

Notes to Chapter 21

1. Venn, *Alumni*
2. TNA, E 134/12Wm3/Mich32 and PCC will of 1684, PROB 11/378
3. Frances was baptised in Saham Toney on 13th May 1660.
4. NRO, ANW 1700, will 409, made in 1686, possibly when or just after Thomas and Frances were married, and proved on 9th July 1700. Frances was sole executrix and the supervisors were Crane's 'brother' Burton and friend Dr Parham.
5. We have not found the date of her brother or father's death but Sarah Calibut widow was buried on 16th April 1681 and was preceded by Philippa Calibut generosa on 10th July 1679, presumably Frances's only other surviving sibling. Crane's family also came from Saham.
6. Mason
7. TNA, C 9/161/9
8. TNA, C 6/333/68
9. NRO, 1700, ANW will 409; Shuckforth was baptised in Saham Toney on 12th May 1662, the son of William Shuckforth gent and his wife Frances Crane, both of Saham, whom he had married on 6th October 1659.
10. TNA C 33/295 and 297
11. NRO, St Peter Hungate parish records, PD 61/31
12. Lease and release and feoffment purchased 2008, now donated to NRO
13. FR Beecheno, *Some Account of St Peter's Hungate Parish, Norwich*, NA, vol 21, 1923, p 128
14. Deeds cited; KI Sandred and B Lindstrom, *The Place Names of Norfolk, Part 1, Norwich*, 1989
15. For photograph see p 63, J Pound, *Tudor and Stuart Norwich*, 1988
16. NRO, PD 61/31
17. R Frostick, *The Printed Plans of Norwich 1558-1840*, 2002
18. NRO, DCN 115/1-3
19. NRO, DCN 47/4-8; DCN 115/1-3; *Norwich Chapter Books, 1566-1649*, NRS vol 24,1953
20. Denny was buried in the Cathedral in 1642.
21. Roberta Gilchrist, *Norwich Cathedral Close*, Boydell, 2005
22. Blom vol 4 p31
23. NRO, ANW will 1695, will 107
24. Arthur Branthwayt esq of Norwich was the second son but heir of William Branthwayt esq of Hethel and his wife Julyan the daughter of Thomas Berney of Swardeston (a younger brother of the 1st Baronet Sir Richard Berney and thus distantly related to Berney the MP). Blom; Visitations. Our Arthur was known as of Norwich to distinguish him from his eldest son, also a lawyer, then known as Arthur of Hethel, who died in 1724. TNA, PCC will of 1724, PROB 11/600. William died in 1710 leaving his wife

as executrix of his will. TNA, PCC will of 1711, PROB 11/523 One of Arthur's several brothers was named 'Barney'. Arthur was an eminent lawyer who worked for many of the families in this story and who was Steward of Norwich from 1691 to 1703, in addition to his role for the Dean and Chapter. He died at his house in Norwich in 1717 and was buried at the family church of Hethel. TNA, PCC will of 1717, PROB 11/561 He was married to Anne the daughter of Thomas Bacon, second son of Sir Francis Bacon the famous judge. Arthur was doubly connected to the Berney family by marriage. He was referred to as 'my brother in law' and made one of the trustees and a supervisor in the will of Sir Richard Berney bt made in 1705 and proved in 1714. TNA, PCC will of 1714, PROB 11/538. Sir Richard, the 3rd baronet, had married and had a number of children by Arthur's sister Dorothy. *Debrett's Baronetage of England*, 1839. From this it seems likely that he would have been close to his cousin Richard Berney esq the Tory MP. As it happens Sir Richard, like Branthwayt, voted Whig in 1710 and thus against Richard Berney esq.

25. *Catalogue of a Valuable Collection of Books in most Faculties; Most of which were brought out of the Study of the late Sir Charles Potts at Mannington* printed by William Chase, 1737 bookseller of Norwich, NRO, NNAS 1/1/5/46; photocopy in Norfolk and Norwich Millennium Heritage Library
26. Talk given to Aylsham Local History Society, November 2007
27. The Online Library of Liberty, www.oll.libertyfund.org
28. BL, Add 22466
29. See MCW Hunter and others, *A Radical's Books: The Library Catalogue of Samuel Jeake of Rye 1623-90*, 1999; S Eliot and J Rose, *A Companion to the History of the Book*, 2007
30. Norfolk and Norwich Subscription Library, *A Catalogue of the books belonging to the Public Library and to the City*, 1825; *Norwich City Library 1608-1737*, NRS vol 72, 2008
31. Wolterton archives 19/36 Potts letters
32. This, and all other analysis of the publication details of books in the library, has been sourced from the British Library's online catalogue.
33. The wall, which no longer exists, and the guardhouse are clearly depicted in a sketch of 1832 (probably by Robert Blake Humphrey) and a painting of 1863 by Frederick Brett Russell taken from it - both in private possession.
34. Wolterton archives, 10/26
35. Described as: the gardens; two meadows totalling 5 acres - probably the 2 wooded meadows around the chapel; the long walks 5 acres - the avenues shown by Hawkes; gravel pit pightle and another pightle by a wall near the Hall, 4 acres. Wolterton archives, 8/11
36. Wolterton archives, 3/1/1, 3/1/3
37. *East Anglian Pedigrees*, Harleian Society Vol 91, 1939
38. Tanner, 305.198
39. *ODNB*
40. BL, Shelf mark 978.d.35
41. BL, Add 23204 f.16
42. Venn, *Alumni*
43. HMC Reports, *Portland Papers Vol VI*, page 526
44. Oct 1720 BL, Add 4253 f.70

45. *ODNB* and the introduction on *The Life of the Author* in the 1836 New York Edition of one of Prideaux's major works *The Old and New Testament Connected in the History of the Jews and Neighbouring Nations ...* Google Books His diaries and letters on political matters have also been drawn on by various authors including *HofC 1690-1715*.
46. *ODNB*
47. *ODNB*
48. GS Holmes, *British Politics in the Age of Anne*
49. *HofC 1690-1715*
50. Nottingham University Mss Dept, Papers of the Harley Family in the Portland (Welbeck) Collection, PW 2 Hy 654
51. HMC Reports, *Portland Papers, Vol IV*, page 561
52. *Visitations*; *HofC 1690-1715*
53. *ODNB*
54. HMC Reports, *Portland Papers, Vol IV*, page 685
55. Mason
56. *HofC*
57. HMC Reports, *Portland Papers, Vol IV*
58. When considering the 'Bever' in Algernon's letter to Robert Harley, at one point we wondered if Preston had brought a case against a friend of Algernon's or perhaps someone involved in his circle's scholarly pursuits. As a stationer freeman of London since 1689 and a long established publisher Thomas Bever had printed various legal works and religious books and sermons. British Library Catalogue; HR Plomer, *A Dictionary of the Printers and Booksellers who were at work in England, Scotland and Ireland from 1668 to 1725*, OUP, 1922. In 1703 John Dunton (the eccentric bookseller and creator of the *Athenian Gazette*) described him as:

Mr Bever in Fleet Street. He had ever the character of being a very merciful, just and peaceable man, never intermeddling with state matters. He is a constant hearer at St Dunstan's church; and I doubt not, as his charities are free and large, "the blessing of him that is ready to perish will come upon him"; neither are any of his virtues blemished by vanity or affectation, for he is liberal from a principle of conscience, and humble to the last degree. I shall only add, he has a large acquaintance amongst the lawyers, and is himself a very thriving man.

J Nichols, *The Life and Errors of John Dunton*, 1818, being an edition of Dunton's own book written in 1703 and published in 1705. Further speculation might be that Preston was trying to exploit the Statute of Anne on copyright, effective from April 1710, in some way against Bever. There was a clause in it, for example, that allowed complaints when a publication was deemed by a gentleman to be unreasonably priced. Such a complaint could be made to various senior officials including the Lord Keeper. Daniel Defoe, having suffered from 'pirate printers' had written to Harley in 1707 and 1709 in support of a change to copyright to give greater protection to the writer and had applauded the 1710 Act for the Encouragement of Learning for making a new and fundamental shift towards authors' rights. Harley would certainly have been engaged in this issue given his patronage of various writers throughout his career and no doubt many of them would have lobbied him. However, in the end we came down on 'Bever' being a Norfolk Beevor.

59. Originally of a Yorkshire family TNA, E 134/11Anne/Mich 8, 9 & 11; J Chambers, *History of Norfolk*, 1829; NRO catalogue contains various deed references to the family; NRO, NCC will 1716 of Margaret the first wife of Thomas, 270 Bokenham; K Wilson, *The Sense of the People ... , 1715-85*, 1995; Debrett's *Baronetage of England ... , 1809,1815,1840* editions; NRO, NRS 2843-46, 12E6. John's brother Thomas Beevor esq was a Norfolk landowner and in due course Thomas's eldest son married a Branthwayt heiress and took over the Hethel estate of the Branthwayts and was to become Sir Thomas the first baronet. Before that, in the 1760s, Thomas the father had made an unsuccessful attempt to become a MP. John and Thomas had a brother James who was a Norwich brewer with a substantial business there.

60. *HofC*

61. Norfolk and Norwich Millennium Library, Norwich Poll Book 1710, 59B. Unfortunately the County Poll Book for 1710 seems not to have survived.

62. Ed. Lord Dover, *Letters of Horace Walpole, Earl of Orford, to Sir Horace Mann ... ,* vol 12, fn p416, New York, 1933

63. Thanks to Dr C Wilkins-Jones for this suggestion.

64. *ODNB*

65. Anthony Page, *John Jebb and the Enlightenment Origins of British Radicalism*, Education, 2003, page 28

66. *ODNB*

67. *ODNB*

68. The Devon County Libraries Local Studies Service website

69. *ODNB*

70. *HofC*

71. *HofC*

72. British Library, and digital copy available to read online at the UEA Library, via Metalib's E books section and the catalogue for Eccobooks

73. Ed. C Rawcliffe and R Wilson, *Norwich Since 1550*, Hambledon and London, 2004, Mark Knight's article on *Politics 1660-1835*

74. NRO, C/Sda 1/5

75. NRO, C/Sda 1/4

76. An original copy is held by the Norfolk and Norwich Millennium Library.

77. *HMC Report on the Townshend Papers*

78. NRO, BUL 2/4, 604x7

79. Venn, *Alumni*

80. Of the tenants in the Hall, we know that two Le Neve baptisms were held at the 'chapel' in the months of May and August and a third at Little Barningham, also August. Perhaps Mannington was usable only if the weather was fine; Venn, *Alumni*

81. Antiquarian snippets NRO, NAS/1/2/6

82. Benjamin may have been related to Richard Knight patron of Little Barningham around 1700.

83. NRO, Antiquarian snippets as above. Blom wrote November 1717 but without any substantiation and this seems to be simply a minor typing error. A letter of April 1717 noted in chapter 23 on Sir Charles shows him then running Mannington. The wording of Algernon's will also supports late 1716 as the date of death. The will was proved by the end of March 1717, but the precise date has not survived.

84. Tanner 305.177 [old 126/7]

85. Herts Record Office, ref Vlll B79

86. The bequests were to her nieces Frances Repps (born 1681) and Anne Russell (the elder daughter of Francis and Lucy Repps who married William Russell of Norwich) and her cousins Anne Brown, Katherine Burton, Frances Raney and Susanna Wright. Further research on these relations is needed, but it is likely that Susanna Wright was related to the Robert Wright in the house deeds.
87. NRO, ANW will 1700, no.409
88. Microfilm at the Norfolk and Norwich Millennium Library
89. NRO, BRA 505/5/1-3, 715x6 and NRO, MC 44/50, 500x2
90. NRO, NCC will of 1716, 222 Bokenham

Notes to Chapter 22

1. Spelling is largely as written, but with some modernisation to make the meaning clear and the whole easier to read.
2. NRO, WAL 1141, 286x4
3. Wolterton archives, 19/36
4. NRO, NAS 1/1/12/Hickling/11
5. Guildhall Lib, Ms 14727 and Ms 7194 - the latter shows Naked Boy Court near Ludgate Hill and Belle Sauvage Court, close by the old prison site. The postal stamp of 5E over 2 might date the letter.
6. NRO, DUN 170, 108x4
7. NRO, NCC 1709 will, 259 Famme
8. NRO, DUN 64/2, 3, & 6, 105x6
9. An underlying distrust of Sir Roger's intentions may be implied by the clause in Israel Long's will (made in 1703) that bequeathed £500 to Matthew payable only after the deaths of both Sir Roger and Lady Potts and which sum was not to accrue any interest either until after their deaths.
10. NRO, WAL 1604/3, 292x2
11. It probably preceded the June 1710 correspondence and seems to fit logically here. It is just possible that it is the letter referred to in the 25th August letter below.
12. NRO, NRS 26679, 149x3
13. Possibly Edward Lomb of Cawston d 1720
14. NRO, ANF 1727, will 225/564
15. NRO, MC 44/50, 500x2
16. NRO, WLS V/7, 407x7
17. NRO, EVL 309, 458x5
18. NRO, WAL 379-386, 273x3 for the trail of mortgages and assignments since 1693 involving Danvers, Wallis and others
19. TNA, C 9/442/16
20. NRO, WAL 407, 273x5
21. NRO, WAL 327/7, 10, 11, 272x5; WAL 1126, 286x2
22. TNA, PCC will 1709, PROB 11/507. The name is sometimes spelt Founds.
23. NRO, WAL 327/11, 272x5
24. NRO, WAL 1034, 284x6
25. NRO, WAL 619, 276x5
26. Venn, *Alumni*
27. NRO, NCC will 1711, 593 Famme

28. NRO, WAL 1444, 290x3
29. TNA, PCC will 1711, PROB 11/521
30. TNA, PCC will 1723, PROB 11/592
31. TNA, PCC will 1753, PROB 11/799
32. NRO, WAL 387, 273x4 and WAL 1138/4, 286x3
33. NRO, WAL 1138/5, 286x3
34. NRO, NRS 1871
35. *Visitation*; *East Anglian Pedigrees* and Rebecca Harbord's will quoted above
36. NRO, NRS 1876 & 1877, 11A4
37. NRO, WAL1031/1-6, 284x6
38. Subsequently, in June 1718, Sir Charles assigned it to John Muston gent of Watton. In November 1720 the mortgage was assigned to William Barker gent of Edgefield who, as we have seen, had provided another more substantial mortgage. By this time the property was in the occupation of Thomas Plane. In this four-part deed Barker appears to have put it into trust with the local cleric John Rush who receipted a number of interest payments on the back of the mortgage deed. In the following year Rush was to take up the parishes of Wolterton and Itteringham. We have not followed this property subsequently but WAL 1031/1 has on its reverse: 'assigned by Mrs Barker to Mr Fowle on Mr [Horatio] Walpole's purchase' - presumably a mortgage continued as part of Walpole's funding arrangements.
39. NRO, WAL 1604/4, 292x2
40. NRO, WAL 1604/1, 292x2
41. NRO, NRS 1880, 11A4
42. NRO, NRS 1884, 11A4
43. NRO, MS 9030 and 9031, 7F5
44. As above and relating to Crane lands: NRO, BRA 505/5/1-3, 715x6 and BRA 505/6/1-16, 715x6
45. NRO, WAL 390, 273x4

Notes to Chapter 23

1. Blom: MI in Great Ellingham church. Farrer's *Church Heraldry of Norfolk* says a stone to her in Baconsthorpe gave 2nd September 1705 aged 20.
2. Tanner 305.178
3. *ODNB*; Blom
4. Frances Tanner had two infant daughters buried in September 1715 and February 1716, one 15 days old and the other not even named on the memorial inscription in the Bishop's Chapel in Norwich Cathedral. Blom. Her son Thomas was baptised on 11th March 1718 in St Mary in the Marsh Norwich and she died exactly three months later aged 40.
5. NRO, COL/13/192. Burke gave her as the daughter of Thomas Smith a *London* merchant.
6. TNA, PCC will 1730, PROB 11/637
7. TNA, PCC will 1726 Edward Parre, PROB 11/611. There is no mention of Lydia or the Potts family in his will and nothing to help identify Lydia or Mary's origins.
8. TNA, PCC will 1763, PROB 11/890

9. Guildhall Lib, Ms 10091/27. As a 'bachelor' not a widower, he was not previously married and so Mary could not have had a half-brother or sister if she was the daughter of this Thomas.

10. Guildhall Lib, Ms 6668/1, Ms 6667/4; they did not marry in either of their own Westminster parishes

11. TNA, RG7; Guildhall Lib parish registers

12. St Margaret registers in *Harleian Society Parish Registers* vols 64, 88, 89

13. If so, there are two strong possibilities for William Smith's marriage and the baptism of a Catherine if we assume that Catherine was also her mother's name. A William Smith married a Catherine Usher 16th June 1694 in St James's Dukes Place London; another married Catherine Coggan 6th February 1697/98 in Lincoln's Inn Chapel. Although the latter is attractive for the law court chapel venue, this man may have died after Lydia thus ruling him out - a William Smith gent of Barking Essex died around 1732. TNA, PCC will 1732, PROB 11/653. Everything was left to his wife who was joint executrix with their friend Ann Cogan also of Barking. The Cogan reference hints at the Smith/Coggan marriage. There seem to have been no children. The dates mean he could not be Lydia's son. A Catherine was baptised to a William and Catherine Smith 18th September 1702 in St Nicholas Cole Abbey London.

14. Tomes's published booklet and his own notebook in the Wolterton archives 20/3/50; NRO, Rye MSS for the Martin notebook itself

15. *The Visitation of Lancashire, 1567*, Chetham Society, 1871

16. This Richard was the third son of Sir William Torbock of Torbock and his wife Margery the sister of Sir James Stanley. His eldest brother was Thomas Torbock esq and this generation was alive in the first half of the sixteenth century. The Torbocks of Torbock had an ancient lineage but fell on hard times during the seventeenth century. Their manor was sold to the Sutton family in 1611 and the main line seems to have died out. *Victoria County History*. However, the Torbock surname was still to be found in the area in the eighteenth century.

17. IGI

18. Guildhall Lib, *Challen's Parish Register Transcripts Vol 1*, a high quality transcription of marriages there

19. The Harebred family show up in late Elizabethan Feet of Fines in Yorkshire as an affluent gentry family involved in a variety of manorial and other land transactions. British History Online, *Yorkshire Fines* from 1581 to 1597. Initially these show a William and his wife Margaret and later Richard Harebred. Richard Harebred esq of Selby had his will proved in February 1664. TNA, PCC will 1664, PROB 11/313. Apart from a deceased son, William, he had six married daughters. Anne was the wife of Thomas Norman gent of Burton in the parish of Fryston Yorkshire. So, Harebred Norman was no doubt their eldest son.

20. *Harleian Society Parish Registers* vol 25

21. TNA, C 11/1433/4 and C 11/474/53

22. TNA, PCC 1732, PROB 11/651

23. For general histories see for example: Malcolm Balen, *A Very English Deceit*, Fourth Estate, 2002; Virginia Cowles, *The Great Swindle*, Collins,1960

24. *South Sea Company Subscription Shares and Warrant Values in 1720* by Gary S.Shea, Department of Economics University of St. Andrews, June 2004

25. TNA, C 33/341, C 33/342 and C 33/345

26. TNA, C 33/345 f.93
27. More research on Sir Charles's exposure could probably be done by examining the South Sea Company registers that have survived in the House of Lords Record Office but here we have established a reasonable estimate of the effect of the bubble on Sir Charles.
28. NRO, C/Sda 1/8 and 1/9
29. NRO, WAL 392, 273x4
30. TNA, PCC will 1732, PROB 11/651
31. NRO, WAL 393-6, 273x4; WAL 406, 273x5; WAL 409, 273x6 and others
32. TNA, PCC will 1706, PROB 11/490
33. NRO, WAL 1441/8, 290x3
34. Seven letters survive in the Wolterton archive that show how assiduously Horatio Walpole endeavoured to buy the Mannington estate from at least 1731 onwards. Wolterton archives, 8/14. Most were addressed to Walpole personally, with one going to one of his men: The Honourable John Fowle esq at the Excise Office London. As elsewhere, where transcribed we have adjusted spelling occasionally and added a little punctuation to help the flow.
35. NRO, DUN 170, 108x4
36. Roger Howman's 1705 will and those of his sons Erasmus 1712, Roger 1722 and daughter Ellen 1714 make repeated reference to three named Longs as kin or cousins. NRO, NCC 1705 will, 670 Piddocke; ANW 1712, will 262; ANW 1722, will 523; ANW 1714 will 359. Edward had been joint executor of his father's will and since his elder brothers died was head of the family. The precise nature of the relationship is not clear but the Howmans were possibly related by marriage to the Cambridgeshire branch of the Long family, or possibly to Thomas Long apothecary of Norwich.
37. *Gents Mag.* 1732 p627
38. TNA, C 33/360 and C 11/1840/51
39. TNA, C 11/1027/21
40. TNA, C 11/1283/48, /51 and /60. Other parts of the case can be found on the TNA catalogue variously under Walpole, Spelman, Naish, Bence and Britiffe. Among these items is correspondence from Spelman's kinsman and attorney Robert Bence with a few related mortgage deeds in C 112/193.
41. Wolterton archives, 17/1/4. Transcribed sections include minor amendments to spellings and a little added punctuation to make the flow clearer.
42. TNA, PCC will 1735, PROB 11/674 'Laurence Charteris gent' had been in Queen Anne's army from 1702-12, but had left the service on getting married in Burda. This would raise the possibility of he and Horatio having been friends when young men in the Low Countries. A copy of this Charteris's account of his actions as a rebel in the Scottish rebellion of 1715 survives in the Wolterton archive. Wolterton archives, 17/1/30. He was taken prisoner by King George's troops at Preston and seems to have written the account in 1718 in Holland.
43. NRO, WAL 1166/5 and /7-11, 287x1
44. Wolterton archives 8/11
45. Norfolk and Norwich Millennium Heritage Library
46. NRO, WAL 1166/6
47. NRO, WAL 1444, 290x3
48. TNA, PCC 1763 will, PROB 11/890

49. NRO, 1737 sale catalogue as before, NNAS 1/1/5/46; photocopy in Norfolk and Norwich Millennium Heritage Library
50. A McLaren, *Impotence: a Cultural History*, University of Chicago Press, 2007
51. A 'pair of organs' at the time normally meant one instrument - like a 'pair of scissors' - although it could have two faces. Alternatively they may have been two small portative or small table-top organs often favoured by ladies. None would have had pedals or wind reservoirs so were quite moveable.

Notes to Chapter 24

1. Prince Duleep Singh, *Portraits in Norfolk Houses*, Ed. Rev Edm Farrer, 1927
2. BL, Add 22466
3. NRO, DUN (C) 64-66, DUN (C) 70 & 71, 499x5

Index

This is a selective person and place index only, with some minor or repeated names excluded. Place-names where no county is given (except for county towns) are in Norfolk. Standard indexing rules have been relaxed to assist with differentiation of families and individuals. Married women central to the story are indexed under maiden name with sequential married names eg Willoughby/Spelman/Potts, Ursula and are not therefore shown in alphabetical groupings. Knights are also listed separately. Occasionally a husband and wife may be shown as 'Jane and John' for ease of identification.

Cooke family 101, 104, 141, 144, 552-3, 574, Maud 103-4, Richard 102, 104, Thomas 102-5, 504, 516, 519-20, 522-3, 527, Sir William 368, William 103-5

Cooke/Bedingfield, Agnes 368

Cooper, Edward 327-8, Thomas cleric 294, 327-8

Coopers, Company of 599

Coote family 75, 88, 102, 613, Christopher 5, 102-3, 613

Coote/Fermour/Bettes, Anne 75

Cootes, John 611

Copland, George 529

Copmanthorpe, Yorks 544

Corbett, Mary 226, Miles 230, 242, 258, 265, 271, 279, 281-2, 284-7, 291, 294-300, 304-6, 324-6, 363-5, Sir John 213-4, 233, Sir Miles 183-4, 218, 294, Sir Thomas 294

Corbett/Richers, Elizabeth 218

Corfe Castle, Dorset 127

Cornwall, Eleanor 580, Sir Thomas 580

Cornwallis family 376, 654, Frederick 230, Sir Charles 187, 216, 376-7, 638, Thomas 374-6

Cornwallis/Leigh/Potts, Anne 374-7, 379

Corpusty 89, 110, 212

Corrance/Long, Elizabeth 530, 569

Cory family 644, Francis 268, 280, 295-6, John 208, 239, 242, 254, 261, 269, 279-80, 289-90, 295, 297, 304, William 301, 304

Cosins, John 231

Cosyn, Nicholas 63, Thomas, clerk 66

Cotterell, Robert 96

Cottesbrook, Northants 56

Cotton family 571, 639, Alice 181, 193, Dr John 193, Sir John 131, 193, Sir John 3rd baronet 220-1, Sir Robert 5, Sir Robert 1st baronet 220-1, Thomas 22

Cotton/Huddleston, Bridget 5

Coulson, Mrs Elizabeth 480, 501-2

Covil, _ 264

Cowlie, Harry 587

Crane, family 642, Captain 268, Joan 455, Sir Robert 230-1, 242, 246, 251, 283, 305

Crane, Thomas 454-7, 463, 480, merchant house inventory 456, Thomas senior 455

Crane/Smith/Clopton/Heydon/Clere, Agnes (Lady) 141, 182, 199, 218

Cranfield, James 2nd Earl of Middlesex 315-6

Cranham, Essex 345

Cranworth 81, 90, 105

Cremer, Sir John 364, 387

Cresset, (Edward?) 320, 324

Cressett family 647

Cressey Hall, Lincs 447

Crew, Carey 389, John 389-91, John MP 390, Randolph junior 390-1, Sir Clippesby 390, Sir Randolph 390

Crew, John 1st Baron Crew of Stene 315-6, 319, 322, 324, 362

Crewe, Cheshire 389-90

Crisp, Anne 273, Sir Nicholas 272-3

Crofts family of Herefords 579-80, Sir James 579-80

Croket, Alice 598, Thomas 598

Crome, John baker 552-3

Cromer 90, 94, 97-8, 147, pier 96

Cromwell family 655

Cromwell, Oliver 231, 234, 271, 274, 280-1, 283, 285, 287, 291, 295-7, 305, 331-2

Cromwell, Thomas 559

Crosby, Sir John 538, William 538

Crossgrove, Henry 474

Crostwight 78, 261-2

Crouch (Crich etc), Henry 59, 65, 587-8

Crowe, Anne 208, 219, Christopher 370, 423, 427, 431, 433, 439, 444, William 208, 219, 260, 288, 344-5, 360

Croxton 81

Croydon, Surrey 566

Crumwell, Anne 574

Culpepper, Thomas 2nd Baron Thoresway 332, 334-5, 337

Curson, John 103, 620

Curtis, Elizabeth 483, 504

Cussyng, John cleric 76

Cutlack, Thomas 276, 284

Cutts family 559, Richard 204, Thomas 345

Cutts/Bendish, Dorothy 204

Cutts/Godsalve, Barbara 199, 201, 203-5

Dacres, Sir Thomas 330-1, Thomas 305

Daker, Henry 601

Dalben, William 342-3, 370

Dale, John 546

Dalham, Suffolk 537

Danvers, Samuel 494

Darcy, Sir Francis 583-4, 642

Darcy/Willoughby, Lettice 583

Darnall, John 562

Davy, Gregory 73, Henry 357, 454, Henry junior 443, Henry senior 442-3, Henry of Mangreen 530, 569, John 569, Margaret 604, Richard 73, Robert 474, Thomas 67, William 357, 391-2, 433, 442-4, 447

Davy/Churchman, Anne 530

Davy/Heigham, Anne 444

Davy/Potts, Mary 348, 356-7, 359, 395, 421, 424, 433, 442, 444, 446-7, 450, 532

676

Grand, William 335

Graveley, George 21, Rowland 29, 164

Graveley, Herts 29, 165

Graver, Thomas 593-4, William 338

Great Barrington, Gloucs 543

Great Burstead, Essex 507, 525, 527

Great Chesham, Bucks 32

Great Cressingham 231

Great Levermere, Suffolk 617

Great Oakley, Essex 345

Great Torrington, Devon 92

Great Warley, Essex 340

Great Witchingham 445, 573

Great Yarmouth 122, 184, 201, 203, 230, 280, 297, 363-9, 378, 391, 469, 471-2, 505

Green, Daniel 212, 396-7, Robert 557

Greenacre, Elizabeth 411-3, Philip 412-3, Robert 411-3, William 412-3

Greenwich, Kent 140

Grendon, Robert 18, Roger 18, Thomas 18, Walter 18

Gresham, Sir John 611, William 611

Gresley, Derbys 65

Grey, Anchetil (Anchitel) 336, 583-6, Elizabeth 583, Henry 1st Earl of Stamford 583

Grey, James 499-500, 506

Grey, Sir Thomas Lord Grey of Richemount 5

Grey, William 1st Baron Grey of Warke 273, 279-80, 284

Griffith, Sir Henry 583

Grimston 109, 431

Grimston, Sir Harbottle 242, 252, 309-10, 315-6, 319, 325, 362, 365

Grocers, Company of 8, 11, 13, 18, 24, 26, 59, 63, 65, 127, 130-1, 133, 540, 547

Grove, Richard 15-6

Growte of Aylsham 108

Grymer, James 214

Guernsey 67, 82, 85, 106-7, 111-126, 621-5, Abbey of Mount St Michael 112, Castle Cornet 113-5, 121, manors/fiefs 555, St Peter Port 114, 117, 119, 126, St Sampson 115, 555

Guestwick 223

Guiana, South America 568

Guildford, Sir Henry 93

Guildford, Surrey 555

Guile, James 118

Guist 288

Gunthorpe 66-7, 73, 442, 608

Gunton 503

Gunton, James 105

Gurdon, Thornhaugh 454, 469-70, 480, 482, 522

Gurney (Gourney) family 572, Edward 443, Frances 443, Helen 443-4, Henry 443, John 498

Gurney/Davy, Margaret 443

Guybon family 72, 81, 219, 572, 611, Clippesby 390-4, 421, 441, Francis 572-3, Gregory 80, Humphrey 390, 574, John 390, 393-4, Sir Francis 450, Thomas 72, 80-2, 390, Thomas junior 81, William 81, 102-3, 142, 147, 390, 449, 582

Guybon/Lumner, Anne 72, 81-2

Gwinne, Sir Adam 41

Gwynne, Rice 148

Hackford 90, 217

Hackshaw, John 431, 433, 440-1, 444

Hacon, Thomas 640

Hadley, Herts 330

Hainford 110, 574

Hales Hall 588

Halford, Charles 486-7

Hall, Bryan 532-3

Hall, Joseph Bishop of Norwich 294

Hall, Mr of Norwich 238

Halman see Alman

Hamilton, Marquess of 223-4

Hamond family 653

Hamond, a murderer 215

Hampden family 655, John 230-1, 239

Hanbury, Alice and Richard 42

Hanchett, Frances 623

Handford, Robert 16

Hanger, George 330, Mary 330

Hanger/Buller Mary 330

Hanneman, Adrian 531

Hanworth 377, 387-9

Happisburgh 210-1

Harbord, Colonel 451, Harbord 503, 520, Philip 449

Harborne, Staffs 376-7

Harding, Humphrey 43-6

Hare, Alice 483, 504-5, Audrey 588, John 216, Ralph 448, 453, 505, Sir Nicholas 136, Sir Ralph 233, 478

Harebred family 687

Hargham 449, 453, 505

Harington, Lady Anne 192

Harley, Abigail 470, Colonel Edward 362, Robert 2nd Earl of Oxford 463-5, 467-75

Harman, Richard mayor 230, 243, 296, 456, Thomas 456

Harper, William 105

Harrington, William 134

Harris, Jane 556, John 380-1, Thomas 350

Harrison, James 483, 504, John 497, 504, Mary 148, William 134

Harrop, Cheshire 535

Hartley Wood, battle of, Kent 99

Hartwell, Thomas 379

Hartwell/Potts, Anne 379-81

Harvey, Edmund 63, Philip 212

Harward family 94-6, Clement 581, Robert 94-5, Robert of Aldborough 617, Thomas 94

Harward/Arnold, Bridget 94

Harward/Hawe, Anne 581

Hascombe, Gloucs 560-1

Haselrig, Arthur 300

Hassall, Dr John 457-8

Hasset, Rolf (Blennerhasset) 274

Hatherton, Cheshire 508

Hatton, Dame Elizabeth *see* Cecil

Hatton, Sir Christopher 44, 100, 111-2, 127-30, 132, 135, 137, 144, 153, 159, 390

Hatton, Sir Robert 230-1, 305, Lady 231

Hatton, Sir William 127-8, 130, 144, 153

Haustand, John 21

Havering atte Bower, Essex 99

Haveringland 214, 482, 498-9

Hawes (Hawe) family 205, 230, 581-3

Hawes/Willoughby, Frances 205, 336

Hawkes, Thomas 462

Hawkyn, Thomas 59

Hawkyn/Lumner, Joan (Johanna) 59-60

Hawkyns, Richard draper 12

Hawstead, Essex 438

Hawstead, Suffolk 29, 107, 166

Hayes, Andrew Norwich apothecary 439, Sir James 377, Thomas 92, William 92

Haywood, Yorks 240

Heckham Heath, Little Barningham 101, 103

Hedenham 410, 567

Hedgerley, Bucks 166

Heigham 280

Heling (Heylyn) family 167, 542-3

Helme, Miles 50

Helmingham, Suffolk 466

Helston, Cornwall 135

Hempstead 203, 445

Hempstead, Essex 599

Heneage, Sir Thomas 115

Henry, Andrew 123

Hereford 579

Heron, Henry 447

Hertford 562

Hertingfordbury, Herts 29, 562

Hervey family 654, Francis 369, 372, John 444-5, 496, Mr (Francis?) 423, 428, Rebecca 273, Sir Thomas 496, Thomas 445

Hervey/Hackshaw, Annabella 369, 427, 431, 444-5

Heston, Middx 566

Hethel 459

Hethersett, Wormley 450

Heveningham family 187, 216, 219, 365, 385, Abigail 385, 447, Anthony 610, Arthur 365, 386, Lady Mary 365, Sir Arthur 216, 219, Sir John 216, 219, 365, 385-6, Sir William 447, William 226, 229-30, 242-3, 295, 298, 316-7, 326, 365, 385-6

Heveningham, Suffolk 365, 385-6

Heveningham/Gawdy/Spelman, Anne 385

Heveningham/Potts, Susan 219, 326, 329, 385-6, 419, 442

Heveningham/Spelman, Anne 219

Hevingham 79, 94, 96, 276

Hewitt, Gardiner 447, Sir John 332, 334-5, Sir William 447

Hewitt/Baldock, Ursula (Lady) 447

Hexham, Henry 566

Heydon 59, 136-7, 214, 370, 478, 500, 628-9, Ollands 218, 262, Stinton Hall 137, 220, 263

Heydon family 62, 66, 564-8, 604, 607

Heydon, Agnes *see* Crane

Heydon, Anne (Lady) of Thursford 90, 100

Heydon, Anne (Lady) *see* Dodge

Heydon, Anne (Lady) *see* Wodehouse

Heydon, Charles 288

Heydon, Christopher (idiot) 184, 564

Heydon, Henry 59, 65-6, 72, 76, 78, 587, Sir Henry 62, 65-6

Heydon, Jane 181

Heydon, Lt 310

Heydon, Miles 181, 196, 207-8, 564, 567

Heydon, Sir Christopher junior 50-1, 79, 135, 143, 155, 165-70, 181-208, 219, 226, 235, 339, 344, 346, 372, 376, 531, 541-2, 557-8, 564-8, Sir Christopher senior 68, 79, 90, 100, 105, 182-4, 195, 224, 294, 605

Heydon, Sir John (pre-1547) 65-6, 80, Sir John junior 181, 185, 208, 237, 288, 565-6, Sir John senior 185-8, 190

Heydon, Sir William junior 181, 184, 192-3, 208, 288, 564-7, Sir William senior 181-4, 187, 190, 224, 226, 557, 625

Heydon, Thomas 181

Heydon/Corbett, Katherine 183

Heydon/Crowe, Martha 208, 219, 344

Heydon/Draper/Vincent, Frances 567-8

Heydon/Lomax, Mirabel 565

Moundeford family 136, Edmund 216, Francis 80, 136, John 136, Sir Edmund 226, 229-32, 237-8, 241-3, 245-6, 271-2, 276, 283, 293

Mount, Thomas 46

Mountney, Richard 552

Mowbray *see* Howard, Henry

Moxon, Mary 570

Muddiclift, Daniel 212, 335, 368, 387, 392-5, 397, 429-35, 439-40, 552-3, Grace 430, 552

Mulbarton 184

Murford, Captain Peter 238, 240

Muston, James 337-8, John 492, 505

Myghte, Geoffrey 608

Mynne family 562, Anna 29, John 80

Myrthe, Elizabeth and Thomas 15

Nabbs family 221, 640, Edward 208, 221, John 367

Naish family 523

Nanseglos family 37-8, Robert 37, Thomas 36-7, William 36-7

Naples, Italy 220

Narborough 205-7, 216, 219, 253, 260-1, 264, 294, 305, 331, 337, 385, 444, 493, 557, 581, 585

Naylor, Francis 496, George 496

Neale, John 420, 439

Neave, Francis 302, Fyrmyn 104

Necton 480, 502

Nedham, Francis 352

Ness, Richard 592-4

Nevell, William 15

Neville family 4-5

New England, USA 568

New Windsor, Berks 100, 378-81

Newark 304, 327

Newbury, Berks 296

Newcastle-under-Lyme, Staffs 508, 577-8

Newell, Mrs 459

Newman family 602, 647, Thomas 427-8, 430-1, 504, 506, Thomas cleric 370-1, Thomas stationer 128, William 307-9, 329

Newman/Potts, Elizabeth 504, 506, 515

Newmarket, Cambs 4, 245, 537

Newport Pagnell, Bucks 298, 327

Newport, IOW 316-8

Newton Flotman 494, 569

Nicholas, Raynold (Reginald) 541-3

Nicholls, Nicholas 342-3, 355, 370

Nicolls, Edmond 154

Nix, Bishop of Norwich 580

Norcot, Sir John 270

Norfolk, Duke of *see* Howard

Norgate, Nicholas 448

Norman als Smith, Lydia *see* Underhill

Norman, Harebred 508, Thomas 508

Norris, James 480, 501, John 433, 435, Sir William 4

North Creake 458, 608

North Elmham 614

North Lenham 460

North Mimms, Herts 30-1

North Tuddenham 155

North Walsham 284

North, Sir Dudley 230, 323-4

Northrepps 96, 98, 223, 276

Northumberland, Earl of *see* Percy

Northwich, Cheshire 576

Norton, Colonel 373

Norwich 56, 71, 185, 196, 203, 206, 207, 209, 219, 223, 228, 242-4, 249-50, 269, 279-80, 327, 385, 387, 394, 448, 450-1, 453-4, 456-7, 466, 469-70, 476-8, 518, 525, 560-1

Norwich Castle 470, Museum 185, 565

Norwich Cathedral 181, 192, 367, 428, 457-60, 463, 466, 478, 498, Almary Green 457-8, Erpingham Gate 456-7, The Close 456-60, 462-3, 466, 470, 478, 480, 492, 497, 503, 507, Upper Green 459

Norwich City Library 462

Norwich inns, The Rose 434, The Sign of the Goat 430, The Three Tuns 427

Norwich parishes, St Andrew 271, St Botolph 572, St George Tombland 507, St Giles 493, St Gregory 430, 560, St John Maddermarket 553, St Margaret 573, St Martin at Palace Gates 609, St Mary in the Marsh 560, St Michael at Plea 454, St Michael Coslany 572, St Peter Hungate 454, 456, St Peter Mancroft 314, St Peter Parmentergate 434, St Simon and St Jude 456, St Stephen 199, 314, 427, 559-60

Norwich streets, Chapel Field 215, Cockey Lane 528, Elm Hill 456, Princes Inn Lane 456, Waggon and Horses Lane 456 Norwich, Conisford 434

Norwich, New Hall 257

Norwich, the Great Blow at 314, 328

Nottingham 207

Nuthurst, 33

Oby 389-90, 393-4

Ockley, Martha 465, Simon cleric 463-7, 474, 476, Thomas 464, Thomazin 464

Offerton, Cheshire 98, 558, 618

Offley, Mr Alderman 598

Oliver, Mrs William 465, 474

Olivier, John 380

Olly, Widow 271, 277, 327

Prestbury, Cheshire 535
Preston family 506, 519, Isaac 360, 448, Jacob junior 469, 471, 482, 485, 500, 506-7, 518-20, 522, Mr 271, Sir Isaac 519
Preston/Tanner, Frances 506-7
Price, Thomas 377
Pride, Colonel Thomas 325
Prideaux, Edmund 463, Humphrey 450-2, 457, 459-60, 463-7, 474-8, 506
Prittlewell, Essex 527
Proudfoot, Edmund 412
Pudding Norton 599
Puller (Poullard), John 41, 46
Purdy, Thomas 412
Purefoy, George 333, 337, 584, Sir Henry 1st baronet 584
Puttenham, Margaret 112
Pye, Richard 65, 70, 72, 609, Thomas 68-70, 148
Pym, John 231, 233, 235, 252, 281, 293
Pynchester, Elizabeth and Roger 38
Pynchon, Nicholas 616
Python, Monty, Flying Circus 606
Quidenham 86, 196, 226, 248, 449
Rainham, Essex 346
Rainow, Cheshire 535
Rainton, Sir Nicholas 330
Ralegh, Sir Walter 134, 184-5, 187, Lady Bess 191
Rant, Dr 202
Ranworth 581
Ratcliffe, Anne 607, Henry Earl of Sussex 610
Rawlyns, John 195
Raynham 4, 202
Raynton family 541-3
Read, Peter 94-5
Reade, Francis 620
Redenhall 136
Redfans manor, Shalford, Essex 37
Redyng, Edmund grocer 17
Reede, Richard 59
Reepham 79, 217, 439, 642, manor of Burgleons 90
Reeve, John 434, Thomas cleric 294
Repps with Bastwick 344, 369, 389-91, 395, 420, 422, 425, 427, 431, 493
Repps, Francis 448, 480, John 480
Rest family 38, 46, Agnes 38, Alice 38, Edward 38, John 38
Reymerston 450, 472
Reymes, Major John 294
Reynolds, Joseph 412, Robert 236-7
Rich, Robert Earl of Warwick 236, 240, 242, 252, 257, 267-8, 303, 309

Rich, Sir Edwin 184-5
Rich/Montagu, Anne 252
Richardson, Annie 74, Philippa 163-4, Richard 164
Richardson, Sir Thomas 257, 266, 269, 274, 277, 279-80, 282-3
Richardson, Thomas Lord Cramond 363
Richers, Henry 218, John 218, 572
Richers/Houghton, Mary 218
Riches, Mr 526
Richmond, Surrey 133
Riddlesworth 166
Risley, Derbys 205, 247, 255, 287, 303, 305, 336, 581-4
Rivers, Countess 251
Rivett, Sir Thomas 181, 192
Rivett/Heydon, Mirabel 181-2, 193
Roades (Reade), Francis 103
Roberts, Fulk 458
Robins family 446, Richard 447, 502-3, Thomas 447
Robinson, Francis grocer 131, Rookewood 299, William grocer 134
Robsart, Amy 111
Roche Monastery, Yorks 35
Roche, William Mayor of London 64
Rockland 447
Rogers, Mr 483, 504, Robert 73-4, 105
Rollesby 390
Romyng, John 602, Juliana 38
Rookwood, Roger 107
Roper family 652, Thomas (Rooper) 352-3, 357, 359-61
Rose, Robert 489
Rothewoode, Isabel 615, Thomas 615
Rotterdam, The Netherlands 282, 291
Rougham 68, 105, 573
Roughton 96, 260, 278, 573, 579, 614
Rous, _ 264, Francis 231, 297, Sir Thomas 567
Rouswell, William 123
Rowith, John 603
Rowland, Francis 353
Rowse, Mr 353
Roxburgh, Earl of 565
Ruddell, Mr cleric 359
Rupert, Prince 274, 374, 377-8
Rush, John cleric 658
Rushall 110
Rushall, Staffs 374-6, 379
Rushbrooke, Suffolk 80
Russell, Edward 3rd Earl of Bedford 232, Francis 4th Earl of Bedford 232, 331-2, 334, Francis junior 232, William, 5th Earl of Bedford 331-2
Ryall, William 444